THE JOSEPH SMITH
REVELATIONS
TEXT & COMMENTARY

Profile of Joseph Smith from an engraving in Frederick Piercy's *Route from Liverpool to Great Salt Lake Valley*, edited by James Linforth (Liverpool and London, 1855). Courtesy Utah State Historical Society

THE JOSEPH SMITH
REVELATIONS
TEXT & COMMENTARY

H. MICHAEL MARQUARDT

SIGNATURE BOOKS · SALT LAKE CITY

COVER DESIGN: BRIAN BEAN

The Joseph Smith Revelations: Text and Commentary
was printed on acid-free paper and was composed, printed,
and bound in the United States of America.

Published by Signature Books. Signature Books is a registered
trademark of Signature Books, Inc.

04   03   02   01   2000   99   6   5   4   3   2   1

LIBRARY OF CONGRESS CATALOGING-IN-PUBLICATION DATA
Marquardt, H. Michael.
    The Joseph Smith revelations : texts and commentary /
by H. Michael Marquardt.
       p.   cm.
    Includes bibliographical references and index.
    ISBN 1-56085-126-0
    1. Doctrine and Covenants—Criticism, interpretation, etc.
2. Smith, Joseph, 1805-1844.   3. Private revelations.   I. Smith,
Joseph, 1805-1844.   II. Title..
BX8628.M37   1999
289.3'2—dc21   98-46500
                                             CIP

CONTENTS

Preface xi

Introduction xiii

Common Abbreviations. xvii

Writings Not Included in this Study. xix

Map: Mormon Country. xxi

Cross-References. xxii

I. HISTORICAL BACKGROUND

1. *Evolution of the Canon.*   3

II. THE DOCUMENTS

2. *Book of Mormon Period, July 1828 - March 1830* 23

   1. Sets at Nought the Counsels of God (LDS D&C 3) 23

   2. O Ye That Embark in the Service of God (D&C 4). 25

   3. He Hath a Gift to Translate the Book (D&C 5) 26

   4. He That Hath Eternal Life Is Rich (D&C 6) 31

   5. Thou Shall Tarry till I Come in My Glory (D&C 7) 33

   6. Spirit of Revelation (D&C 8) 35

   7. Be Patient My Son (D&C 9). 37

   8. That You May Conquer Satan (LDS D&C 10) 38

   9. Behold It Is I That Speaketh (LDS D&C 11) 42

  10. Establish the Cause of Zion (LDS D&C 12). 43

  11. Keep My Commandments in All Things (LDS D&C 14) 44

  12. Hearken My Servant John (LDS D&C 15). 45

  13. Hearken My Servant Peter (LDS D&C 16) 45

  14. Rely upon the Things Which Are Written (LDS D&C 18) . . . 46

  15. It Is by Your Faith that You Shall Obtain a View of Them
     (LDS D&C 17). 49

  16. Pay the Printer's Debt (LDS D&C 19) 51

   Introduction to Chapters 3 to 6.
   Church of Christ Years, April 1830 - May 1834. 55

3. *Laying the Foundation, April 1830 - January 1831* 57

  17. Beware of Pride (LDS D&C 23) 57

18. Thy Duty Is unto the Church Forever (LDS D&C 23) 59

19. Strengthen the Church (LDS D&C 23) 59

20. Thou Also Art Under No Condemnation (LDS D&C 23) 60

21. It Is Your Duty to Unite with the True Church
(LDS D&C 23) 60

22. The Gates of Hell Shall Not Prevail Against You
(LDS D&C 21) 60

23. This Is a New and an Everlasting Covenant (LDS D&C 22) . . . 62

24. The Rise of the Church of Christ (LDS D&C 20) 62

25. Go Thy Way and Sin No More (LDS D&C 24) 69

26. Thou Art an Elect Lady (LDS D&C 25) 70

27. All Things You Shall Receive by Faith (LDS D&C 26) 71

28. Listen to the Voice of Jesus Christ (LDS D&C 27) 72

29. The Hour Is Nigh (LDS D&C 29) 80

30. Thou Shalt Be Obedient (LDS D&C 28) 83

31. You Have Feared Man (LDS D&C 30) 89

32. Give Heed unto These Things (LDS D&C 30) 89

33. Your Whole Labor Shall Be in My Zion (LDS D&C 30) 90

34. Pray Always (LDS D&C 31) 91

35. Be Meek and Lowly of Heart (LDS D&C 32) 92

36. Be Ready at the Coming of the Bridegroom (LDS D&C 33) . . 92

37. I Come Quickly (LDS D&C 34) 94

38. Thou Shalt Preach My Gospel (LDS D&C 35) 95

39. I Will Suddenly Come to My Temple (LDS D&C 36) 97

40. Ye Shall Go to the [State of] Ohio (D&C 37) 97

41. Behold the Kingdom Is Yours (D&C 38) 98

42. The Kingdom of Heaven Is at Hand (D&C 39) 101

43. His Heart Was Right Before Me (D&C 40) 102

4. *Receiving the Laws, February 1831 - September 1831* . . 105

44. Hearken and Hear, O Ye My People (D&C 41) 105

45. Behold I Speak unto the Church (D&C 42) 107

46. Labor Ye in My Vineyard for the Last Time (D&C 43) 115

47. Preach Repentance unto the People (D&C 44) 118

48. He Shall Be Delivered Up unto the Law (D&C 42) 118

49. Be Watchful and Careful with All Inquiry (D&C 42) 120

50. I Am Alpha & Omega (D&C 45) 121

51. Seek Ye Earnestly the Best Gifts (D&C 46) 124

52. Write and Keep a Regular History (D&C 47) 126

53. Save All the Money that Ye Can (D&C 48)............... 127

54. I Have Sent unto You Mine Everlasting Covenant (D&C 49) . 128

55. There Are Many Spirits Which Are False Spirits (D&C 50) ... 130

56. Receive the Properties of This People (D&C 51)........... 133

57. Hearken unto My Words 135

58. I Will Cut My Work Short in Righteousness (D&C 52) 136

59. You Shall Forsake the World (D&C 53) 138

60. Take Your Journey into the Regions Westward (D&C 54) ... 139

61. Ordained by the Hand of My Servant Joseph (D&C 55)...... 140

62. I the Lord Command & Revoke as It Seemeth Me Good
(D&C 56).................................... 140

63. Independence Is the Center Place (D&C 57) 142

64. My Laws Shall Be Kept on This Land (D&C 58) 145

65. The Fulness of the Earth Is Yours (D&C 59) 149

66. Let Them Lift Up Their Voice (D&C 60) 150

67. There Are Many Dangers upon the Waters (D&C 61) 152

68. Rejoice Together in the Land of Missouri (D&C 62)........ 154

69. Let the Church Repent of Their Sins (D&C 63) 155

70. I Will Have Compassion upon You (D&C 64) 158

5. Publishing the Revelations, October 1831 - April 1832 163

71. Blessed Are You for Receiving Mine Everlasting Covenant
(D&C 66) 163

72. May the Kingdom of God Go Forth (D&C 65) 164

73. This Is Mine Authority (D&C 1)....................... 165

74. Let Not Your Minds Turn Back (D&C 67) 167

75. The Testimony of the Witnesses 168

76. I the Lord Am with You (D&C 68) 169

77. Go Ye Out from Babylon (LDS D&C 133).............. 173

78. None Shall Be Exempt from the Justice and the Laws of God
(LDS D&C 107)................................ 177

79. Send Forth the Accounts of Their Stewardships to the Land of
Zion (D&C 69) 179

80. Stewards over the Revelations, and Commandments (D&C 70) 180

81. Confound Your Enemies (D&C 71) 181

82. It Is Expedient in Me for a Bishop to Be Appointed
(D&C 72)..................................... 181

83. To Receive the Funds of the Church (D&C 72) 182

84. Continue Preaching the Gospel (D&C 73) 183

85. According to the Revelations and Commandments
   (D&C 75). 184
86. Supporting the Families (D&C 75) 185
87. The Eyes of Our Understanding (D&C 76) 186
88. To Be a Servant unto Me 194
89. In the Days of the Apostles (D&C 74) 194
90. All Things Be Done unto My Glory (LDS D&C 78) 195
91. Go Ye into the World & Preach the Gospel (LDS D&C 80) . . 198
92. Equal in All Things. 199
93. Glad Tidings of Great Joy (LDS D&C 79) 200
94. Proclaiming the Gospel in the Land of the Living & among
   Thy Brethren (LDS D&C 81) 200
95. The Spirit of Man in the Likeness of His Person
   (LDS D&C 77). 204
96. Let Whatsoever Is Done Be Done in the Name of the Lord. . . 206
97. When Ye Do Not What I Say, Ye Have No Promise
   (LDS D&C 82). 207
98. All Children Have Claim upon Their Parents Untill They Are
   of Age (LDS D&C 83) 209

6. *Priesthood Development, August 1832 - April 1834*. . . . 211
99. Whoso Receiveth You as a Little Child Receiveth My
   Kingdom (LDS D&C 99) 211
100. This Is the Word of the Lord (LDS D&C 84) 212
101. Set in Order the House of God (LDS D&C 85). 219
102. The Angels Are Crying unto the Lord (LDS D&C 86). 220
103. Stand Ye in Holy Places (LDS D&C 87) 221
104. I Now Send upon You Another Comforter (LDS D&C 88). . . 222
105. In Token of the Everlasting Covenant (LDS D&C 88). 229
106. Called to Be a Councellor. 231
107. Enoch of Old 231
108. A Word of Wisdom (LDS D&C 89) 232
109. Set in Order the Churches (LDS D&C 90) 234
110. The Apocrypha (LDS D&C 91) 236
111. Ye Shall Receive Him into the Firm (LDS D&C 92). 236
112. Man Is the Tabernacle of God (LDS D&C 93). 237
113. The Building of Mine House (LDS D&C 95) 239
114. Bringing Forth My Word (LDS D&C 96) 241
115. For This Is Zion the Pure in Heart (LDS D&C 97) 241

116. According to the Pattern (LDS D&C 94)................. 243

117. Renounce War and Proclaim Peace (LDS D&C 98) 244

118. A Pure People (LDS D&C 100) 247

119. Avenge Me of Mine Enemies (LDS D&C 101) 248

120. Restoration and Redemption of Zion (LDS D&C 103) 253

121. Properties Which Belong to the Firm (LDS D&C 104) 255

122. Let There Be Reserved Three Thousand Dollars 260

7. Church of the Latter Day Saints Period, May 1834 - April 1838

.... 263

123. Wait for a Little Season for the Redemption of Zion
(LDS D&C 105)................................... 263

124. Separated Himself from the Crafts of Men (LDS D&C 106) ... 266

125. Condemnation Resteth upon You 266

126. The High Priest, and Elder, Are to Administer in Spiritual
Things (LDS D&C 107) 267

127. Shall Have Wisdom Given Him 273

128. If He Repent Not................................. 273

129. Flee the Wrath to Come............................ 274

130. Let Them Repent Speedily.......................... 274

131. Their Sins Are Forgiven Them 275

132. Are Under Condemnation 275

133. He Shall See Much of My Ancient Records 276

134. He Shall Be Restored unto His Former State............. 276

135. Had Better Not Be Baptised Here..................... 277

136. Receive Counsel of Him Whom I Have Appointed
(LDS D&C 108)................................... 277

137. I Beheld the Celestial Kingdom of God (LDS D&C 137)..... 278

138. I Have Accepted This House (LDS D&C 110) 279

139. Concern Not Yourselves about Zion (LDS D&C 111)....... 281

140. Rebel Not against My Servant Joseph (LDS D&C 112) 281

141. Things Which Are Not Pleasing in My Sight............. 283

142. Awake My Shepherds and Warn My People 284

143. Let the First Presidency of My Church Be Held in Full
Fellowship 284

144. Except It Be Dedicated by This Presidency 285

145. Get Out of This Place.............................. 286

146. Put on the Authority of the Priesthood (LDS D&C 113) 286

147. Others Shall Be Planted in Their Stead (LDS D&C 114) 287

148. Provide for His Family 288

8. Early Church of Jesus Christ of Latter Day Saints Period, April 1838 - November 1843 289

149. The Ground upon Which Thou Standest Is Holy
 (LDS D&C 115) 289
150. Let the Twelve Be Organized (LDS D&C 118) 292
151. Their Former Standing Has Been Taken Away 292
152. This Shall Be a Standing Law unto Them Forever
 (LDS D&C 119) 293
153. It Shall Be Disposed Of (LDS D&C 120) 293
154. Let Them Settle Up Their Business (LDS D&C 117) 294
155. Council of the Eternal God of All Other Gods
 (LDS D&C 121-122) 295
156. I Am Well Pleased with Your Offering (LDS D&C 124) 299
157. Let Them Gather Themselves Together (LDS D&C 125) 311
158. Take Stock in the [Nauvoo] House 311
159. Your Offering Is Acceptable to Me (LDS D&C 126) 312
160. I the Lord Will Bless Them 312
161. A Mission to Preach My Gospel 313
162. Beautify the Place of My Sanctuary 313
163. Take in Hand the Editorial Department 314
164. The Kingdom of God and His Law 314
165. I Am the Lord Thy God 314
166. Shall Be Crowned upon Your Heads 315
167. I Shall Triumph over All My Enemies (LDS D&C 127) 316
168. The Key of Knowledge (LDS D&C 128) 318
169. For Time and for All Eternity (LDS D&C 132) 323
170. Labor Diligently in Proclaiming My Gospel 329

Conclusion 331
Illustrations 337
Appendices 347
 A. Corrected Dates and Locations of Joseph Smith's Revelations 348
 B. Book of Commandments Manuscript Fragments 349
 C. Revelations Printed in *The Evening and the Morning Star* 366
 D. Locations of Manuscript Revelations 368
 E. Six Additional Revelations Given through Joseph Smith 372
 F. A Commandment to Oliver Cowdery Received in 1829 379
Select Bibliography 383
Index 403

PREFACE

Revelation is so central to Mormonism that one might assume the study of original texts is an exhausted field. The truth is that, with few exceptions, such a study has yet to begin. What makes this all the more surprising is that the "Upgrading [of] revelations and retrospectively editing the past are hallmarks of early Mormonism."[1] Mormon books and scriptures give primacy to emended texts, while the originals remain largely ignored. An analysis of the earliest documents helps us better understand the original setting and intention of a revelation, which in many instances is altered—sometimes greatly—by later textual modifications.

The historical study of the texts not only helps us interpret the original meaning but assists in appreciating the richness of a living text as it is transformed over time. Scriptures do not exist without a community of believers that cherishes them as the word of God. Thus the history of scriptural texts reveals the changing world view of the Mormon community. By knowing more of the history of the early church, including events that effected alterations of texts, we hope to reveal important, fundamental vistas regarding the nature of early Mormonism and its canon.

This book arranges in chronological order the revelations received by Mormonism's founding prophet, Joseph Smith, in their earliest available form. Important textual revisions that appeared in the canonized 1835 Doctrine and Covenants are included at the end of each revelation affected. If the basic word in the revision is the same or if there is a minor spelling difference, no attention is drawn to the change. Word(s) in *italics* represent new language that was added in 1835.

A commentary for some of the revelations is included at the end of pertinent passages. I have not commented on every textual change but have highlighted the most significant—those which elucidate how people understood these revelatory pronouncements at the time they were first given. Where manuscripts are available and relevant to this study, I provide transcriptions of the complete documents. Transcriptions of the manuscripts were made from photographic reproductions, microfilm copies, and Book of Commandments fragments. For revelatory texts recorded in the Book of the Law of the Lord, I have consulted the transcription by Dean C. Jessee in *The Papers of Joseph Smith: Journal, 1832-1842*. I have retained the style and spelling of the original scribes.

My selection of "revelations" follows the canonical tradition. It includes not only foundational doctrinal assertions and visions but also pronouncements regarding the duties of church leaders. Specific instructions to church members were an important aspect of early Mormonism, as were explanations of scriptures, episto-

---

1. Richard S. Van Wagoner, *Sidney Rigdon: A Portrait of Religious Excess* (Salt Lake City: Signature Books, 1994), 129n5.

lary advice, and decisions about practical matters regarding property and money. These items are more formally called revelations (148), commandments (6), letters (4), explanations of scripture (3), visions (3), prophecies (2), testimony (1), a song in the gift of tongues (1), instruction (1), and the Articles and Covenants (1). One half of the revelations were written during the formative period of the church before the Quorum of Twelve Apostles was organized in 1835 (125 documents, 73.5 percent). They were given to the general membership, to elders and high priests, to church conferences, or in response to individual inquiries. They were mainly for men. Only five documents are directly related to women: to Emma Hale Smith, Vienna Jacques, Mary Bailey Smith, Nancy Marinda Hyde, and Sarah Ann Whitney.

Versification has been deleted since most of the manuscripts have no verses. References to current editions of the scriptures are given at the beginning of each document. Brackets are used for editorial insertions, to make fragmentary or misspelled words intelligible. Sometimes the manuscripts were difficult to read, especially the endings of words. Rather than complete the intended word, brackets were added. Brackets are also included to identify individuals mentioned. Unless otherwise indicated, words that were crossed out by the original scribes are omitted.

In a number of instances where the meaning is ambiguous, punctuation and capital letters are supplied within brackets to facilitate readability. The Book of Commandments had a few obvious typographical errors that have been corrected. The first word of each revelation, which appeared in capital letters, has been rendered in lower case. In manuscripts, words that appear above lines are included if they were part of the original manuscript and were not late additions.

Most of the manuscripts have been divided into shorter paragraphs for easier reading. Source notations for the texts are at the beginning of each document. Footnotes are given where appropriate. References to Mormon scripture are usually provided in their standard abbreviations; thus BC refers to the Book of Commandments, D&C to the Doctrine and Covenants (usually preceded by LDS or RLDS), etc.

I would like to give a special thanks to the three major repositories containing manuscripts relating to the Restoration movement: the historical department of the Church of Jesus Christ of Latter-day Saints (LDS archives), Salt Lake City, Utah; the library-archives of the Reorganized Church of Jesus Christ of Latter Day Saints (RLDS archives), Independence, Missouri; and Special Collections, Harold B. Lee Library, Brigham Young University, Provo, Utah. Research was conducted at the LDS Family History Library; Manuscripts Division, J. Willard Marriott Library, University of Utah; and the Utah State Historical Society library, all in Salt Lake City; the Kansas State Historical Society, Topeka; the Mercantile Library Association and Missouri Historical Society, both in St. Louis; and the Western Reserve Historical Society in Cleveland, Ohio. I express my appreciation to these institutions and their staffs.

INTRODUCTION

Revelation is usually thought of as the imparting of truth to men and women by Deity. How this wisdom has been communicated between heaven and earth and how it is different from ordinary human thought remains a mystery. For instance, Mormon church founder Joseph Smith (1805-44) was accompanied by scribes who sometimes recorded his most casual observations. For Smith, revelation seemed to come from day-to-day experience, from interactions with other people, and from the study of biblical texts.

In the early years of his life, Smith was a treasure seer who divined where precious things were hidden. As he acquired a prophetic mantle, he used the same methods, including seer-stone gazing, to produce his church's foundational scripture, the Book of Mormon, and his first fifteen revelations.[1]

Smith began his ministry in the spring of 1828 at age twenty-two by dictating the content of ancient gold plates to his scribe Martin Harris. When over one hundred manuscript pages of the dictated text were lost, Smith inquired of God about this matter. In July his prayer was answered, and this response became his first revelation: "The works, and the designs, and the purposes of God, can not be frustrated, neither can they come to nought, for God doth not walk in crooked paths; neither doth he turn to the right hand nor to the left; neither doth he vary from that which he hath said: Therefore his paths are strait and his course is one eternal round."[2]

While these words were reportedly uttered by God through Smith, there is no first-person emphasis. The language is matter of fact and relates directly to the subject at hand: the lost manuscript of the dictated Book of Mormon text. However, in April 1829 one of Smith's revelations to another scribe, Oliver Cowdery, uses the first person: "Behold I am Jesus Christ" and "Verily, verily, I say unto you."[3]

While Smith did not comment on the manner in which he perceived God's mind, the linguistic idiosyncracies are assumed to be his own. Whether he believed that the ideas or the words themselves were God's is not completely understood. For instance, expressions that are borrowed from the King James Version (KJV) of the Bible seem to highlight the importance of the message.

Smith frequently revised the revelations in accordance with his developing the-

---

1. See Dean C. Jessee, ed., *The Papers of Joseph Smith: Autobiographical and Historical Writings* (Salt Lake City: Deseret Book Co., 1989), 1:287, 289, 292, 294. See also H. Michael Marquardt and Wesley P. Walters, *Inventing Mormonism: Tradition and the Historical Record* (San Francisco: Smith Research Associates, 1994), 104, 188-89, 195n49-51.

2. BC 2:1; LDS D&C 3:1-2; RLDS D&C 2:1.

3. The words "Verily, verily, I say unto you" are in the Gospel of John (KJV) and in the Book of Mormon. The shorter wording "verily I say unto you" is in the New Testament Gospels.

ology. God's word, relayed through fallible prophets, was neither inerrant nor static in Smith's view—so as the need arose he revised the Bible and his own autobiography as well as the revelations.

However, in June 1829 instructions were given to twelve future apostles called to serve in the ministry:

> And I Jesus Christ, your Lord and your God, have spoken it. These words are not of men, nor of man, but of me: Wherefore you shall testify they are of me, and not of man; for it is my voice which speaketh them unto you: For they are given by my Spirit unto you: And by my power you can read them one to another; and save it were by my power, you could not have them: Wherefore you can testify that you have heard my voice, and know my words. ... Behold I Jesus Christ, your Lord and your God, and your Redeemer, by the power of my Spirit, have spoken it: Amen.[4]

And on 6 April 1830, the day the church was organized, a revelation referred to Smith's authority as spokesman: "For his word ye shall receive, as if from mine own mouth."[5]

One early disciple, Parley P. Pratt, wrote about the process of revelation:

> After we had joined in prayer in his [Smith's] translating room, he dictated in our presence the following revelation:—(Each sentence was uttered slowly and very distinctly, and with a pause between each, sufficiently long for it to be recorded, by an ordinary writer, in long hand. This was the manner in which all of his written revelations were dictated and written. There was never any hesitation, reviewing, or reading back, in order to keep the run of the subject; neither did any of these communications undergo revisions, interlinings, or corrections. As he dictated them so they stood, so far as I have witnessed; and I was present to witness the dictation of several communications of several pages each. This inquiry was made and the answer given in May, 1831.)[6]

William E. McLellin was the scribe for Smith's October 1831 revelation and for David Whitmer's September 1847 illumination. McLellin wrote of the revelatory process:

> I, as scribe, have written revelations from the mouth of both the Revelators, Joseph Smith and David Whitmer. And I have been present many times when others wrote for Joseph; therefore I speak as one having experience. The scribe seats himself at a desk or table, with pen, ink and paper. The subject of enquiry being understood, the Prophet and Revelator enquires of God. He spiritually sees, hears and feels, and then speaks as he is moved upon by the Holy Ghost, the "thus saith the Lord," sentence after sentence, and waits for his amanuenses to write and then read aloud each sentence. Thus they proceed until the revelator says Amen, at the close of what is then communicated.[7]

Note that McLellin has each sentence read aloud by the scribe while Pratt states that there was no reading back. Many of the manuscripts do not have punctuation marks, perhaps indicating they were dictated too rapidly to have been read back

4. BC 15:36-41, 50; LDS D&C 18:33-36, 47; RLDS D&C 16:5, 7.
5. BC 22:5; LDS D&C 21:5; RLDS D&C 19:2.
6. Parley P. Pratt [Jr.], ed., *Autobiography of Parley P. Pratt* (Salt Lake City: Deseret Book Co., 1994), 48. See LDS and RLDS D&C 50.
7. William E. McLellin, ed., *The Ensign of Liberty* 1 (Aug. 1849): 98, Kirtland, Ohio.

and corrected. In any case, the revelations were written as nearly as possible as Smith spoke them. The early manuscripts have crossed-out words with substituted words above lines, which appear to have been written near the time of the first composition. The orthography is unique for each particular scribe. Smith, on the other hand, was responsible for the content of every message.

Many of the revelations are explicitly attributed to God, as illustrated by the following salutations:

> thus saith the Lord (OT; BOM; 1830-43)
> saith the Lord (OT; NT; BOM; 1830-43)
> Verily thus saith the Lord (1831-43)
> Behold thus saith the Lord (NT; BOM; 1831-38)
> verily I say unto you (NT; BOM; 1829-43)
> Verily, verily, I say unto you (NT; BOM; 1829-1843)
> I am God (OT; BOM; 1829-33)
> I am Alpha and Omega (NT; BOM; 1830-43)
> Listen to the voice (NT; 1830-32)
> I the Lord have spoken it (OT; 1831-33)
> Behold I am Jesus Christ (BOM; 1829-31)
> listen to the words of Jesus Christ (1829)
> give heed unto my word (1829)

In a revelation received on 25 January 1832, the wording commences: "Verily verily I say unto you I who speak even by the voice of my spirit even Alpha and Omega your Lord and your God ... behold this is the will of the Lord your God concerning you even so Amen."[8] Smith stated this was a "commandment of Jesus Christ."[9] In another revelation, he dictated, "these are the words of Alpha & Omega even Jesus Christ."[10] William W. Phelps underscored Smith's role as God's voice in a song, a portion of which reads: "The commandments to the church,/ Which the saints will always search,/ (Where the joys of heaven perch,)/ Came through him from Jesus Christ."[11]

A peculiarity in the revelations is that when there are minor differences between the original and subsequent versions, the meaning has usually remained the same. Theological and historical revisions are more apparent. The most drastic alterations were made in 1835, when the texts were amended, added to, excised, and in some cases assigned different historical settings. About a third of the texts from July 1828 to 23 April 1834 were revised. Among other emendations, the changes softened language, reinterpreted economic matters, added offices existing at the time of revision, and inserted references to priesthood restoration.

The earliest prophetic statements were addressed to individuals as a comfort or

---

8. See LDS D&C 75:1, 12; RLDS D&C 75:1-2.

9. Smith to W. W. Phelps, 31 July 1832, LDS archives. See Dean C. Jessee, ed., *The Personal Writings of Joseph Smith* (Salt Lake City: Deseret Book Co., 1984), 244.

10. See LDS D&C 81; RLDS D&C 80 (15 Mar. 1832).

11. *Latter Day Saints' Messenger and Advocate* 2 (Oct. 1835): 208; *A Collection of Sacred Hymns, for the Church of the Latter Day Saints* (Kirtland, OH: Printed by F. G. Williams & Co., 1835 [1836]), 33-34.

chastisement or to the church regarding organizational issues. Economic ideals, religious expectations, and millennial warnings were also prominent features. Missionaries were called to preach to the world for the last time.

The majority (51.7 percent) of the commandments, revelations, and instructions were received in Kirtland and Hiram, Ohio (1831-38), as doctrines, ordinances, and authority structures were solidified. From the revelations, it becomes clear that dissent was common and forgiveness was often offered to those who transgressed.

Some of the revelations were not only for a specific recipient, but were specifically withheld from the public. Martin Harris was instructed in March 1830: "And I command you, that you preach nought but repentance; and show not these things, neither speak these things unto the world, for they can not bear meat, but milk they must receive[.]"[12] Almost a year later in March 1831 the church was told: "& now I say unto you keep these things from going abroad unto the world that ye may accomplish this work in the eyes of the people & in the eyes of your enemies that they may not know your works untill ye have accomplished the thing which I have commanded you[.]"[13]

At the 1 November 1831 church conference, a revelation authorized publication of the Book of Commandments: "What I the Lord have spoken, I have spoken, and I excuse not myself, and though the heavens and the earth pass away, my word shall not pass away, but shall all be fulfilled, whether by mine own voice, or by the voice of my servants, it is the same[.]"[14] Originally the commandments were to be kept from the world—"And for this cause these commandments were given; they were commanded to be kept from the world in the d[a]y that they were given, but now [November 1831] are to go forth unto all flesh."[15]

Realizing that some of the revelations were not intended for the world underscores the importance of the early texts. Joseph Smith together with a few associates selected the revelations from the original handwritten copies for canonization. Chapter 1 discusses these manuscripts as it explores the historical development of the canon.

12. BC 16:22. For the 1835 D&C the instruction to Harris deleted "neither speak these things," while adding "until it is wisdom in me," to read: "show not these things unto the world until it is wisdom in me; for they cannot bear meat now, but milk they must receive" (1835 D&C 44:2). See LDS D&C 19:21-22; RLDS D&C 18:2.

13. Manuscript in LDS archives. After the words "keep these things from going abroad unto the world," six words were added for the BC: "until it is expedient in me" (BC 48:68; LDS D&C 45:72; RLDS D&C 45:15). The manuscript written by Edward Partridge does not contain these words nor does a copy made by William E. McLellin. See Jan Shipps and John W. Welch, eds., *The Journals of William E. McLellin 1831-1836* (Provo, UT: BYU Studies/Urbana: University of Illinois Press, 1994), 240.

14. BC 1:7; LDS D&C 1:38; RLDS D&C 1:8.

15. *The Evening and the Morning Star* 1 (May 1833): [2; whole page no. 90], Independence, MO; LDS D&C 133:60; RLDS D&C 108:11 (3 Nov. 1831).

COMMON ABBREVIATIONS

1830 BOM . . . . Joseph Smith, *The Book of Mormon: An Account Written by the hand of Mormon, Upon Plates Taken from the Plates of Nephi. By Joseph Smith, Junior, author and proprietor* (Palmyra, NY: Printed by E. B. Grandin for the author, 1830), cited with page number and followed by versification of both LDS and RLDS churches

1835 D&C . . . . . *Doctrine and Covenants of the Church of the Latter Day Saints* (Kirtland, OH: Printed by F. G. Williams & Co., 1835)

BC . . . . *A Book of Commandments, for the Government of the Church of Christ* (Zion [Independence, Missouri]: Published by W. W. Phelps & Co., 1833)

BLL . . . . Book of the Law of the Lord, archives, First Presidency, LDS church

BOM . . . . Book of Mormon

D&C . . . . Doctrine and Covenants

E&M Star . . . . . *The Evening and the Morning Star*

JS Journal . . . . . . Joseph Smith 1835-36 Journal, LDS archives

JST . . . . *The Holy Scriptures* (Independence, MO: Herald Publishing House, Reorgranized Church of Jesus Christ of Latter Day Saints, 1991); also Joseph Smith Translation of the Bible

KJV . . . . King James Version of the Bible

KRB . . . . Kirtland Revelations Book, LDS archives

LDS . . . . Church of Jesus Christ of Latter-day Saints (Mormon) headquartered in Salt Lake City, Utah

LDS D&C . . . . . *The Doctrine and Covenants of The Church of Jesus Christ of Latter-day Saints* (Salt Lake City: Church of Jesus Christ of Latter-day Saints, 1981)

NKW . . . . Newel K. Whitney Collection, Special Collections, Harold B. Lee Library, Brigham Young University, Provo, Utah

NT . . . . New Testament

OT . . . . Old Testament

PGP . . . . *The Pearl of Great Price* (Salt Lake City: Church of Jesus Christ of Latter-day Saints, 1981)

RLDS . . . . Reorganized Church of Jesus Christ of Latter Day Saints, headquartered in Independence, Missouri

RLDS archives . . Library-Archives, RLDS church

RLDS D&C . . . *Book of Doctrine and Covenants* (Independence, MO: Herald Publishing House, Reorganized Church of Jesus Christ of Latter Day Saints, 1990)

SB . . . . Scriptory Book of Joseph Smith, LDS archives

WRITINGS NOT
INCLUDED IN THIS STUDY

I. *Items in the LDS D&C*[1]

ADDED TO THE D&C IN 1876:

D&C 2	the priesthood by the hand of Elijah the prophet
D&C 13	ordination prayer by John the Baptist
D&C 109	dedication prayer of the Kirtland Temple
D&C 116	Adam to visit his people at Adam-ondi-Adam, Daviess County, Missouri
D&C 123	instructions
D&C 129-31	instructions

OTHER:

D&C 102	minutes of the organization of the High Council (1835 D&C 5)
D&C 134	Article on Governments and Laws in General (1835 D&C 102)

II. *Items in the 1835 D&C Omitted from Subsequent Editions*

A. The Lectures on Faith
   removed, RLDS D&C 1897 edition; removed, LDS D&C 1921 edition
B. Article on Marriage (1835 D&C 101)
   removed, LDS D&C 1876 edition and replaced with LDS D&C 132, 1876 edition; contained in RLDS D&C 111
C. General Assembly (17 Aug. 1835)
   removed, D&C 1844 edition (Nauvoo, Illinois)
   added, RLDS D&C 1894 edition; removed, RLDS D&C 1990 edition

III. *Items in the RLDS D&C*

D&C 22	introductory revelation prior to revision of Genesis added to RLDS D&C 1864 edition; in LDS PGP
D&C 36	part of inspired correction of the Holy Scriptures added to RLDS D&C 1864 edition; in LDS PGP
D&C 99	minutes of the organization of the High Council
D&C 111	Article on Marriage
D&C 112	Article on Governments and Laws in General

---

1. These include narrative, the minutes of a meeting, a prayer, and instructions.

IV. Items Outside the D&C

A. The Book of Mormon

B. Correction of the KJV of the Bible, part of which is in the LDS PGP as Selections from the Book of Moses

   1. "A Revelation given to Joseph the Revelator June 1830" (OT MS #1, 1, RLDS archives)

   2. "A Revelation given to the Elders of the Church of Christ On the first Book of Moses ~~given to Joseph the Seer~~ Chapter first" (ibid., 3)

   3. "Chapter 2 A Revelation concerning Adam after he had been driven out of the garden of Eden" (ibid., 8). Note: The handwriting of Oliver Cowdery ends at Genesis 5:28 in the RLDS Bible (Gen. 4:18, KJV; LDS PGP, Moses 5:43).

C. The Book of Abraham, Smith's writings from Egyptian papyrus (LDS PGP)

D. Joseph Smith-Matthew, Smith's correction of Matthew 23:39 and chap. 24 (PGP)

E. Joseph Smith-History, which includes Smith's early visionary experiences (PGP)

F. The Articles of Faith (PGP)

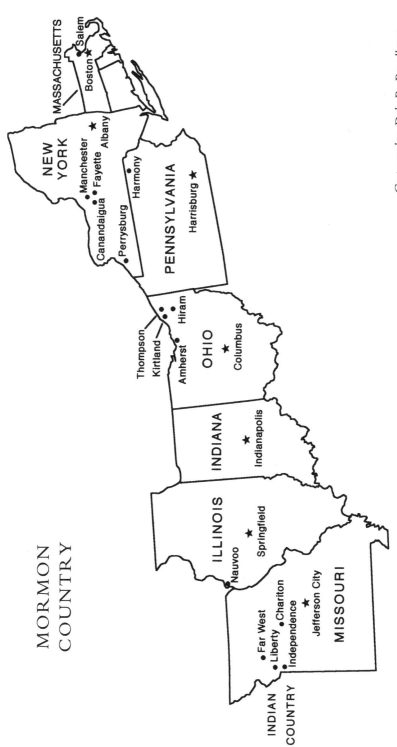

MORMON
COUNTRY

MASSACHUSETTS
Salem
Boston ★

NEW
YORK
Manchester
Fayette Albany ★
Canandaigua
Perrysburg
Harmony

PENNSYLVANIA
Harrisburg ★

Thompson
Kirtland
Amherst
Hiram
OHIO
Columbus ★

INDIANA
Indianapolis ★

ILLINOIS
Springfield ★
Nauvoo

Far West
Liberty ● Chariton
Independence
Jefferson City ★
MISSOURI

INDIAN
COUNTRY

Cartography: Dale R. Broadhurst

CROSS-REFERENCES

Document Number	Day	Month	Year	BC 1833★	D&C 1835★	LDS D&C 1876/1981	RLDS D&C 1864/1990	Source Used
Book of Mormon Period:								
1	[1-31]	July	1828	2	30	3	2	BC 2
2	[1-28]	Feb.	1829	3	31	4	4	BC 3
3	[1-31]	Mar.	1829	4	32	5	5	NKW
4	[7-30]	Apr.	1829	5	8	6	6	BC 5
5	[7-30]	Apr.	1829	6	33	7	7	Manuscript
6	[7-30]	Apr.	1829	7	34	8	8	BC 7
7	[7-30]	Apr.	1829	8	35	9	9	BC 8
8	[1-31]	May	1829	9	36	10	3	BC 9
9	[1-31]	May	1829	10	37	11	10	BC 10
10	[1-31]	May	1829	11	38	12	11	BC 11
11	[1-14]	June	1829	12	39	14	12	BC 12
12	[1-14]	June	1829	13	40	15	13	BC 13
13	[1-14]	June	1829	14	41	16	14	BC 14
14	[1-14]	June	1829	15	43	18	16	BC 15
15	[14-30]	June	1829		42	17	15	1835 D&C 42
16	[26-31]	Mar.	1830	16	44	19	18	BC 16
Church of Christ Years:								
17	6	Apr.	1830	17	45	23:1-2	21:1	BC 17
18	6	Apr.	1830	18	45	23:3	21:2	BC 18
19	6	Apr.	1830	19	45	23:4	21:3	BC 19
20	6	Apr.	1830	20	45	23:5	21:4	BC 20
21	6	Apr.	1830	21	45	23:6-7	21:5	BC 21
22	6	Apr.	1830	22	46	21	19	BC 22
23	16	Apr.	1830	23	47	22	20	Manuscript
24	[1-9]	June	1830	24	2	20	17	Manuscript
25	[4-31]	July	1830	25	9	24	23	BC 25
26	[4-31]	July	1830	26	48	25	24	BC 26
27	[4-31]	July	1830	27	49	26	25	BC 27
28	4	Sept.	1830	28	50	27	26	BC 28
29	[5-26]	Sept.	1830	29	10	29	28	BC 29
30	[5-26]	Sept.	1830	30	51	28	27	BC 30
31	[26-28]	Sept	1830	31	52	30:1-4	29:1	BC 31

Document Number	Day	Month	Year	BC 1833★	D&C 1835★	LDS D&C 1876/1981	RLDS D&C 1864/1990	Source Used
32	[26-28]	Sept.	1830	32	52	30:5-8	29:2	BC 32
33	[26-28]	Sept.	1830	33	52	30:9-11	29:3	BC 33
34	[26-28]	Sept.	1830	34	53	31	30	BC 34
35	[ca 17]	Oct.	1830		54	32	31	KRB, 83-84
36	[18-31]	Oct.	1830	35	55	33	32	BC 35
37	4	Nov.	1830	36	56	34	33	BC 36
38	[7-11]	Dec.	1830	37	11	35	34	BC 37
39	[11-15]	Dec.	1830	38	57	36	35	BC 38
40	[30]	Dec.	1830	39	58	37	37	BC 39
41	2	Jan.	1831	40	12	38	38	BC 40
42	[5]	Jan.	1831	41	59	39	39	BC 41
43	[6]	Jan.	1831	42	60	40	40	BC 42
44	4	Feb.	1831	43	61	41	41	BC 43
45	9	Feb.	1831	44	13	42:1-72	42:1-19	Manuscript
46	[9-23]	Feb.	1831	45	14	43	43	BC 45
47	[9-23]	Feb.	1831	46	62	44	44	BC 46
48	23	Feb.	1831	47:1-20	13	42:78-93	42:21-23	Manuscript
49	23	Feb.	1831	47:21-24	13	42:74-77	42:20	Manuscript
50	[6-7]	Mar.	1831	48	15	45	45	Manuscript
51	8	Mar.	1831	49	16	46	46	BC 49
52	8	Mar.	1831	50	63	47	47	BC 50
53	[8-31]	Mar.	1831	51	64	48	48	BC 51
54	[ca 26]	Mar.	1831	52	65	49	49	BC 52
55	9	May	1831	53	17	50	50	BC 53
56	20	May	1831		23	51	51	KRB, 87-89
57	[1-31]	May	1831					KRB, 91-92
58	6	June	1831	54	66	52	52	BC 54
59	[6-15]	June	1831	55	66	53	53	NKW
60	[6-15]	June	1831	56	67	54	54	BC 56
61	[15]	June	1831	57	68	55	55	BC 57
62	15	June	1831	58	69	56	56	Manuscript
63	20	July	1831		27	57	57	KRB, 89-91
64	[1-2]	Aug.	1831	59	18	58	58	BC 59
65	7	Aug.	1831	60	19	59	59	NKW
66	8	Aug.	1831	61	70	60	60	BC 61
67	12	Aug.	1831	62	71	61	61	BC 62
68	13	Aug.	1831	63	72	62	62	BC 63
69	[30-31]	Aug.	1831	64	20	63	63	NKW
70	11	Sept.	1831	65:1-47	21	64	64	NKW
71	29	Oct.	1831		74	66	66	Manuscript
72	30	Oct.	1831		24	65	65	Manuscript
73	1	Nov.	1831		1	1	1	BC 1

Document Number	Day	Month	Year	BC 1833*	D&C 1835*	LDS D&C 1876/1981	RLDS D&C 1864/1990	Source Used
74	1	Nov.	1831		25	67	67	1835 D&C 25
75	1	Nov.	1831					Manuscript
76	[1-3]	Nov.	1831		22	68	68	E&M Star
77	3	Nov.	1831		100	133	108	E&M Star
78	[11]	Nov.	1831		3	107:59-92, 99-100	104:31-42, 44	NKW
79	[12]	Nov.	1831		28	69	69	1835 D&C 28
80	12	Nov.	1831		26	70	70	1835 D&C 26
81	1	Dec.	1831		90	71	71	NKW
8	24	Dec.	1831		89	72:1-8	72:1-2	NKW
83	4	Dec.	1831		89	72:9-26	72:3-5	NKW
84	10	Jan.	1832		29	73	73	NKW
85	25	Jan.	1832		87	75:1-22	75:1-3	NKW
86	25	Jan.	1832		87	75:23-36	75:4-5	NKW
87	16	Feb.	1832		91	76	76	E&M Star
88	27	Feb.	1832					KRB, 10
89	[Feb.-Mar.]		1832		73	74	74	KRB, 94-95
90	1	Mar.	1832		75	78	77	NKW
91	7	Mar.	1832		77	80	79	KRB, 18-19
92	[ca 8]	Mar.	1832					NKW
93	12	Mar.	1832		76	79	78	KRB, 12
94	15	Mar.	1832		79	81	80	Manuscript
95	[ca 20]	Mar.	1832			77		Manuscript
96	20	Mar.	1832					NKW
97	26	Apr.	1832		86	82	81	1835 D&C 86
98	30	Apr.	1832		88	83	82	NKW
99	29	Aug.	1832		78	99	96	KRB, 19-20
100	22-23	Sept.	1832		4	84	83	NKW
101	27	Nov.	1832			85		Manuscript
102	6	Dec.	1832		6	86	84	KRB, 31-32
103	25	Dec.	1832			87		KRB, 32-33
104	27-28	Dec.	1832		7	88:1-126	85:1-38	KRB, 33-46
105	3	Jan.	1833		7	88:127-137, 141	85:39-44, 46	KRB, 47-48
106	6	Jan.	1833					Manuscript
107	27	Feb.	1833					KRB,48-49
108	27	Feb.	1833		80	89	86	KRB,49-51
109	8	Mar.	1833		84	90	87	NKW
110	9	Mar.	1833		92	91	88	KRB, 55
111	15	Mar.	1833		93	92	89	KRB, 55
112	6	May	1833		82	93	90	NKW
113	[1-3]	June	1833		95	95	92	KRB, 59-60

Document Number	Day	Month	Year	BC 1833*	D&C 1835*	LDS D&C 1876/1981	RLDS D&C 1864/1990	Source Used
114	4	June	1833		96	96	93	KRB, 60-61
115	2	Aug.	1833		81	97	94	Manuscript
116	2	Aug.	1833		83	94	91	Manuscript
117	6	Aug.	1833		85	98	95	Manuscript
118	12	Oct.	1833		94	100	97	NKW
119	16	Dec.	1833		97	101	98	KRB, 73-83
120	24	Feb.	1834			103	100	Manuscript
121	23	Apr.	1834		98	104	101	Manuscript
122	28	Apr.	1834					Manuscript

Church of the Latter Day Saints Period:

Document Number	Day	Month	Year	BC 1833*	D&C 1835*	LDS D&C 1876/1981	RLDS D&C 1864/1990	Source Used
123	22	June	1834			105	102	KRB, 97-100
124	25	Nov.	1834		99	106	103	KRB, 116
125	5	Dec.	1834					Manuscript
126	[28-30]	Apr.	1835		3	107	104	1835 D&C 3
127	27	Oct.	1835					JS Journal
128	1	Nov.	1835					JS Journal
129	2	Nov.	1835					JS Journal
130	3	Nov.	1835					JS Journal
131	7	Nov.	1835					JS Journal
132	8	Nov.	1835					JS Journal
133	14	Nov.	1835					JS Journal
134	16	Nov.	1835					JS Journal
135	16	Nov.	1835					JS Journal
136	26	Dec.	1835			108		JS Journal
137	21	Jan.	1836			137		JS Journal
138	3	Apr.	1836			110		JS Journal
139	6	Aug.	1836			111		Manuscript
140	23	July	1837			112	105	SB
141	4	Sept.	1837					SB
142	7	Jan.	1838					Manuscript
143	12	Jan.	1838					Manuscript
144	12	Jan.	1838					Manuscript
145	12	Jan.	1838					Manuscript
146	[14-31]	Mar.	1838			113		SB
147	11	Apr.	1838			114		SB
148	17	Apr.	1838					SB

Early Church of Jesus Christ of Latter Day Saints Period:

Document Number	Day	Month	Year	BC 1833*	D&C 1835*	LDS D&C 1876/1981	RLDS D&C 1864/1990	Source Used
149	26	Apr.	1838			115		SB
150	8	July	1838			118		SB
151	8	July	1838					SB

Document Number	Day	Month	Year	BC 1833*	D&C 1835*	LDS D&C 1876/1981	RLDS D&C 1864/1990	Source Used
152	8	July	1838			119	106	SB
153	8	July	1838			120		SB
154	8	July	1838			117		SB
155	20	Mar.	1839			121–122		Manuscript
156	19	Jan.	1841			124		1844 D&C103
157	[1-6]	Mar.	1841			125		Manuscript
158	20	Mar.	1841					Manuscript
159	9	July	1841			126		BLL
160	2	Dec.	1841					BLL
161	22	Dec.	1841					BLL
162	22	Dec.	1841					BLL
163	28	Jan.	1842					BLL
164	7	Apr.	1842					Manuscript
165	19	May	1842					BLL
166	27	July	1842					Manuscript
167	1	Sept.	1842			127		Manuscript
168	6	Sept.	1842			128		BLL
169	12	July	1843			132		Manuscript
170	[ca 25]	Nov.	1843					Manuscript

*Appears as Roman numerals in the original volumes.

HISTORICAL
BACKGROUND

1. Evolution of the Canon

Individual followers of Joseph Smith's revelations believe them to be God's word but are often ignorant of the original text. The originals are not only generally the most authentic and uncontaminated, they also best represent the milieu of and open a window on human consciousness for that particular time and place. Yet so little thought is given today to the original texts because, in part, Smith's revelations are assumed to be unchanged. They are considered sacrosanct—beyond scholarship—and if church leaders made changes, they must have had good reason. But who can study these old manuscripts and rare books without sensing something new in the original intent and recognizing how different it often is from later interpretations? Who can read these documents without detecting the human striving for an encounter with the divine that is reflected in the revelations in their historical setting? It is the original, fresh prophetic voice which is encountered in this work. This chapter outlines the history of the original texts. The details of this historical setting help explain how and why the texts were subsequently changed. The remaining chapters contain the texts themselves, with analysis of selected variants as warranted.

On 6 April 1830 at Manchester, New York, a revelation regarding Joseph Smith, Jr., and the Church of Christ declared: "Wherefore, meaning the church, thou shalt give heed unto all his [Joseph Smith's] words, and commandments, which he shall give unto you, as he receiveth them, walking in all holiness before me."[1] This emphasis on heeding Smith's words as they are given to him by God underscores the importance of understanding the revelations in their historical context and original import. Unfortunately, for the majority of the documents, there appear to be no extant original manuscripts as they were first recorded. However, we have the next best thing: handwritten copies and early printed editions. By examining these texts, one can often reconstruct the original wording.

Many of these documents were printed by William W. Phelps and Company in 1832 and 1833 in Independence, Missouri. They appeared in the Mormon periodical *The Evening and the Morning Star*. Before that, in July 1830, at Harmony, Pennsylvania, the revelations were arranged and copied with the assistance of John Whitmer. These included what became BC 2-27.[2]

---

1. BC 22:4; also in LDS D&C 21:4; and RLDS D&C 19:2; subparagraph letters of RLDS D&C not included.

2. See Manuscript History, Book A-1:50, written in 1839, LDS archives; Dean C. Jessee, ed., *The Papers of Joseph Smith: Autobiographical and Historical Writings* (Salt Lake City: Deseret Book Co., 1989), 1:319; and Dan Vogel, ed., *Early Mormon Documents* (Salt Lake City: Signature Books, 1996), 1:127.

In a revelation dictated at Fayette, New York, in September, Smith was likened to Moses in his prophetic primacy: "no one shall be appointed to received commandments and revelations in this church, excepting my servant Joseph, for he receiveth them even as Moses."[3] In this same revelation Oliver Cowdery was called to "go unto the Lamanites and preach" and establish the church among them.[4] A city called New Jerusalem was to be built "on the borders by the Lamanites." Later three others were called to accompany Cowdery. Cowdery himself stated that he was going "to rear up a pillar as a witness where the Temple of God shall be built, in the glorious New-Jerusalem."[5]

After receiving correspondence from Cowdery, Smith had another revelation in March 1831 instructing church members to gather up their riches so they could purchase an inheritance to be designated later: "[I]t shall be called the New Jerusalem, a land of peace, a city of refuge, a place of safety for the saints of the most high God ... And it shall come to pass that the righteous shall be gathered out from among all nations, and shall come to Zion singing, with songs of everlasting joy."[6]

Another revelation in June, in Kirtland, Ohio, stated that Phelps, a recent convert but not yet baptized, should be "ordained to assist my servant Oliver [Cowdery] to do the work of printing."[7] The instructions were: "let my servant William ... be established as a printer unto the church ... and let my servant Oliver assist him even as I have commanded in whatsoever place I shall appoint unto him to copy and to correct and select" the writings to be published.[8] Land was to be purchased at Independence, Missouri, the new Zion, "for the house of the printing."[9]

During the first half of November in Hiram, Ohio, a series of church conferences were held. Three of these dealt with printing the revelations. On 1 November it was voted that 10,000 copies of the revelations should be published in a book known as the Book of Commandments. As stated in the minutes: "[B]r[other] Oliver Cowdery made a request desiring the mind of the Lord through this conference of Elders to know how many copies of the Book of commandments it was the will of the Lord should be published in the first edition of that work. Voted that there be ten thousand copies struck."[10] The preface to the manuscript was then received which began: "Behold, this is mine authority, and the authority of my ser-

---

3. BC 30:2; LDS D&C 28:2; RLDS D&C 27:2.

4. BC 30:7; LDS D&C 28:8; RLDS D&C 27:3. "Lamanites" is a Book of Mormon term for Native Americans.

5. Statement signed by Oliver Cowdery, 17 Oct. 1830; see Ezra Booth to Rev. Ira Eddy, 29 Nov. 1831, in the *Ohio Star* (Ravenna, OH) 2 (8 Dec. 1831: 1; quoted in Richard L. Anderson, "The Impact of the First Preaching in Ohio," *BYU Studies* 11 (Summer 1971): 477.

6. BC 48:59, 67; also published in *Evening and the Morning Star* 1 (June 1832): [2]. Independence, Missouri; see LDS D&C 45:66, 71; RLDS D&C 45:12, 14.

7. BC 57:5; LDS D&C 55:4; RLDS D&C 55:2.

8. KRB, 90, 91; LDS D&C 57:11, 13; RLDS D&C 57:5.

9. BC 59:49; LDS D&C 58:37; RLDS D&C 58:7.

10. "The Conference Minutes and Record Book of Christ's Church of Latter Day Saints" (known as the "Far West Record"), 15, manuscript in possession of LDS church. See Donald Q. Cannon and Lyndon W. Cook, eds., *Far West Record: Minutes of the Church of Jesus Christ of Latter-day Saints, 1830-1844* (Salt Lake City: Deseret Book Co., 1983), 27.

vants, and my Preface unto the Book of my Commandments, which I have given them to publish unto you, O inhabitants of the earth."[11]

In the afternoon "A number of the brethren arose and said that they were willing to testify to the world that they knew that they [the revelations] were of the Lord."[12] A revelation was received which said: "And now I the Lord give unto you a testimony of these commandments which are lying before you."[13] The next day "the brethren then arose in turn and bore witness to the truth of the Book of Commandments."[14] On 3 November Joseph Smith received a revelation designated as the "Appendix."[15] And at an 8 November meeting, it was "Resolved by this conference that Br[other] Joseph Smith Jr correct those errors or mistakes which he may discover by the holy Spirit while reviewing the revelations & commandments & also the fulness of the scriptures."[16]

On 12 November it was made known with regard to Oliver Cowdery's trip to Independence, Missouri, that: "[I]t is not wisdom in me that he should be entrusted with the commandments and the moneys which he shall carry unto the land of Zion, except one go with him who will be true and faithful: wherefore I the Lord willeth that my servant John Whitmer, should go with my servant Oliver Cowdery."[17] Subsequently Cowdery and Whitmer were commissioned: "Voted that Joseph Smith jr. be appointed to dedicate & consecrate these brethren & the sacred writings & all they have entrusted to their care, to the Lord: done accordingly."[18]

On the same date Joseph Smith, Jr., Martin Harris, Oliver Cowdery, John Whitmer, Sidney Rigdon, and William W. Phelps were made "stewards over the revelations and commandments which I have given unto them, and which I shall hereafter give unto them," to manage the publishing business and receive the benefits thereof.[19] Whitmer and Cowdery left Ohio on 20 November and arrived in Independence on 5 January 1832.[20] Cowdery wrote to Smith: "We expect soon

---

11. BC 1:2; LDS D&C 1:6; RLDS D&C 1:2.

12. Cannon and Cook, *Far West Record*, 27. David Whitmer wrote fifty-five years later that he objected to the printing of the revelations. See *An Address To All Believers in Christ* (Richmond, MO: author, 1887), 54-55. It appears that Whitmer went along with the consensus of the conference. Both Whitmer and William E. McLellin were present when the testimony to the revelations was given at the church conference.

13. 1835 D&C 25:2; LDS D&C 67:4; RLDS D&C 67:2.

14. Cannon and Cook, *Far West Record*, 28. Cf. Manuscript History, Book A-1:162-63; Jessee, *Papers of Joseph Smith*, 1:367-68.

15. "Having given, in a previous number, the Preface to the book of Commandments now in press, we give below the close, or as it has been called, the Appendix" (*The Evening and the Morning Star* 1 [May 1833]: 1 [89]). The manuscript of most of this revelation is in RLDS archives.

16. Cannon and Cook, *Far West Record*, 29.

17. 1835 D&C 28:1; LDS D&C 69:1-2; RLDS D&C 69:1.

18. Cannon and Cook, *Far West Record*, 32.

19. 1835 D&C 26:1; LDS D&C 70:3; RLDS D&C 70:1.

20. "The Book of John Whitmer Kept by Commandment," chapter 10, p. 38, RLDS archives; published in *Journal of History* 1 (Apr. 1908): 135. Regarding the date of 20 November, Richard P. Howard has written: "it appears to have been originally 20; but later was made into 10 by someone making a wide old 1 covering all but the presumed tail of the 2" (Howard to Marquardt, 6 Feb. 1981).

to be ready to print and hope that brother Martin [Harris] can supply with paper."[21]

"Shall we procure the paper required of our breatheren [brethren] in thus [their] letter and carry it with us or not and if we do what moneys shall we use for that purpose[?]" Smith asked God in Hiram, Ohio, on 20 March 1832. The answer was: "It is expedient saith the Lord unto you that the paper shall be purchased for the printing of the book of the Lord[']s commandments and it must needs be that you take it with [you] for it is not expedient that my servant Martin [Harris] should as yet go up unto the land of Zion[.] let the purchase be made by the Bishop of [if] it must needs be by hire[;] let whatsoever is done be done in the name of the Lord[.]"[22] The next month Smith and counselors Jesse Gause and Sidney Rigdon traveled to Independence and brought paper with them for publishing *The Evening and the Morning Star* and the Book of Commandments.

At a council of the Literary Firm on 30 April, it was "Ordered by the Council that three thousand copies of the book of Commandments be printed the first edition." Phelps, Cowdery, and Whitmer were "appointed to review the Book of Commandments & select for printing such as shall be deemed by them proper, as dictated by the Spirit & make all necessary verbal corrections."[23] Copies of revelations received since November 1831 were brought to Independence by the presidency of the High Priesthood. These included the vision of the three degrees of glory and a revelation to Gause as Smith's counselor which were copied by Whitmer for the BC.[24]

The Evening and the Morning Star was published for the first time in June 1832. On the first page, under the title "Revelations," appeared "The Articles and Covenants of the Church of Christ." In the July issue Smith and Rigdon's "Vision" of the three degrees of glory was published. Each issue from June 1832 to July 1833 had either a complete revelation or a portion of one, most of which were subsequently published in the BC.[25]

The printing of "A Book of Commandments, for the Government of the Church of Christ" (BC) commenced, but was a slow project.[26] Type was set on sheets of thirty-two pages each, sixteen pages per side, to be folded into signatures as follows:

---

21. Oliver Cowdery to Joseph Smith, 28 Jan. 1832, LDS archives. See Cannon and Cook, *Far West Record*, 238.

22. Manuscript in NKW.

23. Cannon and Cook, *Far West Record*, 46.

24. BC manuscript fragments in RLDS archives.

25. Peter Crawley, "A Bibliography of The Church of Jesus Christ of Latter-day Saints in New York, Ohio, and Missouri," *BYU Studies* 12 (Summer 1972): 477-78; also Affidavit of W. W. Phelps, 28 Sept. 1832. On this same press, the *Upper Missouri Advertiser*, a weekly newspaper, was published.

26. *The Evening and the Morning Star* 1 (Dec. 1832): 8 [56] and 1 (May 1833): 1 [89]. On 1 December 1832 Joseph Smith recorded in his diary: "wrote and corrected revelations &c."(Joseph Smith 1832-34 Diary, 3, LDS archives; Dean C. Jessee, ed., *The Papers of Joseph Smith: Journal, 1832-1842* [Salt Lake City: Deseret Book Co., 1992], 2:4).

Sheet A, pages 1– 32	Title page and BC 1:1 to 12:5
Sheet B, pages 33– 64	BC 12:5 to 29:40
Sheet C, pages 65– 96	BC 29:40 to 45:6
Sheet D, pages 97-128	BC 45:6 to 56:3
Sheet E, pages 129-160	BC 56:4 to 65:47[27]

On 20 July 1833 citizens of Jackson County, Missouri, met at the court house in Independence and formed a committee to ask the Mormons to shut down the printing office and leave the county.[28] When the latter proved unwilling to do so, the non-Mormon community voted to demolish the printing office. On Saturday, 20 July, about 400 people went to the residence and printing house of W. W. Phelps and Company, threw the press from the upper-story, scattered the type, and destroyed most of the building.[29]

The mob thus succeeded in stopping publication of the *Evening and the Morning Star*, the BC, and the *Upper Missouri Advertiser* (published weekly by Phelps). The last verse on sheet E of the BC read: "For verily I say that the rebellious are not of the blood of Ephraim."[30] The Mormons' press was later used when "Davis and Kelly" took it to Liberty, Missouri, to publish the *Upper Missouri Enquirer*.[31]

Sheets of the unfinished BC were salvaged from the wreckage of the office and collected as they blew about the streets of Independence. From these sheets a small number of copies of the book were assembled, though the five printed sheets (160 pages) represented only a portion of the anticipated final work.[32] The few copies thus assembled were used by church members in reading and studying Smith's revelations.[33] Though the books had different title pages and bindings, they constituted "the first book printed in the immense territory between St. Louis and the Pacific coast."[34]

---

27. John McDonnell to the Editor, *Saints Herald* 124 (Dec. 1977): 44.

28. Warren A. Jennings, "Factors in the Destruction of the Mormon Press in Missouri, 1833," *Utah Historical Quarterly* 35 (Winter 1967): 57-76.

29. Petition dated 28 Sept. 1833 in *The Evening and the Morning Star* (Kirtland, OH) 2 (Dec. 1833): 114; in *History of the Church of Jesus Christ of Latter-day Saints*, ed. B. H. Roberts (Salt Lake City: Deseret Book Co., 1959), 1:412; and *Times and Seasons* 1 (Dec. 1839): 18 in *History of the Church*, 1:390, footnote.

30. BC 65:47 (page 160); also BC manuscript in RLDS archives. The surviving manuscript pages are in RLDS church archives. They were obtained with the David Whitmer papers in 1903 and included some items brought to Independence by John Whitmer and Oliver Cowdery early in 1832. For a photo of a page used for Sheet E see: *Journal of History* 14 (Apr. 1921), opposite page 129, and *Restoration Scriptures: A Study of Their Textual Development* (Independence, MO: Herald Publishing House, 1969), 266 and (2nd ed., 1995), 311. See Appendix B.

31. Manuscript History, Book A–1:412, in *History of the Church*, 1:470.

32. Peter Crawley and Chad J. Flake, *Notable Mormon Books 1830-1857* (Provo, UT: Friends of the Brigham Young University Library, 1974), 6. See also Peter Crawley, "Joseph Smith and A Book of Commandments," *The Princeton University Library Chronicle* 42 (Autumn 1980): 18-32.

33. Elden J. Watson, comp., *The Orson Pratt Journals* (Salt Lake City: comp., 1975), 38, entry for 2 Apr. 1834; *The Evening and the Morning Star* (Kirtland, OH) 2 (Aug. 1834): 184, an Appeal dated July 1834; also Lectures on Theology, "Lecture Third," 1835 D&C, 36, 42. See also John Whitmer's Account Book, LDS archives.

34. "Missouri History Not Found in Textbooks," *Missouri Historical Review* 44 (Oct. 1949): 94; extract from the *Kansas City Star*, 1 July 1949, by John Edward Hicks.

By October plans were underway to get another press to publish the revelations at church headquarters in Kirtland. Frederick G. Williams wrote, "The book of commandments were nearly half finished at the time of the riot but were destroyed with the press and will probably be reprinted here as we have sent to New York for a press."[35] Although only a few BC manuscript pages survived, the five printed sheets were an invaluable primary source used in preparing the Doctrine and Covenants along with the "Kirtland Revelations" book. This manuscript book contains documents recorded beginning in the fall of 1832.

Besides portions of the BC manuscript, there are early manuscript copies of revelations in the papers of Newel K. Whitney, the "Bishop at Kirtland." These copies were written as early as 1831-32 and are among the earliest extant. It is possible that some of the Whitney manuscripts were the original texts for some of the revelations.[36]

The Kirtland Revelations Book contains manuscript copies of revelations, as well. The book was begun in late 1832 with all but thirteen pages recorded by 18 August 1834, and for many of the revelations, this is the only manuscript known to exist. However, the texts were copied into the KRB months or years after they were first received. Some of these revelations were additionally corrected at a later date in Smith's handwriting.[37]

Other manuscripts, books, or journals that contain copies of Smith's revelations and were written by early church members include William E. McLellin's journal and manuscripts, from 1831-32; Zebedee Coltrin's journal containing two documents copied in Independence on 12 January 1832; the "Book of Commandments, Laws and Covenants" designated "Book A," made in 1832; "Book B" containing revelations copied by 12 June 1833; and "Book C" made in 1834.[38]

The above works were evidently intended more for private use than as sources for the 1835 D&C. However, the BC manuscript was a printer's manuscript for the forthcoming publication and the Kirtland Revelations Book, with its handwritten changes in the texts, was a church manuscript book with notations that certain documents were to be included in the D&C.

For the period after the 1835 D&C was published, I have consulted the Joseph Smith journal for the years 1835-36 and the Scriptory Book of Joseph Smith for 1838. "The Book of the Law of the Lord," 1841-42, contains revelatory documents as well. All sources (and their locations) used in this book are identified in the following table:

---

35. Williams to John Murdock, Kirtland, Ohio, 10 Oct. 1833, Joseph Smith Letterbook 1:62, LDS archives.

36. Chad J. Flake, "The Newell K. Whitney Collection," *BYU Studies* 11 (Summer 1971): 325.

37. Frederick G. Williams [III], "Frederick Granger Williams of the First Presidency of the Church," *BYU Studies* 12 (Spring 1972): 250n21. At the end of the revelation of 29 August 1832, it is stated: "by Joseph the seer and writ[t]en by F. G. Williams Scribe." Most of the copies of revelations up to 15 March 1833 are in Frederick G. Williams's handwriting.

38. Earl E. Olson, "The Chronology of the Ohio Revelations," *BYU Studies* 11 (Summer 1971):332-35. See also Robert J. Woodford, "The Historical Development of the Doctrine and Covenants," Ph.D. diss., Brigham Young University, 1974, 98-106.

Textual Sources Used in This Study

Printed Sources

A Book of Commandments (1833)
1835 Doctrine and Covenants
1844 Doctrine and Covenants
The Evening and the Morning Star

Manuscript Sources

LDS Archives

"Book of Commandments, Law and Covenants, Book B"
"Book of Commandments, Law and Covenants, Book C"
Zebedee Coltrin Journal
Kirtland Revelations Book
William E. McLellin Journal
William E. McLellin Collection
Manuscript History, Book A-1; Book C-1
Manuscript revelations
William W. Phelps Journal
Scriptory Book of Joseph Smith
Joseph Smith 1835-36 Journal
Joseph Smith Letterbook 1
Frederick G. Williams Papers

Archives of the First Presidency, LDS Church

Book of the Law of the Lord
William Clayton Journal

Harold B. Lee Library, Brigham Young University

Newel K. Whitney Collection

RLDS Archives

Book of Commandments manuscript pages
Manuscript letter to John E. Page

With the destruction of the church's press in Independence, a council of the United Firm met in Kirtland on 11 September 1833. Frederick G. Williams, Joseph Smith, Sidney Rigdon, and Newel K. Whitney, along with Oliver Cowdery (who was a "delegate to represent the residue of the said firm in Independence") conceived two publications to be printed by Williams. These were to be titled "The Latter-day Saints Messenger and Advocate" and "the Star formerly published in Jackson County, Missouri." Cowdery was designated the editor of both. The expectation was that the printing would eventually be transferred back to Independence.[39]

---

39. Kirtland Council Minute Book [3 Dec. 1832-27 Nov. 1837], LDS archives, typescript, 24.; see also Manuscript History, Book A-1:345; *History of the Church* 1:409; Lyndon W. Cook, *The Revelations of the Prophet Joseph Smith* (Provo, UT: Seventy's Mission Bookstore, 1981), 114-15.

On 19 April 1834 in the "wilderness" at Norton, Ohio, Cowdery and Rigdon were commissioned to assist each other "in arranging the church covenants which are to be soon published."[40] A conference of elders would be held at Norton two days later. Soon afterwards a revelation dated 23 April 1834 called on the United Firm's Kirtland printing office under Williams and Cowdery to print "the revelations which I have given unto you, & which I shall hereafter, from time to time, give unto you."[41] Also they were instructed to secure copyrights, "that others may not take the blessings away from you which I have confer[r]ed upon you."[42]

At a high council meeting held on 24 September:

> The council then proceeded to appoint a committee to arrange the items of the doctrine of Jesus Christ for the government of the church of Latter-Day Saints which church was organized and commenced its rise on the 6th of April 1830. These items are to be taken from the Bible, book of mormon, and the revelations which have been given to the church up to this date or shall be, until such arrangement is made. Brother Samuel H. Smith then nominated brothers Joseph Smith Junr[,] Oliver Cowdery[,] Sidney Rigdon and Frederick G. Williams to compose said committee which was seconded by brother Hyrum Smith. The Counselors then gave their vote which was also agreed to by the whole conference. The council then decided that said committee, after arranging and publishing said book of covenants, have the avails [royalties] of the same.[43]

The council thus sustained Cowdery and Rigdon who had been appointed four months previously at Norton.

In the September 1834 issue of the *Evening and the Morning Star*—printed in Kirtland—a "Prospectus for Re-printing the First and Second Volumes of The Evening and the Morning Star" appeared. According to the editor, the twenty-four numbers were to be reprinted with typographical corrections: "There are many typographical errors in both volumes, and especially in the last, which we shall endeavor carefully to correct, as well as principle, if we discover any.—It is also proper for us to say, that in the first 14 numbers, in the Revelations, are many errors, typographical, and others, occasioned by transcribing manuscript; but as we shall have access to originals, we shall endeavor to make proper corrections."[44]

Whether or not this was Cowdery's initial intent, careful study shows that if any original manuscripts (previous to 1835) were used, their exact wording was not ad-

---

40. Joseph Smith 1832-34 Diary, 76-79, handwriting of Oliver Cowdery; Jessee, *Papers of Joseph Smith*, 2:31-32. See also Manuscript History, Book A-1:460; and *History of the Church*, 2:50-51.

41. "Book of Commandments, Law and Covenants; Book C," LDS archives; 1835 D&C 98:10; LDS D&C 104:58; RLDS D&C 101:10. Cf. LDS D&C 104:58 with LDS D&C 70:3; RLDS D&C 70:1.

42. "Book of Commandments, Law and Covenants; Book C." See also Kirtland Revelations Book, 105, LDS archives. The copyright wording was not included in the 1835 D&C after 98:10.

43. Kirtland Council Minute Book, 76. See also Manuscript History, Book B-1:556-57; *History of the Church*, 2:165.

44. Prospectus dated Kirtland, Ohio, 26 Sept. 1834, in *The Evening and the Morning Star* 2 (Sept. 1834): 192. The prospectus was dated two days after the 24 September 1834 high council meeting.

hered to. *The Evening and the Morning Star*, reprinted in Kirtland between January and June 1835 under the title *Evening and Morning Star*, altered the texts, deleted previously published material, and inserted editorial comments by Cowdery.

For instance, in the January 1835 reissue for June 1832, the following remarks concerning Smith's revelations were added:

> On the revelations we merely say, that we were not a little surprised to find the previous print so different from the original. We have given them a careful comparison, assisted by individuals whose known integrity and ability is uncensurable. Thus saying we cast no reflections upon those who were entrusted with the responsibility of publishing them in Missouri, as our own labors were included in that important service to the church, and it was our unceasing endeavor to have them correspond with the copy furnished us. We believe they are now correct. If not in every word, at least in principle. For the special good of the church we have also added a few items from other revelations.[45]

Concerning these remarks, RLDS church historian Richard P. Howard has written:

> It may be that Cowdery's surprise at the remarkable differences between the "original" and that which had been previously published arose from the fact that in late 1834 or early 1835, as he was beginning to republish the revelations, he was working from a *different* "original"—different, that is, from the one he and John Whitmer had copied from in 1831 in preparing the Book of Commandments manuscript for the Independence printer.[46]

The new copy was probably the manuscript being prepared for the 1835 D&C.

On 4 February 1835 Cowdery wrote to Bishop Newel K. Whitney requesting the original manuscript known as the Law of the Church:

> Bishop Whitney:
> Will you have the kindness to send us, by the bearer, the original copy of the Revelation given 12 elders Feb. 1831 called "The Law of the Church"? We are preparing the old Star for re-printing, and have no copy from which to correct, and kno[w] of no other beside yours.
> Your Ob't Serv't.
> Kirtland, Feb. 4, 1835.   Oliver Cowdery.[47]

It is not known if Cowdery received the original from Whitney. But the revised, expanded text contained material anachronistic to the original 1831 setting. Cowdery wrote in the March reprint: "Those who read this paper will see that it contains items of covenant of deep interest to the church of the saints, and as they have frequently been ridiculed in consequence of certain items contained in the one setting forth their faith on the subject of bestowing temporal gifts for the benefit of the poor, it is a matter of joy to us to be able to present this document accord-

---

45. *Evening and Morning Star* (Kirtland reprint) 1 (June 1832): 16, reprinted Jan. 1835.
46. Howard, *Restoration Scriptures* (1969), 202; see also (2nd ed., 1995), 150.
47. NKW. See photo of letter in Chad J. Flake, "The Newell K. Whitney Collection," *BYU Studies* 11 (Summer 1971): 325.

ing to the original."[48] Cowdery's statement that he was presenting the 9 February 1831 revelation, "according to the original," makes sense only if by "original" he meant a new printer's manuscript prepared for the forthcoming D&C. The changes in many of the revelations reflected later theology, modifications in church government, recognition of former discrepancies, and sensitivity to criticism engendered by the originals.

In reconstructing the events of 1835, it may be helpful to know something about the key players, specifically members of the First Presidency. Joseph Smith, Jr., was the prophet through whom the revelations came, and most of the D&C, whether revelations or other documents, is believed to have been originally dictated by him. His own handwriting appears in the entry of a 4 December 1831 revelation copied into the Kirtland Revelations Book. Corrections for a number of sections previously recorded in 1832 are in his hand, as well. He blessed Sidney Rigdon and Oliver Cowdery for their work in arranging the revelations and was the presiding officer both of the Kirtland High Council and of the church.

Smith, and evidently Rigdon, assembled seven Lectures on Faith for use in the elders school during the winter of 1834-35. These were "delivered before a Theological class" in Kirtland.[49] In January 1835 Smith was engaged "in preparing the Lectures on Theology for publication in the Book of Doctrine and covenants, which the committee[,] appointed last September[,] were now compiling."[50] The preface to the 1835 D&C, drafted by the committee, said: "The first part of the book will be found to contain a series of Lectures as delivered before a Theological class in this place, and in consequence of their embracing the important doctrine of salvation, we have arranged them into the following work."[51]

Cowdery had been a close associate of Smith since April 1829 and a number of early revelations are in his handwriting. Though he was not in Ohio when many of the revelations were originally given, he copied a few of them into the Kirtland Revelations Book. He was set apart in April 1834 to assist Rigdon in compiling the book of covenants and was publicly selected for the committee on 24 September. On 5 December 1834 he was ordained an assistant president to Smith and thus became a member of the First Presidency. As a member of the D&C committee, his name appears on the preface to the 1835 edition. He edited the newspapers at Kirtland, including the *Messenger and Advocate*, until June 1835. At that time he relinquished the paper to church historian John Whitmer. Cowdery also edited the reprint of the *Evening and Morning Star* and, in February 1835, the short-lived community-oriented *Northern Times*. As one of the three witnesses to the Book of Mormon, he helped select the first twelve apostles of the church. In addition, he

---

48. *Evening and Morning Star* (Kirtland reprint) 1 (Aug. 1832): 48, reprinted Mar 1835.

49. Alan J. Phipps, "The Lectures on Faith: An Authorship Study," M.A. thesis, Brigham Young University, 1977, and Leland H. Gentry, "What of the Lectures on Faith," *BYU Studies* 19 (Fall 1978): 5-19. See also Richard S. Van Wagoner, Steven C. Walker, and Allen D. Roberts, "'The Lectures on Faith': A Case Study in Decanonization," *Dialogue: A Journal of Mormon Thought* 20 (Fall 1987): 71-77.

50. Manuscript History, Book B-1:563, written in 1843, LDS archives; *History of the Church,* 2:180.

51. 1835 D&C, [iii].

served on the Kirtland High Council.

Rigdon was a noted religious personality in his own right before joining with the Mormons. He became closely associated with Joseph Smith soon after they first met in December 1830; by March 1832 he had become a counselor to Smith. Since he was one of Smith's scribes, his handwriting appears in early drafts. Along with Cowdery, he was set apart to assist in compiling the book of covenants. He also worked on the Lectures on Faith, wrote theological articles for church publications, and, as a member of the First Presidency, attended Kirtland High Council meetings.

Frederick G. Williams was a scribe whose work started in July 1832 at a time when Rigdon for a short period was out of harmony with the church. In the winter of 1832-33, Williams was made a counselor to Smith. Most of the Kirtland Revelations Book is in his handwriting. As a member of the First Presidency, he was also involved in Kirtland High Council meetings.

Although not a member of the revision committee, William W. Phelps, former editor of the *Evening and the Morning Star*, came to Kirtland in mid-May 1835 "and assisted the Committee in compiling the Book of Doctrine and Covenants."[52] The next month he copied revelations into his diary and compared documents for the D&C. With his experience in operating a press, he also worked at the printing office on the D&C and the *Northern Times*.

As members of the First Presidency of the church, and especially as members of the committee in whose charge the revelations were placed, these men were responsible for the 1835 publication. A preface prepared by this committee guaranteed that as presiding elders they had "carefully selected" and "compiled" the *Doctrine and Covenants of the Church of the Latter Day Saints*. The copyright was obtained on 14 January 1835.[53]

On 17 August a General Assembly was called in Kirtland. In this period of church history, the term "General Assembly" meant a gathering "of the several [priesthood] quorums which constitute the spiritual authorities of the church."[54] One of the purposes was to determine if the D&C then at press would be approved by church authorities.

The minutes are recorded in the Kirtland Council Minute Book, and a printed version was published in the August 1835 issue of the *Messenger and Advocate* with an abbreviated version in the 1835 D&C. Errors in the minutes were noticed too late to be corrected as they "escaped the eye of the proof reader" and were placed at the end of the book (xxv) as "Notes to the Reader."[55] The Kirtland Council Minute Book contains the following:

52. Manuscript History, Book B-1:592; *History of the Church*, 2:227.
53. Woodford, "The Historical Development of the Doctrine and Covenants," 48.
54. 1835 D&C 3:11, ([28-30] Apr. 1835); LDS D&C 107:32; RLDS D&C 104:11.
55. The minutes were deleted from the 1844 Nauvoo edition of the D&C. The assembly minutes were first printed in RLDS D&C in the 1894 edition. In the 1911 RLDS edition, the minutes were numbered section "108A," and in the 1970 RLDS D&C they were moved to the Introduction (9-12). They were subsequently removed altogether and are not included in the 1990 RLDS edition.

Convened in Kirtland August 17th A.D. 1835 by the presidency of the Church of the Latter-Day Saints, for the purpose of Examining a book of commandments and covenants which has been compiled and written. ... This committee having finished said Book according to the instructions given them, it was deemed necessary to call the general assembly of the Church to see whether the book be approved or not by the Authoroties [Authorities] of the church, that it may, if approved, become a law unto the church, and a rule of faith and practice unto the same.[56]

The presiding officers, Cowdery and Rigdon, were of course members of the committee that had prepared the D&C. Smith and Williams were in Michigan, and all of the newly ordained apostles were absent on a mission.[57] Cowdery and Rigdon "proceeded to organize the whole assembly," including at least 118 priesthood members, into their respective quorums and non-priesthood groups.

Since not all twelve members of the Kirtland High Council could attend the assembly, eight substitutes stood in their place. In the Missouri High Council, as well, there were only three regular members present; four had been appointed apostles. Thus nine other priesthood holders served as substitutes for the Missouri council for the General Assembly. The seven presidents of the Seventy were represented by four regular members with three substitutes to fill this quorum. The bishop of Kirtland was present with his two counselors. Edward Partridge, bishop from Zion, was absent, but his position was represented by John Corrill. Other substitutes filled in for absentees among the elders, priests, teachers, and deacons presidencies.

In the morning session, ordinations and blessings took place. In the afternoon there was a vote on the D&C. President Cowdery "in behalf of the committee"[58] "arose with the Book of Doctrine and Covenants (284 pages) contain[in]g the faith[,] articles and covenants of the Latter Day Saints."[59] President Rigdon then "explained the manner by which they intended to obtain the voice of the assembly for or against said book."[60] William W. Phelps commented on the book and said "he had examined it carefully, that it was well arranged and calculated to govern

---

56. Kirtland Council Minute Book, 98.

57. The *History of the Church* manuscript for the 17 August 1835 General Assembly states that Smith and Williams were "absent on a visit to the Saints in Michigan." The words "Joseph absent" are in the side margin (Manuscript History, Book B-1:600). See also *History of the Church,* 2:243.

Max H. Parkin has written: "Some elders were dispatched on short-term tours of only a few weeks while others were sent out for longer durations" ("Conflict at Kirtland: A Study of the Nature and Causes of External and Internal Conflict of the Mormons in Ohio between 1830 and 1838" [Salt Lake City: author, 1966], 142). Whereas the *History of the Church* manuscript describes the Michigan trip as a "mission" (Manuscript History, Book B-1:606), the printed version (2:253) changes the word "mission" to "visit." Why such an important meeting did not occur previous to Smith's and Williams's departure is not known. Richard S. Van Wagoner wrote: "For whatever reason, Smith planned a brief missionary venture to Michigan to coincide with the 17 August meeting" ("Mormon Polyandry in Nauvoo," *Dialogue: A Journal of Mormon Thought* 18 [Fall 1985]: 71).

58. *Latter Day Saints' Messenger and Advocate* 1 (Aug. 1835): 161, Kirtland, Ohio.

59. Kirtland Council Minute Book, 103. This 284-page book included articles on "Marriage" and "Of Governments and Laws in General," minutes of the General Assembly, Index, Contents, and Notes to the Reader.

60. *Messenger and Advocate* 1 (Aug. 1835): 161.

the church in righteousness, [and] if followed would bring the members to see eye to eye. And further that he had received the testimony from God, that the Revelations and commandments contained therein are true ..." John Whitmer testified "that he was well acquainted with the work & knew it to be true and from God."[61] John Smith, "taking the lead of the high council in Kirtland," stated "that the lectures were judiciously arranged and compiled, and were profitable for doctrine."[62]

Voting took place as John Smith presented the following: "That they would receive the Book as the rule of theire [their] faith & practice and put themselves under the guidance of the same and also that they were satisfied with the committee that were chosen to compile it, as having discharged their duty faithfully." Levi Jackman "said that he had examined as many of the revelations contained in the book as were printed in Zion, & firmly believes them as he does the Book of Mormon or the Bible and also the whole contents of the Book." Neither set of minutes stated that Jackman actually compared the new document with the BC or any other record. The First Presidency and two high councils voted in favor of the book and the committee.

Phelps again arose and "read the written testimony of the Twelve Apostles in favor of the Book and the Committee who compiled it."[63] Other leaders stated, as they passed the book to each other, that they knew the book was true and were satisfied with it and the committee that compiled it. Votes of the different priesthood quorums were taken, all in the affirmative. Thomas Gates "took the book and expressed his satisfaction with it, and also called a vote of all the members present, both male & female, & They gave a decided voice in favor of it & also of the committee."[64] The *Messenger and Advocate* minutes stated: "The several authorities, and the general assembly, by a unanimous vote accepted of the labors of the committee."[65]

After this vote of confidence, Phelps read an article on marriage. It was voted upon and accepted. Cowdery then read an article on governments and laws in general. This was accepted as well. Both articles were "ordered to be printed in said book, by a unanimous vote."[66] After a hymn and prayer, the assembly was dismissed by Rigdon, having accepted the book as a whole but not having voted on the individual revelatory documents. Don H. Compier commented about this manner of canonizing the D&C:

It was the work of the committee—not the specific content of the Book of Doctrine and Covenants—that was considered by the quorums of the church on August 17, 1835. Their unanimous acceptance of the book that had not yet been published was in effect a decision to include the forthcoming publication in the church's canon of scripture. It is interesting to note that their action thus "canonized" not only Smith's revelations (se-

61. Kirtland Council Minute Book, 103.
62. *Messenger and Advocate* 1 (Aug. 1835): 161.
63. Kirtland Council Minute Book, 104.
64. Ibid., 106.
65. *Messenger and Advocate* 1 (Aug. 1835): 162.
66. Ibid., 162-63.

lected and worded as he chose) but also non-revelatory material, namely the "Lectures on Faith" and the articles on government and marriage.[67]

The following accounts reflect the attitudes of the people present at the General Assembly. Ira Ames wrote twenty-three years later: "I was present at a General Assembly of the Church on the 17th August 1835 to accept the Book of Doctrine & Covenants as our rule of faith. And gave my vote as president of the Priests Quorum. See D&C page 257 1st Edition."[68] Ebenezer Robinson, who worked in the printing office after his arrival in Kirtland in May 1835 (though not a member of the church until October), recorded fifty-three years later:

> On the 17th day of August, 1835, a general assembly of the church convened in the lower part of the temple, to hear the report of the compiling committee of said book, and determine, by vote, whether they "accepted and acknowledged it as the doctrine and covenants of their faith.["]
> After the only two members of the committee, who were present, viz: Oliver Cowdery and Sidney Rigdon, had reported, several official members of the church, Presidents of quorums, arose, one after another, and testified to the truth of the book, and they and their quorums "accepted and acknowledged it as the doctrine and covenants of their faith." Afterwards the question was put to the whole assembly and carried, unanimously.
> We attended that meeting, and noticed that a majority of those voting did so upon the testimony of those who bore record to the truth of the book, as they had neither time or opportunity to examine it for themselves. They had no means of knowing whether any alterations had been made in any of the revelations or not.
> Neither Joseph Smith jr. [n]or Frederick G. Williams, were present at this general assembly, as they had gone to Michigan.[69]

In September 1835 copies of the book arrived from the binder in Cleveland. William W. Phelps wrote: "We got some of the Commandments from Cleveland last week."[70] Wilford Woodruff received a copy on 23 September 1835 "as A Present from O[liver] Cowdery."[71]

There is no indication that anyone realized that the texts of some of the revelations had been revised, deleted, or enlarged. The revelations were accepted in their altered form without comment, apparently in the belief that they were identical to those originally given to the Saints. There was no explanation made by the committee, either in the preface or within the text of the revelations, as to why alterations had been made. Based on Cowdery's editorial comments, it seems that reve-

67. "Canonization in the Reorganized Church of Jesus Christ of Latter Day Saints," *Restoration Studies III* (Independence, MO: Herald Publishing House, 1986), 179.

68. "Journal and Record of the Life & Family of Ira Ames," microfilm A-311, Utah State Historical Society, Salt Lake City; original in LDS archives.

69. Ebenezer Robinson, ed., "Items of Personal History of the Editor," *The Return* 1 (June 1889): 88-89, Davis City, Iowa.

70. Phelps to Sally Phelps, 16 Sept. 1835; as cited in Bruce A. Van Orden, ed., "Writing to Zion: The William W. Phelps Kirtland Letters (1835-1836)," *BYU Studies* 33 (1993): 566.

71. Scott G. Kenney, ed., *Wilford Woodruff's Journal*, typescript, 1833-1898, 9 vols., 1983-85, (Midvale, UT: Signature Books) 1:43; original in LDS archives.

latory texts differing from those that had been previously published were changed without regard for earlier documents.

Seven years later Smith read proof sheets with Phelps in Nauvoo, Illinois, for a new edition of the D&C.[72] In September 1844, two months after Smith's murder, the second edition was referenced in the *Times and Seasons* showing that it was available by that time.[73] This edition had eight additional sections, including two pre-1835 revelations; God's word to Smith in 1837, 1838, and 1841; two letters of 1842; and a testimonial regarding the martyrdom of the prophet and his brother Hyrum on 27 June 1844.

In early histories of the church, the primary source of Smith's revelations was the 1835 D&C. More recently, the two major Latter-day Saint churches have published their own retrospectively updated editions of the D&C and based their histories on these publications.

It is a well-established canon of textual criticism that in order to uncover the original text one must follow the earliest and best manuscripts available.[74] In biblical textual criticism, the text critic works with versions from various scribes in attempting to determine which reading is closest to the original. Among the most significant conventions are assumptions that the shortest reading is probably closest to the original, since a scribe more often adds than takes away, and that the most difficult reading is probably nearest to the original wherever this rule can reasonably be applied. The possibility of transcription errors such as dittography must be kept in mind, as well.

In applying these principles to the revelations given by Joseph Smith, we must apply two distinctly different approaches to the texts themselves. The first involves comparing the various versions of the printed texts. Instead of peeling back layers of scribal variations, as one would do with biblical texts in an attempt to restore the original, the critic here peels back various layers of editing in an attempt to restore the original text of the revelation. The second approach is much like biblical text criticism. It involves examining the various extant scribal manuscripts of Joseph Smith's revelations and comparing them in an attempt to uncover the text of the revelation as Smith originally received it. Applying these principles to Smith's revelations allows us to re-establish the original text and to better understand the revelations in the context in which they were originally given.

The history of the Mormon church, in a passage compiled in 1839, recalled a time in 1830 when Oliver Cowdery suggested a change in the Articles and Cove-

---

72. Scott H. Faulring, ed., *An American Prophet's Record: The Diaries and Journals of Joseph Smith* (Salt Lake City: Signature Books in association with Smith Research Associates, 1987), 305, entry of 14 Feb. 1843. See *History of the Church*, 5:273.

73. *Times and Seasons* 5 (2 Sept. 1844): 636. The 1844 edition was printed in Nauvoo, church headquarters.

74. For text critical methods, see Kurt and Barbara Aland, *The Text of the New Testament, An Introduction to the Critical Edition and to the Theory and Practice of Modern Textual Criticism* (Grand Rapids, MI: Eerdmans/E.J. Brill, 1987); Bruce M. Metzger, *The Text of the New Testament, Its Transmission, Corruption, and Restoration*, 3rd ed. (New York: Oxford University Press, 1992); and Bruce M. Metzger, *A Textual Commentary on the Greek New Testament*, 2nd ed. (Stuttgart, Ger.: German Bible Society, 1994).

nants of the church. Joseph Smith replied, asking Cowdery: "by what authority he [Cowdery] took upon him to command me [Smith] to alter, or erase, to add or diminish to or from a revelation or commandment from Almighty God[.]"[75] Yet it appears that for the 1835 D&C, Smith and Cowdery were both involved in this sort of editing.

On 31 July 1832 Smith wrote a letter to William W. Phelps concerning copies of the commandments and of the vision of three degrees of glory. Smith wrote: "I will send them to you as soon as possable [possible], but I will exhort you to be careful not to alter the sense of any of them for he that adds or diminishes to the prop[h]ecies must come under the condemnation writ[t]en therein[.]"[76] Indeed, this understanding of the unalterable nature of the revelatory text is found in the BC. There it says concerning lost Book of Mormon manuscript pages: "I will confound those who have altered my words."[77]

In recent years there has been a growing willingness on the part of some writers to admit the existence of variant readings of the early revelations.[78] Part of this openness responds to the criticisms of some early rank-and-file members who harbored grievances against church leaders, including charges of textual revision. William Harris, for instance, who left the church, published a book in 1841, *Mormonism Portrayed*, in which he addressed textual changes: "Let me digress for one moment, and ask why this alteration? It does appear to have been done by command of God, but purports to be the same revelation as was first published."[79]

This important point has both historical and theological ramifications. Jonathan B. Turner in his 1842 book also dealt with changes in the 1835 D&C:

> It would have been well for the world if Smith's divinity, instead of giving him a pair of stone spectacles, had given him a divine printer, and a divine press, and such types that he might have been enabled to fix the meaning of his inspired revelations, so that it would be possible to let them stand, at *least two years*, without abstracting, interpolating, altering, or garbling, to suit the times. But the ways of Smith's providence are indeed mysterious. We will not pretend to judge.[80]

---

75. Manuscript History, Book A-1:51. See Jessee, *Papers of Joseph Smith*, 1:260, 320. See also *Times and Seasons* 4 (15 Feb. 1843): 108, and *History of the Church*, 1:105.

76. Smith to Phelps, 31 July 1832, LDS archives. See Dean C. Jessee, ed., *The Personal Writings of Joseph Smith* (Salt Lake City: Deseret Book Co., 1984), 247-48. See also Jessee, "Reliability of Joseph Smith's History," *Journal of Mormon History* 3 (1976): 28, and Donna Hill, *Joseph Smith the First Mormon* (Garden City, NY: Doubleday and Co., 1977), 142. The vision of three glories was published in the July 1832 issue of *The Evening and the Morning Star*, as Phelps already possessed a copy.

77. BC 9:10; LDS D&C 10:42; RLDS D&C 3:9.

78. See, for example, Robert J. Woodford, "How the Revelations in the Doctrine and Covenants were Received and Compiled," *Ensign* 15 (Jan. 1985): 27-33, and Melvin J. Petersen, "Preparing Early Revelations for Publication," ibid., 15 (Feb. 1985): 14-20.

79. William Harris, *Mormonism Portrayed* (Warsaw, IL: Sharp & Gamble, Publishers, 1841), 29. Thomas C. Sharp prepared this work for publication.

80. J[onathan]. B. Turner, *Mormonism in All Ages: or the Rise, Progress, and Causes of Mormonism* (New York: Published by Platt and Peters, 1842), 226, emphasis in original. Another early writer on Mormonism, Englishman Henry Caswall, closely followed Turner's account in his book *The Prophet of the Nineteenth Century; or, the Rise, Progress, and Present State of the Mormons, or Latter-Day Saints* (London: Printed for J.G.F. and J. Rivington, 1843), 79-80.

He further declared: "The revelations in the Book of Covenants cannot be understood without carefully comparing them with the history and position of the Mormon church at the time they were given."[81]

As far as is known, Joseph Smith made no response to these specific charges. He did state in Nauvoo that "there is no error in the revelations which I have taught."[82] It is not certain if he meant by this the original text, the 1835 revisions, or his teachings about the revelations. In any event, in this study the earliest text is preferred over the revised 1835 version for clarity and historical consistency, and the earliest revelatory text is best understood when used in conjunction with contemporary letters and journals of the persons involved.

---

81. Turner, *Mormonism in All Ages*, 244.

82. Report by Thomas Bullock of a discourse delivered on 12 May 1844, in Andrew F. Ehat and Lyndon W. Cook, eds., *The Words of Joseph Smith: The Contemporary Accounts of the Nauvoo Discourses of the Prophet Joseph* (Provo, UT: Religious Studies Center, Brigham Young University, 1980), 369.

THE
DOCUMENTS

THE

BOOK OF MORMON:

AN ACCOUNT WRITTEN BY THE HAND OF MOR-
MON, UPON PLATES TAKEN FROM
THE PLATES OF NEPHI.

Wherefore it is an abridgment of the Record of the People of Nephi; and also of
the Lamanites; written to the Lamanites, which are a remnant of the House of
Israel; and also to Jew and Gentile; written by way of commandment, and also
by the spirit of Prophesy and of Revelation. Written, and sealed up. and hid
up unto the LORD, that they might not be destroyed; to come forth by the gift
and power of GOD, unto the interpretation thereof; sealed by the hand of Moroni, and hid up unto the LORD, to come forth in due time by the way of Gentile;
the interpretation thereof by the gift of GOD; an abridgment taken from the
Book of Ether.

Also, which is a Record of the People of Jared, which were scattered at the time
the LORD confounded the language of the people when they were building a
tower to get to Heaven: which is to shew unto the remnant of the House of
Israel how great things the LORD hath done for their fathers; and that they may
know the covenants of the LORD, that they are not cast off forever; and also to
the convincing of the Jew and Gentile that JESUS is the CHRIST, the ETERNAL
GOD, manifesting Himself unto all nations. And now if there be fault, it be the
mistake of men; wherefore condemn not the things of GOD, that ye may be
found spotless at the judgment seat of CHRIST.

BY JOSEPH SMITH, JUNIOR,
AUTHOR AND PROPRIETOR.

PALMYRA:
PRINTED BY E. B. GRANDIN, FOR THE AUTHOR.

1830.

Title Page of 1830 Book of Mormon

2. Book of Mormon Period, July 1828–March 1830

Joseph Smith, Jr., with his wife Emma were living in Harmony, Pennsylvania, in the summer of 1828. The writing of the early portion of the book of Lehi occupied about two months before Smith allowed Martin Harris, an early scribe and benefactor, to take the manuscript to show it to family members. It is not clear if Lucy Harris, Martin's wife, destroyed the manuscript or gave it to others. The result was that the pages were lost and Smith asked God how this could be. He was told that Harris and he transgressed. A couple of other persons helped take dictation from Smith until a new scribe, Oliver Cowdery, assisted Smith and the work progressed rapidly from then on. They were instructed not to rewrite the lost manuscript pages. Revelations were given to Cowdery and other new acquaintances impressing upon them the marvelous work to come forth. In June 1829 Smith went to the home of Peter Whitmer, Sr., in Fayette, New York, to finished the Book of Mormon. The revelations he received are considered inspired instructions relating to the forthcoming Book of Mormon and to early followers of Smith. Once the Book of Mormon was completed, Harris mortgaged his farm to pay for the book. The idea of a church organization was considered during this period.

1. Sets at Nought the Counsels of God
From BC 2 (cf. LDS D&C 3; RLDS D&C 2)

Revelation received at Harmony [now Oakland], Pennsylvania,
in [1-31] July 1828 for Joseph Smith, Jr.,
regarding the lost manuscript pages of the
forepart of the Book of Mormon[1]

A Revelation given to Joseph [Smith, Jr.], in Harmony, Pennsylvania, July, 1828, after Martin [Harris] had lost the Manuscript of the forepart of the book of Mormon, translated from the book of Lehi, which was abridged by the hand of Mormon, saying:

---

1. This is Joseph Smith's first recorded revelation. The revelation is believed to have been given through the seer stone that Joseph had in his possession. Smith was twenty-two years old at this time.

The works, and the designs, and the purposes of God, can not be frustrated, neither can they come to nought, for God doth not walk in crooked paths; neither doth he turn to the right hand nor to the left; neither doth he vary from that which he hath said: Therefore his paths are strait and his course is one eternal round.

Remember, remember, that it is not the work of God that is frustrated, but the work of men: for although a man may have many revelations, and have power to do many mighty works, yet, if he boasts in his own strength, and sets at nought the counsels of God, and follows after the dictates of his own will, and carnal desires, he must fall and incur the vengeance of a just God upon him.

Behold, you have been intrusted with these things, but how strict were your commandments; and remember, also, the promises which were made to you, if you did not transgress them; and behold, how oft you have transgressed the commandments and the laws of God, and have gone on in the persuasions of men: for behold, you should not have feared man more than God, although men set at nought the counsels of God, and despise his words, yet you should have been faithful and he would have extended his arm, and supported you against all the fiery darts of the adversary; and he would have been with you in every time of trouble.

Behold thou art Joseph, and thou wast chosen to do the work of the Lord, but because of transgression, if thou art not aware thou wilt fall, but remember God is merciful: Therefore, repent of that which thou hast done, and he will only cause thee to be afflicted for a season, and thou art still chosen, and wilt again be called to the work; and except thou do this, thou shalt be delivered up and become as other men, and have no more gift.

And when thou deliveredst up that which God had given thee sight and power to translate, thou deliveredst up that which was sacred, into the hands of a wicked man,[2] who has set at nought the counsels of God, and has broken the most sacred promises, which were made before God, and has depended upon his own judgment, and boasted in his own wisdom, and this is the reason that thou hast lost thy privileges for a season, for thou hast suffered the counsel of thy director to be trampled upon from the beginning.

Nevertheless, my work shall go forth and accomplish my purposes, for as the knowledge of a Savior has come into the world, even so shall the knowledge of my people, the Nephites, and the Jacobites, and the Josephites, and the Zoramites, come to the knowledge of the Lamanites, and the Lemuelites and the Ishmaelites,[3] which dwindled in unbelief, because of the iniquities of their fathers, who have been suffered to destroy their brethren, because of their iniquities, and their abominations: and for this very purpose are these plates preserved which contain these records, that the promises of the Lord might be fulfilled, which he made to his people; and that the Lamanites might come to the knowledge of their fathers,

2. Martin Harris was the principle scribe for Joseph Smith from about 12 April to 14 June 1828. Harris was forty-five years old.
3. The names Nephites, Jacobites, Josephites, Zoramites, Lamanites, Lemuelites, and Ishmaelites are found in three places in the Book of Mormon. See 1830 BOM, 124, 517, 519; LDS and RLDS Jacob 1:13; LDS 4 Ne. 1:36-38/RLDS 1:40-42 and LDS and RLDS Morm. 1:8-9.

and that they might know the promises of the Lord, and that they may believe the gospel and rely upon the merits of Jesus Christ, and be glorified through faith in his name; and that through their repentance they might be saved: Amen.

Revision

1835 D&C 30
(cf. LDS D&C 3:10, 16-18; RLDS D&C 2:4, 6)

therefore, repent of that which thou hast done, *which is contrary to the commandment which I gave you*, and thou art still chosen, and *art* again called to the work

.   .   .

Nevertheless my work shall go forth, for, *inasmuch* as the knowledge of a Savior has come *unto* the world, *through the testimony of the Jews*, even so shall the knowledge of *a Savior come unto* my people; *and to* the Nephites, and the Jacobites, and the Jose-phites, and the Zoramites, *through the testimony of their fathers; and this testimony shall* come to the knowledge of the Lamanites, and the Lemuelites, and the Ishmaelites, *who* dwindled in unbelief because of the *iniquity* of their fathers, *whom the Lord has* suffered to destroy their brethren *the Nephites*, because of their iniquities and their abominations

2. O Ye That Embark in the Service of God
From BC 3 (cf. LDS and RLDS D&C 4)

Revelation received at Harmony, Pennsylvania,
in [1-28] February 1829 for Joseph Smith, Sr.

A Revelation given to Joseph [Smith, Sr.], the father of Joseph [Smith, Jr.], in Har-mony, Pennsylvania, February, 1829, saying:

Now, behold, a marvelous work is about to come forth among the children of men, therefore, O ye that embark in the service of God, see that ye serve him with all your heart, might, mind and strength, that ye may stand blameless before God at the last day: Therefore, if ye have desires to serve God, ye are called to the work, for behold, the field is white already to harvest, and lo, he that thrusteth in his sickle with his might, the same layeth up in store that he perish not, but bringeth salvation to his soul, and faith, hope, charity, and love, with an eye single to the glory of God, qualifies him for the work.

Remember temperance, patience, humility, diligence, &c., ask and ye shall re-ceive, knock and it shall be opened unto you: Amen.

Revision

1835 D&C 31
(cf. LDS D&C 4:6-7; RLDS D&C 4:2)

Remember *faith, virtue, knowledge,* temperance, patience, *brotherly kindness, godliness, charity,* humility, diligence. - Ask and ye shall receive, knock and it shall be opened unto you. Amen.

Commentary: Personal Traits Added

BC 3 is a revelation dated February 1829, for Joseph Smith, Sr. Verse 2 reads: "Remember temperance, patience, humility, diligence, &c., ask and ye shall receive, knock and it shall be opened unto you: Amen." The 1835 D&C added other virtuous personality traits. The words added are: "faith, virtue, knowledge" and "brotherly kindness, godliness, charity" (see 2 Pet. 1:5-7). At the same time the symbol "&c" was not in the 1835 D&C. While this is perhaps a small and seemingly insignificant change, it is not supported by either the BC or a manuscript in the handwriting of Edward Partridge located in LDS archives. The manuscript has a small lacuna where a brief background to the revelation was given. The altered portion of the text is not in the area effected by the hole and can be clearly read. It is reasonably certain that the additional words would not have been in the revelation of February 1829. Therefore the earliest text and shortest text all favor the BC reading.

3. He Hath a Gift to Translate the Book
From NKW Collection (cf. LDS and RLDS D&C 5)

*Revelation received at Harmony, Pennsylvania,
in [1-31] March 1829 for Joseph Smith, Jr., and Martin Harris
when Harris wanted to know if Joseph Smith
had in his possession the record of the Nephites*[4]

Behold I say unto you that my servant hath desired A witness that my servant Joseph [Smith, Jr.] hath got the things which he hath testified that he hath got

and now Behold this shall ye say unto him I the Lord am God I have given these things unto him & I have commanded him that he should stand as a witness of these things nevertheless I have caused him that he should enter into a covenant with me that he should not show them except I command him & he hath no power over them e[x]cept I grant it unto him & he hath A gift to translate the Book & I have commanded him that he shall pretend to no other gift for I will grant unto him no other gift

and verily I say unto you that woe shall come unto the Inhabitents of the Earth if they will not hearken unto my words for Behold if they will not believe my

---

4. Martin Harris traveled from Palmyra, New York, to Harmony to see the plates. The heading of BC 4 indicates that "Martin desired of the Lord to know whether Joseph had, in his possession, the record of the Nephites." Harris did not see the plates at this time but was promised he would be one of three witnesses to view the plates. On Harris wanting a greater witness, see affidavit of Isaac Hale, 20 Mar. 1834, in *Susquehanna Register, and Northern Pennsylvanian* 9 (1 May 1834): 1.

words they would not believe my servants if it were possible he could show them all things O ye unbelieving ye stiffnecked Generation

Behold I have reserved the things which have been spoken of which I have entrusted to my servant for a wise purpose in me & it shall be made known unto future Generations but for this Generation they shall have my word yea & the testimony of three of my servants shall go forth with my word unto this Generation yea three shall know of a surety that those things are true for I will give them power that they may Behold & view those things as they are & to none else will I grant this power among this Generation & the testimony of three Witnesses will I send forth & my word & behold whosoever believeth in my word him will I visit with the manifestations of my spirit & they shall be Born of me & their testimony Shall also go forth

& thus if the People of this Generation harden not their hearts I will work a reformation among them & I will put down all lieings & deceivings & Priestcraft & envyings & strifes & Idolatries and sorceries & all manner of Iniquities & I will establish my Church yea even the church which was taught by my Desiples [Disciples]

& now if this Generation do harden their hearts against my words Behold I deliver them up unto Satan for he reigneth & hath much Power at this time for he hath got great hold upon the hearts of the People of this Generation & how far from the iniquities of Sodom and Gomorrah do they come at this time & Behold the Sword of justice doth hang above their heads & if they persist in the hardness of the[i]r hearts the time cometh that it must fall upon them Behold I tell you these things even as I also told the People of the destruction of Jerusalem & my word shall be verified at this time as it hath hitherto been verrified

& now I command my Servant Joseph [Smith, Jr.] that he repenteth & walketh more uprightly before me & yield to the persuations [persuasions] of men no more & that he be firm in keeping the commandments which I have commanded him & if he do this Behold I grant unto him Eternal life even if he should be slain

And now I speak again concerning the man[5] that desireth the Witness Behold I say unto him if he exalteth himself & doth not humble himself sufficiently before me I will grant unto him no such v[i]ews but if he will go out & bow down before me & humble himself in mightly prayer & faith in the sincerity of his heart then will I grant unto him a v[i]ew of the things which he desireth to v[i]ew then shall he say unto the People of this Generation Behold I have seen the things & I know of a surety that they are true for I have seen them & they have been shone [shown] unto me by the Power of God & I command him that he shall say no more except I have seen them & they have been shone [shown] un[to] me by the Power of God

& these are the words which he shall say but if he deny this he shall break the covenant which he hath covenanted with me & Behold he is condemned & now except he humble himself & acknowledge unto me the things which he hath done that is wrong & covenant with me that he will keep my commandments & exercise

---

5. Martin Harris.

faith in me Behold I say unto him he shall have no such v[i]ews for I will grant unto him no such v[i]ews of which I have spoken & if this be the case I command him that he shall do no more nor trouble me no more concerning this matter

& if this be the case Behold I say unto you Joseph [Smith, Jr.] when thou hast translated a few more pages & then shalt thou stop for a season even untill I command thee again then thou mayest translate & excep[t] thou do this Behold thou shalt have no more gift & I will take away the things which I have entrusted with thee

& now because I forsee the lieing in wait to destroy thee yea I forsee that if my Servant humbleth not himself & receive a witness from my hand that he will fall into transgression & there are many that lie in wait to destroy thee off the face of the Earth & for this cause that thy days may be proulounged [prolonged] I have given unto you these Commandments yea for this Cause have I said stop & stand still untill I Command thee & I will provide means whereby thou mayest accomplish the thing I have commanded thee & if thou art faithful in keeping my Commandments ye shall be lifted up at the last day[6]

Revision

1835 D&C 32
(cf. LDS D&C 5:1-19; RLDS D&C 5:1-3)

Behold I say unto you, that *as* my servant *Martin Harris* has desired a witness *at my hand*, that *you*, my servant Joseph Smith, jr. *have* got the *plates of* which *you have* testified *and borne record* that *you have received of me*:

and now behold, this shall you say unto him, *He who spake unto you said unto you*, I the Lord am God, *and* have given these things unto *you, my servant Joseph Smith, jr.* and have commanded *you* that *you shall* stand as a witness of these things, *and* I have caused *you* that *you* should enter into a covenant with me that *you* should not show them except *to those persons to whom* I commanded *you*; and *you* have no power over them except I grant it unto *you*.

And *you* have a gift to translate the *plates; and this is the first gift that I bestowed upon you*, and I have commanded that *you should* pretend to no other gift *until my purpose is fulfilled in this*; for I will grant unto *you* no other gift *until it is finished*.

Verily I say unto you, that wo shall come unto the inhabitants of the earth if they will not hearken unto my words: for *hereafter you shall be ordained and go forth and deliver my words unto the children of men*. Behold if they will not believe my words, they would not believe *you*, my *servant Joseph*, if it were possible that *you* could show them all *these* things *which I have committed unto you*.

O *this* unbelieving *and* stiffnecked generation, *mine anger is kindled against them*. Behold *verily*, *I say unto you*, I have reserved *those* things which I have entrusted *unto*

---

6. The revelation ends with the word "Amen" in the BC.

you, my servant *Joseph*, for a wise purpose in me, and it shall be made known unto future generations; but this generation shall have my word *through you*;

and *in addition to your testimony* the testimony of three of my servants, *whom I shall call and ordain, unto whom I will show these things: and they* shall go forth with my *words that are given through you*, yea, *they* shall known of a surety that these things are true: for *from heaven will I declare it unto them*: I will give them power that they may behold and view *these* things as they are; and to none else will I grant this power, *to receive this same testimony*, among this generation, *in this, the beginning of the rising up, and the coming forth of my church out of the wilderness - clear as the moon and fair as the sun and terrible as an army with banners*. And the testimony of three witnesses will I send forth *of* my word. And behold, whosoever believeth *on* my *words*, them will I visit with the manifestation of my Spirit; and they shall be born of me, *even of water and of the Spirit. And you must wait yet a little while; for ye are not yet ordained* - and their testimony shall also go forth *unto the condemnation* of this generation *if they* harden their hearts *against* them:

for a desolating scourge shall go forth among the inhabitants of the earth, and shall continue to be poured out, from time to time, if they repent not, until the earth is empty, and the inhabitants thereof are consumed away, and utterly destroyed by the brightness of my coming.

Commentary: No Other Gift; Judgements upon the People of this Generation

Jonathan B. Turner, nearly seven years after the publication of the 1835 D&C, commented on the revelation given in March 1829:

> By turning to that same revelation, as it stands on the tenth page of the first edition of the Book of Commandments, published in 1833, before the prophet saw fully what powers it would be convenient for him to assume in the church, the reader will see that, at the end of the second verse, God commands Smith to pretend to *"no other gift"* except to translate [the Book of Mormon], and expressly declares that he will *"grant* [unto] *him no other gift."* Doubtless the prophet thought this sufficient at the time. But, in publishing the second edition, two years after, it was found expedient to add a saving clause or two, so as effectually to annihilate at once the command and the promise, and leave Smith still free to usurp whatever power he pleased. The second edition is made to read thus: "I have commanded that you should pretend to no other gift" (save to translate) *"until my purpose is fulfilled in this,"* "for I will grant [unto] you no other gift *until it is finished."* The words in italics are interpolated in the second edition, but not found in the first ... Smith did not see the necessity of correcting the type in '33, but in '35 it became apparent.[7]

William E. McLellin, a former apostle, and Book of Mormon witness David Whitmer also noticed the alteration of this text.[8]

There is an early manuscript copy of this revelation to Joseph Smith and Martin

---

7. J[onathan]. B. Turner, *Mormonism in All Ages: or the Rise, Progress, and Causes of Mormonism* (New York: Published by Platt and Peters, 1842), 225-26, emphasis in original.

8. McLellin to Joseph Smith III, July 1872, original in RLDS archives; and David Whitmer, *An Address to All Believers in Christ* (Richmond, MO: author, 1887), 57-58.

Harris that contains this passage. There are four major variations. First, there is a minor substitution of the word "plates" for "book." Second, an additional phrase was added: "and this is the first gift that I bestowed upon you." In March 1829 Smith was not told that this was his "first gift" but that he would have no other. The other additions are, third, "until my purpose is fulfilled in this," and, fourth, "until it is finished." David Whitmer emphasized the significance: "they change and reverse the original meaning: as if God had commanded Joseph to pretend to no other gift but to translate the Book of Mormon, that he would 'grant [unto] *him no other gift*,' and then afterwards God had changed his mind and concluded to grant him another gift."[9]

To summarize, Joseph Smith was commanded to translate the book or plates, which would be his only work, as, indeed, the project consumed most of his time for the next several months. The revelation indicated that Smith should pretend to no other gift/work, as he would not receive another.

But after Smith completed the Book of Mormon dictation and had it published, he started to revise the Bible without any knowledge of Hebrew or Greek, which would be considered another gift. When he revised the ending of Genesis in 1832, he included material from the Book of Mormon which has been assumed to refer to himself: "he shall do none other work, save the work which I shall command him,"[10] but dropped the words "none other" for the new text to read, "and he shall do whatsoever work I shall command him."[11]

The change in the March 1829 revelation appears to have been made to eliminate problems with Smith's later involvement with the Bible revision. Since the Bible revision was still in manuscript form in 1835, three of the additions made sure that no work would be excluded from Smith. The textual additions changed the meaning of the revelation's original 1829 intent.

Included in the March 1829 instructions to Smith and Martin Harris is an apocalyptic passage.[12] The 1835 D&C, however, presented a largely reworked version of this. This later version is much shorter than the earlier one. In comparing the 1835 D&C with the early manuscript copy, a number of features have been deleted from the earlier version, namely: (1) Satan "hath got great hold upon the hearts of the People of this Generation"; (2) the current generation of 1829 are not "far from the iniquities of Sodom and Gomorrah"; and (3) "Behold the Sword of justice doth hang above their heads & if they persist in the hardness of the[i]r hearts the time cometh that it must fall upon them." These items are also found in the BC.

It is clear that the 1835 D&C also adds to what is found in the manuscript. In

---

9. Whitmer, *An Address to All Believers in Christ*, 57, emphasis in original.

10. 1830 BOM, 66; LDS 2 Ne. 3:8; RLDS 2:13.

11. OT MS #2, 64, RLDS archives. This work is variously known as the Inspired Version, the Joseph Smith Bible Revision, and the JST. Gen. 50:28 (JST). The JST is Joseph Smith's doctrinal correction ("translation") of the OT and NT and does not restore the Hebrew or Greek biblical text.

12. See BC 4:5-6. Cf. 1830 BOM, 487, 499-501; LDS 3 Ne. 16:10; 21:6, 19-22; RLDS 3 Ne. 7:34; 9:92, 105-106.

particular, the "desolating scourge" would occur periodically until the inhabitants are destroyed "by the brightness of my coming." It is not clear how the editorial decision was made that resulted in the 1835 version, nor how it would have affected Martin Harris. But it is clear in this case that the uniformity of the manuscript and the BC against the later 1835 version argues that the earliest was closer to the original. Even though the later text is shorter, it shows evidence of being a revision.

4. He That Hath Eternal Life Is Rich
From BC 5 (cf. LDS and RLDS D&C 6)

Revelation received at Harmony, Pennsylvania,
in [7-30] April 1829 for Oliver Cowdery[13]

A Revelation to Oliver [Cowdery], given in Harmony, Pennsylvania, April, 1829, when employed a scribe for Joseph [Smith, Jr.], while translating the book of Mormon.

A great and marvelous work is about to come forth unto the children of men: behold I am God, and give heed unto my word, which is quick and powerful, sharper than a two-edged sword, to the dividing asunder of both joints and marrow:— Therefore give heed unto my words.

Behold the field is white already to harvest, therefore whoso desireth to reap, let him thrust in his sickle with his might and reap while the day lasts, that he may treasure up for his soul everlasting salvation in the kingdom of God: Yea, whosoever will thrust in his sickle and reap, the same is called of God; therefore, if you will ask of me you shall receive; if you will knock it shall be opened unto you.

Now as you have asked, behold I say unto you, keep my commandments, and seek to bring forth and establish the cause of Zion: seek not for riches but for wisdom, and behold the mysteries of God shall be unfolded unto you, and then shall you be made rich. Behold he that hath eternal life is rich.

Verily, verily I say unto you, even as you desire of me, so shall it be unto you; and, if you desire, you shall be the means of doing much good in this generation. Say nothing but repentance unto this generation; keep my commandments and assist to bring forth my work according to my commandments, and you shall be blessed.

Behold thou hast a gift, and blessed art thou because of thy gift. Remember it is sacred and cometh from above; and if thou wilt inquire, thou shalt know mysteries which are great and marvelous: therefore thou shalt exercise thy gift, that thou mayest find out mysteries, that thou mayest bring many to the knowledge of the

---

13. Oliver Cowdery arrived at Harmony on 5 April 1829 with Samuel Harrison Smith. Two days later on 7 April Cowdery commenced as Joseph Smith's scribe. Cowdery was twenty-two years old.

truth; yea, convince them of the error of their ways. Make not thy gift known unto any, save it be those which are of thy faith.—Trifle not with sacred things. If thou wilt do good, yea and hold out faithful to the end, thou shalt be saved in the kingdom of God, which is the greatest of all the gifts of God; for there is no gift greater than the gift of salvation.

Verily, verily I say unto thee, blessed art thou for what thou hast done, for thou hast inquired of me, and behold as often as thou hast inquired, thou hast received instruction of my Spirit. If it had not been so, thou wouldst not have come to the place where thou art at this time.

Behold thou knowest that thou hast inquired of me, and I did enlighten thy mind; and now I tell thee these things, that thou mayest know that thou hast been enlightened by the Spirit of truth; yea, I tell thee, that thou mayest know that there is none else save God, that knowest thy thoughts and the intents of thy heart: I tell thee these things as a witness unto thee, that the words or the work which thou hast been writing is true:

Therefore be diligent, stand by my servant Joseph [Smith, Jr.] faithfully in whatsoever difficult circumstances he may be, for the word's sake. Admonish him in his faults and also receive admonition of him. Be patient; be sober; be temperate; have patience, faith, hope and charity.

Behold thou art Oliver [Cowdery], and I have spoken unto thee because of thy desires, therefore, treasure up these words in thy heart. Be faithful and diligent in keeping the commandments of God, and I will incircle [encircle] thee in the arms of my love.

Behold I am Jesus Christ, the Son of God. I am the same that came unto my own and my own received me not. I am the light which shineth in darkness, and the darkness comprehendeth it not.

Verily, verily I say unto you, if you desire a further witness, cast your mind upon the night that you cried unto me in your heart, that you might know concerning the truth of these things; did I not speak peace to your mind concer[n]ing the matter?— What greater witness can you have than from God? And now behold, you have received a witness, for if I have told you things which no man knoweth, have you not received a witness? And behold I grant unto you a gift if you desire of me, to translate even as my servant Joseph [Smith, Jr.].

Verily, verily I say unto you, that there are records which contain much of my gospel, which have been kept back because of the wickedness of the people; and now I command you, that if you have good desires, a desire to lay up treasures for yourself in heaven, then shall you assist in bringing to light, with your gift, those parts of my scriptures which have been hidden because of iniquity.

And now behold I give unto you, and also unto my servant Joseph [Smith, Jr.], the keys of this gift, which shall bring to light this ministry; and in the mouth of two or three witnesses, shall every word be established.

Verily, verily I say unto you, if they reject my words, and this part of my gospel and ministry, blessed are ye, for they can do no more unto you than unto me; and if they do unto you, even as they have done unto me, blessed are ye, for you shall dwell with me in glory: but if they reject not my words, which shall be established by the testimony which shall be given, blessed are they; and then shall ye have joy in the fruit of your labors.

Verily, verily I say unto you, as I said unto my disciples, where two or three are gathered together in my name, as touching one thing, behold there will I be in the midst of them: even so am I in the midst of you. Fear not to do good my sons, for whatsoever ye sow, that shall ye also reap: therefore, if ye sow good, ye shall also reap good for your reward:

Therefore fear not little flock, do good, let earth and hell combine against you, for if ye are built upon my Rock, they cannot prevail. Behold I do not condemn you, go your ways and sin no more: perform with soberness the work which I have commanded you: look unto me in every thought, doubt not, fear not: behold the wounds which pierced my side, and also the prints of the nails in my hands and feet: be faithful; keep my commandments, and ye shall inherit the kingdom of heaven: Amen.

5. Thou Shall Tarry till I Come in My Glory

From a manuscript in LDS archives
(cf. LDS and RLDS D&C 7)

Revelation received at Harmony, Pennsylvania, in [7-30] April 1829 for Joseph Smith, Jr., and Oliver Cowdery[14]

A revelation concerning John the beloved deciple [disciple]

And the Lord said unto me John my beloved, what desirest thou[?] And I said Lord give unto me power that I may bring souls unto thee, and the Lord said unto me verily I say unto thee becau[se] thou desirest this; thou shalt tarry till I come in my glory

and for this cause the Lord said unto Peter if I will that he tarry till I come, what is that to thee[?] for he desirest of me that he might bring souls unto me, but thou desirest that thou might speedely come unto me in my kingdom I say unto thee Peter this was a good desire, But my beloved hath undertaken a greater work;

verily I say unto you ye shall both have according to your desires for ye hath Joy in th[at] which ye have desired &c &c &c

Revision

1835 D&C 33
(cf. LDS D&C 7:1-3, 5-7; RLDS D&C 7:1-2)

---

14. The BC has in its heading: "they [Smith and Cowdery] desired to know whether John, the beloved disciple, tarried on earth. Translated from parchment, written and hid up by himself [John]." There is no evidence that the ancient manuscript was physically present for Smith to translate. A revelation was given to him concerning the essence of the hidden text. See John 21:20-24.

And the Lord said unto me, John, my beloved, what desirest thou? *For if ye shall ask, what you will, it shall be granted unto you.* And I said *unto him,* Lord, give unto me power *over death,* that I may *live and* bring souls unto thee. And the Lord said unto me, Verily, *verily,* I say unto thee, because thou desirest this thou shalt tarry until I come in my glory, *and shall prophesy before nations, kindreds, tongues and people.*

.   .   .

I say unto thee, Peter, this was a good desire, but my beloved *has desired that he might do more, or a greater work, yet among men than what he has before done; yea, he has undertaken a greater work; therefore, I will make him as flaming fire and a ministering angel: he shall minister for those who shall be heirs of salvation who dwell on the earth; and I will make thee to minister for him and for thy brother James: and unto you three I will give this power and the keys of this ministry until I come.*

Commentary: John the Beloved Disciple

In April 1829 a revelation was received which was called "A revelation concerning John the beloved deciple [disciple]." There are two early manuscripts which agree in wording.[15] When this revelation was published in the BC, the following background information was given: "A Revelation given to Joseph and Oliver, in Harmony, Pennsylvania, April, 1829, when they desired to know whether John, the beloved disciple, tarried on earth. Translated from parchment, written and hid up by himself."[16] This idea of a translation from parchment fits the time frame when they were working on the Book of Mormon.

The 1839 Manuscript History explains that Cowdery and Smith wanted to know if John the Apostle "died, or whether he continued" on the earth.[17] When this revelation was prepared for republication, to the question, "John my beloved, what desirest thou," the following words were added: "For if ye shall ask, what you will, it shall be granted unto you." This promise is more than what was originally offered. In the original version the Lord simply asked John what he wanted. Being granted whatever he asked is outside the scope of the original revelation.

In the manuscript version John requests "power that I may bring souls unto thee." This was expanded in just two words, to power "over death," which is beyond his original request.

To the wording that John would "tarry till I come in my glory" was added words which appear to follow the promise that his request would be granted. The 1835 text reads at this point: "and shall prophesy before nations, kindreds, tongues and people." The early text has the Lord tell Peter that John "has undertaken a greater work." To this was made an important addition that John had become a

---

15. Robert J. Woodford, "The Historical Development of the Doctrine and Covenants," Ph.D. diss., Brigham Young University, 1974, 182-83.

16. BC 6:1. *The Evening and the Morning Star* 1 (May 1833): [6; whole page no. 94], contains the last part of the text of this early document and was probably based upon the BC manuscript then in Independence, Missouri.

17. Dean C. Jessee, ed., *The Papers of Joseph Smith: Autobiographical and Historical Writings* (Salt Lake City: Deseret Book Co., 1989), 1:289.

ministering angel who, with Peter and James, holds "this power and the keys of this ministry until I come." The complete interpolation is as follows:

> therefore, I will make him as flaming fire and a ministering angel: he shall minister for those who shall be heirs of salvation who dwell on the earth; and I will make thee to minister for him and for thy brother James: and unto you three I will give this power and the keys of this ministry until I come.

The manuscript ending has "&c &c &c." This is at the end of the text of the document. The added words are previous and not after BC 6:3. Since the earlier text is the shorter of the two and BC follows the manuscript version, in terms of text criticism this appears to support the early text. One of the manuscripts (Woodford's #1) needs to be made available for further study.[18] While there is space at the bottom of BC page 18 for additional material, this would be after the last words and, like page 21 or 30, would not mean that there was more text to be added.

The additions refer to a presidency of three, which might relate to the establishment of a church presidency in 1832. A March 1832 revelation states, "unto whom I have given the keys of the Kingdom which belongs always to the presidency of the high Priest Hood."[19]

At a meeting held on 17 February 1834, Joseph Smith established the Kirtland High Council. He taught: "The apostle, Peter, was the president of the Council and held the keys of the Kingdom of God on the earth[,] was appointed to this office by the voice of the Savior and acknowledged in it by the voice of the Church. He had two men appointed as Counsellors with him, and in case Peter was absent, his counsellors could transact business, or either one of them."[20] In 1834 the presidency was given additional responsibilities in presiding over the twelve members of the high council. They became known as the First Presidency of the church.

The change regarding Peter being one of the "three" with John and James would seem to be a later addition arising from a time when the church had three presiding officers, appealing to Peter's alleged position as head of the high council in the New Testament church.

6. Spirit of Revelation
From BC 7 (cf. LDS and RLDS D&C 8)

Revelation received at Harmony, Pennsylvania, in [7-30] April 1829 for Oliver Cowdery

A Revelation given to Oliver, in Harmony, Pennsylvania, April, 1829.

Oliver [Cowdery], verily, verily I say unto you, that assuredly as the Lord liveth, which is your God and your Redeemer, even so sure shall you receive a

---

18. Woodford, "Historical Development of the Doctrine and Covenants," 177-83.
19. Document no. 94; LDS D&C 81:2; RLDS D&C 80:1.
20. Kirtland Council Minute Book, 30, LDS archives.

knowledge of whatsoever things you shall ask in faith, with an honest heart, believing that you shall receive a knowledge concerning the engravings of old records, which are ancient, which contain those parts of my scripture of which have been spoken, by the manifestation of my Spirit; yea, behold I will tell you in your mind and in your heart by the Holy Ghost, which shall come upon you and which shall dwell in your heart.

Now, behold this is the Spirit of revelation:— behold this is the spirit by which Moses brought the children of Israel through the Red sea on dry ground: therefore, this is thy gift; apply unto it and blessed art thou, for it shall deliver you out of the hands of your enemies, when, if it were not so, they would slay you and bring your soul to destruction.

O remember, these words and keep my commandments. Remember this is your gift. Now this is not all, for you have another gift, which is the gift of working with the rod: behold it has told you things: behold there is no other power save God, that can cause this rod of nature, to work in your hands,[21] for it is the work of God; and therefore whatsoever you shall ask me to tell you by that means, that will I grant unto you, that you shall know.

Remember that without faith you can do nothing. Trifle not with these things. Do not ask for that which you ought not. Ask that you may know the mysteries of God, and that you may translate all those ancient records, which have been hid up, which are sacred, and according to your faith shall it be done unto you.

Behold it is I that have spoken it, and I am the same which spake unto you from the beginning:— Amen.

<u>Revision</u>

1835 D&C 34
(cf. LDS D&C 8:6-11; RLDS D&C 8:3)

Now this is not all *thy gift*; for you have another gift, which is the gift of *Aaron*: Behold it has told you *many* things: behold, there is no other power save *the power of* God that can cause this *gift* of *Aaron* to *be with you; therefore, doubt not, for it is the gift of God, and you shall hold it* in your hands, *and do marvelous works; and no power shall be able to take it away out of your hands*; for it is the work of God. And therefore, whatsoever you shall ask me to tell you by that means, that will I grant unto you *and* you shall *have knowledge concerning it*: remember, that without faith you can do nothing. *Therefore, ask in faith.*

Trifle not with these things: do not ask for that which you ought not: ask that you may know the mysteries of God, and that you may translate *and receive knowledge from* all those ancient records which have been hid up, *that* are sacred, and according to your faith shall it be done unto you.

<u>Commentary: Rod of Nature</u>

In BC 7 Oliver Cowdery is told that he has the gift of the Spirit of revelation.

---

21. The "rod of nature" in Cowdery's "hands" refers to his possession of a divining rod.

He is also told that he has "another gift, which is the gift of working with the rod." Cowdery is told that God can "cause this rod of nature, to work in your hands." In the 1835 D&C the wording "rod of nature, to work in your hands" has been replaced by "gift of Aaron to be with you."

This addition, which is not in the BC, still identifies Cowdery's gift as being in his hands. The deletion of the words "working with the rod" and the "rod" of "nature" makes the meaning less clear as to how he might work his gift in obtaining revelations. It seems that Cowdery obtained revelations as he worked with a divining rod, but, with the change, the allusion to Aaron's rod which budded (Num. 17:8), is obscurantist.

7. Be Patient My Son
From BC 8 (cf. LDS and RLDS D&C 9)

Revelation received at Harmony, Pennsylvania,
in [7-30] April 1829 for Oliver Cowdery

A Revelation given to Oliver, in Harmony, Pennsylvania, April, 1829.

Behold I say unto you, my son, that, because you did not translate according to that which you desired of me, and did commence again to write for my servant Joseph [Smith, Jr.], even so I would that you should continue until you have finished this record, which I have intrusted unto you: and then behold, other records have I, that I will give unto you power that you may assist to translate.

Be patient my son, for it is wisdom in me, and it is not expedient that you should translate at this present time. Behold the work which you are called to do, is to write for my servant Joseph [Smith, Jr.]; and behold it is because that you did not continue as you commenced, when you begun to translate, that I have taken away this privilege from you. Do not murmur my son, for it is wisdom in me that I have dealt with you after this manner.

Behold you have not understood, you have supposed that I would give it unto you, when you took no thought, save it was to ask me; but behold I say unto you, that you must study it out in your mind; then you must ask me if it be right, and if it is right, I will cause that your bosom shall burn within you: therefore, you shall feel that it is right; but if it be not right, you shall have no such feelings, but you shall have a stupor of thought, that shall cause you to forget the thing which is wrong: therefore, you cannot write that which is sacred, save it be given you from me.

Now if you had known this, you could have translated: nevertheless, it is not expedient that you should translate now. Behold it was expedient when you commenced, but you feared and the time is past, that it is not expedient now: for, do you not behold that I have given unto my servant Joseph [Smith, Jr.] sufficient strength, whereby it is made up? and neither of you have I condemned.

Do this thing which I have commanded you, and you shall prosper. Be faithful, and yield to no temptation. Stand fast in the work wherewith I have called you, and a hair of your head shall not be lost, and you shall be lifted up at the last day: Amen.

8. That You May Conquer Satan
From BC 9 (cf. LDS D&C 10; RLDS D&C 3)

Revelation received at Harmony, Pennsylvania,
in [1-31] May 1829 for Joseph Smith, Jr., regarding the
alteration of the lost manuscript pages of the forepart
of the Book of Mormon[22]

A Revelation given to Joseph, in Harmony, Pennsylvania, May, 1829, informing him of the alteration of the Manuscript of the fore part of the book of Mormon.

Now, behold I say unto you, that because you delivered up so many writings, which you had power to translate, into the hands of a wicked man,[23] you have lost them, and you also lost your gift at the same time, nevertheless it has been restored unto you again: therefore, see that you are faithful and go on unto the finishing of the remainder of the work as you have begun. Do not run faster than you have strength and means provided to translate, but be diligent unto the end, that you may come off conquerer [conqueror]; yea, that you may conquer satan, and those that do uphold his work.

Behold they have sought to destroy you; yea, even the man in whom you have trusted, and for this cause I said, that he is a wicked man, for he has sought to take away the things wherewith you have been intrusted; and he has also sought to destroy your gift, and because you have delivered the writings into his hands, behold they have taken them from you: therefore, you have delivered them up; yea, that which was sacred unto wickedness. And behold, satan has put it into their hearts to alter the words which you have caused to be written, or which you have translated, which have gone out of your hands; and behold I say unto you, that because they have altered the words, they read contrary from that which you translated and caused to be written; and on this wise the devil has sought to lay a cunning plan, that he may destroy this work; for he has put it into their hearts to do this, that by lying they may say they have caught you in the words which you have pretended to translate.

Verily I say unto you, that I will not suffer that satan shall accomplish his evil design in this thing, for behold he has put it into their hearts to tempt the Lord their God; for behold they say in their hearts, We will see if God has given him power to translate, if so, he will also give him power again; and if God giveth him power again, or if he translate again, or in other words, if he bringeth forth the same words, behold we have the same with us, and we have altered them: Therefore, they will not agree, and we will say that he has lied in his words, and that he has no gift, and that he has no power: therefore, we will destroy him, and also the work,

---

22. For various ideas on the dating of this document, see Max H. Parkin, "A Preliminary Analysis of the Dating of Section 10," *The Seventh Annual Sidney B. Sperry Symposium: The Doctrine and Covenants* (Provo, UT: Brigham Young University, 1979), 68–84.
23. Martin Harris. See document no. 1, dated July 1828. The writing of the early portion of the BOM was not recovered by May 1829.

and we will do this that we may not be ashamed in the end, and that we may get glory of the world.

Verily, verily I say unto you, that satan has great hold upon their hearts; he stirreth them up to do iniquity against that which is good, that he may lead their souls to destruction, and thus he has laid a cunning plan to destroy the work of God; yea, he stirreth up their hearts to anger against this work; yea, he saith unto them, Deceive and lie in wait to catch, that ye may destroy: behold this is no harm, and thus he flattereth them and telleth them that it is no sin to lie, that they may catch a man in a lie, that they may destroy him, and thus he flattereth them, and leadeth them along until he draggeth their souls down to hell; and thus he causeth them to catch themselves in their own snare; and thus he goeth up and down, to and fro in the earth, seeking to destroy the souls of men.

Verily, verily I say unto you, wo be unto him that lieth to decieve [deceive], because he supposeth that another lieth to decieve [deceive], for such are not exempt from the justice of God.

Now, behold they have altered those words, because satan saith unto them, He hath decieved [deceived] you, and thus he flattereth them away to do iniquity, to tempt the Lord their God.

Behold I say unto you, that you shall not translate again those words which have gone forth out of your hands; for behold, they shall not lie any more against those words; for behold, if you should bring forth the same words, they would say that you have lied; that you have pretended to translate, but that you have contradicted your words; and behold they would publish this, and satan would harden the hearts of the people, to stir them up to anger against you, that they might not believe my words: thus satan would overpower this generation, that the work might not come forth in this generation: but behold here is wisdom, and because I show unto you wisdom, and give you commandments concerning these things, what you shall do, show it not unto the world until you have accomplished the work.

Marvel not that I said unto you, here is wisdom, show it not unto the world, for I said, show it not unto the world, that you may be preserved. Behold I do not say that you shall not show it unto the righteous; but as you cannot always judge the righteous, or as you cannot always tell the wicked from the righteous: therefore, I say unto you, hold your peace until I shall see fit to make all things known unto the world concerning the matter.

And now, verily I say unto you, that an account of those things that you have written, which have gone out of your hands, are engraven upon the plates of Nephi; yea, and you remember, it was said in those writings, that a more particular account was given of these things upon the plates of Nephi.

And now, because the account which is engraven upon the plates of Nephi, is more particular concerning the things, which in my wisdom I would bring to the knowledge of the people in this account: therefore, you shall translate the engravings which are on the plates of Nephi, down even till you come to the reign of king Benjamin, or until you come to that which you have translated, which you have retained; and behold, you shall publish it as the record of Nephi, and thus I will confound those who have altered my words. I will not suffer that they shall destroy my work; yea, I will show unto them that my wisdom is greater than the cunning of the devil.

Behold they have only got a part, or an abridgment of the account of Nephi. Behold there are many things engraven on the plates of Nephi, which do throw greater views upon my gospel: therefore, it is wisdom in me, that you should translate this first part of the engravings of Nephi, and send forth in this work. And behold, all the remainder of this work, does contain all those parts of my gospel which my holy prophets; yea, and also my disciples desired in their prayers, should come forth unto this people. And I said unto them, that it should be granted unto them according to their faith in their prayers; yea, and this was their faith, that my gospel which I gave unto them, that they might preach in their days, might come unto their brethren, the Lamanites,[24] and also, all that had become Lamanites, because of their dissensions.

Now this is not all, their faith in their prayers were, that this gospel should be made known also, if it were possible that other nations should possess this land; and thus they did leave a blessing upon this land in their prayers, that whosoever should believe in this gospel, in this land, might have eternal life; yea, that it might be free unto all of whatsoever nation, kindred, tongue, or people, that may be.

And now, behold, according to their faith in their prayers, will I bring this part of my gospel to the knowledge of my people. Behold, I do not bring it to destroy that which they have received,[25] but to build it up.

And for this cause have I said, if this generation harden not their hearts, I will establish my church among them.[26] Now I do not say this to destroy my church, but I say this to build up my church: therefore, whosoever belongeth to my church need not fear, for such shall inherit the kingdom of heaven: but it is they who do not fear me, neither keep my commandments, but buildeth up churches unto themselves, to get gain; yea, and all those that do wickedly, and buildeth up the kingdom of the devil; yea, verily, verily I say unto you, that it is they that I will disturb, and cause to tremble and shake to the centre [center].

Behold, I am Jesus Christ, the Son of God: I came unto my own, and my own received me not. I am the light which shineth in darkness, and the darkness comprehendeth it not. I am he who said other sheep have I which are not of this fold, unto my disciples, and many there were that understood me not.

And I will show unto this people, that I had other sheep, and that they were a branch of the house of Jacob; and I will bring to light their marvelous works, which they did in my name; yea, and I will also bring to light my gospel, which was ministered unto them, and behold they shall not deny that which you have received, but they shall build it up, and shall bring to light the true points of my doctrine: Yea, and the only doctrine which is in me; and this I do, that I may establish my gospel, that there may not be so much contention: Yea, satan doth stir up the

---

24. "Lamanites" is a BOM term for the Native American Indians.
25. The Bible.
26. 1830 BOM, 501; LDS 3 Ne. 21:22/RLDS 10:1.

hearts of the people to contention, concerning the points of my doctrine; and in these things they do err, for they do wrest the scriptures, and do not understand them: therefore, I will unfold unto them this great mystery, for behold, I will gather them as a hen gathereth her chickens under her wings, if they will not harden their hearts: Yea, if they will come, they may, and partake of the waters of life freely.

Behold this is my doctrine: whosoever repenteth, and cometh unto me, the same is my church: whosoever declareth more or less than this, the same is not of me, but is against me: therefore, he is not of my church.

And now, behold whosoever is of my church, and endureth of my church to the end, him will I establish upon my Rock, and the gates of hell shall not prevail against them.

And now, remember the words of him who is the life and the light of the world, your Redeemer, your Lord and your God: Amen.

Revision

1835 D&C 36
(cf. LDS D&C 10:1-5, 20-23; RLDS D&C 3:1, 3)

Now, behold I say unto you, that because you delivered up *those* writings which you had power *given unto you* to translate, *by the means of the Urim and Thummim*, into the hands of a wicked man, you have lost them; and you also lost your gift at the same time, *and your mind became darkened*; nevertheless, it *is now* restored unto you again, therefore see that you are faithful and *continue* on unto the finishing of the remainder of the work *of translation* as you have begun: do not run faster, *or labor more* than you have strength and means provided to *enable you to* translate; but be diligent unto the end: *pray always*, that you may come off conquerer; yea, that you may conquer satan and *that you may escape the hands of the servants of satan*, that do uphold his work.

. . .

Verily, verily I say unto you, that satan has great hold upon their hearts; he stirreth them up to iniquity against that which is good, *And their hearts are corrupt, and full of wickedness and abominations, and they love darkness rather than light, because their deeds are evil: therefore they will not ask of me. Satan stirreth them up*, that he may lead their souls to destruction. And thus he has laid a cunning plan, *thinking* to destroy the work of God, *but I will require this at their hands, and it shall turn to their shame and condemnation in the day of judgment*

9. Behold It Is I That Speaketh
From BC 10 (cf. LDS D&C 11; RLDS D&C 10)

Revelation received at Harmony, Pennsylvania,
in [1-31] May 1829 for Hyrum Smith[27]

A Revelation given to Hyrum, in Harmony, Pennsylvania, May, 1829.

A great and marvelous work is about to come forth among the children of men: behold I am God and give heed to my word, which is quick and powerful, sharper than a two-edged sword, to the dividing asunder of both joints and marrow: therefore, give heed unto my word.

Behold the field is white already to harvest, therefore, whoso desireth to reap, let him thrust in his sickle with his might, and reap while the day lasts, that he may treasure up for his soul everlasting salvation in the kingdom of God; yea, whosoever will thrust in his sickle and reap, the same is called of God: therefore, if you will ask of me, you shall receive; if you will knock, it shall be opened unto you.

Now as you have asked, behold I say unto you, keep my commandments, and seek to bring forth and establish the cause of Zion. Seek not for riches but for wisdom, and behold the mysteries of God shall be unfolded unto you, and then shall you be made rich; behold he that hath eternal life is rich.

Verily, verily I say unto you, even as you desire of me, so shall it be done unto you; and, if you desire you shall be the means of doing much good in this generation. Say nothing but repentance unto this generation. Keep my commandments, and assist to bring forth my work according to my commandments, and you shall be blessed.

Behold thou has a gift, or thou shalt have a gift, if thou wilt desire of me in faith, with an honest heart, believing in the power of Jesus Christ, or in my power which speaketh unto thee: for behold it is I that speaketh: behold I am the light which shineth in darkness, and by my power I give these words unto thee.

And now, verily, verily I say unto thee, put your trust in that Spirit which leadeth to do good: Yea, to do justly; to walk humbly; to judge righteously; and this is my Spirit.

Verily, verily I say unto you, I will impart unto you of my Spirit, which shall enlighten your mind, which shall fill your soul with joy, and then shall you know, or by this shall you know, all things whatsoever you desire of me, which is pertaining unto things of righteousness, in faith believing in me that you shall receive.

Behold I command you, that you need not suppose that you are called to preach until you are called: wait a little longer, until you shall have my word, my Rock, my church, and my gospel, that you may know of a surety my doctrine; and then behold, according to your desires, yea, even according to your faith, shall it be done unto you.

Keep my commandments; hold your peace; appeal unto my Spirit: Yea, cleave

---

27. The opening portion of this revelation contains the same words as document no. 4.

unto me with all your heart, that you may assist in bringing to light those things of which have been spoken: Yea, the translation of my work: be patient until you shall accomplish it.

Behold this is your work, to keep my commandments: Yea, with all your might, mind, and strength: seek not to declare my word, but first seek to obtain my word, and then shall your tongues be loosed; then, if you desire you shall have my Spirit, and my word: Yea, the power of God unto the convincing of men: but now hold your peace; study my word which hath gone forth among the children of men; and also study my word which shall come forth among the children of men; or that which you are translating: Yea, until you have obtained all which I shall grant unto the children of men in this generation; and then shall all things be added thereunto.

Behold thou art Hyrum, my son; seek the kingdom of God and all things shall be added according to that which is just. Build upon my Rock, which is my gospel; deny not the Spirit of revelation, nor the Spirit of prophecy, for wo unto him that denieth these things: therefore, treasure up in your hearts until the time which is in my wisdom, that you shall go forth: Behold I speak unto all who have good desires, and have thrust in their sickles to reap.

Behold I am Jesus Christ, the Son of God: I am the life and the light of the world: I am the same which came unto my own, and my own received me not: but verily, verily I say unto you, that as many as receiveth me, them will I give power to become the sons of God, even to them that believe on my name: Amen.

10. Establish the Cause of Zion
From BC 11 (cf. LDS D&C 12; RLDS D&C 11)

*Revelation received at Harmony, Pennsylvania,
in [1-31] May 1829 for Joseph Knight, Sr.*[28]

A Revelation given to Joseph (K.,) in Harmony, Pennsylvania, May, 1829, informing him how he must do, to be worthy to assist in the work of the Lord.

A great and marvelous work is about to come forth among the children of men: behold I am God, and give heed to my word, which is quick and powerful, sharper than a two-edged sword, to the dividing asunder of both joints and marrow: therefore, give heed unto my word.

Behold the field is white already to harvest, therefore whoso desireth to reap, let him thrust in his sickle with his might, and reap while the day lasts, that he may treasure up for his soul everlasting salvation in the kingdom of God: Yea, whosoever will thrust in his sickle and reap, the same is called of God: therefore, if you will ask of me you shall receive; if you will knock it shall be opened unto you.

---

28. The first part of this revelation to Joseph Knight, Sr., contains the same wording as documents 4 and 9.

Now as you have asked, behold I say unto you, keep my commandments, and seek to bring forth and establish the cause of Zion.

Behold I speak unto you, and also to all those who have desires to bring forth and establish this work, and no one can assist in this work, except he shall be humble and full of love, having faith, hope and charity, being temperate in all things, whatsoever shall be intrusted to his care.

Behold I am the light and the life of the world, that speaketh these words: therefore, give heed with your might, and then you are called: Amen.

11. Keep My Commandments in All Things
From BC 12 (cf. LDS D&C 14; RLDS D&C 12)

Revelation received at Fayette, New York,
in [1-14] June 1829 for David Whitmer[29]

A Revelation given to David, in Fayette, New-York, June, 1829.

A great and marvelous work is about to come forth unto the children of men: behold I am God, and give heed to my word, which is quick and powerful, sharper than a two-edged sword, to the dividing asunder of both joints and marrow: therefore, give heed unto my word.

Behold the field is white already to harvest, therefore, whoso desireth to reap, let him thrust in his sickle with his might, and reap while the day lasts, that he may treasure up for his soul everlasting salvation in the kingdom of God: Yea, whosoever will thrust in his sickle and reap, the same is called of God: therefore, if you will ask of me you shall receive; if you will knock it shall be opened unto you.

Seek to bring forth and establish my Zion.— Keep my commandments in all things, and if you keep my commandments, and endure to the end, you shall have eternal life; which gift is the greatest of all the gifts of God.

And it shall come to pass, that if you shall ask the Father in my name, in faith believing, you shall receive the Holy Ghost, which giveth utterance, that you may stand as a witness of the things of which you shall both hear and see; and also, that you may declare repentance unto this generation.

Behold I am Jesus Christ the Son of the living God, which created the heavens and the earth; a light which cannot be hid in darkness: wherefore, I must bring forth the fulness of my gospel from the Gentiles unto the house of Israel. And behold thou art David, and thou art called to assist: Which thing if ye do, and are faithful, ye shall be blessed both spiritually and temporally, and great shall be your reward: Amen.

---

29. David Whitmer transported Joseph Smith and Oliver Cowdery from Harmony, Pennsylvania, to the residence of his father Peter Whitmer, Sr., in the township of Fayette, New York, about 1 June 1829. This revelation as well as the two which follow were given shortly after their arrival. The opening part of this revelation to David Whitmer contains the same words as documents 4, 9, and 10.

12. Hearken My Servant John
From BC 13 (cf. LDS D&C 15; RLDS D&C 13)

Revelation received at Fayette, New York,
in [1-14] June 1829 for John Whitmer[30]

A Revelation given to John, in Fayette, New-York, June, 1829.

Hearken my servant John [Whitmer], and listen to the words of Jesus Christ, your Lord and your Redeemer, for behold I speak unto you with sharpness and with power, for mine arm is over all the earth, and I will tell you that which no man knoweth save me and thee alone: for many times you have desired of me to know that which would be of the most worth unto you.

Behold, blessed are you for this thing, and for speaking my words which I have given you, according to my commandments:

And now behold I say unto you, that the thing which will be of the most worth unto you, will be to declare repentance unto this people, that you may bring souls unto me, that you may rest with them in the kingdom of my Father. Amen.

13. Hearken My Servant Peter
From BC 14 (cf. LDS D&C 16; RLDS D&C 14)

Revelation received at Fayette, New York,
in [1-14] June 1829 for Peter Whitmer, Jr.[31]

A Revelation given to Peter, in Fayette, New-York, June, 1829.

Hearken my servant Peter [Whitmer, Jr.], and listen to the words of Jesus Christ, your Lord and your Redeemer, for behold I speak unto you with sharpness and with power, for mine arm is over all the earth, and I will tell you that which no man knoweth save me and thee alone: for many times you have desired of me to know that which would be of the most worth unto you.

Behold, blessed are you for this thing, and for speaking my words which I have given you, according to my commandments:

And now behold I say unto you, that the thing which will be of the most worth unto you, will be to declare repentance unto this people, that you may bring souls unto me, that you may rest with them in the kingdom of my Father. Amen.

---

30. John Whitmer became a scribe to Smith for a portion of the BOM manuscript. Whitmer was twenty-seven years old.

31. The wording of this revelation is the same as that given to his brother John Whitmer (document no. 12).

14. Rely upon the Things Which Are Written
From BC 15 (cf. LDS D&C 18; RLDS D&C 16)

Revelation received at Fayette, New York, in [1-14] June 1829
for Joseph Smith, Jr., Oliver Cowdery, and David Whitmer[32]

A Revelation to Joseph, Oliver and David, making known the calling of twelve disciples in these last days, and also, instructions relative to building up the church of Christ, according to the fulness of the gospel: Given in Fayette, New-York, June, 1829.

Now behold, because of the thing which you have desired to know of me, I give unto you these words:

Behold I have manifested unto you, by my Spirit in many instances, that the things which you have written are true:

Wherefore you know that they are true; and if you know that they are true, behold I give unto you a commandment, that you rely upon the things which are written; for in them are all things written, concerning my church, my gospel, and my rock.

Wherefore if you shall build up my church, and my gospel, and my rock, the gates of hell shall not prevail against you.

Behold the world is ripening in iniquity, and it must needs be, that the children of men are stirred up unto repentance, both the Gentiles, and also the house of Israel:

Wherefore as thou hast been baptized by the hand of my servant, according to that which I have commanded him:

Wherefore he hath fulfilled the thing which I commanded him.

And now marvel not that I have called him unto mine own purpose, which purpose is know in me:

Wherefore if he shall be diligent in keeping my commandments, he shall be blessed unto eternal life, and his name is Joseph [Smith, Jr.].

And now Oliver [Cowdery], I speak unto you, and also unto David [Whitmer], by the way of commandment:

For behold I command all men every where to repent, and I speak unto you, even as unto Paul mine apostle, for you are called even with that same calling with which he was called.

Remember the worth of souls is great in the sight of God:

For behold the Lord your God suffered death in the flesh: wherefore he suffered the pain of all men, that all men might repent and come unto him.

And he hath risen again from the dead, that he might bring all men unto him on conditions of repentance.

---

32. This revelation was given by 14 June 1829 as a letter written by Oliver Cowdery to Hyrum Smith which contains similar wording. It was not until 6 April 1830 that the Church of Christ was organized at Manchester, New York. It was here that Oliver Cowdery ordained Joseph Smith an elder, prophet, and seer.

And how great is his joy in the soul that repenteth.

Wherefore you are called to cry repentance unto this people.

And if it so be that you should labor in all your days, in crying repentance unto this people, and bring save it be one soul only unto me, how great shall be your joy with him in the kingdom of my Father?

And now if your joy will be great with one soul, that you have brought unto me into the kingdom of my Father, how great will by your joy, if you should bring many souls unto me?

Behold you have my gospel before you, and my rock, and my salvation:

Ask the Father in my name in faith believing that you shall receive, and you shall have the Holy Ghost which manifesteth all things, which is expedient unto the children of men.

And if you have not faith, hope and charity, you can do nothing.

Contend against no church, save it be the church of the devil.

Take upon you the name of Christ, and speak the truth in soberness, and as many as repent, and are baptized in my name, which is Jesus Christ, and endure to the end, the same shall be saved.

Behold Jesus Christ is the name which is given of the Father, and there is none other name given whereby man can be saved:

Wherefore all men must take upon them the name which is given of the Father, for in that name shall they be called at the last day:

Wherefore if they know not the name by which they are called, they cannot have place in the kingdom of my Father.

And now behold, there are others which are called to declare my gospel, both unto Gentile and unto Jew: Yea, even unto twelve:

And the twelve shall be my disciples, and they shall take upon them my name:

And the twelve are they which shall desire to take upon them my name, with full purpose of heart:

And if they desire to take upon them my name, with full purpose of heart, they are called to go into all the world to preach my gospel unto every creature:

And they are they which are ordained of me to baptize in my name, according to that which is written; and you have that which is written before you:

Wherefore you must perform it according to the words which are written.

And now I speak unto the twelve:

Behold my grace is sufficient for you: You must walk uprightly before me and sin not.

And behold you are they which are ordained of me to ordain priests and teachers to declare my gospel, according to the power of the Holy Ghost which is in you, and according to the callings and gifts of God unto men:

And I Jesus Christ, your Lord and your God, have spoken it.

These words are not of men, nor of man, but of me:

Wherefore you shall testify they are of me, and not of man; for it is my voice which speaketh them unto you:

For they are given by my Spirit unto you:

And by my power you can read them one to another; and save it were by my power, you could not have them:

Wherefore you can testify that you have heard my voice, and know my words.

And now behold I give unto you, Oliver [Cowdery], and also unto David [Whitmer], that you shall search out the twelve which shall have the desires of which I have spoken; and by their desires and their works, you shall know them:[33]

And when you have found them you shall show these things unto them.

And you shall fall down and worship the Father in my name:

And you must preach unto the world, saying, you must repent and be baptized in the name of Jesus Christ:

For all men must repent and be baptized; and not only men, but women and children, which have arriven [arrived] to the years of accountability.

And now, after that you have received this, you must keep my commandments in all things:

And by your hands I will work a marvelous work among the children of men, unto the convincing of many of their sins, that they may come unto repentance; and that they may come unto the kingdom of my Father:

Wherefore the blessings which I give unto you are above all things.

And after that you have received this, if you keep not my commandments, you cannot be saved in the kingdom of my Father. Behold I Jesus Christ, your Lord and your God, and your Redeemer, by the power of my Spirit, have spoken it: Amen.

Revision

1835 D&C 43
(cf. LDS D&C 18:3-5, 11; RLDS D&C 16:1, 3)

behold I give unto you a commandment, that you rely upon the things which are written; for in them are all things written concerning *the foundation of* my church, my gospel and my rock; wherefore, if you shall build up my church *upon the foundation of* my gospel and my rock, the gates of hell shall not prevail against you.

.　　　.　　　.

for behold the Lord your *Redeemer* suffered death in the flesh: wherefore he suffered the pain of all men, that all men might repent and come unto him.

---

33. On 26 October 1831, "The Clerk [Oliver Cowdery] said that the directions which himself & his br[other]. David Whitmer had received this morning respecting the choice of the twelve was that they would be ordained & sent forth from the Land of Zion [Missouri]" (Donald Q. Cannon and Lyndon W. Cook, eds., *Far West Record: Minutes of The Church of Jesus Christ of Latter-day Saints, 1830-1844* [Salt Lake City: Deseret Book Co., 1983], 26). Five and a half years later, on 14 February 1835, Cowdery and David Whitmer with the addition of Martin Harris (the three witnesses to the Book of Mormon) chose twelve men to be ordained as apostles in Kirtland, Ohio (Kirtland Council Minute Book, 149).

15. It Is by Your Faith
that You Shall Obtain a View of Them
From 1835 D&C 42 (cf. LDS D&C 17; RLDS 15)

*Revelation received at Fayette, New York, in [14-30] June 1829
for Oliver Cowdery, David Whitmer, and Martin Harris*[34]

Revelation to Oliver Cowdery, David Whitmer and Martin Harris, June, 1829, given previous to their viewing the plates containing the book of Mormon:

Behold I say unto you, that you must rely upon my word, which if you do, with full purpose of heart, you shall have a view of the plates, and also the breastplate, the sword of Laban, the Urim and Thummim,[35] which were given to the brother of Jared upon the mount, when he talked with the Lord face to face, and the miraculous directors which were given to Lehi while in the wilderness, on the borders of the red sea; and it is by your faith that you shall obtain a view of them, even by that faith which was had by the prophets of old.

And after that you have obtained faith, and have seen them with your eyes, you shall testify of them, by the power of God; and this you shall do that my servant Joseph Smith, jr. may not be destroyed, that I may bring about my righteous purposes unto the children of men, in this work. And ye shall testify that you have seen them, even as my servant Joseph Smith, jr. has seen them, for it is by my power that he has seen them, and it is because he had faith: and he has translated the book, even that part which I have commanded him, and as your Lord and your God liveth it is true.

Wherefore you have received the same power, and the same faith, and the same gift like unto him; and if you do these last commandments of mine, which I have given you, the gates of hell shall not prevail against you; for my grace is sufficient for you: and you shall be lifted up at the last day.— And I, Jesus Christ, your Lord and your God, have spoken it unto you, that I might bring about my righteous purposes unto the children of men. Amen.

Commentary: Urim and Thummim

In two 1829 revelations, as published in the 1835 D&C, mention is made of the "Urim and Thummim." BC 9, dated May 1829, states that Smith delivered to Martin Harris writings "which you had power to translate." This was expanded to include (in italic) that Smith had power "to translate, *by the means of the Urim and Thummim.*" This addition, using the names of biblical instruments of divination, appears to be an anachronism for an 1829 revelation.

Of interest is that the second revelation, though in manuscript form, was not published in the BC. When it was copied into the Kirtland Revelations Book in

---

34. This revelation was written for the three witnesses but was not included in the BC. Ezra Booth mentioned that he examined it while he was in Missouri (Booth to Rev. Ira Eddy, 24 Oct. 1831, *Ohio Star* 2 [27 Oct. 1831]:3, Ravenna, Ohio).

35. The term "Urim and Thummim" as published in 1835 was not in use in 1829.

1834-35, the text had already been changed to reflect the current understanding. The three witnesses to the Book of Mormon were to see certain artifacts, such as "a view of the plates, and also the breastplate, the sword of Laban, the Urim and Thum[m]im."[36] The Kirtland Revelations Book manuscript copy thus reflects a later tradition not known in June 1829. The printed testimony of the three witnesses only mentioned the plates. It is of interest that while the term "Urim and Thummim" is contained in the Bible, it is not found in the Book of Mormon.

It was not until about 1832, over two years after the revelation, that the new term was used in church literature. In the *Evening and the Morning Star*, January 1833, is a brief tentative allusion to two biblical objects, Teraphim and Urim and Thummim: "It [the Book of Mormon] was translated by the gift and power of God, by an unlearned man, through the aid of a pair of Interpreters, or spectacles—(known, perhaps, in ancient days as Teraphim, or Urim and Thummim)[.]"[37]

Teraphim, it should be noted, were probably some sort of figurines or statues representing the image of idols. Worship of Teraphim was forbidden by the ten commandments. When mentioned in Israelite context, they are almost always condemned.[38] Teraphim were used for divination by opening up the liver and examining it.[39] It would be an odd quirk of historical fate for someone to suggest that the Teraphim would be used as a means for translating the Book of Mormon. One also wonders if the writer of the *Evening and the Morning Star* article knew the nature of biblical Urim and Thummim. There is no evidence that these were used for translation, as the term is presently understood. They were to obtain answers to specific questions which could be answered with a simple yes or no.[40]

The use of Urim and Thummim in connection with translating the Book of Mormon became a fact by the end of 1834. Oliver Cowdery wrote: "he [Joseph Smith] translated, with the *Urim* and *Thummim*, or, as the Nephites whould [would] have said, 'Interpreters,' the history, or record, called 'The book of Mormon.'"[41]

36. KRB, 119.
37. *The Evening and the Morning Star* 1 (Jan. 1833): [2; whole page 58]. See also the July 1832 issue [6; whole page 14] that mentions "Teraphim, [Urim & Thummim, perhaps] or sacred spectacles or declarers."
38. See J. D. Douglas, ed., *The New Bible Dictionary* (Grand Rapids, MI: Wm. B. Eerdmans Publishing Co., 1978), "Teraphim," 1,253; "Urim and Thummim," 1,306. Teraphim in the King James Version (KJV): Judg. 17:5; 18:14, 17-18, 20, and Hosea 3:4. "Urim" and "Thummim" in KJV in the following passages: Ex. 28:30; Lev. 8:8; Deut. 33:8; Ezra 2:63; Neh. 7:65. "Urim" in Num. 27:21; 1 Sam. 28:6.
39. Ezek. 21:21.
40. Douglas, *New Bible Dictionary*, 1,306; Kenneth Sowers, "The Mystery and History of the Urim and Thummim," *Restoration Studies II* (Independence, MO: Herald Publishing House, 1983), 75-79. See also "Urim and Thummim" in *The Interpreter's Dictionary of the Bible: An Illustrated Encyclopedia* (New York: Abingdon Press, 1962), 4:739-40.
41. Cowdery to William W. Phelps, 7 Sept. 1834, in *Messenger and Advocate* 1 (Oct. 1834): 14, emphasis in original. Phelps wrote on 15 January 1831 that he heard that the Book of Mormon "was interpreted by Joseph Smith, through a pair of silver spectacles, found with the plates" (Phelps to E. D. Howe, 15 Jan. 1831, in E. D. Howe, *Mormonism Unvailed* [Painesville (OH): Printed and Published by the Author, 1834], 273).

That "Urim and Thummim" was an addition to the text is evident since it was a development in early church history and culminated in its inclusion in the 1835 D&C.[42] Primary sources tell us that a seer stone was used in the translation process. But the wording here does not clear up questions about what objects were used in producing the Book of Mormon.

16. Pay the Printer's Debt
From BC 16 (cf. LDS D&C 19; RLDS D&C 18)

*Commandment received at Manchester, New York,
in [26-31] March 1830 for Martin Harris*[43]

A commandment of God and not of man to you, Martin, given (Manchester, New-York, March, 1830,) by him who is eternal:

Yea, even I, I am he, the beginning and the end: Yea, Alpha and Omega, Christ the Lord, the Redeemer of the world:
I having accomplished and finished the will of him whose I am, even the Father:
Having done this, that I might subdue all things unto myself:
Retaining all power, even to the destroying of satan and his works at the end of the world, and the last great day of judgment, which I shall pass upon the inhabitants thereof, judging every man according to his works, and the deeds which he hath done.
And surely every man must repent or suffer, for I God am endless:
Wherefore, I revoke not the judgments which I shall pass, but woes shall go forth, weeping, wailing and gnashing of teeth:
Yea, to those who are found on my left hand, nevertheless, it is not written, that there shall be no end to this torment; but it is written endless torment.
Again, it is written eternal damnation: wherefore it is more express than other scriptures, that it might work upon the hearts of the children of men, altogether for my name's glory:
Wherefore, I will explain unto you, this mystery, for it is mete unto you, to know even as mine apostles.
I speak unto you that are chosen in this thing, even as one, that you may enter into my rest.

---

42. See Charles A. Davies in *Question Time* (Independence, MO: Herald House, 1967), 2: 111-12; and Richard P. Howard, *Restoration Scriptures: A Study of Their Textual Development* (Independence, MO: Herald House, 1969), 207-209; (2nd ed., 1995), 152-53. The BOM mentions two stones being received by the brother of Jared. See 1830 BOM, 545; LDS Ether 3:23, 28/RLDS 1:88, 93.

43. The BOM was advertised as being available for purchase on 26 March 1830 in the *Wayne Sentinel* (Palmyra, NY). Shortly afterwards, Martin Harris was at the Smith home in Manchester and insisted on having a commandment. See Dean C. Jessee, ed., "Joseph Knight's Recollection of Early Mormon History," *BYU Studies* 17 (Autumn 1976): 37. The revelation would have been given between 26 and 31 March 1830.

For behold, the mystery of Godliness how great is it? for behold I am endless, and the punishment which is given from my hand, is endless punishment, for endless is my name:

Wherefore— Eternal punishment is God's punishment: Endless punishment is God's punishment:

Wherefore, I command you by my name, and by my Almighty power, that you repent: repent, lest I smite you by the rod of my mouth, and by my wrath, and by my anger, and your sufferings be sore:

How sore you know not!

How exquisite you know not!

Yea, how hard to bear you know not!

For behold, I God have suffered these things for all, that they might not suffer, if they would repent, but if they would not repent, they must suffer even as I:

Which suffering caused myself, even God, the greatest of all, to tremble because of pain, and to bleed at every pore, both body and spirit:

And would that I might not drink the bitter cup and shrink:

Nevertheless, glory be to the Father, and I partook and finished my preparations unto the children of men:

Wherefore, I command you again by my Almighty power, that you confess your sins, lest you suffer these punishments of which I have spoken, of which in the smallest, yea, even in the least degree you have tasted at the time I withdrew my Spirit.

And I command you, that you preach nought but repentance; and show not these things, neither speak these things unto the world, for they can not bear meat, but milk they must receive:

Wherefore, they must not know these things lest they perish:

Wherefore, learn of me, and listen to my words; walk in the meekness of my Spirit and you shall have peace in me, Jesus Christ by the will of the Father.

And again: I command you, that thou shalt not covet thy neighbor's wife.

Nor seek thy neighbor's life.

And again: I command you, that thou shalt not covet thine own property, but impart it freely to the printing of the book of Mormon, which contains the truth and the word of God, which is my word to Gentile, that soon it may go to the Jew, of which the Lamanites are a remnant; that they may believe the gospel, and look not for a Messiah to come which has already come.

And again: I command you, that thou shalt pray vocally as well as to thyself:

Yea, before the world as well as in secret; in public as well as in private.

And thou shalt declare glad tidings; yea, publish it upon the mountains, and upon every high place, and among every people which thou shalt be permitted to see.

And thou shalt do it with all humility, trusting in me, reviling not against revilers.

And of tenets thou shalt not talk, but thou shalt declare repentance and faith on the Savior and remission of sins by baptism and by fire; yea, even the Holy Ghost.

Behold this is a great and the last commandment which I shall give unto you:
For this shall suffice for thy daily walk even unto the end of thy life.

And misery thou shalt receive, if thou wilt slight these counsels; Yea, even destruction of thyself and property.

Impart a portion of thy property; Yea, even a part of thy lands and all save the support of thy family.

Pay the printer's debt.

Release thyself from bondage.

Leave thy house and home, except when thou shalt desire to see them.

And speak freely to all: Yea, preach, exhort, declare the truth, even with a loud voice; with a sound of rejoicing, crying hosanna! hosanna! blessed be the name of the Lord God.

Pray always and I will pour out my Spirit upon you, and great shall be your blessing:

Yea, even more than if you should obtain treasures of earth, and corruptibleness to the extent thereof.

Behold, canst thou read this without rejoicing, and lifting up thy heart for gladness; or canst thou run about longer as a blind guide; or canst thou be humble and meek and conduct theyself wisely before me:

Yea, come unto me thy Savior. Amen.

Revision

1835 D&C 44
(cf. LDS D&C 19:13-15, 20-26, 32, 35; RLDS D&C 18:2-3, 5)

wherefore, I command you *to repent, and keep the commandments which you have received* by *the hand of my servant Joseph Smith, jr. in* my name: and *it is* by my almighty power that you *have received them: therefore I command you to* repent, repent, lest I smite you by the rod of my mouth, and by my wrath, and by my anger, and your sufferings be sore: how sore you know not! how exquisite you know not! yea, how hard to bear you know not!

.   .   .

wherefore, I command you again *to repent lest I humble you* by my almighty power, *and* that you confess your sins lest you suffer these punishments of which I have spoken, of which in the smallest, yea, even in the least degree you have tasted at the time I withdrew my Spirit.

And I command you, that you preach nought but repentance; and show not these things unto the world *until it is wisdom in me*; for they cannot bear meat *now*, but milk they must receive: wherefore, they must not know these things lest they perish: learn of me, and listen to my words; walk in the meekness of my Spirit and you shall have peace in me: *I am* Jesus Christ: *I came* by the will of the Father, *and I do his will.*

And again: I command *thee*, that thou shalt not covet thy neighbor's wife. Nor seek thy neighbor's life. And again: I command *thee*, that thou shalt not covet thine own property, but impart it freely to the printing of the book of Mormon

.   .   .

Behold, this is a great, and the last commandment which I shall give unto you *concerning this matter*

.   .   .

Pay the debt *thou hast contracted with the* printer.

Commentary: Stress on Joseph Smith's Revelations

BC 16 is a commandment to Martin Harris previous to the church's organization. A comparison shows that the emphasis "I [God] command you by my name" is subordinated to Smith's authority as revelator. The additional wording in the text would not have been what Harris had heard in 1830. The change emphasizes Harris's need to obey the commandments he received through Smith.

Another textual addition qualifies the command to "show not these things, neither speak these things unto the world" with the words "until it is wisdom in me," implying that Harris was to be silent on certain matters but that the 1835 committee was free of such a proscription. That this is a correct understanding may be seen in a later revelation dated 3 November 1831 wherein it states clearly: "And for this cause these commandments were given; they were commanded to be kept from the world in the d[a]y that they were given, but now are to go forth unto all flesh[.]"[44] This phrase "until it is wisdom in me" was probably added to the revelation for Martin Harris because it would now be published to the world.

---

44. Document no. 77; *The Evening and the Morning Star* 1 (May 1833): [2; whole page no. 90]; LDS D&C 133:60; RLDS D&C 108:11.

Introduction to Chapters 3 to 6.
Church of Christ Years, April 1830–May 1834

At Manchester, New York, early members received guidance as Joseph Smith, Jr., spoke words of encouragement. Three church conferences were held in Fayette, New York. Instructions were given to relocate to the state of Ohio. Sidney Rigdon, a recent convert, became a scribe and friend of Smith. The two worked periodically on a revision of the Bible, and revelations concerning their progress were received during this time. A communal law of consecration instructed members to consecrate their property and receive an inheritance from the church bishop. Kirtland, Ohio, was now church headquarters. A major emphasis was locating the New Jerusalem (Zion) in Jackson County, Missouri. Missionaries were called to preach to outsiders from the Bible, Book of Mormon, and Smith's revelations. For about one year, Smith lived at John Johnson Sr.'s residence in Hiram, Ohio. Problems with church members were solved by revelations from Smith. Financial matters accelerated as the church borrowed money to purchase equipment and food items for its United Firm. Church members were forced to leave Jackson County. The concepts of Zion, temples, and priesthood were developed. The majority of Smith's pronouncements were given in Ohio during these early years.

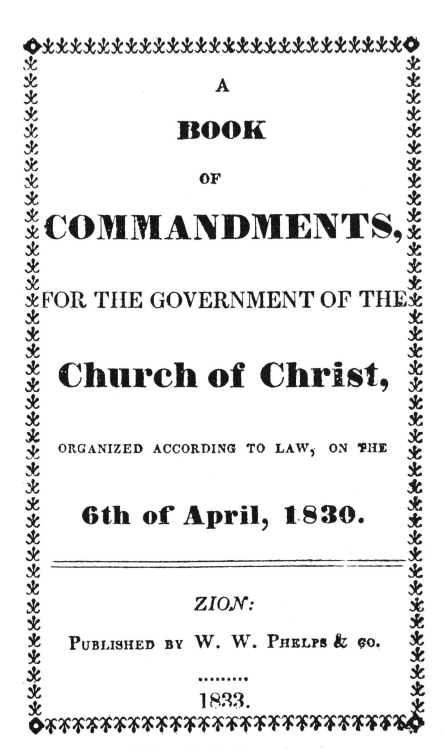

A

BOOK

OF

COMMANDMENTS,

FOR THE GOVERNMENT OF THE

Church of Christ,

ORGANIZED ACCORDING TO LAW, ON THE

6th of April, 1830.

ZION:

PUBLISHED BY W. W. PHELPS & CO.

....

1833.

Title Page of Book of Commandments

3. Laying the Foundation, April 1830-January 1831

17. Beware of Pride
From BC 17 (cf. LDS D&C 23:1-2; RLDS D&C 21:1)

Revelation received at Manchester, New York,
on 6 April 1830 for Oliver Cowdery[1]

A Revelation to Oliver, given in Manchester, New-York, April 6, 1830.

Behold I speak unto you, Oliver [Cowdery], a few words: Behold thou art blessed, and art under no condemnation.

But beware of pride, lest thou shouldst enter into temptation.

Make known thy calling unto the church, and also before the world; and thy heart shall be opened to preach the truth from henceforth and forever. Amen.

Commentary: Revelations of 6 April 1830

Five of the 6 April 1830 revelations "given in Manchester, New-York" were combined into one revelation given to five individuals. The 1835 D&C retained the same basic wording but dropped the location where the Church of Christ was organized from the headings. Six revelations (BC 17-22) were originally dated 6 April.

Only one of these retained the same date when published in the 1835 D&C. This was BC 22 (1835 D&C 46) which mentions that a record should be kept and that Smith should be ordained by Cowdery. All indications confirm that Smith and Cowdery were present at the Smith residence at the time of this historic meeting.[2] The time-line below will help clarify the events for March to June 1830.

---

1. The Church of Christ was established in the township of Manchester on 6 April 1830. See H. Michael Marquardt and Wesley P. Walters, *Inventing Mormonism: Tradition and the Historical Record* (San Francisco: Smith Research Associates, 1994), 153-72.

2. H. Michael Marquardt, "An Appraisal of Manchester as Location for the Organization of the Church," *Sunstone* 16 (Feb. 1992): 49-57.

Palmyra, New York
26 March   The *Wayne Sentinel* advertises the Book of Mormon for sale.
Manchester, New York
[26-31] March   Joseph Smith arrives in Manchester with Joseph Knight, Sr.;
                 a commandment is given to Martin Harris (BC 16; LDS D&C
                 19; RLDS D&C 18).
6 April   The Church of Christ is organized; six revelations are received
                 (BC 17-22; LDS D&C 21, 23; RLDS D&C 19, 21). Oliver
                 Cowdery is ordained an elder. Joseph Smith is ordained an
                 elder, prophet, and seer by Cowdery. Joseph Smith, Sr., Lucy
                 Mack Smith, Martin Harris and Sarah Rockwell are baptized in
                 Crooked Brook.
Fayette, New York
11-16 April   A Fayette, New York, branch of the church is established.
                 Cowdery delivers the first public discourse of the church and
                 performs baptisms. A revelation is received regarding individuals
                 who have been baptized in other Christian churches (BC 23;
                 LDS D&C 22; RLDS D&C 20).
18 April   More baptisms are performed by Cowdery.
9 June   The first conference of the church is held; articles and covenants
                 are presented (BC 24; LDS D&C 20; RLDS D&C 17). Baptisms
                 are performed. Joseph Sr. and Hyrum Smith are ordained priests.

Joseph Knight, Sr., wrote an account concerning some of the events of 6 April
(original spelling retained):

> Now in the Spring of 1830 I went with my Team and took Joseph [Smith] out to
> Manchester to his Father. When we was on our way he told me that there must be a
> Church formed But did not tell when. ... I stay[e]d a few Days wa[i]ting for some Books
> [of Mormon] to Be Bound. Joseph said there must Be a Church B[u]iltup. I had Be[e]n
> there several Days. Old Mr Smith and Martin Harris Come forrod [forward] to Be Bap-
> tise[d] for the first. They found a place in a lot a small Stream ran thro[ugh] and they
> ware Babtized in the Evening Because of persecution. They went forward and was Bab-
> tized Being the first I saw Babtized in the new and everlasting Covenant. ...
> There was one thing I will mention that evening that old Brother Smith and Martin
> Harris was Babtised. Joseph was fil[le]d with the Spirit to a grate Degree to see his Father
> and Mr Harris that he had Bin [been] with so much he Bast [Burst] out with greaf and
> Joy and seamed as tho[ugh] the world Could not hold him. He went out into the Lot
> and appear[e]d to want to git [get] out of site of every Body and would sob and Crie and
> seamed to Be so full that he could not live. Oliver and I went after him and Came to him
> and after a while he Came in. But he was the most wrot [wrought] upon that I ever saw
> any man. But his joy seemed to Be full. I think he saw the grate [great] work he had Be-
> gun and was Desirus [Desirous] to Carry it out. On the sixth Day of April 1830 he Be-
> gun the Church with six members and received the following Revelation Book of
> Covenants Page 177. [BC 22][3]

---

3. Dean C. Jessee, ed., "Joseph Knight's Recollection of Early Mormon History," *BYU Studies* 17 (Autumn 1976): 36–37. Minimal punctuation and editing have been added to clarify the
account. See LDS D&C 21; RLDS D&C 19.

There are several possible explanations for the 1835 change of venue. It is possible that memories of these momentous events became conflated over time. It is also possible that image-consciousness played a role. It may have seemed impressive to advertise the church's founding at a distant location, away from the Smiths' humble log cabin and critics of the family. More likely was a motivation to render ambiguous the church's legal history at a time when creditors were demanding satisfaction—a rationale which might also explain why the church's name was changed in mid-1834.

18. Thy Duty Is unto the Church Forever
From BC 18 (cf. LDS D&C 23:3; RLDS D&C 21:2)

Revelation received at Manchester, New York,
on 6 April 1830 for Hyrum Smith

A Revelation to Hyrum, given in Manchester, New-York, April 6, 1830.

Behold I speak unto you, Hyrum [Smith], a few words:
For thou also art under no condemnation, and thy heart is opened, and thy tongue loosed;
And thy calling is to exhortation, and to strengthen the church continually.
Wherefore thy duty is unto the church forever; and this because of thy family. Amen.

19. Strengthen the Church
From BC 19 (cf. LDS D&C 23:4; RLDS D&C 21:3)

Revelation received at Manchester, New York,
on 6 April 1830 for Samuel H. Smith

A Revelation to Samuel, given in Manchester, New-York, April 6, 1830.

Behold I speak a few words unto you, Samuel [H. Smith]:
For thou also art under no condemnation, and thy calling is to exhortation, and to strengthen the church.
And thou art not as yet called to preach before the world. Amen.

20. Thou Also Art Under No Condemnation
From BC 20 (cf. LDS D&C 23:5; RLDS D&C 21:4)

Revelation received at Manchester, New York,
on 6 April 1830 for Joseph Smith, Sr.[4]

A Revelation to Joseph [Smith, Sr.], the father of Joseph [Smith, Jr.], given in Manchester, New-York, April 6, 1830.

Behold I speak a few words unto you, Joseph [Smith, Sr.]:
For thou also art under no condemnation, and thy calling also is to exhortation, and to strengthen the church.
And this is thy duty from henceforth and forever. Amen.

21. It Is Your Duty to Unite with the True Church
From BC 21 (cf. LDS D&C 23:6-7; RLDS D&C 21:5)

Revelation received at Manchester, New York,
on 6 April 1830 for Joseph Knight, Sr.[5]

A Revelation to Joseph (K.,) [Joseph Knight, Sr.] given in Manchester, New-York, April 6, 1830.

Behold I manifest unto you by these words, that you must take up your cross, in the which you must pray vocally before the world, as well as in secret, and in your family, and among your friends, and in all places.
And behold it is your duty to unite with the true church, and give your language to exhortation continually, that you may receive the reward of the laborer. Amen.

22. The Gates of Hell Shall Not Prevail Against You
From BC 22 (cf. LDS D&C 21; RLDS D&C 19)

Revelation received at Manchester, New York, on 6 April 1830
for Joseph Smith, Jr., and the Church of Christ[6]

A Revelation to Joseph [Smith, Jr.], given in Manchester, New-York, April 6, 1830.

Behold there shall be a record kept among you, and in it thou shalt be called a

---

4. Joseph Smith, Sr., was baptized in Crooked Brook, Manchester Township, on 6 April 1830.
5. Joseph Knight, Sr., was not baptized at this time. He had not read the Book of Mormon and wanted to examine it more. See Jessee, "Joseph Knight's Recollection," 37.
6. This revelation gives instructions to proceed with ordaining Joseph Smith as a prophet and seer over the church.

seer, a translator, a prophet, an apostle of Jesus Christ, an elder of the church through the will of God the Father, and the grace of our Lord Jesus Christ;

Being inspired of the Holy Ghost to lay the foundation thereof, and to build it up unto the most holy faith;

Which church was organized and established, in the year of our Lord eighteen hundred and thirty, in the fourth month, and on the sixth day of the month, which is called April.

Wherefore, meaning the church, thou shalt give heed unto all his words, and commandments, which he shall give unto you, as he receiveth them, walking in all holiness before me:

For his word ye shall receive, as if from mine own mouth, in all patience and faith;

For by doing these things, the gates of hell shall not prevail against you:

Yea, and the Lord God will disperse the powers of darkness from before you; and cause the heavens to shake for your good, and his name's glory.

For thus saith the Lord God, him have I inspired to move the cause of Zion in mighty power for good; and his diligence I know, and his prayers I have heard:

Yea, his weeping for Zion I have seen, and I will cause that he shall mourn for her no longer, for his days of rejoicing are come unto the remission of his sins, and the manifestations of my blessings upon his works.

For behold, I will bless all those who labor in my vineyard, with a mighty blessing, and they shall believe on his words, which are given him through me, by the Comforter:

Which manifesteth that Jesus was crucified by sinful men for the sins of the world;

Yea, for the remission of sins unto the contrite heart.

Wherefore, it behooveth me, that he should be ordained by you, Oliver [Cowdery], mine apostle;

This being an ordinance unto you, that you are an elder under his hand, he being the first unto you, that you might be an elder unto this church of Christ, bearing my name;

And the first preacher of this church, unto the church, and before the world; yea, before the Gentiles:

Yea, and thus saith the Lord God, lo, lo, to the Jews, also. Amen.

23. This Is a New and an Everlasting Covenant
From the William E. McLellin Collection,
LDS archives (cf. LDS D&C 22; RLDS D&C 20)

Commandment received at Fayette, New York, on 16 April 1830 for the Church of Christ[7]

A commandment to the church of Christ which was established in these last days in the year of our Lord 1830 on the fourth month and on the sixth day of the month which is called April

Behold I say unto you that all old covenants have I caused to be done away in this thing and this is a new and an everlasting covenant even the same which was from the beginning

Wherefore although a man should be baptized a hundred times it availeth him nothing for ye cannot enter in at the strait gate by the Law of Moses neither by your dead works

for it is because of your dead works that I have caused this last Covenant and this church to be built up unto me wherefore enter ye in at the gate as I have commanded you and seek not to counsel your God. Amen.

April 16th 1830 Joseph Smith

24. The Rise of the Church of Christ
From the Zebedee Coltrin Journal, LDS archives
(cf. LDS D&C 20; RLDS D&C 17)

The Articles and Covenants of the Church of Christ composed at Fayette, New York, in [1-9] June 1830[8]

The rise of the Church of Christ in thes[e] last days being 1830 years since the coming of our lord & saveiour [Savior] Jesus Christ in the flesh it being regularly

---

7. The Fayette branch of the church was established on 11 April 1830. Baptisms were also performed at Fayette on 18 April 1830 (see Dean C. Jessee, ed., *The Papers of Joseph Smith: Autobiographical and Historical Writings* [Salt Lake City: Deseret Book Co., 1989], 1:244, 304). The BC contains the following in the introduction to this document: "Given in Fayette, New-York, April, 1830, in consequence of some desiring to unite with the church without re-baptism, who had previously been baptized." This commandment concerns itself with individuals who had been baptized in other Christian churches. These converts wanted to know if it was necessary to be baptized again in order to unite with the new church founded by Joseph Smith, Jr.

8. The first conference of the Church of Christ was held in Fayette Township, New York, on 9 June 1830. The conference minutes of that date were copied into a record book called the Far West Record. The minutes state that the "Articles and Covenants [were] read by Joseph Smith jr. and received by unanimous voice of the whole congregation" (Donald Q. Cannon and Lyndon W. Cook, eds., *Far West Record: Minutes of the Church of Jesus Christ of Latter-day Saints, 1830-1844* [Salt Lake City: Deseret Book Co., 1983], 1). Though copied in 1832, the text in the Zebedee Coltrin Journal compares favorably with three other manuscripts.

organized & established agreeable to the laws of our Country by the will & commandments of God in the fourth Month & on the Sixth day of the Month which is
called April which commandments were given to Joseph [Smith, Jr.] the seer who
was called of God & ordained an Apostle of Jesus Christ an Elder of the Church &
also to Oliver [Cowdery] who was also called of God an Apostle of Jesus Christ an
Elder of the Church & ordained under his hand & this according to the grace of
our Lord & Saveiour [Savior] Jesus Christ to whom be all glory both now & for
ever Amen

For after that it was truly manifested unto this first Elder[9] that he had received a
remission of his Sins he was entangled again in the vanities of the world but after
truly repenting god ministered unto him by an Holy angel whose countenance was
as lightning & whose garments were pure & white above all whiteness & gave unto
him commandments which inspired him from on high & gave unto him power by
the means which was before prepa[red] that he should translate a Book which
Book contained a Record of a fallen people & also the fullness of the gospel of Jesus
Christ to the gentiles & also to the Jews proving unto them that the Holy Scriptures are true & also that God doth inspire men & call them to his holy work in
these last days as well as in days of old that he might be the same God for ever Amen

Which Book was given by inspiration & is called the Book of Mormon & is
confirmed to others by the ministering of Angels & declared unto the world by
them wherefore having so great witnesses by them shall the world be Judged even
as many as shall hereafter receive this work either to faith & righteousness or to the
hardness of heart in unbelief to their own condemnati[on] for the Lord god hath
spoken it for we the Elders of the Church have heard & bear witness to the words
of his glorious majesty on high to whom be glory for ever & ever Amen

Wherefore by these things we know that there is a god in heaven who is infinite
& eternal from everlasting to everlasting the same unchang[e]able God the maker
of heaven & Earth & all things that in them is & that he created man male & female
& after his own image And in his likeness created he them & that he gave unto the
children of men a commandment that they Should love & Serve him the only being whom they should worship but by the transgression of these holy laws man became sensual & devilish & became fallen man

Wherefore the almighty God gave his only begotten Son as it is written in those
Scriptures which have been given of him that he suffered temptations but gave no
heed unto them that he was crucified died & rose again the third day & that he as-
cended into Heaven to sit down on the right hand of the father to reign with almighty power according to the will of the father therefore as many as would believe & were baptized in his holy name & endured in faith to the end should be
saved yea even as many as were before he came in the flesh from the begin[n]ing
which believed in the words of the Holy Prophets which were inspired by the gift
of the Holy Ghost which truly testify of him in all things as well as those who
should come after who should believe in the gifts & callings of God by the Holy

---

9. Joseph Smith, Jr.

ghost which beareth record of the father & of the Son which father & Son & holy ghost is one god infinite & eternal without end Amen

And we know that all men must repent & believe on the name of Jesus christ & worship the father in his name & endure in faith on his name to the end or they cannot be saved in the kingdom of God & we know that Justification through the grace of our Lord & saveiour [Savior] J[e]sus Christ is Just & true

& we also know that Sanctification through the grace of our Lord & saveiour [Savior] Jesus christ is Just & true to all those who love & serve God with all their mights minds & strength but there is a pos[s]ibility that men may fall from grace & depart from the living God therefore let the church take heed & pray always lest they fall into temptation yea & even he that is san[c]tified also

& we know that these things are true & agreeable to the revelations of John neither adding nor diminishing to the Prophecy of his book neither to the Holy Scriptures neither to the revelations of God which Shall come hereafter by the gift & power of the holy ghost neither by the voice of God neither by the ministering of Angels & the Lord god hath spoken it & honour power & glory be rendered to his holy name both now & ever Amen

And again by way of commandment to the church concerning the manner of Baptism Book of Mormon Page 576[10]

The duty of the Elders Priests Teachers Deacons & Members of the Church of Christ an Apostle is an Elder & it is his calling to Baptize & to ordain other Elders Priests Teachers & Deacons & to administer the flesh & blood of Christ according to the Scriptures & to teach expound exhort & to Baptize & to watch over the Church & to confirm the Church by the laying on of the hands & the giving of the Holy Ghost & to take the lead of all meetings &c

The Elders are to conduct the meetings according as they are led by the Holy Ghost

The Priests duty is to Preach teach expound exhort & baptize & administer the sacrament & visit the house of each member & exhort them to pray vocally & in Secret & also to attend all family duties & ordain other Priests Teachers & Deacons & take the lead in meetings but none of these offices are they to do when there is an Elder Present but in all cases are to assist the Elders &c

The Teachers duty is to watch over the church always & be with them & strengthen them & see that there is no iniquity in the church nor hardness with each other nor lying nor backbiting nor evil speaking & see that the Church meets together often & also that every member does his duty & he is to take the lead of Meetings in the absence of Elder or Priest & is to be assisted always & in all his duties in the Church by the deacons but neither the Teachers nor the Deacons have authority to Baptize nor administer the Sacrament but are to warn expound exhort & teach & invite all to come to Christ

Every Elder Priest Teacher or Deacon is to be ordained according to the gifts & callings of God unto him by the Power of the holy Ghost which is in the one who ordains him

---

10. See 1830 BOM, 576; LDS Moro. 6:1–4/RLDS 6:1–5.

The several Elders composing this Church of Christ are to meet in conference one [once] in three month[s] to [do] Church business whatsoever is nessessary [necessary] &c

& each Priest or Teacher who is ordained by any Priest is to take a cirtificate [certificate] from him at the time which when shown to an Elder he is to give him a licence [license] which shall authorize him to perform the duty of his calling

The Duty of the members after they are received by Baptism the Elders or Priests are to have a sufficient time to expound all things concerning this Church of Christ to their understanding previous to their partaking of the Sacrament & being confirmed by the laying on of the hands of the Elders so that all things may be done in order & the members shall manifest before the Church & also before the Elders by a Godly walk & conversation that they are worthy of it that there may be works & faith agreeable to the Holy Scriptures walking in holyness before the Lord

Every member of this Church of Christ having children is to bring them unto the Elders before the Church who is to lay their hands on them in the name of the Lord & bless them in the name of Christ

There cannot any one be received into this church of Christ who has not ariven [arrived] to the years of accountability before God & is not capable of repentance And Baptism is to be administered in the following manner[11] unto all those who repent whosoever being called of God & having authority given them of Jesus Christ shall go down into the water with them & shall say calling them by name having authority given me of Jesus Christ I baptize you in the name of the father & of the Son & of the Holy Ghost Amen then shall he immerse them in the water & come forth again out of the water

& it is expedient that the Church meet together often to partake of bread & wine in remembrance of the Lord Jesus & the Elder or Priest shall minister it & after this manner shall he do Book of Mormon Page 175 [575]

Any member of this church of christ transgressing or being over taken in a fault shall be dealt with according as the Scriptures direct &c

It shall be the duty of the Several Churches composing this church of Christ to send one or more of their Teachers to attend the Several conferences held by the Elders of this Church with a list of the names of the Several members uniting themselves to the Church since the last conference or send by the hand of some Priest so that there can be kept a regular list of all the names of the members of the whole Church in a book kept by one of the Elders whomsoever the other Elders shall appoint from time to time & also if any have been expelled from the Church so that their names may be blotted out of the general Church record of names

---

11. *The Telegraph*, a newspaper in Painesville, Ohio, published a copy of the Articles and Covenants which was obtained from Martin Harris. The wording for this part is as follows: "And the manner of baptism & the manner of administering the sacrament are to be done as it is written in the Book of Mormon" (*The Telegraph* 2 [19 Apr. 1831]:4; cf. 1830 BOM, 478; LDS 3 Ne. 11:23-26/RLDS 5:24-26 and 1830 BOM, 575; LDS and RLDS Moro. chaps. 4 and 5). This portion of the Articles and Covenants of the Church of Christ should be compared with the text in Appendix F, "A commandment of God unto Oliver" written in 1829, where the baptismal and sacramental prayers are included and also the ordination prayer as written in the Book of Mormon.

Any Member removing from the Church where he belongs if going to a Church where he is not known may take a letter certifying that he is a regular member & in good standing which certificate may be signed by any Elder or Priest if the member receiving the letter is Personally acquainted with the Elder or Priest or it may be signed by the Teacher[s] or Deacons of the Church

Revision

1835 D&C 2
(cf. LDS D&C 20:6-19, 25-28, 32-34, 38-41, 45, 64-67, 72-73; RLDS D&C 17:2-6, 8-9, 15-17, 21)

but after repenting, *and humbling himself, sincerely, through faith* God ministered unto him by an holy angel whose countenance was as lightning, and whose garments were pure and white above all *other* whiteness, and gave unto him commandments which inspired him, and gave him power from on high, by the means which *were* before prepared, *to* translate the book of Mormon, which *contains* a record of a fallen people, and the fulness of the gospel of Jesus Christ to the Gentiles, and to the Jews also, which was given by inspiration, and is confirmed to others by the ministering of angels, and *is* declared unto the world by them, proving *to the world* that the holy scriptures are true, and that God does inspire men and call them to his holy work in *this age and generation*, as well as in *generations* of old, *thereby showing* that he *is* the same God *yesterday, to-day, and* forever. - Amen.

Therefore, having so great witnesses, by them shall the world be judged, even as many as shall hereafter *come to a knowledge of* this work; *and those who receive it in* faith and *work* righteousness, *shall receive a crown of eternal life; but those who harden their hearts* in unbelief *and reject it, it shall turn* to their own condemnation, for the Lord God has spoken it; *and* we, the elders of the church, have heard and bear witness to the words of *the* glorious Majesty on high, to whom be glory forever and ever. Amen.

By these things we know that there is a God in heaven who is infinite and eternal, from everlasting to everlasting the same unchangeable God, the *framer* of heaven and earth and all things *which are* in them, and that he created man male and female: after his own image and in his own likeness created he them, and gave unto *them commandments* that they should love and serve him *the only living and true God, and that he should be* the only being whom they should worship.

.   .   .

that as many as would believe and *be* baptized, in his holy name, and endure in faith to the end should be saved: *not only those who believed after he came in the meridian of time* in the flesh, *but all those*, from the beginning, even as many as were before he came, who believed in the words of the holy prophets, who *spake as they* were inspired by the gift of the Holy Ghost, who truly testified of him in all things, *should have eternal life*, as well as those who should come after, who should believe in the gifts and callings of God by the Holy Ghost, which beareth record of the Father, and of the Son, which Father, Son, and Holy Ghost *are* one God, infinite and eternal, without end. Amen.

.   .   .

but there is a possibility that *man* may fall from grace and depart from the living God. Therefore let the church take heed and pray always, lest they fall into *temptations*; yea, and even *let those who are* sanctified, *take heed* also.

.   .   .

The duty of the elders, priests, teachers, deacons, and members of the church of Christ. An apostle is an elder, and it is his calling to baptize, and to ordain other elders, priests, teachers, and deacons, and to administer *bread and wine - the emblems of* the flesh and blood of Christ - *and to confirm those who are baptized into the church, by the laying on of hands for the baptism of fire and the Holy Ghost,* according to the scriptures

.   .   .

The elders are to conduct the meetings as they are led by the Holy Ghost, according *to the commandments and revelations of God.*

.   .   .

Each priest, teacher, or *deacon,* who is ordained by *a* priest, *may* take a certificate from him at the time, which *certificate* when *presented* to an elder, *shall entitle* him *to* a license, which shall authorize him to perform the *duties* of his calling - *or he may receive it from a conference. No person is to be ordained to any office in this church, where there is a regularly organized branch of the same, without the vote of that church; but the presiding elders, travelling bishops, high counsellors, high priests, and elders, may have the privilege of ordaining, where there is no branch of the church, that a vote may be called. Every president of the high priesthood, (or presiding elder,) bishop, high counsellor, and high priest, is to be ordained by the direction of a high counsel* [council], *or general conference.*

.   .   .

Baptism is to be administered in the following manner unto all those who repent: *The person who is* called of God and *has* authority *from* Jesus Christ *to baptize,* shall go down into the water with *the person who has presented him or herself for baptism,* and shall say, calling *him or her* by name: Having *been commissioned* of Jesus Christ, I baptize you in the name of the Father, and of the Son, and of the Holy Ghost. Amen.

Commentary: Offices in the Early Church

In the Articles and Covenants of the Church of Christ is listed the following offices in the church: elder, priest, teacher, and deacon. The Articles and Covenants were read and received by a vote of the congregation at the first church conference on 9 June 1830 at Fayette, New York. At this time some men had been ordained to three of the four offices: elder, priest, and teacher. It was prior to 25 October 1831 when the first known deacons were ordained.[12] As the church grew, additional offices or callings became part of the ecclesiastical structure. By 1835 it was felt necessary to add these offices to the Articles and Covenants, though such a step created an anachronism.

There are at least four early manuscripts which do not contain the additional offices in the church.[13] One document was published twice in the *Evening and the Morning Star* and in BC 24.[14]

In three subsequent revelations mention is made to church members to remember and observe the church articles. This would refer to the early text that was voted upon in June 1830, not to the 1835 text.[15]

Three offices not mentioned in this addition are those of the patriarch, twelve apostles, and seventy. The office of twelve apostles was not established until 14 February 1835.[16] By this omission one can determine the earliest date when the addition was written. It would have been after the Kirtland High Council was established and before any ordinations to the last two offices. The first published source of the revised text was in the reprint of the *Evening and Morning Star* (Kirtland, Ohio) published in January 1835, a month before the Council of the Twelve Apostles was established.[17]

Offices mentioned in the revised text were developed as follows: bishop, 4 February 1831; high priests (ordained to the high priesthood), 3 June 1831;[18] president of the high priesthood, 25 January 1832; traveling bishops, 22-23 September 1832; high council, 17 February 1834; and high counselors, 17 February 1834.

12. Cannon and Cook, *Far West Record*, 19. At the general conference held on 3 June 1831, no deacons were listed as functioning in the church. Some scholars wonder if the office of deacon was in the original Articles and Covenants. See G. St. John Stott, "Ordination and Ministry in the Book of Mormon," *Restoration Studies III* (Independence, MO: Herald Publishing House, 1986), 253n14; and Dan Vogel, *Religious Seekers and the Advent of Mormonism* (Salt Lake City: Signature Books, 1988), 149. What is known is that the office of deacon would have been in the June 1830 text by 19 April 1831 when a copy of the document was published in the Painesville *Telegraph*. All extant manuscripts mention the teacher's duties "to be assisted always & in all his duties in the Church by the deacons" (Zebedee Coltrin Journal, LDS archives). The words "or deacon" were added once in 1835 D&C 2:15.

13. Robert J. Woodford, "The Historical Development of the Doctrine and Covenants," Ph.D. diss., Brigham Young University, 1974, 294-95.

14. *The Evening and the Morning Star* 1 (June 1832): [1-2]; 2 (June 1833): [1-2; whole page nos. 97-98].

15. LDS D&C 33:14; RLDS D&C 32:3 ([18-31] Oct. 1830); LDS D&C 42:13; RLDS D&C 42:5 (9 Feb. 1831); and KRB, 10 (27 Feb. 1832).

16. See Kirtland Council Minute Book, 147-51, LDS archives; Joseph Smith et al., *History of the Church of Jesus Christ of Latter-day Saints,* ed. B. H. Roberts (Salt Lake City: Deseret Book Co., 1959), 2:181-89.

17. *Evening and Morning Star* 1 (June 1832): 4, (Kirtland, Ohio), reprinted January 1835.

18. See William E. McLellin Journal, 25 Oct. 1831, LDS archives, in Jan Shipps and John W. Welch, eds., *The Journals of William E. McLellin 1831-1836* (Provo, UT: BYU Studies, Brigham Young University; Urbana: University of Illinois Press, 1994), 45.

25. Go Thy Way and Sin No More
From BC 25 (cf. LDS D&C 24 and RLDS D&C 23)

Revelation received at Harmony, Pennsylvania,
in [4-31] July 1830 for Joseph Smith, Jr., and Oliver Cowdery

A Revelation to Joseph, and also to Oliver, given in Harmony, Pennsylvania, July, 1830.

Behold thou wast called and chosen to write the book of Mormon, and to my ministry;

And I have lifted thee up out of thine afflictions, and have counseled thee, that thou hast been delivered from all thine enemies, and thou hast been delivered from the powers of satan, and from darkness!

Nevertheless, thou art not excusable in thy transgressions; nevertheless go thy way and sin no more.

Magnify thine office;

And after thou hast sowed thy fields and secured them go speedily unto the church, which is in Colesville, Fayette and Manchester, and they shall support thee; and I will bless them both spiritually and temporally;

But if they receive thee not, I will send upon them a cursing instead of a blessing.

And thou shalt continue in calling upon God in my name, and writing the things which shall be given thee by the Comforter;

And expounding all scriptures unto the church, and it shall be given thee in the very moment, what thou shalt speak and write;

And they shall hear it, or I will send unto them a cursing instead of a blessing:

For thou shalt devote all thy service in Zion.

And in this thou shalt have strength.

Be patient in afflictions, for thou shalt have many:

But endure them, for lo, I am with you, even unto the end of thy days.

And in temporal labors thou shalt not have strength, for this is not thy calling.

Attend to thy calling and thou shalt have wherewith to magnify thine office, and to expound all scriptures.

And continue in the laying on of the hands, and confirming the churches.

And thy brother Oliver [Cowdery] shall continue in bearing my name before the world; and also to the church.

And he shall not suppose that he can say enough in my cause;

And lo I am with him to the end.

In me he shall have glory, and not of himself, whether in weakness or in strength, whether in bonds or free:

And at all times and in all places, he shall open his mouth and declare my gospel as with the voice of a trump, both day and night.

And I will give unto him strength such as is not known among men.

Require not miracles, except I shall command you; except casting out devils; healing the sick; and against poisonous serpents; and against deadly poisons:

And these things ye shall not do, except it be required of you, by them who desire it, that the scriptures might be fulfilled, for ye shall do according to that which is written.

And in whatsoever place ye shall enter, and they receive you not, in my name, ye shall leave a cursing instead of a blessing, by casting off the dust of your feet against them as a testimony, and cleansing your feet by the wayside.

And it shall come to pass, that whosoever shall lay their hands upon you by violence, ye shall command to be smitten in my name, and behold I will smite them according to your words, in mine own due time.

And whosoever shall go to law with thee shall be cursed by the law.

And thou shalt take no purse, nor scrip, neither staves, neither two coats, for the church shall give unto thee in the very hour what thou needest for food, and for raiment, and for shoes, and for money, and for scrip:

For thou art called to prune my vineyard with a mighty pruning, yea, even for the last time.

Yea, and also, all those whom thou hast ordained.

And they shall do even according to this pattern. Amen.

26. Thou Art an Elect Lady
From BC 26 (cf. LDS D&C 25; RLDS D&C 24)

*Revelation received at Harmony, Pennsylvania,
in [4-31] July 1830 for Emma Hale Smith*[19]

A Revelation to Emma, given in Harmony, Pennsylvania, July, 1830.

Emma, my daughter in Zion, a revelation I give unto you, concerning my will:

Behold thy sins are forgiven thee, and thou art an elect lady, whom I have called.

Murmur not because of the things which thou hast not seen, for they are withheld from thee, and from the world, which is wisdom in me in a time to come.

And the office of thy calling shall be for a comfort unto my servant Joseph [Smith, Jr.], thy husband, in his afflictions with consoling words, in the spirit of meekness.

And thou shalt go with him at the time of his going, and be unto him for a scribe, that I may send Oliver [Cowdery] whithersoever I will.

And thou shalt be ordained under his hand to expound scriptures, and to exhort the church, according as it shall be given thee by my Spirit:

For he shall lay his hands upon thee, and thou shalt receive the Holy Ghost, and thy time shall be given to writing, and to learning much.

And thou needest not fear, for thy husband shall support thee from the church:

---

19. Ezra Booth wrote, "I have in my possession the '27th commandment to Emma my daughter in Zion'" (Booth to Rev. Ira Eddy, 2 Oct. 1831, *Ohio Star* 2 [20 Oct. 1831]: 3). Booth's manuscript copy predated the BC manuscript.

For unto them is his calling, that all things might be revealed unto them, whatsoever I will according to their faith.

And verily I say unto thee, that thou shalt lay aside the things of this world, and seek for the things of a better.

And it shall be given thee, also, to make a selection of sacred Hymns,[20] as it shall be given thee, which is pleasing unto me, to be had in my church:

For my soul delighteth in the song of the heart; Yea, the song of the righteous is a prayer unto me.

And it shall be answered with a blessing upon their heads.

Wherefore lift up thy heart and rejoice, and cleave unto the covenants which thou hast made.

Continue in the spirit of meekness, and beware of pride.

Let thy soul delight in thy husband, and the glory which shall come upon him.

Keep my commandments continually, and a crown of righteousness thou shalt receive.

And except thou do this, where I am you cannot come.

And verily, verily I say unto you, that this is my voice unto all. Amen.

27. All Things You Shall Receive by Faith
From BC 27 (cf. LDS D&C 26; RLDS D&C 25)

Revelation received at Harmony, Pennsylvania,
in [4-31] July 1830 for Joseph Smith, Jr.,
Oliver Cowdery, and John Whitmer

A Revelation to Joseph, Oliver and John, given in Harmony, Pennsylvania, July, 1830.

Behold, I say unto you, that you shall let your time be devoted to the studying of the scriptures, and to preaching, and to co[n]firming the church at Colesville;[21]

And to performing your labors on the land, such as is required, until after you shall go to the west,[22] to hold the next conference; and then it shall be made known what you shall do.

And all things shall be done by common consent in the church, by much prayer and faith;

For all things you shall receive by faith. Amen.

---

20. On 14 September 1835 it was decided "that Sister Emma Smith proceed to make a selection of sacred hymns according to the revelation, and that President W. W. Phelps be appointed to revise and arrange them for printing" (Kirtland Council Minute Book, 108). Selected by Emma Smith, *A Collection of Hymns for the Church of the Latter Day Saints* (Kirtland, OH: Printed by F. G. Williams & Co., 1835). Though the hymnal was dated 1835, it was published in early 1836.

21. After this revelation was received, Joseph Smith and Oliver Cowdery went to Colesville to confirm those baptized. They were unable to accomplish the confirmations at this time. Cowdery then went to visit the Fayette branch of the church.

22. Fayette, New York.

28. Listen to the Voice of Jesus Christ
From BC 28 (cf. LDS D&C 27; RLDS D&C 26)

Commandment received at Harmony, Pennsylvania,
on 4 September 1830 for the Church of Christ[23]

A Commandment to the church of Christ, given in Harmony, Pennsylvania, September 4, 1830.

Listen to the voice of Jesus Christ, your Lord, your God and your Redeemer, whose word is quick and powerful.

For behold I say unto you, that it mattereth not what ye shall eat, or what ye shall drink, when ye partake of the sacrament, if it so be that ye do it with an eye single to my glory;

Remembering unto the Father my body which was laid down for you, and my blood which was shed for the remission of your sins:

Wherefore a commandment I give unto you, that you shall not purchase wine, neither strong drink of your enemies:

Wherefore you shall partake of none, except it is made new among you, yea, in this my Father's kingdom which shall be built up on the earth.

Behold this is wisdom in me, wherefore marvel not, for the hour cometh that I will drink of the fruit of the vine with you, on the earth, and with all those whom my Father hath given me out of the world:

Wherefore lift up your hearts and rejoice, and gird up your loins and be faithful until I come:—even so. Amen.

<u>Revision</u>

1835 D&C 50
(cf. LDS D&C 27:5-18; RLDS D&C 26:2-3)

Behold this is wisdom in me: wherefore marvel not for the hour cometh that I will drink of the fruit of the vine with you on the earth, and with *Moroni, whom I have sent unto you to reveal the book of Mormon, containing the fulness of my everlasting gospel; to whom I have committed the keys of the record of the stick of Ephraim;*

and also with Elias, to whom I have committed the keys of bringing to pass the restoration of all things, or the restorer of all things spoken by the mouth of all the holy prophets since the world began, concerning the last days: and also John the son of Zacharias, which Zacharias he (Elias) visited and gave promise that he should have a son, and his name should be John, and he should be filled with the spirit of Elias;

which John I have sent unto you, my servants, Joseph Smith, jr. and Oliver Cowdery, to or-

---

23. Soon after this commandment was given, Joseph Smith returned to Colesville to confirm those baptized in June who had not yet received confirmation. Afterwards he and Emma Smith went to Fayette, New York, from Harmony to live with the Whitmer family.

dain you unto this first priesthood which you have received, that you might be called and or-dained even as Aaron:

and also Elijah, unto whom I have committed the keys of the power of turning the hearts of the fathers to the children and the hearts of the children to the fathers, that the whole earth may not be smitten with a curse: and also, with Joseph, and Jacob, and Isaac, and Abraham your fathers; by whom the promises remain; and also with Michael, or Adam, the father of all, the prince of all, the ancient of days:

And also with Peter, and James, and John, whom I have sent unto you, by whom I have or-dained you and confirmed you to be apostles and especial witnesses of my name, and bear the keys of your ministry: and of the same things which I revealed unto them: unto whom I have committed the keys of my kingdom, and a dispensation of the gospel for the last times; and for the fulness of times, in the which I will gather together in one all things both which are in heaven and which are on earth: and *also* with all those whom my Father hath given me out of the world:

wherefore lift up your hearts and rejoice, and gird up your loins, and take upon you my whole armor, that ye may be able to withstand the evil day, having done all ye may be able to stand.
Stand, therefore, having your loins girt about with truth; having on the breastplate of right-eousness; and your feet shod with the preparation of the gospel of peace which I have sent mine angels to commit unto you, taking the shield of faith wherewith ye shall be able to quench all the fiery darts of the wicked; and take the helmet of salvation, and the sword of my Spirit, which I will pour out upon you, and my word which I reveal unto you, and be agreed as touching all things whatsoever ye ask of me, and be faithful until I come, *and ye shall be caught up that where I am ye shall be also.* Amen.

Commentary: Restoration of All Things

In BC 28 is a commandment to the church dated 4 September 1830. In the 1835 D&C additional wording has been added. The commandment was published in the *Evening and the Morning Star* in March 1833 and reads the same as the BC,[24] which is based on a handwritten manuscript of November 1831. The text was published in a non-Mormon newspaper, *The Telegraph* (Painesville, Ohio), on 19 April 1831. Once again the text compares closely with what later appeared in BC 28. In the one surviving manuscript in the handwriting of Edward Partridge, the text is close to all pre-1835 versions.[25]

In the shorter text it states: "Behold this is wisdom in me, wherefore marvel not, for the hour cometh that I will drink of the fruit of the vine with you, on the earth, and with all those whom my Father hath given me out of the world[.]"[26]

In the 1835 D&C, after the words "drink of the fruit of the vine with you, on the earth, and with" and before the words "all those whom my Father hath given

24. *The Evening and the Morning Star* 2 (Mar. 1833): [6; whole page no. 78].
25. Edward Partridge manuscript, LDS archives.
26. BC 28:6.

me out of the world" is inserted a major block of material dealing with "the keys of bringing to pass the restoration of all things."[27]

The following will help sort those who are to drink of the fruit of the vine:

1. Moroni, who was sent to reveal the Book of Mormon and has the keys of the stick of Ephraim.
2. Elias [Gabriel[28]], who has the keys of the restoration of all things and visited Zacharias and promised that John the Baptist would be filled with his spirit.
3. John the Baptist, who was sent to Smith and Cowdery "to ordain you unto this first priesthood ... that you might be called and ordained even as Aaron."

The text at this point deals with many other faithful who would celebrate when the Lord comes:

4. Elijah, who has the keys of Malachi 4:6.
5. Joseph, Jacob, Isaac, and Abraham.
6. Michael (or Adam).
7. Peter, James, and John, "by whom I have ordained you and confirmed you to be apostles" and "bear the keys of your ministry." Peter, James, and John have "the keys of my kingdom and a dispensation of the gospel for the last times; and for the fulness of times."

A strong indication that this is an embellished text is the phrase "Michael, or Adam, the father of all, the prince of all, the ancient of days." A letter written by Oliver Cowdery on 1 January 1834 states: "Since I came down I have been informed from a proper source that the Angel Michael is no less than our father Adam, and Gabriel is Noah."[29] This idea was not known to Cowdery until the end of 1833.

After a few words from the early text, another addition begins after the words "gird up your loins" and before "and be faithful until I come." The majority of this is borrowed from Ephesians 6:13-17 (KJV) with minor differences. The point of including these words seems to be that Smith and Cowdery had taken upon them the "whole armor" and that the angels had sent to them the necessary equipment (keys) to protect them from the "fiery darts of the wicked." This emphasis from Ephesians on the "preparation of the gospel of peace" (6:15) refers in its new context to angelic visits listed above with the words: "which I have sent mine angels to commit unto you."

It appears that all the added material dates from after the time when the com-

---

27. 1835 D&C 50:2.
28. Luke 1:19.
29. Cowdery to John Whitmer, 1 Jan. 1834, Oliver Cowdery Letterbook, 15, Henry E. Huntington Library, San Marino, California. See also discourse by Joseph Smith before 8 August 1839 in Andrew F. Ehat and Lyndon W. Cook, eds., *The Words of Joseph Smith: The Contemporary Accounts of the Nauvoo Discourses of the Prophet Joseph* (Provo, UT: Religious Studies Center, Brigham Young University, 1980), 8.

mandment was received. The additions are too developed, the product of a later stage of theological evolution.

The title page of the 1835 edition states that the documents were selected from the revelations of God. Section 50 of the 1835 D&C is titled "Revelation given September, 1830" with no location given. Joseph Smith's church history uses the 1835 text and mentions that a messenger appeared to Smith and that there were two sections to this revelation. The draft history of 1839 states:

> Early in the month of August [1830] Newel Knights [Knight] and his wife paid us a visit at our place in Harmony. Neither his wife nor mine had been as yet confirmed, and it was proposed that we should have sacrament together & confirm them; before he & his wife should leave us. and that we In order to prepare for these things I set out—to go to procure some wine for the occasion. I had however gone but a short distance when I was met by a heavenly messenger, and had the following revelation. the first paragraph of which was written at this time, & the remainder in Septer [September] following Page 179 [LDS D&C 27; RLDS D&C 26] ... We arrived at Fayette, during the last week of August ... As a conference meeting had been appointed for the 1rst [1st] September[30]

It is possible that Newel Knight helped James Mulholland with this portion of the history.[31] The published Newel Knight journal states that Joseph Smith "received the first four verses of the revelation given on page 138, of the Doctrine and Covenants (new edition), the remainder being given in the September following at, Fayette, New York."[32] This reference to the new edition is to the 1879 edition of the LDS D&C which contains the heading: "The first four verses of the following Revelation, were given through Joseph, the Seer, in Harmony, Penn., August, 1830, and the remainder in Fayette, New York, September, 1830."[33]

The first paragraph of the 1835 printing of this commandment ends with the words "in this my Father's kingdom which shall be built up on the earth." In BC 28 this phrase ends verse 5 and there are two more short verses before the end of the document. The second paragraph in the 1835 D&C contains thirty words that were in BC 28:6. In addition, the earliest printing in the *Evening and the Morning Star* has sixty-three words after "built up on the earth" and ends with "Amen."[34]

The manuscript history draft is incorrect that "the first paragraph of which was written at this time, & the remainder in Septer [September] following." Interpretations that either two separate revelations were put together to complete the text or two separate revelations were given in different months and possibly at different locations do not fit the BC, the *Evening and Morning Star*, or an early manuscript of the text of this 4 September 1830 commandment.

30. Jessee, *Papers of Joseph Smith*, 1:260-61, 263. Manuscript History, Book A-1:51 was taken from this draft and contains the 1835 revision of the commandment introduced as a "Revelation given at Harmony Penn, August 1830."

31. Dean C. Jessee, ed., *The Papers of Joseph Smith: Journal, 1832-1842* (Salt Lake City: Deseret Book Co., 1992), 2:326.

32. "Newel Knight's Journal," in *Scraps of Biography. Tenth Book of the Faith-Promoting Series* (Salt Lake City: Juvenile Instructor Office, 1883), 62. Newel Knight died in 1847.

33. The wording "the first four paragraphs" appears in *History of the Church*, 1:106.

34. *The Evening and the Morning Star* 1 (Mar. 1833): [6; whole page no. 78].

The draft of Joseph Smith's history has Newel Knight and his wife Sally visiting Harmony in early August, but it dates their arrival with Smith "at Fayette, during the last week of August" as a conference was scheduled for 1 September 1830. Since the conference started on 26 September, the draft history is twenty-five days too early. It appears that James Mulholland changed the September date of the revelation in the 1835 D&C to "August 1830" in the manuscript history. This was done to reconcile what he had previously written concerning the Knights visiting Smith in Harmony early in August since the second church conference had been incorrectly dated as 1 September.[35] Mulholland moved back the visit of Newel and Sally Knight to early August when it should have been early September.

The 1835 text mentions drinking the fruit of the vine (wine) with Christ on the earth and with "Elias" who has "the keys of bringing to pass the restoration of all things, or the restorer of all things."[36] Mentioned next is John, son of Zacharias (known as John the Baptist who baptized Jesus). This "Elias" promised Zacharias that he would "have a son, and his name should be John" and that John would "be filled with the spirit of Elias." In Luke 1:13 and 17 is recorded the name of the child and the promise of going forth "in the spirit of Elias," meaning the spirit and power of Elijah.

That this refers to the spirit of Elijah is evident since in the New Testament the John the Baptist material applies to the passage in Malachi 4:5-6 about turning the hearts of the fathers to the children. In the New Testament John the Baptist is said to have put Malachi 4:5-6 into effect.[37] Luke 1:19 records that the angel told Zacharias that his name was Gabriel. The angel Gabriel is mentioned in the Old Testament book of Daniel.[38] If the passage about the angel promising Zacharias that his son would be "filled with the spirit of Elias" meant filled with the spirit of Gabriel, then this passage is in error.

In essence, the Elias in this 1835 revision was Gabriel, who on earth was Noah in the book of Genesis. Having a deceased person who lived come back to minister to people on earth is evidently another problem.

The revision of 1835 mentions that John the Baptist was sent to Joseph Smith and Oliver Cowdery to ordain them that they "might be called and ordained even as Aaron." This first priesthood would by 1835 be called the Aaronic Priesthood or the Priesthood of Aaron though it did not require recipients to be descendants of Aaron or of the tribe of Levi.

Next mentioned to attend with Jesus on the earth is Elijah who has "the keys of the power of turning the hearts of the fathers to the children, and the hearts of the children to the fathers." Here in the additional material we have Elias and Elijah as two distinct persons.

In the King James Version of the Bible, the proper names appear in the Hebrew form in the Old Testament (Elijah) and in Greek form in the New Testament

---

35. Manuscript History, Book A-1:51; Jessee, *Papers of Joseph Smith*, 1:321.
36. The words "or the restorer of all things" do not appear in LDS D&C 27:6.
37. Matt. 11:14; 17:10-13; Mark 9:11-13; Luke 1:17.
38. Dan. 8:16; 9:21.

(Elias).[39] Elias and Elijah are the same person, the Tishbite of the Old Testament. They are not separate persons. When the Hebrew scriptures were translated into Greek in the Septuagint, the reading of Malachi 4:5 in English read: "I will send to you Elias the Thesbite,"[40] clearly meaning Elijah the Tishbite.

To Joseph Smith, a number of people were considered an "Elias," being a forerunner/preparer or a restorer. In addition to Gabriel, there was John the Baptist, Jesus, and John the Revelator. Smith spent time during 1830-33 correcting the Bible. This work is known variously as the Inspired Version, Joseph Smith Revision, or the Joseph Smith Translation (JST). The JST is Joseph Smith's doctrinal correction ("translation") of the Old and New Testaments and does not restore the Hebrew or Greek biblical text.

The New Testament KJV records that John the Baptist was to go before the Lord in the spirit and power of Elias [Elijah].[41] Jesus explained that, for those who understood, John the Baptist was the Elijah they were waiting for.[42] John the Baptist was understood by Christ's disciples as the Elias (Elijah) who would "restore all things."[43]

Joseph Smith dictated his revision of Matthew 17 in the spring of 1831. It tells about Jesus being transfigured on a high mountain before Peter, James, and John. While Smith had the text refer to John the Baptist, he also had the name Elias used for "another which should come and restore all things." His scribe Sidney Rigdon wrote (italics are added words to the KJV):

> and his disciples asked him [Jesus] saying why then say the Scribes that Elias must first come[?] and Jesus answered and said unto them Elias truly shall first come and restore all things *as the prophets have written and again* I say unto you that Elias *has* come already and they knew him not *and* have done unto him whatsoever they listed likewise shall also the son of Man suffer of them
> *but I say unto you who is Elias*[?] *behold this is Elias who I send to prepare the way before me* Then the disciples understood that he spake unto them of John the Baptist *and also of another which should come and restore all things as they were written by the prophets*[44]

In August 1831 Joseph Smith was told the "day of transfiguration shall come when the earth shall be transfigured even according to the pattern which was shown unto mine apostles upon the mount of which account the fulness ye have not yet received."[45] When Smith and Sidney Rigdon revised Mark in the fall of 1831 concerning the transfiguration, Smith interpreted the Elias who appeared

---

39. Luke 4:25-27 (Elias) = 1 Kgs. 17:1 (Elijah the Tishbite). See also 1 Kgs. 17:9; 21:17, 28; 2 Kgs. 1:3, 8; 9:36. Known also as Elijah the prophet, see 1 Kgs. 18:36; 2 Chron. 21:12.

40. *The Septuagint Version of the Old Testament, with an English Translation; and with Various Readings and Critical Notes* (Grand Rapids, MI: Zondervan Publishing House, 1970), 1,130.

41. Luke 1:17.

42. Matt. 11:14, KJV. This verse was revised in 1831 by Joseph Smith as having Jesus say that he was Elias.

43. Cf. Matt. 17:11-13; Mark 9:11-13, KJV.

44. Matt. 17:9-14, JST; NT MS #1, 42, RLDS archives, cf. Matt. 17:10-13, KJV. See NT MS #2, folio 1, 32 for additional revision to this passage.

45. Document no. 69; LDS D&C 63:20-21; RLDS D&C 63:6.

before the four men not as the prophet Elijah but as John the Baptist. The King James Version reads, "And there appeared unto them Elias with Moses: and they were talking with Jesus."[46] But Smith's revision reads, "And there appeared unto them Elias with Moses, or in other words, John the baptist and Moses; and they were talking with Jesus."[47] The words "or in other words" help us to understand this is commentary by Smith.[48] The mention of Moses and Elias in Matthew means Moses and Elijah, representatives of the law and the prophets.[49]

When Smith first revised Matthew 11 in 1831, the manuscript had Jesus saying: "and if ye will receive me I am Elias which was for to come."[50] This reading was also copied onto the second New Testament manuscript shortly after with the same reading. A number of changes were made to this manuscript, and this reading was revised in December 1832 or January 1833 with the words "me I am Elias" being crossed through and the passage now applying to John the Baptist.[51]

John 1 describes John the Baptist being questioned. Sidney Rigdon originally wrote in January or February 1832 the following:

and he [John the Baptist] confessed and denied [denied] not but confessed I am not the christ and they asked him what then art thou Elias[?] and he saith I am not[.] art thou that prophet[?] and he answered no ... and they asked him and said unto him why baptisest thou then if thou be not the christ nor Elias neither that prophet[?] John answered ... he it is *of whom I bear record he is that Prophet, even Elias*[52]

This passage was further revised in December 1832 or January 1833 on a note pinned to the manuscript as follows:

And he [John the Baptist] confessed, and denied [denied] not *that he was Elias*, but confessed, *saying*; I am not the christ. And they asked him, *saying*; *How* then art thou Elias?

---

46. Mark 9:4, KJV; cf. Matt. 17:3 and Luke 9:30.

47. NT MS #2, folio 2, 24, RLDS archives; Mark 9:3, JST.

48. Philip L. Barlow wrote, "A third category is 'interpretive additions,' often signaled by the phrase 'or in other words,' which the Prophet [Joseph Smith] appended to a passage he wished to clarify. Thus, to Jesus' counsel to turn one's other cheek if smitten (Luke 6:29), Smith added 'or, in other words, it is better to offer the other [cheek], than to revile again.' The interpretive phrase 'or in other words' (often shortened to 'in other words' or simply 'or') is common in Smith's sermons as well as in the Book of Mormon, the Doctrine and Covenants, and the revision of the Bible" (Barlow, *Mormons and the Bible: The Place of the Latter-day Saints in American Religion* [New York: Oxford University Press, 1991], 51-52).

49. Compare with modern translations such as the New Revised Standard Version, New International Version, and Contemporary English Version of Mark 9:4.

50. NT MS #1, 28, RLDS archives, Matt. 11:15, JST; cf. Matt. 11:14, KJV.

51. NT MS #2, folio 1, 21, RLDS archives. Robert J. Matthews wrote, "It is evident that the Prophet [Joseph Smith] was working with an idea that he developed and then discarded. He compared and contrasted John [the Baptist] with Jesus and then decided to speak only of John. He identified Jesus as Elias and then identified John as Elias. It is, however, interesting to note that the doctrinal ideas and identifications here introduced and then discarded were reintroduced in Matthew 17:9-14 on a partial basis and then more fully in John 1" (Matthews, "A Plainer Translation" Joseph Smith's Translation of the Bible: A History and Commentary [Provo, UT: Brigham Young University Press, 1975], 217).

52. NT MS #2, folio 4, 106, RLDS archives, emphasis added; John 1:21-22, 26-28, JST. Cf John 1:20-21, 26-27, KJV.

And he saith, I am not *that Elias who was to restore all things. And they asked him, saying;* Art thou that Prophet? And he answered; No ... And they asked him, and said unto him; why baptisest thou then, if thou be not *the* christ, nor Elias *who was to restore all things,* neither that prophet?[53]

In March 1832, when Joseph Smith first revised the biblical book of Revelation, a number of questions were asked concerning the interpretation of passages in that book. To the question relating to the angel of Revelation 7:2, Smith answered, "the angel ascending from the east is he to whom is given the seal of the living God over the twelve tribes of Israel ... And, if you will receive it, this is Elias which was to come to gather together the tribes of Israel." To a question about Revelation 10, the answer was, "We are to understand that it was a mission, and an ordinance, for him to gather the tribes of Israel; behold, this is Elias, who, as it is written, must come and restore all things."[54] In June 1831 Smith prophesied "that John the Revelator was then among the ten tribes of Israel."[55] Levi Hancock who attended the same meeting wrote, "Joseph said that John was to tarry until Christ came. He is now with the ten tribes preaching to them and when we can get ready for them they will come."[56]

While Joseph Smith was trying to make it clear to himself who various biblical personages were as he interpreted the text, he also created a number of confused passages. For example, in LDS D&C 76:100; RLDS D&C 76:7 (16 Feb. 1832), he used New Testament names of Elias [Elijah] and Esaias [Isaiah] and used the Old Testament name of Isaiah: "some of Moses, and some of Elias, and some of Esaias, and some of Isaiah, and some of Enoch." Later it was said that "Esaias also lived in the days of Abraham."[57] In LDS D&C 110:12 mention is made of a vision when "Elias appeared, and committed the dispensation of the gospel of Abraham." Some have interpreted this to mean the Old Testament prophet Noah (Elias = Gabriel = Noah), or it may refer to Esaias who "lived in the days of Abraham."

Smith's doctrine of Elias developed further, and Elias was applied in the revision of 1835 to the angel Gabriel. This application does not fit an 1830 context as the 1835 revision seemingly implies.

The 1835 addition to the September 1830 commandment also mentioned Abraham, Isaac, Jacob, and Joseph. Then there would be "Michael, or Adam, the father of all, the prince of all, the ancient of days."[58]

The final persons named to gather with Jesus were the apostles Peter, James, and John, who were sent "unto whom I have committed the keys of the kingdom, and

53. NT MS #2, folio 4, 106, RLDS archives; John 1:21-22, 26, JST, emphasis added; cf. John 1:20-21, 25, KJV.
54. Document no. 95, LDS D&C 77:9, 14.
55. Bruce N. Westergren, ed., *From Historian to Dissident: The Book of John Whitmer* (Salt Lake City: Signature Books, 1995), 69; original manuscript in RLDS archives.
56. *The Life of Levi Hancock* (n.p., ca. 1968), 33, original in LDS archives.
57. Document no. 100; LDS D&C 84:13; RLDS D&C 83:2.
58. Biblical references to Michael are in Dan. 10:13, 21; 12:1; Jude 1:9; Rev. 12:7. On the ancient of days, see Dan. 7:9, 13, 22.

a dispensation of the gospel for the last times; and for the fulness of times." This 1835 addition is the earliest known record of Christ's apostles being sent to visit Joseph Smith and Oliver Cowdery.[59] Smith and Cowdery ordained each other elders (apostles) on 6 April 1830.

29. The Hour Is Nigh
From BC 29 (cf. LDS D&C 29; RLDS D&C 28)

*Revelation received at Fayette, New York,
in [5-26] September 1830 for the Church of Christ*[60]

A Revelation to the church of Christ, given in the presence of six elders, in Fayette, New-York, September, 1830.

Listen to the voice of Jesus Christ, your Redeemer, the Great I AM, whose arm of mercy hath atoned for your sins;

Who will gather his people even as a hen gathereth her chickens under her wings, even as many as will hearken to my voice, and humble themselves before me, and call upon me in mighty prayer.

Behold, verily, verily I say unto you, that at this time your sins are forgiven you; therefore ye receive these things:

But remember to sin no more, lest perils shall come upon you.

Verily I say unto you, that ye are chosen out of the world to declare my gospel with the sound of rejoicing, as with the voice of a trump:

Lift up your hearts and be glad for I am in your midst, and am your advocate with the Father; and it is his good will to give you the kingdom;

And as it is written, Whatsoever ye shall ask in faith, being united in prayer according to my command, ye shall receive;

And ye are called to bring to pass the gathering of mine elect, for mine elect hear my voice and harden not their hearts:

Wherefore the decree hath gone forth from the Father, that they shall be gathered in unto one place, upon the face of this land, to prepare their hearts, and be prepared in all things, against the day when tribulation and desolation are sent forth upon the wicked:

For the hour is nigh, and the day soon at hand, when the earth is ripe:

And all the proud, and they that do wickedly, shall be as stubble, and I will burn them up, saith the Lord of Hosts, that wickedness shall not be upon the earth:

For the hour is nigh, and that which was spoken by mine apostles must be fulfilled; for as they spoke so shall it come to pass;

---

59. Brian Q. Cannon and others wrote, "In 1835 the original edition of the Doctrine and Covenants gave the first precise published account of the appearance of Peter, James, and John to Joseph and Oliver" ("Priesthood Restoration Documents," *BYU Studies* 35 [1995-96]: 167).

60. This revelation was received prior to the second conference of the church that commenced on 26 September 1830. The total membership of the church reported at the conference was sixty-two. See Cannon and Cook, *Far West Record*, 3.

For I will reveal myself from heaven with power and great glory, with all the hosts thereof, and dwell in righteousness with men on earth a thousand years, and the wicked shall not stand.

And again, verily, verily I say unto you, and it hath gone forth in a firm decree, by the will of the Father, that mine apostles, the twelve which were with me in my ministry at Jerusalem, shall stand at my right hand at the day of my coming in a pillar of fire, being clothed with robes of righteousness, with crowns upon their heads, in glory even as I am, to judge the whole house of Israel, even as many as have loved me and kept my commandments, and none else;

For a trump shall sound both long and loud, even as upon mount Sinai, and all the earth shall quake, and they shall come forth:

Yea, even the dead which died in me, to receive a crown of righteousness, and to be clothed upon, even as I am, to be with me, that we may be one.

But behold, I say unto you, that before this great day shall come, the sun shall be darkened, and the moon shall be turned into blood, and the stars shall fall from heaven;

And there shall be greater signs in heaven above, and in the earth beneath; and there shall be weeping and wailing among the hosts of men;

And there shall be a great hailstorm sent forth to destroy the crops of the earth:

And it shall come to pass, because of the wickedness of the world, that I will take vengeance upon the wicked, for they will not repent:

For the cup of mine indignation is full; for behold, my blood shall not cleanse them if they hear me not.

Wherefore I the Lord God will send forth flies upon the face of the earth, which shall take hold of the inhabitants thereof, and shall eat their flesh, and shall cause maggots to come in upon them, and their tongues shall be stayed that they shall not utter against me, and their flesh shall fall from off their bones, and their eyes from their sockets:

And it shall come to pass, that the beasts of the forests, and the fowls of the air, shall devour them up:

And that great and abominable church, which is the whore of all the earth, shall be cast down by devouring fire, according as it was spoken by the mouth of Ezekiel the prophet, which spoke of these things, which have not come to pass, but surely must, as I live, for abominations shall not reign.

And again, verily, verily I say unto you, that when the thousand years are ended, and men again begin to deny their God, then will I spare the earth but for a little season;

And the end shall come, and the heaven and the earth shall be consumed, and pass away, and there shall be a new heaven and a new earth;

For all old things shall pass away, and all things shall become new, even the heaven and the earth, and all the fulness thereof, both men and beasts;

The fowls of the air, and the fishes of the sea, and not one hair, neither mote, shall be lost, for it is the workmanship of mine hand.

But behold, verily I say unto you, before the earth shall pass away, Michael mine archangel, shall sound his trump, and then shall all the dead awake, for their graves shall be opened, and they shall come forth; yea, even all;

And the righteous shall be gathered on my right hand unto eternal life;

And the wicked on my left hand will I be ashamed to own before the Father:

Wherefore I will say unto them, depart from me ye cursed into everlasting fire, prepared for the devil and his angels.

And now behold I say unto you, never at any time, have I declared from mine own mouth, that they should return, for where I am they cannot come, for they have no power;

But remember, that all my judgments are not given unto men;

And as the words have gone forth out of my mouth, even so shall they be fulfilled, that the first shall be last, and that the last shall be first in all things, whatsoever I have created by the word of my power, which is the power of my Spirit;[61]

For by the power of my Spirit, created I them:

Yea, all things both spiritual and temporal:

Firstly spiritual, secondly temporal, which is the beginning of my work:

And again, firstly temporal, and secondly spiritual, which is the last of my work:

Speaking unto you, that you may naturally understand, but unto myself my works have no end, neither beginning; but it is given unto you, that ye may understand, because ye have asked it of me and are agreed.

Wherefore, verily I say unto you, that all things unto me are spiritual, and not at any time have I given unto you a law which was temporal, neither any man, nor the children of men:

Neither Adam your father, whom I created; behold I gave unto him that he should be an agent unto himself;

And I gave unto him commandment, but no temporal commandment gave I unto him; for my commandments are spiritual;

They are not natural, nor temporal, neither carnal nor sensual.

And it came to pass, that Adam being tempted of the devil, for behold the devil was before Adam, for he rebelled against me saying, Give me thine honor, which is my power: and also a third part of the hosts of heaven turned he away from me because of their agency:

And they were thrust down, and thus came the devil and his angels; and behold, there is a place prepared for them from the beginning, which place is hell:

And it must needs by that the devil should tempt the children of men, or they could not be agents unto themselves, for if they never should have bitter, they could not know the sweet.

Wherefore, it came to pass, that the devil tempted Adam and he partook the forbidden fruit, and transgressed the commandment, wherein he became subject to the will of the devil, because he yielded unto temptation.

---

61. The dictated manuscript (OT MS #1) relating to a vision of Moses, a revision and addition to the book of Genesis concerning the creation of the world, the garden of Eden, Adam, and the rebellion of the devil was written prior to this revelation. Similar ideas are expressed at the end of this instruction to the early church. The manuscripts of the revision and the King James Bible (that has markings on some pages) are in RLDS archives.

Wherefore, I the Lord God caused that he should be cast out from the garden of Eden, from my presence, because of his transgression;

Wherein he became spiritually dead; which is the first death, even that same death, which is the last death, which is spiritual, which shall be pronounced upon the wicked when I shall say, Depart ye cursed.

But behold I say unto you, that I the Lord God gave unto Adam and unto his seed, that they should not die as to the temporal death, until I the Lord God should send forth angels to declare unto them repentance and redemption, through faith on the name of mine only begotten Son:

And thus did I the Lord God appoint unto man the days of his probation; that by his natural death he might be raised in immortality unto eternal life, even as many as would believe, and they that believe not, unto eternal damnation, for they cannot be redeemed from their spiritual fall, because they repent not, for they will love darkness rather than light, and their deeds are evil, and they receive their wages of whom they list to obey.

But behold I say unto you, that little children are redeemed from the foundation of the world, through mine only Begotten:

Wherefore they cannot sin, for power is not given unto satan to tempt little children, until they begin to become accountable before me;

For it is given unto them even as I will, according to mine own pleasure, that great things may be required at the hand of their fathers.

And again I say unto you, that whoso having knowledge, have I not commanded to repent? and he that hath no understanding, it remaineth in me to do according as it is written. And now, I declare no more unto you at this time. Amen.

30. Thou Shalt Be Obedient
From BC 30 (cf. LDS D&C 28; RLDS D&C 27)

*Revelation received at Fayette, New York,
in [5-26] September 1830 for Oliver Cowdery*

A Revelation to Oliver, given in Fayette, New-York, September, 1830.

Behold I say unto you, Oliver [Cowdery], that it shall be given unto thee, that thou shalt be heard by the church, in all things whatsoever thou shalt teach them by the Comforter, concerning the revelations and commandments which I have given.

But behold, verily, verily I say unto you, no one shall be appointed to receive commandments and revelations in this church, excepting my servant Joseph [Smith, Jr.], for he receiveth them even as Moses:

And thou shalt be obedient unto the things which I shall give unto him, even as Aaron, to declare faithfully the commandments and the revelations, with power and authority unto the church.

And if thou art led at any time by the Comforter to speak or teach, or at all times by the way of commandment unto the church, thou mayest do it.

But thou shalt not write by way of commandment, but by wisdom:

And thou shalt not command him who is at thy head, and at the head of the church, for I have given him the keys of the mysteries and the revelations which are sealed, until I shall appoint unto them another in his stead.

And now, behold I say unto you, that you shall go unto the Lamanites and preach my gospel unto them, and cause my church to be established among them. And thou shalt have revelations but write them not by way of commandment.

And now behold I say unto you, that it is not revealed, and no man knoweth where the city shall be built, but it shall be given hereafter.[62]

Behold I say unto you, that it shall be on the borders by the Lamanites.

Thou shalt not leave this place until after the conference, and my servant Joseph [Smith, Jr.] shall be appointed to rule the conference by the voice of it, and what he saith to thee, that thou shalt tell.

And again, thou shalt take thy brother Hiram [Page] between him and thee alone, and tell him that those things which he hath written from that stone are not of me, and that satan deceiveth him:

For behold these things have not been appointed unto him:

Neither shall any thing be appointed unto any of this church contrary to the church covenants, for all things must be done in order and by common consent in the church, by the prayer of faith.

And thou shalt settle all these things according to the covenants of the church before thou shalt take thy journey among the Lamanites.

And it shall be given thee from the time that thou shalt go, until the time that thou shalt return, what thou shalt do.

And thou must open thy mouth at all times declaring my gospel with the sound of rejoicing.— Amen.

Revision

1835 D&C 51
(cf. LDS D&C 28:8, 10; RLDS D&C 27:3-4)

And now, behold I say unto you, that you shall go unto the Lamanites and preach my gospel unto them; and *inasmuch as they receive thy teachings, thou shalt* cause my church to be established among them

.   .   .

Thou shalt not leave this place until after the conference and my servant Joseph shall be appointed to *preside over* the conference by the voice of it, and what he saith to thee thou shalt tell.

---

62. This city refers to the New Jerusalem soon to be located in Jackson County, Missouri. See 1830 BOM, 501; LDS 3 Ne. 21:23/RLDS 10:2.

Commentary: Failed Mission to the Lamanites

In September 1830, prior to the second conference of the church held at Fayette, one of the eight witnesses to the Book of Mormon, Hiram Page, a teacher in the church, claimed to receive revelations through the medium of a seer stone just as Joseph Smith had done. These revelations dealt with "the upbuilding of Zion, the order of the Church," and other matters.[63]

"Finding, however, that many (especially the Whitmer family and Oliver Cowdery) were believing much in the things set forth by this stone," Smith inquired of God concerning the matter and was told that Page's revelations were not from heaven.[64]

In the same revelation, Cowdery, second elder to Smith, was called to "go unto the Lamanites [American Indians] and preach my gospel unto them, and cause my church to be established among them."[65]

Peter Whitmer, Jr., was instructed to accompany Cowdery.[66] In October, Parley P. Pratt and Ziba Peterson were called as well. The instructions stated that "nothing shall prevail" against them.[67] This revelation was not published in the BC.

The missionaries traveled to the Cattaraugus tribe near Buffalo, New York, through the state of Ohio, to the Delaware Nation in the territory west of Missouri. But, lacking credentials, they were reduced to preaching to the white population in Jackson and Lafayette counties, Missouri. In essence, the mission failed—the Church of Christ was not "established" among the Indians. So in the 1835 D&C the words "inasmuch as they receive thy teachings, thou shalt" were inserted to explain the failure.

It is important to give some of the known details of this adventure. The revelation for Cowdery stated: "it is not revealed, and no man knoweth where the city [New Jerusalem] shall be built, but it shall be given hereafter. Behold I say unto you, that it shall be on the borders by the Lamanites."[68] There is a question as to whether "borders by the" was an addition to the text, since it was published as "among" in the *Ohio Star* in December 1831. Except for this instance, other New York revelations used the word "among."[69]

While there were Indians living in New York, the four elders "were appointed to go into the wilderness through the western States, and to the Indian territory."[70] The western states were those west of New York, including Ohio, Indiana, Illinois, and Missouri. The Indian country, where some of the woodland tribes had

---

63. Manuscript History of the Church, A-1:54, written in 1839; Jessee, *Papers of Joseph Smith*, 1:323. See also "Newel Knight's Journal," in *Scraps of Biography*, 64.

64. BC 30:11; LDS D&C 28:11; RLDS D&C 27:4.

65. BC 30:7; LDS D&C 28:8; RLDS D&C 27:3.

66. Document no. 32; LDS D&C 30:5-6; RLDS D&C 29:2.

67. Document no. 35; LDS D&C 32:3; RLDS D&C 31:1.

68. Document no. 30; LDS D&C 28:9; RLDS D&C 27:3.

69. See Document nos. 30 and 32; LDS D&C 28:8, 14; 30:6; RLDS D&C 27:3, 5; 29:2.

70. Parley P. Pratt [Jr.], ed., *Autobiography of Parley P. Pratt* (Salt Lake City: Deseret Book Co., 1994), 35.

been relocated west of the Missouri River, was at that time unorganized. On 17 October 1830 at Manchester, New York, Cowdery was further told to "go forth unto the Lamanites ... to rear up a pillar as a witness where the Temple of God shall be built, in the glorious New-Jerusalem."[71] These missionaries knew the general location of where they were going prior to their departure. Their destination would be outside the states in Indian territory.

In BC 32 Peter Whitmer, Jr., was instructed to accompany Cowdery, "For I have given unto him [Cowdery] to build up my church among your brethren, the Lamanites."[72] In 1835 the wording was changed to read: "for I have given unto him power to build up my church among the Lamanites." This one word addition weakens the promise. With the deletion of "your brethren," the 1835 D&C accounts for the fact that no Lamanite brethren had been organized into a church.

An October 1830 revelation for Parley P. Pratt stated "he shall go with my servant Oliver and Peter into the wilderness among the Lamanites and Ziba [Peterson] also shall go with them and I myself will go with them and be in their midst and I am their advocate with the Father and nothing shall prevail."[73] Pratt said that they called on the Catteraugus Indians.[74] They stayed a few hours and left two copies of the Book of Mormon.

The missionaries arrived at Kirtland, Ohio, on 29 October 1830.[75] They preached and baptized seventeen people into the church on 5 November. A few days later Pratt's former minister Sidney Rigdon was baptized. One of the converts, Frederick G. Williams, went with them on their journey. As they were preparing to depart, the Painevsille *Telegraph* reported, "We understand that he [Cowdery] is bound for the regions beyond the Mississippi, where he contemplates founding a 'City of Refuge' for his followers, and converting the Indians, under his prophetic authority."[76] The five men traveled to Sandusky, Ohio, called upon the Wyandot Indians, and spent several days there. Then they continued on to Cincinnati on the Ohio River and walked to St. Louis, Missouri. From St. Louis they continued to Independence, Jackson County, Missouri, arriving about 13 January 1831. Of their arrival Peter Whitmer, Jr. wrote:

> we came to independence on the twelfth [sic; first] month on the 13 d[ay] of the month on the 14 daye of the month began to Labour with mine owne hands Brother Oliver & Parley and Frederick started to see the deleware tribe in a few dayes they came to see me & brother Ziba and they declared that the Lamanites received them with great joy my brethren started againe to the deleweres- and also to the Shayney[77]

---

71. *Ohio Star* 2 (8 Dec. 1831): 3, Ravenna, Ohio.
72. Document no. 32; LDS D&C 30:6; RLDS 29:2.
73. Document no. 35; LDS D&C 32:2-3; RLDS D&C 31:1.
74. "History of Parley P. Pratt," *Deseret News* 8 [19 May 1858]: 53.
75. Copy of Oliver Cowdery letter, dated 12 Nov. 1830, in a Newel Knight journal currently in private possession.
76. *Telegraph* 2 (16 Nov. 1830): 3.
77. Statement of Peter Whitmer, Jr., 13 Dec. 1831, LDS archives. That Whitmer is incorrect as to their arrival in "the twelfth month" is clear from the writings of Pratt and Cowdery. Pratt wrote that they were near St. Louis in "the beginning of 1831" (*Autobiography of Parley P. Pratt*, 40). Cowdery reported on 29 January 1831 "we ar[r]ived at this place a few days since" (Dean C. Jessee, ed., *The Personal Writings of Joseph Smith* [Salt Lake City: Deseret Book Co., 1984], 230).

Pratt mentions that "Two of our number [Whitmer and Peterson] now commenced work as tailors in the village of Independence, while the others crossed the frontier line and commenced a mission among the Lamanites, or Indians."[78] Cowdery wrote that he

> had two interviews with the Chief of the delewares[,] who is a very old & venerable looking man[.] after laying before him & eighteen or twenty of the Council of that nation the truth[,] he said that he he [sic] and they were very glad for what I their Brother had told them and they had received it in their hearts &c- But how the matter will go with this tribe to me is uncirtain [uncertain] ne[i]ther Can I at present Conclude mutch [much] about it[.][79]

Cowdery, Pratt, and Frederick G. Williams started to preach and instruct the Shawnee and Delaware, but lacking a government license, they were ordered off the reservation by Indian agent Richard Cummins. They were told they could obtain a permit from Gen. William Clark, who was in charge of Indian affairs in St. Louis.

Both Pratt and Cummins wrote to Clark in St. Louis. Clark was away from 30 November 1830 through 31 March 1831, and his business was being conducted by John Ruland, sub-agent.[80] Cowdery's letter written on 14 February read: "As I have been appointed by a society of Christians in the State of New York to superintend the establishing Missions among the Indians I doubt not but I shall have the approbation of your honour and a permit for myself and all who may be recommended to me by that Society to have free intercourse with the several tribes in establishing schools for the instruction of their children and also teaching them the Christian religion without intruding or interfering with any other Mission now established."[81]

Cummins's letter to Clark of 15 February read:

> A few days agoe three Men all Strangers to me went among the Indians Shawanees & Delawares, they say for the purpose of preaching to and Instructing them in Religious Matters, they say they are sent by God and must proceed, ... I have refused to let them stay or, go among the Indians unless they first obtain permission from you or, some of the officers of the Genl. Government who I am bound to obey. I am informed that they intend to apply to you for permission to go among the Indians, if you refuse, then they will go to the Rocky Mountains.[82]

Pratt wrote in his autobiography: "Passing through the tribe of Shawnees we tarried one night with them, and the next day crossed the Kansas river and entered among the Delawares,"[83] where they met Chief William Anderson.

---

78. *Autobiography of Parley P. Pratt*, 41.

79. Jessee, *Personal Writings of Joseph Smith*, 230.

80. Warren A. Jennings, "The First Mormon Mission to the Indians," *Kansas Historical Quarterly* 37 (Autumn 1971): 298.

81. "U.S. Superintendency of Indian Affairs," Vol. 6:103; William Clark Papers, MS 95, [microfilm edition], Manuscript Division, Kansas State Historical Society, Topeka, Kansas.

82. Ibid., 113-14.

83. *Autobiography of Parley P. Pratt*, 41.

We continued for several days to instruct the old chief and many of his tribe. ... The excitement now reached the frontier settlements in Missouri, and stirred up the jealousy and envy of the Indian agents and sectarian missionaries to that degree that we were soon ordered out of the Indian country as disturbers of the peace; and even threatened with the military in case of non-compliance. We accordingly departed from the Indian country, and came over the line, and commenced laboring in Jackson County, Missouri, among the whites. We were well received, and listened to by many; and some were baptized and added to the Church. Thus ended our first Indian Mission in which we had preached the gospel in its fulness, and distributed the record of their forefathers among three tribes, viz: the Catteraugus Indians, near Buffalo, N.Y., the Wyandots of Ohio, and the Delawares west of Missouri.[84]

It was agreed that Pratt should travel to St. Louis.

In a letter to Smith of 8 April, Cowdery reported the following:

we had been long looking for [a] letter from you with the hope that the news we should received wou[l]d give our friend[s] who reside in this Land joy by confirming them in the belief that we were men of truth and the Lord God of hosts has not forsaken the earth but is in very deed about to redeem his ancien[t] covenant people & lead them with the fulness of the Gentiles to springs[,] yea[,] fountain of living waters to his holy hill of Zion[.][85]

Cowdery said

the principl[e] chief says he believes ev[e]ry word of the Book [of Mormon] & there are many more in the Nation who believes & we understand there are many among the Shawnees who also believe & we trust that when the Lord shall open our way we shall have glorious times ... the agent for the Lamanites is very strict with us and we think some what strenuous respecting our having liberty to visit our brethren the Lamanites but we trust that when our brother Parley returns we shall have a permit from General Clark[,] who is the Superintendent of Indian affairs west of the Missi[ssi]ppi who must have a recommend or security before he can give a permit for any stranger or foreigner to go among them to teach or preach.[86]

While Cowdery stated that his teachings were received with gladness, there was no mention of any baptisms.

It is possible that Pratt carried Cowdery's letter to Clark personally. Another letter from Cowdery of 16 April is not extant. On 7 May he wrote to Smith, "I have nothing particular to write as concerning the Lamanites."[87] Pratt had left St. Louis and arrived in Kirtland, Ohio, near the end of March, and from there embarked on a mission to the Shakers.

Smith's history contains the following: "From P. P. Pratt, who had returned from the expedition of last fall, during the spring we had verbal information; and from letters from the still remaining elders we had written intelligence," and also

84. Ibid., 44.
85. Copy of letter in Joseph Smith Letterbook 1:10, LDS archives.
86. Ibid., 11-12.
87. Ibid., 12.

that "this was the most important subject which then engrossed the attention of the saints."[88]

Two of the first converts among the white population in Jackson County were Joshua Lewis and his wife who lived in Kaw Township, west of Independence. They were baptized in early 1831.[89] Peter Whitmer, Jr., stated, "then [we] resorted among the gentiles and declared the word and Babtized 7."[90]

31. You Have Feared Man
From BC 31 (cf. LDS D&C 30:1-4; RLDS D&C 29:1)

*Revelation received at Fayette, New York,
in [26-28] September 1830 for David Whitmer*

A Revelation to David, given in Fayette, New-York, September 1830.

Behold I say unto you, David [Whitmer], that you have feared man and have not relied upon me for strength, as you ought:

But your mind has been on the things of the earth more than on the things of me, your Maker, and the ministry whereunto you have been called; and you have not given heed unto my Spirit, and to those who were set over you, but have been persuaded by those whom I have not commanded:

Wherefore you are left to inquire for yourself, at my hand, and ponder upon the things which you have received.

And your home shall be at your father's house, until I give unto you further commandments.

And you shall attend to the ministry in the church, and before the world, and in the regions round about. Amen.

32. Give Heed unto These Things
From BC 32 (cf. LDS D&C 30:5-8; RLDS D&C 29:2)

*Revelation received at Fayette, New York,
in [26-28] September 1830 for Peter Whitmer, Jr.*

A Revelation to Peter, given in Fayette, New-York, September, 1830.

Behold I say unto you, Peter [Whitmer, Jr.], that you shall take your journey

88. *Times and Seasons* 5 (15 Feb. 1844): 432. For a change in the manuscript history after the 1844 publication, see Jessee, *Papers of Joseph Smith*, 1:354, and *History of the Church*, 1:181-82.
89. Jessee, "Joseph Knight's Recollection," 39; see also Journal History of the Church, 3 Feb. 1831, LDS archives.
90. Statement of Peter Whitmer, Jr., 13 Dec. 1831, LDS archives.

with your brother Oliver [Cowdery], for the time has come, that it is expedient in me, that you shall open your mouth to declare my gospel:

Therefore, fear not but give heed unto the words and advice of your brother, which he shall give you.

And be you afflicted in all his afflictions, ever lifting up your heart unto me in prayer, and faith, for his and your deliverance:

For I have given unto him to build up my church among your brethren, the Lamanites.

And none have I appointed to be over him in the church, except it is his brother Joseph [Smith, Jr.].

Wherefore give heed unto these things and be diligent in keeping my commandments, and you shall be blessed unto eternal life. Amen.

Revision

1835 D&C 52
(cf. LDS D&C 30:6-7; RLDS D&C 29:2)

And be you afflicted in all his afflictions, ever lifting up your heart unto me in prayer, and faith, for his and your deliverance: for I have given unto him *power* to build up my church among the Lamanites: and none have I appointed to be *his counsellor*, over him, in the church, *concerning church matters*, except it is his brother Joseph Smith, jr.

33. Your Whole Labor Shall Be in My Zion
From BC 33 (cf. LDS D&C 30:9-11; RLDS D&C 29:3)

Revelation received at Fayette, New York,
in [26-28] September 1830 for John Whitmer

A Revelation to John, given in Fayette, New-York, September, 1830.

Behold I say unto you my servant, John [Whitmer], that thou shalt commence from this time forth to proclaim my gospel, as with the voice of a trump.

And your labor shall be at your brother Philip's [Burroughs], and in that region round about:

Yea, wherever you can be heard, until I command you to go from hence.

And your whole labor shall be in my Zion, with all your soul, from henceforth; yea, you shall ever open your mouth in my cause not fearing what man can do, for I am with you. Amen.

34. Pray Always
From BC 34 (cf. LDS D&C 31; RLDS D&C 30)

Revelation received at Fayette, New York,
in [26-28] September 1830 for Thomas B. Marsh

A Revelation to Thomas, given in Fayette, New-York, September, 1830.

Thomas [B. Marsh], my son, blessed are you because of your faith in my work.

Behold you have had many afflictions because of your family: nevertheless I will bless you, and your family:

Yea, your little ones, and the day cometh that they will believe and know the truth and be one with you in my church.

Lift up your heart and rejoice for the hour of your mission is come; and your tongue shall be loosed: and you shall declare glad tidings of great joy unto this generation.

You shall declare the things which have been revealed to my servant Joseph [Smith, Jr.].

You shall begin to preach from this time forth; yea, to reap in the field which is white already to be burned:

Therefore thrust in your sickle with all your soul; and your sins are forgiven you; and you shall be laden with sheaves upon your back, for the laborer is worthy of his hire.

Wherefore your family shall live.

Behold, verily I say unto you, go from them only for a little time, and declare my word, and I will prepare a place for them; yea, I will open the hearts of the people and they will receive you.

And I will establish a church by your hand; and you shall strengthen them and prepare them against the time when they shall be gathered.

Be patient in afflictions, and in sufferings, revile not against those that revile.

Govern your house in meekness, and be steadfast.

Behold I say unto you, that you shall be a physician unto the church, but not unto the world, for they will not receive you.

Go your way whithersoever I will, and it shall be given you by the Comforter what you shall do, and whither you shall go.

Pray always, lest you enter into temptation, and loose your reward.

Be faithful unto the end, and lo, I am with you.

These words are not of man nor of men, but of me, even Jesus Christ, your Redeemer, by the will of the Father. Amen.

35. Be Meek and Lowly of Heart
From KRB, 83-84 (cf. LDS D&C 32; RLDS D&C 31)

Revelation received at Manchester, New York,
in [ca. 17] October 1830 for Parley P. Pratt
and Ziba Peterson[91]

Revelation to Parley Pratt to go to th[e] wilderness

And now concerning my servant Parley [P. Pratt] behold I say unto him that as I live I will that he shall declare my gospel and Learn of me and be meek and lowly of heart and that which I have appointed unto him is that he shall go with my servant Oliver [Cowdery] and Peter [Whitmer, Jr.] into the wilderness among the Lamanites and Ziba [Peterson] also shall go with them and I myself will go with them and be in their midst and I am their advocate with the Father and nothing shall prevail and they shall give heed to that which is writ[t]en and pretend to no other revelation and they shall pray always that I may unfold them to their understanding and they shall give heed [u]nto these words and trifle not and I will bless them amen.

Manchester Oct 1830

36. Be Ready at the Coming of the Bridegroom
From BC 35 (cf. LDS D&C 33; RLDS D&C 32)

Revelation received at Fayette, New York,
in [18-31] October 1830 for Ezra Thayer and Northrop Sweet[92]

A Revelation to Ezra, and Northrop, given in Fayette, New-York, October, 1830.

Behold I say unto you, my servants Ezra [Thayer], and Northrop [Sweet], open ye your ears and hearken to the voice of the Lord your God, whose word is quick and powerful, sharper than a two-edged sword, to the dividing asunder of the joints and marrow, soul and spirit; and is a discerner of the thoughts and intents of the heart.

For verily, verily I say unto you, that ye are called to lift up your voices as with the sound of a trump, to declare my gospel unto a crooked and a perverse generation:

---

91. This revelation was received in Manchester about the time that a missionary covenant was signed at the same place on 17 October 1830. (See *Ohio Star* 2 [8 Dec. 1831]: 1.) The missionaries to the Native Americans (Lamanites) arrived in Kirtland, Ohio, on 29 October 1830. They traveled to Independence, Missouri, arriving in January 1831. This revelation was not included in the BC.

92. Ezra Thayer and Northrop Sweet were baptized at Manchester that same month by Parley P. Pratt. See "Testimony of Brother E. Thayre [Thayer]," *True Latter Day Saints' Herald* 3 (Oct. 1862): 83.

For behold the field is white already to harvest; and it is the eleventh hour, and for the last time that I shall call laborers into my vineyard. And my vineyard has become corrupted every whit: and there is none which doeth good save it be a few; and they err in many instances, because of priestcrafts, all having corrupt minds.

And verily, verily I say unto you, that this church have I established and called forth out of the wilderness:

And even so will I gather mine elect from the four quarters of the earth, even as many as will believe in me, and hearken unto my voice:

Yea, verily, verily I say unto you, that the field is white already to harvest:

Wherefore thrust in your sickles, and reap with all your might, mind, and strength.

Open your mouths and they shall be filled; and you shall become even as Nephi of old, who journeyed from Jerusalem in the wilderness:

Yea, open your mouths and spare not, and you shall be laden with sheaves upon your backs, for lo I am with you:

Yea, open your mouths and they shall be filled, saying Repent, repent and prepare ye the way of the Lord, and make his paths strait: for the kingdom of heaven is at hand:

Yea, repent and be baptized every one of you, for a remission of your sins; yea, be baptized even by water, and then cometh the baptism of fire and of the Holy Ghost.

Behold, verily, verily I say unto you, this is my gospel, and remember that they shall have faith in me, or they can in no wise be saved:

And upon this Rock I will build my church; yea, upon this Rock ye are built, and the gates of hell shall not prevail against you; and ye shall remember the church articles and covenants to keep them:

And whoso having faith you shall confirm in my church, by the laying on of the hands, and I will bestow the gift of the Holy Ghost upon them.

And the book of Mormon, and the holy scriptures, are given of me for your instruction; and the power of my Spirit quickeneth all things:

Wherefore be faithful, praying always, having your lamps trimmed and burning, and oil with you, that you may be ready at the coming of the Bridegroom; for behold, verily, verily I say unto you, that I come quickly; even so: Amen.

Revision

1835 D&C 55
(cf. LDS D&C 33:13-14; RLDS D&C 32:3)

and upon this Rock I will build my church; yea, upon this rock ye are built, and *if ye continue*, the gates of hell shall not prevail against you; and ye shall remember the church articles and covenants to keep them

Commentary: If Ye Continue

To BC 35 was added, after "And upon this Rock I will build my church; yea, upon this Rock ye are built, and," the words, "if ye continue." This was a mission-ary revelation to Ezra Thayer and Northrop Sweet, given in October 1830, in-structing them what to say when preaching.

It is probable that the reason for the addition "if ye continue" applied to North-rop Sweet, since he left the church in 1831 and joined with Wycom Clark who or-ganized the Pure Church of Christ.[93]

37. I Come Quickly
From BC 36 (cf. LDS D&C 34; RLDS D&C 33)

Revelation received at Fayette, New York,
on 4 November 1830 for Orson Pratt[94]

A Revelation to Orson (P.) given in Fayette, New-York, November, 1830.

My son Orson [Pratt], hearken and hear and behold what I the Lord God shall say unto you, even Jesus Christ your Redeemer, the light and the life of the world:

A light which shineth in darkness and the darkness comprehendeth it not:

Who so loved the world that he gave his own life, that as many as would believe might become the sons of God:

Wherefore you are my son, and blessed are you because you have believed, and more blessed are you because you are called of me to preach my gospel; to lift up your voice as with the sound of a trump, both long and loud, and cry repentance unto a crooked and perverse generation; preparing the way of the Lord for his sec-ond coming: for behold, verily, verily I say unto you, the time is soon at hand, that I shall come in a cloud with power and great glory, and it shall be a great day at the time of my coming, for all nations shall tremble.

But before that great day shall come, the sun shall be darkened, and the moon be turned into blood, and the stars shall refuse their shining, and some shall fall, and great destructions await the wicked:

Wherefore lift up your voice and spare not, for the Lord God hath spoken.

Therefore prophesy and it shall be given by the power of the Holy Ghost; and if you are faithful behold I am with you until I come:

And verily, verily I say unto you, I come quickly.

I am your Lord and your Redeemer; even so: Amen.

---

93. Lyndon W. Cook, *The Revelations of the Prophet Joseph Smith: A Historical and Biographical Commentary of the Doctrine and Covenants* (Provo, UT: Seventy's Mission Bookstore, 1981), 48. See also Steven L. Shields, *Divergent Paths of the Restoration: A History of the Latter Day Saint Move-ment,* 4th ed. (Los Angeles, CA: Restoration Research, 1990), 21.

94. This revelation was originally given through a seer stone placed in a hat by Joseph Smith and recorded by John Whitmer. See James R. B. Vancleave to Joseph Smith III, 29 Sept. 1878, "Miscellaneous Letters and Papers," RLDS archives, and John Logan Traughber to "Dear Friend," 10 Oct. 1881, Schroeder Collection, State Historical Society of Wisconsin, Madison.

38. Thou Shalt Preach My Gospel
From BC 37 (cf. LDS D&C 35; RLDS D&C 34)

Revelation received at Fayette, New York,
in [7-11] December 1830 for Joseph Smith, Jr.,
and Sidney Rigdon[95]

A Revelation to Joseph, and Sidney, given in Fayette, New-York, December, 1830.

Listen to the voice of the Lord your God, even Alpha and Omega, the beginning and the end, whose course is one eternal round, the same today as yesterday and forever.

I am Jesus Christ, the Son of God, who was crucified for the sins of the world, even as many as will believe on my name, that they may become the sons of God, even one in me as I am in the Father, as the Father is one in me, that we may be one:

Behold, verily, verily I say unto my servant Sidney [Rigdon], I have looked upon thee and thy works.

I have heard thy prayers and prepared thee for a greater work.

Thou art blessed for thou shalt do great things.

Behold thou wast sent forth, even as John, to prepare the way before me, and before Elijah which should come, and thou knew it not.

Thou didst baptize by water unto repentance, but they received not the Holy Ghost; but now I give unto thee a commandment, that thou shalt baptize by water, and they shall receive the Holy Ghost by the laying on of hands, even as the apostles of old.

And it shall come to pass, that there shall be a great work in the land even among the Gentiles, for their folly and their abominations shall be made manifest, in the eyes of all people:

For I am God and mine arm is not shortened and I will show miracles, signs and wonders, unto all those who believe on my name.

And whoso shall ask it in my name, in faith, they shall cast out devils; they shall heal the sick; they shall cause the blind to receive their sight, and the deaf to hear, and the dumb to speak, and the lame to walk:

And the time speedily cometh, that great things are to be shown forth unto the children of men:

But without faith shall not any thing be shown forth except desolations upon Babylon, the same which has made all nations drink of the wine of the wrath of her fornication.

---

95. The date of this revelation is given as "Dec. 7th, 1830" in the *Ohio Star*, 5 Jan. 1832, 3. Sidney Rigdon was baptized on 8 November 1830 in Ohio. He was thirty-seven years old. See Richard S. Van Wagoner, *Sidney Rigdon: A Portrait of Religious Excess* (Salt Lake City: Signature Books, 1994), 62, 66-67n61. The date for the baptism of Edward Partridge is recorded as 11 December 1830 (Jessee, *Papers of Joseph Smith*, 1:348).

And there are none that doeth good except those who are ready to receive the fullness of my gospel, which I have sent forth to this generation:

Wherefore, I have called upon the weak things of the world, those who are unlearned and despised, to thresh the nations by the power of my Spirit:

And their arm shall be mine arm, and I will be their shield and their buckler, and I will gird up their loins, and they shall fight manfully for me:

And their enemies shall be under their feet; and I will let fall the sword in their behalf; and by the fire of mine indignation will I preserve them.

And the poor and the meek shall have the gospel preached unto them, and they shall be looking forth for the time of my coming, for it is nigh at hand:

And they shall learn the parable of the fig-tree: for even now already summer is nigh, and I have sent forth the fulness of my gospel by the hand of my servant Joseph [Smith, Jr.]:

And in weakness have I blessed him, and I have given unto him the keys of the mystery of those things which have been sealed, even things which were from the foundation of the world, and the things which shall come from this time until the time of my coming, if he abide in me, and if not, another will I plant in his stead.

Wherefore watch over him that his faith fail not, and it shall be given by the Comforter, the Holy Ghost, that knoweth all things:

And a commandment I give unto thee, that thou shalt write for him:

And the scriptures shall be given even as they are in mine own bosom, to the salvation of mine own elect:[96]

For they will hear my voice, and shall see me, and shall not be asleep, and shall abide the day of my coming, for they shall be purified even as I am pure. And now I say unto you, tarry with him and he shall journey with you; forsake him not and surely these things shall be fulfilled.

And inasmuch as ye do not write, behold it shall be given unto him to prophesy.

And thou shalt preach my gospel, and call on the holy prophets to prove his words, as they shall be given him.

Keep all the commandments and covenants by which ye are bound, and I will cause the heavens to shake for your good:

And satan shall tremble; and Zion shall rejoice upon the hills, and flourish; and Israel shall be saved in mine own due time.

And by the keys which I have given, shall they be led and no more be confounded at all.

Lift up your hearts and be glad: your redemption draweth nigh.

Fear not little flock, the kingdom is yours until I come.

Behold I come quickly; even so: Amen.

---

96. Sidney Rigdon became a scribe for Smith while he was revising Genesis. Rigdon's handwriting commences on page 15 of the dictated manuscript of the Bible revision (manuscript in RLDS archives).

39. I Will Suddenly Come to My Temple
From BC 38 (cf. LDS D&C 36: RLDS D&C 35)

Revelation received at Fayette, New York,
in [11-15] December 1830 for Edward Partridge[97]

A Revelation to Edward, given in Fayette, New-York, December, 1830.

Thus saith the Lord God, the mighty One of Israel, behold I say unto you, my servant Edward [Partridge], that you are blessed, and your sins are forgiven you, and you are called to preach my gospel as with the voice of a trump; and I will lay my hand upon you by the hand of my servant Sidney [Rigdon], and you shall receive my Spirit, the Holy Ghost, even the Comforter, which shall teach you the peaceable things of the kingdom:
And you shall declare it with a loud voice saying, Hosanna, blessed be the name of the most high God.
And now this calling and commandment give I unto all men, that as many as shall come before my servant Sidney [Rigdon] and Joseph [Smith, Jr.], embracing this calling and commandment, shall be ordained and sent forth to preach the everlasting gospel among the nations, crying repentance, saying, Save yourselves from this untoward generation, and come forth out of the fire, hating even the garment spotted with the flesh.
And this commandment shall be given unto the elders of my church, that every man which will embrace it with singleness of heart, may be ordained and sent forth, even as I have spoken.
I am Jesus Christ, the Son of God:
Wherefore gird up your loins and I will suddenly come to my temple; even so: Amen.

40. Ye Shall Go to the [State of] Ohio
From BC 39 (cf. LDS and RLDS D&C 37)

Revelation received at Canandaigua, New York,
in [30] December 1830 for Joseph Smith, Jr., and Sidney Rigdon[98]

A Revelation to Joseph and Sidney, given in Canandaigua, New-York, December, 1830.

Behold I say unto you, that it is not expedient in me that ye should translate any

---

97. Edward Partridge accompanied Rigdon to see Smith. Partridge was thirty-seven years old and was ordained an elder on 15 December 1830 by Rigdon (copy of license in LDS archives).
98. This revelation is dated 30 December 1830 by William E. McLellin, in *The Ensign of Liberty* 1 (Mar. 1847): 2, Kirtland, Ohio.

more until ye shall go to the Ohio;[99] and this because of the enemy and for your sakes.

And again, I say unto you, that ye shall not go until ye have preached my gospel in those parts, and have strengthened up the church whithersoever it is found, and more especially in Colesville:

For behold they pray unto me in much faith.

And again a commandment I give unto the church, that it is expedient in me that they should assemble together at the Ohio, against the time that my servant Oliver [Cowdery] shall return unto them.

Behold here is wisdom, and let every man choose for himself until I come; even so: Amen.

41. Behold the Kingdom Is Yours
From BC 40 (cf. LDS and RLDS D&C 38)

Revelation received at Fayette, New York,
on 2 January 1831 for the churches in New York[100]

A Revelation to the churches in New-York, commanding them to remove to Ohio, given in Fayette, New-York, January, 1831.

Thus saith the Lord your God, even Jesus Christ, the Great I AM, Alpha and Omega, the beginning and the end, the same which looked upon the wide expanse of eternity, and all the seraphic hosts of heaven, before the world was made, the same which knoweth all things, for all things are present before mine eyes:

I am the same which spake and the world was made, and all things came by me:

I am the same which hath taken the Zion of Enoch into mine own bosom:[101]

And verily I say, even as many as have believed on my name, for I am Christ, and in mine own name, by the virtue of the blood which I have spilt, have I plead before the Father for them:

But behold the residue of the wicked have I kept in chains of darkness until the judgment of the great day, which shall come at the end of the earth, and even so will I cause the wicked to be kept, that will not hear my voice but harden their hearts, and wo, wo, wo is their doom.

But behold, verily, verily I say unto you, that mine eyes are upon you; I am in

---

99. The text of Joseph Smith's revision of Genesis dictated in New York ends at Genesis 5:32 (KJV); Gen. 7:85 (JST); LDS Moses 8:12. John Whitmer's copy of the manuscript, taken by him to Ohio in January 1831, ends at this point. Both manuscripts are in the RLDS archives. Though in the revelation this work is termed a "translation," no ancient biblical manuscripts were used and Joseph Smith did not know Hebrew at the time. This work is better understood as an inspired correction of the Bible rather than a translation.

100. This revelation was given at the third conference of the church. See Cannon and Cook, *Far West Record*, 5.

101. This refers to a city built during the days of Enoch. The city was taken up into heaven, according to Smith's addition to Genesis.

your midst and ye cannot see me, but the day soon cometh that ye shall see me and know that I am:

For the vail of darkness shall soon be rent, and he that is not purified shall not abide the day:

Wherefore gird up your loins and be prepared.

Behold the kingdom is yours and the enemy shall not overcome.

Verily I say unto you, ye are clean but not all; and there is none else with whom I am well pleased, for all flesh is corruptible before me, and the powers of darkness prevail upon the earth, among the children of men, in the presence of all the hosts of heaven, which causeth silence to reign, and all eternity is pained, and the angels are waiting the great command, to reap down the earth, to gather the tares that they may be burned:

And behold the enemy is combined.

And now I show unto you a mystery, a thing which is had in secret chambers, to bring to pass even your destruction, in process of time, and ye knew it not, but now I tell it unto you, and ye are blessed, not because of your iniquity, neither your hearts of unbelief, for verily some of you are guilty before me; but I will be merciful unto your weakness.

Therefore, be ye strong from henceforth; fear not for the kingdom is yours:

And for your salvation I give unto you a commandment, for I have heard your prayers, and the poor have complained before me, and the rich have I made, and all flesh is mine, and I am no respecter to persons. And I have made the earth rich, and behold it is my footstool: wherefore, again I will stand upon it:

And I hold forth and deign to give unto you greater riches, even a land of promise; a land flowing with milk and honey, upon which there shall be no curse when the Lord cometh, and I will give it unto you for the land of your inheritance, if you seek it with all you hearts:

And this shall be my covenant with you, ye shall have it for the land of your inheritance, and for the inheritance of your children forever, while the earth shall stand, and ye shall possess it again in eternity, no more to pass away:

But verily I say unto you, that in time ye shall have no king nor ruler, for I will be your King and watch over you.

Wherefore, hear my voice and follow me, and you shall be a free people, and ye shall have no laws but my laws, when I come, for I am your Lawgiver, and what can stay my hand.

But verily I say unto you, teach one another according to the office wherewith I have appointed you, and let every man esteem his brother as himself, and practice virtue and holiness before me.

And again I say unto you, let every man esteem his brother as himself:

For what man among you, having twelve sons, and is no respecter to them, and they serve him obediently, and he saith unto the one, be thou clothed in robes and sit thou here; and to the other, be thou clothed in rags and sit thou there, and looketh upon his sons and saith I am just.

Behold, this I have given unto you a parable, and it is even as I am, I say unto you, be one; and if ye are not one, ye are not mine. And again I say unto you, that the enemy in the secret chambers, seeketh your lives:

Ye hear of wars in far countries, and you say in your hearts there will soon be great wars in far countries, but ye know not the hearts of them in your own land:

I tell you these things because of your prayers:

Wherefore, treasure up wisdom in your bosoms, lest the wickedness of men reveal these things unto you, by their wickedness, in a manner which shall speak in your ears, with a voice louder than that which shall shake the earth:

But if ye are prepared, ye shall not fear.

And that ye might escape the power of the enemy, and be gathered unto me a righteous people, without spot and blameless:

Wherefore, for this cause I gave unto you the commandment, that ye should go to the Ohio: and there I will give unto you my law, and there you shall be endowed with power from on high, and from thence, whomsoever I will shall go forth among all nations, and it shall be told them what they shall do, for I have a great work laid up in store:

For Israel shall be saved, and I will lead them whithersoever I will, and no power shall stay my hand.

And now I give unto the church in these parts, a commandment, that certain men among them shall be appointed, and they shall be appointed by the voice of the church; and they shall look to the poor and the needy, and administer to their relief, that they shall not suffer; and send them forth to the place which I have commanded them; and this shall be their work, to govern the affairs of the property of this church. And they that have farms, that can not be sold, let them be left or rented as seemeth them good.

See that all things are preserved, and when men are endowed with power from on high, and are sent forth, all these things shall be gathered unto the bosom of the church.

And if ye seek the riches which it is the will of the Father to give unto you, ye shall be the richest of all people, for ye shall have the riches of eternity:

And it must needs be that the riches of the earth is mine to give:

But beware of pride, lest ye become as the Nephites of old.

And again: I say unto you, I give unto you a commandment, that every man both elder, priest, teacher and also member, go to with his might, with the labor of his hands, to prepare and accomplish the things which I have commanded.

And let your preaching be the warning voice, every man to his neighbor, in mildness and in meekness.

And go ye out from among the wicked. Save yourselves.

Be ye clean that bear the vessels of the Lord; even so: Amen.

42. The Kingdom of Heaven Is at Hand
From BC 41 (cf. LDS and RLDS D&C 39)

Revelation received at Fayette, New York,
in [5] January 1831 for James Covill[102]

A Revelation to James (C.,) given in Fayette, New-York, January, 1831.

Hearken and listen to the voice of him who is from all eternity to all eternity, the Great I AM, even Jesus Christ, the light and the life of the world; a light which shineth in darkness and the darkness comprehendeth it not:

The same which came in the meridian of time unto my own, and my own received me not; but to as many as received me, gave I power to become my sons, and even so will I give unto as many as will receive me, power to become my sons.

And verily, verily I say unto you, he that receiveth my gospel, receiveth me; and he that receiveth not my gospel, receiveth not me.

And this is my gospel: Repentance and baptism by water, and then cometh the baptism of fire and the Holy Ghost, even the Comforter, which showeth all things, and teacheth the peaceable things of the kingdom.

And now behold I say unto you, my servant James [Covill], I have looked upon thy works and I know thee:

And verily I say unto thee, thine heart is now right before me at this time, and behold I have bestowed great blessing upon thy head:

Nevertheless thou hast seen great sorrow, for thou hast rejected me many times because of pride, and the cares of the world:

But behold the days of thy deliverance are come.

Arise and be baptized, and wash away your sins, calling on my name and you shall receive my Spirit, and a blessing so great as you never have known. And if thou do this, I have prepared thee for a greater work.

Thou shalt preach the fulness of my gospel which I have sent forth in these last days; the covenant which I have sent forth to recover my people, which are of the house of Israel.

And it shall come to pass that power shall rest upon thee; thou shalt have great faith and I will be with thee and go before thy face.

Thou art called to labor in my vineyard, and to build up my church, and to bring forth Zion, that it may rejoice upon the hills and flourish.

Behold, verily, verily I say unto thee, thou art not called to go into the eastern countries, but thou art called to go to the Ohio.

And inasmuch as my people shall assemble themselves to the Ohio, I have kept in store a blessing such as is not known among the children of men, and it shall be poured forth upon their heads.

And from thence men shall go forth into all nations.

Behold, verily, verily I say unto you, that the people in Ohio call upon me in

---

102. James Covill had been a Baptist minister (Jessee, *Papers of Joseph Smith*, 1:346).

much faith, thinking I will stay my hand in judgment upon the nations, but I can not deny my word:

Wherefore lay to with your might and call faithful laborers into my vineyard, that it may be pruned for the last time.

And inasmuch as they do repent and receive the fulness of my gospel, and become sanctified, I will stay mine hand in judgment:

Wherefore go forth, crying with a loud voice, saying, The kingdom of heaven is at hand; crying Hosanna! blessed be the name of the most high God.

Go forth baptizing with water, preparing the way before my face, for the time of my coming; for the time is at hand:

The day nor the hour no man knoweth, but it surely shall come, and he that receiveth these things receiveth me; and they shall be gathered unto me in time and in eternity.

And again, it shall come to pass, that on as many as ye shall baptize with water, ye shall lay your hands, and they shall receive the gift of the Holy Ghost, and shall be looking forth for the signs of my coming, and shall know me.

Behold I come quickly; even so: Amen.

<u>Revision</u>

1835 D&C 59
(cf. LDS D&C 39:10; RLDS D&C 39:3)

but behold the days of thy deliverance are come, *if thou wilt hearken to my voice, which saith unto thee,* Arise and be baptized

<u>Commentary: James Covill</u>

In BC 41 a revelation was given instructing James Covill: "But behold the days of thy deliverance are come. Arise and be baptized[.]"[103] BC 42 explains why Covill, who had been a Baptist minister, did not obey the revelation and join the church. While this should have settled the matter for Smith and his followers in January 1831, evidently the revision committee of 1834-35 felt that the issue was still alive. The words "if thou wilt hearken to my voice, which saith unto thee" were added without regard for the historical context.

43. His Heart Was Right Before Me
From BC 42 (cf. LDS and RLDS D&C 40)

*Revelation received at Fayette, New York,
in [6] January 1831 for Joseph Smith, Jr., and Sidney Rigdon*

A Revelation to Joseph, and Sidney, given in Fayette, New-York, January, 1831, explaining why James (C.,) [James Covill] obeyed not the revelation which was given unto him.

---

103. BC 41:8-9.

Behold, verily I say unto you, that his heart was right before me, for he covenanted with me, that he would obey my word.

And he received the word with gladness, but straitway [straightway] satan tempted him; and the fear of persecution, and the cares of the world, caused him to reject the word:

Wherefore he broke my covenant, and it remaineth in me to do with him as seemeth me good. Amen.

4. Receiving the Laws,
February 1831–September 1831

44. Hearken and Hear, O Ye My People
From BC 43 (cf. LDS and RLDS D&C 41)

Revelation received at Kirtland, Ohio,
on 4 February 1831 for the Church of Christ[1]

A Revelation to the church in Kirtland, Ohio, and also the calling of Edward [Partridge] to the office of bishop, given February, 1831.

Hearken and hear, O ye my people, saith your Lord and your God, ye whom I delight to bless with the greatest of blessings, ye that hear me:

And ye that hear me not will I curse, that have professed my name, with the heaviest of all cursings.

Hearken, O ye elders of my church whom I have called;

Behold I give unto you a commandment, that ye shall assemble yourselves together to agree upon my word, and by the prayer of your faith ye shall receive my law, that ye may know how to govern my church, and have all things right before me.

And I will be your Ruler when I come: and behold, I come quickly: and ye shall see that my law is kept.

He that receiveth my law and doeth it the same is my disciple;

And he that saith he receiveth it and doeth it not, the same is not my disciple, and shall be cast out from among you:

For it is not meet that the things which belong to the children of the kingdom, should be given to them that are not worthy, or to dogs, or the pearls to be cast before swine.

And again, it is meet that my servant Joseph [Smith, Jr.] should have a house built, in which to live and translate.

---

1. Joseph Smith arrived in Kirtland, Ohio, about 1 February 1831. He and his wife, Emma, resided at the home of Newel K. Whitney for several weeks. Edward Partridge was the first bishop appointed and ordained in the Church of Christ. He received his ordination on 4 February 1831 by Sidney Rigdon. Partridge's license as bishop was signed by Rigdon and Smith, and a number of times between August 1831 and about January 1832 (license in LDS archives).

And again, it is meet that my servant Sidney [Rigdon] should live as seemeth him good.

And again, I have called my servant Edward [Partridge], and give a commandment, that he should be appointed by the voice of the church, and ordained a bishop unto the church, to leave his merchandise and to spend all his time in the labors of the church; to see to all things as it shall be appointed unto him, in my laws in the day that I shall give them.

And this because his heart is pure before me, for he is like unto Nathaniel of old, in whom there is no guile.

These words are given unto you, and they are pure before me:

Wherefore beware how you hold them, for they are to be answered upon your souls in the day of judgment; even so: Amen.

Revision

1835 D&C 61
(cf. LDS D&C 41:8; RLDS D&C 41:3)

And again it is meet that my servant Sidney Rigdon should live as seemeth him good, *inasmuch as he keepeth my commandments.*

Commentary: Sidney Rigdon, Live as Seemeth Him Good

In the first revelation received in Kirtland, Ohio, dated 4 February 1831 (BC 43:10), it says, "And again, it is meet that my servant Sidney [Rigdon] should live as seemeth him good." In the 1835 D&C after the word "good" was added "inasmuch as he keepeth my commandments." This addition changes the tone from praise to reproach.

In July 1832 Rigdon stated that "the keys of the kingdom are rent from the church and there shall not be a prayer put up in this place to day ... the keys of [the] kingdom are wrent [rent] from you and you never will have them again untill you build me a new house."[2] Reynolds Cahoon recalled that "Br Sidney remarked that he had a revelation from the Lord & said that the kingdom was taken from the Church and left with him."[3] It may have been this incident that inspired the committee to make Rigdon's living conditions provisional.

---

2. Lucy Mack Smith, Preliminary Manuscript, 160, LDS archives; *Biographical Sketches of Joseph Smith the Prophet, and His Progenitors for Many Generations* (Liverpool, Eng.: Published for Orson Pratt by S.W. Richards, 1853), 195; *History of Joseph Smith By His Mother, Lucy Mack Smith* (Salt Lake City: Bookcraft, 1958), 222.

3. Reynolds Cahoon Journal, 5 July 1832, LDS archives.

45. Behold I Speak unto the Church

From "Book of Commandments, Law and Covenants; Book B," LDS archives (cf. LDS D&C 42:1-72 and RLDS D&C 42:1-19)

Revelation received at Kirtland, Ohio,
on 9 February 1831 for twelve elders also containing
the Laws of the Church of Christ[4]

Laws of the Church of Christ received in the presence of twelve Elders February 9th 1831

Question 1st. = Shall the Church come together into one place or remain as they are in separate bodies?

Answer = Hearken Oh! ye Elders of my Church who have assembled yourselves together in my name, even Jesus Christ the Son of the living God the Saviour of the world, inasmuch as they believe on my name & keep my Commandments, again I say unto you hearken and he[a]r obey the laws which I shall give unto you for verily I say as ye have assembled yourselves together according to the Commandment wherewith I commanded you, and are agreed as touching this one thing and have asked me in my name, even so ye shall receive

Behold verily I say unto you, I give unto you this first commandment that ye shall go forth in my name every one of you, together with[5] my Servants Joseph [Smith, Jr.] & Sidney [Rigdon], & I give unto them a Commandment that they shall go forth for a little season & it shall be given by the power of my spirit when they shall return and ye shall go forth in the power of my Spirit, preaching my gospel two by two in my name lifting up your voices as with the voice of a trump, declaring my word like unto Angels of God and ye shall go forth baptizing with water, saying Repent ye, Repent ye, for the Kingdom of Heaven is at hand, and from this place ye shall go forth into the regions westward & inasmuch as ye shall find my disciples ye shall build up my Church in every region untill the time shall come when it shall be revealed unto you from on high, and the City of the New Jerusalem shall be prepared, that ye may be gathered into one, that ye may be my people & I will be your God & again I say unto you that my Servant Edward [Partridge] shall stand in the Office wherewith I have appointed him & it shall come to pass that if he transgress another shall be planted in his stead, even so, Amen

Question 2d. The Law regulating the Church in her present situation till the time of her gathering[?]

Answer – Again verily I say unto you that it shall not be given to any one to go forth to preach my gospel & to build up my Church except he be ordained by some one that hath authority & it be known to the Church that he hath authority & has

---

4. Joseph Smith wrote to Martin Harris, "We have received the laws of the Kingdom since we came here and the Disciples in these parts have received them gladly" (Smith to Harris, 22 Feb. 1831, LDS archives; *The Essential Joseph Smith* [Salt Lake City: Signature Books, 1995], 11).

5. Another early manuscript copy of this revelation has the word "except" rather than the words "together with" (LDS archives).

been regularly ordained by the heads of this Church, & again the Elders, Priests & Teachers of this Church shall teach the scriptures which are in the Bible & Book of Mormon in the which is the fullness of my Gospel & thou shall observe the Covenants & Church Articles to do them, & this shall be thy teaching as thou shalt be directed by the spirit, it shall be given unto thee by the prayer of faith, & if ye receive not the spirit ye shall not teach, and all this ye shall observe to do as I have commanded you concerning your teachings untill the fullness of my scriptures are given and as ye shall lift up your voices by the Comforter, ye shall speak & prophecy as seemeth me good for behold the Comforter knoweth all things and beareth record of the Father & the Son

And now behold I speak unto the Church, thou Shalt not kill, and he that killeth shall not have forgiveness neither in this world nor the world to Come, and again, I say unto you thou shalt not kill, he that killeth shall die Thou shalt not Steal & he that stealeth & will not repent shall be Cast out thou shalt not lie, he that lieth & will not repent shall be cast out.

Thou shalt love thy wife with all thy heart and shall cleave unto her & none else, and he that looketh upon a woman to lust after her shall deny the faith & shall not have the spirit & if he repent not he shall be cast out

Thou shalt not Commit adultery and he that committeth adultery & repenteth not shall be cast out and he that committeth adultery and repenteth with all his heart and forsaketh & doeth it no more, thou shalt forgive him, but if he do it again he shall not be forgiven, but shall be cast out.

Thou shalt not speak evil of thy neighbor nor do him any harm, thou knowest my laws, they are given in my scriptures he that sinneth & repenteth not shall be cast out

If thou lovest me thou shalt serve me & keep all my commandments and behold thou shalt consecrate all thy property that which thou hath unto me with a covenant & a deed which cannot be broken and they shall be laid before the Bishop of my Church & two of the Elders such as he shall appoint and set apart for that purpose[6] and it shall come to pass that the Bishop of my Church after that he hath received the [properties][7] of my Church that it cannot be taken from you, he shall appoint every man a steward over his own property or that which he hath received inasmuch as it shall be sufficient for himself & family and the residue shall be kept to administer to him that hath not, that every man may receive according as he stands in need, & the residue shall be kept in my Store House to administer to the poor & needy as shall be appointed by the Elders of the Church and the Bishop & for the purpose of purchasing lands & the building up the New Jerusalem which is hereafter to be revealed that my Covenant people may be gathered in me in the day that I shall come to my Temple this do for the salvation of my people

---

6. On 3 June 1831 "John Corrill and Isaac Morley were ordained assistants to the Bishop under the hand of Lyman Wight" (Donald Q. Cannon and Lyndon W. Cook, eds., *Far West Record: Minutes of the Church of Jesus Christ of Latter-day Saints, 1830-1844* [Salt Lake City: Deseret Book Co., 1983], 7).

7. The word "properties" is not contained in this manuscript. Three other manuscripts and the BC use "properties."

and it shall come to pass that he that sinneth & repenteth not shall be cast out and shall not receive again that which he hath consecrated unto me for it shall come to pass that which I spake by the mouth of my prophets shall be fulfilled for I will consecrate the riches of the Gentiles unto my people which are of the House of Israel and again thou shalt not be proud in heart, let all thy Garments be plain & their beauty the beauty of the work of thine own hands & let all things be done in decency before me.

Thou shalt not be idle for he that is idle shall not eat the bread nor wear the garments of the Labourer, and whosoever among you that is sick & hath not faith to be healed but believeth shall be nourished in all tenderness with herbs & mild food & that not of the world and the Elders of the church two or more shall be called & shall pray for & lay their hands on them in my name, & if they die, they shall die unto me, & if they live, they shall live unto me, thou shalt live together in love, insomuch that thou shalt weep for the loss of those that die, & more especially those that have not the hope of a glorious resurrection, and it shall come to pass that they that die in me shall not taste of death for it shall be sweet unto them & they that die not in me [wo unto them for][8] their death shall be bitter, & again it shall come to pass that he that hath faith in me to be healed & is not appointed unto death shall be healed, he that hath faith to see shall see, he that hath faith to hear shall hear, the lame that hath faith to leap shall leap, & they that have not faith to do these things but believe in me hath power to become my sons, & inasmuch as they believe in & break not my law, thou shalt bear their infirmities

Thou shalt stand in the place of thy stewardship, thou shalt not take thy brothers garment, thou shalt pay for that which thou shalt receive of thy brother and if thou obtain more than that which would be for thy support, thou shalt give it into my Store house, that it my be done according to that which I have spoken

Thou shalt ask and my scriptures shall be given as I have appointed, and for thy salvation thou shalt hold thy peace concerning them till ye have rec[eive]d. them, and then I give unto you a Commandment that ye shall teach them unto all men & they also shall be taught unto all nations kindreds, tongues & people

Thou shalt take those things which thou hast rec[eive]d. which thou knowest to have been my law & to be [my law][9] to govern my Church & he that doeth according to these things shall be saved & he that doeth them not shall be damned if he continues If thou shalt ask thou shalt receive revelation upon revelation, knowledge upon knowledge that thou mayest know the mysteries of the peaceable things of the kingdom, that which bringeth joy, that which bringeth life Eternal

Thou shalt ask & it shall be revealed unto you in mine own due time, when the New Jerusalem shall be built, thou shalt ask & it shall be revealed in mine own due time,[10] & behold it shall come to pass that my servants shall be sent both to the East

---

8. The words "wo unto them for" are not in this manuscript, but are in other manuscripts and in the BC.

9. The words "my law" are not in this manuscript, but are in other manuscripts and in the BC.

10. The words "thou shalt ask & it shall be revealed in mine own due time" are repeated in this manuscript. The repetition has been retained.

& to the west & to the North & to the south, & even now let him that goeth to the East teach them that are Converted to flee to the west & this because of that which is to come, & secret combinations

Behold thou shalt observe all these things & great shall be thy reward, thou shalt observe to keep the mysteries of the kingdom unto thyself, for it is not given to the world to know the mysteries.

And these laws which ye have rec[eive]d. are sufficient for you both here & in the New Jerusalem but he that lacketh knowledge let him ask of me & I will give him liberally & upbraid him not lift up your hearts & rejoice for unto you the kingdom has been given, even so, Amen

Question 4th [3rd] How the Elders are to dispose of their families while they are proclaiming or otherways engaged in the service of the Church[?]

Answer - That the Priests & Teachers shall have their stewardship given them as the other members, and the Elders are to assist the Bishop in all things & he is to see that their families are supported out of the property consecrated to the Lord either a Stewardship or otherwise as may be thought best by the Elders and Bishop

Question 5th [4th] How far is it the will of the Lord we should have dealings with them[?][11]

Answer, Thou shalt not contract any debts with them & again the Elders and Bishop shall councel [counsel] together and by the direction of the spirit do as it must needs by necessary.

Question 6th [5th] What preparation shall we make for our Brethren from the East & where & how?

Answer - There shall be as many appointed as must needs be necessary to assist the Bishop in obtaining Houses that they may be together as much as can be & is directed by the Holy Spirit, & every family shall have place that they may live by themselves, and every Church shall be organized in as close bodies as they can be for the Enemy

Revision

1835 D&C 13
(cf. LDS D&C 42:12-14, 29-39, 56-59, 62, 65-73; RLDS D&C 42:5, 8-11, 15, 17-19)

the elders, priests and teachers of this church, shall teach the *principles of my gospel* which are in the bible and the book of Mormon, in the which is the fulness of *the* gospel; and *they* shall observe the covenants and church articles to do them, and *these* shall be *their* teachings, as *they* shall be directed by the Spirit: *and the Spirit* shall be given unto you by the prayer of faith, and if ye receive not the Spirit, ye shall not teach.

---

11. In another manuscript the question is: "How far it is the will of the Lord that we should have dealings with the world & how we Should conduct our dealings with them?" (LDS archives)

.   .   .

If thou lovest me thou shalt serve me and keep all my commandments. And be-hold, thou *wilt remember the poor, and* consecrate *of* thy properties *for their support*, that which thou hast *to impart* unto *them*, with a covenant and a deed which cannot be broken—and inasmuch as ye impart of your substance unto the poor, ye will do it unto me—and they shall be laid before the bishop of my church and *his counsel-lors*, two of the elders, *or high priests*, such as he shall *or has* appointed and set apart for that purpose.

And it shall come to pass, that *after they are laid before* the bishop of my church, *and* after that he has received *these testimonies concerning the consecration of* the properties of my church, that *they* cannot be taken from *the church, agreeable to my command-ments*, every man *shall be made accountable unto me*, a steward over his own property, or that which he has received *by consecration*, inasmuch as *is* sufficient for himself and family.

And *again, if there shall be properties in* the *hands of the church, or any individuals of it, more than is necessary for their support, after this first consecration, which is a* residue, *to be consecrated unto the bishop, it* shall be kept to administer to *those who* have not, *from time to time*, that every man *who has* need may *be amply supplied, and* receive accord-ing *to his wants*.

Therefore, the residue shall be kept in my store house, to administer to the poor and *the* needy, as shall be appointed by the *high council* of the church, and the bishop *and his council*, and for the purpose of purchasing lands *for the public benefit of the church, and building houses of worship*, and building up *of* the New Jerusalem which is hereaf-ter to be revealed, that my covenant people may be gathered in *one* in *that* day *when* I shall come to my temple. *And* this *I* do for the salvation of my people.

And it shall come to pass, that he that sinneth and repenteth not, shall be cast out *of the church*, and shall not receive again that which he has consecrated *unto the poor and the needy of my church, or in other words*, unto me, *for inasmuch as ye do it unto the least of these ye do it unto me*—for it shall come to pass, that which I spake by the mouths of my prophets, shall be fulfilled; for I will consecrate *of* the riches of *those who embrace my gospel among* the Gentiles, unto *the poor of* my people *who* are of the house of Israel.

.   .   .

Thou shalt ask, and my scriptures shall be given as I have appointed, and *they shall be preserved in safety*; and *it is expedient that* thou shouldst hold thy peace concerning them, *and not teach them* until ye have received them *in full*. And I give unto you a commandment, that *then* ye shall teach them unto all men; *for* they shall be taught unto all nations, kindreds, tongues and people. Thou shalt take *the* things which thou hast received, which have been *given unto thee in* my *scriptures for a* law, to be my law, to govern my church

.   .   .

Thou shalt ask, and it shall be revealed unto you in mine own due time, *where* the New Jerusalem shall be built.

.   .   .

Behold thou shalt observe all these things, and great shall be thy reward; *for unto you it is given to know* the mysteries of the kingdom, *but* unto the world it is not given to know *them. Ye shall observe the* laws which ye have received, *and be faithful. And ye shall hereafter receive church covenants, such as shall be* sufficient *to establish* you, both here, and in the New Jerusalem. *Therefore,* he that lacketh *wisdom,* let him ask of me, and I will give him liberally, and upbraid him not. Lift up your hearts and rejoice, for unto you the kingdom, *or in other words, the keys of the church, have* been given; even so Amen.

The priests and teachers shall have their stewardships, *even* as the members, and the elders, *or high priests who* are *appointed* to assist the bishop *as counsellors,* in all things *are to have* their families supported out of the property *which is* consecrated to the *bishop, for the good of the poor, and for other purposes, as before mentioned; or they are to receive a just remuneration for all their services*; either a stewardship, or otherwise, as may be thought best, *or decided* by the *counsellors* and bishop. *And the bishop also, shall receive his support, or a just remuneration for all his services, in the church.*

Commentary: The Laws of the Church

On 9 February 1831 the "Laws of the Church of Christ" (also called the Law of the Church) were given in the presence of twelve elders assembled in Kirtland, Ohio. These laws were given in answer to a series of questions that were evidently posed at their meeting.[12] In BC 44 the questions are absent.

The revelation states that "if thou obtain more than that which would be for thy support, thou shalt give it into my Store house."[13] In early 1831, while revising the Old Testament, additions were made to the text in Genesis 14 and mention was made of Melchizedek who "blessed Abram [Abraham] being the high Priest and the keeper of the store house of God him whom God had appointed to receive tithes for the poor wherefore Abram paid unto him [Melchizedek] tithes of all that he had of all the riches which he pos[s]essed which God had given him more than that which he had need."[14]

The requirement of the Saints was that "every man who cometh up to Zion must lay all things before the Bishop in Zion,"[15] or, in other words, to donate all property to the bishop who would allot to the individual and his family what was needed to live. The stewardship form printed in Independence stated that the property was "For the purpose of purchasing lands, and building up the New Jeru-

---

12. "Book of Commandments, Law and Covenants; Book B," LDS archives.
13. Document no. 45; LDS D&C 42:55; RLDS D&C 42:14.
14. OT MS #1, 34, RLDS archives. See Gen. 14:37-39 (JST).
15. Document no. 83; LDS D&C 72:15; RLDS D&C 72:3.

salem, even Zion, and for relieving the wants of the poor and needy." A few copies of this form have survived in LDS archives and have after the words "purchasing lands" the handwritten note "in Jackson County Mo" above the printed line. The printed consecration deed required the individual to "pay yearly" to the bishop or his successor in office "all that I shall make or accumulate more than is needful for the support and comfort of myself and family." Also he would "forfeit all claim to the above described leased and loaned property."[16]

The Evening and the Morning Star stated that a man "can consecrate unto the Lord, all the property that he has, more than he wants for himself and family, for the benefit of the poor and needy."[17] But there was a difference on another page of the same issue, which affirmed that "Members of the church have, or will have, 'deeds' in their own name." The article told of "One Bates from New-London, Ohio, who subscribed fifty dollars for the purpose of purchasing lands, and the necessaries for the saints, after his arrival here, [and] sued [Bishop] Edward Partridge and obtained a judgment for the same."[18]

One of the first references to giving to the church bishop less than one's all was in May 1833. On 2 May Joseph Smith wrote a letter explaining the law given on 9 February 1831, noting that if an individual was no longer in the church he could keep his inheritance. Smith wrote to Bishop Partridge:

> The law of the Lord, binds you to receive, whatsoever property is consecrated, by deed, The consecrated property, is considered the residue kept for the Lord['s] store house, and it is given for this consideration, for to purchase inheritances for the poor, this, any man has a right to do, agreeable to all laws of our country, to donate, give or consecrate all that he feels disposed to give, and it is your duty, to see that whatsoever is given, is given legally, therefore, it must be given for the consideration of the poor saints, and in this way no man can take any advantage of you in law, again, concerning inheritances, you are bound by the law of the Lord, to give a deed, securing to him who receives inheritances, his inheritance, for an everlasting inheritance, or in other words, to be his individual property, his private stewardship, and if he is found a transgressor & should be cut off, out of the church, his inheritance is his still and he is delivered over to the buffetings of satan, till the day of redemption, But the property which he consecrated to the poor, for their benefit, & inheritance, & stewardship, he cannot obtain again by the law of the Lord.[19]

From the above it appears that changing conditions in the church brought about a gradual development in the handling of funds. But rather than seek a new revelation, the old one was reinterpreted.

---

16. Retained copies of stewardship and consecration deeds in LDS archives. See, for example, *History of the Church,* 1:365-67, fn; Leonard J. Arrington, Feramorz Y. Fox, and Dean L. May, *Building the City of God: Community and Cooperation Among the Mormons* (Salt Lake City: Deseret Book, 1976), 28-29, 365-73; and Ronald E. Romig and John H. Siebert, "Jackson County, 1831-1833: A Look at the Development of Zion," *Restoration Studies III* (Independence, MO: Herald Publishing House, 1986), 290-91.

17. *The Evening and the Morning Star* 2 (July 1833): 108.

18. Ibid., 2 (July 1833): 110.

19. Copy of letter of Smith to Edward Partridge, 2 May 1833, LDS archives. See *Essential Joseph Smith,* 41-42.

The 1835 D&C text represents an important departure from the early text which stressed that one was to "consecrate all thy property, that which thou hath unto me with a covenant & a deed which cannot be broken."[20] The altered portion weakened the requirement to demand only that one "consecrate of thy properties," leaving the percentage—all or part—ambiguous. In fact, it seemed to imply that the amount might be a matter of personal preference.

In 1834 Smith and Cowdery stated that they were willing to give a tenth. This covenant was made on 29 November 1834 and recorded in Smith's journal.[21]

The 1835 revision added a concern for providing for the poor which was not part of the original text: "wilt [thou] remember the poor, and" consecrate "for their support" properties which they had "to impart" to "them." Also added was: "and inasmuch as ye impart of your substance unto the poor, ye will do it unto me." This addition has no manuscript support.[22] Because the poor are mentioned elsewhere in this revelation, it is not clear why the addition was made at all.

The early text mentions that when an individual consecrated all his property to the bishop, that property could not be retrieved, although the individual would be made a "steward over his own property," which is to say that he received a sufficient amount for himself and his household. The residue, which was the difference between the consecration and stewardship, was to be kept in the storehouse for the poor, for purchasing land, and for building up the New Jerusalem.

The 1835 D&C changed these concepts from what was published in the BC and newspapers accounts. The revision admonished members to "remember the poor" and to consecrate surplus property. Even though the word "residue" is still in the 1835 text, its meaning is radically changed.

The early text mentioned the "Elders of the Church," but the 1835 revision deletes "Elders" and adds "high council." As it was not until February 1834 that the high council was established at Kirtland, the rewriting could not have happened before 1834, which is when the revision committee commenced its work. To the word "bishop" is added "and his council." In February 1831 there was only one bishop in the church; he had no assistants until 3 June 1831.[23] Added to the 1831 text is an allowance for the residue to be used "for the public benefit of the church, and building houses of worship."

In 1831 the Saints were told that God "will consecrate the riches of the Gentiles unto my people which are of the House of Israel." This was first published by non-church newspapers in Ohio during 1831, then at Independence, Missouri, in July 1832 on the front page of the *Evening and the Morning Star*. Evidently the revision committee saw this as problematic in dealing with neighbors and so reworded it.

20. Concerning the words in the early text, "shalt consecrate all thy property, that thou hath unto me," there are two manuscripts with the word "property" and two with "properties." See Robert J. Woodford, "The Historical Development of the Doctrine and Covenants," Ph.D. diss., Brigham Young University, 1974, 545.

21. Jessee, *Papers of Joseph Smith*, 2:34-35.

22. A January 1831 revelation mentioned the poor, see document no. 41; LDS D&C 38:16, 35; and RLDS D&C 38:4, 8.

23. Cannon and Cook, *Far West Record*, 7.

The last part of this revelation is in answer to three questions. While the BC contained the answers, it did not include the questions. The questions are important in understanding the answers. There is evidence here that there was editing for the BC manuscript beyond dropping the questions.[24] The following questions and answers were entirely omitted in the 1835 Doctrine and Covenants:

> Question 5th [4th] How far is it the will of the Lord we should have dealings with them[?]
> Answer, Thou shalt not contract any debts with them & again the Elders and Bishop shall councel together and by the direction of the spirit do as it must needs be necessary.
> Question 6th [5th] What preparations shall we make for our Brethren from the East & where & how?
> Answer – There shall be as many appointed as must needs be necessary to assist the Bishop in obtaining Houses that they may be together as much as can be & is directed by the Holy Spirit, & every family shall have place that they may live by themselves, and every Church shall be organized in as close bodies as they can be for the Enemy

Deletions from a text for whatever reason are more serious than additions and are more difficult to understand, especially when manuscript evidence agrees that there was text present. The deleted items were originally part of the laws of the church. Included in the omission was a prohibition against contracting debt,[25] as well as material about elders and bishop counseling together and congregations being "organized in as close bodies as they can be."

46. Labor Ye in My Vineyard for the Last Time
From BC 45 (cf. LDS and RLDS D&C 43)

Revelation received at Kirtland, Ohio,
in [9-23] February 1831 for the elders of the church

A Revelation to the elders of the church, assembled in Kirtland, Ohio, given February, 1831.

O Hearken, ye elders of my church, and give ear to the words which I shall speak unto you:

For behold, verily, verily I say unto you, that ye have received a commandment for a law unto my church, through him whom I have appointed unto you, to receive commandments and revelations from my hand.

And this ye shall know assuredly, that there is none other appointed unto you to receive commandments and revelations until he be taken, if he abide in me.

But verily, verily I say unto you, that none else shall be appointed unto this gift except it be through him, for if it be taken from him he shall not have power, except to appoint another in his stead:

---

24. Cf. document no. 45 with BC 44:54-57.
25. It is of interest here that BC 44:55 included the words "except thou art commanded," which are not part of any known manuscript.

And this shall be a law unto you, that ye receive not the teachings of any that shall come before you as revelations or commandments:

And this I give unto you, that you may not be deceived; that you may know they are not of me.

For verily I say unto you, that he that is ordained of me shall come in at the gate and be ordained as I have told you before, to teach those revelations which you have received, and shall receive through him whom I have appointed.

And now behold I give unto you a commandment, that when ye are assembled together ye shall note with a pen how to act,[26] and for my church to act upon the points of my law and commandments, which I have given:

And thus it shall become a law unto you, being sanctified by that which ye have received, that ye shall bind yourselves to act in all holiness before me; that inasmuch as ye do this, glory shall be added to the kingdom which ye have received.

Inasmuch as ye do it not, it shall be taken even that which ye have received.

Purge ye out the iniquity which is among you; sanctify yourselves before me and if ye desire the glories of the kingdom, appoint ye my servant Joseph [Smith, Jr.] and uphold him before me by the prayer of faith.

And again, I say unto you, that if ye desire the mysteries of the kingdom, provide for him food and raiment and whatsoever thing he needeth to accomplish the work, wherewith I have commanded him:

And if ye do it not, he shall remain unto them that have received him, that I may reserve unto myself a pure people before me.

Again I say, hearken ye elders of my church, whom I have appointed:

Ye are not sent forth to be taught, but to teach the children of men the things which I have put into your hands by the power of my Spirit: and ye are to be taught from on high.

Sanctify yourselves and ye shall be endowed with power, that ye may give even as I have spoken.

Hearken ye, for behold the great day of the Lord is nigh at hand.

For the day cometh that the Lord shall utter his voice out of heaven; the heavens shall shake and the earth shall tremble, and the trump of God shall sound both long and loud, and shall say to the sleeping nations:

Ye saints arise and live:

Ye sinners stay and sleep until I shall call again:

Wherefore gird up your loins, lest ye be found among the wicked.

Lift up your voices and spare not.

Call upon the nations to repent, both old and young, both bond and free; saying, Prepare yourselves for the great day of the Lord:

For if I, who am a man, do lift up my voice and call upon you to repent, and ye hate me, what will ye say when the day cometh when the thunders shall utter their voices from the ends of the earth, speaking in the ears of all that live, saying, Repent, and prepare for the great day of the Lord:

---

26. This is a commandment regarding record keeping.

Yea, and again, when the lightnings shall streak forth from the east unto the west, and shall utter forth their voices unto all that live, and make the ears of all tingle, that hear, saying these words:

Repent ye, for the great day of the Lord is come.

And again, the Lord shall utter his voice out of heaven, saying:

Hearken, O ye nations of the earth, and hear the words of that God who made you.

O ye nations of the earth, how often would I have gathered you, together as a hen gathereth her chickens under her wings, but ye would not?

How oft have I called upon you by the mouth of my servants; and by the ministering of angels; and by mine own voice; and by the voice of thunderings; and by the voice of lightnings; and by the voice of tempests; and by the voice of earthquakes; and great hail-storms; and by the voice of famines, and pestilences of every kind; and by the great sound of a trump; and by the voice of judgment; and by the voice of mercy all the day long; and by the voice of glory, and honor, and the riches of eternal life; and would have saved you with an everlasting salvation, but ye would not?

Behold the day has come, when the cup of the wrath of mine indignation, is full.

Behold, verily I say unto you, that these are the words of the Lord your God:

Wherefore, labor ye, labor ye, in my vineyard for the last time:

For the last time call ye upon the inhabitants of the earth, for in mine own due time will I come upon the earth in judgment:

And my people shall be redeemed and shall reign with me on earth:

For the great Millennial [Millennium], which I have spoken by the mouth of my servants, shall come;

For satan shall be bound; and when he is loosed again, he shall only reign for a little season, and then cometh the end of the earth:

And he that liveth in righteousness, shall be changed in the twinkling of an eye;

And the earth shall pass away so as by fire;

And the wicked shall go away into unquenchable fire; and their end no man knoweth, on earth, nor ever shall know, until they come before me in judgment.

Hearken ye to these words; behold I am Jesus Christ, the Savior of the world.

Treasure these things up in your hearts, and let the solemnities of eternity rest upon your minds.

Be sober.

Keep all my commandments; even so: Amen.

Revision

1835 D&C 14
(cf. LDS D&C 43:8-9; RLDS D&C 43:3)

And now behold I give unto you a commandment, that when ye are assembled together, ye shall *instruct and edify each other, that ye may know* how to act and *direct* my church *how* to act upon the points of my law and commandments, which I have given: and thus *ye* shall become *instructed in the* law *of my church, and be* sanctified by that which ye have received, *and* ye shall bind yourselves to act in all holiness before me

47. Preach Repentance unto the People
From BC 46 (cf. LDS and RLDS D&C 44)

Revelation received at Kirtland, Ohio,
in [9-23] February 1831 for Joseph Smith, Jr., and Sidney Rigdon

A Revelation to Joseph, and Sidney, given in Kirtland, Ohio, February, 1831.

Behold thus saith the Lord unto you my servants, it is expedient in me that the elders of my church should be called together, from the east and from the west, and from the north and from the south, by letter or some other way.

And it shall come to pass, that, inasmuch as they are faithful, and exercise faith in me, I will pour out my Spirit upon them in the day that they assemble themselves together.

And it shall come to pass that they shall go forth into the regions round about, and preach repentance unto the people;

And many shall be converted, insomuch that ye shall obtain power to organize yourselves, according to the laws of man;

That your enemies may not have power over you, that you may be preserved in all things;

That you may be enabled to keep my laws, that every band may be broken wherewith the enemy seeketh to destroy my people.

Behold I say unto you, that ye must visit the poor and the needy and administer to their relief, that they may be kept until all things may be done according to my law which ye have received: Amen.

48. He Shall Be Delivered Up unto the Law
From a manuscript in LDS archives
(cf. LDS D&C 42:78-93; RLDS D&C 42:21-23)

Revelation received at Kirtland, Ohio,
on 23 February 1831 for seven elders
also concerning adultery

February 23d 1831 the rules and regulations of the Law How the Elders of the church of Christ are to act upon the points of the Law given by Jesus Christ to the Church in the presence of twelve Elders February 9th 1831 as agreed upon by seven El[ders] Elders Feby 23d 1831 according to to the commandment of God?

1st The first commandment in the law teaches that all the Elders shall go into the regions westward and labour to build up Churches unto Christ wheresoever they should find any to receive them and obey the Gospel of Jesus Christ except Joseph [Smith, Jr.] & Sidney [Rigdon] and Edward [Partridge] and such as the Bishop shall appoint to assist him in his duties according to the Law which we have received this commandment as far as it respects these Elders to be sent to the west is a special one for the time being incumbent on the present Elders who shall return when directed by the Holy Spirit

2d Every person who belongeth to this church of Christ shall observe all the commandments and covenants of the Church and it shall come to pass that if any person among you sh[a]ll kill they shall be delivered up and dealt with according to the laws of the land for remember that he hath no forgiveness and it shall be proven according to the laws of the land

but if any man shall commit Adultery he shall be tried before two Elders of the Church or more and every wo[rd] shall be established against him by two witnesses of the Church and not of the world but if there are more than two witnesses it is better but he shall be condemned by the mouth of two witnesses and the Elders shall lay the case before the Church and the Church shall lift up their hands against them that they may be dealt with according to the Law and if it can be it is necessary that the Bishop is present also and thus ye shall do in all cases which shall come before you and if a man shall rob he shall be delivered up unto the Law and if he shall steal he shall be delivered up unto the Law and if he lie he shall be delivered up unto the Law if he do any manner of iniquity he shall be delivered up unto the Law even that of God and if thy Brother offend thee, thou shalt take him between him and thee alone and if he confess thou shalt be reconciled and if he confess not thou shalt take another with thee and then if he confess not thou shalt deliver him up unto the Church not to the members but to the Elders and it shall be done in a meeting and that not before the world

and if thy Brother offend many he shall be chastened before many and if any one offend openly he shall be rebuked openly that he may be ashamed and if he confess not he shall be delivered up unto the law if any shall offend in secret he shall be rebuked in secret that he may have opportunity to confess in secret to him whom he he has offended and to God that the Brethren may not speak reproachfully of him and thus shall ye conduct in all things

Revision

1835 D&C 13
(cf. LDS D&C 42:80-93; RLDS D&C 42:22-23)

And if any man *or woman* shall commit adultery, he *or she* shall be tried before two elders of the church or more, and every word shall be established against him *or her* by two witnesses of the church, and not of the *enemy.* But if there are more than two witnesses it is better: but he *or she* shall be condemned by the mouth of two witnesses, and the elders shall lay the case before the church, and the church shall lift up their hands against *him or her*, that they may be dealt with according to the law *of God*. And if it can be, it is necessary that the bishop is present also. And thus ye shall do in all cases which shall come before you.

And if a man *or woman* shall rob, he *or she* shall be delivered up unto the law *of the land*. And if he *or she* shall steal, he *or she* shall be delivered up unto the law *of the land*. And if he *or she shall* lie, he *or she* shall be delivered up unto the law *of the land*. If he *or she* do any manner of iniquity, he *or she* shall be delivered up unto the law, even that of God.

And if thy brother *or sister* offend thee, thou shalt take him *or her* between him *or her* and thee alone; and if he *or she* confess, thou shalt be reconciled. And if he *or she* confess not, thou shalt deliver him *or her* up unto the church, not to the members but to the elders. And it shall be done in a meeting, and that not before the world.

And if thy brother *or sister* offend many, he *or she* shall be chastened before many. And if any one offend openly, he *or she* shall be rebuked openly, that he *or she* may be ashamed. And if he *or she* confess not, he *or she* shall be delivered up unto the law *of God*. If any shall offend in secret, he *or she* shall be rebuked in secret, that he *or she* may have opportunity to confess in secret to him *or her* whom he *or she* has offended, and to God, that the *church* may not speak reproachfully of him *or her*. And thus shall ye conduct in all things.

49. Be Watchful and Careful with All Inquiry
From a manuscript in LDS archives
(cf. LDS D&C 42:74-77; RLDS D&C 42:20)

*Revelation received at Kirtland, Ohio,
on 23 February 1831 further concerning adultery*

How to act in cases of adultery

Behold verily I say unto you whatsoever person among you having put away their companion for the cause of fornication or in otherwords if he shall testify before you in all Lowliness of heart that this is the case ye shall not cast them out from among you but if ye shall find that any person hath left their companion for the sake of adultery and they themselves are the offender and their companions are living they shall be cast out from among you and again I say unto you that ye be watchful and careful with all inquiry that ye receive none such among you if they are married and if they are not married they shall repent of all their sins or ye shall not receive them

50. I Am Alpha & Omega
From a manuscript in LDS archives
(cf. LDS and RLDS D&C 45)

Prophecy given at Kirtland, Ohio,
in [6-7] March 1831 for the Church of Christ[27]

A prophecy to the Church of Christ given the 6th March 1831 Saying

hearken O ye people of my Church to whom the kingdom has been given hearken ye & give ear to him who laid the foundation of the earth who made the heavens & all the hosts thereof & by whom all things were made which live & move & have a being & again I say hearken unto my voice lest death shall overtake you in an hour when you think not the summer shall be past & the harvest ended & your souls are not saved

listen to him who is your advocate with the Father who is pleading your cause before him saying Father behold the sufferings & death of him who did no sin in whom thou wast well pleased behold the blood of thy son which was shed the blood of him whom thou gave that thyself might be glorified wherefore Father spare these my brethren that believe on my name that they may come unto me & have everlasting life

Hearken O ye people of my Church & ye Elders listen together & hear my voice whilst it is cal[l]ed to day & harden not your hearts for verily I say unto you that I am Alpha & Omega the beginning & the end the light & the life of the world a light that shineth in darkness & the darkness comprehendeth it not I came unto my own & my own received me not but unto as many as received me gave I power to do many miracles & to become the sons of God & even unto them that believed on my name gave I power to obtain eternal life & even so I have sent mine everlasting covenant into the world to be a light to the world & to be a standard for the people & for the Gentiles to seek to it & to be a messenger before my face to prepare the way before me

wherefore come ye unto it with him that cometh I will reason as with men in days of old & I will shew unto you my strong reasoning wherefore hearken ye together & let me shew it unto you even my wisdom the wisdom of him whom ye say is the God of Enoch & his brethren who was separated from the earth & was reserved unto myself a City reserved untill a day of righteousness shall come a day which was sought for by all holy men & found it not because of wickedness & abominations & confessed that they were strangers & pilgrims on the earth but obtained a promise that they should find it & see it in their flesh

wherefore hearken & I will reason with you & I will speak unto you & prophesy as unto men in days of old & I will shew it plainly as I shewed it unto my Disciples

---

27. This manuscript in the hand of Edward Partridge and a copy made by William E. McLellin are dated 6 March 1831. The *Evening and the Morning Star* 1 (June 1832: [2]) and the Manuscript History has the date as 7 March 1831. See Jessee, *Papers of Joseph Smith*, 1:350. The exact day of the prophecy is not known.

as I stood before them in the flesh & spoke unto them saying as ye have asked of me concerning these signs of my coming in the day when I shall come in my glory in the clouds of heaven to fulfil the promises that I have made unto your Fathers for as you have looked upon the long absence of your spirits from your bodies to be a bondage I will shew unto you how the day of redemption shall come & also the restoration of the scattered Israel

& now ye behold this Temple which is in Jerusalem which ye call the house of God & your enemies say that this house shall never fall but verily I say unto you that desolation shall come upon this generation as a thief in the night & this people shall be destroyed & scattered among all nations & this Temple which ye now see shall be thrown down that there shall not be left one stone upon another & it shall come to pass that this generation of Jews shall not pass away untill every desolation which I have told you concerning them shall come to pass ye say that ye know that the end of the world cometh ye say also that ye know that the heavens & the earth shall pass away & in this ye say truly for so it is but these things which I have told you shall not pass away but all shall be fullfilled

& this I have told you concerning Jerusalem & when that day shall come shall a remnant be scattered among all nations but they shall be gathered again but they shall remain till the times of the Gentiles be fulfilled

& in that day shall be heard of wars & rumors of wars & the whole earth shall be in commotion & mens hearts shall fail them & shall say that Christ delayeth his coming untill the end of the world & the love of men shall wax cold & iniquity shall abound & when the times of the Gentiles is come in a light shall break forth among them that sit in darkness & it shall be the fullness of my gospel but they receive it not for they perceive not the light & they turn their hearts from me because of the precepts of men & in that generation shall the times of the gentiles be fulfilled, & there shall be men standing in that generation that shall not pass untill they shall see an overflowing scourge for a desolating sickness shall cover the land but my Disciples shall stand in holy places & shall not be moved, but among the wicked men shall lift up their voices & curse God & die, & there shall be earthquakes also in divers places & many desolations yet men will harden their hearts against me & they will take up the sword one against another & they will kill one another,

& now when I the Lord had spoke these words unto my Disciples they were troubled & I said unto them be not troubled for when all these things shall come to pass ye may know the promises which have been made unto you shall be fulfilled & when the light shall begin to break forth it shall be with them even like unto a parable which I will shew you, ye look & behold the fig trees & ye see them with your eyes & ye say when they begin to shoot forth & their leaves are yet tender ye say that summer is now nigh at hand even so it shall be in that day when they shall see all these things then shall they know that the hour is nigh

& it shall come to pass that he that feareth me shall be looking for the great day of the Lord to come even for the signs of the coming of the son of man & they shall see signs & wonders for they shall be shown forth in the heavens above & in the earth beneath & they shall behold blood & fires & vapors of smoke & before the day of the Lord shall come the sun shall be darkened & the moon turn to blood & stars shall fall from heaven, & the remnant shall be gathered unto this place & then they shall look for me & behold I will come & they shall see me in the clouds of heaven clothed with power & great glory with all the holy angels & he that watcheth not for me shall be cut off,

but before the arm of the Lord shall fall the Angel shall sound his trump & the saints that have slept shall come forth to meet me in the cloud. wherefore if ye have slept in peace blessed are you for as you now behold me & know that I am, even so shall ye come unto me & your souls shall live & your redemption shall be perfected & the saints shall come forth from the four quarters of the earth

then shall the arm of the Lord fall upon the nations & then shall the Lord set his foot upon this mount & it shall cleave in twain & the earth shall tremble & reel to & fro, & the heavens also shall shake & the Lord shall utter his voice & all the ends of the earth shall hear it, & the nations of the earth shall mourn & they that have laughed shall see their folly, & calamity shall cover the mockers, & the scorner shall be consumed, & they that have watched for iniquity shall be hewn down & cast into the fire.

& then shall the Jews look upon me & say what are these wounds in thine hands & in thy feet then shall they know that I am the Lord for I will say unto them these wounds are the wounds with which I was wounded in the house of my friends. I am he that was lifted up [I] am Jesus which was crucified I am the Son of God. & then shall they weep because of their iniquities then shall they lament because they persecuted their King

& then shall the heathen nations be redeemed & they which knew no law they shall have part in the first resur[r]ection & it shall be tolerable for them. & Satan shall be bound that he shall have no place in the hearts of the children of men.

& at that day when I shall come in my glory shall the parable be fulfilled which I spoke concerning the ten virgins for he that is wise & hath received the truth & have taken the holy Spirit for their guide & have not been deceived verily I say unto you they shall not be hewn down & cast into the fire but shall abide the day. & the earth shall be given unto them for an inheritance & they shall multiply & wax strong & their children shall grow up without sin unto salvation for the Lord shall be in their midst & his glory shall be upon them & he will be their King & their lawgiver

& now behold I say unto you it shall not be given unto you to know any farther than this[28] untill the New Testament be translated & in it all these things shall be made known, wherefore I give unto you that ye may now translate it[29] that ye may be prepared for the things to come

for verily I say unto you that great things await you ye hear of wars in foreign lands but behold I say unto you they are nigh even unto your doors & not many

---

28. Matt. 24.

29. On 8 March 1831 Joseph Smith commenced his correction of Matthew. On top of page one is written, "A Translation of the New Testament translated by the power of God" (NT MS #1, RLDS archives). Though the word translation is used in the title, no ancient manuscript was used and Smith did not know Greek in 1831.

years hence ye shall hear of wars in your own lands,

wherefore I the Lord hath said gather ye out from the eastern lands, assemble ye yourselves together ye Elders of my Church go ye forth into the western countries call up[on] the inhabitants to repent & inasmuch as they do repent build up churches unto me & with one heart & with one mind gather up your riches that ye may purchase an inheritance which shall hereafter be appointed you & it shall be called the New Jerusalem a land of peace a City of refuge a place of safety for the saints of the most high God & the glory of the Lord shall be there & the terror of the Lord also shall be there insomuch that the wicked will not come unto it. & it shall be called Zion, & it shall come to pass among the wicked that every man that will not take his sword against his neighbor must needs flee unto Zion for safety & there shall be gathered unto it out of every nation under heaven & it shall be the only people that shall not be at war one with another,

& it shall be said among the wicked let us not go up to battle against Zion for the inhabitants of Zion are terrible wherefore we cannot stand. & it shall come to pass that the righteous shall be gathered out from among all nations & shall come to Zion singing with songs of everlasting joy.

& now I say unto you keep these things from going abroad unto the world that ye may accomplish this work in the eyes of the people & in the eyes of your enemies that they may not know your works untill ye have accomplished the thing which I have commanded you that when they shall know it. it may be terrible unto them that fear may seize upon them & they shall stand afar off & tremble & all nations shall be affraid because of the terror of the Lord & the power of his might even so Amen

51. Seek Ye Earnestly the Best Gifts
From BC 49 (cf. LDS and RLDS D&C 46)

Revelation received at Kirtland, Ohio,
on 8 March 1831 for the Church of Christ

A Revelation to the church, given in Kirtland, Ohio, March, 1831.

Hearken, O ye people of my church, for verily I say unto you, that these things were spoken unto you for your profit and learning;

But notwithstanding those things which are written, it always has been given to the elders of my church, from the beginning, and ever shall be, to conduct all meetings as they are directed and guided by the Holy Spirit:

Nevertheless ye are commanded never to cast any one out from your public meetings, which are held before the world:

Ye are also commanded not to cast any one, who belongeth to the church, out of your sacrament meetings:

Nevertheless, if any have trespassed, let him not partake until he makes reconciliation.

And again I say unto you, ye shall not cast any one out of your sacrament meetings, who is earnestly seeking the kingdom;

I speak this concerning those who are not of the church.

And again I say unto you, concerning your confirmation meetings, that if there be any that is not of the church, that is earnestly seeking after the kingdom, ye shall not cast them out;

But ye are commanded in all things to ask of God who giveth liberally, and that which the Spirit testifies unto you, even so I would that ye should do in all holiness of heart, walking uprightly before me, considering the end of your salvation, doing all things with prayer and thanksgiving, that ye may not be seduced by evil spirits, or doctrines of devils, or the commandments of men, for some are of men, and others of devils.

Wherefore, beware lest ye are deceived! and that ye may not be deceived, seek ye earnestly the best gifts, always remembering for what they are given;

For verily I say unto you, they are given for the benefit of those who love me and keep all my commandments, and him that seeketh so to do, that all may be benefitted, that seeketh or that asketh of me, that asketh and not for a sign that he may consume it upon his lusts.

And again, verily I say unto you, I would that ye should always remember, and always retain in you minds what those gifts are, that are given unto the church, for all have not every gift given unto them: for there are many gifts, and to every man is given a gift by the Spirit of God;

To some it is given one, and to some is given another, that all may be profited thereby;

To some it is given by the Holy Ghost to know that Jesus Christ is the Son of God, and that he was crucified for the sins of the world; to others it is given to believe on their words, that they also might have eternal life, if they continue faithful.

And again, to some it is given by the Holy Ghost to know the differences of administration, as it will be pleasing unto the same Lord, according as the Lord will, suiting his mercies according to the conditions of the children of men.

And again it is given by the Holy Ghost to some to know the diversities of operations, whether it be of God, that the manifestations of the Spirit may be given to every man to profit withal.

And again, verily I say unto you, to some it is given, by the Spirit of God, the word of wisdom; to another it is given, the word of knowledge, that all may be taught to be wise and to have knowledge.

And again, to some it is given to have faith to be healed, and to others it is given to have faith to heal.

And again, to some it is given the working of miracles;

And to others it is given to prophesy, and to others the discerning of spirits.

And again, it is given to some to speak with tongues, and to another it is given the interpretation of tongues:

And all these gifts cometh from God, for the benefit of the children of God.

And unto the bishop of the church, and unto such as God shall appoint and ordain to watch over the church, and to be elders unto the church, are to have it given unto them to discern all those gifts, lest there shall be any among you professing and yet be not of God.

And it shall come to pass that he that asketh in spirit shall receive in spirit; that unto some it may be given to have all those gifts, that there may be a head, in order that every member may be profited thereby:

He that asketh in the spirit, asketh according to the will of God, wherefore it is done even as he asketh.

And again I say unto you, all things must be done in the name of Christ, whatsoever you do in the spirit;

And ye must give thanks unto God in the spirit for whatsoever blessing ye are blessed with:

And ye must practice virtue and holiness before me continually; even so: Amen.

52. Write and Keep a Regular History
From BC 50 (cf. LDS and RLDS D&C 47)

Revelation received at Kirtland, Ohio,
on 8 March 1831 for Joseph Smith, Jr., and John Whitmer[30]

A Revelation to Joseph and John, given in Kirtland, Ohio, March 1831.

Behold it is expedient in me that my servant John [Whitmer] should write and keep a regular history, and assist you, my servant Joseph [Smith, Jr.], in transcribing[31] all things which shall be given you.

Again, verily I say unto you, that he can also lift up his voice in meetings, whenever it shall be expedient.

And again, I say unto you, that it shall be appointed unto him to keep the church record and history continually, for Oliver [Cowdery] I have appointed to another office:

Wherefore it shall be given him, inasmuch as he is faithful, by the Comforter, to write these things; even so: Amen.

Revision

1835 D&C 63
(cf. LDS D&C 47:1; RLDS D&C 47:1)

Behold it is expedient in me that my servant John should write and keep a regular history, and assist you, my servant Joseph, in transcribing all things which shall be given you, *until he is called to further duties.*

---

30. A special meeting of the elders of the church was held in Kirtland on 9 April 1831 and "John Whitmer was appointed to keep the Church record & History by the voice of ten Elders" (Cannon and Cook, *Far West Record*, 5).
31. The KRB has "translating" rather than "transcribing" (12).

53. Save All the Money that Ye Can
From BC 51 (cf. LDS and RLDS D&C 48)

Revelation received at Kirtland, Ohio, in [8-31] March 1831
for Edward Partridge and the church in Kirtland

A Revelation to the bishop, and the church in Kirtland, given in Kirtland, Ohio, March, 1831.

It is necessary that ye should remain, for the present time, in your places of abode, as it shall be suitable to your circumstances;

And inasmuch as ye have lands, ye shall impart to the eastern brethren,;

And inasmuch as ye have not lands, let them buy, for the present time, in those regions round about, as seemeth them good, for it must needs be necessary that they have places to live for the present time.

It must needs be necessary, that ye save all the money that ye can, and that ye obtain all that ye can in righteousness, that in time ye may be enabled to purchase lands for an inheritance, even the city.[32]

The place is not yet to be revealed, but after your brethren come from the east, there are to be certain men appointed, and to them it shall be given to know the place, or to them it shall be revealed; and they shall be appointed to purchase the lands, and to make a commencement, to lay the foundation of the city;

And then ye shall begin to be gathered with your families, every man according to his family, according to his circumstances, and as is appointed to him by the bishop and elders of the church, according to the laws and commandments, which ye have received, and which ye shall hereafter receive; even so: Amen.

<u>Revision</u>

1835 D&C 64
(cf. LDS D&C 48:6; RLDS D&C 48:2)

and they shall be appointed to purchase the lands, and to make a commencement, to lay the foundation of the city; and then ye shall begin to be gathered with your families, every man according to his family, according to his circumstances, and as is appointed to him by *the presidency* and the bishop of the church, according to the laws and commandments, which ye have received, and which ye shall hereafter receive; even so. Amen.

<u>Commentary: Presidency</u>

BC 51:6 mentions "the bishop and elders of the church," whereas the D&C supplants "elders" with "the presidency" (meaning the presidency of the high priesthood or first presidency of the church). There was no presidency in 1831, therefore the earlier text is considered more authentic.

---

32. New Jerusalem.

54. I Have Sent unto You Mine Everlasting Covenant
From BC 52 (cf. LDS and RLDS D&C 49)

Revelation received at Kirtland, Ohio,
in [ca. 26] March 1831 for Sidney Rigdon,
Parley P. Pratt, and Leman Copley[33]

A Revelation to Sidney, Parley, and Lemon, given in Kirtland, Ohio, March, 1831.

Hearken unto my word, my servant Sidney [Rigdon], and Parley [P. Pratt], and Lemon [Leman Copley], for behold, verily I say unto you, that I give unto you a commandment, that you shall go and preach my gospel, which ye have received, even as ye have received it, unto the Shakers.[34]

Behold I say unto you, that they desire to know the truth in part, but not all, for they are not right before me, and must needs repent:

Wherefore I send you, my servants Sidney [Rigdon] and Parley [P. Pratt], to preach the gospel unto them; and my servant Lemon [Leman Copley] shall be ordained unto this work, that he may reason with them, not according to that which he has received of them, but according to that which shall be taught him by you, my servants, and by so doing I will bless him, otherwise he shall not prosper:

Thus saith the Lord, for I am God and have sent mine only begotten Son into the world, for the redemption of the world, and have decreed, that he that receiveth him shall be saved, and he that receiveth him not, shall be damned:

And they have done unto the Son of man even as they listed;

And he has taken his power on the right hand of his glory, and now reigneth in the heavens, and will reign till he descends on the earth to put all enemies under his feet:

Which time is nigh at hand: I the Lord God have spoken it:

But the hour and the day no man knoweth, neither the angels in heaven, nor shall they know until he come:

Wherefore I will that all men shall repent, for all are under sin, except them which I have reserved unto myself, holy men that ye know not of:

Wherefore I say unto you, that I have sent unto you mine everlasting covenant, even that which was from the beginning, and that which I have promised I have so fulfilled, and the nations of the earth shall bow to it;

---

33. A variant date is 7 May 1831. The *Evening and the Morning Star* 1 (Nov. 1832): [7; whole no. 47] has the date published as "May, 1831." A manuscript copy in "A Mormon interview. Copied from Brother Ashbel Kitchell's Pocket Journal. -(By E.D.B.) [Elisha D. Blakeman]" records the date at the end of the message as "May 7th 1831" (Emma B. King Library, Shaker Museum, Old Chatlam, New York). This date is not considered accurate since Parley P. Pratt arrived at Kirtland circa 26 March 1831 (*Autobiography of Parley P. Pratt*, 45-47).

34. They went to the Shaker community, Sidney Rigdon read this message to them, but it was rejected.

And, if not of themselves, they shall come down, for that which is now exalted of itself, shall be laid low of power:

Wherefore I give unto you a commandment, that ye go among this people and say unto them, like unto mine apostle of old, whose name was Peter:

Believe on the name of the Lord Jesus, who was on the earth, and is to come, the beginning and the end;

Repent and be baptized in the name of Jesus Christ, according to the holy commandment, for the remission of sins;

And whoso doeth this, shall receive the gift of the Holy Ghost, by the laying on of the hands of the elders of this church.

And again, I say unto you, that whoso forbiddeth to marry, is not ordained of God, for marriage is ordained of God unto man:

Wherefore it is lawful that he should have one wife, and they twain shall be one flesh, and all this that the earth might answer the end of its creation; and that it might be filled with the measure of man, according to his creation before the world was made.

And whoso forbiddeth to abstain from meats, that man should not eat the same, is not ordained of God;

For behold the beasts of the field, and the fowls of the air, and that which cometh of the earth, is ordained for the use of man, for food, and for raiment, and that he might have in abundance, but it is not given that one man should possess that which is above another:

Wherefore the world lieth in sin; and wo be unto man that sheddeth blood or that wasteth flesh and hath no need.

And again, verily I say unto you, that the Son of man cometh not in the form of a woman, neither of a man travelling on the earth:

Wherefore be not deceived, but continue in steadfastness, looking forth for the heavens to be shaken;

And the earth to tremble, and to reel to and fro as a drunken man; and for the valleys to be exalted; and for the mountains to be made low; and for the rough places to become smooth:

And all this when the angel shall sound his trumpet.

But before the great day of the Lord shall come, Jacob shall flourish in the wilderness; and the Lamanites shall blossom as the rose:

Zion shall flourish upon the hills, and rejoice upon the mountains, and shall be assembled together unto the place which I have appointed.

Behold I say unto you, go forth as I have commanded you;

Repent of all your sins; ask and ye shall receive; knock and it shall be opened unto you:

Behold I will go before you, and be your rereward [reward]; and I will be in your midst, and you shall not be confounded:

Behold I am Jesus Christ, and I come quickly; even so: Amen.

55. There Are Many Spirits Which Are False Spirits
From BC 53 (cf. LDS and RLDS D&C 50)

Revelation received at Kirtland, Ohio,
on 9 May 1831 for the elders of the church

A Revelation to the elders of the church assembled at Kirtland, Ohio, given May, 1831.

Hearken, O ye elders of my church, and give ear to the voice of the living God; and attend to the words of wisdom which shall be given unto you, according as ye have asked and are agreed as touching the church, and the spirits which have gone abroad in the earth.

Behold verily I say unto you, that there are many spirits which are false spirits, which have gone forth in the earth, deceiving the world:

And also satan hath sought to deceive you, that he might overthrow you.

Behold I the Lord have looked upon you, and have seen abominations in the church, which profess my name;

But blessed are they who are faithful and endure, whether in life or in death, for they shall inherit eternal life.

But wo unto them that are deceivers, and hypocrites, for thus saith the Lord, I will bring them to judgment.

Behold verily I say unto you, there are hypocrites among you, and have deceived some, which has given the adversary power, but behold such shall be reclaimed;

But the hypocrites shall be detected and shall be cut off, either in life or in death, even as I will, and wo unto them who are cut off from my church, for the same are overcome of the world:

Wherefore, let every man beware lest he do that which is not in truth and righteousness before me.

And now come, saith the Lord, by the Spirit, unto the elders of his church, and let us reason together, that ye may understand:

Let us reason even as a man reasoneth one with another face to face:

Now when a man reasoneth, he is understood of man, because he reasoneth as a man; even so will I the Lord reason with you that you may understand:

Wherefore I the Lord asketh you this question, unto what were ye ordained?

To preach my gospel by the Spirit, even the Comforter which was sent forth to teach the truth; and then received ye spirits which ye could not understand, and received them to be of God, and in this are ye justified?

Behold ye shall answer this question yourselves, nevertheless I will be merciful unto you:

He that is weak among you hereafter shall be made strong.

Verily I say unto you, he that is ordained of me and sent forth to preach the word of truth by the Comforter, in the spirit of truth, doth he preach it by the spirit of truth, or some other way? and if by some other way, it be not of God.

And again, he that receiveth the word of truth, doth he receive it by the spirit of truth, or some other way? if it be some other way, it be not of God:

Therefore, why is it that ye can not understand and know that he that receiveth the word by the spirit of truth, receiveth it as it is preached by the spirit of truth?

Wherefore, he that preacheth and he that receiveth, understandeth one another, and both are edified and rejoice together; and that which doth not edify, is not of God, and is darkness:

That which is of God is light, and he that receiveth light and continueth in God, receiveth more light, and that light groweth brighter and brighter, until the perfect day.

And again, verily I say unto you, and I say it that you may know the truth, that you may chase darkness from among you, for he that is ordained of God and sent forth, the same is appointed to be the greatest, notwithstanding he is least, and the servant of all:

Wherefore he is possessor of all things, for all things are subject unto him, both in heaven and on the earth, the life, and the light, the spirit, and the power, sent forth by the will of the Father, through Jesus Christ, his Son;

But no man is possessor of all things, except he be purified and cleansed from all sin;

And if ye are purified and cleansed from all sin, ye shall ask whatsoever you will in the name of Jesus, and it shall be done:

But know this, it shall be given you what you shall ask, and as ye are appointed to the head, the spirits shall be subject unto you:

Wherefore it shall come to pass, that if you behold a spirit manifested that ye can not understand, and you receive not that spirit, ye shall ask of the Father in the name of Jesus, and if he give not unto you that spirit, then you may know that it is not of God:

And it shall be given unto you power over that spirit, and you shall proclaim against that spirit with a loud voice, that it is not of God;

Not with railing accusation, that ye be not overcome; neither with boasting, nor rejoicing, lest you be seized therewith:

He that receiveth of God, let him account it of God, and let him rejoice that he is accounted of God worthy to receive, and by giving heed and doing these things which ye have received, and which ye shall hereafter receive:

And the kingdom is given unto you of the Father, and power to overcome all things, which is not ordained of him:

And behold, verily I say unto you, blessed are you who are now hearing these words of mine from the mouth of my servant, for your sins are forgiven you.

Let my servant Joseph (W.) [Joseph Wakefield] in whom I am well pleased, and my servant Parley [P. Pratt], go forth among the churches and strengthen them by the word of exhortation;

And also my servant John (C.,) [John Corrill] or as many of my servants as are ordained unto this office, and let them labor in the vineyard;

And let no man hinder them of doing that which I have appointed unto them:

Wherefore in this thing my servant Edward [Partridge] is not justified, never-the[le]ss let him repent and he shall be forgiven.

Behold ye are little children, and ye can not bear all things now; ye must grow in grace and in the knowledge of the truth.

Fear not, little children, for you are mine, and I have overcome the world, and you are of them that my Father hath given me;

And none of them which my Father hath given me shall be lost:

And the Father and I are one; I am in the Father and the Father in me:

And inasmuch as ye have received me, ye are in me, and I in you: wherefore I am in your midst; and I am the good Shepherd;

And the day cometh that you shall hear my voice and see me, and know that I am.

Watch, therefore, that ye may be ready; even so: Amen.

Revision

1835 D&C 17
(cf. LDS D&C 50:44; RLDS D&C 50:8)

and inasmuch as ye have received me, ye are in me, and I in you: wherefore I am in your midst: and I am the good Shepherd, (*and the stone of Israel: He that buildeth upon this rock shall never fall.*) And the day cometh that you shall hear my voice and see me, and know that I am.

Commentary: Stone of Israel

BC 53:41–42 states: "And inasmuch as ye have received me, ye are in me, and I in you: wherefore I am in your midst; and I am the good Shepherd; And the day cometh that you shall hear my voice." This 9 May 1831 revelation is supported by two manuscripts copied after the BC manuscript was prepared, with minor word differences. The published text in the *Evening and the Morning Star* (Aug. 1832) is also the same, as is the reprint of the *Star* published in Kirtland in March 1835.

The D&C adds after the words "good Shepherd" the following: "(and the stone of Israel: He that buildeth upon this rock shall never fall)."[35] Here is a clear addition, at variance with the BC, two manuscripts (Books A and B, LDS archives), the *Star*, and the *Star* reprint. The addition must have been created after the March 1835 Kirtland reprint.[36]

---

35. 1835 D&C 17:8. See Gen. 49:24 that includes the wording "the stone of Israel."
36. *Evening and Morning Star* (Kirtland reprint), 1 (Aug. 1832): 44, reprinted Mar. 1835.

56. Receive the Properties of this People
From KRB, 87-89 (cf. LDS and RLDS D&C 51)

*Revelation received at Thompson, Ohio,
on 20 May 1831 for Edward Partridge*

Thomp[s]on May 20, 1831 [37]

Hearken unto me saith the Lord your God and I will speak unto my servant Edward [Partridge] and give unto him directions for it must needs be that he receive directions how to organise this people[38] for it must needs be that they are organized according to my laws if otherwise they will be cut off

wherefore let my servant Edward [Partridge] receive the properties of this people which have covenanted with me to obey the Laws which I have given and let my servant Edward [Partridge] receive the money as it shall be laid before him according to the covenant and go and obtain a deed or article of this land unto himself of him who holdeth it if he harden not his heart[39] for I have appointed him to receive these things and thus through him the properties of the church shall be consecrated unto me

wherefor[e] let my servant Edward [Partridge] and those whom he has chosen in whom I am well pleased appoint unto this people their portion every man alike according to their families according to their wants and their needs

and let my servant Edward [Partridge] when he shall appoint a man his portion give unto him a writing that shall secure unto him his portion that he shall hold it of the church until he transgress and is not counted worthy by the voice of the church according to the Laws to belong to the church and thus all things shall be made sure according to the Laws of the land

and let that which belongeth to this people be appointed unto this people and the money which is left unto this people let there be an agent appointed unto this people to take the money to provide food and raiment according to the wants of this people and let every man deal honestly and be alike among this people and receive alike that ye may be one even as I have commanded you

and let that which belongeth to this people not be taken and given unto that of another church wherefore if another church would receive money of this church let them pay unto this church again according as they shall agree and this shall be done through the Bishop or the agent which shall be appointed by the voice of the church

and again let the Bishop appoint a storehouse unto this church and let all things both in money and in meat which is more than is needful for the wants of this people be kept in the hands of the Bishop and let him also reserve unto himself for his

---

37. The month of May is written over August in the KRB. This revelation was not included in the BC. It was published in the 1835 D&C with revised wording.

38. Members of the Colesville Branch from New York.

39. The phrase "of him who holdeth it if he harden not his heart" is not in "Book of Commandments, Law and Covenants, Book B."

own wants and for the wants of his family as he shall be employed in doing this business and thus I grant unto this people a privelege [privilege] of organizing themselves according to my laws and I consecrate unto them this land for a little season until I the Lord shall provide for them otherwise and command them to go hence and the hour and the day is not given unto them wherefore let them act upon this land as for years and this shall turn unto them for their good

behold this shall be an example unto my servant Edward [Partridge] in other places in all churches and whoso if found a faithful and Just and a wise steward shall enter into the Joy of his lord and shall inherit eternal life verily I say unto you I am Jesus Christ who cometh quickly in an hour you think not Amen

<u>Revision</u>

1835 D&C 23
(cf. LDS D&C 51:3-6; RLDS D&C 51:1)

wherefore let my servant Edward Partridge, and those whom he has chosen, in whom I am well pleased, appoint unto this people their portion, every man *equal* according to their families, according to their *circumstances, and* his wants and needs; and let my servant Edward Partridge, when he shall appoint a man his portion, give unto him a writing that shall secure unto him his portion, that he shall hold it, *even this right and this inheritance in* the church, until he transgresses and is not accounted worthy by the voice of the church, according to the laws *and covenants of the church,* to belong to the church: *and if he shall transgress, and is not accounted worthy to belong in the church, he shall not have power to claim that portion which he has consecrated unto the bishop for the poor and the needy of my church: therefore, he shall not retain the gift, but shall only have claim on that portion that is deeded unto him.* And thus, all things shall be made sure according to the laws of the land.

<u>Commentary: Covenanted Properties</u>

The revelation of 20 May 1831, while not published in the BC or *The Evening and the Morning Star,* is located in two manuscripts.[40] The following is from the Kirtland Revelations Book:

> wherefore let my servant Edward [Partridge] receive the properties of this people which have covenanted with me to obey the Laws which I have given and let my servant Edward receive the money as it shall be laid before him according to the covenant and go and obtain a deed or article of this land unto himself of him who holdest it if he harden not his heart for I have appointed him to receive these things and thus through him the properties of the church shall be consecrated unto me

This text mentions "to obey the Laws"—the laws given on 9 February 1831, three months earlier—and agrees with the text of the Law of Consecration. When the 1835 committee revised this revelation, this opening section was not included

---

40. KRB, 87-89, and "Book of Commandments, Law and Covenants, Book B."

though it is in two manuscripts. It is possible that this was simply an oversight.

However, the committee added wording to the text. This addition has no manuscript support and agrees with Joseph Smith's May 1833 understanding that for a transgressor, "his inheritance is his still."[41] This is a post-1831 concept.[42]

57. Hearken unto My Words
From KRB, 91-92

*Revelation received at Kirtland, Ohio,
in [1-31] May 1831 for Joseph Smith, Sr., and Ezra Thayer*[43]

Revelation given May 1831 in Kirtland concerning the farm owned by Frederick [G. Williams] and also concerning Joseph [Smith, Sr.] & Ezra [Thayer]

Hearken unto my words and behold I will make known unto you what ye shall do as it shall be pleasing unto me for verily I say unto you it must needs be that ye let the bargain stand that ye have made concerning those farms until it be so fulfilled behold ye are holden for the one even so likewise thine advisary is holden for the other wherefore it must needs be that ye pay no more money for the present time until the contract be fulfilled

and let mine aged servant Joseph [Smith, Sr.] and his family go into the house after thine advisary is gone and let my servant Ezra [Thayer] board with him and let all the brethren immediately assemble together to put up an house for my servant Ezra [Thayer] and let my servant Fredericks [G. Williams] family remain and let the house be prepared and their want be supplied and when my servant Frederick [G. Williams] returns from the west[44] behold and lo he desir[e]th to take his family in mine own due time unto the west let that which belongeth unto my servant Frederick [G. Williams] be secured unto him by deed or bond and thus he willeth that the brethren reap the good thereof

let mine aged servant Joseph [Smith, Sr.] govern the things of the farm and provide for the families and let him have healp [help] in as much as he standest in need

let my servant Ezra [Thayer] humble himself and at the conference meeting[45] he shall be ordained unto power from on high and he shall go from thence if he be obedient unto my commandments and proclaim my gospel unto the western regions with my servants that must go forth even unto the borders by the Lamanites for behold I have a great work for them to do and it shall be given unto you to

41. Smith to Partridge, 2 May 1833, LDS archives.
42. Cook, *Revelations of the Prophet Joseph Smith*, 69-70, 135.
43. This revelation was not included in the BC or the 1835 D&C.
44. Frederick G. Williams had accompanied the four missionaries from New York to preach to Native Americans near the western border of Missouri.
45. The next conference was scheduled for the first Saturday in June. But the conference was held on Friday, 3 June 1831, when some of the elders, including Ezra Thayer, were ordained to the high priesthood (Cannon and Cook, *Far West Record*, 5-7). See 1830 BOM, 259-60; LDS Alma 13:6-10, 14, 18/RLDS 9:69-73; 10:1, 7, 12.

know what ye shall do at the conference meeting even so amen.

[Question] What shall the brethren do with the monies[?]

[Answer] ye shall go forth and seek dilligently among the brethren and obtain lands and save the money that it may be consecrated to purchase lands in the west for an everlasting inheritance even so Amen

58. I Will Cut My Work Short in Righteousness
From BC 54 (cf. LDS and RLDS D&C 52)

Revelation received at Kirtland, Ohio,
on 6 June 1831 for the elders of the church

A Revelation to the elders of the church assembled in Kirtland, Ohio, given June, 1831.

Behold, thus saith the Lord unto the elders whom he hath called and chosen, in these last days, by the voice of his Spirit, saying, I the Lord will make known unto you what I will that ye shall do from this time until the next conference, which shall be held in Missouri,[46] upon the land which I will consecrate unto my people, which are a remnant of Jacob, and them who are heirs according to the covenant.

Wherefore, verily I say unto you, let my servants Joseph [Smith, Jr.] and Sidney [Rigdon] take their journey as soon as preparations can be made to leave their homes, and journey to the land of Missouri.

And inasmuch as they are faithful unto me it shall be made known unto them what they shall do:

And it shall also, inasmuch as they are faithful, be made known unto them the land of your inheritance.

And inasmuch as they are not faithful, they shall be cut off, even as I will, as seemeth me good.

And again, verily I say unto you, let my servant Lyman (W.,) [Lyman Wight] and my servant John (C.,) [John Corrill] take their journey speedily:

And also my servant John (M.) [John Murdock] and my servant Hyrum [Smith], take their journey unto the same place by the way of Detroit.

And let them journey from thence preaching the word by the way, saying none other things than that which the prophets and apostles have written, and that which is taught them by the Comforter, through the prayer of faith.

Let them go two by two, and thus let them preach by the way in every congregation, baptizing by water, and the laying on of the hands by the water side:

For thus saith the Lord, I will cut my work short in righteousness:

For the days cometh that I will send forth judgment unto victory.

And let my servant Lyman [Wight] beware, for satan desireth to sift him as chaff.

---

46. The conference was held in Kaw Township, Jackson County, Missouri, on 4 August 1831 (Cannon and Cook, *Far West Record*, 9–10).

And behold, he that is faithful shall be made ruler over many things.

And again, I will give unto you a pattern in all things, that ye may not be deceived, for satan is abroad in the land, and he goeth forth deceiving the nations:

Wherefore he that prayeth whose spirit is contrite, the same is accepted of me, if he obey mine ordinances:

He that speaketh, whose spirit is contrite, whose language is meek, and edifieth, the same is of God, if he obey mine ordinances.

And again, he that trembleth under my power, shall be made strong, and shall bring forth fruits of praise, and wisdom, according to the revelations, and truths which I have given you.

And again, he that is overcome and bringeth not forth fruits, even according to this pattern, is not of me:

Wherefore by this pattern ye shall know the spirits in all cases, under the whole heavens.

And the days have come, according to men's faith it shall be done unto them.

Behold this commandment is given unto all the elders whom I have chosen.

And again, verily I say unto you, let my servant Thomas [B. Marsh], and my servant Ezra [Thayer], take their journey also, preaching the word by the way, unto this same land.

And again, let my servant Isaac [Morley] and my servant Ezra (B.,) [Ezra Booth] take their journey, also preaching the word by the way unto the same land.

And again, let my servant Edward [Partridge] and Martin [Harris] take their journey with my servants Sidney [Rigdon] and Joseph [Smith, Jr.].

Let my servant David [Whitmer] and Harvey [Whitlock], also take their journey, and preach by the way unto this same land.

Let my servants Parley [P. Pratt] and Orson (P.) [Orson Pratt] take their journey, and preach by the way, even unto this same land.

And let my servants Solomon [Hancock] and Simeon [Carter], also take their journey unto this same land, and preach by the way.

Let my servants Edson [Fuller] and Jacob (S.,) [Jacob Scott] also take their journey.

Let my servants Levi [W. Hancock] and Zebidee [Zebedee Coltrin], also take their journey.

Let my servants Reynolds [Cahoon] and Samuel [H. Smith], also take their journey.

Let my servants Wheeler [Baldwin] and William (C.,) [William Carter] also take their journey.

And let my servants Newel (K.) [Newel Knight] and Selah [J. Griffin], both be ordained and also take their journey:

Yea, verily I say, let all these take their journey unto one place, in their several courses, and one man shall not build upon another's foundation, neither journey in another's track.

He that is faithful, the same shall be kept and blessed with much fruit.

And again, I say unto you, let my servant Joseph (W.) [Joseph Wakefield] and

Solomon (H.,) [Solomon Humphrey] take their journey into the eastern lands.

Let them labor with their families, declaring none other things than the prophets and apostles, that which they have seen, and heard, and most assuredly believe, that the prophecies may be fulfilled.

In consequence of transgression, let that which was bestowed upon Heman [Basset], be taken from him, and placed upon the head of Simonds [Symonds Ryder].[47]

And again, verily I say unto you, let Jared [Carter] be ordained a priest, and also George [James] be ordained a priest.

Let the residue of the elders watch over the churches, and declare the word in the regions among them.

And let them labor with their own hands, that there be no idolatry nor wickedness practiced. And remember in all things, the poor and the needy, the sick and the afflicted, for he that doeth not these things, the same is not my disciple.

And again, let my servants Joseph [Smith, Jr.] and Sidney [Rigdon] and Edward [Partridge], take with them a recommend from the church.

And let there be one obtained for my servant Oliver [Cowdery], also:

And thus, even as I have said, if ye are faithful, ye shall assemble yourselves together to rejoice upon the land of Missouri, which is the land of your inheritance, which is now the land of your enemies.

But behold I the Lord will hasten the city in its time;

And will crown the faithful with joy and with rejoicing.

Behold I am Jesus Christ, the Son of God, and I will lift them up at the last day; even so: Amen.

59. You Shall Forsake the World
From NKW Collection (cf. LDS and RLDS D&C 53)

Commandment received at Kirtland, Ohio, in [6-15] June 1831 for Sidney Gilbert[48]

A commandment of the Lord to Sidney

Behold I say unto you my servant Sidney [Gilbert] that I have heard your prayers and ye have called upon me that it should be made known unto you of the Lo[r]d your God concerning your calling and election in this church which I the Lord hath raised up in these last days

---

47. Symonds Ryder was appointed to take the place of Heman Bassett to preach the gospel. On 16 June 1831 Ryder was ordained an elder. The Far West Record has his name spelled "Simonds Rider." Lyndon W. Cook wrote that Ryder's "Letter of appointment and license to preach both misspelled [his] last name. Later used error as pretense to show call was not divinely inspired" (*Revelations of the Prophet Joseph Smith*, 81).

48. Algernon Sidney Gilbert was a business partner with Newel K. Whitney. He was ordained an elder by Joseph Smith, Jr., on 16 June 1831.

behold I the Lord who was crucified for the sins of the world giveth unto you a commandment that you shall forsake the world and take upon you mine ordinances even that of an Elder to preach faith and repentance and remission of sins according to my word and the reception of the Holy Spirit by the laying on of hands and also to be an agent unto this church in the place which shall be appointed by the Bishop according to commandments which shall be given hereafter

and again verily I say unto you you shall take your journey with my servents Joseph [Smith, Jr.] and Sidney [Rigdon] behold these are the first ordinances which you shall receive and the residue shall be made known unto you in a time to come according to your labours in my vin[e]yard And again I would that ye should learn that it is him only who is saved that endureth unto the end even so Amen

60. Take Your Journey into the Regions Westward
From BC 56 (cf. LDS and RLDS D&C 54)

Revelation received at Kirtland, Ohio,
in [6-15] June 1831 for Newel Knight
and the church in Thompson

A Revelation to Newel (K.,) and the church in Thompson, given in Kirtland, Ohio, June, 1831.

Behold, thus saith the Lord, even Alpha and Omega, the beginning and the end, even he who was crucified for the sins of the world.

Behold, verily, verily I say unto you, my servant Newel [Knight], you shall stand fast in the office wherewith I have appointed you:

And if your brethren desire to escape their enemies let them repent of all their sins, and become truly humble before me and contrite:

And as the covenant which they made unto me, has been broken, even so it has become void and of none effect;

And wo to him by whom this offence cometh, for it had been better for him that he had been drowned in the depth of the sea;

But blessed are they who have kept the covenant, and observed the commandment, for they shall obtain mercy:

Wherefore, go to now and flee the land, lest your enemies come upon you:

And take your journey, and appoint whom you will to be your leader, and to pay moneys for you.

And thus you shall take your journey into the regions westward, unto the land of Missouri, unto the borders of the Lamanites.

And after you have done journeying, behold I say unto you, seek ye a living like unto men, until I prepare a place for you.

And again, be patient in tribulation until I come:

And behold I come quickly, and my reward is with me, and they who have sought me early, shall find rest to their souls; even so: Amen.

61. Ordained by the Hand of My Servant Joseph
From BC 57 (cf. LDS and RLDS D&C 55)

Revelation received at Kirtland, Ohio,
in [15] June 1831 for William W. Phelps[49]

A Revelation to William, given in Kirtland, Ohio, June 1831.

Behold thus saith the Lord unto you, my servant William [W. Phelps]; yea, even the Lord of the whole earth,

Thou art called and chosen and after thou hast been baptized by water, which if you do with an eye single to my glory, you shall have a remission of your sins, and a reception of the Holy Spirit, by the laying on of hands:

And then thou shalt be ordained by the hand of my servant Joseph [Smith, Jr.], to be an elder unto this church, to preach rep[e]ntance and remission of sins by way of baptism in the name of Jesus Christ, the Son of the living God;

And on whomsoever you shall lay your hands, if they are contrite before me, you shall have power to give the Holy Spirit.

And again, you shall be ordained to assist my servant Oliver [Cowdery] to do the work of printing, and of selecting, and writing books for schools, in this church, that little children also may receive instruction before me as is pleasing unto me.

And again verily I say unto you, for this cause you shall take your journey with my servants Joseph [Smith, Jr.] and Sidney [Rigdon], that you may be planted in the land of your inheritance, to do this work.

And again let my servant Joseph (C.) [Joseph Coe] also take his journey with them.

The residue shall be made known hereafter; even as I will: Amen.

62. I the Lord Command & Revoke as It Seemeth Me Good
From a manuscript in LDS archives (cf. LDS and RLDS D&C 56)

Revelation received at Kirtland, Ohio, on 15 June 1831
for the Church of Christ and certain elders[50]

Recd. [Received] June 15th 1831

Hearken O ye People which Profess my name Saith the lord your God for be-

---

49. This revelation was evidently received the day before the baptism of William W. Phelps. Phelps was baptized into the Church of Christ on 16 June 1831. See *Latter Day Saints' Messenger and Advocate* 1 (Apr. 1835): 97. Previous to coming to Kirtland, he edited the *Ontario Phoenix* in Canandaigua, New York. On the day of his baptism, Phelps was ordained an elder by Joseph Smith, Jr.

50. The unknown scribe who wrote this revelation also was a scribe for a number of pages of the original dictated manuscript of 1 Nephi (LDS archives). The lower case letters "i" (except in two places where it is written "I") and "l" in Lord are not capitalized in the manuscript.

hold mine anger is kindled against the rebel[l]ious & they shal[l] know mine arm & mine indignation in the day of visitation & of wrath uppon [upon] the nations & he that will not take up his cross & follow me & keep My commandments the same shal[l] not be saved

behold I the lord commandeth & he that will not obey shal[l] be cut of[f] in mine own due time & After that i have commanded & the commandments is broken wharefore [wherefore] I the lord command & revoke as it seemeth me good & all this [to] be Answered uppon [upon] the heads of the rebel[l]ious Saith the lord

wharefore [wherefore] i revoke the Commandment which was given unto my Servant[s] Thomas [B. Marsh] and Ezra [Thayer] & give a new commandment unto my servant thomas [Thomas B. Marsh] that he shal[l] take his journey spe[e]dily to the land of Missurie [Missouri] & my servant sely griffen [Selah J. Griffin] shal[l] also Go with him for beho[ld] i revoke the commandment which was given unto my servant[s] seely griffen [Selah J. Griffin] & newal Knights [Newel Knight] in consequence of the stif[f]neckedness of my people which are in thompson [Thompson] & their rebel[l]ions

wherefore let my servant Newal [Newel Knight] remain with them & as manny [many] as will Go may go that are contrite before me & be led by him to the land which i have appointed

& again verily i say unto you that my servant Ezra Thayer must repent of his pride & of his selfishness & obey the former commandment[51] which i have given him conserning [concerning] the place [upon] [w]hich he lives & if he will not do this as there shal[l] be no division made uppon [upon] the land he shal[l] be appointed still to go to the land of Missorie [Missouri] otherwise he shal[l] receivee [receive] the money which he has paid & shal[l] leave the place & shal[l] be cut of[f] out of my church saith the lord God of hosts & though the he[a]ven & earth pass away these words shal[l] not pass away but shal[l] be fulfilled

& if my servant Joseph [Smith, Jr.] must needs pay the money behold i the lord will pay it unto him again in the land of Missorie [Missouri] & these of whom he shal[l] receive may be rewarded again according to that which they do for according to that which they do they shal[l] receive even in lands for there [their] inheritance

behold thus saith the lord unto my people you have many things to do & repent of for behold your sins have come up unto me & are not pardoned because you seek to counsil [counsel] in your own ways & your hearts are not satisfied & ye obey not the truth but have pleasure in unrighteousness

woe unto you ye rich men that will not give your substance to the Poor for your riches will canker your souls & this shal[l] be your lamentation in the day of visitation & of Judgement & [of] indignation the harvest is past the summer is ended & my soul is not saved

woe unto you poor men whose hearts are not broken whose spirits are not contrite & whose bellies are not satisfied & whose hands are not stayed from laying

---

51. This refers to a revelation given in May 1831, see document no. 57.

hold uppon [upon] other mens goods whose eyes are full of greediness who will
not labour with their own hands

but blessed are the poor who are poor in heart whose hearts are broken And
whose spirits are contrite for they shal[l] see the kingdom of god Comeing in
power & great Glory unto their deliverance for the fatness of the earth shal[l] be
theirs for behold the lord shal[l] come And his reword [reward] shal[l] be with him
& he shal[l] reward every one & the poor shal[l] rejoice & their generations shal[l]
inherit the earth from generation to generation for ever & ever & now i make an
end of speaking unto you even so Amen

63. Independence Is the Center Place
From KRB, 89-91 (cf. LDS and RLDS D&C 57)

*Revelation received at Independence, Jackson County, Missouri,
on 20 July 1831 indicating the place of the City of Zion
and the gathering[52]*

Revelation given in independence July th[e] 20 1831 shewing that to be the place
of the city of Zion and the gathering

Hearken O ye Elders of my church saith the lord your God who have assembled
yourselves together according to my commandments in this land which is the land
of Missouri which is the land which I have appointed and consecrated for the gathering of the saints

Wherefore this is the land of promise and the place for the city of Zion yea and
thus saith the Lord your God if ye will receive wisdom here is wisdom behold the
place which is now called Independence is the center place and the spot for the
temple is lying westward upon a lot which is not far from the courthouse[53]

Wherefore it is wisdom that the Land should be purchased by the saints and also
every tract lying westward even unto the line run[n]ing directly between Jew[54] and
Gentile and also every tract bordering by the prairies in asmuch as my disciples are
enabled to buy lands behold this is wisdom that they may obtain it for an everlasting inheritance

and let my servant Sidney Gilbert stand in the office which I have appointed
him to receive monies to be an agent unto the church to buy lands in all the regions

---

52. Another manuscript has "1st Commandment recd. at Missouri after the arrival of Joseph
Smith Jun = M[artin]. Harris Edwd. Partridge = Joseph Coe & W.W. Phelps" ("Book of Commandments, Law and Covenants; Book B"). This revelation was not included in the BC. It was
published in the 1835 D&C with revised wording.

53. The courthouse mentioned is the brick Jackson County Courthouse located in 1831 on
the public square in the village of Independence. The land and site of the temple was outside the
Independence city boundary. At the time of the dedication, the property was owned by the state
of Missouri. Bishop Edward Partridge purchased some sixty-three acres near Independence on
19 December 1831, including the spot where the contemplated temple was to be erected.

54. Native Americans. See document no. 16, [26-31] March 1830.

round about inasmuch as can be in righteousness and as wisdom shall direct

and let my servant Edward [Partridge] stand in the office which I have appointed unto him to divide unto the saints their inheritance even as I have commanded and also them whom he has appointed to assist him

And again verily I say unto you let my servant Sidney Gilbert plant himself in this place and establish a store that he may sell goods without fraud that he may obtain money to buy lands for the good of the saints and that he may obtain provisions and whatsoever things the di[s]ciples may need to plant them in their inheritance

and also let my servant Sidney [Gilbert] obtain a licence [license] (Behold here is wisdom and whoso readeth let him understand) that he may send goods also unto the Lamanites even by whom I will as clerks employed in his service and thus the gospel may be preached unto them.[55]

And again verily I say unto you let my servant William [W. Phelps] also be planted in this place and be established as a printer unto the church and lo if the world receiveth his writings (Behold this is wisdom) let him obtain whatsoever he can obtain in righteousness for the good of [the] saints and let my servant Oliver [Cowdery] assist him even as I have commanded in whatsoever place I shall appoint unto him to copy and to correct and select &c that all things may be right before me as it shall be proved by the spirit through him And thus let those of whom I have spoken be planted in the land of Zion as speedily as can be with their families to do these things even as I have spoken

And now concerning the gathering let the Bishop and the agent make preparations for those families which have been commanded to come to this land as soon as possable [possible] and plant them in there [their] inheritance and unto the residue of both Elders and members further directions shall be given hereafter even so Amen

Revision

1835 D&C 27
(cf. LDS D&C 57:9-10; RLDS D&C 57:4)

And also let my servant Sidney Gilbert obtain a licence, (behold here is wisdom, and whoso readeth let him understand,) that he may send goods also unto the *people,* even by whom *he* will as clerks, employed in his service, and thus *provide for my saints, that my* gospel may be preached unto *those who sit in darkness and in the region and shadow of death.*

Commentary: Goods to the Lamanites

Two manuscripts exist of the 20 July 1831 revelation regarding the gathering to Missouri, and also concerning A. Sidney Gilbert. This revelation pointed to Inde-

---

55. Here it is understood that clerks will be employed under license in the Gilbert store to bring goods to the Native Americans and thereby obtain entrance and do missionary work among them.

pendence "to be the place of the city of Zion and the gathering."[56] The temple property was designated as "lying westward upon a lot which is not far from the courthouse."

The early text indicated that the gospel would be preached unto the Lamanites (Indians) by "clerks employed" in Gilbert's service, sending goods to the Lamanites under "licence."

Though there were no Indian converts when Joseph Smith and his associates arrived in Independence, it is evident that Smith was still planning to preach to the Indians. He could not have struck upon a doctrine more provocative on the frontier than his belief that the "Lamanites" would unite with the Mormons to prepare the way for Christ's return. Ezra Booth, one of the elders who arrived at Independence, wrote four months later as a former member:

> Another method has been invented, in order to remove obstacles which hitherto have proved insurmountable. "The Lord's store-house," is to be furnished with goods suited to the Indian trade, and persons are to obtain license from the government to dispose of them to the Indians in their own territory; at the same time, they are to disseminate the principles of Mormonism among them. From this smug[g]ling method of preaching to the Indians, they anticipate a favorable result.[57]

The 1835 committee changed the whole thrust of the passage. First, all the goods were now to be sent to the "people," which obscures the meaning. Second, the people are more specifically designated as being the Saints. And third, the purpose was to provide means for preaching to the lost anywhere. A. Sidney Gilbert, it should be noted, died in June 1834 before the revelation was altered in Kirtland. A manuscript copy (found in Book B) was written in Gilbert's own handwriting and again makes clear which is the earliest text. Gilbert's manuscript agrees with the Kirtland Revelations Book, and the revisions are far afield.

Ezra Booth also mentioned another plan to get onto the Indian territory:

> In addition to this, and to co-operate with it, it has been made known by revelation, that it will be pleasing to the Lord, should they form a matrimonial alliance with the Natives; and by this means the Elders, who comply with the thing so pleasing to the Lord, and for which the Lord has promised to bless those who do it abundantly, gain a residence in the Indian territory, independent of the agent.[58]

Years later William W. Phelps transcribed—presumably from memory—a revelation which among other things mentioned taking wives of the Lamanites, though his document contains anachronisms.[59]

---

56. KRB, 89.
57. Booth to Rev. Ira Eddy, 6 Dec. 1831, in *Ohio Star* 2 (8 Dec. 1831): 3.
58. Ibid.
59. See David J. Whittaker, "Mormons and Native Americans: A Historical and Biographical Introduction," *Dialogue: A Journal of Mormon Thought* 18 (Winter 1985): 35; and Richard S. Van Wagoner, *Mormon Polygamy: A History*, 2nd ed. (Salt Lake City: Signature Books, 1989), 12-13. See Appen. E.

64. My Laws Shall Be Kept on This Land
From BC 59 (cf. LDS and RLDS D&C 58)

Revelation received in Jackson County, Missouri,
in [1-2] August 1831 for the elders of the church[60]

A Revelation to the elders of the church, assembled on the land of Zion, given August, 1831.

Hearken O ye elders of my church, and give ear to my word, and learn of me what I will concerning you, and also concerning this land unto which I have sent you:

For verily I say unto you, blessed is he that keepeth my commandments, whether in life or in death;

And he that is faithful in tribulation the reward of the same is greater in the kingdom of heaven.

Ye can not behold with your natural eyes, for the present time, the design of your God concerning those things which shall come hereafter, and the glory which shall follow, after much tribulation.

For after much tribulation cometh the blessings.

Wherefore, the day cometh that ye shall be crowned with much glory, the hour is not yet but is nigh at hand.

Remember this which I tell you before, that you may lay it to heart, and receive that which shall follow. Behold, verily I say unto you, for this cause I have sent you that you might be obedient, and that your hearts might be prepared to bear testimony of the things which are to come;

And also, that you might be honored of laying the foundation, and of bearing record of the land upon which the Zion of God shall stand;

And also, that a feast of fat things might be prepared for the poor;

Yea a feast of fat things, of wine on the lees well refined, that the earth may know that the mouths of the prophets shall not fail;

Yea, a supper of the house of the Lord, well prepared, unto which all nations shall be invited.

Firstly the rich, and the learned, the wise and the noble;

And after that cometh the day of my power:

Then shall the poor, the lame and the blind, and the deaf, come in unto the marriage of the Lamb, and partake of the supper of the Lord, prepared for the great day to come.

Behold I the Lord have spoken it.

And that the testimony might go forth from Zion; yea from the mouth of the

---

60. The Manuscript History inserts the revelation before telling about laying "the first log for a house as a foundation of Zion, in Kaw township, twelve miles west of Independence" on 2 August 1831 (see Jessee, *Papers of Joseph Smith,* 1:358).

city of the heritage of God:

Yea, for this cause I have sent you hither;

And have selected my servant Edward [Partridge] and appointed unto him his mission in this land:

But if he repent not of his sins, which are unbelief and blindness of heart, let him take heed lest he fall.

Behold his mission is given unto him and it shall not be given again.

And whoso standeth in this mission, is appointed to be a judge in Israel, like as it was in ancient days, to divide the lands of the heritage of God unto his children; and to judge his people by the testimony of the just, and by the assistance of his counsellors, according to the laws of the kingdom which are given by the prophets of God:

For verily I say unto you, my laws shall be kept on this land.

Let no man think that he is ruler, but let God rule him that judgeth, according to the counsel of his own will:

Or in other words, him that counselleth, or sitteth upon the judgment seat.

Let no man break the laws of the land, for he that keepeth the laws of God, hath no need to break the laws of the land:

Wherefore be subject to the powers that be, until He reigns whose right it is to reign, and subdues all enemies under his feet.

Behold the laws which ye have received from my hand, are the laws of the church;

And in this light ye shall hold them forth.

Behold here is wisdom.

And now as I spake concerning my servant Edward [Partridge]: this land is the land of his residence, and those whom he has appointed for his counsellors.

And also the land of the residence of him whom I have appointed to keep my storehouse:

Wherefore let them bring their families to this land, as they shall counsel between themselves and me:

For behold it is not meet that I should command in all things, for he that is compelled in all things, the same is a slothful and not a wise servant:

Wherefore he receiveth no reward.

Verily I say, men should be anxiously engaged in a good cause, and do many things of their own free will, and bring to pass much righteousness:

For the power is in them, wherein they are agents unto themselves.

And inasmuch as men do good, they shall in no wise loose their reward.

But he that doeth not any thing until he is commanded, and receiveth a commandment with doubtful heart, and keepeth it with slothfulness, the same is damned.

Who am I that made man, saith the Lord, that will hold him guiltless, that obey not my commandments?

Who am I, saith the Lord, that have promised and have not fulfilled?

I command and a man obeys not, I revoke and they receive not the blessing:

Then they say in their hearts, this is not the work of the Lord, for his promises are not fulfilled.

But wo unto such, for their reward lurketh beneath, and not from above.

And now I give unto you further directions concerning this land.

It is wisdom in me, that my servant Martin [Harris] should be an example unto the church, in laying his moneys before the bishop of the church.

And also, this is a law unto every man that cometh unto this land, to receive an inheritance;

And he shall do with his moneys according as the law directs.

And it is wisdom also, that there should be lands purchased in Independence, for the place of the storehouse:

And also for the house of the printing.

And other directions, concerning my servant Martin [Harris], shall be given him of the Spirit, that he may receive his inheritance as seemeth him good. And let him repent of his sins, for he seeketh the praise of the world.

And also let my servant William [W. Phelps] stand in the office which I have appointed him, and receive his inheritance in the land.

And also, he hath need to repent, for I the Lord am not pleased with him, for he seeketh to exc[e]ll, and he is not sufficiently meek before me.

Behold he who has repented of his sins the same is forgiven, and I the Lord remembereth them no more.

By this ye may know if a man repenteth of his sins.

Behold he will confess them and forsake them.

And now verily I say, concerning the residue of the elders of my church, the time has not yet come for many years, for them to receive their inheritance in this land; except they desire it through prayer, only as it shall be appointed unto them of the Lord.

For behold they shall push the people together from the ends of the earth:

Wherefore assemble yourselves together, and they who are not appointed to stay in this land, let them preach the gospel in the regions round about;

And after that, let them return to their homes.

Let them preach by the way, and bear testimony of the truth in all places, and call upon the rich, the high, and the low, and the poor, to repent;

And let them build up churches inasmuch as the inhabitants of the earth will repent.

And let there be an agent appointed by the voice of the church, unto the church in Ohio, to receive moneys to purchase lands in Zion.

And I give unto my servant Sidney [Rigdon] a commandment, that he shall write a description of the land of Zion,[61] and a statement of the will of God, as it shall be made known by the Spirit, unto him; and an epistle and subscription, to be

---

61. Rigdon wrote the description, but it was not accepted. Another description of Zion was made by Rigdon in an epistle written at Kirtland, Ohio. A copy of the epistle is preserved in John Whitmer's history (RLDS archives). See Westergren, *From Historian to Dissident*, 88-91.

presented unto all the churches, to obtain moneys, to be put into the hands of the bishop, to purchase lands for an inheritance for the children of God, of himself or the agent, as seemeth him good, or as he shall direct.

For behold, verily I say unto you, the Lord willeth that the disciples, and the children of men, should open their hearts, even to purchase this whole region of country, as soon as time will permit.

Behold here is wisdom; let them do this lest they receive none inheritance, save it be by the shedding of blood.

And again, inasmuch as there is land obtained, let there be workmen sent forth, of all kinds, unto this land, to labor for the saints of God.

Let all these things be done in order.

And let the privileges of the lands be made known from time to time, by the bishop, or the agent of the church.

And let the work of the gathering be not in haste, nor by flight, but let it be done as it shall be counselled by the elders of the church at the conferences, according to the knowledge which they receive from time to time.

And let my servant Sidney [Rigdon] consecrate and dedicate this land, and the spot of the temple, unto the Lord.[62]

And let a conference meeting be called,[63] and after that, let my servant Sidney [Rigdon] and Joseph [Smith, Jr.] return, and also Oliver [Cowdery] with them, to accomplish the residue of the work, which I have appointed unto them in their own land:

And the residue as shall be ruled by the conferences.

And let no man return from this land, except he bear record by the way, of that which he knows and most assuredly believes.

Let that which has been bestowed upon Ziba [Peterson], be taken from him:

And let him stand as a member in the church, and labor with his own hands, with the brethren, until he is sufficiently chastened for all his sins, for he confesseth then not, and he thinketh to hide them.

Let the residue of the elders of this church, which are coming to this land, some of whom are exceedingly blessed even above measure, also, hold a conference upon this land.[64]

And let my servant Edward [Partridge] direct the conference, which shall be held by them.

And let them also return, preaching the gospel by the way, bearing record of the things which are revealed unto them:

---

62. The land was consecrated and dedicated as an inheritance for the Saints by Sidney Rigdon on 2 August 1831. Rigdon on 3 August "dedicated the ground where the city [New Jerusalem] is to Stand." Joseph Smith "laid a stone at the North east corner" for the temple, and Sidney Rigdon "pronounced this Spot of ground wholy [wholly] dedicated unto the Lord forever" (Oliver Cowdery's description copied into "The Book of John Whitmer Kept by Commandment," 32; Westergren, *From Historian to Dissident*, 80).

63. This special conference was held at the home of Joshua Lewis in Kaw Township, Jackson County, Missouri, on 4 August 1831 (Cannon and Cook, *Far West Record*, 9-10).

64. On 24 August 1831 a conference was held in Jackson County for these elders who arrived in the land of Zion (Cannon and Cook, *Far West Record*, 13-14).

For verily the sound must go forth from this place into all the world;

And unto the uttermost parts of the earth, the gospel must be preached unto every creature, with signs following them that believe.

And behold the Son of man cometh: Amen.[65]

65. The Fulness of the Earth Is Yours
From NKW Collection (cf. LDS and RLDS D&C 59)

Revelation received in Jackson County, Missouri,
on 7 August 1831 for the Church of Christ

Behold blessed saith the Lord are they who have come up unto this land with an eye single to my glory according to my Commandments for them that live shall inherit the earth and them that die shall rest from all their labours & their works shall follow them they shall receive a crown in the mansions of my Father which I have prepared for them[66]

Yea blessed are they whose feet stand upon the land of Zion who have obeyed my Gospel for they shall receive for their reward the good things of the earth & it shall bring forth in her strength & they also shall be crowned with blessings from above yea & with commandments not a few & with revelations in their time they that are faithful & diligent before me

Wherefore I give unto them a commandment saying thus Thou shalt love the Lord thy God with all thy heart with all thy might mind & strength & in the name of Jesus Christ thou shalt serve him thou shalt love thy neighbour as thyself thou shalt not steal neither commit adult[e]ry nor kill or do any thing like unto it thou shalt thank the Lord thy God in all things thou shalt offer a sacrafice [sacrifice] unto the Lord thy God in righteousness even that of a broken heart & a contrite spirit

And that thou mayest more fully keep thyself unspotted from the world thou shalt go to the house of prayer & offer up thy sacraments upon my holy day for verily this is a day appointed unto you to rest from your labours & to pay thy devotions unto the most high Nevertheless thy vows shall be offered up in righteousness in all days & at all times but remember that on this the Lord[']s day thou shalt offer thine

---

65. Shortly after he left the church, Ezra Booth wrote about the location of the temple: "The next day [3 August 1831] the ground for the Temple was consecrated, and [Joseph] Smith claimed the honor of laying the corner-stone himself. Should the inhabitants of Independence, feel a desire to visit the place, destined at some future time to become celebrated, they will have only to walk one half of a mile out of Town, to a rise of ground, a short distance south of the road. They will be able to ascertain the spot, by the means of a sappling, distinguished from others by the bark being taken off on the north and on the west side. – On the south side of the sappling will be found the letter, T. which stands for Temple; and on the east side ZOM for Zomar; which Smith says is the original word for Zion. Near the foot of the sappling, they will find a small stone, covered over with bushes, which were cut for that purpose. This is the corner-stone for the Temple" (Booth to Rev. Ira Eddy, 14 Nov. 1831, in *Ohio Star* 2 [17 Nov. 1831]: 3).

66. On this day Polly Peck Knight, wife of Joseph Knight, Sr., died. She was the first church member to die in Jackson County, Missouri. (See Dean C. Jessee, ed., "Joseph Knight's Recollection," *BYU Studies* 17 [Autumn 1976]: 36, 39, original in LDS archives).

oblations & thy sacraments unto the most High confessing thy sins unto thy brethren & before the Lord & on this day thou shalt do none other things only let thy
food be prepared with singleness of heart that thy fastings may be perfect or in
other words that thy joy may be full verily this is fasting and prayer or in other
words rejoicing & prayer

And inasmuch as ye do these things with thanksgiving with cheerful hearts &
countenances not with much laughter (for this is sin) but with a glad heart & a
cheerful countenance verily I say that inasmuch as ye do this the fulness of the earth
is yours the beasts of the field & the fowls of the air & that which climbeth upon
trees & walketh upon the earth yea & the herb & the good things which cometh of
the earth whether for food or for raiment or for houses or for barns or for orchards
or for gardens or for vineyards yea all things which cometh of the earth in the season thereof is made for the benefit & the use of man both to please the eye & to
glad[d]en the heart yea for food & for raiment for taste & for smell to strengthen the
body & to enliven the soul & it pleaseth God that he hath given all these things
unto man for unto this end were they made to be used with judgement not to excess neither by extortion & in nothing doth man offend God or against none is his
wrath kindled save those who Confess not his hand in all things & obey not his
commandments behold this is according to the law & the prophets.

Wherefore trouble me no more concerning this matter but learn that he who
doeth the words of righteousness shall receive his reward even peace in this world
& eternal life in the world to come I the Lord hath spoken it & the spirit beareth
record Amen

Given by Joseph [Smith, Jr.] the translation [translator] & written by Oliver [Cow-
dery] August 7 1831 in the land of Zion[67]

66. Let Them Lift Up Their Voice
From BC 61 (cf. LDS and RLDS D&C 60)

*Revelation received in Jackson County, Missouri,
on 8 August 1831 for the elders of the church*

A Revelation to the elders of the church, given in Zion, August, 1831.

Behold, thus saith the Lord unto the elders of his church, who are to return
speedily to the land from whence they came.

Behold it pleaseth me, that you have come up hither;

But with some I am not well pleased, for they will not open their mouths, but
hide the talent which I have given unto them, because of the fear of man.

Wo unto such, for mine anger is kindled against them.

---

67. This document was copied by Samuel Smith who wrote at the end of the revelation,
"Given by Joseph [Smith, Jr.] the translator & written by Oliver [Cowdery] August 7 1831 in
the land of Zion & copied by Samuel H Smith Brother to the Seer" (In "Book of Commandments, Law and Covenants; Book A," LDS archives).

And it shall come to pass, if they are not more faithful unto me, it shall be taken away, even that which they have, for I the Lord ruleth in the heavens above, and among the armies of the earth;

And in the day when I shall make up my jewels, all men shall know what it is that bespeaketh the power of God.

But verily I will speak unto you concerning your journey unto the land from whence you came.

Let there be a craft made, or bought, as seemeth you good, it mattereth not unto me, and take your journey speedily for the place which is called St. Louis.

And from thence let my servants Sidney [Rigdon] and Joseph [Smith, Jr.] and Oliver [Cowdery], take their journey for Cincinnati:

And in this place let them lift up their voice, and declare my word with loud voices, without wrath or doubting, lifting up holy hands upon them.

For I am able to make you holy, and your sins are forgiven you.

And let the residue take their journey from St. Louis, two by two, and preach the word, not in haste, among the congregations of the wicked, until they return to the churches from whence they came.

And all this for the good of the churches; for this intent have I sent them.

And let my servant Edward [Partridge] impart of the money which I have given him, a portion unto mine elders, which are commanded to return: and he that is able, let him return it by the way of the agent, and he that is not, of him it is not required.

And now I speak of the residue which are to come unto this land.

Behold they have been sent to preach my gospel among the congregations of the wicked:

Wherefore, I give unto them a commandment, thus:

Thou shalt not idle away thy time:

Neither shalt thou bury thy talent that it may not be known.

And after thou hast come up unto the land of Zion, and hast proclaimed my word, thou shalt speedily return proclaiming the word among the congregations of the wicked.

Not in haste, neither in wrath, nor with strife:

And shake off the dust of thy feet against those who receive thee not, not in their presence, lest thou provoke them, but in secret, and wash thy feet as a testimony against them in the day of judgment.

Behold this is sufficient for you, and the will of him who hath sent you.

And by the mouth of my servant Joseph [Smith, Jr.], it shall be made known concerning Sidney [Rigdon] and Oliver [Cowdery].

The residue hereafter; even so: Amen.

67. There Are Many Dangers upon the Waters
From BC 62 (cf. LDS and RLDS D&C 61)

Revelation received at McIlwaine's Bend on the bank of the
Missouri River, Missouri, on 12 August 1831 for eleven elders[68]

A Revelation to eleven elders, given upon the bank of the Missouri river, August, 1831.[69]

Behold, and hearken unto the voice of him who has all power, who is from everlasting to everlasting, even Alpha and Omega, the beginning and the end.

Behold, verily thus saith the Lord unto you O ye elders of my church, who are assembled upon this spot, whose sins are now forgiven you, for I the Lord forgiveth sins, and am merciful unto those who confess their sins with humble hearts:

But verily I say unto you, that it is not needful for this whole company of mine elders, to be moving swiftly upon the waters, whilst the inhabitants on either side are perishing in unbelief:

Nevertheless, I suffered it that ye might bear record:

Behold there are many dangers upon the waters and more especially hereafter, for I the Lord have decreed, in mine anger, many destructions upon the waters;

Yea, and especially upon these waters;

Nevertheless, all flesh is in mine hand, and he that is faithful among you, shall not perish by the waters.

Wherefore it is expedient that my servant Sidney (G.) [Sidney Gilbert] and my servant William [W. Phelps] be in haste upon their errand and mission:

Nevertheless I would not suffer that ye should part until you are chastened for all your sins, that you might be one;

That you might not perish in wickedness;

But now verily I say, it behooveth me that ye should part: wherefore let my servants Sidney [Gilbert] and William [W. Phelps], take their former company, and let them take their journey in haste that they may fill their mission, and through faith they shall overcome;

And inasmuch as they are faithful, they shall be preserved, and I the Lord will be with them.

And let the residue take that which is needful for clothing.

Let my servant Sidney [Gilbert] take that which is not needful with him, as you shall agree.

And now behold, for your good I gave unto you a commandment concerning

---

68. On 9 August 1831 Joseph Smith and members of his party left Independence for their homes in Ohio. After arriving at McIlwaine's Bend, William W. Phelps on 11 August "in an open vision, by daylight, saw the Destroyer [the devil], in his most horrible power, ride upon the face of the waters. Others heard the noise, but saw not the vision" (Jessee, *Papers of Joseph Smith*, 1:362).

69. Another manuscript describes this as "a Commandment recd. the 12 Augt 1831 on the Banks of the Missouri about 40 miles above Chairton [Chariton] on our return from Zion" ("Book of Commandments, Law and Covenants; Book B").

these things; and I the Lord will reason with you as with men in days of old.

Behold I the Lord in the beginning, blessed the waters, but in the last days by the mouth of my servant John, I cursed the waters:

Wherefore, the days will come that no flesh shall be safe upon the waters, and it shall be said in days to come, that none is able to go up to the land of Zion, upon the waters, but he that is upright in heart.

And, as I the Lord in the beginning cursed the land, even so in the last days have I blessed it, in its time, for the use of my saints, that they may partake the fatness thereof.

And now I give unto you a commandment, and what I say unto one I say unto all, that you shall forewarn your brethren concerning these waters, that they come not in journeying upon them, lest their faith fail and they are caught in her snares:

I the Lord have decreed, and the destroyer rideth upon the face thereof, and I revoke not the decree:

I the Lord was angry with you yesterday, but today mine anger is turned away:

Wherefore let those concerning whom I have spoken, that should take their journey in haste:

Again I say unto you, let them take their journey in haste, and it mattereth not unto me, after a little, if it so be that they fill their mission, whether they go by water or by land:

Let this be as it is made known unto them according to their judgments, hereafter.

And now, concerning my servants Sidney [Rigdon], and Joseph [Smith, Jr.], and Oliver [Cowdery], let them come not again upon the waters, save it be upon the canal, while journeying unto their homes, or in other words they shall not come upon the waters to journey, save upon the canal.

Behold I the Lord have appointed a way for the journeying of my saints, and behold this is the way:

That after they leave the canal, they shall journey by land, inasmuch as they are commanded to journey and go up unto the land of Zion; and they shall do like unto the children of Israel, pitching their tents by the way.

And behold this commandment, you shall give unto all your brethren: nevertheless unto whom it is given power to command the waters, unto him it is given by the Spirit to know all his ways:

Wherefore let him do as the Spirit of the living God commandeth him, whether upon the land or upon the waters, as it remaineth with me to do hereafter;

And unto you it is given the course for the saints, or the way for the saints of the camp of the Lord, to journey.

And again, verily I say unto you, my servants Sidney [Rigdon], and Joseph [Smith, Jr.], and Oliver [Cowdery], shall not open their mouths in the congregations of the wicked, until they arrive at Cincinnati;

And in that place they shall lift up their voices unto God against that people.

Yea, unto him whose anger is kindled against their wickedness; a people which is well nigh ripened for destruction;

And from thence let them journey for the congregations of their brethren, for their labors, even now, are wanted more abundantly among them, than among the congregations of the wicked.

And now concerning the residue, let them journey and declare the word among the congregations of the wicked, inasmuch as it is given, and inasmuch as they do this they shall rid their garments, and they shall be spotless before me;

And let them journey together, or two by two, as seemeth them good, only let my servant Reynolds [Cahoon], and my servant Samuel [H. Smith], with whom I am well pleased, be not separated until they return to their homes, and this for a wise purpose in me.

And now verily I say unto you, and what I say unto one I say unto all, be of good cheer little children for I am in your midst, and I have not forsaken you, and inasmuch as you have humbled yourselves before me, the blessings of the kingdom are yours:

Gird up your loins and be watchful, and be sober, looking forth for the coming of the Son of man, for he cometh in an hour you think not.

Pray always that you enter not into temptation, that you may abide the day of his coming, whether in life or in death; even so: Amen.

68. Rejoice Together in the Land of Missouri
From BC 63 (cf. LDS and RLDS D&C 62)

Revelation received at Chariton on the bank of the Missouri River, Missouri, on 13 August 1831 for John Murdock, Hyrum Smith, Harvey Whitlock, and David Whitmer[70]

A Revelation to certain elders, while journeying to the land of Zion, given on the bank of the Missouri river, August, 1831.

Behold and hearken, O ye elders of my church, saith the Lord your God; even Jesus Christ, your advocate who knoweth the weakness of man and how to succor them who are tempted:

And verily mine eyes are upon those who have not as yet gone up unto the land of Zion:

Wherefore your mission is not yet full:

Nevertheless ye are blessed, for the testimony which ye have borne, is recorded in heaven for the angels to look upon, and they rejoice over you; and your sins are forgiven you.

And now continue your journey.

Assemble yourselves upon the land of Zion, and hold a meeting and rejoice together, and offer a sacrament unto the Most High;

And then you may return to bear record;

70. These four elders were traveling to the land of Zion in Missouri.

Yea, even all together, or two by two, as seemeth you good;

It mattereth not unto me, only be faithful, and declare glad tidings unto the inhabitants of the earth, or among the congregations of the wicked.

Behold I the Lord have brought you together that the promise might be fulfilled, that the faithful among you should be preserved and rejoice together in the land of Missouri.

I the Lord promised the faithful, and cannot lie.

I the Lord am willing, if any among you desireth to ride upon horses, or upon mules, or in chariots, shall receive this blessing, if he receive it from the hand of the Lord, with a thankful heart in all things.

These things remain with you to do according to judgment and the directions of the Spirit.

Behold the kingdom is yours.

And behold, and lo I am with the faithful always; even so: Amen.

69. Let the Church Repent of Their Sins
From NKW Collection (cf. LDS and RLDS D&C 63)

Revelation received at Kirtland, Ohio, in [30-31] August 1831 for the Church of Christ[71]

Hearken O ye people and open your hearts and give ear from afar and listen you that call yourselves the people of the Lord & hear the word of the Lord & his will concerning you yea verily I say hear the word of him whose anger is kindled against the wicked & rebellious who willeth to take even them whom he will take & preserveth in life them whom he will preserve who buildeth up at his own will & pleasure & destroyeth when he please & is able to cast the soul down to hell

Behold I the Lord uttereth my voice & it shall be obeyed wherefore verily I say let the wicked take heed & let the rebellious fear & tremble & let the unbelieving hold their lips for the day of wrath shall come upon them as a whirlwind & all flesh shall know that I am God And he that seeketh signs shall see signs but not unto salvation

Verily I say unto you There are those among you who seeketh signs & there has been such even from the beginning But behold faith cometh not by signs but signs follow those that believe yea signs cometh by faith not by the will of men nor as they please but by the will of God yea signs cometh by faith unto mighty works for without faith no man pleaseth God & with whom God is angry he is not well pleased wherefore unto such he sheweth no signs only in wrath unto their condemnation

Wherefore I the Lord am not pleased with those among you who have sought

---

71. This manuscript has the date as 31 August 1831. The *Evening and the Morning Star* 1 (Feb. 1833): [6; whole no. 70] and "Book of Commandments, Law and Covenants; Book B," has 30 August 1831. It is not known which day is the correct one.

after signs & wonders for faith & not for the good of men unto my glory Nevertheless I gave commandments & many have turned away from my commandments & have not kept them

There were among you adulterers & adulteresses some of whom have turned away from you & others remain with you that hereafter shall be revealed let such be aware & repent speedily lest judgements shall come upon them as a snare & their folly shall be made manifest & their works shall follow them in the eyes of the people & verily I say unto you as I have said before he that looketh on a woman to lust after her or if any shall commit adultery in his heart they shall not have the spirit but shall deny the faith & shall fear Wherefore I the Lord have said that the fearful & the unbelieving & all liars & whosoever loveth & maketh a lie & the whoarmunger [whoremonger] & the sorcerer should have their part in that lake which burneth with fire & brimstone which is the second death Verily I say that they shall not have part in the first resurrection

And now behold I the Lord saith unto you that ye are not Justified because these things are among you nevertheless he that endureth in faith & doeth my will the same shall overcome & shall receive an inheritance upon the Earth when the day of transfiguration shall come when the earth shall be transfigured even according to the pattern which was shown unto mine apostles upon the mount of which account the fulness ye have not yet received

And now verily I say unto you that as I said that I would make known my will unto you behold I will make it known unto you not by the way of commandment for their [there] are many who observe not to keep my commandments but unto him that keepeth my commandments I will give the mysteries of my Kingdom & the same shall be in him a well of living water springing up unto everlasting life

And now behold this is the will of the Lord your God concerning his saints that they should assemble themselves together unto the land of Zion not in haste lest there should be confusion which bringeth pestilence

Behold the land of Zion I the Lord holdeth it in mine own hands nevertheless I the Lord rendereth unto Cezar [Caesar] the things which are Cezars [Caesar's] Wherefore I the Lord willeth that you should purchase the lands that you may have advantage of the world that you may have claim on the world that they may not be stir[r]ed up unto anger for satan putteth it into their hearts to anger & to the shedding of blood

Wherefore the land of Zion shall not be obtained but by purchase or by blood otherwise there is none inheritance for you & if by purchase behold you are blessed & if by blood as ye are forbidden to shed blood lo your enemies are upon you & ye shall be scourged from city to city & from Synagogue to synagogue & but few shall stand to receive an inheritance

I the Lord am angry with the wicked I am holding my spirit from the inhabitants of the earth I have sworn in my wrath & decreed wars upon the face of the earth & the wicked shall slay the wicked & fear shall come upon every man & the Saints also shall hardly escape nevertheless I the Lord am with them & will come down in Heaven from the presence of God & consume the wicked with unquenchable fire & behold this is not yet but by & by

Wherefore seeing that I the Lord have decreed all these things upon the face of the earth I willeth that my saints should be assembled upon the land of Zion & that every man should take righteousness in his hands & faithfulness upon his loins & lift a warning voice unto the inhabitants of the earth & declare both by word & by flight that desolation shall come upon the wicked

Wherefore let my Desiples [Disciples] in Kirtland arrange their temporal concerns which dwell upon this farm let my servant Titus [Billings] who has the care thereof dispose of the land that he may be prepared in the coming spring to take his Journey up unto the land of Zion with those that dwell upon the face thereof excepting those whom I shall reserve unto myself that shall not go until I shall command them

& let all the moneys which can be spared (it mattereth not unto me whether it be little or much) sent up unto the land of Zion unto them whom I have appointed to receive

Behold I the Lord will give unto my servant Joseph [Smith, Jr.] power that he shall be enable to descern [discern] by the spirit those who shall go up unto the land of Zion & those of my Desiples [Disciples] that shall tarry

Let my servant Newel Whitney retain his store or in otherwords the store yet for a little season nevertheless let him impart all the money which he can impart to be sent up unto the land of Zion behold these things are in his own hands let him do according to wisdom verily I say let him be ordained as an agent unto the Desiples [Disciples] that shall tarry & let him be ordained unto this power & now speedily visit the churches expounding these things unto them with my servant Oliver [Cowdery]

behold this is my will obtaining moneys even as I have directed he that is faithful & endureth shall overcome the world he that sendeth up treasures unto the land of Zion shall receive an inheritance in this world & his works shall follow him & also a reward in the world to come yea & blessed are the dead that die in the Lord from henceforth when the Lord shall come & old things shall pass away & all things become new they shall rise from the dead & shall not die & shall receive an inheritance before the Lord in the Holy City & he that liveth when the Lord shall come & have kept the faith blessed is he nevertheless it is appointed unto him to die at the age of man Wherefore children shall grow up until they become old. Old men shall die but they shall not sleep in the dust but they shall be changed in the twinkling of an eye

Wherefore for this cause preached the Apostles unto the world the resurrection of the dead these things are the things that ye must look for & speaking after the manner of the Lord they are now nigh at hand & in a time to come even in the day of the coming of the Son of man & until that hour there will be foolish virgins among the wise & at that hour cometh an entire separation of the righteous & the wicked & in that day will I send mine angels & pluck out the wicked & cast into unquenchable fire

And now behold verily I say unto you I the Lord am not pleased with my servant Sidney [Rigdon] he exaulted [exalted] himself in his heart & received not counsel but grieved the spirit

Wherefore his writing is not acceptable unto the Lord & he shall make another[72] & if the Lord receive it not behold he standeth no longer in the office which he hath appointed him

And again verily I say unto you let those who desire in their hearts in meekness to warn sinners to repentance let them be ordained unto this power for this is a day of warning & not a day of many words for I the Lord am not to be mocked in the last days

Behold I am from above & my power lieth beneath I am over all & in all & through all & searcheth all things & the days cometh that all things shall be subject unto me Behold I am Alpha & Omega even Jesus Christ

Wherefore let all men be ware how they take my name in their lips for behold verily I say that many there be who are under this condemnation who useth the name of the Lord & useth it in vain having not authority

Wherefore let the church repent of their sins & I the Lord will own them otherwise they shall be cut off remember that that which cometh from above is sacred & must be spoken with care & by constraint of the spirit & in this there is no condemnation and ye receive the spirit through prayer wherefore without this there remaineth condemnation

Let my servants Joseph [Smith, Jr.] & Sidney [Rigdon] seek them a home as they are taught through prayer by the spirit these things remain to overcome through patience that such may receive a more exceeding & eternal weight of glory otherwise a greater condemnation Amen

Given by Joseph the Seer in Kirtland August 31. 1831 and written by Oliver [Cowdery]

70. I Will Have Compassion upon You
From NKW Collection (cf. LDS and RLDS D&C 64)

Revelation received at Kirtland, Ohio, on 11 September 1831 for the elders of the church

given at Kirtland Sept 11th 1831

Behold thus saith the Lord your God unto you oh ye Elders of my church hearken ye & hear & receive my will concerning you for verily I say unto you I will that ye should overcome the world wherefore I will have compassion upon you

---

72. Ezra Booth wrote, "Sidney [Rigdon], since his return, has written a description of the land of Zion" (Booth to Edward Partridge, 20 Sept. 1831, copy in *Ohio Star* 2 (24 Nov. 1831): [1]). Rigdon was told his earlier writing was not acceptable. He then wrote an epistle to the Saints that included a description of Zion written on 31 August 1831 (see Sidney Rigdon Papers, LDS archives; and Westergren, *From Historian to Dissident*, 88-91).

there are those among you who have sinned but verily I say for this once for mine own glory & for the Salvation of souls I have forgiven you your sins I will be mercyfull unto you for I have given unto you the kingdom & the keys of the mysteries of the kingdom Shall not be taken from my Servant Joseph [Smith, Jr.] while he liveth in as much as he obeyeth mine ordinances

there are those who have Sought occation [occasion] against him without a cause nevertheless he has sinned but verily I say unto you I the Lord forgiveth Sins unto those who confess their Sins before me & ask forgiveness who have not sinned unto Death

my Deciples [Disciples] in days of old Sought occation [occasion] against one an other & forgave not one another in their hearts & for this evil they were afflicted & sorely chastened wherefore I say unto you that ye had ought to forgive one another for he that forgiveth not his brother his trespasses standeth condemned before the Lord for there remaineth in him the greater sin

I the Lord will forgive whom I will forgive but of you it is required to forgive all men & ye had ought to say in your hearts let God Judge between me & thee & reward thee according to thy deeds & he that repenteth not of his sins & confess them not then ye shall bring him before the Church & do with him as the Scripture saith unto you either by commandment or by revelation & this ye shall do that god might be glorified not because ye forgive not having not compassion but that ye may be Justified in the eyes of the Law that ye may not offend him who is your lawgiver verily I say for this cause ye shall do these things

Behold I the Lord was angry with him who was my Servent Ezra [Booth] & also my servent Isaac [Morley] for they kept not the Law neither the commandment they sought evil in their hearts & I the Lord withheld my Spirit from them they condemned for evil that thing in which there was no evil nevertheless I have forgiven my servent Isaac [Morley] & also my Servent Edward [Partridge] he hath sinned & Satan Seeketh to destroy his Soul but when these things are made known they repenteth of the evil & they shall be forgiven

And now verily I say that it is expedient in me that my Servent Sidney [Gilbert] after a few weeks should return upon his business & to his agency in the Land of Zion & that which he hath seen & heard may be made known unto my Deciples [Disciples] that they Perish not & for this cause have I spoken these things

& again I say unto you that my servent Isaac [Morley] may not be tempted above that which he is able to bear & council [counsel] wrongfully to your hurt I gave commandment that this farm should be sold I willeth not that my Servent Frederick [G. Williams] should sell his farm for I the Lord willeth to retain a Strong hold in the Land of Kirtland for the space of five years in the which I will not overthrow the wicked that thereby I may save some & after that day I thee [the] Lord will not hold any Guilty that shall go with open hearts up to the Land of Zion for I the Lord requireth the hearts of the Children of men

Behold now it is called to day & verily it is a day of Sacrifice & a day for the thithing [tithing] of my People for he that is tithed shall not be burned for after to day cometh the burning this is speaking after the manner of the Lord for verily I say tomorrow all the Proud & they that do wickedly shall be as stubble & I will burn them up for I am the Lord of hosts & I will not spare any that remaineth in Babylon

Wherefore if ye believe me ye will labour while it is called to day & it is not meet that my Servent Newel [K. Whitney] & Sidney [Gilbert] should sell their store & their Possession[s] here for this is not wisdom untill the residue of the Church which remaineth in this place shall go up unto the Land of Zion

Behold it is said in my Law or forbid[d]en to get in debt to thine enemies[73] but behold it is not said at any time that the Lord should not take when he please & pay as Seemeth him good wherefore as ye are agents & ye are on the Lord['s] errand & whatever ye do according to the will of the Lord is the Lord['s] business & it is the Lord['s] business to provide for his saints in these last days that they may obtain an inheritance in the land of Zion & behold I the Lord declare unto you & my words are shure [sure] & shall not fail that they shall obtain it

But all things must come to pass in its time wherefore be not weary in welldoing for ye are laying the foundation of a great work & out of Small things proceedeth that which is great behold the Lord requireth the heart & a willing mind & the willing & the obedient shall eat the good of the land of Zion in these last days & the rebel[l]ious shall be cut off out of the land of Zion & shall be sent away & shall not inherit the Land for verily I say that the rebel[l]ious are not of the blood of Ephraim[74] wherefore they shall be plucked out

Behold I the Lord have made my church in these last days like unto a Judge sitting on an hill or in an high place to Judge the Nations for it shall come to pass that the inhabitants of Zion shall Judge all things & all liars & hypocrites shall be proved by them & they which are not Apostles shall be known

& even the Judge & his councillors if they are not faithfull in their Stewartship [Stewardship] shall be condemned & others shall be planted in their stead for behold I say unto you that Zion shall flourish & the glory of the Lord shall be upon her & she shall be an ensign unto the People & there shall come unto her out of every Nation under heaven & the days shall come when the Nations of the Earth shall tremble because of her & shall fear because of her terrible ones the Lord hath spoken it Amen

<u>Revision</u>

1835 D&C 21
(cf. LDS D&C 64:4-5, 23, 30-31, 37-40; RLDS D&C 64:2, 5-8)

I have given unto you the kingdom: and the keys of the mysteries of the kingdom, shall not be taken from my servant Joseph Smith, jr. *through the means I have ap-*

---

73. See document no. 45, 9 Feb. 1831.
74. The BC printing was destroyed by a mob on 20 July 1833. The last words printed were "blood of Ephraim," though the manuscript revelation continued to the end (BC manuscript, 111, RLDS archives). At the end of a revelation given for William E. McLellin on 29 October 1831, McLellin was told that he was a descendant from Joseph "through the loins of Ephraim his Son."

pointed, while he liveth, inasmuch as he obeyeth mine ordinances.

.   .   .

Behold now it is called to-day, (*until the coming of the Son of man*) and verily it is a day of sacrifice, and a day for the tithing of my people; for he that is tithed shall not be burned (*at his coming;*)

.   .   .

and *he hath set you* to provide for his saints in these last days, that they may obtain an inheritance in the land of Zion; and behold I the Lord declare unto you, and my words are sure and shall not fail, that they shall obtain it

.   .   .

Behold I the Lord have made my church in these last days, like unto a judge sitting on an hill, or in an high place, to judge the nations: for it shall come to pass, that the inhabitants of Zion shall judge all things *pertaining to Zion*: and liars, and hypocrites shall be proved by them, and they *who* are not apostles *and prophets* shall be known. And even the *bishop, who is a* judge, and his counsellors, if they are not faithful in their stewardships, shall be condemned, and others shall be planted in their stead

Commentary: Judge All Things

One of the earliest manuscripts of the revelation of 11 September 1831 is in the Newel K. Whitney Collection. The BC manuscript page 111 for the last portion of the revelation is extant and in the possession of the RLDS church. The first addition written on the BC manuscript after the words "Judge all things" was the words "pertaining to Zion." The words "Judge all things" appear in all of the manuscripts, but the addition is found only in the BC manuscript (interlinear) and in the 1835 D&C.

The second addition to the BC manuscript, which comes after the word "Apostles," was "& prophets." The shorter reading "Apostles" was in the earliest manuscript in the Whitney Collection, as well as in Book A. The other two manuscripts (Wilford Woodruff's BC and "Book B") have the additional reading.[75] The 1835 publication follows this longer version.

All of the manuscripts have the expression "the Judge & his counsellors" (BC MS). Only the 1835 D&C has instead the phrase "the bishop, who is a judge, and his counsellors." This reading, which contains the additional words "bishop, who is a," is the least defensible of all three additions.

---

75. Wilford Woodruff's copy of the BC, LDS archives.

5. Publishing the Revelations, October 1831–April 1832

71. Blessed Are You for Receiving Mine Everlasting Covenant
From the William E. McLellin Journal, LDS archives
(cf. LDS and RLDS D&C 66)

Revelation received at Hiram, Ohio, on 29 October 1831
for William E. McLellin[1]

Behold thus saith the Lord unto you my servant Wm. [William E. McLellin] blessed are you, in as much as you have turned away from your iniquities and have received my truths, saith the Lord, your Redeemer, The Saviour of the world; even of as many as believe on my name.

Verily I say unto you, blessed are you for receiving mine everlasting Covenant, even the fulness of my Gospel sint [sent] forth unto the children of men, that they might have life, and be made partakers of the glories which are to be revealed in the last days as it was written by the Prophets & Apostles in days of old.

Verily I say unto you my servant William [E. McLellin] that you are clean but not all. Repent therefore of those things which are not pleasing in my sight Saith the Lord; for the Lord will show them unto you. And now, verily I the Lord will show unto you what I will concerning you: or what is my will concerning you.

Behold verily I say unto you that it is my will that you should proclaim my Gospel from land to land, and from city to city: Yea in those regions round about where it hath not been proclaimed Tarry not many days in this place. Go not up unto the land of Zion, as yet. But in as much as you can send; Send otherwise think not of thy property Go unto Eastern lands. Bear testimony in every place, unto every people and in their sinagogues [synagogues]:[2] reasoning with the people.

Let my servant Samuel [H. Smith] go with you; and forsake him not, and give

---

1. McLellin was the scribe for this revelation. He wrote in his journal, "This day the Lord conde[s]cended to hear my pray[e]r and gave me a revelation of his will, through his prophet or seer (Joseph) – And these are the words which I wrote from his mouth, saying," then the text of the revelation follows. After the text he continued, "This revelation give [gave] great joy to my heart because some important questions were answered which had dwelt upon my mind with anxiety yet with uncertainty" (Jan Shipps and John W. Welch, eds., *The Journals of William E. McLellin 1831-1836* (Provo, UT: BYU Studies/Urbana: University of Illinois Press, 1994], 45-46).

2. Churches.

him thine instructions: and he that is faithful shall be made strong in every place. And I the Lord will go with you. Lay your hands upon the sick and they shall recover. Return not until I the Lord shall send you. Be patient in afflictions. Ask and ye shall receive. Knock and it shall be opened unto you.

Seek not to be cumbered. Forsake all unrighteousness. Commit not Adultery. (A temptation with which thou hast been troubled.) Keep these sayings true and faithful and thou shalt magnify thine office, and push many people to Zion, with songs of everlasting Joy upon their heads. Continue in these things even unto the end; and you shall have a crown of Eternal life on the right hand of my Father, who is full of grace and truth. Verily, thus saith the Lord your God, your Redeemer even Jesus Christ Amen

A revelation given to William E. McLel[l]in a true descendant from Joseph who was sold into Egypt down through the loins of Ephraim his Son — Given in Hiram, Portage Co. Ohio. 29th Oct 1831

72. May the Kingdom of God Go Forth
From the William E. McLellin Collection, LDS archives
(cf. LDS and RLDS D&C 65)

Revelation received at Hiram, Ohio, on 30 October 1831
on prayer[3]

A revelation of Joseph the Seer 30 Oct. 1831 on the 6th [chapter of] Matthew 10[th] verse

He[a]rken and lo a voice as one sent down from on high who is mighty and powerfu[l] whose going forth is unto the ends of the earth yea whose voice is unto all men prepare ye the way of the Lord make his paths strait. The keys of the kingdom of God is committed unto man on the earth and from thence shall the gospel roll forth unto the ends of the earth, as the stone which is hewn from the mountain without hands shall roll forth unti[l] it hath filled the whole earth.[4]

Yea a voice crying prepare ye the way of the Lord prepare ye the supper of the Lamb Make ready for the comeing of the bridegroom Pray unto the Lord. Call upon his holy name Make known his wonderful works among the people. Call upon the Lord that his kingdom may go forth upon the earth that the inhabitants thereof may receive it and be prepared for the days to come in the which the son of man shall come down in Heaven Clothed in the brightness of his glory to meet the kingdom of God which is set up on the earth. Wherefore may the kingdom of God go forth that the kingdom of heaven may come, that thou O God may be glorified

---

3. William McLellin wrote in his journal that he "read and copied revelations" in November 1831. He also copied revelations in January 1832 (Shipps and Welch, *Journals of William E. McLellin*, 47, 70).

4. The stone coming from a mountain without hands to fill the earth refers to the dream of King Nebuchadnezzar (see Dan. 2:34-35, 45).

in heaven so on earth that thine enemies may be subdued for thine is the honor, power and glory for ever and ever Amen.

Jos[eph]. Smith Revelator

Revision

1835 D&C 24
(cf. LDS D&C 65:2; RLDS D&C 65:1)

The keys of the kingdom of God are committed unto man on the earth, and from thence shall the gospel roll forth unto the ends of the earth, as the stone which is *cut out of* the mountain without hands shall roll forth, until it has filled the whole earth

Commentary: A stone

A revelation on prayer was given on 30 October 1831 and copied by William E. McLellin. It was also copied by John Whitmer in November onto what would be page 112 of the BC manuscript. The revelation was published in the *Evening and the Morning Star* in September 1832. The wording "stone which is hewn from the mountain without hands" appears in this text, as in the BC manuscript. Later the words "hewn from" were crossed out and the words "cut out of" were added above the line.

The *Evening and Morning Star* reprint at Kirtland has the same text as that published earlier in Independence.[5] The 1835 D&C followed the revision and printed the text as "cut out of." The Kirtland Revelations Book (recorded after December 1833) does not contain this revision and evidently was not used for the 1835 D&C.

73. This Is Mine Authority
From BC 1 (cf. LDS and RLDS D&C 1)

Revelation received at Hiram, Ohio, on 1 November 1831 as the preface to the Book of Commandments

A Preface or instruction unto the Book of Commandments, which were given of the Lord unto his church, through him whom he appointed to this work, by the voice of his saints through the prayer of faith: This church being organized according to the will of him, who rules all things, on the sixth day of April, in the year of our Lord, one thousand eight hundred and thirty:

Hearken, O ye people of my church, saith the voice of Him who dwells, on high, and whose eyes are upon all men; yea, verily I say, hearken ye people from afar, and ye that are upon the islands of the sea, listen together; for verily the voice

---

5. *Evening and Morning Star* 1 (Sept. 1832): 62, reprinted April 1835.

of the Lord is unto all men, and there is none to escape, and there is no eye that shall not see, neither ear that shall not hear, neither heart that shall not be penetrated; and the rebellious shall be pierced with much sorrow, for their iniquities shall be spoken upon the house-tops, and their secret acts shall be revealed; and the voice of warning shall be unto all people, by the mouth of my disciples, whom I have chosen in these last days, and they shall go forth and none shall stay them, for I the Lord have commanded them.

Behold, this is mine authority, and the authority of my servants, and my Preface unto the Book of my Commandments, which I have given them to publish unto you, O inhabitants of the earth:—Wherefore fear and tremble, O ye people for what I the Lord have decreed, in them, shall be fulfilled: And verily, I say unto you, that they who go forth, bearing these tidings unto the inhabitants of the earth, to them is power given, to seal both on earth and in heaven, the unbelieving and rebellious; yea, verily, to seal them up unto the day when the wrath of God shall be poured out upon the wicked, without measure, unto the day when the Lord shall come to recompence [recompense] unto every man according to his work, and measure to every man according to the measure which he has measured to his fellow man.

Wherefore the voice of the Lord is unto the ends of the earth, that all that will hear may hear: Prepare ye, prepare ye for that which is to come, for the Lord is nigh; and the anger of the Lord is kindled, and his sword is bathed in heaven, and it shall fall upon the inhabitants of the earth; and the arm of the Lord shall be revealed; and the day cometh, that they who will not hear the voice of the Lord, neither the voice of his servants, neither give heed to the words of the prophet[s], and apostles, shall be cut off from among the people: For they have strayed from mine ordinances, and have broken mine everlasting covenant, they seek not the Lord to establish his righteousness, but every man walketh in his own way, and after the image of his own god, whose image is in the likeness of the world, and whose substance i[s] that of an idol, which waxeth old and shall perish in Babylon, even Babylon the great, which shall fall:

Wherefore I the Lord, knowing the calamity which should come upon the inhabitants of the earth, called upon my servant Joseph [Smith, Jr.], and spake unto him from heaven, and gave him commandments; and also gave commandments to others, that they should proclaim these things unto the world, and all this that it might be fulfilled, which was written by the prophets: The weak things of the world should come forth and break down the mighty and strong ones; that man should not counsel his fellow man, neither trust in the arm of flesh, but that every man might speak in the name of God, the Lord, even the Savior of the world; that faith also might increase in the earth; that mine everlasting covenant might be established; that the fulness of my gospel might be proclaimed by the weak and the simple, unto the ends of the world; and before kings and rulers.

Behold I am God and have spoken it: these commandments are of me, and were given unto my servants in their weakness, after the manner of their language, that they might come to understanding; and inasmuch as they erred, it might be made known: and inasmuch as they sought wisdom, they might be instructed; and inasmuch as they sinned, they might be chastened, that they might repent; and inasmuch as they were humble, they might be made strong, and blessed from on high, and receive knowledge from time to time: after they, having received the record of the Nephites; yea, even my servant Joseph [Smith, Jr.] might have power to translate through the mercy of God, by the power of [G]od, the book of Mormon:

And also, those to whom these commandments were given, might have power to lay the foundation of this church, and to bring it forth out of obscurity, and out of darkness, the only true and living church upon the face of the whole earth, with which I the Lord am well pleased, speaking unto the church collectively and not individually, for I the Lord can not look upon sin with the least degree of allowance:

Nevertheless, he that repenteth and doeth the commandments of the Lord, shall be forgiven, and he that repenteth not from him shall be taken even the light which he hath received, for my Spirit shall not always strive with man, saith the Lord of hosts.

And again, verily I say unto you, O inhabitants of the earth, for I the Lord am willing to make these things known unto all flesh, for I am no respecter to persons, and willeth that all men shall know that the day speedily cometh, the hour is not yet, but is nigh at hand, when peace shall be taken from the earth, and the devil shall have power over his own dominion; and also, the Lord shall have power over his saints, and shall reign in their midst, and shall come down in judgment upon Idumea, or the world.

Search these commandments, for they are true and faithful, and the prophecies and promises which are in them, shall all be fulfilled. What I the Lord have spoken, I have spoken, and I excuse not myself, and though the heavens and the earth pass away, my word shall not pass away, but shall all be fulfilled, whether by mine own voice, or by the voice of my servants, it is the same: For behold, and lo, the Lord is God, and the Spirit beareth record, and the record is true, and the truth abideth forever and ever: Amen.

74. Let Not Your Minds Turn Back
From 1835 D&C 25 (cf. LDS and RLDS D&C 67)

Revelation received at Hiram, Ohio, on 1 November 1831
for the elders of the church

Revelation given November, 1831.

Behold, and hearken, O ye elders of my church, who have assembled yourselves together, whose prayers I have heard, and whose hearts I know, and whose desires have come up before me. Behold and lo, mine eyes are upon you; and the heavens and the earth are in mine hands, and the riches of eternity are mine to give. Ye endeavored to believe that ye should receive the blessing which was offered unto you, but behold, verily I say unto you, there were fears in your hearts: and verily this is the reason that ye did not receive.

And now I the Lord give unto you a testimony of the truth of these commandments which are lying before you: your eyes have been upon my servant Joseph Smith, jr.: and his language you have known; and his imperfections you have known; and you have sought in your hearts knowledge, that you might express beyond his language: this you also know: now seek ye out of the book of commandments, even the least that is among them, and appoint him that is the most wise among you; or if there be any among you, that shall make one like unto it, then ye are justified in saying that ye do not know that they are true: but if ye cannot make one like unto it, ye are under condemnation if ye do not bear record that they are true: for ye know that there is no unrighteousness in them; and that which is righteous cometh down from above, from the Father of lights.

And again, verily I say unto you, that it is your privilege, and a promise I give unto you that have been ordained unto this ministry, that inasmuch as you strip yourselves from jealousies and fears, and humble yourselves before me, for ye are not sufficiently humble, the vail [veil] shall be rent and you shall see me and know that I am; not with the carnal, neither natural mind, but with the spiritual; for no man has seen God at any time in the flesh, except quickened by the Spirit of God: neither can any natural man abide the presence of God; neither after the carnal mind; ye are not able to abide the presence of God now, neither the ministering of angels: wherefore continue in patience until ye are perfected.

Let not your minds turn back; and when ye are worthy, in mine own due time, ye shall see and know that which was conferred upon you by the hands of my servant Joseph Smith, jr. Amen.

75. The Testimony of the Witnesses
From the Manuscript History, Book A-1:162-63

Testimony to the Book of Commandments given at Hiram, Ohio, on 1 November 1831[6]

The testimony of the witnesses to the book of the Lord[']s commandments, which he gave to his church through Joseph Smith, Jr. who was appointed by the voice of the church for this purpose: we therefore feel willing to bear testimony to all the world of mankind, to every creature upon the face of all the earth, and upon the islands of the sea, that the Lord has borne record to our souls, through the Holy

---

6. Quotation marks omitted. A series of conferences was held in November 1831 relating to the publishing of the revelations of Joseph Smith, Jr., for the BC. The minutes copied in Far West Record state: "A number of the brethren arose and said that they were willing to testify to the world that they knew that they were of the Lord. Revelation received relative to the same" (Donald Q. Cannon and Lyndon W. Cook, eds., *Far West Record: Minutes of the Church of Jesus Christ of Latter-day Saints, 1830-1844* [Salt Lake City: Deseret Book Co., 1983], 27).

Ghost shed forth upon us, that these commandments were given by inspiration of God, and are profitable for all men, and are verily true. We give this testimony unto the world, the Lord being our helper: and it is through the grace of God, the Father, and his Son Jesus Christ, that we are permitted to have this privilege of bearing this testimony unto the world, that the children of men may be profited thereby.

76. I the Lord Am with You

From *The Evening and the Morning Star* 1 (Oct. 1832): [3]
(cf. LDS and RLDS D&C 68)

*Revelation received at Hiram, Ohio, in [1-3] November 1831
for Orson Hyde, Luke S. Johnson, Lyman E. Johnson,
and William E. McLellin*[7]

A Revelation, given November, 1831.

My servant, Orson [Hyde], was called, by his ordinance, to proclaim the everlasting gospel, by the spirit of the living God, from people to people, and from land to land, in the congregations of the wicked, in their synagogues,[8] reasoning with and expounding all scriptures unto them: And behold and lo, this is an ensample [example] unto all those who were ordained unto this priesthood, whose mission is appointed unto them to go forth: And this is the ensample [example] unto them, that they shall speak as they are moved upon by the Holy Ghost; and whatsoever they shall speak, when moved upon by the Holy Ghost, shall be scripture; shall be the will of the Lord; shall be the mind of the Lord; shall be the word of the Lord; shall be the voice of the Lord, and the power of God unto salvation; Behold this is the promise of the Lord unto you, O ye my servants: wherefore, be of good cheer, and do not fear, for I the Lord am with you, and will stand by you; and ye shall bear record of me even Jesus Christ, that I am the Son of the living God; that I was; that I am; and that I am to come.

This is the word of the Lord unto you my servant, Orson [Hyde]; and also unto my servant, Luke [S. Johnson], and unto my servant, Lyman [E. Johnson], and unto my servant William [E. McLellin]; and unto all the faithful elders of my church: Go ye into all the world; preach the gospel to every creature; acting in the authority which I have given you; baptizing in the name of the Father, and of the Son, and of the Holy Ghost; and he that believeth, and is baptized, shall be saved, and he that believeth not shall be damned; and he that believeth shall be blessed with signs following, even as it is written: And unto you it shall be given to know

---

7. This revelation is placed in the Manuscript History prior to document no. 77 received on 3 November 1831. See Dean C. Jessee, ed., *The Papers of Joseph Smith: Autobiographical and Historical Writings* (Salt Lake City: Deseret Book Co., 1989), 1:368. It was published in the 1835 D&C with revised wording.

8. Churches.

the signs of the times, and the signs of the coming of the Son of man; and of as many as the Father shall bear record, to you it shall be given power to seal them up unto eternal life: Amen.

And now, concerning the items in addition to the Laws and commandments, they are these: There remaineth hereafter in the due time of the Lord, other bishops to be set apart unto the church, to minister even according to the first; wherefore it shall be an high priest who is worthy; and he shall be appointed by a conference of high priests.

And again, no bishop or judge, which shall be set apart for this ministry, shall be tried or condemned for any crime, save it be before a conference of high priests; and in as much as he is found guilty before a conference of high priests, by testimony that cannot be impeached, he shall be condemned or forgiv[en], according to the laws of the church.

And again, in as much as parents have children in Zion, that teach them not to understand the doctrine of repentance; f[a]ith in Christ the Son of the living God; and of baptism and the gift of the Holy Ghost by the laying on of the hands, when eight years old:[9] the sin be upon the head of the parents, for this shall be a law unto the inhabitants of Zion, and their children shall be baptized for the remission of their sins when eight years old, and receive the laying on of the hands: and they also shall teach their children to pray, and to walk uprightly before the Lord. And the inhabitants of Zion shall also observe the sabbath day to keep it holy[.] And the inhabitants of Zion, also, shall remember their labors, in as much as they are appointed to labor, in all faithfulness, f[o]r the idler shall be had in remembrance before the Lord.

Now I the Lord am not well pleased with the inhabitants of Zion, for there are idlers among them; and their children are also growing up in wickedness: They also seek not earnestly the riches of eternity, but their eyes are full of greediness. These things ought not to be, and must be done away from among them: wherefore let my servant Oliver [Cowdery], carry these s[a]yings unto the land of Zion. And a commandment I give unto them, that he that observeth not his prayers before the Lord in the season thereof, let him be had in remembrance before the judge of my people. These sayings are true and faithful: wherefore transgress them not, neither take therefrom. Behold I am Alpha and Omega, and I come quickly: Amen.

Revision

1835 D&C 22
(cf. LDS D&C 68:14-26; RLDS D&C 68:2-4)

There remaineth hereafter in the due time of the Lord, other bishops to be set apart unto the church to minister even according to the first: wherefore *they* shall be high

---

9. The age "eight years old" had been added to Genesis 17 during the revision of the OT in early 1831 (OT MS #1, 41, RLDS archives). See Gen. 17:11 (JST).

priests who *are* worthy, and *they* shall be appointed by *the first presidency* of *the Melchizedek priesthood, except they be literal descendants of Aaron; and if they be literal descendants of Aaron, they have a legal right to the bishopric, if they are the first born among the sons of Aaron: for the first born holds the right of presidency over this priesthood, and the keys or authority of the same.*

No man has a legal right to this office, to hold the keys of this priesthood, except he be a literal descendant and the first born of Aaron: but as a high priest of the Melchizedek priesthood has authority to officiate in all the lesser offices, he may officiate in the office of bishop when no literal descendant of Aaron can be found; provided he is called and set apart, and ordained unto this power under the hands of the first presidency of the Melchizedek priesthood.

And a literal descendant of Aaron, also, must be designated by this presidency, and found worthy, and anointed, and ordained under the hands of this presidency, otherwise they are not legally authorized to officiate in their priesthood: but by virtue of the decree concerning their right of the priesthood descending from father to son, they may claim their anointing, if at any time they can prove their lineage, or do ascertain it by revelation from the Lord under the hands of the above named presidency.

And again, no bishop or *high priest, who* shall be set apart for this ministry, shall be tried or condemned for any crime save it be before *the first presidency* of *the church*; and inasmuch as he is found guilty before *this presidency*, by testimony that cannot be impeached, he shall be condemned, *and if he repents he shall be* forgiven, according to the *covenants and commandments* of the church.

And again, inasmuch as parents have children in Zion, *or in any of her stakes which are organized*, that teach them not to understand the doctrine of repentance; faith in Christ the Son of the living God; and of baptism and the gift of the Holy Ghost by the laying on of the hands, when eight years old, the sin be upon the head of the parents, for this shall be a law unto the inhabitants of Zion, *or in any of her stakes which are organized*

Commentary: Melchizedek priesthood and literal descendants of Aaron

Two revelations received at Hiram, Ohio, in November 1831 were preserved during the early years of the church. The first of these, which calls Orson Hyde to the ministry, was first published in the *Evening and the Morning Star* in October 1832.

At the end of the revelation for Orson Hyde, Luke Johnson, Lyman E. Johnson, and William E. McLellin, God warns: "These sayings are true and faithful: wherefore transgress them not, neither take therefrom. Behold I am Alpha and Omega, and I come quickly: Amen." A comparison between the early text and the 1835 D&C shows that a few words were deleted from the revelatory message. In three places the words "conference" and "high priests" were replaced by "presidency."

To this revelation the words "or in any of her stakes which are organized" were added twice. When the committee was appointed to compile the D&C, two stakes had been organized in the church, one at Kirtland, the second in Clay County, Missouri, both in 1834.

The second of these revelations (see document 78) concerns the manner of regulating the Church of Christ in the land of Zion (Missouri). There are two complete manuscripts of document 78, neither of which states that a literal descendant of Aaron has the legal right to the office of bishop. This is not only foreign to the early text, but nothing of this sort was taught in 1831, making this one of the most obvious anachronisms of the revision process.

Even though the early text of document 78 says the bishop's counsellors should be chosen "among the Elders of the church," this was probably interpreted to include high priests. Bishop Edward Partridge himself had been ordained to the high priesthood (high priest) on 3 June 1831. It is unclear what the phrase "whom he hath chosen or will choose" means, since Partridge had already chosen assistants or counselors on 3 June.[10]

The revisions emphasize that someone called from the high priesthood to officiate as a bishop does not have the legal right to hold this office. Why this type of addition was made is not known. It gives the impression that a bishop could be replaced if a literal descendant of Aaron (firstborn among the sons of Aaron) could be found. The addition states, "for the first born holds the right of presidency over this priesthood, and the keys or authority of the same."[11] What if someone happened to make this claim for himself? This was resolved in the following words which were added to document 76: "but by virtue of the decree concerning their right of the priesthood descending from father to son, they may claim their annointing, if at any time they can prove their lineage, or do ascertain it by revelation from the Lord under the hands of the above named presidency."[12]

The emphasis here is on Old Testament concepts. The revision also states: "but as a high priest of the Melchizedek priesthood, has authority to officiate in all the lesser offices, he may officiate in the office of bishop when no literal descendant of Aaron can be found; provided he is called and set apart, and ordained unto this power under the hands of the first presidency of the Melchizedek priesthood."[13] Almost identical instructions were incorporated into document 78.[14] The publication of the revised text in the June 1835 reprint of the *Evening and Morning Star* neither indicated that the text was different nor hinted at what the motivation for the change might be.

---

10. Cannon and Cook, *Far West Record*, 6-7.
11. 1835 D&C 22:2; LDS D&C 68:17; RLDS D&C 68:2.
12. 1835 D&C 22:2; LDS D&C 68:21; RLDS D&C 68:2.
13. 1835 D&C 22:2; LDS D&C 68:19; RLDS D&C 68:2.
14. See 1835 D&C 3:8; LDS D&C 107:17; RLDS D&C 104:8.

77. Go Ye Out from Babylon

From *The Evening and the Morning Star* 1 (May 1833): [1-2]
(cf. LDS D&C 133; RLDS D&C 108)

*Revelation received at Hiram, Ohio, on 3 November 1831
for the Church of Christ*[15]

Hearken, O ye people of my church, saith the Lord your God, and hear the word of the Lord concerning you; the Lord who shall suddenly come to his temple; the Lord who shall come down upon the world with a curse to judgment; yea, upon all the nations that forget God, and upon all the ungodly among you.

For he shall make bare his holy arm in the eyes of all the nations, and all the ends of the earth shall see the salvation of their God:

Wherefore, prepare ye, prepare ye, O my people; sanctify yourselves; gather ye together, O ye people of my church, upon the land of Zion, all you that have not been commanded to tarry.

Go ye out from Babylon. Be ye clean that bear the vessels of the Lord. Call your solemn assemblies, and speak often one to another.

And let every man call upon the name of the Lord; yea, verily I say unto you, again, the time has come when the voice of the Lord is unto you, Go ye out of Babylon; gather ye out from among the nations, from the four winds, from one end of heaven to the other.

Send forth the elders of my church unto the nations which are afar off; unto the islands of the sea; send forth unto foreign lands; call upon all nations; firstly, upon the Gentiles, and then upon the Jews.

And behold and lo, this shall be their cry, and the voice of the Lord unto all people: Go ye forth unto the land of Zion, that the borders of my people may be enlarged, and that her stakes may be strengthened, and that Zion may go forth unto the regions round about:

Yea let the cry go forth among all people: Awake and arise and go forth to meet the Bride-groom:

Behold and lo the Bride-groom cometh, go ye out to meet him. Prepare yourselves for the great day of the Lord. Watch, therefore, for ye know neither the day nor the hour.

Let them, therefore, which are among the Gentiles, flee unto Zion. And let them who be of Judah, flee unto Jerusalem, unto the mountains of the Lord's house.

Go ye out from among the nations, even from Babylon, from the midst of wickedness, which is spiritual Babylon.

But verily thus saith the Lord, let not your flight be in haste, but let all things be

---

15. The May 1833 issue of the *Evening and the Morning Star* stated, "we give below, the close, or as it has been called, the Appendix." Originally this revelation ended the BC manuscript compilation. Additional documents were considered for inclusion for publication after the BC manuscript was taken to Independence, Missouri.

prepared before you: and he that goeth, let him not look back, lest sudden destruction shall come upon him.

Hearken and hear O ye inhabitants of the earth. Listen ye elders of my church together, and hear the voice of the Lord, for he calleth upon all men and he commandeth all men every where to repent: for behold the Lord God hath sent forth the angel crying through the midst of heaven, saying: Prepare ye the way of the Lord, and make his paths strait, for the hour of his coming is nigh, when the Lamb shall stand upon mount Zion, and with him a hundred and forty-four thousand, having his Father's name written in their foreheads:[16]

Wherefore, prepare ye for the coming of the Bride-groom: go ye, go ye out to meet him, for behold he shall stand upon the mount of Olivet, and upon the mighty ocean, even the great deep, and upon the islands of the sea, and upon the land of Zion; and he shall utter his voice out of Zion, and he shall speak from Jerusalem, and his voice shall be heard among all people, and it shall be a voice as the voice of many waters, and as the voice of a great thunder, which shall break down the mountains, and the valleys shall not be found:

He shall command the great deep and it shall be driven back into the north countries, and the islands shall become one land, and the land of Jerusalem and the land of Zion, shall be turned back into their own place, and the earth shall be like as it was in the days before it was divided.

And the Lord even the Savior shall stand in the midst of his people, and shall reign over all flesh. And they who are in the north countries shall come in remembrance before the Lord, and their prophets shall hear his voice, and shall no longer stay themselves, and they shall smite the rocks, and the ice shall flow down at their presence.

And an high way shall be cast up in the midst of the great deep. Their enemies shall become a prey unto them, and in the barren deserts there shall come forth pools of living water; and the parched ground shall no longer be a thirsty land. And they shall bring forth their rich treasures unto the children of Ephraim my servants.

And the boundaries of the everlasting hills shall tremble at their presence.— And then shall they fall down and be crowned with glory, even in Zion, by the hands of the servants of the Lord, even the children of Ephraim; and they shall be filled with songs of everlasting joy.

Behold this is the blessing of the everlasting God upon the tribes of Israel, and the richer blessing upon the head of Ephraim and his fellows.

And they also of the tribe of Judah, after their pain, shall be sanctified in holiness before the Lord to dwell in his presence day and night for ever and ever.

And now verily saith the Lord, that these things might be known among you, O inhabitants of the earth, I have sent forth mine angel, flying through the midst of heaven, having the everlasting gospel, who hath appeared unto some, and hath committed it unto man, who shall appear unto many that dwell on the earth, and this gospel shall be preached unto every nation, and kindred, and tongue, and peo-

16. See Rev. 14:1.

ple, and the servants of God shall go forth, saying, with a loud voice:

Fear God and give glory to him: for the hour of his judgment is come: and worship him that made heaven, and earth, and sea, and the fountain of waters, calling upon the name of the Lord day and night, saying:

O that thou wouldst rend the heavens, that thou wouldst come down, that the mountains might flow down at thy presence. And it shall be answered upon their heads, for the presence of the Lord shall be as the melting fire that burneth, and as the fire which causeth the waters to boil.

O Lord, thou shalt come down to make thy name known to thine adversaries, and all nations shall tremble at thy presence. When thou doeth terrible things, things they look not for; yea, when thou comest down and the mountains flow down at thy presence, thou shalt meet him who rejoiceth and worketh righteousness, who remember thee in thy ways:

For since the beginning of the world have not man heard nor perceived by the ear, neither hath any eye seen, O God, besides thee, how great things thou hast prepared for him that waiteth for thee.

And it shall be said, Who is this that cometh down from God in heaven with died garments: yea, from the regions which are not known, clothed in his glorious apparrel [apparel], travelling in the greatness of his strength?

And he shall say, I am he who spake in righteousness, mighty to save. And the Lord shall be red in his apparrel [apparel], and his garments like him that treadeth in the wine vat, and so great shall be the glory of his presence, that the sun shall hide his face in shame; and the moon shall withhold its light; and the stars shall be hurled from their places:

And his voice shall be heard, I have trodden the wine-press alone, and have brought judgment upon all people; and none was with me; and I have trampled them in my fury, and I did tread upon them in mine anger, and their blood have I sprinkled upon my garments, and stained all my raiment: for this was the day of vengeance which was in my heart.

And now the year of my redeemed is come, and they shall mention the loving kindness of their Lord, and all that he has bestowed upon them, according to his goodness, and according to his loving kindness, forever and ever. In all their afflictions he was afflicted.

And the angel of his presence saved them; and in his love, and in his pity, he redeemed them, and bare them, and carried them all the days of old; yea, and Enoch also, and they who were with him; the prophets which were before him, and Noah also, and they who were before him, and Moses also, and they who were before him, and from Moses to Elijah, and from Elijah to John, who were with Christ in his resurrection, and the holy apostles, with Abraham, Isaac and Jacob, shall be in the presence of the Lamb.

And the graves of the saints shall be opened, and they shall come forth and stand on the right hand of the Lamb, when he shall stand upon mount Zion, and upon the holy city, the New Jerusalem, and they shall sing the song of the Lamb day and night forever and ever.

And for this cause, that men might be made partakers of the glories which were to be revealed, the Lord sent forth the fulness of his gospel, his everlasting covenant, reasoning in plainness, and simplicity, to prepare the weak for those things which are coming on the earth; and for the Lord's errand in the day when the weak should confound the wise, and the little one become a strong nation, and two should put their tens of thousands to flight; and by the weak things of the earth, the Lord should thresh the nations by the power of his Spirit.

And for this cause these commandments were given; they were commanded to be kept from the world in the d[a]y that they were given, but now are to go forth unto all flesh.

And this according to the mind and will of the Lord, who ruleth over all flesh; and unto him that repenteth and sanctifieth himself before the Lord, shall be given eternal life. And upon them that hearken not to the voice of the Lord, shall be fulfilled that which was written by the prophet Moses, That they should be cut off from among the people.

And also that which was written by the prophet Malachi: For behold the day cometh that shall burn as an oven, and all the proud; yea, and all that do wickedly, shall be stubble: and the day that cometh shall burn them up saith the Lord of Hosts, that it shall leave them neither root nor branch.

Wherefore this shall be the answer of the Lord unto them: In that day when I came unto my own, no man among you received me, and you were driven out.— When I called again, there was none of you to answer, yet my arm was not shortened at all, that I could not redeem, neither my power to deliver.

Behold at my rebuke I dry up the sea. I make the rivers a wilderness: their fish stinketh, and dieth for thirst. I clothe the heavens with blackness, and make sackcloth their covering.

And this shall ye have of my hand, ye shall lay down in sorrow.

Behold and lo there are none to deliver you, for ye obeyed not my voice when I called to you out of the heavens, ye believed not my servants; & when they were sent unto you ye received them not: wherefore they sealed up the testimony and bound up the law, and ye were delivered over unto darkness: these shall go away into outer darkness, where there is weeping, and wailing, and gnashing of teeth.— Behold the Lord your God hath spoken it. Amen.

78. None Shall Be Exempt
from the Justice and the Laws of God

From NKW Collection (cf. LDS D&C 107:59-75, 78-92, 99-100;
RLDS D&C 104:31-33, 35-42, 44)

Revelation received at Hiram, Ohio, in [11] November 1831
to the Church of Christ in the Land of Zion[17]

To the church of christ in the land of Zion in addition to the church laws respecting church business. Verily I say unto you saith the Lord of hosts; there must needs be presiding Elders to preside over those who are of the office of an Elder, and also priests over those who are of the office of a Priest, and also Teachers over those who are of the office of a Teacher in like manner and also the deacon; wherefore from Deacon to Teacher and from teacher to priest and from priest to Elder severally as they are appointed according to the church articles and covenants.

Then cometh the High priesthood which is the greatest of all; wherefore it must needs be that one be appointed of the high priesthood to preside over the priesthood and he shall be called president of the high priesthood of the church, or in other words the presideing [presiding] high priest over the high priesthood of the church from the same cometh the administering of ordinances and blessings upon the church by the laying on of the hands, wherefore the office of a Bishop is not equal unto it, for the office of a Bishop is in administering all temporal things,

nevertheless a Bishop must be chosen from the high priesthood that he may be set apart unto the ministering of temporal things, haveing a knowledge of them by the spirit of truth and also to be a Judge in israel to do the business of the church to sit in judgment upon transgressors upon testimony as it shall be laid before him according to the laws by the assistance of his counsellors whom he hath chosen or will choose among the Elders of the church, thus shall he be a judge even a common judge among the inhabitants of Zion until the borders are enlarged and it becomes necessary to have other Bishops or judg[es] and in asmuch as there are other Bishops appointed they shall act in the same office

and again verily I say unto you the most important business of the church and the most difficult cases of the church inasmuch as there is not satisfaction upon the decission [decision] of the judges it shall be handed over and carried up unto the court of the church before the president of the high priesthood and the president of the court of the Highpriesthood shall have power to call other high priests even twelve to assist as counsellors and thus the president of the high priesthood and his counsellors shall have power to decide upon testimony according to the laws of the

---

17. This revelation was referred to in a meeting held in Independence, Missouri. On 3 July 1832 it was "Resolved that the mode and manner of regulating the Church of Christ Take effect from this time, according to a Revelation received in Hiram Portage County Ohio Nov 11, 1831" (Cannon and Cook, *Far West Record*, 51). This document was copied into the KRB and titled, "Revelation given November 1831 Cuyahoga [Portage] Co Ohio regulating the Presidency of the Church" (84). The revelation was published with revised wording in section 3 of the 1835 D&C. See document no. 126.

church and after this decision it Shall be had in remembrance no more before the Lord for this is the highest court of the church of God and a final decission [decission] upon controversies,

There is not any person belonging to the church who is exempt from this court of the church and inasmuch as the president of the high priesthood shall transgress, he shall be had in remembrance before the common court of the church who shall be assisted by twelve counsellors of the high priesthood and their decision upon his head shall be an end of controversy concerning him, Thus none shall be exempt from the justice and the laws of God, that all things may be done in order and in solemnity before me according to truth and righteousness Amen.

A few more words in addition to the laws of the church And again verily I say unto you, the duty of a president over the office of a Deacon is to preside over twelve Deacons to sit in council with them and to teach them their duty, edifying one another as it is given according to the covenants and also the duty of the president over the office of the Teachers is to preside over twenty four of the Teachers and to sit in council with them teaching them the duties of their office as given in the covenants, also the duty of the president over the priesthood [priests] is to preside over forty eight priests and to sit in council with them and to teach them the duties of their office as given in the covenants, and again the duty of the president over the office of the Elders is to preside over ninety six Elders and to sit in council with them and to teach them according to the covenants,

and again the duty of the president of the office of the high priesthood is to preside over the whole church and to be like unto moses. Behold here is wisdom yea to be a Seer a revelator a translator and a prophet, haveing all the gifts of God which he bestoweth upon the head of the church.

wherefore now let every man learn his duty and to act in the office in which he is appointed in all dilligence. He that is slothful shall not be counted worthy to stand, and he that learneth not his duty and showeth himself not approved shall not be counted worthy to stand even so Amen

Revision

1835 D&C 3
(cf. LDS D&C 107:63, 69-71, 74, 78-80; RLDS D&C 104:31-33, 35)

wherefore, from deacon to teacher, and from teacher to priest, and from priest to elder, severally as they are appointed, according to the covenants and *commandments of the* church

.   .   .

nevertheless, a bishop must be chosen from the high priesthood, *unless* he *is a literal descendant of Aaron; for unless he is a literal descendant of Aaron he cannot hold the keys of that priesthood. Nevertheless, a high priest, that is after the order of Melchizedek*, may be set apart unto the ministering of temporal things, having a knowledge of them by the Spirit of truth

. 　　　　. 　　　　.

Thus shall he be a judge, even a common judge among the inhabitants of Zion, *or in a stake of Zion, or in any branch of the church where he shall be set apart unto this ministry,* until the borders *of Zion* are enlarged, and it becomes necessary to have other bishops, or judges *in Zion, or elsewhere*:

. 　　　　. 　　　　.

Again, verily, I say unto you: The most important business of the church, and the most difficult cases of the church, inasmuch as there is not satisfaction upon the decision of the *bishop, or* judges, it shall be handed over and carried up unto the *council* of the church, before the *presidency* of the high priesthood; and the *presidency* of the *council* of the high priesthood shall have power to call other high priests, even twelve, to assist as counsellors; and thus the *presidency* of the high priesthood, and *its* counsellors shall have power to decide upon testimony according to the laws of the church. And after this decision it shall be had in remembrance no more before the Lord; for this is the highest *council* of the church of God, and a final decision upon controversies *in spiritual matters.*

79. Send Forth the Accounts of Their Stewardships to the Land of Zion
From 1835 D&C 28 (cf. LDS and RLDS D&C 69)

Revelation received at Hiram, Ohio, in [12] November 1831 for Oliver Cowdery and John Whitmer

Revelation given November, 1831.

Hearken unto me, saith the Lord your God, for my servant Oliver Cowdery's sake, it is not wisdom in me that he should be entrusted with the commandments and the moneys which he shall carry unto the land of Zion, except one go with him who will be true and faithful: wherefore I the Lord willeth that my servant John Whitmer, should go with my servant Oliver Cowdery. And also that he shall continue in writing and making a history of all the important things which he shall observe and know, concerning my church, and also that he receive counsel and assistance from my servant Oliver Cowdery, and others.

And also, my servants who are abroad in the earth, should send forth the accounts of their stewardships to the land of Zion; for the land of Zion shall be a seat and a place to receive and do all these things; nevertheless, let my servant John Whitmer travel many times from place to place, and from church to church, that he may the more easily obtain knowledge: preaching and expounding, writing, copying, selecting and obtaining all things which shall be for the good of the church, and for the rising generations, that shall grow up on the land of Zion, to possess it from generation to generation, forever and ever. Amen.

80. Stewards over the Revelations, and Commandments
From 1835 D&C 26 (cf. LDS and RLDS D&C 70)

Revelation received at Hiram, Ohio, on 12 November 1831
for Joseph Smith, Jr., Martin Harris, Oliver Cowdery,
John Whitmer, Sidney Rigdon, and William W. Phelps

Revelation given November, 1831.

Behold and hearken, O ye inhabitants of Zion, and all ye people of my church, who are far off, and hear the word of the Lord which I give unto my servant Joseph Smith, jr.; and also unto my servant Martin Harris; and also unto my servant Oliver Cowdery; and also unto my servant John Whitmer; and also unto my servant Sidney Rigdon; and also unto my servant Wm. W. Phelps: by the way of commandment unto them, for I give unto them a commandment: wherefore hearken and hear, for thus saith the Lord unto them, I the Lord have appointed them, and ordained them to be stewards over the revelations, and commandments which I have given unto them, and which I shall hereafter give unto them; and an account of this stewardship will I require of them in the day of judgment: wherefore I have appointed unto them, and this is their business in the church of God, to manage them and the concerns thereof, yea, the benefits thereof:

Wherefore a commandment I give unto them, that they shall not give these things unto the church, neither unto the world, nevertheless; inasmuch as they receive more than is needful for their necessities, and their wants, it shall be given into my storehouse, and the benefits shall be consecrated unto the inhabitants of Zion, and unto their generations, inasmuch as they become heirs according to the laws of the kingdom.

Behold this is what the Lord requires of every man in his stewardship; even as I the Lord have appointed, or shall hereafter appoint unto any man. And behold none are exempt from this law who belong to the church of the living God; yea, neither the bishop, neither the agent, who keepeth the Lord's storehouse; neither he who is appointed in a stewardship over temporal things: He who is appointed to administer spiritual things, the same is worthy of his hire, even as those who are appointed to a stewardship, to administer in temporal things; yea, even more abundantly, which abundance is multiplied unto them through the manifestations of the Spirit: nevertheless, in your temporal things you shall be equal, and this not grudgingly, otherwise the abundance of the manifestations of the Spirit, shall be withheld.

Now this commandment I give unto my servants for their benefit while they remain, for a manifestation of my blessings upon their heads, and for a reward of their diligence; and for their security for food and for raiment, for an inheritance; for houses and for lands, in whatsoever circumstances I the Lord shall place them, and whithersoever I the Lord shall send them: for they have been faithful over many things, and have done well inasmuch as they have not sinned. Behold I the Lord am merciful and will bless them, and they shall enter into the joy of these things: even so. Amen.

81. Confound Your Enemies
From NKW Collection (cf. LDS and RLDS D&C 71)

Revelation received at Hiram, Ohio, on 1 December 1831
for Joseph Smith, Jr., and Sidney Rigdon

Hiram Portage county Ohio Dec 1 1831

Behold thus saith the Lord unto you my servents that the time has verily come that it is necessary and expedient in me that you should open your mouths in proclaiming my gospel the things of the kingdom expounding the misteries [mysteries] thereof out of the Scriptures [Scriptures] according to that portion of spirit and power which shall be given unto you as I will

Verily I say unto you proclaim unto the world in the regions round about and in the church also for the space of a season even untill it shall be made known unto you verily this is a mission for a season which I give unto you Wherefore labour ye in my vin[e]yard call upon the inhabitants of the earth and bear record and prepare the way for the commandments and the revelations which are to come

Now behold this is wisdom whoso readeth let him understand and receive also for unto him who receiveth it shall be given more abundantly even power wherefore confound your enemies call upon them to meet you both in publick and in private and inasmuch as ye are faithfull their shame shall be made manifest wherefore let them bring forth their strong reasons against the Lord Verily thus saith the Lord unto you there is no weapon that is formed against you shall prosper and if any man lift his voice against you he shall be confounded in mine own due time wherefore keep these commandments for they are true and faithful even so Amen

82. It Is Expedient in Me for a Bishop to Be Appointed
From NKW Collection (cf. LDS D&C 72:1-8; RLDS D&C 72:1-2)

Revelation received at Kirtland, Ohio, on 4 December 1831
for Newel K. Whitney[18]

Kirtland December 4th 1831

Hearken and listen to the voice of the Lord o ye who have assembled yourselves together who are the high priests of my church to whom the kingdom and power have been given for Verily thus saith the Lord it is expedient in me for a Bishop to be appointed unto you or of you unto the church in this part of the Lord[']s Vineyard and verily in this thing ye have done wisely for it is required of the Lord at the hand of every steward to render an account of his stewardship both in time and in

---

18. On this date two revelatory messages were given. The index to the KRB explains, "A Revelation given to choose a Bishop. N. K. Whitney was chosen & was sanctioned by th[e] lord and also another in addition to th[e] Law making known the duty of th[e] Bishop."

eternity for he who is faithfull and wise in time is accounted worthy to inherit the mantions [mansions] prepared for them of my father

Verily I say unto you the Elders of the church in this part of my vineyard shall render an account of their stewardship unto the Bishop which shall be appointed of me in this part of my vin[e]yard these things shall be had on record to be handed over unto the Bishop in Zion and the duty of the Bishop shall be made known by the commandments which have been given and by the voice of the conference

And now I say unto you my servent Newel [K. Whitney] is the man who shall be appointed and ordained unto this power this is the will of the Lord your God your Redeemer even so Amen

83. To Receive the Funds of the Church
From NKW Collection (cf. LDS D&C 72:9-26; RLDS D&C 72:3-5)

Revelation received at Kirtland, Ohio, on 4 December 1831
on the duty of the bishop

The duty of the Bishop as made known at the same time

The word of the Lord in addition to the law which has been given making known the duty of the Bishop which has been ordained unto the church in this part of the vin[e]yard which is verily this To keep the Lord[']s storehouse to receive the funds of the church in this part of the vin[e]yard to take an account of the Elders as before has been commanded and to administer to their wants who shall pay for that which they receive inasmuch as they have wherewith to pay that this also may be consecrated to the good of the church to the poor and needy and he who hath not wherewith to pay an account shall be taken and handed over to the Bishop in Zion who shall pay the debt out of that which the Lord shall put into his hands and the labours of the faithfull who labour in spiritual things in administering the gospel and the things of the kingdom unto the church and unto the world shall answer the debt unto the Bishop in Zion thus it cometh out of the church for according to the law every man who cometh up to Zion must lay all things before the Bishop in Zion.

And now verily I say unto you that as every Elder in this part of the Vin[e]yard must give an account of his stewardship unto the Bishop in this part of the vin[e]yard a certificate from the judge or Bishop in this part of the vin[e]yard unto the Bishop in Zion rendereth every man acceptable and answereth all things for an inherit[a]nce and to be received as a wise steward and as a faithfull labourer otherwise shall not be accepted of the Bishop in Zion. And now verily I say unto you let every Elder who shall give an account unto the Bishop of the church in this part of the vin[e]yard be recommended by the church or churches in which he labours that he may render himself and his accounts approved in all things

And again let my servents who are appointed as stewards over the litterary [literary] concerns of my church have claim for assist[a]nce upon the Bishop or Bishops in all things that the revelations may be published and go forth unto the ends of the earth that they also may obtain funds which shall benefit the church in all things that they also may render themselves approved in all things and be accounted as wise stewards. And behold this shall be an ensample [example] for all the extensive branches of my church in whatsoever land they shall be established and now I make an end of my sayings Amen

A few words in addition to the laws of the kingdom respecting the members of the church they who are appointed by the holy spirit to go up unto Zion & they who are priviledged [privileged] to go up unto Zion let them carry up unto the bishop a certificate from three Elders of the church or a certificate from the Bishop otherwise he who shall go up unto the land of Zion shall not be accounted a wise steward this also an ensample [example] Amen

84. Continue Preaching the Gospel
From NKW Collection (cf. LDS and RLDS D&C 73)

Revelation received at Hiram, Ohio, on 10 January 1832
for Joseph Smith, Jr., and Sidney Rigdon

Hiram Portage county ohio Jan 10th 1832
A Revelation to Joseph and Sidney. The word of the Lord unto them concerning the Elders of the church of the Living God established in the last days making known the will of the Lord unto the Elders what they should do untill conference

For verily thus saith the Lord it is expedi[e]nt in me that they should continue preaching the gospel and in exhortation to the churches in the reagions [regions] round about untill conference and behold then it shall be made known unto them by the voice of the conference their severall [several] missions

Now verily I say unto my servents Joseph [Smith, Jr.] and Sidney [Rigdon] saith the Lord it is expedient to translate again and in asmuch as it is practicable to preach in the reagions [regions] round about untill conference and after that it is expedient to continue the work of translation untill it be finished. And let this be a pattern unto the Elders untill further knowledge even as it is written and now I give no more unto you at this time gird up you loines [loins] and be sober even so Amen

85. According to the Revelations and Commandments
From NKW Collection (cf. LDS D&C 75:1-22; RLDS D&C 75:1-3)

Revelation received at Amherst, Ohio, on 25 January 1832
for the elders of the church[19]

Verily verily I say unto you I who speak even by the voice of my spirit even Alpha and Omega your Lord and your God Hearken o ye who have giv[e]n your names to go forth to proclaim my gospel and to prune my vin[e]yard behold I say unto you that it is my will that you should go fo[r]th and not tarry neither be idle but labour with you mights lifting up your voices as with the sound of a trump proclaiming the truth according to the revelations and commandments which I have given you and thus if ye are faithfull ye shall be laden with many she[a]ves and crouned [crowned] with honor and glory and immortality and eternal life

Therefore verily I say unto my servent William [E. McLellin] I revoke the commission which I gave unto him to go unto the eastern countries and I give unto him a new commission and a new commandment in the which I the Lord chasteneth him for the murmurings of his heart and he sinned nevertheless I forgive him and say unto him again go ye into the south countries and let my servent Luke [S. Johnson] go with him and proclaim the things which I have commanded them calling on the name of the Lord for the comforter which shall teach them all things that is expedient for them praying always that they faint not and inasmuch as they do this I will be with them even unto the end behold this is the will of the Lord your God concerning you even so Amen

And again verily thus saith the Lord let my servent Orson Hyde and my servent Samuel [H. Smith] take their journey into the eastern countries and proclaim the things which I have commanded them and inasmuch as they are faithfull lo I will be with them even unto the end

And again verily I say unto my servent Lyman [E. Johnson] and unto my servent orson Pratt they shall also take their Journey into the eastern countries and behold and lo I am with them also even unto the end

And again I say unto my servent Asa [Dodds] and unto my servent Calves [Wilson] that they also shall take their journey unto the western countries and proclaim my gospel even as I have commanded them and he who is faithfull shall over come all things and shall be lifted up at the last day

and again I say unto my servent Major [N. Ashley] and my Servent Burr [Riggs] take their journey also into the south countries yea let all these take their journey as I have commanded them going from house to house and from village to village and from City to City and in whatsoever house ye enter and they receive you leave your blessing upon that house and in whatsoever house ye enter and they receive

---

19. On 25 January 1832 a conference was held at Amherst, Ohio. Orson Pratt who attended wrote: "At this conference, the Prophet Joseph [Smith, Jr.] was acknowledged President of the High Priesthood, and hands were laid on him by Elder Sidney Rigdon, who sealed upon his head the blessings which he had formerly received" (Elden Jay Watson, comp., *The Orson Pratt Journals* [Salt Lake City: comp., 1975], 11).

you not ye shall depart speedily from that house and shake off the dust of your feet as a testimony against them and you shall be filled with joy and gladness and know this that in the day of judgement you shall be judges of that house and condemn them and it shall be more tollarable [tolerable] for the heathen in the day of judgement than for that house therefore gird up your loines [loins] and be faithfull and ye shall overcome all things and be lifted up at the last day even so Amen

86. Supporting the Families

From NKW Collection (cf. LDS D&C 75:23-36; RLDS D&C 75:4-5)

Revelation received at Amherst, Ohio, on 25 January 1832 for the elders of the church

And again thus saith the Lord unto you o ye Elders of my church who have given your names that you might know his will concerning you behold I say unto you that it is the duty of the church to assist in supporting the families of those and also to support the families of those who are called and must needs be sent unto the world to proclaim the gospel unto the world wherefore I the Lord give unto you this commandment that ye obtain places for your families inasmuch as your breathren [brethren] are willing to open their hearts and let all such as can obtain places for their families and support of the church for them not fail to go into the world wheather [whether] to the east or to the west or to the north or to the South let them ask and they shall receive knock and it shall be opened unto them and made known from on high even by the comforter whither they shall go

And again verily I say unto you that every man who is obliged to provide for his own family let him provide and he shall in no wise loose his crown and let him labour in the church let every man be dilligent in all things and the idler shall not have place in the church except he repents and mends his ways

wherefore let my servant Simeon [Carter] and my servant Emer [Harris] be united in their ministry and also my servant Ezra [Thayer] and my servant Thomas [B. Marsh] also my servant Hiram [Hyrum Smith] and my servant Reynolds [Cahoon] and also my servant Daniel [Stranton] and my servant Seymore [Seymour Brunson] and also my servant Selvester [Sylvester Smith] and my servant Gideon [Carter] and also my servant Ruggles [Eames] and my servant Stephen [Burnett] and also my servant Micha [Micah B. Welton] and also my servant Eden [Smith] even so Amen

87. The Eyes of Our Understanding

From *The Evening and the Morning Star* 1 (July 1832): [2-3] (cf. LDS and RLDS D&C 76)

Vision of Joseph Smith, Jr., and Sidney Rigdon received at Hiram, Ohio, on 16 February 1832[20]

A VISION.

Hear, O ye Heavens, and give ear, O earth, and rejoice ye inhabitants thereof, for the Lord he is God, and beside him there is none else; and great is his wisdom; marvelous are his ways; and the extent of his doings, none can find out; his purposes fail not, neither are there any who can stay his hand: from eternity to eternity, he is the same, and his years never fail.

I the Lord am merciful and gracious unto them who fear me, and delight to honor them who serve me in righteousness, and in truth; great shall be their reward, and eternal shall be their glory; and unto them will I reveal all mysteries; yea, all the hidden mysteries of my Kingdom from days of old; and for ages to come will I make known unto them the good pleasure of my will concerning all things; yea, even the wonders of eternity shall they know, and things to come will I show them, even the things of many generations; their wisdom shall be great, and their understanding reach to Heaven; before them the wisdom of the wise shall perish, and the understanding of the prudent shall come to nought; for by my Spirit will I enlighten them, and by my power will I make known unto them the secrets of my will; yea, even those things which eye has not seen, nor ear heard, nor yet entered into the heart of man.

We, Joseph [Smith, Jr.] and Sidney [Rigdon], being in the Spirit on the sixteenth of February, in the year of our Lord, one thous[a]nd eight hundred and thirty two, and through the power of the Spirit, our eyes were opened, and our understandings were enlightened, so as to see and understand the things of God; even things which were from the beginning before the world was, which was ordained of the Father, through his only begotten Son, who was in the bosom of the Father, even from the beginning, of whom we bear record, and the record which we bear is the fulness of the Gospel of Jesus Christ, which is in the Son whom we saw and with whom we conversed in the Heavenly Vision; for as we sat doing the work of translation, which the Lord had appointed unto us, we came to the twenty ninth verse of the fifth chapter of John, which was given unto us thus:

---

20. This vision was opened to Smith and Rigdon after they had revised John 5:29 and were reflecting upon the change in wording. It is known as the vision of the three degrees of glories. The text is from the *Evening and the Morning Star* which was based on a copy made as an addition to the November 1831 manuscript of the BC. An extant page [139] of the ending of the vision is in the RLDS archives. The KRB has the following introduction: "A vision of Joseph [Smith, Jr.] & Sidney [Rigdon] February 16th 1832 given in Portage County Hiram Township state of Ohio in North Americ[a] which they saw concerning the church of the first born and concerning the economy of God and his vast creation throughout all eternity" (1). See similar wording in "Book of Commandments, Law and Covenants," Book A, LDS archives, also copied in 1832.

speaking of the resurrection of the dead who should hear the voice of the Son of m[a]n, and shall come forth; they who have done good in the resurrection of the just, and they who have done evil in the resurrection of the unjust.

Now this caused us to marvel, for it was given us of the Spirit; and while we meditated upon these things, the Lord touched the eyes of our understandings, and they were opened, and the glory of the Lord shone round about; and we beheld the glory of the Son, on the right hand of the Father, and received of his fulness; and saw the holy angels, and they who are sanctified before his throne, worshiping God and the Lamb forever and ever.

And now after the many testimonies which have been given of him, this is the testimony, last of all, which we give of him, that he lives; for we saw him, even on the right hand of God; and we heard the voice bearing record that he is the only begotten of the Father; that by him, and through him, and of him, the worlds are made, and were created; and the inhabitants thereof are begotten sons and daughters unto God.

This we saw also and bear record, that an angel of God, who was in authority in the presence of God, who rebelled against the only begotten Son, (whom the Father loved, and who was in the bosom of the Father,) and was thrust down from the presence of God and the Son, and was called Perdition; for the Heavens wept over him; for he was Lucifer, even the son of the morning; and we beheld and lo, he is fallen! is fallen! even the son of the morning. And while we were yet in the Spirit, the Lord commanded us that we should write the Vision; for behold satan, that old serpant [serpent], even the devil, who rebelled against God, and sought to take kingdoms of our God, and of his Christ; wherefore he maketh war with the saints of God, and encompasses them about: And we saw a vision of the eternal sufferings of those with whom he maketh war and overcometh, for thus came the voice of the Lord unto us.

Thus saith the Lord, concerning all those who know my power, and who have been made partakers thereof, and suffered themselves, through the power of the devil, to be overcome unto the denying of the truth, and the defying of my power: they are they who are the sons of perdition, of whom I say it had been better for them never to have been born; for they are vessels of wrath doomed to suffer the wrath of God, with the devil and his angels, throughout eternity: concerning whom I have said there is no forgiveness for them in this world nor in the world to come; having denied the Holy Ghost after having received it, and having denied the only begotten Son of the Father, crucifying him unto themselves, and putting him to an open shame:

these are they who shall go away into the lake of fire and brimstone, with the devil and his angels, and the only ones on whom the second death shall have any power; yea, verily the only ones who shall not be redeemed in the due time of the Lord, after the sufferings of his wrath, who shall be brought forth by the resurrection of the dead, through the triumph & the glory of the Lamb; who was slain, who was in the bosom of the Father before the worlds were made.

And this is the Gospel, the glad tidings which the voice out of the heavens bore record unto us, that he came into the world, even Jesus to be crucified for the world, and to bear the sins of the world, and to sanctify the world, and to cleanse it from all unrighteousness; that through him all might be saved, whom the Father had put into his power; and made by him who glorifieth the Father; and saveth all the work of his hands, except those sons of perdition, who denieth the Son after the Father hath revealed him: wherefore he saveth all save them, and these shall go away into everlasting punishment, which is endless punishment, which is eternal punishment, to reign with the devil and his angels throughout eternity, where their worm dieth not and the fire is not quenched, which is their torment, but the end thereof, neither the place thereof, and their torment, no man knoweth, neither was revealed, neither is, neither will be revealed unto man, save to them who are made partakers thereof:

nevertheless I the Lord showeth it by vision unto many, but straightway shutteth it up again: wherefore the end, the width, the height, the depth, and the misery thereof, he understandeth not, neither any man save them who are ordained unto this condemn[a]tion. And we heard the voice saying, Write the Vision for lo, this is the end of the vision of the eternal sufferings of the ungodly!

And again, we bear record for we saw and heard, and this is the testimony of the Gospel of Christ, concerning them who come forth in the resurrection of the just: they are they who received the testimony of Jesus, and believed on his name, and were baptized after the manner of his burial, being buried in the water in his name, and this according to the comm[a]ndment which he hath given, that, by keeping the commandment, they might be washed and cleansed from all their sins, and receive the Holy Ghost by the laying on of the hands of him who is ord[a]ined and sealed unto this power; and who overcome by faith, and are sealed by that Holy Spirit of promise, which the Father shedeth forth upon all those who are just and true:

they are they who are the church of the first-born: they are they into whose hands the Father hath given all things: they are they who are priests and kings, who having received of his fulness, and of his glory, are priests of the most High after the order of Melchisedek, which was after the order of Enoch, which was after the order of the only begotten Son: wherefore, as it is written, they are gods, even the sons of God: wherefore all things are theirs, whether life or death, or things present, or things to come, all are theirs, and they are Christ's and Christ is God's; and they shall overcome all things: wherefore let no man glory in man, but rather let him glory in God, who shall subdue all enemies under his feet:

these shall dwell in the presence of God and his Christ forever and ever: these are they whom he shall bring with him, when he shall come in the clouds of heaven, to reign on the earth over his people: these are they who shall have part in the first resurrection: these are they who shall come forth in the resurrection of the just: these are they who are come unto mount Zion, and unto the city of the living God, the heavenly place, the holiest of all: these are they who have come to an innumerrable company of angels; to the general assembly and church of Enoch, and of the first born: these are they whose names are written in Heaven, where God and Christ is the judge of all: these are they who are just men made perfect through Jesus the Mediator of the new covenant, who wrought out this perfect atonement through the shedding of his own blood: these are they whose bodies are celestial, whose glory is that of the Son, even of God the highest of all; which glory the Sun of the firmament is written of as being typical.

And again, we saw the Terrestrial world, and behold and lo! these are they who are of the terrestrial, whose glory differeth from that of the church of the first born, who have received of the fulness of the Father, even as that of the Moon differeth from the Sun of the firmament.

Behold, these are they who died without law; and also they who are the spirits of men kept in prison, whom the Son visited and preached the Gospel unto them, that they might be judged according to men in the flesh, who received not the testimony of Jesus in the flesh, but afterwards received it: these are they who are honorable men of the earth, who were blinded by the craftiness of men: these are they who receive of his glory, but not of his fulness: these are they who receive of the presence of the Son, but not of the fulness of the Father: wherefore they are bodies terrestrial, and not bodies celestial, and differeth in glory as the Moon differeth from the Sun: these are they who are not valiant in the testimony of Jesus: wherefore they obtained not the crown over the kingdoms of our God. And now this is the end of the vision which we saw of the terrestrial, that the Lord commanded us to write while we were yet in the Spirit.

And again, we saw the glory of the Telestial, which glory is that of the lesser, even as the glory of the stars differeth from that of the glory of the Moon in the firmament: these are they who receive not the Gospel of Christ, neither the testimony of Jesus: these are they who deny not the Holy Ghost: these are they who are thrust down to hell: these are they who shall not be redeemed from the devil, until the last resurrection, until the Lord, even Christ the Lamb, shall have finished his work: these are they who receive not of his fulness in the eternal world, but of the Holy Ghost through the administration of the terrestrial; and the terrestrial through the administration of the celestial; and also the telestial receive it of the administering of angels, who are appointed to minister for them, or who are appointed to be ministering spirits for them, for they shall be heirs of salvation.—

And thus we saw in the Heavenly vision, the glory of the telestial which surpasseth all understanding; and no man knoweth it except him to whom God hath revealed it. And thus we saw the glory of the terrestrial, which excelleth in all things the glory of the telestial, even in glory, and in power, and in might, and in dominion. And thus we saw the glory of the celestial, which excelleth in all things where God, even the Father, reigneth upon his throne forever and ever: before whose throne all things bow in humble reverence and giveth him glory forever and ever.

They who dwell in his presence are the church of the first born; and they see as they are seen, and know as they are known, having received of his fulness and of his grace; and he maketh them equal in power, and in might, and in dominion. And the glory of the celestial is one, even as the glory of the Sun is one. And the glory of the Terrestrial is one, even as the glory of the Moon is one. And the glory of the

Telestial is one, even as the glory of the stars is one: for as one star differeth from another star in glory, even so differeth one from another in glory in the telestial world:

for these are they who are of Paul, and of Apollos, and Cephas: they are they who say, there are some of one and some of annother [another]; some of Christ; and some of John; and some of Moses; and some of Elias; and some of Esaias; and some of Isaiah; and some of Enoch, but received not the Gospel; neither the testimony of Jesus; neither the prophets; neither the everlasting covenant; last of all: these are they who will not be gathered with the saints, to be caught up into the church of the first born, and received into the cloud: these are they who are liars, and sorcerers, and adulterers, and whoremungers [whoremongers], and whosoever loveth and maketh a lie: these are they who suffer the wrath of God on the earth: these are they who suffer the vengeance of eternal fire: these are they who are cast down to hell and suffer the wrath of Almighty God until the fulness of times, when Christ shall have subdued all enemies under his feet, and shall have perfected his work, when he shall deliver up the kingdom and present it unto his Father spotless, saying:

I have overcome and trodden the wine-press alone, even the wine-press of the fierceness of the wrath of Almighty God: then shall he be crowned with the crown of his glory, to sit on the throne of his power to reign forever and ever.

But behold and lo, we saw the inhabitants of the telestial world, that they were in number as innumerable as the stars in the firmament of Heaven, or as the sand upon the sea shore, and heard the voice of the Lord saying: These all shall bow the knee, and every tongue shall confess to him who sitteth upon the throne forever and ever: for they shall be judged according to their works; and every man shall receive according to his own works, and his own dominion, in the mansions which are prepared; and they shall be servants of the most High, but where God and Christ dwells they cannot come, worlds without end. This is the end of the vision which we saw, which we were commanded to write while we were yet in the Spirit.

But great and marvelous are the works of the Lord and the mysteries of his kingdom which he showed unto us, which surpasseth all understanding in glory, and in might, and in dominion, which he commanded us we should not write, while we were yet in the Spirit, and are not lawful for man to utter; neither is man capable to make them known, for they are only to be seen and understood by the power of the Holy Ghost; which God bestows on those who love him and purify themselves before him; to whom he grants this privilege of seeing and knowing for themselves; that through the power and manifestation of the Spirit, while in the flesh, they may be able to bear his presence in the world of glory. And to God and the Lamb be glory, and honor, and dominion, forever and ever. Amen.

Revision

1835 D&C 91
(cf. LDS D&C 76:1, 26, 30, 33-34, 44, 49, 68, 116; RLDS D&C 76:1, 3-5, 8)

Hear, O ye heavens, and give ear, O earth, and rejoice ye inhabitants thereof, for the Lord is God, and beside him there is *no Savior*

.   .   .

and was called Perdition; for the heavens wept over him; he was Lucifer, *a* son of the morning; and we beheld and lo, he is fallen! is fallen! even *a* son of the morning.

.   .   .

And we saw a vision of the sufferings of those with whom he made war and over- came, for thus came the voice of the Lord unto us.

.   .   .

for they are vessels of wrath doomed to suffer the wrath of God, with the devil and his angels, *in* eternity: concerning whom I have said there is no forgiveness in this world nor in the world to come

.   .   .

wherefore he saves all *except* them; *they* shall go away into everlasting punishment, which is endless punishment, which is eternal punishment, to reign with the devil and his angels *in* eternity, where their worm dieth not and the fire is not quenched, which is their torment, and the end thereof, neither the place thereof, *nor* their tor- ment, no man knows, neither was *it* revealed, neither is, neither will be revealed unto man, *except* to them who are made partakers thereof

.   .   .

And we heard the voice saying, Write the vision for lo! this is the end of the vision of the sufferings of the ungodly!

.   .   .

these are they whose names are written in heaven, where God and Christ *are* the judge of all

.   .   .

neither is man capable to make them known, for they are only to be seen and un- derstood by the power of the Holy *Spirit*, which God bestows on those who love him and purify themselves before him

Commentary: Vision of the glories

Joseph Smith's and Sidney Rigdon's vision of glory was written down, probably by Sidney Rigdon, on 16 February 1832 at Hiram, Ohio, and later that year copied into the Kirtland Revelations Book by Frederick G. Williams. The vision (actually a series of visions) was published in the *Evening and the Morning Star* in the July issue probably from a copy brought to Independence, Missouri, for publication in the

BC. A portion of the printer's manuscript, which contains the concluding part of the vision, is in the possession of the RLDS church; it is in the handwriting of John Whitmer.[21]

The vision was revised for the *Evening and Morning Star* reprint published in Kirtland in February 1835. Some of the textual changes are found in the KRB, apparently in Joseph Smith's handwriting. The altered text was published in the 1835 D&C as section 91, and copied from there into the manuscript history of the church in 1843.[22]

There are two full texts of the vision: one in the "Book of Commandments, Law and Covenants, Book B," the other in the KRB. The later was altered by deleting words and inserting additional words above the lines.

The early text reads "for the Lord he is God, and besides him there is none else." In the KRB the word "none" was shortened to "no" and the word "else" was crossed out. Above the line the word "Savior" was added. At that point the later text reads "besides him there is no Savior." Book B does not support the later text. The *Evening and Morning Star* reprint for the passage had the latest reading, it being published in February 1835, three years after the vision was originally written. The D&C has "no Savior."

The process of change seems fairly straightforward. The text was recorded in the KRB in the latter part of 1832 and the crossouts and additions were probably done after the members of the D&C committee were appointed. The early text was basically the same as the three earliest documents.

In the vision of eternal sufferings, Smith and Rigdon said that they saw the sons of perdition. They recorded that "he [God] saveth all save them, and these shall go away into everlasting punishment, which is endless punishment, which is eternal punishment, to reign with the devil and his angels throughout eternity, where their worm dieth not and the fire is not quenched, which is their torment, but the end thereof, neither the place thereof, and their torment, no man knoweth, neither was revealed, neither is, neither will be revealed unto man, save to them who are made partakers thereof."[23]

The text in several areas was then altered to delete words such as "eternal" from "eternal sufferings" and "throughout" from "throughout eternity," which became "in eternity." Most of this was done after the text was copied into the KRB. Some of the changes are cosmetic, but some are important because they affect our understanding of doctrine.

The background for the vision is as follows: Smith and Rigdon were working on a correction of the King James Version of the New Testament; Smith would read the text, and any revisions were related to Rigdon, his scribe, who would rec-

---

21. BC Manuscript, [139], RLDS archives. See LDS D&C 76:109-119; RLDS 76:7-8.
22. Manuscript History, Book A-1:183-92. The background to D&C 76 and the text of the vision from the 1835 D&C was written into the manuscript history by Willard Richards before 8 May 1843. See Willard Richards Journal, LDS archives. See also Jessee, *Papers of Joseph Smith,* 1:372.
23. *The Evening and the Morning Star* 1 (July 1832): [2; whole page no. 10]; LDS D&C 76:44-46; RLDS D&C 76:4.

ord them in the working manuscript. The *Evening and the Morning Star* published the vision with the following background:

> for as we sat doing the work of translation, which the Lord had appointed unto us, we came to the twenty ninth verse of the fifth chapter of John, which was given unto us thus: speaking of the resurrection of the dead who should hear the voice of the Son of man, and shall come forth; they who have done good in the resurrection of the just, and they who have done evil in the resurrection of the unjust. Now this caused us to marvel, for it was given us of the Spirit; and while we meditated upon these things, the Lord touched the eyes of our understanding, and they were opened[24]

When Rigdon and Smith came to the passage of John 5:29, it apparently brought to mind concepts in 1 Corinthians 15:40 and Hebrews 12:22-24. The former reads: "And shall come forth; they that have done good, unto the resurrection of life; and they that have done evil, unto the resurrection of damnation" (John 5:29, KJV).[25]

There are three passages in the Book of Mormon that are based on John 5:29 regarding the resurrection of the just and unjust. All three include the word "damnation."[26] However, as Smith and Rigdon pondered John 5:29,[27] they were no longer comfortable with the traditional concept of heaven and hell.

---

24. *The Evening and the Morning Star* 1 (July 1832): [2; whole page 10]. See LDS D&C 76:15-19; RLDS D&C 76:3. If the words "speaking of the resurrection of the dead who should hear the voice of the Son of man" are considered a part of the revision of John, they were not added to the text of John 5:29 in NT MS #2, folio 4, page 114. The words "and shall all be judged of the son of man" were added after John 5:29; see John 5:30 (JST).

25. No major textual problems in these verses are noted in *The Greek New Testament,* ed. Barbara Aland, Kurt Aland, Johannes Karavidopulos, Carlo M. Martini, and Bruce M. Metzger (Stuttgart, Ger.: German Bible Society, 4th rev. ed., 1994), 332, or in Bruce M. Metzger, *A Textual Commentary on the Greek New Testament* (Stuttgart, Ger.: German Bible Society, 2nd ed., 1994), 180. The Bodmer Papyrus, which contains the gospel of John, was written about 200 C.E. and reads basically the same as the KJV. The reading "of damnation" is currently rendered "of judgment" or "of condemnation."

26. LDS Hel. 12:26/RLDS 4:73 (no word "resurrection"); LDS Mosiah 16:11/RLDS 8:84; and LDS 3 Ne. 26:5/RLDS 6:33. Two previous revelations also included the word damnation ("eternal damnation"), see LDS D&C 19:7; RLDS D&C 18:2 and LDS D&C 29:44; RLDS D&C 28:12. The wording of Acts 24:15 evidently influenced Smith in revising John 5:29 where the word "just" replaces "life" and "unjust" replaces "damnation." See Luke 14:14, "resurrection of the just." The New Testament manuscript of Smith's revision reads: "and shall come forth they who have done good ~~unto~~ <in> the resur[r]ection of ~~life~~ <the just> and they who have done evil, ~~unto~~ <in> the resur[r]ection of ~~damnation~~ the unjust and shall be judged of the son of man" (NT MS #2, folio #4, 114, RLDS archives). Angle brackets are for word(s) written above the line. This reading of the text is not a restoration of the biblical text.

27. NT Manuscript #2, folio #4, 114 (NT Dictated MS, 114), original in RLDS archives. See photo of manuscript page in Richard P. Howard, *Restoration Scriptures: A Study of Their Textual Development* (Independence, MO: Herald House, 1969), 180; (2nd ed., 1995), 295; and Stephen R. Knecht, *The Story of Joseph Smith's Bible Translation* (Salt Lake City: Associated Resea[r]ch Consultants Publication, 1977), 35a. Except for the word "who" replacing "that" twice, the text of John 5:29 is identical to the Phinney 1828 King James Bible that was used during the revision process.

88. To Be a Servant unto Me
From KRB, 10

Revelation received at Hiram, Ohio, on 27 February 1832
for Lincoln Haskins[28]

Hyrum [Hiram] Portage County Ohio Feby. 27th 1832

Behold thus saith the Lord unto you my servants that I have chosen Lincoln [Haskins] to be a servant unto me wherefore verely [verily] I say unto you lit [let] him be ordained and receive the articles and covenants which I have givin [given] unto you and some of the commandments that he may go forth and proclaim my gospel whitherso[e]ver I will send him in the congregation[s] of the wicked and in asmuch as he is faithful I will prosper him even so Amen

89. In the Days of the Apostles
From KRB, 94-95 (cf. LDS and RLDS D&C 74)

Explanation of 1 Corinthians 7:14, given at
Hiram, Ohio, in [ca. 17 February-early March] 1832[29]

An explanation of the 14th verse of the 7 chap[ter] of the first [epistle to the] corinthians

Now in the days of the Apostles the law of circum[cision] was had among the Jews which believed not the Gospel of Jesus Christ And it came to pass that there arose a great contention among the people concerning the law of circumcission for the unbelieving husband was desirous that his children should be circumcised and become subject to the law of Moses which law was fulfilled

and it came to pass that the children being brought up in subjection to the law of Moses and gave heed to the traditions of their fathers and believed not the gospel of Christ wherein they became unholy wherefore for this cause the apostle wrote unto the church giving unto them a commandment not of the Lord but of himself

---

28. Lincoln Haskins was baptized on 21 February 1832. Orson Hyde and Samuel H. Smith visited Haskins near Westfield, New York, on 21 March 1832. Samuel Smith recorded in his journal, "Came across a man by the name of Haskins. He told us that he had been in Kirtland and to Hiram (for he was a brother) and that he had been ordained an elder of the Church, and he told us that he has aeen [seen] Joseph [Smith, Jr.] and Sidney [Rigdon] and that they had had a vision and that they had seen great and marvelous things, and that they had got along wonderfully well on translating. Haskins was strong in the faith" (Samuel H. Smith Journal, typescript, original in LDS archives). This revelation was crossed out with an "X" in the KRB. It was not included in the 1835 D&C.

29. This explanation of scripture has no date even though it was recorded twice in the KRB. The 1835 D&C also has no date as to when the explanation was given. The manuscript history when including the explanation in the narrative for January 1832 dates it to "this period" (Jessee, *Papers of Joseph Smith*, 1:371). The approximate date of 17 February-early March 1832 is based on the revision of the NT that Smith and Rigdon were working on. They were revising John 5 on 16 February and by 20 March had proceeded to about Revelation 11.

that a believer should not be united to an unbeliever except the law of Moses should be done away among them that their children might remain without circumcision and that the tradition might be done away which saith that little children are unholy for it was had among the Jews but little children are holy being sanctified through the atonement of Jesus Christ and this is what these scriptures mean

90. All Things Be Done unto My Glory
From NKW Collection (cf. LDS D&C 78; RLDS D&C 77)

Revelation received at Kirtland, Ohio, on 1 March 1832 concerning the United Firm[30]

Kirtland March 1st 1832

Hearken unto me saith the Lord your God O ye who are ordained unto the High Priesthood of my church who have assembled yourselves together & listen to the councel [counsel] of him who has ordained you from on high who shall speak in your ears the words of wisdom that salvation may be with you in that thing which you have presented before me saith the Lord God

for verily I say unto you the time has come and and is now at hand and behold & lo it must needs be that there be an organization of the Literary and Merchantile establishments of my church both in this place and in th[e] land of Zion for a permient [permanent] and everlasting establishment and firm unto my church to advance the cause which ye have espaused [espoused] to the salvation of man and to th[e] glory of your Father who is in heaven that you may be equal in the bonds of heavenly things yea and earthly things also for the obtaining of heavenly things for if ye are not equal in earthly things ye cannot be equal in obtaining heavenly thing[s] for if ye will that I give unto you a place in the celestial world you must prepare yourselves by doing the thing[s] which I have commanded & required of you

& now verily thus saith the Lord it is expedient that all things be done unto my glory that ye should who are joined together in this firm or in other words that my Servant Newel [K. Whitney] and my servant Joseph [Smith, Jr.] and my servant Sidney [Rigdon] sit in councel [council] with the saints who are in zion otherwise satan seeketh to turn there [their] hearts away from the truth that they become blinded & understand not the things which are prepared for them wherefore a commandment I give unto you to prepare an[d] organize yourselves by an everlasting covenant which cannot be broken

---

30. The KRB also records this revelation as received at Kirtland (11, 15). The 1835 D&C has as a title "The order given of the Lord to Enoch, for the purpose of establishing the poor." In 1835 the revelation to Joseph Smith, Jr., was made to appear to have been given to ancient Enoch. The United Firm had as members high priests (ordained to the High Priesthood) and leaders in the church.

& he who breaketh it shall loose his office & standing in the church and shall be delivered over unto the buffitings of satan untill th[e] day of redemption Behold this is the preparation wherewith I prepare you and the foundation & th[e] ensample [example] which I give unto you whereby you may accomp[l]ish the commandments which are given to you that through the providenc[e] of your Father notwithstanding the tribulation which shall descend upon you you may stand independent above all other creatures beneath the Celestial world that you may come up unto the crown prepared for you and be made rulers over many Kingdoms saith the Lord God the holy one of Israel

Verily Verily I say unto you ye are little children and ye have not as yet understood how great blessings the father has put into his own hands and prepared for you and ye cannot bear all things now nevertheless be of good cheer for I will lead you a long the Kingdom is yours and the blessing thereof are yours and the riches of Eternity ar[e] yours & he who receiveth all things with thankfulness shall be made glorious in the things of this world even an hundred fold yea more wherefore do the things which I have commanded you saith your redeemer even Jesus Christ who prepareth all things before he cometh and then he will come even with the church of the first born & receive you in the cloud and appoint ev[e]ry man his portion & he that is a faithful & wise steward shall inherit all things Amen

<u>Revision</u>

1835 D&C 75
(cf. LDS D&C 78:1, 3-4, 8-9, 14-16, 19-22; RLDS D&C 77:1-4)

The Lord spake unto Enoch, saying, Hearken unto me saith the Lord your God, who are ordained unto the high priesthood of my church, who have assembled yourselves together

.   .   .

for verily I say unto you, the time has come, and is now at hand, and behold, and lo, it must needs be that there be an organization of my *people, in regulating and establishing the affairs* of the *storehouse for the poor of my people,* both in this place and in the land of Zion, *or in other words, the city of Enoch,* for a permanent and everlasting establishment and *order* unto my church, to advance the cause which ye have espoused, to the salvation of man, and to the glory of your Father who is in heaven

.   .   .

And now, verily thus saith the Lord, it is expedient that all things be done unto my glory, that ye should, who are joined together in this *order;* or, in other words, *let* my servant Ahasdah, and my servant *Gazelam, or Enoch,* and my servant *Pelagoram,* sit in council with the saints which are in Zion

.   .   .

that through *my* providence, notwithstanding the tribulation which shall descend upon you, *that the church* may stand independent above all other creatures beneath the celestial world, that you may come up unto the crown prepared for you, and be made rulers over many kingdoms, saith the Lord God, the Holy One of *Zion, who hath established the foundations of Adam-ondi-Ahman; who hath appointed Michael, your prince, and established his feet, and set him upon high; and given unto him the keys of salvation under the counsel and direction of the Holy One, who is without beginning of days or end of life.*

> .   .   .

and he who receiveth all things, with thankfulness, shall be made glorious, *and* the things of this *earth shall be added unto him*, even an hundred fold, yea, more: wherefore do the things which I have commanded you, saith your Redeemer, even *the Son Ahman*, who prepareth all things before he *taketh you; for ye are* the church of the first born, and *he will take* you *up* in the cloud, and appoint every man his portion. And he that is a faithful and wise steward shall inherit all things. Amen.

Commentary: Michael Your Prince

This revelation of 1 March 1832 has one interesting addition. The early text reads: "saith the Lord God the holy one of Israel." The same reading is in the Kirtland Revelations Book. But in the 1835 publication, the word "Israel" was changed to "Zion" and the following added text appeared for the first time: "who hath established the foundations of Adam-ondi-Ahman; who hath appointed Michael, your prince, and established his feet, and set him upon high; and given unto him the keys of salvation under the counsel and direction of the Holy One, who is without beginning of days or end of life."[31]

The wording "Adam-ondi-Ahman" first appeared in the literature of the early church in 1835 when instruction was given on antediluvian priesthood (Document 126). After listing the patriarchs from Adam to Noah, along with their ages when ordained, an accounting is given of a meeting presided over by Adam in the valley of Adam-ondi-Ahman. This information was said to have been recorded in the "book of Enoch." This passage in the D&C contains material that was put together from a number of sources[32] and presented by Joseph Smith to members of the newly formed Council of the Twelve Apostles.

Heber C. Kimball made a general statement on the twelve apostles hearing Joseph Smith: "One evening when we were assembled to receive instructions, the revelation contained in the third section [LDS D&C 107; RLDS D&C 104] of the Book of Doctrine and Covenants, on priesthood was given to brother Joseph as he

---

31. 1835 D&C 75:3; LDS D&C 78:15-16; RLDS D&C 77:3. See Dan. 10:13, 21, and 12:1. Cf. two manuscripts, the KRB, 17, and NKW Collection, neither of which shows this addition.

32. Robert J. Woodford, "How the Revelations in the Doctrine and Covenants Were Received and Compiled," *Ensign* 15 (Jan. 1985): 31.

was instructing us and we praised the Lord."[33] The first part of the section contains material relating to priesthood. Then instructions are related to other sources such as the book of Enoch, a revelation for Zion given in November 1831 and then revised, and a vision of the Seventy.

The 1835 D&C says that Enoch was "430 years old when he was translated."[34] The revision of the KJV Bible adds the following words to the dictated Old Testament manuscript above the line: "& al[l] the days of Enoch were 430 years."[35] The manuscript text was to read: "Zion is fled. <& al[l] the days of Enoch were 430 years> and it came to pass that Mathusalah[.]"[36] Joseph Smith had Enoch's age when translated as 430, while in Genesis 5:23 he was 365 years old. Changes that appear to have been done in 1835 have Adam dying at the age of 1,000 instead of 930 years as in the Bible.

The words "foundations of Adam-ondi-Ahman" were an addition to the text of document 90. William W. Phelps composed a hymn titled "Adam-ondi-Ahman," and recorded in his journal under the date of 3 June 1835, "Com[posed]. a hymn - Adam-ondi-Ahman."[37] This was written a few weeks after his arrival in Kirtland and was published in the next issue of the *Messenger and Advocate*.[38]

So the stimulus for altering the ages of the patriarchs came from 1835 when additional revisions were made to the Old Testament dictated manuscript. The change in the age of Enoch in the Bible revision and included in document 126 was done about the same time. The phrase Adam-ondi-Ahman is a post-1832 term that church members learned was associated with Michael the prince. The 1832 revelation would not have had this term.

91. Go Ye into the World & Preach the Gospel
From KRB, 18-19 (cf. LDS D&C 80; RLDS D&C 79)

*Revelation received at Hiram, Ohio, on 7 March 1832
for Stephen Burnett*

Hiram Portage County Ohio March 7th 1832

Verily thus saith the Lord u[n]to you my se[r]vant Stephen [Burnett] go ye go

---

33. Heber C. Kimball Journal, quoted in Robert J. Woodford, "The Historical Development of the Doctrine and Covenants," Ph.D. diss., Brigham Young University, 1974, 1,399; see also "Extracts from H. C. Kimball's Journal," *Times and Seasons* 6 (15 Apr. 1845): 869; and Stanley B. Kimball, ed., *On the Potter's Wheel: The Diaries of Heber C. Kimball* (Salt Lake City: Signature Books in association with Smith Research Associates, 1987), 207.

34. 1835 D&C 3:24; LDS D&C 107:49; RLDS D&C 104:24.

35. OT MS #1, 19, RLDS archives.

36. See Gen. 7:78-79 (JST); Moses 8:1-2 in PGP.

37. William W. Phelps Journal, LDS archives.

38. *Messenger and Advocate* 1 (June 1835): 144. This issue was probably not published until July. Since Phelps helped with the 1835 D&C, he could have read the revised revelations that mention the place "Adam-Ondi-Ahman." Joseph Smith's "Grammar & A[l]phabet of the Egyptian Language" has interpreted for the "5th Degree," "Beth, The place appointed of God for the residence of Adam; Adam ondi= Ahman" ("Egyptian Alphabet," [1835], 23, LDS archives).

ye into the world & preach the Gospel to every creature that cometh under the Sound of your voice and inasmuch as you desire a companion I will give unto you my servant Eden Smith therefore go ye and preach my gospel whither to the North or to th[e] South, to the East or to the west it mattereth not for you can not go amiss therefore declare th[e] things which you have heard and verily believe and know to be true Behold this is the will of him who hath called you Your Redeemer even Jesus Christ Amen

92. Equal in All Things
From NKW Collection

Revelation received at Hiram, Ohio, in [ca. 8] March 1832
for Sidney Rigdon and Joseph Smith, Jr.,
on the duty of the bishops[39]

Verily thus saith the Lord unto you my servent Sidney [Rigdon] and Joseph [Smith, Jr.] I reveal unto you for your own prophet [profit] and instruction concerning the Bishops of my church what is their duty in the church

behold it is their duty to stand in the office of their Bishoprick [Bishopric] and to fill the judgement seat which I have appointed unto them to administer the benef[i]ts of the church or the overpluss [overplus] of all who are in their stewardships according to the commandments as they are sever[al]ly appointed and the property or that which they receive of the church is not their own but belongeth to the church wherefore it is the property of the Lord and it is for the poor of the church to be administered according to the law

for it is the will of the Lord that the church should be made equal in all things wherefore the bishops are accountable before the Lord for their stewardships to administer of their stewardship in the which they are appointed by commandment jointly with you my servents unto the Lord as well as you my servents or the rest of the church that the benef[i]ts of all may be dedicated unto the Lord that the Lord['s] storehouse may be filled always that ye may all grow in temporal as well as spiritual things

and now verily I say unto you the bishops must needs be seperated [separated] unto their bishoppricks [bishoprics] and judgement seats from care of business but not from claim neither from council wherefore I have given unto you commandment that you should be joined together by covenent [covenant] and bond wherefore see that ye do even as I have commanded

and unto the office of the presidency of the high Priest hood I have given authority to preside with the assistance of his councellers [counselors][40] over all the

---

39. This revelation was not published in the 1835 D&C.

40. Two counselors were chosen on 8 March 1832 to assist Joseph Smith, Jr., as president of the high priesthood. The following note was copied into the KRB: "March 8th 1832 Chose this day and ordained brother Jesse Gause and Broth[er] Sidney [Rigdon] to be my councellors [counselors] of the ministry of the presidency of th[e] high Pri[e]sthood" (10-11).

concerns of the church wherefore stand ye fast claim your Priest hood in authority yet in meekness and I am able to make you abound and be fruitfull and you shall never fall for unto you I have given the keys of the kingdom and if you transgress not they shall never be taken from you wherefore feed my sheep even so amen

93. Glad Tidings of Great Joy
From KRB, 12 (cf. LDS D&C 79; RLDS D&C 78)

Revelation received at Hiram, Ohio, on 12 March 1832 for Jared Carter

A Revelation given to Jerad [Jared] Carter March 12th 1832 in Hiram Portage County Ohio,

Verily verily I say unto you that it is my will that my Servant Jerad [Jared Carter] should go again into the eastern countries from place, to place, and from City, [to] City, in the power of the ordinan[ce] where with he has been ordained proclaiming glad tidings of great joy even the everlasting gospel and I will send upon him the comforter which shall teach him the truth and his way whither he shall go and in as much as he is faithful I will crown him again with sheaves wherefore let your heart be glad my servant Jerad [Jared Carter] and fear not saith your Lord even Jesus Christ Amen

94. Proclaiming the Gospel in the Land of the Living & among Thy brethren
From BC manuscript, RLDS archives (cf. LDS D&C 81; RLDS D&C 80)

Revelation received at Hiram, Ohio, on 15 March 1832 for Jesse Gause[41]

Revelation given to Jesse Gause Hiram Portage March 15 1832 Co. Ohio

Verily verily I say unto you my servant Jesse [Gause] listen to the voice of him who speaketh, to the word of the Lord your God, & hearken to the calling wherewith you are called, even to be a high Priest in my Church & counsellor unto my Servant Joseph [Smith, Jr.], unto whom I have given the keys of the Kingdom which belongs always to the presidency of the high Priest Hood, therefore verily I acknowledge him & will bless him, & also thee, in as much as thou art faithful in

---

41. The text of the revelation for Jesse Gause is from the manuscript of the BC ([139]-140). The KRB contains a copy of the revelation to Gause, who was ordained as a counselor to Joseph Smith, Jr., on 8 March 1832, and after having gone on a mission with Zebedee Coltrin in August 1832, left the church.

Counsel, in the office which I have appointed unto you, & in prayer always vocally & in thy heart in publick & in private also in thy ministry, in proclaiming the gospel in the Land of the Living & among thy brethren; and in doing these things thou wilt do the greatest good unto thy fellow beings, & will promote the glory of him who is your Lord.

wherefore be faithful, stand in the office I have appointed you succor the weak, lift up the hands which hang down, & strengthen the feeble knees; & if thou art faithful unto the end thou shalt have a crown of immortality & eternal life in the mansion which I have prepared in the house of my father behold & lo these are the words of Alpha & Omega even Jesus Christ Amen

Revision

1835 D&C 79
(cf. LDS D&C 81:1; RLDS D&C 80:1)

Verily, verily I say unto you my servant *Frederick G. Williams*, listen to the voice of him who speaketh, to the word of the Lord your God

Commentary: Jesse Gause

This revelation was given on 15 March 1832 at Hiram, Ohio. There are two manuscripts. The first is an additional part of the BC manuscript which originally read: "Verily <verily>I say unto you my servant Jesse[.]"[42] The other is the Kirtland Revelations Book that read when first recorded: "Verily Verily I say unto you my servant Jesse."[43] In both manuscripts the name "Jesse" has been crossed out and the name "Frederick G Williams" inserted in its place. The revelation originally was for Jesse Gause who had been ordained a counselor to Joseph Smith on 8 March 1832.[44] Williams's name was published in the 1835 D&C as indicated in the changed text after Gause was excommunicated from the church.[45]

Some historical background relating to the presidency of the High Priesthood may be helpful. In November 1831, in a revelation dealing with the Church of Christ in Missouri, Joseph Smith was appointed to the presidency of the High Priesthood:

Then cometh the High priesthood which is the greatest of all; wherefore it must needs be that one be appointed of the high priesthood to preside over the priesthood and he shall be called president of the high priesthood of the church, or in other words the presideing [presiding] high priest over the high priesthood of the church ... and again the

---

42. The BC manuscript, [139], in RLDS archives.
43. KRB, 17.
44. See ibid., 10-11.
45. For further study, see Woodford, "Historical Development of the Doctrine and Covenants," 1,017-25; Cook, *Revelations of the Prophet Joseph Smith*, 171-72, 314-15; Robert J. Woodford, "Jesse Gause Counselor to the Prophet," *BYU Studies* 15 (Spring 1975): 262-64; and D. Michael Quinn, "Jesse Gause: Joseph Smith's Little-Known Counselor," ibid. 23 (Fall 1983): 487-93.

duty of the president of the office of the high priesthood is to preside over the whole church and to be like unto [M]oses.[46]

Accordingly, on 25 January 1832, at general conference, Smith was officially ordained president of the High Priesthood by Sidney Rigdon. Orson Pratt recorded the incident in these words: "At this conference, the Prophet Joseph was acknowledged President of the High Priesthood, and hands were laid on him by Elder Sidney Rigdon, who sealed upon his head the blessings which he had formerly received."[47]

Soon after this conference Rigdon and Gause were chosen to be Smith's counselors and were ordained to this high position on 8 March: "March 8th 1832 Chose this day and ordained brother Jesse Gause and Broth[er] Sidney to be my councellors of the ministry of the presidency of th[e] high Pri[e]sthood[.]"[48]

Seven days later a revelation confirmed Gause's call to be both a high priest and counselor: "Verily verily I say unto you my servant Jesse listen to the voice of him who speaketh, to the word of the Lord your God, & hearken to the calling wherewith you are called, even to be a high Priest in my Church & counsellor unto my Servant Joseph, unto whom I have given the keys of the Kingdom which belongs always to the presidency of the high Priest Hood[.]"[49]

This position elevated Gause and Rigdon to a place of authority second only to Smith. Another revelation in March 1832 made this privileged status clear: "and unto the office of the presidency of the high Priest hood I have given authority to preside with the assistance of his councellers [counselors] over all the concerns of the church[.]"[50]

As counselors, these men joined Smith in managing the day-to-day affairs of the church. In April, for example, they went to Independence, Missouri, with President Smith. John Whitmer recorded in his history: "And it came to pass that Joseph the seer and Sidney the Scribe and N. W. [K.] Whitney and one Jesse Gause came to Zion to comfort the Saints and set[t]le some little dif[f]iculties, and regulate the church and affairs concerning it[.]"[51]

While at Independence, Smith's authority was consolidated. According to the minutes recorded in the Far West Record, on 26 April, at a council meeting there, "Joseph Smith jr [was] acknowledged by the High priests in the land of Zion to be President of the High Priesthood, according to commandment and ordination in

46. NKW. See document no. 78; LDS D&C 107:64-66, 91; RLDS D&C 104:31, 42.

47. "History of Orson Pratt. (Written by himself, March, 1858.)," *Deseret News* 8 (2 June 1858): 62, Fillmore City [U.T.]; also Watson, *Orson Pratt's Journals*, 11. Reynolds Cahoon recorded the following: "Wednesday the Elders assemble[d] for Conference the first business ordained the President of the high Preashood [Priesthood] and others then returned holm [home]" (in Reynolds Cahoon Journal, typed copy, original in LDS archives).

48. KRB, 10-11.

49. "Revelation given to Jesse Gause Hiram Portage March 15 1832 Co. Ohio," BC Manuscript, [139], RLDS archives.

50. Document no. 92.

51. Bruce N. Westergren, ed., *From Historian to Dissident: The Book of John Whitmer* (Salt Lake City: Signature Books, 1995), 102.

Ohio."[52] At two other meetings in Independence, Gause was listed as "one of the President's councillors" and "Counsillor to the President."[53]

After Gause served on a mission with Zebedee Coltrin in August, nothing more was heard about him except that he denied the faith.[54] An entry in Joseph Smith's Diary for 3 December 1832 clearly refers to Gause: "held a conference in the Evening Br Jese and Mogan and William Mclelen was excommunicated from the church &c[.]"[55]

The Kirtland Council Minute Book as early as 22 January 1833 mentions Frederick G. Williams as a counselor,[56] and a revelation calling him to this position is dated 6 January.[57] In March Williams was formally ordained as a counselor.

When the revelations were copied into the Kirtland Revelations Book, the office of counselor was listed by Williams's name three times:

1. Revelation of 6 December 1832: "given by Joseph the seer and writ[t]en by Sidney the scribe and Councellor & Transcribed by Frederick assistant scribe and councellor."[58]
2. Revelation of 27-28 December 1832: "Given by Joseph the seer and writ[t]en by F.G. Williams assistan[t] scribe and councellor to s[ai]d Joseph."[59]
3. Revelation of 3 January 1833: "Given by Joseph the seer, and writ[t]en by Frederick assistant scribe and councellor."[60]

All of these dates fall before 22 January and well before 8 March 1833 when Williams and Rigdon were said to be equal with Smith in holding the "keys of this Last Kingdom."[61]

Williams was ordained to the high priesthood (a high priest) on 25 October 1831,[62] but was not ordained to the presidency until a year after the revelation was given to Gause.[63] The BC manuscript indicated by the superscription that "Jesse Gause" was the "Jesse" referred to in the text, and the handwritten index to the Kirtland Revelations Book designates page 17 as a "Revelation to Jesse Gauze March 15 - 1832." The index of the 1835 D&C lists the March 1832 document as a revelation "to F. G. Williams."

52. Cannon and Cook, *Far West Record*, 44.

53. Ibid., 46-47.

54. Zebedee Coltrin Journal. The Far West record has added after listing Gause's position for the meeting of 30 April: "(denied the faith)."

55. Jessee, *Papers of Joseph Smith*, 2:4. It is evident that Gause had already left the church while William McLellin was still functioning as a high priest in Missouri.

56. Kirtland Council Minute Book, 6, LDS archives.

57. Document no. 106. The revelation stated, "thou art called to be a councellor and scribe unto my servant Joseph." Williams had already been acting as a scribe to Smith since 20 July 1832.

58. KRB, 32.

59. Ibid., 46.

60. Ibid., 48.

61. Document no. 109; See LDS D&C 90:6; RLDS D&C 87:3; Kirtland Council Minute Book, 17.

62. Cannon and Cook, *Far West Record*, 19.

63. Kirtland Council Minute Book, 17; Ordination Certificate, LDS archives, reproduced in Frederick G. Williams [III], "Frederick G. Williams, 'Veteran in the Work of the Lord'," *The Carpenter: Reflections of Mormon Life* 1 (Spring 1969): 19.

The 1981 edition of the LDS D&C states in the historical heading to section 81, "Frederick G. Williams is called to be a high priest and a counselor in the First Presidency," though it also mentions the 1835 textual inaccuracy: "The historical records show that when this revelation was received in March 1832, it called Jesse Gause to the office of counselor to Joseph Smith in the First Presidency." Then, in the face of the historical records and in order to perpetuate the 1835 published variant and to justify it, the heading continues: "However, when he failed to continue in a manner consistent with this appointment, the call was subsequently transferred to Frederick G. Williams."[64]

The call could not have been "transferred" to Williams who was already a high priest, whereas Gause's call was to become a high priest and counselor. Williams's call came separately in January 1833, two months prior to his ordination as a counselor. The March 1832 revelation states that the recipient would be blessed as he proclaimed the gospel "among thy brethren," which refers to Gause's former Shaker brethren. The revelation ends: "these are the words of Alpha and Omega, even Jesus Christ." Why the text would be altered and published through the years as referring to Williams is not known, but it demonstrates again that the 1835 D&C committee was not primarily concerned with historical accuracy.

95. The Spirit of Man in the Likeness of His Person
From the Manuscript History, Book A-1:192-95
(cf. LDS D&C 77)

*Explanation of part of Revelation, chapters 4-11
given at Hiram, Ohio, in [ca. 20] March 1832*[65]

[Question] What is the sea of glass spoken of by John 4th chapter, and 6th verse of the Revelation?

[Answer] It is the earth in its sanctified, immortal and eternal state.

[Question] What are we to understand by the four beasts spoken of by John in the 4th chapter, and 6th verse of Revelation?

[Answer] They are figurative expressions, used by the Revelator, John, in describing heaven, the paradise of God, the happiness of men, and of beasts, and of creeping things, and of the fowls of the air; that which is spiritual being in the likeness of that which is temporal, and that which is temporal in the likeness of that which is spiritual the spirit of man in the likeness of his person; as also the spirit of the beast, and every other creature which God has created.

[Question] Are the four beasts limited to individual beasts, or do they represent classes or orders?

---

64. 1981 edition of LDS D&C, p. 149.

65. Smith and Rigdon had revised the NT up to Revelation 11 prior to this explanation. They were told to "omit the translation for the present time" on 20 March 1832. This explanation was published in the 1876 LDS D&C.

[Answer] They are limited to four individual beasts, which were shown to John to represent the glory of the classes of beings in their destined order, or sphere of creation, in the enjoyment of their eternal felicity.

[Question] What are we to understand by the eyes and wings which the beasts had?

[Answer] Their eyes are a representation of light and knowledge, that is, they are full of knowledge; and their wings are a representation of power, to move, to act &c.

[Question] What are we to understand by the four and twenty elders spoken of by John?

[Answer] We are to understand that these elders whom John saw, were elders who had been faithful in the work of the ministry, and were dead, who belonged to the seven churches, and were then in the Paradise of God.

[Question] What are we to understand by the book which John saw, which was sealed on the back with seven seals?

[Answer] We are to understand that it contains the revealed will, mysteries and works of God: the hidden things of his economy concerning this earth during the seven thousand years of its continuance or its temporal existence.

[Question] What are we to understand by the seven seals with which it was sealed?

[Answer] We are to understand that the first seal contains the things of the first thousand years, and the second also of the second thousand years, and so on until the seventh.

[Question] What are we to understand by the four angels spoken of by John 7th chapter and first verse of Revelations?

[Answer] We are to understand that they are four angels sent forth from God, to whom is given power over the four parts of the earth, to save life and to destroy; these are they who have the everlasting gospel to commit to every Nation, kindred, tongue, and people, having power to shut up the heavens, to seal up unto life, or to cast down to the regions of darkness.

[Question] What are we to understand by the angel ascending from the east, Revelations, seventh chapter, and sechond [second] verse?

[Answer] We are to understand that the angel ascending from the east is he to whom is given the seal of the living God over the twelve tribes of Israel, wherefore he crieth unto the four angels having the everlasting gospel, saying, hurt not the earth, neither the sea, nor the trees till we have sealed the servants of our God in their foreheads; and if you will receive it, this is Elias which was to come, to gather to gether the tribes of Israel, and restore all things.

[Question] What time are the things spoken of in this chapter to be accomplished?

[Answer] They are to be accomplished in the sixth thousandth year, or the opening of the sixth seal.

[Question] What are we to understand by sealing the one hundred and forty four thousand out of all the tribes of Israel, Twelve thousand out of every tribe?

[Answer] We are to understand that those who are sealed are high priests ordained unto the holy order of God to administer the everlasting gospel, for they are they who are ordained out of every nation, kindred, tongue and people by the angels to whom is given power over the nations of the earth to bring as many as will come, to the church of the first born.

[Question] What are we to understand by the sounding of the trumpets mentioned in the eighth chapter of Revelations?

[Answer] We are to understand that as God made the world in six days, and on the seventh day he finished his work and sanctified it, and also formed man out of the dust of the earth; even so in the beginning of the seven thousandth year will the Lord God sanctify the earth and complete the salvation of man, and Judge all things and shall redeem all things, except that which he hath not put into his power when he shall have sealed all things unto the end of all things: and the sounding of the trumpets of the seven angels, are the preparing and finishing of his work in the beginning of the seven thousandth year, the preparing of the way before the time of his coming.

[Question] When are the things to be accomplished which are written in the ninth chapter of Revelations?

[Answer] They are to be accomplished after the opening of the seventh seal, before the coming of Christ.

[Question] What are we to understand by the little book, which was eaten by John, as mentioned in the tenth chapter of Revelations?

[Answer] We are to understand that it was a mission and an ordinance for him to gather the tribes of Israel. Behold this is Elias, who, as it is written, must come and restore all things.

[Question] What is to be understood by the two witnesses in the el[e]venth chapter of Revelations?

[Answer] They are two prophets that are to be raised up to the Jewish nation in the last days, at the time of the restoration, and to prophecy to the Jews after they are gathered and have built the City of Jerusalem, in the land of their fathers.

96. Let Whatsoever Is Done
Be Done in the Name of the Lord
From NKW Collection

Revelation received at Hiram, Ohio, on 20 March 1832
concerning paper for the Book of Commandments
and the translation of the New Testament[66]

[Question] First Shall we procure the paper required of our breatheren [brethren] in thus [their] letter and carry it with us or not and if we do what moneys shall we use for that purpose[?]

---

66. This revelation was not included in the 1835 D&C.

[Answer] It is expedient saith the Lord unto you that the paper shall be purchased for the printing of the book of the Lord[']s commandments and it must needs be that you take it with [you] for it is not expedient that my servent Martin [Harris] should as yet go up unto the land of Zion let the purchase be made by the Bishop of [if] it must needs be by hire let whatsoever is done be done in the name of the Lord

[Question] Second shall we finish the translation of the New Testament before we go to Zion or wait till we return[?]

[Answer] It is expedient saith the Lord that there be no delays and this saith the Lord for the greatest good and benef[i]t of the church Wherefore omit the translation for the present time

97. When Ye Do Not What I Say, Ye Have No Promise
From 1835 D&C 86 (cf. LDS D&C 82; RLDS D&C 81)

Revelation received at Independence, Missouri, on 26 April 1832 concerning the United Firm[67]

Revelation given April, 1832, showing the order given to Enoch and the church in his day.

Verily, verily I say unto you, my servants, that inasmuch as you have forgiven one another your trespasses, even so I the Lord forgive you; nevertheless there are those among you who have sinned exceedingly; yea, even all of you have sinned, but verily I say unto you, beware from henceforth and refrain from sin lest sore judgments fall upon your heads: for unto whom much is given much is required; and he who sins against the greater light shall receive the greater condemnation. Ye call upon my name for revelations, and I give them unto you; and inasmuch as ye keep not my sayings which I give unto you, ye become transgressors, and justice and judgment is the penalty which is affixed unto my law: therefore, what I say unto one I say unto all, watch, for the adversary spreadeth his dominions and darkness reigneth; and the anger of God kindleth against the inhabitants of the earth; and none doeth good, for all have gone out of the way.

And now verily I say unto you, I the Lord will not lay any sin to your charge: go your ways and sin no more: but unto that soul who sinneth shall the former sins return, saith the Lord your God.[68]

And again, I say unto you, I give unto you a new commandment, that you may

67. When this document was published in 1835, certain names were used instead of individuals' real names as though this document was "showing the order given to Enoch and the church in his day." No known manuscript exits. The names of those individuals who can be identified are given in brackets. See David J. Whittaker, "Substituted Names in the Published Revelations of Joseph Smith," *BYU Studies* 23 (Winter 1983): 103-12. At the meeting held in Independence, "A Revelation [was] received through him [Joseph Smith, Jr.] whom the Church has appointed respecting organization" (Cannon and Cook, *Far West Record*, 45).
68. See document no. 64; LDS and RLDS D&C 58.

understand my will concerning you; or, in other words, I give unto you directions
how you may act before me, that it may turn to you for your salvation. I the Lord
am bound when ye do what I say, but when ye do not what I say, ye have no
promise.

Therefore, verily I say unto you, that it is expedient for my servant Alam [Ed-
ward Partridge] and Ahashdah [Newel K. Whitney], Mahalaleel [Sidney Gilbert]
and Pelagoram [Sidney Rigdon], and my servant Gazelam [Joseph Smith, Jr.], and
Horah [John Whitmer], and Olihah [Oliver Cowdery], and Shalemanasseh [Wil-
liam W. Phelps], and Mehemson,[69] be bound together by a bond and covenant
that cannot be broken by transgression except judgment shall immediately follow,
in your several stewardships, to manage the affairs of the poor, and all things pertaining to the bishopric both in the land of Zion, and in the land of Shinehah [Kirt-
land], for I have consecrated the land of Shinehah [Kirtland] in mine own due time
for the benefit of the saints of the Most High, and for a stake to Zion:

for Zion must increase in beauty, and in holiness: her borders mush be enlarged;
her stakes must be strengthened: yea, verily I say unto you, Zion must arise and put
on her beautiful garments: therefore I give unto you this commandment, that ye
bind yourselves by this covenant, and it shall be done according to the laws of the
Lord. Behold here is wisdom, also, in me, for your good. And you are to be equal,
or in other words, you are to have equal claims on the properties, for the benefit of
managing the concerns of your stewardships, every man according to his wants and
his needs, inasmuch as his wants are just: and all this for the benefit of the church of
the living God, that every man may improve upon his talent, that every man may
gain other talents; yea, even an hundred fold, to be cast into the Lord's storehouse,
to become the common property of the whole church, every man seeking the interest of his neighbor, and doing all things with an eye single to the glory of God.

This order[70] I have appointed to be an everlasting order unto you and unto your
successors, inasmuch as you sin not: and the soul that sins against this covenant, and
hardeneth his heart against it, shall be dealt with according to the laws of my
church, and shall be delivered over to the buffitings of satan until the day of
redemption.

And now verily I say unto you, and this is wisdom, make unto yourselves
friends with the mammon of unrighteousness, and they will not destroy you. Leave
judgment alone with me, for it is mine and I will repay. Peace be with you; my
blessings continue with you, for even yet the kingdom is yours, and shall be forever
if you fall not from your steadfastness; even so. Amen.

69. The text probably had the name Jesse or Jesse Gause when originally recorded. It is not
known if the 1835 pseudonym "Mehemson" was used in place of United Firm member Gause
or for Martin Harris. A pseudonym spelled "Mahemson" was used for Harris in the 1835 D&C
for an April 1834 revelation. Gause was a high priest and counselor to Joseph Smith, Jr., and in
attendance at the 26 April 1832 meeting at Independence. Harris was not in attendance at the
1832 meeting when this revelation was received. Later Harris became a member of the United
Firm.

70. The United Firm at Independence was named the Gilbert, Whitney & Company at a
meeting held on 27 April 1832 (Cannon and Cook, *Far West Record*, 45).

98. All Children Have Claim upon Their Parents Untill They Are of Age
From NKW Collection (cf. LDS D&C 83; RLDS D&C 82)

Revelation received at Independence, Missouri, on 30 April 1832 in addition to the laws of the Church of Christ[71]

Zion May [1st?] 1832

Verily thus saith the Lord in addition to the laws of the church concerning women and children who belong to the church who have lost their husbands or fathers women have claim on their husbands untill they are taken and if they are not found transgressors they remain upon their inheritences [inheritances] all children have claim upon their parents untill they are of age and after that they have claim upon the church or in otherwords the Lord[']s storehouse for inheritences [inheritances]

Revision

1835 D&C 88
(cf. LDS D&C 83:1-6; RLDS D&C 82:1-2)

Verily thus saith the Lord, in addition to the laws of the church concerning women and children, *those* who belong to the church, who have lost their husbands or fathers: women have claim on their husbands *for their maintainance* until *their husbands are taken*; and if they are not found transgressors they *shall have fellowship in the church, and if they are not faithful, they shall not have fellowship in the church*; yet they may remain upon their inheritances *according to the laws of the land.*

All children have claim upon their parents *for their maintainance* until they are of age; and after that, they have claim upon the church; or, in other words *upon* the Lord's storehouse, *if their parents have not wherewith to give them* inheritances. *And the storehouse shall be kept by the consecrations of the church, that widows and orphans shall be provided for, as also the poor. Amen.*

Commentary: Women and children have claim

In a revelation received at Independence, Missouri, on 30 April 1832, instructions were given concerning the inheritances of women and children. The text is the same in the Newel K. Whitney Collection, Book B, and in the *Evening and the*

---

71. The date is recorded as "30 apr. 1832" on the reverse side of this manuscript. Book B and the KRB (93) have the date 30 April 1832. A few minor word changes were made soon after this copy was made. The text follows the final reading.

Morning Star, published in January 1833.[72]

The text of this revelation was copied into the Kirtland Revelations Book by Frederick G. Williams. This text would have been written at the earliest in December 1833 and the latest by 18 August 1834. The text in the Kirtland Revelations Book is already revised as recorded in that volume,[73] which agrees with the revised text of the 1835 D&C. The revision was completed before the formal committee was appointed on 24 September 1834. This is one of the earliest revisions known to have been made that later appeared in the 1835 D&C.

The added words "according to the laws of the land" are not in the early text but are evidently related to a case mentioned in the *Evening and the Morning Star* (July 1833), which states: "When a disciple comes to Zion for an inheritance, it is his duty, if he has any thing to consecrate to the Lord, for the benefit of the poor and the needy, or to purchase lands, to consecrate it according to the law of the Lord, and also according to the law of the land; and the Lord has said, that in keeping his laws, we have no need to break the laws of the land."[74]

---

72. Robert J. Woodford wrote about the copy of the revelation found in "Book of Commandments, Law and Covenants; Book B" (handwriting of Sidney Gilbert), as follows: "In fact, his copy contains some significant changes that were not made until after January 1833" (Woodford, "Historical Development of the Doctrine and Covenants," 1,042). This should refer to the KRB and not Book B. Book B contains the same wording as the NKW Collection and the *Evening and the Morning Star* (Jan. 1833). The only difference is between the early text and what is recorded in the KRB (93) and published in the 1835 D&C.

73. KRB, 93.

74. "The Elders Stationed in Zion to the Churches Abroad, in Love Greeting," *The Evening and the Morning Star* 2 (July 1833): 110.

6. Priesthood Development,
August 1832–April 1834

99. Whoso Receiveth You
as a Little Child Receiveth My Kingdom
From KRB, 19-20 (cf. LDS D&C 99; RLDS D&C 96)

Revelation received at Hiram, Ohio, on 29 August 1832
for John Murdock

Hiram Portage County Ohio August 29th 1832

Behold thus saith the Lord unto you my servant John [Murdock] thou art called to go unto the eastern countries from house to hous[e] and from Village to Village and from City to City to proclai[m] mine everlasting Gospel unto the in habitants thereof in the midst of persecution and wickedness and whos[o] receivet[h] you receiveth me and you shall have power to declare my word in the demonstration of my holy Spirit and whoso receiveth you as a little child receiveth my Kingdom and blessed are they for they shall obtain mercy, and whoso rejecteth you shall be rejected of my Father and his house and you shall cleanse your feet in the secret places by the way for a testamony against them and behold and lo I come quickly to Judgment to convince all of their ungodly deeds which they have commit[t]ed against me as it is writ[t]en of me in the volum[e] of the book

and now verily I say unto you that it is not expedient that you should go untill your children are provided for and kindly sent up unto the Bishop in Zion, and after a few years if thou desirest of me thou mayest go up also unto the goo[d]ly land to possess thin[e] in heritence otherwise thou shalt continue proclaiming my gospel untill thou be taken Amen

by Joseph the seer and writ[t]en by F.G. Williams Scribe[1]

---

1. Frederick G. Williams became a scribe for Joseph Smith, Jr., on 20 July 1832 (Statement of Frederick G. Williams, LDS archives). Williams was forty-four years old.

100. This Is the Word of the Lord
From NKW Collection (cf. LDS D&C 84; RLDS D&C 83)

Revelation received at Kirtland, Ohio,
on 22 and 23 September 1832 concerning
the city New Jerusalem and the two priesthoods[2]

A revelation given in Kirtland the 22d & 23d day of Sept AD 1832

A revelation of Jesus Christ unto his servant Joseph [Smith, Jr.] and six Elders as they united there [their] hearts in lifting there [their] voice on high, yea the word of the Lord concerning his church established in the last days for the restoration of his people as he has spoken by the mouth of his prophets and for the gathering, of his saints to stand upon mount Zion which shall be called the city New Jerusalem, which city shall be built begin[n]ing at the temple lot which is appointed by the finger of the Lord in the western boundaries of the State of Misso[uri] and dedicated by the hand of Joseph [Smith, Jr.] and others with whom the Lord was well pleased,

verily this is the word of the Lord, that the city New Jerusalem shall be built by the gath[e]ring of the saints begin[n]ing at this place, even the place of the Temple, which Temple shall be reared in this generation for verely [verily] this generation shall not all pass away untill an house shalt be built unto the Lord and a cloud shall rest upon it which cloud shall be even the glory of the Lord which shall fill the house,

and the sons of Moses according to the holy Priesthood which he received under the hand of his father in Law Jethro, and Jethro received it u[n]der the hand of Caleb and Caleb received it under the hand of Elihu and Elihu und[er] the hand of Jeremy[3] and Jeremy under the hand of Gad and Gad under the hand of Esaius[4] and Esaius received it under the hand of God, Esaius also lived in the days of Abraham and was blessed of him which Abraham received the Priesthood from Melchesedec who received it through the lin[e]age of his fathers even till Noah, and from Noah till Enoch, through the lin[e]age of those fathers and from Enoch to abel who was slain by the conspiracy of his brother who received the Priesthood by the commandment of God by the hand of his father Adam who was the first man, which Priesthood continueth in the church of God in all generations and is without begin[n]ing of days or end of years

and the Lord confirmed a priesthood also upon Aaron and his seed throughout all the generation[s] of the Jews which priesthood also continueth and abideth for ever with the Priesthood which is after the holiest order of God, and this greater

---

2. The index for the KRB has as a description of this revelation, "explaining the two priest hoods and commissioning the Apostles to preach the gospel." The apostles were evidently those high priests at the meeting.

3. In the NT, Jeremy is the name for Jeremiah the prophet.

4. The name Esaius is not in the OT. It is possible that Esaius is a scribal error and the name should be Esaias as in the 1835 D&C 4. In the KJV NT, Esaias is used for the prophet Isaiah. The person named in this text is said to have "lived in the days of Abraham."

Priesthood adminestereth [administereth] the gospel and holdeth the key of the misteries [mysteries] of the kingdom, even the key of the knowledge of God therefore in the ordinences [ordinances] thereof the power of Godliness is manifest and without the ordinences [ordinances] thereof, and the authority of the Priesthood, the power of Godliness is not manifest unto man in the flesh, for without this no man can see the face of God even the father and live,

now this Moses plainly taught to the children of Israel in the wilderness, and saught [sought] diligently to sanctify his people that they might behold the face of God, but they hardened the[i]r hearts and could not endure his presence therefore the Lord in his wrath (for his anger was kindled against them) swore that they should not enter into his rest, which rest is the fulness of his glory while in the wilderness, therefore he took Moses out of there [their] midst and the holy Priesthood also, and the lesser Priesthood continued, which Priesthood holdeth the keys of the minist[e]ring of Angels and the preparitory [preparatory] gospel, which gospel is the gospel of repentance and of Baptism, and the remission of sins, and the Law of carnal commandments which the lord in his wrath caused to continue with the house of Aaron among the children of Israel until John whom God raised up being fillid [filled] with the holy ghost from his Mother['s] womb, for he was baptised while he was yet in the womb and was ordained by the Angel of God at the time he was eight days old unto this power to overthrow the kingdom of the Jews and to make straight the way of the Lord before the face of his people to prepare them for the coming of the Lord in whose hand is given all power,

and again, the offices of Elder & Bishop are necessary appendages belon[g]ing unto the high Priesthood, and again the offices of Teacher and Deacon are necessary appendages belonging to the lesser Priesthood, which priesthood was confirmed upon Aaron and his sons

therefore as I said, concerning the Sons of Moses, for the sons of Moses, and also the sons of Aaron shall offer an acceptable offering and sacrifice in the house of the Lord which house shalt be built unto the Lord in this generation upon the consecrated spot as I have appointed and the sons of Moses, and of Aaron shall be filled with the glory of the Lord upon mount Zion in the Lord['s] house whose sons are ye, and also many whom I have called and sent forth to build up my church

for whoso is faithful unto the attaining of these two Priesthoods of which I have spoken and the magnifying there [their] calling are sanctified by the spir[i]t unto the renewing of there [their] bodies that they become the sons of Moses and of Aaron and the seed of Abraham, and the church and kingdom and the elect of God and also all they who receive this Priesthood receiveth me saith the Lord for he that receiveth my servants, rece[i]veth me, and he that receiveth me receiveth my father, and he that receiveth my father, receiveth my father's kingdom, therefore all that my father hath shall be given unto him

and this according to the oath and the covenant which belongeth to the Priesthood, therefore all those who receive the Priesthood, receiveth this oath and covenant of my father which he cannot break neither can it be mooved [moved], but whoso breaketh this covenant after he hath received it, and altogether turneth therefrom shall not have forgiv[e]ness in this world nor in the world to come and all those who come not unto this Priesthood, which ye have received, which I now confirm upon you who are present this day viz the 23d, day of September AD 1832 Eleven high Priests save one[5] by by mine own voice out of the heavens and even I have given the heavenly hosts and mine Angels charge concerning you,

and I now give unto you a commandment to beware concerning yourselves to give heed dilligently to the words of eternal life for you shall live by ev[e]ry word that proce[e]deth forth from the mouth of God

for the word of the Lord is truth and whatsoever is truth is light, and whatsoever is light is spirit even the spirit of Jesus Christ, and the spirit giveth light to ev[e]ry man that cometh into the world, and the spirit enlight[e]neth ev[e]ry man through the world that h[e]ark[e]neth to the voice of the spirit, and ev[e]ry one that h[e]ark[e]neth to the voice of the spirit cometh unto God even the father and the father teacheth him of the covenant which he hath renewed and confirmed upon you which is confirmed upon you for your sakes and not for your sakes only, but for the sake of the whole world, and the whole world lieth in sin and groaneth under darkness and under the bondage of sin and by this you may know they are under the bondage of sin because they come not unto me for whoso cometh not unto me is under the bondage of sin, and whoso receiveth not my voice is not acqua[i]nted with my voice and is not of me, and, by this you may know the righteous from the wicked, and that the whole world groaneth under sins and darkness even now,

and your minds in times past have been darkened because of unbelief and because you have treated lightly the things you have received which vanity and unbelief hath brought the whole church under condemnation and this condemnation resteth upon the children of Zion even all, and they shall remain under this condemnation until they repent and remember the new covenant even the book of Mormon and the former commandments which I have given them, not only to say but to do according to that which I have writ[t]en that they may bring forth fruit meet for there [their] father[']s kingdom otherwise there remaineth a sco[u[rge and a Judgment to be poured out upon the children of Zion for shall the children of the kingdom pollute my holy land [?] verily verily I say unto you na[y].

verily, verily, I say unto you who now hear my words which is my voice blessed are you inasmuch as you receive these things for I will forgive you of your sins with this commandment that you remain steadfast in your minds in solemnity and the spirit of p[r]ayer in bearing testamony [testimony] to all the world of those things which are communicated unto you,

therefore go ye into all the world and whatsoever place ye cannot go into ye shall send, that the testamony [testimony] may go from you into all the world unto every creature, and as I said unto mine apostles even so I say unto you, for you are mine Apostles, even God[']s High priests ye are they whom my father hath given

---

5. The earlier portion of this revelation obtained on 22 September 1832 was received in the presence of six elders. On the next day, 23 September, ten high priests were present. Rather than writing that there were ten high priests, the text reads, "Eleven high Priests save one."

me, ye are my friends therefore as I said unto mine Apostles I say unto you again that ev[e]ry soul who believeth on your words and are baptized by water for the remission of their sins shall receive the holy-ghost, and these signs shall follow them,

in my name they shall do many wonderful works, in my name they shall cast out devels [devils] in my name they shall heal the sick in my name they shall open the eyes of the blind and unstop the ears of the deaf, and the tongue of the dumb shall speak, and if any man shall administer poison unto them it shall not hurt them, and the poison of a serpent shall not have power to harm them, but a commandment I give unto them that they shall not boast themselves of these things, neither speak them before the world for these things are given unto you for your proffet [profit] and for salvation,

verily, verily I say unto you he who beleiveth not on your words, and are not baptized by water in my name for the remission of there [their] sins, that they may receive the holy ghost Shall be damned and shall not come into my father['s] kingdom where my father and I am and this revelation unto you and commandment is in force from this very hour upon all the world, and this gospel is unto all who have not received it, but verily I say unto all those to whom the kingdom has been given from you it must be preached unto them that they shall repent of the[i]r former evil works for they are to be upbra[i]ded for there [their] evil hearts of unbelief and your brethren in Zion for there [their] rebellion against you at the time I sent you,

and again I say unto you my friends, for from henceforth I shall call you friends, it is expedient that I give unto you this commandment that you become even as my friends in days when I was with them in trav[e]lling to preach this gospel in my power for I suffered them not to have purse or scrip, neither two coats behold I send you out to proove [prove] the world, and the Laborer is worthy of his hire and any man that shall go and preach this gospel of the kingdom, and fail not to continue faithful in all things shall not be weary in mind neither darkened neither body limb, or Joint and an hair of your head shall not fall to the ground unnoticed and they shall not go hungry, neither athirst,

therefore take no thought for the morrow for what ye shall eat or what ye shall drink or wherewithall ye shall be clothed for consider the lillies of the field how they grow they toil not neither do they spin and the kingdoms of the world in all the[i]r glory are not ar[r]ayed like one of these for your father who art in heaven knoweth that you have need of all these thing[s] therefore let the morrow take thought for the things of itself, neither take ye thought before hand what ye shall say but treasure up in your minds continually the words of Life and it shall be given you in the very hour that po[r]tion that shall be meeted unto ev[e]ry man

therefore let no man among you (for this commandment is unto all the faithful who are called of God in the church unto the ministry) therefore let no man from this hour take purse or scrip that goeth forth to proclaim this gospel of the kingdom behold I send you out to reproove [reprove] the world of all there [their] unrighteous deeds and to teach them of a Judgment which is to come and whoso receiveth you there I will be also for I will go before your face I will be on your right hand and on your lift [left] and my spirit shall be in your hearts and mine Angels round about you to bear you up whoso receiveth you receiveth me and the same will feed you and clothe you, and give you money and he who feedeth you or clothe you or giveth you money shall in no wise loose his reward and he that doeth not these things is not my deciple [disciple], by this you may know my deciples [disciples] he that receiveth you not, go away from him, alone by yourselves and cleanse your feet even with water, pure water, whether in heat or in cold and bare testamony [testimony] of it unto your father which is in heaven and return not again unto that man, and in whatsoever village or city ye enter do likewise, nevertheless search dilligently and spare not,

wo unto that house, or that village or city that rejecteth you or your words or testamony [testimony] concerning me, wo I say again unto that house or that village or city that rejecteth you or your words or your testamony [testimony] of me for I the Almighty have laid my hand upon the nations to sco[u]rge them for the[i]r wickedness and plagues shall go forth and it shall not be taken from the earth untill I have completed my work which shall be cut short in righteousness until all shall know me who remain even from the least unto the greatest and shall be filled with the knowledge of the Lord and shall see eye to eye, and shall lift up the voice, and with the voice together sing this new song, saying

the lord hath brought again Zion the Lord hath redeemed his people Israel, according to the election of grace which was brought to pass by the faith and covenant of the[i]r fathers, the Lord hath redeemed his people and Satan is bound and time is no longer the Lord hath gathered all things in one the Lord hath brought down Zion from above the Lord hath brought up Zion from beneath the earth hath travailed and brought forth her strength and truth is established in her bowels and the heavens hath smiled upon her and she is clothed with the glory of her God for he standeth in the midst of his people, glory and honor and power and might be ascribed to our God for he is full of mercy Justice grace and truth and peace for ever and ever Amen

And again verily verily I say unto you it is expedient that ev[e]ry man who goes forth to proclaim mine everlasting gospel that in as much as they have families and receive monies by gift they should send it unto them or make use of if for there [their] benefit as the Lord shall direct them for thus it seemeth me good and let all those who have not families who receive monies send it up unto the Bishop in Zion or unto the Bishop in Ohio that it may be consecrated for the bringing forth of the revelations and the printing thereof and for the establishing of Zion

and if any man shall give unto any of you a coat, or a suit take the old and cast it unto the poor and go your way rejoicing and if any man among you be strong in the spirit let him take with him he that is weak that he may be edified in all meekness that he may become strong also

therefore take with you those who are ordained unto the lesser Priesthood, and send them before you to make appointments and to prepare the way, and to fill appointments that yourselves are not able to fill, behold this is the way that mine Apostles in ancient days built up my church unto me,

therefore let ev[e]ry man stand in his own office, and labour in his own calling and let not the head say unto the feet it hath no need of the feet for with out the feet how shall the body be able to stand, also the body hath ne[e]d of ev[e]ry member that all may be edified together that the system may be kept perfect,

and behold the high Priest[s] should travel and also the Elders and also the lesser Priests, but the Teachers and deacons should be appointed to watch over the church to be a standing minister unto the church,

and the Bishop also should travel round about and among all the churches searching after the poor to administer to the[i]r wants by humbling the rich and the proud he should also imploy [employ] an agent for to take charge and to do his secular [secular] business as he shall direct nevertheless let the Bishop[6] go unto the city of New York and also to the city of Albany and also to the city of Boston and warn the people of those cities with the sound of the gospel with a loud voice of the desolation and utter abolishment which awaits them if they do reject these things, for if they do reject these things the hour of the[i]r Judgment is nigh and there [their] house shall be left unto them desolate, let him trust in me and he shall not be confounded and an hair of his head shall not fall to the ground unnoticed;

and verily I say unto you the rest of my servants go ye forth as your circumstances shall permit in your several callings unto the great and notable cities and villages reprooving [reproving] the world in righteousness of all the[i]r unrighteous and ungodly deeds setting forth clearly and understandingly the desolation of abomination in the last days for with you saith the Lord Almighty I will rend there [their] kingdoms I will not only shake the earth but the star[r]y heavens shall tremble also for I the Lord have put forth mine hand to exhert [exert] the powers of heaven ye cannot see it now, yet a little while and ye shall see it and know that I am and that I will come and reign with my people I am Alpha and Omega the begin[n]ing and the end Amen

Transcribed by F[rederick]. G. Williams for N[ewel]. K. Whitney and Joseph the Seer

Revision

1835 D&C 4
(cf. LDS D&C 84:27-28; RLDS D&C 83:4)

the Lord, in his wrath, caused to continue with the house of Aaron among the children of Israel until John, whom God raised up, being filled with the Holy Ghost from his mother's womb: for he was baptized while he was yet in *his childhood*, and was ordained by the angel of God at the time he was eight days old unto this power—to overthrow the kingdom of the Jews

Commentary: John the Baptist baptized in the womb

In a revelation concerning the priesthood given over a two-day period, 22-23 September 1832, we find one of the most interesting texts in Joseph Smith's revela-

---

6. Newel K. Whitney, bishop in Kirtland.

tions. The early manuscripts of this revelation were written by Frederick G. Williams, since there are two manuscripts of this revelation in his handwriting. The difficult reading is in the early text. The revelation in the Kirtland Revelations Book originally read like the manuscript cited above, but then was revised with the words "the womb" crossed out and "his childhood" added above the line.[7] The 1835 D&C follows this revision of the text.[8]

It appears that this portion of the revelation is trying to answer the question of who baptized John and where he got his authority. The answer given in 1832 has never been published as such in the canonical D&C.

Early Text		1835 D&C	
Holy Ghost	womb	Holy Ghost	womb
Baptized	womb	baptized	childhood
Ordained	eight days old	ordained	eight days old

The September 1832 text is problematic in having John the Baptist "baptised while he was yet in the womb" of his mother before he was born. Did the baptism take place in the watery amniotic fluid? It is understandable why Joseph Smith would want to change the reading of "the womb" to "his childhood." One reason to change the early text is because anyone could claim that he or she had already received baptism in the womb. But this would appear to be a type of pre-infant baptism before birth. Members of the Jewish faith did not practice infant baptism, but may have practiced Mikveh for converts. The exact dating of Jewish proselyte baptism is a matter of debate.

The revelation has John the Baptist's ordination when he was eight days old. Yet with the 1835 D&C revision, when he was to have been baptized is put at a later time and is out of sequence within the context. Retaining John's ordination at eight days old makes it clear that this revision was an afterthought and tried to solve the perceived problem of John being baptized in the womb. But in solving this problem, the 1835 revision now seemed to have John the Baptist being baptized after being ordained.

The revelation to Smith, besides mentioning that John was filled with the Holy Ghost from his mother's womb (see Luke 1:15), then baptized, notes that he was "ordained by the Angel of God at the time he was eight days old." Here is another problem relating to what the text says in Luke 1:59, "on the eighth day they came to circumcise the child." Circumcision when John was eight days old may therefore be related to the presumed ordination to ministry by the angel. This is strange since there is nothing in the gospel accounts about John needing to be either baptized or ordained—nor does the angel appear in the family tradition—because Zacharias was an Aaronic priest "of the course of Abia [Abijah]." Zacharias and Elisabeth were descended from Aaron, brother of Moses.[9] Zacharias had been cho-

---

7. KRB, 23, line 2.

8. 1835 D&C 4:4. See LDS D&C 84:28; RLDS D&C 83:4.

9. Luke 1:5, 8. The sons of Aaron through Eleazar and Ithamar were later divided into twenty-four orders or divisions of which Abijah is the eighth. See 1 Chron. 24:1-5, 10.

sen by lot to offer incense in the holy place in the temple at Jerusalem.[10]

So whether John the Baptist needed baptism to preach repentance and baptize converts is an interesting question. The revised text has John baptized in "his childhood." In the New Testament there is no indication of who baptized the Baptist, if indeed he received such a rite.

101. Set in Order the House of God
From the Joseph Smith Letterbook 1:1A-3 (cf. LDS D&C 85)

Excerpt from a letter of instructions by Joseph Smith, Jr., to William W. Phelps, written at Kirtland, Ohio, on 27 November 1832[11]

firstly, it is the duty of the lord['s] clerk[12] whom he has appointed to keep a hystory [history] and a general church receord [record] of all things that transpire in Zion and of all those who consecrate properties and receive inher[i]tance legally from the bishop and also there [their] manner of life and the faith and works and also of all the apostates who apostatize after receiving the[i]r inher[i]tances

seccondly [secondly] it is conterary [contrary] to the will and commandment of God that those who receive not the[i]r inheriten[ce] by consecration agre[e]able to his law which he has given th[at] he may tithe his people to prepare them against the day of venge[a]nce and burning should have there [their] names enrolled with the people of God, neithe[r] is the[ir] genealogy to be kept or to be had where it may be found on any of the reccords [records] or hystory [history] of the church there [their] names shall not be found neithe[r] the names of the[ir] fathers or the names of the[ir] children writ[t]en in the book of the Law of God saith the Lord of hosts

yea thus saith the still small voice which whispereth through and pierceth all things and often times it maketh my bones to quake while it maketh manifest saying

and it shall come to pass that I the Lord God will send one mighty and strong[13] holding the scepter of power in his hand clothed with light for a covering whose mouth shall utter words Eternal words while his bowels shall be a fountain of truth to set in order the house of God and to ar[r]ange by lot the inheritance of the saints whose names are found and the names of their fathers and of their children enrol[l]ed in the Book of the Law of God while that man[14] who was called of God

---

10. Luke 1:8-9.
11. Published in 1876 LDS D&C.
12. John Whitmer, clerk and church historian.
13. Joseph Smith, Jr., appears to refer to himself.
14. Evidently Edward Partridge, bishop of the church in Jackson County, Missouri. Joseph Smith wrote in a previous letter to William W. Phelps, "now this is a warning to all to whom this knowledge may come, and he that thinks he stands, let him take heed least he fall, tell Bro[ther] Edward it is very dangerous for men who have received the light he has received to be a seeking

and appointed that put[t]eth forth his hand to steady the ark of God shall fall by the shaft of death like as a tree that is smitten by the viv[i]d shaft of lightning

and all they who are not found writ[t]en in the book of remmenberance [remembrance] shall find none inheritence [inheritance] in that day but they shall be cut assunder [asunder] and their portion shall be appointed them among unbelievers where is wailing and gnashing of teeth these things I say not of myself therefore as the Lord speaketh he will also fulfill

and they who are of the high Priesthood whose names are not found writ[t]en in the book of the Law or that are found to have appostitised [apostatized] or to have been cut off out of the church as well as the lesser Priesthood or the members in that day shall not find an inheritence [inheritance] among the saints of the most high therefore it shall be done unto them as unto the children of the Priest as you will find recorded in the second chapter and sixty first and second verses of Ezra[15]

102. The Angels Are Crying unto the Lord
From KRB, 31-32 (cf. LDS D&C 86; RLDS D&C 84)

Revelation received at Kirtland, Ohio, on 6 December 1832 as an explanation of the parable of the wheat and tares in Matthew 13[16]

A Revelation explaining the parable of the wheat & the [tares]

Verily thus saith the Lord unto you my servants concerning the parable of the wheat and of the tears [tares], Behold verily I say that the field was the world and the Apostles were the sowers of the seed and after they have fallen asleep the great persecutor of the church the apostate, the whore, even Babylon, that maketh all nations to drink of her cup, in whose hearts the enemy even Satan sitteth to reign, behold he soweth the tears [tares], wherefore the tears [tares] choke the wheat and drive the church in to the wilderness,

---

a after [sic; after a] sign, for there shall no sign be given for a sign except as it was in the days of Lot" (Smith to Phelps, 31 July 1832, LDS archives). Later Oliver Cowdery, who was residing in Missouri at the time the November 1832 letter was written, wrote: "Brother Joseph [Smith, Jr.] says, that the item in his letter that says, that the man that is called &c. and puts forth his hand to steady the ark of God, does not mean that any one had at the time, but it was given for a caution to those in high standing to beware, lest they, should fall by the shalf of death as the Lord had said" (Cowdery to John Whitmer, 1 Jan. 1834, Oliver Cowdery Letterbook, 15, Henry E. Huntington Library, San Marino, California).

15. Smith (with Frederick G. Williams as scribe) had completed the revision of NT by 31 July 1832. Smith wrote to William W. Phelps: "Brother Frederick is employed to be a scribe for me of the Lord –we have finished the translation of the New testament great and glorious things are revealed, we are making rapid strides in the old book" (Smith to Phelps, 31 July 1832, LDS archives). By 27 November 1832 Smith had revised to about Nehemiah 10 in the OT.

16. Smith had turned his attention from the OT revision to Matthew in the New when he received this revelation. The following was recorded by Smith: "translating and received a revelation explaining the Parable [of] the wheat and the tears [tares] &c" (Joseph Smith Journal, 6 Dec. 1832, LDS archives; see Dean C. Jessee, ed., *The Papers of Joseph Smith: Journal, 1832-1842* [Salt Lake City: Deseret Book Co., 1992], 2:5).

but behold in th[e] last days, even now while the Lord is begin[n]ing to bring forth the word, and the blade is springing up and is yet tender, behold verily I say unto you the angels are crying unto the Lord, day and night who are ready, and waiting to be sent forth to reap down the fields, but the Lord saith unto them pluck not up the tears [tares] while the blade is yet tender (for verily your faith is weak) least you destroy the wheat also, therefore let the wheat and the tears [tares] grow together untill the harvest is fully ripe then ye shall first gather out the wheat from among the tears [tares] and after the gathering of the wheat, behold and lo the tears [tares] are bound in bund[l]es, and the field remaineth to be burned

therefore thus saith the Lord unto you with whom the priesthood hath continued through the lineage of your fathers, for ye are lawful heirs according to the flesh and have been hid from the world with christ in God therefore your life, and the Priesthood hath remained and must needs remain through you and your lineage untill the restoration of all thing[s] spoken by the mouth of all the holy Prophets since the world began,

therefore blessed are ye if ye continue in my goodness, a light unto the Gentiles and through this Priesthood a saviour unto my people Israel the Lord hath said it

Kirtland December 6th AD 1832 given by Joseph th[e] seer and writ[t]en by Sidney [Rigdon] the scribe an[d] Councellor [Counsellor] & Transcribed by Frederick [G. Williams] assistant scribe and councellor [counselor]

103. Stand Ye in Holy Places
From KRB, 32-33 (cf. LDS D&C 87)
Prophecy given at Kirtland, Ohio, on 25 December 1832 concerning wars[17]

A Prophecy given Decm [December] 25th 1832

Verily thus saith the Lord, concerning the wars that will shortly come to pass begin[n]ing at the rebellion of South Carolina which will eventually terminate in the death and misery of many souls, and the days will come that war will be poured out upon all Nations begin[n]ing at this place for behold the southern states shall be divided against the Northern States, and the Southern States will call on other Nation[s] even the Nation of Great Britian [Britain] as it is called and they shall also

17. Though this prophecy on wars was copied by early members of the church, it was not published in the 1835 D&C. It was first published in the 1851 PGP and in the 1876 LDS D&C. In January 1833 Smith wrote: "And now I am prepared to say by the authority of Jesus Christ, that not many years shall pass away before the United States shall present such a scene of bloodshed as has not a parallel in the hystory [history] of our nation pestalence [pestilence] hail famine and earthquake will sweep the wicked of this generation from off the face of this Land to open and prepare the way for the return of the lost tribes of Israel from the north country" (Smith to N. C. Saxton, 4 Jan. 1833, Joseph Smith Letterbook 1:18, LDS archives). The understanding at the time was that wars and destruction would occur that would make "a full end of all Nations."

call upon other Nations in order to defend themselves against other Nations and thus war shall be poured out upon all Nations

and it shall come to pass after many days Slaves shall rise up against the[i]r Masters who shall be Martialed [Marshaled] and disc[i]plined for war

and it shall come to pass also that the remnants who are left of the land will martial [marshal] themselves also and shall become exce[e]ding angry and shall vex the Gentiles with a soar [sore] vexation

and thus with the sword and by bloodshed the inhabitants of the earth shall mourn and with famine and plague, and Earthquake and the thunder of heaven and the fierce and vivid lightning also shall the inhabitants of the earth be made to feel the wrath and indignation and chast[e]ning hand of an Almighty God untill the consumption decreed hath made a full end of all Nations that the cry of the saints and of the blood of the saints shall cease to come up into the ears of the Lord of Sabaoth from the earth to be avenged of their enemies wherefor[e] stand ye in holy places and be not moved untill the day of the Lord come, for be hold it cometh quickly saith the Lord Amen

Given by Joseph th[e] Seer writt[en] by F G Williams

104. I Now Send upon You Another Comforter
From KRB, 33-46 (cf. LDS D&C 88:1-126; RLDS D&C 85:1-38)

*Revelation received at Kirtland, Ohio, on 27 and 28 December 1832
for the first elders of the Church of Christ*[18]

A Revelation given to the first Elders of this Church of Christ in the last days Dec 27th 1832

Verily thus saith the Lord unto you, who have assembled yourselves together, to receive his will concerning you, behold this is pleasing unto unto your lord, and the Angels rejoice over you, the alms of your prayers have come up into the ears of the Lord of Sabaoth, and are recorded in the book of the names of the sanctified, even they of the celestial world, wherefore, I now send upon you another comforter, even upon you my friends; that it may abide in your hearts, even the holy spirit of promis[e] which other comforter, is the same that I promised unto my deciples [disciples], as is recorded in the testamony [testimony] of John,

This comforter is the promise which I give unto you of eternal life; even the glory of the celestial kingdom, which glory is that of the church of the first born; even of God the holiest of all; through Jesus Christ, his son. he that assended [as-

---

18. This revelation was given at a conference of high priests (Kirtland Council Minute Book, 3-4, LDS archives). The text follows the manuscript reading, including corrections made near the time of recording. Minor revisions for the 1835 D&C are omitted. Some punctuation marks in the manuscript are not included for easier reading. The bottom of pages 43 and 44 were not readable on a microfilm copy of the revelation. Wording has been added in brackets.

cended] up on high, as also he de[s]cended below all things; in that he comprehended all things, that he might be in all, and through all things; the light of truth,
which truth shineth – this is the light of Christ as also he is in the sun, and the light
of the sun, and the power thereof by which it was made, as also he is in the moon,
& is the light of the moon, and the power thereof, by which it was made, as also the
light of the stars, and the power thereof; by which they were made; and the earth
also, and the power thereof, even the earth upon which you stand,

and the light which now shineth, which giveth you light, is through him which
enlight[e]neth you[r] eyes; which is the same light that guick[e]neth your understanding, which light proce[e]deth forth from the presence of God; to fill the em-
encity [immensity] of space; the light which is in all thing[s] which giveth life to all
things, which is the law by which all things are governed, even the power of God,
who sitteth upon his throne; who is in the bosom of eternity, who is in the midst of
all things

Now verily I say unto you, that through th[e] redemption, which is made for
you; is brought to pass the resur[r]ection from the dead; (and the spirit and the
body is the soul of man) and the resur[r]ection from the dead, is the redemption of
the soul; and the redemption of the soul, is through him who quick[e]neth all
things, in whose bosom, it is decreed, that the poor and the meek of the earth, shall
inherit it, therefor[e] it must needs be sanctified, from all unrighteousness, that it
may be prepared for th[e] celestial glory; for after it hath filled the measure of its
creation, it shall be crowned with glory, even with the presence of God, the father,
that bodies, who are of the celestial kingdom may posses[s] it, for ever & ever; for,
for this intent was it made, and created, and for this intent, are they sanctified,

and they who are not sanctified through the law which I have given unto you;
even the law of Christ, must inherit another kingdom even that of a Ter[r]estrial
kingdom or that of a telestial Kingdom, for he that is not able to abide the law of a
celestial kingdom cannot abide a celestial glory, and he who cannot abide the law
of a Ter[r]estrial kingdom cannot abide a Ter[r]estrial glory, he who cannot abide
the law of a Telestial kingdom cannot abide a Telestial glory; therefore he is not
meet for a kingdom of glory, therefor[e] he must abide a kingdom which is not a
kingdom of glory.

And again, verily I say unto you, the earth abideth the law of a celestial kingdom, for it filleth the measure of its creation; and transgresseth not the law wherefore it shall be sanctified, yea notwithstanding it shall die, it shall be quickened
again, and shall abide the power by which it is quickened, and the righteous shall
inherit it, for notwithstanding they die, they also shall rise again, a spiritual body,
they who are of a celestial spirit, shall receive the same body which was a natural
body, even ye shall receive your bodies and your glory shall be that glory by which
your bodies are quickened, ye who ar[e] quickened by a portion of the celestial
glory shall then receive of the same, even a fulness, and they who are quickened by
a portion of the Ter[r]estiall glory, shall then receive of the same even a fulness; and
also they who are quickened by a portion of the Telestial glory, shall then receive
of the same, even a fulness, and they who remain, shall also be quickened, nevertheless they shall return again, to there [their] own place to enjoy that which they

are willing to receive, because they were not willing to enjoy that which they might have received;

for what doth it proffit [profit] a man, if a gift is bestowed upon him and he receive not the gift[?] behold he rejoiceth not in that which is given unto him, neither rejoices in him, who is the giver of the gift;

and again verily I say unto you, that which is governed by law, is also preserved by law, and perfected, and sanctified by the same; that which breaketh a law, and abideth not by law, but seeketh to become a law unto itself, and willeth to abide in sin; and altogether adideth in sin, can not be sanctified by law; neither [of] mercy, Justice, or Judgment; therefore they must remain filthy still,

all kingdoms have a law given; and there are many kingdoms; for there is no space in the which there is no kingdom; and there is no kingdom in which there is no space, eather [either] a greater or lesser kingdom, and unto ev[e]ry kingdom is given a law, and unto ev[e]ry law there are certain bounds also, and conditions,

all beings who abide not in those conditions, are not Justified, for intel[l]igenc[e] cleaveth unto intel[l]igenc[e], wisdom receiveth wisdom, truth embraceth truth, virtue Loveth virtue, light cleaveth unto light, mercy hath compassion on mercy and claimeth her own, Justice continueth its course and claimeth its own, Judgment goeth before the face of him who sitteth upon the throne and gove[r]neth and executeth all things, he comprehendeth all things, and all things are before him, and all things are round about him, and he is above all things, and in all things, and is through all things, and is round about all thing[s] and all things are by him, and of him, even God for ever and ever,

And again verily I say unto you he hath given a law unto all things, by which they moove [move] in there [their] times, and there [their] seasons, and there [their] courses are fixed, even the courses of the heavens and the earth which comprehend the earth, and all the planets, and they give light to each other in there [their] times, and in there [their] seasons, in there [their] minuits [minutes] in there [their] hours, in there [their] days, in there [their] weeks in there [their] months, in there [their] years; all these are one year with God but not with man;

the Earth rolls upon her wings, and the sun giveth his light by day, and the moon giveth her light by night, and the stars also giveth there [their] light as they roll upon there [their] wings in there [their] glory in the midst of the power of God, unto what shall I liken th[e]se kingdoms, that ye may understand[?]

behold all these are kingdoms, and any man who hath seen any or the least of these have seen God moving in his magesty [majesty] and power; I say unto you, he hath seen him, nevertheless, he who came unto his own was not comprehended, the light shineth in darkness, and the darkness compre[hen]deth it not, nevertheless, the day shall come when you shall comprehend even God, being quickened in him, and by him, then shall ye know, that ye have seen me, that I am, and that I am the true light that is in you, and that you are in me, otherwis[e] ye could not abound,

Behold I will liken these kingdoms unto a man having a field, and he send forth his servants into the field to dig in the field, and he said unto the first, go ye and labour in the field and in the first hour I will come unto you, and ye shall behold the

Joy of my countenance, and he said unto the second, go ye also into the field, and in the second hour I will visit you with the Joy of my countenance, and also unto the third saying, I will visit you; and unto the fourth, and so on unto the twelth [twelfth],

and the lord of the field went unto the first, in the first hour, and tarried with him all that hour, and he was made glad, with the light of this countenance of his lord, and then he withdrew from the first that he might visit the second also, and the third, and the fourth, and so on unto the twelveth [twelfth], and thus they all received the light of the countenance of there [their] Lord, every man in his hour, and in his time, and in his season, begin[n]ing at the first, and so on unto the last, and from the last unto the first and from the first unto the Last, ev[e]ry man in his own order, untill his hour was finished, even according as his lord had commanded him, that his Lord might by glor[i]fied in him; and he in him that they all might be glorified

therefore unto this parable will I liken all th[e]se kingdoms; and the inhabitants thereof, ev[e]ry kingdom, in its hour, and in its time, and in its season, even according to th[e] decree which God hath made;

and again; verily I say unto you, my friends, I leave these sayings with you for to ponder in your hearts; with this commandment which I give unto you, that ye shall call upon me, while I am near, draw near unto me, and I will draw near unto you, seek me diligently and ye shall find me, ask and ye shall receive, knock, and it shall be opened unto you; whatsoever ye ask the father, in my name, it shall be given unto you, that is expedient for you, and if ye ask any thing that is not expedient for you, it shall turn unto your condem[na]tion,

behold that which you hear is as the voice of one crying in the wilderness, In the wilderness, because you cannot see him; my voice, because my voice is spirit, my spirit is truth, truth abideth and hath no end, and if it be in you it shall abound,

and if your eye be single to my glory, your whole bodies shall be filled with light, and there shall be no darkness in you, and that body which is filled with light comprehendeth all things; therefore sanctify yourselves that your minds become single to God, and The days will come that you shall see him, for he will unveil his face unto you, and it shall be in his own time, and in his own way, and according to his own will;

Remember the great and last promise which I have made unto you, cast away your Idille [Idle] thoughts, and your excess of Laughter far from you; tarry ye, tarry ye in this place, and call a solemn assembly, even of those who are the first labourers in this last kingdon [kingdom], and let those whom they have warned in there [their] trav[e]ling call on the Lord and ponder the warning in there [their] hearts; which they have received, for a little season, behold and lo I will take care of your flocks, and will raise up elders and send unto them,

behold I will hasten my work, in its time, and I give unto you, who are the first labourers [laborers] in this last kingdom, a commandment that you assembl[e] yourselves together, and organize yourselves, and prepare yourselves, and sanctify yourselv[es] yea purify your hearts, and clea[n]se your hands, and your feet, before me, that I may make you clean, that I may testify unto your father, and your God and my God, that you are clean from the blood of this wicked generation, that I may fulfil this promise, this great and last promise, which I have made unto you, when I will,

also I give unto you a commandment, that ye shall continue in prayer, and fasting, from this time forth; and I give unto you a commandment, that you shall teach one another, the doctrines of the kingdom, teach ye diligently, and my grace shall attend you, that ye may be inst[r]ucted more perfectly, in theory, in principle, in doctrine in the law of the Gospel, in all things that pertain unto the kingdom of God, that is expedient for you to understand, of things both in heaven and in the earth, and under the earth, things which have been, things which are, things which must shortly come to pass, things which are at home, things which are abroad; the wars and the perplexities of th[e] nations, and the Judgment[s] which are on th[e] land, and a knowledge also of Countries, and of Kingdoms; that ye may be prepared in all things when I shall send you again to magnify th[e] calling whereunto I have called you, and th[e] mission with which I have commissioned you,

behold I send you out to testify and warn the people, and it becometh ev[e]ry man who hath been warned to warn his neighbour, therefor[e] they are left without excuse, and there [their] sins are upon there [their] own heads, he that seeketh me early shall find me, and shall not be forsaken,

therefore tarry ye, and labour diligently, that you may be perfected in your ministry to go forth among the gentiles, for the last time, as many as the mouth of the Lord shall name, to bind up the law, and seal up the testamoy [testimony] and to prepare the saints for the hour of Judgments which is to come, that there [their] souls may escape the wrath of God, the desolation of abomination which awaiteth the wicked, both in this world, and in the world to come, verily I say unto you, let those who are not th[e] first elders continue in the vineyard untill the mouth of the Lord shall call them, for there [their] time is not yet come, there [their] garments are not clean from the blood of this generation,

abide ye in the liberty wherewith ye are made free, entangle not yourselves in sin, but let your hands be clean, untill the lord come, for not many days hence and the earth shall tremble and real [reel] to and fro as a drunken man, and the sun shall hide his face, and shall refuse to give light, and the moon shall be bathed in blood, and the stars shall become exce[e]ding angry and shall cast themselves down as a fig that falleth from off a fig tree,

and after your testamony [testimony] cometh wrath and indignation upon th[e] people, for after your testamony [testimony] cometh th[e] testamony [testimony] of earthquakes, that shall cause gro[a]nings in the midst of her, and men shall fall upon the ground and shall not be able to stand, and also cometh the testamony [testimony] of the voice of thunder[i]ngs, and the voice of lightnings, and th[e] voice of tempests, and th[e] voice of the waves of th[e] sea heaving themselves beyond there [their] bounds, and all things shall be in commotion; and surely men[']s hearts shall fail them, for fear shall come upon all people, and Angels shall fly through the midst of heaven crying with a loud voice, sounding the trump of God, saying prepare ye, prepare ye, O inhabitants of the earth, for the Judgment of our God is come, behold and lo, the bridegroom cometh, go ye out to meet him and immediately there shall appear a great sign in heaven, and all people shall see it together, & another Angel shall sound his trump, saying that great Church, the mother of abominations that made all nations drink of the wine of the warth [wrath] of its fornication, that per[se]cuteth the saints of God, that shed there [their] blood, her who sitteth upon many waters, and upon the Is[l]ands of the sea behold she is the tears [tares] of the earth, she is bound in bundles, her bands are made strong no man can loose them, therefore she is ready to be burned and he shall sound his trump both long and loud, and all nations shall hear it,

and there shall be silence in heaven for the space of a[n] half an hour, & im[m]ediately after shall the curtain of heaven be unfolded as a scroll is unfolded after it is rolled up and the face of the Lord shall be unveiled and the saints that are upon the earth, who are alive, shall be quickened, and be caught up to meet him, and they who have slept in there [their] graves shall come forth, for there [their] graves shall be opened, and they also shall be caught up to meet him in the midst of the pillar of heaven they are Christ['|s the first fruits, they who shall de[s]cend with him first, and they who are on the earth and in there [their] graves, who are first caught up to meet him, and all this by the voice of the sounding of the trump of the Angel of God,

and after this another trump shall sound, which is the second trump and then cometh the redemption of those who are [Christ's] at his coming, who have rece[i]ved [the]re [their] par[t in] that prision [prison] which is prepared for them [that] they [mig]ht receive the gospel and be judged according to men in the fless [flesh],

and again, another trump shall sound, which is the third trump, and then cometh the spirits of men who are to be judged, and are found under condemnation and these are the rest of the dead, and they live not again untill the thousand years are ended, neither again, untill the end of the earth,

and another trump shall sound, which is the fo[u]rth trump, saying: there are found among those who are to remain untill that great and last day, even the end, who shall remain filthy still, and another trump shall sound, which is the fifth trump, which is the fifth angel who com[m]itteth the everlasting gospel, flying through the midst of heaven, unto all Nations, Kindred Tongue[s], & people, and this shall be the sound of his trump, saying to all people, both in heaven and in earth, and that are under the earth, for ev[e]ry ear shall hear it, and ev[e]ry knee shall bow, and ev[e]ry tongue shall confess, while they hear the sound of the trump, saying fear God, and give glory to him who sitteth upon the throne for ever and ever, for the hour of his Judgment is come;

and again another angel shall sound his trump, which is the sixth Angel, saying, [she] is fallen who made all Nations drink of the wine of the wrath of her fornication; she is fallen, is fal[le]n,

and again, another Angel shall sound his [trump] which is the seventh Angel, saying, it i[s] fin[ished] it is finished, the lamb of God ha[th ov]erc[ome] and trod[d]en the wine press allone [alone], eve[n the] wi[ne press] of the fierceness of the wrath of Al[migh]ty [G]o[d and] then shall the Angels be crowned [with t]he glor[y of h]is might, and the saints shall b[e filled] with h[is glo]ry, and receive their inheritance and be made equal with him and then shall the first Angel again sound his trump in the ears of all living, and reveal the secret acts of men, and the mighty works of God in the first thousandth year,

and then shall the second Angel sound his trump, and reveal the secret acts of men, and the thoughts and intents of their hearts, and the mighty works of God in the second thousandth year; and so on untill the seventh Angel shall sound his trump, and he shall stand forth upon the land and upon the sea, and sware [swear] in the name of him who sitteth upon the throne, that there shall be time no longer,

and satan shall be bound, that old serpent who is called the devle [devil], and shall not be loosed for the space of a thousand years; and then he shall be loosed for a little season, that he may gather together his armies, and Michael, the seventh Angel, even the archangel, shall gather together his armies, even the hosts of heaven, and the Devel [Devil] shall gather his armies, even the hosts of hell, and shall come up to battle against Michael and his armies; and then cometh the battle of the Great God, and the Devell [Devil] and his armies shall be cast away into there [their] own place; that they shall not have power over the saints any more at all, for Michael shall fight their battles, and shall ove[r]come him who seeketh the throne of him who sitteth upon the throne, even the Lamb, this is the glory of God, and the sanctified, and they shall not any more see death,

Therefore verily I say unto you my friends, call your solemn assembly, as I have commanded you, and as all have not faith, seek ye diligently and teach one another words of wisdom, yea seek ye out of the best books words of wisdom, seek Learning even by study and also by faith organize yourselves, prepare ev[e]ry needful thing and establish an house, even an house of prayer an house of fasting, an house of faith, an house of Learning, an house of glory, an house of orde[r] an house of God, that your incomings may be in the name of the Lord, that your outgoing[s] may be in the name of the Lord, that all your salutations may be in the name of the Lord, with uplifted hands unto the most high,

therefore cease from all your light speaches [speeches], from all laughter from all your lustful des[ir]es, from all your pride and lightmindness, and from all your wicked doings, appoint among yourselves a teacher, and and let not all be spokesmen at once, but let one speak at a time and let all listen unto his sayings that when all have spoken that all may be edified of all, and that ev[e]ry man may have an equal privilege,

see that ye love one another ceace [cease] to be covetous, learn to impart one to another as the gospel requires, ceace [cease] to be Idle, ceace [cease] to be unclean, ceace [cease] to find fault one with another ceac[e] [cease] to sleep longer than is needful, retire to thy bed early that ye may not be weary, arise early, that your bodies and your minds may be invigorated, and above all things, clothe yourselves with the bonds of charity, as with a mantle, which is the bonds of perfectness and peace, pray always, that you may not faint until I come, behold, and lo, I will come quickly and receive you unto myself Amen

Given by Joseph the seer and writ[t]en by F. G. Williams assistan[t] scribe and councellor [counselor] to Sd [Said] Joseph

105. In Token of the Everlasting Covenant
From KRB, 47-48 (cf. LDS D&C 88:127-137, 141; RLDS D&C 85:39-44, 46)

Revelation received at Kirtland, Ohio, on 3 January 1833 on the order of the house for the presidency[19]

Kirtland January 3d 1833. Revelation given to for a [illegible word]

The order of the house prepared for the presidency, and instruction in all things that is expedient for the officers; or in other words, them who are called to the ministry in the Church, begin[n]ing at the high Priests, even down to the deacon, and this shall be the order of the house, he that is appointed to be a teacher, shall be found standing in his place, which shall be prepared for him in the house of God, in a place that the congregation in the house may hear his words correctly and distinctly; not with loud speach [speech]; and when he cometh into the house of God, (for he should be first in the house, be hold this is beautiful that he may be an example)

let him offer himself in prayer upon his knees before God, in token of the everlasting covenant and when any shall come in after him, let the teacher arise, and with uplifted hands to heaven, yea even directly, salute his brother or brethren with thes[e] words saying

art thou a brother or brethren, I salute you in the name of the Lord Jesus Christ, in token of the everlasting covenant, in which covenant I receive you to fellowship, in a determination that is fixed immovable, and unchang[e]able, to be your friend and brother through the grace of God in the bonds of Love, to walk in all the commandments of God blameless, in thanksgiving for ever and ever; Amen.

and he that cometh in and is a brother or brethren shall salute the teacher with uplifted hands to heaven, with this same prayer and covenant or by saying amen; in token of the same,

Behold verily I say unto you, this is a sample unto you for a salutation to one another in the house of God, and ye are called to do this by prayer and thanksgiving, as the spirit shall give utterance in all your doings in the house of the Lord, that it may become a sanctu[a]ry, a tabernacle of the holy spirit to your edification Amen

Given by Joseph th[e] seer, and writ[t]en by Frederick [G. Williams] assistant scribe and Councellor [Counselor]

Revision

1835 D&C 7
(cf. LDS D&C 88:127-129, 136-141; RLDS D&C 85:39, 44-46)

And again, the order of the house prepared for the presidency *of the school of the*

---

19. Some punctuation marks are not included for easier reading.

prophets, established for their instruction in all things that are expedient *for them, even* for *all* the officers *of the church,* or in other words, those who are called to the ministry in the church, beginning at the high-priests, even down to the deacons: and this shall be the order of the house *of the presidency of the school*: He that is appointed to be *president, or* teacher, shall be found standing in his place, *in the house,* which shall be prepared for him. *Therefore, he shall be first* in the house of God, in a place that the congregation in the house may hear his words *carefully* and distinctly, not with loud speech.

.   .   .

Behold, verily I say unto you, this is a sample unto you for a salutation to one another in the house of God, *in the school of the prophets.* And ye are called to do this by prayer and thanksgiving as the Spirit shall give utterance, in all your doings in the house of the Lord, *in the school of the prophets,* that it may become a sanctuary, a tabernacle, of the Holy Spirit to your edification. *And ye shall not receive any among you, into this school save he is clean from the blood of this generation: and he shall be received by the ordinance of the washing of feet; for unto this end was the ordinance of the washing of feet instituted. And again, the ordinance of washing feet is to be administered by the president, or presiding elder of the church. It is to be commenced with prayer: and after partaking of bread and wine he is to gird himself, according to the pattern given in the thirteenth chapter of John's testimony concerning me.* Amen.

Commentary: Washing feet

On 3 January 1833 a revelation was given concerning the "order of the house prepared for the presidency" of the church. Two records have the complete early text of this revelation. They are the *Evening and the Morning Star* of March 1833 and the Kirtland Revelations Book.[20] This revelation was combined with another of December 1832 to make one complete document for the 1835 D&C. At the end of the 3 January 1833 revelation is an addition to the text about the washing of feet.

The washing of feet is not found in the manuscript preserved in the Kirtland Revelations Book or in *The Evening and the Morning Star.* This was likely added to the text after a meeting of the School of the Prophets on 23 January 1833 where the first washing of feet took place.[21] A copy of this revelation was sent to Independence soon after it was written and was published in the March 1833 issue.

This addition was made part of the January revelation by having the word "Amen" of the 3 January revelation placed at the end of the addition. There is no evidence that this addition was ever a part of the 3 January 1833 revelatory text.

---

20. *The Evening and the Morning Star* 1 (Mar. 1833): [6; whole page no. 78]; KRB, 47–48.
21. Kirtland Council Minute Book, 7–8.

106. Called to Be a Councellor

From the Frederick G. Williams Papers, LDS archives

Revelation received at Kirtland, Ohio, on 6 January 1833
for Frederick G. Williams

Revelation given at Kirtland, Ohio, through Joseph, the Seer, on January 6, 1834 [1833] [22]

Behold I say unto you my servant Frederick [G. Williams] Listen to the word of the Lord Jesus Christ your lord and your rede[e]mer: thou hast designed [desired] of me to know which wou[l]d be the most worth unto you: behold, blessed are thou for this thing. Now I say unto you, my servant Joseph [Smith, Jr.] is called to do a great work and hath needs that he may do the work of translation for the salvation of souls. verily, verily I say unto you, thou art called to be a councellor [counselor] and scribe unto my servant Joseph [Smith, Jr.]. Let thy farm be consecrated for bringing forth of the revelations, and thou shalt be blessed, and lifted up at the last day: even so. Amen.

107. Enoch of Old

From KRB, 48-49

Song in the gift of tongues received and interpreted
at Kirtland, Ohio, on 27 February 1833[23]

Sang by the gift of Tongues & Translated

age after age has rolled away, according to the sad fate of man, countless millions for ever gone at length the period of time has come that oft was seen by a prophetic eye and writ[t]en too by all holy men Inspired of the Lord

a time which was seen by Enoch of Old at a time when he stood upon the mount which was called the mountain of God as he gazed upon nature and the corruption of man of man and mourned their sad fate and wept and cried with a

22. The text follows the wording of the manuscript before minor alterations. Versification deleted. Frederick G. Williams was a scribe since 20 July 1832 and became a counselor to Smith in December 1832 or early January 1833. The Kirtland Council Minute Book for 22 January 1833 mentions that Williams is an assistant scribe to Rigdon and a counselor (6). This revelation was not published in the 1835 D&C.

23. On 14 November 1832 Zebedee Coltrin wrote that he heard Joseph Smith speak and sing in tongues (Zebedee Coltrin Journal, LDS archives). At a conference of high priests in Kirtland, Ohio, on 22 January 1833, it was recorded that Smith "spake in an unknown tongue" (Kirtland Council Minute Book, 7). It appears that Smith sang this praise by the gift of tongues and then interpreted it. One of the songs of Zion composed by William W. Phelps was evidently based upon this experience. See *The Evening and the Morning Star* 1 (May 1833): [8; whole page no. 96]; and Michael Hicks, *Mormonism and Music: A History* (Urbana: University of Illinois Press, 1989), 36. Not included in 1835 D&C.

loud voice and heaved forth his sighs Omnipotence Omnipotence O may I see thee – and with his finger he touched his eyes and he saw heaven he gazed on eternity and sang an Angelic song and mingled his voice with the heavenly throng Hosan[n]a Hosan[n]a the sound of the trump around the throne of God echoed & echoed again and rang and reechoed until eternity was filled with hi[s] voice

he saw yea he saw and he glorif[i]ed God the salvation of his people his city caught up through the gospel of Christ

he saw the begin[n]ing the ending of man he saw the time when Adam his fath[er] was made and he saw that he was in eternity before a grain of dust in the ballance was weighed

he saw that he emenated [emanated] and came down from God he saw what had passed and then was and is present and to come

therefore he saw the Last days the Ang[e]l that came down to John and the Angel that is now flying having the everlasting Gospel to commit unto men – which in my soul I have received and from death and bondage from the Devil I[']m freed and am free in the gospel of Christ and I[']m waiting and with patience I[']ll wait on the Lord Hosan[n]a loud sound the trump cause eternity to ring hosan[n]a for ever I[']m waiting the coming of Christ a mansion on high a celestial abode a seat on the right hand of God

Angels are coming the holy Ghost is falling upon the saints and will continue to fall the saviour is coming yea the Bridegroom prepar[e] ye prepare yea the cry has gone forth go wait on the Lord the Angels in glory will soon be descending go join you in singing the praises of God the trump Loud shall sound the dark vail [veil] soon shall rend heaven shall shake the earth shall tremble and all nature shall feel the power of God, gase [gaze] ye saints gase [gaze] ye upon him, gase [gaze] upon Jesus hosan[n]a loud sound the trump his church is caught up

hosan[n]a praise him ye saints they stand at his feet behold they are weeping they strike hands with Enoch of Old they inherit a city as it is writ[t]en the City of God. Loud sound the trump, they receive a celestial crown hozana [hosanna] hozana [hosanna] the heaven of heavens, and the heavens are filled with the praises of God Amen

Given February 27 – 1833

108. A Word of Wisdom
From KRB, 49-51 (cf. LDS D&C 89 and RLDS D&C 86)

Revelation received at Kirtland, Ohio, on 27 February 1833
for the temporal salvation of the Saints

A Revelation for the benefit of the saints &c

a word of wisdom for the benefit of th[e] council of high Priests assembled in Kirtland and Church and also the saints in Zion to be sent greeting not by commandment or constraint but by revelation and the word of wisdom shewing forth the order and will of God in the temporal salvation of all saints in the last days given for a principle with promise adapted to the capasity [capacity] of the weak and the weakest of all saints who are or can be called saints

behold verily thus saith the Lord unto you in consequence of evils and designs which do and will exist in the hearts of conspiring men in the last days I have warned you and forewarn you by giving unto you this word of wisdom by revelation that inasmuch as any man drinketh wine or strong drink among you behold it is not good neither meet in the sight of your father only in assembling yourselves together to offer up your sacrament before him and behold this should be wine yea pure wine of the grape of the vine of your own make,

and again strong drinks are not for the belly but for the washing of your bodies,

and again, Tobacco is not for the body neither for the belly and is not good for man, but is an herb for bruises and all sick cattle to be used with Judgment and skill

and again hot drinks are not for the body or belly

and again verily I say unto you all whol[e]some herbs God hath ordained for the constitution nature and use of man ev[e]ry herb in the season thereof and ev[e]ry fruit in the season thereof, all these to be used with prudence and thanksgiving yea flesh also of beasts and of the fowls of the are [air] I the Lord hath ordained for the use of man with thanksgiving nevertheless they are to be used sparingly, and it is pleasing unto me that they should not be used only in times of winter or of cold [or] famine,

all grain is ordained for the use of man and of beasts to be the staff of life not only for man but for the beasts of the field and the fowls of heaven and all wild animals that run or creap [creep] on the earth and these hath God made for the use of man only in times of famine and excess of hunger

all grain is good for the food of man as also the fruit of the vine that which yieldeth fruit whether in the ground or above the ground nevertheless wheat for man and corn for the ox and oats for the horse and rye for th[e] fowls & for swine and for all beasts of the field and barley for all useful animals and for mild drink[s] as also other grain,

and all saints who remember to keep and do these sayings walking in obedience to the commandments shall receive health in their naval and marrow to their bones and shall find wisdom and great treasure of knowledge even hid[d]en treasures and shall run and not be weary and shall walk and not faint and I the Lord give unto them a promise that the destroying angel shall pass by them as the Children of Israel and not slay them Amen

Given February 27 - 1833

109. Set in Order the Churches
From NKW Collection (cf. LDS D&C 90; RLDS D&C 87)

*Commandment received at Kirtland, Ohio, on 8 March 1833
concerning the keys of the kingdom
and certain church members*

Kirtland 8th of March 1833

A Commandment given unto Joseph [Smith, Jr.] saying, thus saith the Lord; verily, verily, I say unto you my son, thy sins are forgiven thee, according to thy petition: for thy prayers, and the prayers of thy brethren, have come up into my ears; therefore, thou art blessed from henceforth that bear the keys of the kingdom, given unto you; which kingdom is coming forth for the Last time.

verily I say unto you, the keys of this kingdom shall never be taken from you, while thou art in the world; neither in the world to come, never[the]less through you shall the oricles [oracles] be given unto another, yea, even unto the church: and all they who receiv[e] the oricles [oracles] of God, let them be aware how they hold them, Lest they are accounted as a light thing and are brought under condemnation thereby and stumble and fall when the storms descend & the winds blow and the rains descend and beat upon their hous[e]

and again verily I say unto thy brethren Sidney [Rigdon] and Fred[e]rick [G. Williams] their sins are forgiven them also and they are accounted as equal with thee in holding the keys of this Last Kingdom[24] as also through your administration the Keys of the school of the prophets which I have commanded to be organized that thereby they may be perfected in their ministry for the salvation of Zion and of the Nations of Israel and of the Gentiles as many as will believe that through your administration they may receive the word and through their administration the word may go forth unto th[e] ends of the earth unto the Gentiles first and then behold and Lo they shall turn unto the Jews and then cometh the day when the arm of the Lord shall be reveiled [revealed] in power in convincing the nations the heathen nations the house of Joseph of the Gospel of their salvation

for it shall come to pass in that day that ev[e]ry man shall hear the fulness of the Gospel in his own Tongue and in his own Language through those who are ordained unto this power by the administration of the comforter shed forth upon them for the revelation of Jesus Christ

and now verely [verily] I say unto you I give unto you a commandment that you continue in this ministry and presidency and when you have finished the translation of th[e] prophets[25] you shall from thenceforth preside over the affairs of

---

24. On 18 March 1833 the presidency was reorganized. Rigdon and Williams were ordained by Smith "to be equal with him in holding the keys of the Kingdom and also the Presidency of the high Priesthood" (Kirtland Council Minute Book, 17).

25. In February Smith had completed his review of the NT revision. A notation to this effect was recorded in the Kirtland Council Minute Book for 2 February 1833: "This day completed the translation and the reviewing of the New Testament and sealed up no more to be broken till it goes to Zion" (8). This revelation gives instruction to finish the revision of the OT prophets.

the Church and the school and from time to time as shall be manifest by the comfo[r]ter receive revelations to unfold the myste[ries] of the Kingdom and set in order the Churches and study and Learn and become acquainted with all good books and with Languages tongues and people &c &c and this shall be your busin[e]ss and mission in all your Lives to preside in council and set in order all the affairs of this Church and kingdom be not ashamed neither confounded but be admonished in all your high mindedn[e]ss and pride for it bringeth a snare upon your souls set in order your houses keep slothfulness and uncleanlin[e]ss far from you

now verily I say unto you let there be a place provided as soon as it is possable [possible] for the family of thy councellor [counselor] & scribe even Frederick [G. Williams]

and Let mine Aged servant Joseph [Smith, Sr.] continue with his family upon th[e] place wher[e] he now lives and let it not be sold untill the mouth of the Lord shall name

and let thy councellor [counselor] even Sidney [Rigdon] remain where he now resides untill the mouth of the Lord shall nam[e]

and let the Bishop search dilligently to obtain an agent and let it be a man who has got riches in store a man of God and of strong faith that thereby he may be enabled to discharge ev[e]ry debt that the store house of the Lord may not be brought into disrepute before the eyes of the people search diligently pray always and be believing and all thing[s] shall work together for your good if ye walk uprightly and remember the covenant wherewith ye have covenanted one with another

let your families be small especially mine aged Servant Joseph [Smith, Sr.] as pertaining to thos[e] who do not belong to your families that those thing[s] that are provided for you to bring to pass my work are not taken from you and given to thos[e] that ar[e] not worthy and thereby you be hindered in accomplishing those things which I have commanded you

and again verely [verily] I say unto you it is my will that my hand maid Vienna [Jaques] should receive money to bear her expenses and go up unto the Land of Zion and the residue of her money I will consecrate unto myself and reward her in min[e] own due time verely [verily] I say unto you that it is meet in mine eyes that she should go up un to the Land of Zion and receive an inheritance from the hand of the Bishop that she may settle down in peace in as much as she is faithful and not be Idle in her days from thenceforth

and behold verely [verily] I say unto you that ye shall write this commandment and say unto your brethren in Zion in Love greeting that I have called you also to preside over Zion in mine own due time therefore let them cease wearying me concerning this matter behold I say unto you that your brethren in Zion begin to repent and the Angels rejoice over them

nevertheless I am not well pleased with many things and I [am] not well please[d] with my servant William [E] McLel[l]in, neithe[r] with my servant Sidney Gilbert, and th[e] Bishop also and others have many things to repent of but verely [verily] I say unto you that I the Lord will contend with Zion and plead with her strong ones and chasten her untill she overcome[s] and are clean before me for she shall not be removed out of her place I the Lord hav[e] spoken it - Am[en]

Revision

1835 D&C 84
(cf. LDS D&C 90:29; RLDS D&C 87:7)

and the residue of *the* money *may be* consecrated unto *me,* and *she be* rewarded in mine own due time

110. The Apocrypha
From KRB, 55 (cf. LDS D&C 91; RLDS D&C 88)

Revelation received at Kirtland, Ohio, on 9 March 1833 concerning the Apocrypha in the King James Bible

Kirtland 9th of March 1833
A Revelation given concerning [the] Apocrypha

Verily thus saith the Lord unto you concerning the Apocrypha there are many things contained therein that are true and it is mostly translated correct - there are many things contained therein that are not true which are interpolation[s] by the hands of men

verily I say unto you that it is not needful that the Apocrypha should be translated therefore whoso readeth it let him understand for the spirit manifesteth truth and and whoso is enlightened by the spirit shall obtain benefit therefrom and whoso receiveth not the spirit cannot be benefited Therefore it is not needful that it should be translated Amen

111. Ye Shall Receive Him into the Firm
From KRB, 55 (cf. LDS D&C 92; RLDS D&C 89)

Revelation received at Kirtland, Ohio, on 15 March 1833 for Frederick G. Williams to be received into the United Firm[26]

Kirtland 15th March 1833

Verily thus saith the Lord I give unto the united firm organized agreeable to the commandment previously given a revelation & commandment concerning my servant Frederick [G. Williams] that ye shall receive him into the firm what I say

---

26. The Kirtland Council Minute Book records, "Thursday [Friday, 15 March] received a revelation making known that F.G.W. should be received into the United firm in full partnership agreeable to the specification of the bond" (11). The 1835 D&C has: "Revelation to Enoch, on the order of the Church for the benefit of the poor, given to the saints in Kirtland, March, 1833."

unto one I say unto all and again I say unto you my servant Frederick [G. Williams] thou shalt be a lively member in this firm and inas much as thou art faithful in keeping all former commandments thou shalt be blessed for ever Amen[27]

112. Man Is the Tabernacle of God
From NKW Collection (cf. LDS D&C 93; RLDS D&C 90)

Revelation received at Kirtland, Ohio, on 6 May 1833 concerning light and truth

Kirtland May 6 - 1833

Verely [Verily] thus saith the Lord, it shall come to pass, that ev[e]ry soul who forsaketh their sin[s] and cometh unto me and calleth on my name and obeyeth my voice and keepeth all my commandments shall see my face and know that I am and that I am the true light that lighteth ev[e]ry man who cometh into the world; and that I am in the fathe[r] and the fathe[r] in me and the fath[er] and I ar[e] one the fath[er] becaus[e] he gave me of his fulness and the son becaus[e] I was in the world and made flesh my tabernacl[e] and dwelt among the sons of men I was in the world and received of my father, and the works of him were plainly manifest

and John saw and bear [bore] record of the fulness of my glory and the fulness of John[']s record is hereafte[r] to be revealed and he bear [bore] record saying

I saw his glory that he was in the begin[n]ing befor[e] the world was therefore in the begig [beginning] the word was for he was the word even th[e] messenge[r] of salvation the light and th[e] redeeme[r] of the world the spirit of truth who came into the world becaus[e] th[e] world was made by him and in him was the Life of men and the light of men the worlds were made by him men were made by him all things were made by him and through him and of him

and I, John bear record that I beheld his glory as the glory of the only begotten of th[e] fath[er] full of grac[e] and truth even the spirit of truth which came and dwelt in [the] flesh and dwelt among us

and I John saw that he received not of the fulness at the first but received grac[e] for grace and he received n[o]t of the fulness but continued from grace to grace until he received a fulness and thus he was called the son of God because he received not of the fulness at the first

and I John bear record and lo the heaven[s] were opened and the holy ghost de[s]cended upon him in the form of a dove and sat upon him and there came a voice out of heaven saying this is my beloved son,

and I John bear record that he received a fulness of the glory of the father and he received all power both in heaven and on earth and the glory of the father was with him for he dwelt in him

---

27. This is the text prior to minor revisions in the manuscript book.

and it shall come to pass that if you ar[e] faithful you shall receive the fulness of th[e] record of John[28]

I give unto you thes[e] saying[s] that you may understand and know how to worship and know what you worship that you may come unto the fath[er] in my nam[e] and in due time receive of his fulness for if you keep my commandment[s] you shall receive of his fulness and be glor[i]fied in me as I am glor[i]fied in the fathe[r], therefore I say unto you you shall receive grace for grac[e]

and now verely [verily] I say unto you I was in the begin[n]ing with the fath[er] and am the first born and all thos[e] who are begotten through me are partakers of the glory of the sam[e] and ar[e] the church of the first born ye were also in the begin[n]ing with the fath[er] that which is spirit even the spirit of truth and truth is knowledge of thing[s] as they ar[e] and as they were, and as they are to come and whatsoev[er] is more or less than these is the spirit of that wicked one who was a liar from the begin[n]ing the spirit of truth is of God, I am the spirit of truth

and John bear [bore] record of me saying he received a fullness of truth yea even all truth and no man receiveth a fulness unless he keepeth his commandments he that keepeth his commandments receiveth truth and light untill he is glor[i]fied in truth and knoweth all things

man was also in th[e] begin[n]ing with God, intel[l]ige[nce] or the Light of truth was not created or mad[e] neith[er] indeed can be all truth is independent in that sphere in which God has placed it to act for itself as all intel[l]igen[ce] also otherwis[e] ther[e] is no existence behold her[e] is the agency of man and here is the condemnation of man becaus[e] that which was from th[e] begin[n]ing is plainly manifest unto them and they receive not th[e] light and ev[e]ry man whos[e] spirit rec[e]ivet[h] not the light[29] for man is spirit the Elements ar[e] eternal and spirit and element inseparably connected rec[e]iveth a fulness of Joy and when separated man cannot receiv[e] a fulness of Joy the elements are the tabernacle of God, yea man is the tabernacl[e] of God even temples and whatsoev[er] templ[e] is defiled God shall destroy that temple,

the glory of God is intel[l]igenc[e] or in other words light & truth light and truth forsaketh that evil one ev[e]ry spirit of man was innocent in th[e] begin[n]ing, and God having redeemed man from the fall man became again in their inf[ant] state innocent before God and that wicked one cometh and taketh away light and truth through disobeidien[ce] [disobedience] from the childre[n] of men and becaus[e] of the tradition of their fathers

but I have commanded you to bring up your Children in light and truth, but verely [verily] I say unto you my servant Frederick [G. Williams] you have continued under this condemnation you have not taught your Children light and truth according to the commandments and that wicked on[e] hath power as yet over you

---

28. The text is unclear if the "record of John" to be revealed is that of the gospel writer John (revision already completed) or John the Baptist. See John 1:1-34 and Robert J. Matthews, *A Burning Light: The Life and Ministry of John the Baptist* (Provo, UT: Brigham Young University Press, 1972), 79-83.

29. The KRB completes this phrase by adding above the line the words "is under condemnation" (57).

and this is the caus[e] of your affliction and now a commandment I give unto you and if ye will be delivered you shall set in order your own house for there are many things that are not right in your house

verely [verily] I say unto my servant Sidney [Rigdon] that in some things he hath not kept the commandments concerning his children therefor[e] firstly set in order thy hou[se]

and verely [verily] I say unto my servant Joseph [Smith, Jr.], (or in othe[r] word[s], I will call you friends) for ye ar[e] my friends) and ye shall have an inheritan[ce] with me I called you servants for the world[']s sake and ye are their servants for my sake and now verely [verily] I say unto you Joseph [Smith, Jr.] you have not kept th[e] commandments and must needs stand rebuked before the lord your family must needs repent and forsake some things and give mor[e] earnest heed unto your sayings or be remooved [removed] out of their place what I say unto one I say unto all pray always lest that wicked one hav[e] power in you and remove you out of you[r] pla[ce]

my servant Newel [K. Whitney] also the Bishop of my church hath need to be chastened and set in order his family and see that they are more diligent and concerned at home and pray always or they shall be removed out of their plac[e]

now I say unto you my friends let my servant Sidney [Rigdon] go on his Journey and make haste and also proclai[m] the acceptabl[e] year of the Lord and the gospel of salvation as I shall give him utterence and by your praye[r] of faith with one consent I will uphold him

and let my servants Josep[h] [Smith, Jr.] & Frederick [G. Williams] make hast[e] also and it shall be given them even according to the pray[er] of faith and inasmu[ch] as you keep my saying[s] you shall not be confounded in this world nor in the world to come

and verely [verily] I [s]ay unto you that it is my will that y[ou] should hasten to translat[e] my script[ure]s[30] and to obtain a knowledg[e] of history and of countries and of kingdom[s] and of laws, [of] God & man and all th[is] for the salvation of Zion Amen

113. The Building of Mine House
From KRB, 59-60 (cf. LDS D&C 95; RLDS D&C 92)

Revelation received at Kirtland, Ohio, in [1-3] June 1833
concerning building a house unto the Lord[31]

Kirtland June 1st 1833

Verily thus saith the Lord unto you whom I love, and whom I love I also chasten that their sins may be forgiven, for with the chastisement I prepare a way for

---

30. The initial revision of the OT was finished on 2 July 1833.

31. The Kirtland Council Minute Book records under the date 3 June 1833 that "A Conference of high Priests convened in Kirtland ... received a revelation on the size of the house" (12).

their deliverance in all things out of temptation and I have loved you therefore ye must needs be chasten[e]d and stand rebuked before my face, for ye have sinned against me a verry [very] grievous sin in that ye have not considered the great commandment in all things that I have given unto you concerning the building of mine house for the preparation wherewith I design to prepare mine Apostles to prune my vineyard for the last time that I may bring to pass my strange act that I may pour out my spirit upon all flesh.

But behold verily I say unto you there are many who have been ordained among you whom I have called but few of them are chosen. they who are not chosen have sinned a verry [very] grievous sin in that they are walking in darkness at noon day, and for this cause I gave unto you a commandment that you should call your solem[n] assembly that your fastings and your mourning might come up into the ears of the Lord of Sabaoth which is by interpretation the creator of the first day the beginning and the end.

Yea verily I say unto you I gave unto you a commandment that you should build an hous[e] in the which house I design to endow those whom I have chosen with power from on high, for this is the promise of the Father unto you.

Therefore, I commanded you to tarry even as mine Apostles at Jerusalem. nevertheless my servants sinned a verry [very] grievous sin and contentions arose in the school of the prophets, which was verry [very] grievous unto me saith your Lord. therefore I sent them forth to be chastened.

Verily I say unto you, it is my will that you should build an house. If ye keep my commandments ye shall have power to build it. If ye keep not my commandments the love of the fath[er] shall not continue with you therefore ye shall walk in darkness.

now here is wisdom and the mind of the Lord, Let the house be built not after the manner of the world, for I give not unto you that ye shall live after the manner of the world. Therefore let it be built after the manner which I shall show unto three of you whom ye shall appoint and ordain unto this pow[er] and the size thereof shall be fifty and five feet in width and let it be sixty and five feet in length in the inner court thereof, and let the lower part of the inner court be dedicated unto me for your sacrament offering and for your preaching and your fasting and your praying and the offering up your most holy desires unto me saith your lord,

and let the higher part of the inner court be dedicated unto me for the school of mine Apostles saith Son ah man [Ahman], or in otherwords Alphos, or in other words Omegos[32] even Jesus Christ your lord Amen

---

32. The 1835 D&C has "Alphus" and "Omegus." Other revelations end with Alpha and Omega.

114. Bringing Forth My Word
From KRB, 60-61 (cf. LDS D&C 96; RLDS D&C 93)

*Revelation received at Kirtland, Ohio, on 4 June 1833
concerning the Peter French farm and John Johnson*[33]

Kirtland June 4th 1833

Behold I say unto you here is wisdom whereby ye may know how to act concerning this matter. for it is expedient in me that this stake that I have set for the strength of Zion should be made strong.

Therefore let my servant Newel [K. Whitney] take charge of the place which is named among yo[u] upon which I design to build mine holy house, and again let it be divided into lots according to wisdom for the benefit of those who seek inheritances as it shall be determined in council among you.

Therefore take heed that ye see to this matter, and that portion that is necessary to benefit the firm for the purpose of bringing forth my word to the children of men, for Behold verily I say unto you, this is the most expedient in me that my word should go forth unto the children of men for the purpose of subdueing [subduing] the hearts of the children of men for your good even so Amen

and again verily I say unto you it is wisdom and expedient in me that my servant John Johnson whose offering I have accepted and whose prayers I have heard, unto whom I give a promise of Eternal life inasmuch as he keepeth my commandments from hence forth, for he is a descendant of Joseph and a partaker of the blessings of the promise made unto his fathers. Verily I say unto you it is expedient in me that he should become a member of this firm that he may assist in bringing forth my word unto the children of men. Therefore ye shall ordain him unto this blessing,[34] and he shall seek dilligently to take away incumbrances that are upon the house named among you that he may dwell therein even so Amen

115. For This Is Zion the Pure in Heart
From a letter of Joseph Smith, Jr., et al. to Beloved Brethren, 6 August 1833, LDS archives (cf. LDS D&C 97; RLDS D&C 94)

*Revelation received at Kirtland, Ohio, on 2 August 1833
concerning building a house [temple] in the Land of Zion*[35]

The word of the Lord unto Joseph [Smith, Jr.] Sidney [Rigdon] and Fred[e]rick [G. Williams]

Verily I say un to my friends I speak unto you with my voice, even the voice of

---

33. This text follows the wording in the KRB before later revision.
34. The Kirtland Council Minute Book for 4 June 1833 notes that John Johnson "was ordained unto the high Priesthood and admit[t]ed" as a member of the united firm (13).
35. Some punctuation marks added to the original letter are included.

my spirit, that I may shew unto you my will concerning your breatheren [brethren] in the land of Zion, many of whom are truly humble, and are seeking dilligently to learn wisdom, and to find truth. verily verily I say un to you blessed are all such for they shall obtain for I the Lord sheweth mercy unto all the meek, and upon all whomsoever I will, that I may be justified when I shall bring them unto judgement.

Behold I say unto you concerning the school in Zion, I the Lord am well pleased that there should be a school in Zion, and also with my servent Parley [P. Pratt], for he abideth in me. and inasmuch as he continue to abide in me, he shall continue to preside over the school in the land of Zion, and I will bless him with a multiplicity of blessings in expounding all Schriptures [Scriptures] and mysteries to the edification of [the] school and of the church in Zion.

And to the residue of the school I the Lord am willing to shew mercy nevertheless there are those that must needs be chastened, and their works shall be made known, the axe [ax] is laid at the roots of the trees, and every tree that bringeth not forth good fruit shall be hewn down and cast into the fire, I the Lord have spoken it: verily I say unto you; all among them who know their hearts are honest, and are broken, and their spirits contrite, and are willing to observe their covenant[s] by sacrafice [sacrifice], yea, every sacrafice [sacrifice] which I the Lord shall command them are all accepted of me; for I the Lord will cause them to bring forth as a very fruitfull tree which is planted in a goodly land by a pure stream that yieldeth much precious fruit.

Verily I say unto you that it is my will that an house should be built unto me in the land of Zion[36] like unto the pattern which I have given you.[37] Yea, let it be built speedily by the tithing of my people, behold this is the tithing, and the sacrafice [sacrifice] which I the Lord require at their hand, that there may be a hous[e] built unto me for the salvation of Zion, and for a place of thanksgiving for all saints, and for a place of instruction for all those who are called to the work of the ministry in all their several calling[s] and offices, that they may be perfected in the understanding of their ministry, in theory, and principle, and in doctrine, in all things pertaining to [the] kingdom of God on the earth. (the keys of which kingdom have been confer[r]ed upon you)

And inasmuch as my people build an house unto me in the name of the Lord and do not suffer any unclean thing to come into it that it be not defiled, my glory shall rest upon it yea and my presence shall be there, for I will come into it and all

---

36. That a house or temple should be built in Missouri was mentioned in a revelation received in September 1832 (see document no. 100; LDS D&C 84; RLDS D&C 83).

37. At this point the letter contains the words: "(which pattern we have sent to Zion in a former package)[.]" This was an explanatory note and not part of the revelatory text. These words were not included in the copy preserved in the KRB (62). During this period the thought was that only one temple would be built in Zion. In June 1833 Smith worked on a draft containing a plat of the city of Zion with explanations regarding the city center and plans for a number of houses called temples. This included a draft for "the house of the Lord which is to be built first in Zion" (Joseph Smith Letterbook, 1:41). The plat designated and numbered twenty-four "temples" which were to be twenty-four buildings for the purpose of "houses of worship" and "schools." In August 1833 corrections were made to the plat and the house for the presidency.

the pure in heart that shall come into it shall see God; but if it be defiled I will not come into it, and my glory shall not be there, for I will not come into an unholy temple.

And now behold if Zion do these things she shall prosper and sp[r]ead herself and become very glorious very great and very terable [terrible], and the nations of the earth shall honor her, and shall say surely Zion is the City of our God, and surely Zion cannot fall neither be removed, out of her place, for God is there, and the hand of the Lord is there and he hath sworn by the power of his might, to be her salvation and her high tower.

therefore verily thus saith the Lord let Zion rejoice for this is Zion the pure in heart Therefore let Zion rejoice while all the wicked shall mourn, for behold and lo! vengence [vengeance] cometh speedily upon the ungodly as the whirlwind and who shall escape, it, the Lord['] s scourge shall pass over, by night, and by day, and the report thereof shall vex all people, yet it shall not be staid [stayed] untill the Lord come; for the indignation of the [Lord] is kindled against their abominations, and all their wicked works; nevertheless Zion shall escape if she observe to do all things whatsoever I have commanded her, but if she observe not [to do] whatso- ever I have commanded her, I will visit her according to all her works, with sore affliction, with pestilence, with plague with sword, with vengence [vengeance], with devouring fire, nevertheless let it be read this once in their ears that I the Lord have accepted of their offering and if she sin no more none of these things shall come upon her, but I will bless her with blessings and multiply a multiplicity of blessings upon her and upon her generations forever and ever saith th[e] Lord your God Amen.

116. According to the Pattern
From a letter of Joseph Smith, Jr., et al. to Beloved Brethren, 6 August 1833, LDS archives (cf. LDS D&C 94; RLDS D&C 91)

Commandment received at Kirtland, Ohio, on 2 August 1833 concerning building houses for the presidency and for printing[38]

And again verily I say unto you my friends, a commandment I give unto you that ye shall commence a work of laying out and preparing a begin[n]ing and foun- dation of the City of the stake of Zion here in the land of Kirtland; begin[n]ing at my house, and behold it must be done according to the pattern which I have given you unto you,

and let the first lot on the south be consecrated unto me for the building of an house for the presidency,[39] in obtaining revelations and for the work of the minis- try of the presidency in all things pertaining to the church and kingdom;

38. A few punctuation marks added to the original letter are included.
39. Here the KRB contains the words "for the work of the presidency" (65).

Verily I say unto you it shall[40] that it shall be built fifty five by sixty five [feet] in the width thereof and in the length thereof in the inner court, and there shall be a lower court and a higher court according to the pattern, which shall be given unto you hereafter; and it shall be dedicated unto the Lord from the foundation thereof according to the order of the priesthood according to the pattern which shall be given unto you hereafter and it shall be whol[l]y dedicated unto the Lord, for the work of the presidency; and ye shall not suffer any unclean thing to come into it and my glory shall be there, and my presence shall be there, but if there shall come into it any unclean thing my glory shall not be there and my presence shall not come into it.

And again verily I say unto you the second lot on the south shall be dedicated unto me for the work of the printing of the translation of my schriptures [scriptures], and all things whatsoever I shall command you; and it shall be fifty five by sixty five [feet] in the width thereof and in the length thereof in the inner court, and there shall be a lower and higher court, and this house shall be whol[l]y dedicated unto the Lord from the foundation thereof for the work of the printing in all thing[s] whatsoever I shall command you to be holy and undefiled according to the pattern, in all things as it shall be given unto you,

and on the thir[d] lot shall my servant Hiram [Hyrum Smith] receive his inheritance

and on the first and second lots on the north shall my servents Reynolds Cahoon and Jared Carter receive their inheritance that they may do the work which I have appointed unto them to be a committee to build my houses according to the commandment which I the Lord God have given unto you and now I give unto you no more at this time.[41]

117. Renounce War and Proclaim Peace

From a letter of Joseph Smith, Jr., et al. to Beloved Brethren, 6 August 1833, LDS archives (cf. LDS D&C 98; RLDS D&C 95)

Revelation received at Kirtland, Ohio, on 6 August 1833 concerning the law of vengeance

Kirtland August 6th 1833

verily I say unto you my friends fear not let your heart[s] be comforted yea rejoice ever more & in every thing give thanks waiting patiently on the Lor[d] for your prayer[s] have entered into the ears of the Lord of sabboth [sabaoth] and are recorded with this seal and testament the Lord hath sworn and decreed that they shall be granted therefor[e] he giveth this promis[e] unto you with an immutable

---

40. The first "it shall" is evidently a copying error as the KRB words are "that it shall" (65).

41. The KRB has added in small handwriting: "These two houses are not to be bui[l]t ti[ll] I give you a commandment concerning them" (66). It is not known if this was part of the early text. The text ends with "Amen."

covenant that they shall be fulfilled and all things wherewith you have been afflicted shall work togethe[r] for your good and to my name[']s glory saith the Lord God.

And now verily I say unto you concerning the Laws of the Land it is my will that my peopl[e] should observe to do all things whatsoeve[r] I command them and that law of the Land which is constitutional supporting the principles of freedom in maintaining right[s] and privileges belongs to all mankin[d] and is Justifyable before me therefore I the Lord Justifieth you and your brethren of my church in befriending that law which is the constitutional law of the Land and as pertaining to law of men whatsoever is more or less than this cometh of evil.

I the Lord your God maketh you free therefore you are free indeed and the law also maketh you free nevertheless when the wicked rule the people mourn wherefor[e] honest men and wise men should be saught [sought] for dilligently and good men and wise men ye should observe to uphold otherwise whatsoever is less than this cometh of evil

and I give unto you a commandment that ye shal[l] forsake all evil and cleave unto all good that ye shall live by every word that proceedeth out forth out of the mouth of God for he will give unto the faithful line upon lin[e] precept upon precept and I will try you and prove you herewith and whoso layeth down his life in my caus[e] for my nam[e's] sake shall find it again even life eternal therefor[e] be not affraid [afraid] of your enemies for I have decreed in my heart saith the Lord that I will prove you in all things whether you will abide in my covenant even unto death that you may be found worthy for if you will not abide in my covena[n]t ye are not worthy of me

therefor[e] renounce war and proclaim peace and seek dilligently to turn the hearts of the children to their fathers and the hearts of the fathers to the children and again the hearts of [the] Jews to the prophets and the prophets unto the Jews lest I come and smite the whole earth with a curse and all flesh be consumed before me let not your hearts be troubled for in my father[']s house are many mansions and I have prepared a place for you and where my father and I am there you shall be also,

Behold I the Lord am not well pleased with many who are in the church at Kirtland for they do not forsake their sins and their wicked ways the pride of their hearts and their covetousness and all their detestable things and observ[e] the words of wisdom and eternal life which I have given unto them verily I say unto you that I the Lord will chasten them and will do whateve[r] I list if they do not repent and observe all thing[s] whatsoever I have said unto them

And again I say unto you if ye observe to do whatsoever I command you I the Lord will turn away all wrath and indignation from you and the gates of hell shall not prevail against you

Now I speak unto you concerning your families if men will smite you or your families once and ye bear it patiently and revile not against them neithe[r] seek revenge ye shall be rewarded but if ye bear it not patiently it shall be accounted unto you as being meeted [meted] out [as] a Just measur[e] unto you, and again if your enemies shall smite you a second time and you revile not against your enemies and bear it patiently your reward shall be an hundredfold and again if he shall smite you a third time and ye bear it patiently your reward shall be doubled unto you four fold and these three testamones [testimonies] shall stand against your enemy if he repent not and shall not be blotted out

and now verily I say unto you if that enemy shall escape my venge[a]nce that he be not broug[h]t into Judgment before me then you shall see to it that ye warn him in my name that he come no more upon you [n]either upon your families [n]either your children or your children['s] children unto the thir[d] and fourth generation and then if he shall come upon you or your children or your children[']s children unto the third and fo[u]rth generation I have delivered thine enemy into thine hands and then if thou wilt spare him thou shalt be rewarded for thy righteousness and thy children and thy children[']s children unto the third and fourth generation nevertheless thine enemy is in thine hands and if thou rewardest him according to his works thou art Justified if he has sought thy life and thy life is endangered by him thine enemy is in thine hands and thou art Justified.

Behold this is the Law I gave unto my servant Nephi and thy father[s] Joseph and Jacob and Isaac and Abram [Abraham] and all mine ancient prophets and Apostles and again this is the Law that I gave unto mine ancients that they should not go out unto battle against any nation kindred tongue or people save I the Lord commanded them

and if any Nation tongue or people should proclaim war against them they should first lift a standard of peace unto that people Nation or tongue and if that peoper [people] did not ecept [accept] the offering of peace neither the second nor the third time they should bring those testimonies before the Lord then I the Lord would give unto them a commandment and Justify them in going out to battle against that nation tongue or people and I the Lord will fight their battles and their children[']s battles and their children[']s children untill they have avenged themselves on all their enemies to the third and fourth generation behold this is an ensample [example] unto all people saith the Lord your God for justification before me.

And again Verily I say unto you if after thine enemies has come upon you the first time he repents and come unto thee praying thy forgiveness thou shall forgive him and shall hold it no more as a testimony against thine enemy and so on unto the second and the third time and as oft as thine enemy repent of the trespass wherewith he has trespassed against thee thou shalt forgive him unto seventy times seven

and if he trespass against thee and repent not the first time nevertheless thou shalt forgive him and if he trespass against thee the second time and repent not nevertheless thou shalt forgive him and if he trespass against thee the third time and repent not thou shalt also forgive him

but if he trespass against him the fourth time thou shalt not forgive him but shalt bring these testimonies before the Lord and they shall not be blotted out till he repent and reward thee four fould [fold] in all things wherewith he has trespasses against you and if he do this thou shalt forgive him with all thine heart and if he do no[t] this I the Lord will avenge thee of thine enemy an hundred fold and upon his children and upon his children[']s children of all them that hate me unto the third and fourth generation but if the children shall repent or the children[']s children and turn unto the Lord their God with all their heart and with all their might mind and strength and restore four fold for all their trespasses wherewith they have trespassed or wherewith their fathers have trespassed or their father[']s fathers then thine indignation shall be turned away and vengeance shall no more come upon them saith the Lord your God and their trespasses shall never be brought any more as a testimony before the Lord against them Amen.

118. A Pure People

From NKW Collection (cf. LDS D&C 100; RLDS D&C 97)

Revelation received at Perrysburg [now South Dayton], New York, on 12 October 1833 for Sidney Rigdon and Joseph Smith, Jr.[42]

Prereysburg [Perrysburg] Chatoegua [Cattaraugus] Co[ounty] N[ew] Y[ork] Saturday October 12th 1833

Verily thus saith the Lord unto you my friends, Sidney [Rigdon], & Joseph [Smith, Jr.] your families are well; they are in mine hands, and I will do with them as seemeth me good; for in me there is all power. therefore, follow me and listen to the council [counsel] which I shall give unto you: behold, and lo, I have much people in this place in the regions round about, and an effectual door shall be opened in the regions round about in this eastern land.

therefore, I the Lord have suffered you to come unto this place, for thus it was expedient in me for the salvation of souls. therefore, verily I say unto you, lift up your voices unto this people, speak the thoughts that I shall put into your hearts, and ye shall not be confounded before men; for it shall be given you in the very hour, yea, in the very moment what ye shall say.

but a commandment I give unto you, that ye shall declare whatsoever things ye declare in my name in solemnity of heart in the spirit of meekness in all things. and I give unto you this promise, that inasmuch as ye do this the holy Ghost shall be shed forth in bearing record unto all things whatsoever ye shall say.

and it is expedient in me, that you, Sidney [Rigdon], should be a spokesman unto this people; yea, verily I will ordain you unto this calling, even to be a spokesman unto my servant Joseph [Smith, Jr.]. and I will give unto him power to be mighty in testimony. and I will give unto thee power to be mighty in expounding all schriptures [scriptures] that thou mayest be a spokesman unto him, and he shall be a revelator unto thee that thou mayest know the certa[i]nty of all things pertaining to the things of my kingdom on the earth. Therefore, continue your journey and let your hearts rejoice, for behold, and lo, I am with you even unto the end.

---

42. Smith recorded on this day, "I feel very well in my mind the Lord is with us but have much anxiety about my family &c" (Joseph Smith Journal, 12 Oct. 1833; Jessee, *Papers of Joseph Smith*, 2:6).

And now I give unto you a word concerning Zion: Zion shall be redeemed altho[ugh] she is chastened for a little season: thy brethren, my servants, Orson [Hyde], and John [Gould], are in my hands, and inasmuch as they keep my commandments they shall be saved. therefore let your hearts be comforted, for all things shall work together for good to them that walk uprightly and to the sanctifycation of the church for I will raise up unto myself a pure people that will serve me in righteousness and all that call on the name of the Lord and keep his commandments shall be saved even so Amen

119. Avenge Me of Mine Enemies
From KRB, 73-83 (cf. LDS D&C 101; RLDS D&C 98)

Revelation received at Kirtland, Ohio, on 16 December 1833 concerning the redemption of Zion in Jackson County, Missouri

Verily I say unto you concerning your brethren who have been afflicted, and persecuted, and cast out from the land of their inheritanc[e] I the Lord have suffered the affliction to come upon them, wherewith they have been afflicted, in consequence of their transgressions; yet, I will own them and they shall be mine in that day when I shall come to make up my jewels.

Therefor[e], they must needs be chastened, and tried, even as Abraham, who was commanded to offer up his only son; for all those who will not endure chastening but deny me, cannot be sanctified.

Behold I say unto you, there were jar[r]ings, and contention[s], & envyings, and strifes, and lustful and covetous desires among them; Therefore by these things they pol[l]uted their inheritance; they were slow to hearken unto the voice of the Lord their God. Therefore the Lord their God is slow to hearken unto their prayers, to answer them in the day of their trouble: In the day of their peace they esteemed lightly my counsel; but in the day of their trouble, of necessity they feel after me.

Verily, I say unto you, notwithstanding their sins, my bowels are filled with compassion toward[s] them; I will not utterly cast them off; and in the day of wrath I will remember mercy, I have sworn and the decree hath gone forth by a former commandment which I have given unto you, that I would Let fall the sword of mine indignation in th[e] behalf of my people.[43] and even as I have said it shall come to pass, mine indignation is soon to be poured out without measure upon all nations. and this will I do when the cup of their eniquity [iniquity] is full; and in that day, all who are found upon th[e] watch tower, or in other words, all mine Israel shall be saved; and they that have been scattered shall be gathered; and all they who have mourned shall be comforted, and all they who have given their lives for my name shall he crowned,

43. See document no. 38; LDS D&C 35; RLDS D&C 34.

Therefore, let your hearts be comforted concerning Zion, for all flesh is in mine hands: be still and know that I am God: Zion shall not be moved out of her place, notwithstanding, her children are scattered, they that remain and are pure in heart shall return and come to their inheritances, they and their children, with songs of everlasting Joy, to build up the waste places of Zion; and all these things that the prophets might be fulfilled.

and behold, the[re] is none other place appointed than that which I have appointed, neithe[r] shall the[re] be any othe[r] place appointed than that which I have appointed for the work of the gathering of my saints until th[e] day cometh when there is found no more room for them, & then I have other places which I will appoint unto them and they shall be called stakes for the curtains or strength of Zion.

Behold it is my will that all they who call on my name and worship me according to mine everlasting gospel, should gather to gether and stand in holy places and prepare for the revelation which is to come when the veil of the covering of my temple in my tabernacle which hidet[h] the earth shall be taken off and all flesh shall see me together and ev[e]ry coruptable [corruptible] thing; both of man, or of the beasts of the field or of the fowls of heaven or of the fish of the sea, that dwell upon all the face of the earth shall be consumed. And also that of element shall melt with fervent heat and all things shall be come new that my knowledge and glory may dwell upon all the earth and in that day the enmity of man and the enmity of beasts yea the enmity of all flesh shall cease from before my face.

And in that day whatsoever any man shall ask it shall be given unto him and in that day Satan shall not have power to tempt any man; and there shall be no sorrow becaus[e] ther[e] is no death, In that day an infant shall not die until he is old, and his life shall be as the age of a tree; and when he dies he shall not sleep, (that is to say in th[e] earth,) but shall be changed in the twinkling of an eye, and shall be caught up; and his rest shall be glorious,

yea, verily I say unto you, in that day when the Lord shall come he shall reveal all things, things which have passed and hidden things which no man kn[e]w things of the earth by which it was made and the purpos[e] and the end thereof; things most precious; things that are above, and thing[s] that are beneath; things that are in the earth and upon the earth, and in heaven; And all they that suffe[r] persecution for my name and endure in faith, though they are called to lay down their lives for my sake yet shall they partak[e] of all this glory wherefore fea[r] not even unto death for in this world your Joy is not full but in me your Joy is full therefor[e] car[e] not for the body neithe[r] for the Life of th[e] body but car[e] for the soul and for th[e] life of the soul and seek th[e] face of th[e] Lord always that in patience ye may possess your souls and ye shall have eternal life

When men are called unto mine everlasting gospel and covenant with an everlasting covenant they are accounted as the salt of the earth and the savor of men; they are called to be the savor of men; therefor[e] if that salt of the earth lose its savor behold it is thenceforth good for nothing only to be cast out and trod[d]en unde[r] th[e] feet of men. Behold here is wisdom concerning the children of Zion even many but not all they were found transgressors therefor[e] they must needs be chastened he that exalteth himself shall be abased and he that abaseth himself shall be exalted

And now I will shew unto you a parable that you may know my will concerning the redemption of Zion A certain nobleman had a spot of Land very choice and he said unto his servants go ye into my vineyard even upon this very choice piece of land and plant twelve olive trees and set watchmen round about them and build a tower that one may overlook the Land round about to be a watchman upon th[e] tower that mine olive trees may not be broken down when the enemy shall come to spoil and take unto themselves the fruit of my vineyard

Now the servants of this nobleman went and did as their Lord commanded them and planted th[e] olive trees and built a hedge round about and set watchmen and began to build the tower and whil[e] they were yet Laying the foundation thereof they began to say among themselves and what need hath my Lord of this tower[?] and consulted for a long time saying among themselves what need hath my Lord of this tower seeing this is a time of peace[?] might not this money be given to the exchanges[?] for ther[e] is no need of thes[e] things and while they were at variance one with anothe[r] they became very slothful and they h[e]arkened not unto the commandment[s] of their Lord and the enemy came by night and broke down the hedge and the servant[s] of the nobleman aros[e] and were affrighted and fled and th[e] enemy distroyed [destroyed] their works and broke down the Olive trees

Now behold the nobleman the Lord of the vineyard called upon his servants and said unto them why what is the cause of this great evil[?] ought ye not to have done even as I commanded you and after you had planted the vineyard and built the hedge round about and set watchmen upon the walls thereof built the tower also and set a watchman upon the tower and watched for my vineyard and not have fallen asleep lest the enemy should come upon you[?] And behold the watchman upon the tower would have seen the enemy while he was yet afar off and then ye could have made ready and kept th[e] enemy from breaking down th[e] hedge thereof and saved my vineyard from the hands of the distroyer [destroyer].

And th[e] Lord of the vineyard said unto one of his servants go and gathe[r] togethe[r] the residue of my servants and take all the strength of mine hous[e] which are my war[r]iors my young men and they that are of middl[e] age also among all my servants who are the strength of mine house save th[o]se only whom I have appointed to tarry and go ye strai[gh]tway unto the Land of my vineyard and redeem my vineyard for it is mine I have bought it with money therefor[e] get ye strai[gh]tway unto my Land break down the walls of mine enemies th[r]ow down their tower and scatte[r] their watchmen and inasmuch as they gathe[r] to gethe[r] against you avenge me of mine enemies that by and by I may com[e] with the residue of mine house and possess the Land

And the servant said unto his Lord when shall thes[e] things be[?] And h[e] said unto his servant when I will. go ye strai[gh]t way and do all things whatsoever I have commanded you and this shall be my seal and blessing upon you: A faithful and wise steward in th[e] midst of mine house, a ruler in my kingdom. And his servant went strai[gh]tway and done all things whatsoeve[r] his Lord commanded him and after many days all things were fulfilled

And again verily I say unto you I will shew unto you wisdom in me concerning all the churches inasmuch as they are willing to be guided in a right and prope[r] way for their salvation that the work of the gathering togeth[er] of my saints may continue that I may build them up unto my name upon holy places for the time of harvest is come and my word must needs be fulfilled

therefor[e] I must gather to geth[er] my people according to the parable of the wheat and the tares that the wh[e]at may be secured in the garner to possess eternal Life and be crowned with celestial glory when I shall come in the kingdom of my father to reward ev[e]ry man according as his work shall be while the tares shall be bound in bundles and their bands made strong that they may be burned with unquenchable fire,

therefore a commandment I give unto all the churches that they shall continue to gather to gether unto the places which I have appointed, nevertheless as I have said unto you in a former commandment — let not your gathering be in haste nor by flight but let all things be prepared before you[44] and in order that all things be prepared befor[e] you observe the commandments which I have given concerning those things, which saith or teacheth to purchas[e] all the Land by money whic[h] can be purchased for money in the region round about the Land which I have appointed to be the Land of Zion for the begin[n]ing of the gathering of my saints all the Land which can he purchased in Jackson County and the counties round about and leave th[e] residu[e] in mine hand

Now verily I say unto you let all the churches gathe[r] to gether all their monies let thes[e] things be done in their time bu[t] not in haste and observe to have all things prepared before you and let honorable men be appointed even wise men and send them to purchas[e] th[e] lands and every church in the eastern counties when they are built up if they will h[e]arken unto this council [counsel] they may buy Land[s] and gather together upon them and in this way they may establish Zion ther[e] is even now already in store a sufficient yea even [an] abundance to redeem Zion and establish her waste places no more to be thrown down were the churches who call thems[e]lves afte[r] my name willing to hearken to my voice

and again I say unto you thos[e] who have been scattered by their enemies it is my will that they should continue to importune for redress and redemption by the hand of those who are placed as rulers and are in authority over you according to th[e] Law and constitution of th[e] people which I have suffered to be established and should be maintained for the rights and protectio[n] of all flesh according to Just and holy principl[e]s, that ev[e]ry man may act in doctrine and principle pertaining to futurity according to the moral agency which I have given unto them that ev[e]ry man may be accountable for his own sins in the day of Judgment therefor[e] it is not right that any man should be in bondage one to another and for this purpos[e] have I established the constitution of this Land by the hands of wise men whom I raised up unto this very purpos[e] and redeemed the Land by the shedding of blood,

---

44. See document no. 64; LDS and RLDS D&C 58.

Now unto what shall I liken the children of Zion[?] I will liken them unto the parable of the woman and the unjust Judge (for men ought always to pray and not to faint) which saith there was in a city a Judge which feared not God neithe[r] regarded man and there was a widow in that city and she came unto him saying avenge me of mine adversary and he would not for a while but afterward he said within himself though I fear not God nor regard man yet becaus[e] this widow troubleth me I will avenge her lest by her continual coming she weary me thus will I liken th[e] children of Zion

let them importune at the feet of the Judge and if he heed them not let them importune at the feet of the Govoner [Governor] and if the Govone[r] [Governor] heed them not let them importun[e] at the feet of th[e] President and if th[e] President heed them not then will the Lord arise and come forth out of his hiding place & in his fury vex the nation and in his hot displeasur[e] and in his fierc[e] anger in his time will cut off these wicked unfaithful and unjust stewards and appoint them their portion among hypocrit[e]s and unbelieve[r]s even in oute[r] darkness where there is weeping and wailing and gnashing of teeth

pray ye therefor[e] that their ears may be opened unto your cries that I may be merciful unto them that these things may not come upon them what I have said unto you must need[s] be that all men may be left without excus[e] that wise men and rulers may hear and know that which they have never considered that I may proceed to bring to pass my act my strange act and perform my work my strange work that men may desern [discern] between th[e] righteous and the wicked saith your God

and again I say unto you it is contrary to my commandment and my will that my servant Algernon Sidney Gilbert should sell my store house which I have appointed unto my people into the hand[s] of mine enemies let not that which I have appointed be pol[l]uted by mine enemies by the consent of those who call themselves afte[r] my name — for this is a very sore and grievou[s] sin against me —and against my people in consequence of thos[e] things which I have decreed and are soon to befall the nations therefor[e] it is my will that my people should claim and hold claim upon that which I have appointed unto them though they should not be permit[t]ed to dwell thereon nevertheless I do not say they shall not dwell thereon for in as much as they bring forth fruit and works meet for my kingdom they shall dwell thereon they shall build and anothe[r] shall not inherit it they shall plant vineyards and they shall eat the fruit thereof even so amen

120. Restoration and Redemption of Zion

From "Book of Commandments, Law and Covenants; Book C,"
LDS archives (cf. LDS D&C 103; RLDS D&C 100)

Revelation received at Kirtland, Ohio, on 24 February 1834
to organize men to travel to Missouri
and redeem the Land of Zion[45]

Verily I say unto you my Friends behold, I will give unto you a revelation & commandment, that you may know how to act in the discharge of your duties concerning the salvation & redemption of your brethren who have been scattered from the land of Zion: being driven & smitten by the hands of mine enemies on whom I will pour out of my wrath without measure in mine own time for I have suffered them thus far. that they might fill up the measure of their iniquities that their cup might be full, & that those who call themselves after my name might be chastened for a little season, with a sore & grievous chastisement; because they did not hearken all together unto the precepts & commandments which I gave unto them.

But verily I say unto you, that I have decreed a decree which my people shall realize inasmuch as they hearken from this hour unto the counsel which I the Lord their God shall give unto them. Behold, they shall, for I have decreed it, begin to prevail against mine enemies; from this verry [very] hour, & by hearkening to observe all the words which I the Lord their God shall speak unto them, they shall never cease to prevail untill the kingdoms of the world are subdued under my feet, & the earth is given unto the saints to possess it forever, & ever.

But inasmuch as they keep not my commandments & hearken not to observe all my words, the kingdoms of the world shall prevail against them; for they were set to be a light unto the world, & to be the Saviours of men: & inasmuch as they are not the Saviours of men they are as salt that has lost its savor, & is thenceforth good for nothing but to be cast out & to be trodden under the feet of men.

But verily, I say unto you, I have decreed that your brethren who have been scattere[d] shall return to the lands of their inheritances & build up the waste places of Zion. for after much tribulation, as I have said unto you in a former commandment, cometh the blessing:[46] behold this is the blessing which I promised after your tribulations, & the tribulations, of your brethren; your redemption & the redemption of your brethren, even their restoration to the land of Zion, to be established no more to be thrown down.

Nevertheless if they shall pollute their inheritances they shall be thrown down; for I will not spare them if they shall pollute their inheritances. Behold I say unto you, that the redem[p]tion of Zion must needs come by power; therefore, I will raise up unto my people a man who shall lead them like as Moses led the children

---

45. This revelation was not included in the 1835 D&C. It was published in the 1844 D&C. The group that traveled to Missouri was known as Zion's Camp.

46. See document no. 64; LDS and RLDS D&C 58.

of Israel; for ye are the children of Israel, & of the seed of Abraham; & ye must needs be led out of bondage by power, & with a stretched out arm.

And as your Fathers were led at the first even so shall the redem[p]tion of Zion be. Therefore let not your hearts faint; for I say not unto you as I said unto your fathers, mine Angel shall go up before you, but not my presence; but I say unto you, mine Angel shall go up before you, & also my presence. And in time ye shall possess the goodly land.

Verily, Verily, I say unto you, that my servant Joseph [Smith, Jr.] is the man to whom I likened the servant to whom the Lord of the vin[e]yard spake in the parable which I have given unto you.[47]

Therefore, let my servant Joseph [Smith, Jr.], say unto the strength of my house, my young men, & the middle aged, Gather ye together unto the land of Zion, upon the lands which I have bought with moneys that have been consecrated unto me; & let all the churches send up wise men with their moneys & purchase lands, even as I have commanded them.

And inasmuch as mine enemies com[e] against you to drive you from my goodly land which I have consecrated to be the land of Zion; even from your own lands after these testimonies which ye have brought before me against them, ye shall curse them; & whomsoever ye curse I will curse, And ye shall avenge me of mine enemies; and my presence shall be with you even in avenging me of mine enemies, unto the third & fourth generation of them that hate me.

Let no man be afraid to lay down his life for my sake; for whoso layeth down his life for my sake shall find it again; & whoso is not willing to lay down his life for my sake is not my disciple.

It is my will that my servant Sidney [Rigdon] shall lift up his voice in the congregations in the eastern countries in preparing the churches to keep the commandments which I have given unto them concerning the restoration & redemption of Zion.

It is my will that my Servant Parley [P. Pratt], & my servant Lyman [Wight] should not return to the land of their brethren until they have obtained Companies to go up unto the land of Zion, by tens, or by twenties or by fifties, or by a hundred, until they have obtained unto the number of five hundred of the strength of my house.

Behold, this is my will; ask & ye shall receive; but men do not always do my will; therefore if ye cannot obtain five hundred, seek diligently, that peradventure ye may obtain three [hundred]; & if ye cannot obtain three hundred, seek diligently that peradventure ye may obtain one hundred: But verily I say unto you, a commandment I give unto you that you shall not go up unto the Land of Zion until you have obtained a hundred of the strength of my house, to go up with you unto the land of Zion.

Therefore as I said unto you, ask & you shall receive; pray earnestly, that peradventure my servant Joseph [Smith, Jr.] may go up with you & preside in the midst of my people & organize my kingdom upon the consecrated land, & establish the

47. See document no. 119; LDS D&C 101; RLDS D&C 98.

children of Zion upon the laws & commandments which have been given & which shall be given unto you.

All victory and Glory is brought to pass unto you through your diligence, faithfulness, & prayers of faith.

Let my Servant Parley [P. Pratt] journey with my servant Joseph [Smith, Jr.] let my servant Lyman [Wight] Journey with my servant Sidney [Rigdon]: let my servant Hyrum [Smith] Journey with my servant Frederick [G. Williams]: let my servant Orson Hyde Journey with my servant Orson Pratt, whithersoever my servant Joseph [Smith, Jr.] shall counsel them in obtaining the fulfillment of these commandments which I have given unto you, & leave the residue in my hands; even so, Amen.

121. Properties Which Belong to the Firm

From "Book of Commandments, Law and Covenants; Book C," LDS archives (cf. LDS D&C 104; RLDS D&C 101)

Revelation received at Kirtland, Ohio, on 23 April 1834 appointing to each member of the United Firm their stewardship

April 23, 1834

Verily, I say unto you my friend[s], I give unto you counsel & a commandment concerning all the properties which belong to the Firm, which I commanded to be organized & established to be a United Firm, & an everlasting Firm, for the benefit of my church, & for the salvation of men until I come. with promise immutible [immutable] & unchangeable, that inasmuch as those whom I commanded were faithful, they should be blessed with multiplicity of blessings; but inasmuch as they were not faithful, they were nigh unto cursing.

Therefore inasmuch as some of my servants have not kept the commandment but have broken the covenant, by covetousness & with feigned words, I have cursed them with a verry [very] sore & grievous curse; for I the Lord have decreed in my heart, that inasmuch as any man belonging to the Firm, shall be found a transgressor, or in other words, shall brake [break] the covenant with which ye are bound, he shall be cursed in his life & shall he trodden down by whom I will; for I the Lord am not to be mocked in these things; & all this that the in[n]ocent among you may not be condemned with the unjust, & that the guilty among you may not escape because, I the Lord have promised unto you a crown of glory at my right hand. Therefore, inasmuch as ye are found transgressors, ye cannot escape my wrath in your lives; & inasmuch as ye are cut off by transgression ye cannot escape the buffetings of Satan unto the day of Redemption.

And I now give unto you power from this verry [very] hour, that if any man among you, of the Firm, is found a transgressor, & repenteth not of the evil, that ye shall deliver him over unto the buffetings of Satan, & he shall have no more power to bring evil upon you; but as long as ye hold communion with transgressors, behold, they bring evil upon you.

It is wisdom in me, therefore, a commandment I give unto you, that ye shall organize yourselves, & appoint every man his stewardship, that every man may give an account unto me of the stewardship which is appointed unto him;

for it is expedient, that I the Lord should make every man accountable, as stewards over earthly Blessings, which I have made & prepared for my creatures.

I the Lord stretched out the heavens; & builded the earth as a verry [very] handy work, & all things therein are mine, & it is my business to provide for my saints, for all things are mine; but it must needs be done in mine own way: & behold, this is the way that I the Lord hath decreed to provid[e] for my saints, that the poor shall be exalted in that the rich are made low; for the earth is full, & there is enough & to spare; yea, I have prepared all things, & have given unto the children of men to be agents unto themselves.

Therefore if any man shall take of the abundance which I have made, & impart not his portion according to the law of my gospel unto the poor & the needy, he shall with [the] Divel [Devil] lift up his eyes in hell, being in torment.

And now verily, I say unto you concerning the properties of the Firm, Let my servant Sidney [Rigdon] have appointed unto him the place where he now resides, & the lot of the Tan[n]ery for his stewardship for his support while he is labouring in my vin[e]yard, even as I will, when I shall command him; & let all things be done according to the counsel of the Firm, & united consent, or voice of the Firm which dwells in the land of Kirtland. And this stewardship & blessing, I the Lord confer upon my servant Sidney [Rigdon] for a blessing upon him, & upon his seed after him, & I will multiply blessings upon him & upon his seed after him inasmuch as he shall be humble before me.

And again let my servant Martin [Harris] have appointed unto him for his stewardship the lot of land which my servant John [Johnson] obtained in exchange for his farm, for him & his seed after him; & inasmuch as he is faithful I will multiply blessings upon him & his seed after him. And let my servant Martin [Harris] devote his moneys for the printing of my word, according as my servant Joseph [Smith, Jr.] shall direct.

And again let my servant Frederick [G. Williams] have the place upon which he now dwells; & let my servant Oliver [Cowdery] have the Lot which is set off joining the house which is to be for the printing office which is lot number one; & also the lot upon which his father[48] resides; & let my servants Frederick [G. Williams] & Oliver [Cowdery] have the printing office & all things that pertain unto it; & this shall be their stewardship which shall be appointed unto them; & inasmuch as they are faithful, behold, I will bless them, & multiply blessings upon them, & this is the beginning of the stewardship which I have appointed unto them for them & their seed after them; & inasmuch as they are faithful I will multiply blessings upon them & their seed after them, even a multiplicity of blessings.

And again, let my servant John [Johnson] have the house in which he lives, & the farm all save the ground which has been reserved for the building of my houses, which pertains to that farm, & those lots which have been named for my servant

---

48. William Cowdery.

Oliver [Cowdery]; & inasmuch as he is faithful I will multiply blessings upon him. And it is my will that he should sell the lots that are laid off for the building up of the city of my saints, inasmuch as it shall be made known to him by the voice of the spirit & according to the counsel of the Firm, & by the voice of the Firm, & this is the beginning of the stewardship which I have appointed unto him, for a blessing unto him & his seed after him; & inasmuch as he is faithful I will multiply a multiplicity of blessings upon him.

And again let my servant Newel [K. Whitney] have appointed unto him the houses & lot where he now resides, & the lot & building on which the store stands, & the lot also which is on the corner south of the store, & also the lot in which th[e] Ashery is situated. And all this I have appointed unto my servant Newel [K. Whitney] for his stewardship, for a blessing upon him & his seed after him, for the benefit of the mercantile establishment of my Firm, which I have established for my Stake in the land of Kirtland; yea, verily. this is th[e] stewardship which I have appointed unto my servant Newel [K. Whitney], even this whole mercantile establishment, him & his agent, & his seed after him, & inasmuch as he is faithful in keeping the commandments which I have given unto him, I will multiply blessings upon him, & his seed after him, even a multiplicity of blessings.

And again let my servant Joseph [Smith, Jr.] have appointed unto him the lot which is laid off for the building of my houses, which is forty rods long and twelve wide, & also the farm upon which his father now reside[s] & this is the beginning of the Stewardship which I have appointed unto him, for a blessing upon him & upon his father; for behold, I have reserved an inheritanc[e] for his father, for his support; therefore he shall be reckoned in the house of my servant Joseph [Smith, Jr.]: & I will multiply blessings upon the house of my servant Joseph [Smith, Jr.] inasmuch as he is faithful, even a multiplicity of blessings.

And now a commandment I give unto you concerning Zion, that you shall no longer be bound as a United Firm, to your brethren of Zion, only on this wise: after you are organized, you shall be called, The United Firm of the Stake of Zion, the City of Kirtland, among yourselves. And your brethren, after they are organized, shall be called, The United Firm of the City of Zion, & they shall be organized in their own names, & in their own name; & they shall do their business in their own name, & in their own names; & you shal[l] do your business in your own name, & in your own names.

And this I have commanded to be done for your salvation, as also for their salvation, in consequence of their being driven out, and that which is to come. The covenant being broken throug[h] transgression, by covetousness & feigned words, therefore, you are dissolved as a United Firm with your brethren, that you are not bound only up to this hour unto them, only on this wise, as, I said, By loan, as shall be agreed by this Firm in counsel [council] as your circumstances will admit, & the voice of the council direct.

And again, a commandment I give unto you concerning your Stewardship which I have appointed unto you, behold, all these properties are mine, or else, your faith is vain, & ye are found hypocrites, & the covenants which you have made unto me are broken, & if these properties are mine, then, ye are stewards, otherwise ye are no stewards.

But, verily, I say unto you, I have appointe[d] unto you to be Stewards over mine house, even Stewards indeed, & for this purpose have I commanded you to organize yourselves, even to print my word, the fulness of my scriptures, the revelations which I have given unto you, & which I shall hereafter fro[m] time to time give unto you, for the purpose of building up my church & kingdom on the earth & to prepare my people for th[e] time of my coming which is nigh at hand.

Therefore a commandment I give unto you that ye shall take the books of Mormon, & also the copyright, & also the copy-right which shall be secured of the articles & covenants, in which covenants, all my commandments, which it is my will should be printed, shall be printed, as it shall be made known unto you; & also the copy-right to the new translation of the scriptures; & this I say that others may not take the blessings away from you which I have confer[r]ed upon you.

And ye shall prepare for yourselves a place for a Treasury, & consecrate it unto my name, & ye shall appoint one among you to keep the treasury & he shall be ordained unto this blessing; & there shall be a seal upon the Treasury, & all these sacred things shall be delivered into the Treasury, & no man among you shall call it his own or any part of it; for it shall belong to you all with one accord; & I give it unto you from this very hour; & now see to it, that ye go to & make use of the stewardship which I have appointed unto you, exclusive of these sacred things, for the purpose of printing these sacred things, according as I have said; & the avails of these sacred thing[s] shall be had in the Treasury, & a seal shall be upon it, & it shall not be used or taken out of the Treasury by any one neither shall the seal be loosed which shall be placed upon it only by the voice of the Firm, or by commandment.

And thus shall ye preserve all the avails of these sacred things in the Treasury, for sacred & holy purposes, & this shall be called, The Sacred Treasury of the Lord, & a seal shall be kept upon it, that it may be holy & consecrated unto the Lord.

And again, there shall be another Treasury prepared & a Treasurer appointed to keep the Treasury, & a seal shall be placed upon it, & all monies that you receive in your stewardships by improving upon the properties which I have appointed unto you, in houses, or in lands, or in cattle, & in all things save it be the holy & sacred writings, which I have reserved unto myself for holy & sacred purposes, shall be cast into the Treasury as fast as you receive monies, by hundreds, or by fifti[es] or by twenties, or by tens, or by fives, or in other words, if any man among you, obtain five dollars, let him cast it into the Treasury, or if he obtain ten, or twenty, or fifty or a hundred, let him do likewise; & let not any man among you say that it is his own; for it shall not be called his; nor any part of it, & there shall not any part of it be used, or taken out of the Treasury only by the voice & common consent of the Firm.

And this shall be the voice & common consent of the Firm that any man among you; say unto the Treasurer, I have need of this to help me in my stewardship, if it be five dollars, or if it be ten dollars, or twenty, or fifty, or a hundred [dollars].

The Treasurer shall give unto him the sum which he requires, to help him in his stewardship, until he be found a transgressor, & it is manifest before the counsel [council] of the Firm, plainly that he is an unfaithful & an unwise steward; but so long as he is in full fellowship & is faithful & wise in his stewardship, this shall be his token unto the Treasurer, that the Treasurer shall not withhold; but in case of transgression the Treasurer shall be subject unto the counsel [council] & voice of the Firm, & in case the Treasurer is found an unfaithful & an unwise steward, he shall be subject to the counsel [council] & voice of the Firm, & shall be removed out of his place & another shall be appointed in his stead.

And again, verily I say unto you concerning your debts, behold, it is my will that you should pay all your debts; & it is my will that you should humble your-selves befor[e] me, & obtain this blessing by your diligence, & humility & the prayer of faith; & inasmuch as you are diligent & humble, & exercise the prayer of faith; behold, I will soften the hearts of those to whom you are in debt, until I shall send means unto you for your deliverance.

Therefore, write spe[e]dily unto New York, & write according to that which shall be dictated by my Spirit, & I will soften the hearts of those to whom you are in debt, that it shall be taken away out of their minds to bring afflictio[n] upon you. And inasmuch as ye are humble & faithful & call on my name, behold, I will giv[e] you the victory; I give unto you a promise, that you shall be delivered this once, out of your bondage.

Inasmuch as you obtain a chance to loan money by hundreds, or by thousands, even until you shall loan enough to deliver yourselves from bondage, it is your privilege, & pledge the properties which I have put into your hands this once by giving your names by common consent, or otherwise as it shall seem good unto you, I give unto you the privilege this once, & behold, if you proceed to do the things which I have laid before you, according to my commandment, all these things are mine, & ye are my Stewards, & the Master will not suffer his house to be broken up; even so, Amen.

copied from the origional [original] by O[rson]. Pratt[49]

Revision

1835 D&C 98
(cf. LDS D&C 104:10, 43, 59; RLDS D&C 101:2, 8, 10)

And I now give unto you power from this very hour, that if any man among you, of the *order*, is found a transgressor, and repenteth not of the evil, that ye shall de-liver him over unto the buffetings of satan; and he shall *not* have power to bring evil upon you.

.   .   .

And again, let my servant *Gazelam* have appointed unto him, the lot which is laid off for the building of my *house*, which is forty rods long, and twelve wide, and also the *inheritance* upon which his father now resides

49. Orson Pratt wrote, "I copied revelations for Brother Joseph" (Elden J. Watson, comp., *The Orson Pratt Journals* [Salt Lake City: comp., 1975], 39, entry for 26 Apr. 1834). Pratt's copy was written three days after the revelation was received.

.   .   .

to prepare my people for the time *when I shall dwell with them*, which is nigh at hand.

Commentary: Copyrights to be secured

In a revelation given on 23 April 1834, the United Firm is instructed to undertake a number of actions. The following text was omitted from the revelation:

> Therefore a commandment I give unto you that ye shall take the books of Mormon, & also the copyright, & also the copy-right which shall be secured of the articles & covenants, in which covenants, all my commandments, which it is my will should be printed, shall be printed, as it shall be made known unto you; & also the copy-right to the new translation of the scriptures; & this I say that others may not take the blessings away from you which I have confer[r]ed upon you.[50]

Apparently, in April 1834 the title "articles and covenants" was being considered for what later was titled *Doctrine and Covenants*. Joseph Smith's journal for 19 April mentions Sidney Rigdon and Oliver Cowdery assisting each other in arranging the church covenants.[51]

There are two manuscripts of this revelation extant. Book C was copied from the original by Orson Pratt; the Kirtland Revelations Book has this text recorded by Orson Hyde. Both manuscripts were written in 1834.[52] The 1835 D&C did not print this portion of the text.[53] There is no indication in the Kirtland Revelations Book that these words were to be omitted. It is possible that this was an oversight on the part of the D&C committee. While this was known to be part of the revelatory text, it was not included in the 1981 LDS edition of the D&C.[54]

122. Let There Be Reserved Three Thousand Dollars
From "Book of Commandments, Law and Covenants; Book C," LDS archives

Revelation received at Kirtland, Ohio, on 28 April 1834 concerning the United Firm[55]

Kirtland 28 April 1834.

Verily thus saith the Lord concerning the division and settlement of the United Firm: Let there be reserved three Thousand Dollars for the right and claim

---

50. "Book of Commandments, Law and Covenants; Book C," LDS archives.
51. Jessee, *Papers of Joseph Smith*, 2:31-32.
52. The revelation was copied into the KRB on 18 August 1834 (107).
53. 1835 D&C 98:10-11. See LDS D&C 104:59-60; RLDS D&C 101:10-11.
54. See Woodford, "Historical Development of the Doctrine and Covenants," 1,353, 1,366; and Cook, *Revelations of the Prophet Joseph Smith*, 212.
55. This revelation was not included in the 1835 D&C.

of the Firm in Kirtland for inheritances in due time, even when the Lord will; and with this claim to be had in rememberanc[e] when the Lord shall reveal it for a right of inheritance, Ye are made free from the Firm of Zion and the Firm in Zion is mad[e] free from the firm in Kirtland: Thus saith the Lord. Amen

Copied from the original by Orson Hyde

DOCTRINE AND COVENANTS

OF

THE CHURCH OF THE

LATTER DAY SAINTS:

CAREFULLY SELECTED

FROM THE REVELATIONS OF GOD,

AND COMPILED BY

JOSEPH SMITH Junior.
OLIVER COWDERY,
SIDNEY RIGDON,
FREDERICK G. WILLIAMS,

[*Presiding Elders of said Church.*]

PROPRIETORS.

KIRTLAND, OHIO.

PRINTED BY F. G. WILLIAMS & CO

FOR THE

PROPRIETORS.

1835.

Title Page of 1835 Doctrine and Covenants

7. Church of the Latter Day Saints Period, May 1834–April 1838

Zion's Camp in 1834 was to redeem Zion and replant the Saints in their inheritances in Jackson County, Missouri. This did not happen. Joseph Smith, Jr., said the Saints would need to wait a little season for Zion's redemption. Out of the failure of the camp came major organizational changes with a Quorum of Twelve Apostles and a group known as the Seventy. The Saints purchased four Egyptian mummies and some papyri in 1835. A revelation appointed Warren Parrish as a new scribe for Joseph Smith. At Kirtland, Ohio, the building of the House of the Lord (temple) took resources in time and money. The Kirtland temple was dedicated in March 1836. Many spiritual experiences were reported by church members in the temple. Smith traveled to Salem, Massachusetts, on business to obtain funds in a quest to alleviate debt. Internal dissent occurred over Kirtland banking activities. Disagreement with Smith caused apostasy among some leaders and members. Smith received revelations in January 1838 including one to leave Ohio for Far West, Missouri.

123. Wait for a Little Season for the Redemption of Zion
From KRB, 97-100 (cf. LDS D&C 105; RLDS D&C 102)
Revelation received near Fishing River, Clay County, Missouri, on 22 June 1834 concerning the men who went to redeem Zion[1]

Clay County, Missouri, June 22, 1834

Verily, I say unto you, who have assembled yourselves together that you may learn my will concerning the redemption of mine afflicted people:

Behold, I say unto you, were it not for the transgressions of my people, speaking concerning the church and not individuals, they might have been redeemed, even now; but, behold, they have not learned to be obedient to the things which I require at their hands, but are full of all manner of evil, and do not impart of their substance as becometh saints, to the poor and afflicted among them, and are not united according to the union required by the law of the Celestial kingdom; and

---

1. This text follows the wording in the KRB before later changes were made in the manuscript. The revelation was not published in the 1835 D&C. It was published in the 1844 D&C.

Zion cannot be built up unless it is by the principles of the law of the Celestial Kingdom, otherwise I can not receive her unto myself. And my people must needs be chastened until they learn obedience, if it must needs be by the things which they suffer.

I speak not concerning those who are appointed to lead my people, who are the first elders of my church, for they are not all under this condemnation; but I speak concerning the Churches abroad: there are many who will say, Where is their God? Behold, he will deliver in time of trouble, otherwise we will not go up unto Zion, and will keep our moneys.

Th[e]refore, in consequence of the transgressions of my people, it is expedient in me that mine elders should wait for a little season for the redemption of Zion, that they themselves may be prepared, and that my people may be taught mor[e] perfectly, and have experience, and know more perfectly concerning their duty and the things which I require at their hands. And this can not be brought to pass until mine elders are endowed with power from on high; for behold, I have prepared a greater endowment and blessing to be poured out upon them, inasmuch as they are faithful, and continue, in humility before me.

Therefore, it is expedient in me that mine elders should wait for a little season for the redemption of Zion; for behold, I do not require at their hands to fight the battles of Zion; for as I have said in a former commandment, even So I will fulfil: I will fight your battles.[2]

Behold, the destroyer I have already sent forth to destroy and lay waste mine enemies, and not many years hence they shall not be left to pollute mine heritage, and to blaspheme my name upon the lands which I have consecrated for the gathering together of my saints.

Behold, I have commanded my servant Joseph [Smith, Jr.] to say to the strength of my house even my warriors, my young men and middleaged, to gather together for the redemption of my people, and throw down the towers of mine enemies, and scatter their watchmen; but the strength of mine house has not hearkened unto my words: but inasmuch as there are those that have hearkened unto my word I have prepared a blessing and an endowment for them I have heard their prayers and will accept their offering. And it is expedient in me that they should be brought thus far for a trial of their faith.

And now, verily I say unto you, a commandment I give unto you, that as many as have come hither that can stay in the regions round about, let them stay, and those who cannot stay, who have families in the east, let them tarry for a little season, inasmuch as my servant Joseph [Smith, Jr.] shall appoint unto them; for I will counsel him concerning this matter, and all things whatsoever he shall appoint unto them, shall be fulfilled.

And let all may [my] people who dwell in the regions round about be very faithful, and prayerful, and humble before me, and reveal not the things which I have revealed unto them, and talk not of judgments, neither boast of faith no[r] of mighty works, but carefully gather together as much in one region as can be consis-

---

2. See document no. 117; LDS D&C 98; RLDS D&C 95.

tantly with the feelings of the people; and behold, I will give unto you favor and grace in their eyes, that you may rest in peace and safety, while you are saying unto the people, Execute judgment and justice for us, according to law, and redress us of our wrongs.

Now behold, I say unto you my friends, in this way you may find favor in the eyes of the people until the army of Israel has become very great, and I will soften the hearts of the people as I did the heart of Pharaoh, from time to time, until my servant Joseph [Smith, Jr.], and mine elders, whom he shall appoint, shall have time to gather up the strength of mine house, and to have sent wise men to fulfill that which I have commanded concerning the purchasing of all the lands in Jackson county that can be purchased, and in the adjourning [adjoining] counties round about; for it is my will that these lands should be purchased; and after they are purchased, that my saints should possess them according to the law of consecration which I have given.

And after these lands are purchased I will hold the armies of Israel guiltless in taking possession of their own lands, and of throwing down the towers of mine enemies that may be upon them, and scattering their watchmen and avenging me of mine enemies, unto the third and fo[u]rth generation of them that hate me.

But firstly let my army become very great, and let it be sanctified before me, that it may become fair as the sun, and clear as the moon, and that her banners may be terrible unto all nations, that the kingdoms of this world may be constrained to acknowledge that the kingdom of Zion, is, in very deed, the kingdom of our God and his Christ; therefore, let us become subject unto her laws.

Verily, I say unto you, it is expedient in me that the first elders of my church should receive their endowment from on high in mine house which I have commanded to be built unto my name in the land of Kirtland, and let those commandments which I have given concerning Zion, and her law, be executed and fulfilled after her redemption.[3]

There has been a day of calling, but the time has come for a day of choosing, and let those be chosen that are worthy: and it shall be manifest unto my servant Joseph [Smith, Jr.] by the voice of the Spirit those who are chosen, and they shall be sanctified: and inasmuch as they follow the counsels which they receive, they shall have power after many days to accomplish all things pertaining to Zion.

And again, I say unto you, sue for peace, not only the people that have smitten you, but also to all people; and lift up an ensign of peace, and make a proclamation for peace unto the ends of the earth: and make proposals for peace unto those who

---

3. The date for the redemption of Zion was set as 11 September 1836. Joseph Smith, Jr., wrote from Kirtland, Ohio, in August 1834: "in case the excitement continues to be allayed and peace prevails use every effort to prevail on the churches to gather to those regions and situate themselves to be in readiness to move into Jackson Co[unty]. in two years from the Eleventh of September next which is the appointed time for the redemption of Zion" (Smith to Lyman Wight et al., 16 Aug. 1834, Joseph Smith Letterbook, 1:86, LDS archives). The 11 September date refers to an earlier revelation which stated, "I the Lord willeth to retain a Strong hold in the Land of Kirtland for the space of five years" (see document no. 70 [11 Sept. 1831]; LDS D&C 64:21; RLDS D&C 64:4). See also Dean C. Jessee, ed., *The Papers of Joseph Smith: Journal, 1832-1842* (Salt Lake City: Deseret Book Co., 1992), 2:41-42, 58, 91, 188, 203-206.

have smitten you, according to the voice of the Spirit which is in you; and all things shall work together for your good; and be faithful: and behold, and lo; I am with you even unto the end, even so; Amen.

124. Separated Himself from the Crafts of Men
From KRB, 116 (cf. LDS D&C 106; RLDS D&C 103)

Revelation received at Kirtland, Ohio, on 25 November 1834 for Warren A. Cowdery[4]

Kirtland, November 25, 1834

It is my will that my servant Warren [A. Cowdery] should be appointed and or-dained a presiding High Priest over my church in the land of Freedom [New York] and the regions round about; and should preach my everlasting gospel, and lift up his voice and warn the people, not only in his own place, but in the adjoining countries [counties], and devote his whole time in this high and holy calling which I now give unto him; seeking dilligently the kingdom of heaven and its righteous-ness, and all things necessary shall be added thereunto; for the laborer is worthy of his hire.

And again, verily I say unto you, the coming of the Lord draweth nigh, and it overtaketh the world as a thief in the night: therefore, gird up your loins, that ye may be the children of the light, and that day shall not ove[r]take you as a thief.

And again, verily I say unto you, there was joy in heaven when my servant Warren [A. Cowdery] bowed to my scepter and separated himself from the crafts of men. Therefore, blessed is my servant Warren [A. Cowdery], for I will have mercy on him, and notwithstanding the vanity of his heart, I will lift him up, and inasmuch as he will humble himself before me; I will give him grace and assurance wherewith he may stand; and if he continues to be a faithful witness, and a light unto the church, I have prepared a crown for him in the mansion of my Father: even so, Amen.

125. Condemnation Resteth upon You
From the Manuscript History, Book A-1:17 [separate section]

Revelation received at Kirtland, Ohio, on 5 December 1834 concerning repentance and reformation of the church[5]

Verily, condemnation resteth upon you, who are appointed to lead my Church, and to be saviors of men: and also upon the church:

---

4. This text follows the wording in the KRB before a few minor changes were made for the 1835 D&C.

5. This revelation was not published in the 1835 D&C.

And there must needs be a repentance and a refor[m]ation among you, in all things, in your ensamples [examples] before the Church, and before the world, in all your manners, habits and customs, and salutations one toward another - rendering unto every man the respect due the office, calling, and priesthood, whereunto I the Lord have appointed and ordained you. Amen.

126. The High Priest, and Elder, Are to Administer in Spiritual Things
From the 1835 D&C 3 (cf. LDS D&C 107; RLDS D&C 104)

Instructions given at Kirtland, Ohio, [28-30] April 1835 concerning two priesthoods in the church[6]

There are, in the church, two priesthoods, namely: the Melchizedek, and the Aaronic, including the Levitical priesthood. Why the first is called the Melchizedek priesthood, is because Melchizedek was such a great high priest: before his day it was called *the holy priesthood, after the order of the Son of God*; but out of respect or reverence to the name of the Supreme Being, to avoid the too frequent repetition of his name, they, the church, in ancient days, called that priesthood after Melchizedek, or the Melchizedek priesthood.

All other authorities, or offices in the church are appendages to this priesthood; but there are two divisions, or grand heads—one is the Melchizedek priesthood, and the other is the Aaronic, or Levitical priesthood.

The office of an elder comes under the priesthood of Melchizedek. The Melchizedek priesthood holds the right of presidency, and has power and authority over all the offices in the church, in all ages of the world, to administer in spiritual things.

The presidency of the high priesthood, after the order of Melchizedek, have a right to officiate in all the offices in the church.

High priests, after the order of the Melchizedek priesthood, have a right to officiate in their own standing, under the direction of the presidency, in administering spiritual things, and also in the office of an elder, priest, (of the Levitical order,) teacher, deacon and member.

An elder has a right to officiate in his stead when the high priest is not present.

The high priest, and elder, are to administer in spiritual things, agreeably to the

---

6. These instructions are a composite of several documents originally written on different dates; brackets are inserted to separate the documents. The April date is based on the journal of William E. McLellin who recorded that Joseph Smith and others of the twelve apostles left Kirtland and went to nearby Huntsburg, Ohio, being there on 26-30 March 1835. There is no record of Smith or the apostles returning to Kirtland. The traditional date of 28 March 1835 is based on a letter dated 28 March 1836 [sic], recorded in the Kirtland Council Minute Book, LDS archives (198). It appears that the March date is in error and that the meeting where the Twelve "had a time of general confession" was held on the afternoon of 28 April 1835 ("A record of the transactions of the Twelve apostles," 1835, in Patriarchal Blessing Book 1, LDS archives).

covenants and commandments of the church; and they have a right to officiate in all these offices of the church when there are no higher authorities present.

The second priesthood is called the priesthood of Aaron, because it was conferred upon Aaron and his seed, throughout all their generations. Why it is called the lesser priesthood, is because it is an appendage to the greater, or the Melchizedek priesthood, and has power in administering outward ordinances. The bishopric is the presidency of this priesthood and holds the keys, or authority of the same. No man has a legal right to this office, to hold the keys of this priesthood, except he be a litteral [literal] descendant of Aaron. But as a high priest, of the Melchizedek priesthood, has authority to officiate in all the lesser offices, he may officiate in the office of bishop when no literal descendant of Aaron can be found; provided he is called and set apart and ordained unto this power by the hands of the presidency of the Melchizedek priesthood.

The power and authority of the higher or Melchizedek priesthood, is to hold the keys of all the spiritual blessings of the church—to have the privilege of receiving the mysteries of the kingdom of heaven—to have the heavens opened unto them—to commune with the general assembly and church of the first born, and to enjoy the communion and presence of God the Father, and Jesus the Mediator of the new covenant.

The power and authority of the lesser, or Aaronic priesthood, is, to hold the keys of the ministering of angels, and to administer in outward ordinances—the letter of the gospel—the baptism of repentance for the remission of sins, agreeably to the covenants and commandments.

Of necessity there are presidents, or presiding offices growing out of, or appointed of, or from among those who are ordained to the several offices in thess [these] two priesthoods.

Of the Melchizedek priesthood, three presiding high priests, chosen by the body, appointed and ordained to that office, and upheld by the confidence, faith and prayer of the church, form a quorum of the presidency of the church.

The twelve travelling counsellors are called to be the twelve apostles,[7] or special witnesses of the name of Christ, in all the world: thus differing from other officers in the church in the duties of their calling. And they form a quorum equal in authority and power to the three presidents, previously mentioned.

The seventy[8] are also called to preach the gospel, and to be especial witnesses unto the Gentiles and in all the world. Thus differing from other officers in the church in the duties of their calling: and they form a quorum equal in authority to that of the twelve especial witnesses or apostles, just named.

And every decision made by either of these quorums, must be by the unanimous voice of the same; that is, every member in each quorum must be agreed to

---

7. The first members of the twelve apostles were ordained on 14 February 1835 at Kirtland, Ohio. The names and dates of ordination are: Lyman E. Johnson, Brigham Young, Heber C. Kimball (14 Feb. 1835); Orson Hyde, David W. Patten, Luke S. Johnson, William E. McLellin, John F. Boynton, William Smith (15 Feb. 1835); Parley P. Pratt (21 Feb. 1835); and Thomas B. Marsh and Orson Pratt (26 April 1835). (See Kirtland Council Minute Book, 149-58.)

8. The first Seventies in the church were ordained on 28 February 1835.

its decisions in order to make their decisions of the same power or validity one with the other. [A majority may form a quorum when circumstances render it impossible to be otherwise.]⁹ Unless this is the case, their decisions are not entitled to the same blessings which the decisions of a quorum of three presidents were anciently, who were ordained after the order of Melchizedek, and were righteous and holy men.

The decisions of these quorums, or either of them are to be made in all righteousness; in holiness and lowliness of heart; meekness and long suffering; and in faith and virtue and knowledge; temperance, patience, godliness, brotherly kindness and charity, because the promise is, if these things abound in them, they shall not be unfruitful in the knowledge of the Lord. And in case that any decision, of these quorums, is made in unrighteousness, it may be brought before a general assembly of the several quorums which constitute the spiritual authorities of the church, otherwise there can be no appeal from their decision.

The twelve are a travelling, presiding high council, to officiate in the name of the Lord, under the direction of the presidency of the church, agreeably to the institution of heaven; to build up the church, and regulate all the affairs of the same, in all nations: first unto the Gentiles, and secondly unto the Jews.

The seventy are to act in the name of the Lord, under the direction of the twelve, or the travelling high council, in building up the church and regulating all the affairs of the same, in all nations: first unto the Gentiles and then to the Jews:—the twelve being sent out, holding the keys, to open the door by the proclamation of the gospel of Jesus Christ; and first unto the Gentiles and then unto the Jews.

The standing high councils, at the stakes of Zion, form a quorum equal in authority, in the affairs of the church, in all their decisions, to the quorum of the Presidency, or to the travelling high council.

The high council in Zion, forms a quorum equal in authority, in the affairs of the church, in all their decisions, to the councils of the twelve at the stakes of Zion.

It is the duty of the travelling high council to call upon the seventy, when they need assistance, to fill the several calls for preaching and administering the gospel, in stead of any others.

It is the duty of the twelve in all large branches of the church, to ordain evangelical ministers,¹⁰ as they shall be designated unto them by revelation.

The order of this priesthood was confirmed to be handed down from father to son, and rightly belongs to the literal descendants of the chosen seed, to whom the promises were made. This order was instituted in the days of Adam, and came down by lineage in the following manner:¹¹

From Adam to Seth, who was ordained by Adam at the age of 69 years, and was blessed by him three years previous to his (Adam's) death, and received the promise of God by his father, that his posterity should be the chosen of the Lord, and that

---

9. Brackets in 1835 D&C.
10. Evangelical ministers are understood to be patriarchs.
11. Included here is a list of ordinations from Adam to Noah said to be written in the book of Enoch.

they should be preserved unto the end of the earth, because he [Seth][12] was a perfect man, and his likeness was the express likeness of his father's, insomuch that he seemed to be like unto his father in all things; and could be distinguished from him only by his age.

Enos was ordained at the age of 134 years, and four mouths, by the hand of Adam.

God called upon Cainan in the wilderness, in the fortieth year of his age, and he met Adam in journeying to the place Shedolamak: he was eighty seven years old when he received his ordination.

Mahalaleel was 496 years and seven days old when he was ordained by the hand of Adam, who also blessed him.

Jared was 200 years old when he was ordained under the hand of Adam, who also blessed him.

Enoch, was 25 years old when he was ordained under the hand of Adam, and he was 65 and Adam blessed him—and he saw the Lord: and he walked with him, and was before his face continually: and he walked with God 365 years: making him 430 years old when he was translated.[13]

Methuselah was 100 years old when he was ordained under the hand of Adam.

Lamech was 32 years old when he was ordained under the hand of Seth.

Noah was 10 years old when he was ordained under the hand of Methuselah.

Three years previous to the death of Adam, he called Seth, Enos, Cainan, Mahalaleel, Jared, Enoch and Methuselah, who were all high priests, with the residue of his posterity, who were righteous, into the valley of Adam-ondi-Ahman, and there bestowed upon them his last blessing. And the Lord appeared unto them, and they rose up and blessed Adam, and called him Michael, the Prince, the Arch angel. And the Lord administered comfort unto Adam, and said unto him, I have set thee to be at the head: a multitude of nations shall come of thee; and thou art a prince over them for ever.

And Adam stood up in the midst of the congregation, and notwithstanding he was bowed down with age, being full of the Holy Ghost, predicted whatsoever should befall his posterity unto the latest generation. These things were all written in the book of Enoch, and are to be testified of in due time.

It is the duty of the twelve, also, to ordain and set in order all the other officers of the church, agreeably to the revelation which says:

[revision of part of revelation received (11) November 1831:][14]

To the church of Christ in the land of Zion, in addition to the church laws, respecting church business: Verily, I say unto you, says the Lord of hosts, There must

---

12. Brackets in 1835 D&C.

13. The age of Enoch when he was translated appears to have been added while changing the ages of the patriarchs in reviewing the Genesis revision text in 1835. The words added above the line are: "& al[l] the days of Enoch were 430 years" (OT MS #1, 19, RLDS archives). See Gen. 7:78 (JST); Moses 8:1 (PGP).

14. See document no. 78 given at Hiram, Ohio, [11] November 1831.

needs be presiding elders, to preside over those who are of the office of an elder; and also priests, to preside over those who are of the office of a priest; and also teachers to preside over those who are of the office of a teacher, in like manner; and also the deacons: wherefore, from deacon to teacher, and from teacher to priest, and from priest to elder, severally as they are appointed, according to the covenants and commandments of the church; then comes the high priesthood, which is the greatest of all.

Wherefore, it must needs be that one be appointed, of the high priesthood, to preside over the priesthood; and he shall be called president of the high priesthood of the church, or, in other words, the presiding high priest over the high priesthood of the church. From the same comes the administering of ordinances and blessings upon the church, by the laying on of the hands.

Wherefore the office of a bishop is not equal unto it; for the office of a bishop is in administering all temporal things: nevertheless, a bishop must be chosen from the high priesthood, unless he is a literal descendant of Aaron; for unless he is a literal descendant of Aaron he cannot hold the keys of that priesthood. Nevertheless, a high priest, that is after the order of Melchizedek, may be set apart unto the ministering of temporal things, having a knowledge of them by the Spirit of truth, and also to be a judge in Israel, to do the business of the church to sit in judgment upon transgressors, upon testimony, as it shall be laid before him, according to the laws, by the assistance of his counsellors, whom he has chosen, or will choose among the elders of the church. This is the duty of a bishop who is not a literal descendent of Aaron, but has been ordained to the high priesthood after the order of Melchizedek.

Thus shall he be a judge, even a common judge among the inhabitants of Zion, or in a stake of Zion, or in any branch of the church where he shall be set apart unto this ministry, until the borders of Zion are enlarged, and it becomes necessary to have other bishops, or judges in Zion, or elsewhere: and inasmuch as there are other bishops appointed they shall act in the same office. [end of revision]

But a literal descendant of Aaron has a legal right to the presidency of this priesthood, to the keys of this ministry, to act in the office of bishop independently, without counsellors, except in a case where a president of the high priesthood, after the order of Melchizedek, is tried; to sit as a judge in Israel.—And the decision of either of these councils, agreeable, to the commandment which says;

[revision of part of revelation of (11) November 1831:]

Again, verily, I say unto you: The most important business of the church, and the most difficult cases of the church, inasmuch as there is not satisfaction upon the decision of the bishop, or judges, it shall be handed over and carried up unto the council of the church, before the presidency of the high priesthood; and the presidency of the council of the high priesthood shall have power to call other high priests, even twelve, to assist as counsellors; and thus the presidency of the high priesthood, and its counsellors shall have power to decide upon testimony according to the laws of the church. And after this decision it shall be had in remembrance no more before the Lord; for this is the highest council of the church of God, and a final decision upon controversies, in spiritual matters.

There is not any person belonging to the church, who is exempt from this council of the church.

And in as much as a president of the high priesthood shall transgress, he shall be had in remembrance before the common council of the church, who shall be assisted by twelve counsellors of the high priesthood; and their decision upon his head shall be an end of controversy concerning him. Thus, none shall be exempted from the justice and the laws of God; that all things may be done in order and in solemnity, before him, according to truth and righteousness.

And again, verily I say unto you, the duty of a president over the office of a deacon, is to preside over twelve deacons, to sit in council with them, and to teach them their duty—edifying one another, as it is given according to the covenants.

And also the duty of the president over the office of the teachers, is to preside over twenty four of the teachers, and to sit in council with them—teaching them the duties of their office, as given in the covenants.

Also the duty of the president over the priesthood of Aaron, is to preside over forty eight priests, and sit in council with them, to teach them the duties of their office, as is given in the covenants. This president is to be a bishop; for this is one of the duties of this priesthood.

Again, the duty of the president over the office of elders is to preside over ninety six elders, and to sit in council with them, and to teach them according to the covenants. This presidency is a distinct one from that of the seventy, and is designed for those who do not travel into all the world.

And again, the duty of the president of the office of the high priesthood is to preside over the whole church, and to be like unto Moses. Behold, here is wisdom—yea, to be a seer, a revelator, a translator and a prophet—having all the gifts of God which he bestows upon the head of the church. [end of revision]

[vision concerning the Seventy:]

And it is according to the vision, showing the order of the seventy, that they should have seven presidents to preside over them, chosen out of the number of the seventy, and the seventh president of these presidents is to preside over the six; and these seven presidents are to choose other seventy beside the first seventy, to whom they belong, and are to preside over them; and also other seventy until seven times seventy, if the labor in the vineyard of necessity requires it. And these seventy are to be travelling ministers unto the Gentiles, first, and also unto the Jews,

whereas other offices of the church who belong not unto the twelve neither to the seventy, are not under the responsibility to travel among all nations, but are to travel as their circumstances shall allow, notwithstanding they may hold as high and responsible offices in the church.

[part of revelation of (11) November 1831:]

Wherefore, now let every man learn his duty, and to act in the office in which he is appointed, in all diligence. He that is slothful shall not be counted worthy to stand, and he that learns not his duty and shows himself not approved, shall not be counted worthy to stand; even so. Amen.

127. Shall Have Wisdom Given Him
From JS Journal

Revelation received at Kirtland, Ohio, on 27 October 1835 concerning Mary Bailey Smith

Tuesday 27th in the morning I was called to visit at Br[other] Samuel Smith[']s his wife was confined and in a verry [very] dangerous situation, Br[other]. Carloss [Don Carlos Smith] took one of my horses and went to Chardon after Doct[or]. [Frederick G.] Williams I went out into the field and bowed before the Lord and called upon him in mighty prayer in her behalf the word of the Lord came unto me saying

my Servant Fred[e]rick [G. Williams] shall come and shall have wisdom given him to deal prudently and my handma[i]den[15] shall be delivered of a living child & be spared[16]

128. If He Repent Not
From JS Journal

Revelation received at Kirtland, Ohio, on 1 November 1835 for Reynolds Cahoon

Sunday morning November 1st 1835

Verily thus Saith the Lord unto me, his servant Joseph Smith jr min[e] anger is kindle[d] against my servant Reynolds Cahoon because of his iniquities his covetous and dishonest principles in himself and family and he doth not purge them away and set his house in order therefore if he repent not chastis[e]ment awaiteth him even as it seemeth good in my sight therefore go and declare unto him these words[17]

---

15. Mary Bailey Smith, wife of Samuel H. Smith.
16. The journal then states: "he come [came] in a bout one hour after that and in the course of about 2 hours she was delivered and thus what God had manifested to me was fulfilled every whit." The child born was Susanna Bailey Smith. See Jessee, *Papers of Joseph Smith*, 2:55.
17. The journal entry continues: "I went im[m]ediately and del[i]vered this message according as the Lord commanded me I called him in & read what the Lord had said concerning him, he acknowledged that it was verily so & expressed much humility." See Jessee, *Papers of Joseph Smith*, 2:62.

129. Flee the Wrath to Come
From JS Journal

Revelation received at Kirtland, Ohio, on 2 November 1835
for Frederick G. Williams

the question was agitated whether Frederick G. Williams or Oliver Cowdery Should go to New York to make arrangements respecting a book bindery they refer[r]ed to me for a decision, and thus cam[e] the word of the Lord unto me saying

it is not my will that my servant Frederick [G. Williams] should go to New York, but inasmuch as he wishes to go and visit his relatives that he may warn them to flee the wrath to come let him go and see them, for that purpose and let that be his only business, and behold in this thing he shall be blessed with power to overcome their prejudices, Verily thus saith the Lord Amen.

130. Let Them Repent Speedily
From JS Journal

Revelation received at Kirtland, Ohio, on 3 November 1835
concerning the Quorum of Twelve Apostles

Tuesday 3d Thus came the word of the Lord unto me concerning the Twelve saying

behold they are under condemnation, because they have not been sufficiently humble in my sight, and in consequence of their covetous desires, in that they have not dealt equally with each other in the division of the moneys which came into their hands, nevertheless some of them dealt equally therefore they shall be rewarded, but verily I say unto you they must all humble themselves before me, before they will be accounted worthy to receive an endowment to go forth in my name unto all nations,

as for my Servant William [Smith] let the Eleven humble themselves in prayer and in faith and wait on me in patience and my servant William [Smith] shall return, and I will yet make him a polished shaft in my quiver, in bringing down the wickedness and abominations of men and their [there] shall be none mightier than he in his day and generation, nevertheless if he repent not spe[e]dily he shall be brought low and shall be chastened sorely for all his iniquities he has commit[t]ed against me. nevertheless the sin which he hath sin[n]ed against me is not even now more grevious [grievous] than the sin with which my servant David W. Patten and my servant Orson Hyde and my servant Wm E. McLellen [William E. McLellin] have sinded [sinned] against me, and the residue are not sufficiently humble before me,

behold the parable which I spake concerning a man having twelve Sons,[18] for

---

18. See document no. 41; LDS and RLDS D&C 38.

what man amon[g] you having twelve Sons and is no respecter to them and they serve him obediantly [obediently] and he saith unto the one be thou clothed in robes and sit thou here, and to the other be thou clothed in rages [rags] and sit thou there, and looketh upon his sons and saith I am just, ye will answer and say no man, and ye answer truly,

therefore Verely [Verily] thus saith the Lord your God I appointed these twelve that they should be equal in their ministry and in their portion and in their evangelical rights, wherefore they have sin[n]ed a verry [very] grevious sin, in asmuch as they have made themselves unequal and have not hearkned unto my voice ther[e]for[e] let them repent speedily and prepare their hearts for the solem[n] assembly and for the great day which is to come Verely [Verily] thus saith the Lord Amen.

131. Their Sins Are Forgiven Them
From JS Journal

Revelation received at Kirtland, Ohio, on 7 November 1835
for Isaac Morley and Edward Partridge

The word of the Lord came to me saying,

behold I am well pleased with my servant Isaac Morley and my servant Edward Partridge, because of the integrity of their h[e]arts in laboring in my vin[e]yard for the salvation of the souls of men, Verely [Verily] I say unto you their sins are forgiven them, therefore say unto them in my name that it is my will that they should tarry for a little season and attend the school, and also the solem[n] assembly for a wise purpose in me, even so amen

132. Are Under Condemnation
From JS Journal

Revelation received at Kirtland, Ohio, on 8 November 1835
for William W. Phelps and John Whitmer[19]

The word of the Lord cam[e] unto me saying

that President [William W.] Phelps & President J[ohn]. Whitmer are under condemnation before the Lord, for their errors

---

19. This text follows what was recorded in 1835. An added explanation by William W. Phelps is not included. After the word "errors" Phelps added, "for which they made satisfaction the same day" (Joseph Smith 1835-36 Journal, 22, LDS archives). See Jessee, *Papers of Joseph Smith*, 2:68.

133. He Shall See Much of My Ancient Records
From JS Journal

Revelation received at Kirtland, Ohio, on 14 November 1835
for Warren Parrish

Saturday morning 14th Thus came the word of the Lord unto me saying:

verily thus saith the Lord unto my servant Joseph [Smith, Jr.] concerning my servant Warren [Parrish] behold his sins are forgiven him because of his desires to do the works of righteousness therefore in as much as he will continue to hearken unto my voice he shall be blessed with wisdom and with a sound mind even above his fellows,

behold it shall come to pass in his day that he shall see great things shew forth themselves unto my people, he shall see much of my ancient records,[20] and shall know of hid[d]en things, and shall be endowed with a knowledge of hid[d]en languages, and if he desires and shall seek it at my hand, he shall be privileged with writing much of my word, as a scribe[21] unto me for the benefit of my people, therefore this shall be his calling until I shall order it otherwise in my wisdom and it shall be said of him in a time to come, behold Warren [Parrish] the Lord[']s Scribe, for the Lord[']s Seer whom he hath appointed in Israel: Therefore if he will keep my commandments he shall be lifted up at the last day, even so Amen

134. He Shall Be Restored unto His Former State
From a letter of Smith to Whitlock, 16 November 1835, in JS Journal

Revelation received at Kirtland, Ohio, on 16 November 1835
for Harvey Whitlock

I have inquired of the Lord concerning your case, these words came to me

Verily thus saith the Lord unto you: let him who was my servant Harvey [Whitlock], return unto me;— and unto the bosom of my Church, and forsake all the

---

20. The church purchased some Egyptian papyri together with four Egyptian mummies from Michael H. Chandler in July 1835. Warren Parrish was called as a scribe to Smith for work on the Book of Abraham. In 1838 Parrish wrote, "I have set [sat] by his [Smith's] side and penned down the translation of the Egyptian Hierogyphicks [Hieroglyphics] as he claimed to receive it by direct inspiration from Heaven" (Parrish to Editor, 5 Feb. 1838 in *Painesville Republican* 2 (15 [i.e., 22] Feb. 1838). See Jay M. Todd, *The Saga of the Book of Abraham* (Salt Lake City: Deseret Book Co., 1969), 185.

21. Parrish became a scribe to Smith on 29 October 1835. He kept Smith's journal at various times during 1835-36. Parrish wrote in February 1838, "I have been Smith's private secretary, called to fill this high and responsible station by revelation which I wrote myself as it dropped from the lips of the prophet" (Parrish to Editor, 5 Feb. 1838, in *Painesville Republican* 2 (15 [i.e., 22] Feb. 1838).

sins wherewith he has offended against me and persue [pursue] from hence forth a virtuous and upright life, and remain under the direction of those whom I have appointed to be pillars, and heads of my church, and behold, saith the Lord, your God; his sins shall be blotted out from under heaven, and shall be forgotten from among men, and shall not come up in mine ears, nor be recorded as a memorial against him, but I will lift him up as out of deep mire, and he shall be exalted upon the high places, and shall be counted worthy to stand ammong [among] princes, and shall yet be made a polished shaft in my quiver, of bringing down the strong holds of wickedness, among those who set themselves up on high, that they may take council against me, and against annointed ones in the last days.

Therefore let him prepare himself speedily and come unto you; even to Kirtland and inasmuch as he shall h[e]arken unto all your council [counsel] from henceforth he shall be restored unto his former state, and shall be saved unto the uttermost, even as the Lord your God livith [liveth] Amen.

135. Had Better Not Be Baptised Here
From JS Journal

Revelation received at Kirtland, Ohio, on 16 November 1835
for Erastus Holmes

The same night [16 November 1835] I received the word of the Lord on Mr. H[o]lmes case, he had desired that I would inquire at the hand of the Lord whether it was his duty to be baptised here, or wait until he returned home:— The word of the Lord came unto me saying,

that Mr. [Erastus] Holmes had better not be baptised here, and that he had better not return by water, also that there were three men that were seeking his destruction, to be ware of his eneys [enemies]

136. Receive Counsel of Him Whom I Have Appointed
From JS Journal (cf. LDS D&C 108)

Revelation received at Kirtland, Ohio, on 26 December 1835
for Lyman Sherman

The following is a revelation given to Lyman Sherman this day 26 Dec 1835

Verily thus saith the Lord unto you my servant Lyman [Sherman] your sins are forgiven you because you have obeyed my voice in coming up hither this morning to receive councel [counsel] of him whom I have appointed

Therefore let your soul be at rest concerning your spiritual standing, and resist no more my voice, and arise up and be more careful henceforth in observing your vows which you have made and do make, and you shall be blessed with exce[e]ding great blessings. Wait patiently untill the solemn assembly shall be called of my servants then you shall be numbered with the first of mine elders and receive right by ordination with the rest of mine elders whom I have chosen

Behold this is the promise of the father unto you if you continue faithful — and it shall be fulfilled upon you in that day that you shall have right to preach my gospel wheresoever I shall send you from henceforth from that time. Therefore strengthen your brethren in all your conversation in all your prayers, and in all your exhortations, and in all your doings, and behold and lo I am with you to bless you and deliver you forever Amen

137. I Beheld the Celestial Kingdom of God
From JS Journal (cf. LDS D&C 137)

Vision received at Kirtland, Ohio, on 21 January 1836
of the Celestial Kingdom

The heavens were opened upon us and I [Joseph Smith, Jr.] beheld the celestial kingdom of God, and the glory thereof, whether in the body or out I cannot tell, — I saw the transcendant [transcendent] beauty of the gate through which the heirs of that Kingdom will enter, which was like unto circling flames of fire, also the blasing [blazing] throne of God, whereon was seated the Father and the Son, — I saw the beautiful streets of that Kingdom, which had the appearance of being paved with gold — I saw father Adam, and Abraham and Michael[22] and my father and mother, my brother Alvin [Smith] that has long since slept, and marv[el]led how it was that he had obtained an inheritance in that Kingdom, seeing that he had departed this life, before the Lord had set his hand to gather Israel the second time[23] and had not been baptised for the remission of sins

Thus came the voice of the Lord unto me saying

all who have died with[out] a knowledge of this gospel, who would have received it, if they had been permitted to tarry, shall be heirs of the celestial kingdom of God — also all that shall die henseforth [henceforth], without a knowledge of it, who would have received it, with all their hearts, shall be heirs of that kingdom, for I the Lord will judge all men according to their works according to the desires of their hearts

and I also beheld that all children who die before they ar[r]ive to the years of accountability, are saved in the celestial kingdom of heaven

I saw the 12, apostles of the Lamb, who are now upon the earth who hold the keys of this last ministry, in foreign lands, standing together in a circle much fa-

---

22. The text in the journal says that Smith also saw Michael in this vision. Prior to this time, it was taught that Michael was another name for Adam. Oliver Cowdery wrote in a letter in January 1834, "I have been informed from a proper source that the Angel Michael is no less than our father Adam" (Cowdery to John Whitmer, 1 Jan. 1834, Oliver Cowdery Letterbook, 15, Henry E. Huntington Library, San Marino, California).

23. Alvin Smith died on 19 November 1823 at age twenty-five.

tiegued [fatigued], with their clothes tattered and feet swol[l]en, with their eyes cast downward, and Jesus standing in their midst, and they did not behold him, the Saviour looked upon them and wept

I also beheld Elder McLellen [William E. McLellin] in the south, standing upon a hill surrounded with a vast multitude, preaching to them, and a lame man standing before him, supported by his crutches, he threw them down at his word, and leaped as an heart [hart], by the mighty power of God

Also [beheld] Eld[er] Brigham Young[24] standing in a strange land, in the far southwest, in a desert place, upon a rock in the midst of about a dozen men of colour [color], who, appeared hostile He was preaching to them in their own toung [tongue], and the angel of God standing above his head with a drawn sword in his hand protec[t]ing him, but he did not see it,

and I finally saw the 12 in the celestial kingdom of God, —I also beheld the redemption of Zion, and many things which the toung [tongue] of man, cannot discribe [describe] in full.[25]

138. I Have Accepted This House
From JS Journal (cf. LDS D&C 110)

Visions received by Joseph Smith, Jr., and Oliver Cowdery
in the House of the Lord at Kirtland, Ohio,
on 3 April 1836[26]

In the P.M. he [Joseph Smith, Jr.] assisted the other Presidents in distributing the elements of the Lord[']s Supper to the church, receiving them from the "Twelve" whose privilige [privilege] it was to officiate in the sacred desk this day. After having performed this service to his brethren, he retired to the pulpit, the vails [veils] being dropped, and bowed himself with O[liver]. Cowdery, in solemn, but silent prayer to the Most High. After rising from prayer the following vision was opened to both of them.[27]

---

24. Brigham Young became the second president of the LDS church. In December 1847 the First Presidency was organized with Young as president.

25. Smith's journal also states, "and I saw in my vision all of the presidency in the Celestial Kingdom of God, and, many others who were present."

26. This account was copied into Smith's journal by Warren A. Cowdery who arrived in Kirtland on 25 February 1836. He edited Smith's first-person journal to a third-person history for the dates of 22 September to 18 November 1835. The entries of 2 and 3 April 1836 are written in third-person. It appears that Cowdery used a first-person account but recorded the entries in the third-person as he did for the 1835-36 History.

27. Stephen Post recorded the events in the Kirtland temple: "P.M. partook of the sacrament confirmed a large number & blessed those little children that had not been blessed. the curtains were unfolded & confirmation, sacrament &c was attended to in 4 parts at the sa[me] time, the presidency took the pulpit during the confirmation & blessing of the children after which the curtains were raised & the people dismissed" (Stephen Post Journal, 3 Apr. 1836, LDS archives).

The vail [veil] was taken from their minds and the eyes of their understandings were opened. They saw the Lord standing upon the breast work of the pulpit before them, and under his feet was a paved work of pure gold, in color like amber: his eyes were as a flame of fire; the hair of his head was like the pure snow, his countenance shone above the brightness of the sun, and his voice was as the sound of the rushing of great waters, even the Voice of Jehovah, saying,

I am the first and the last, I am he who liveth, I am he who was slain. I am your Advocate with the Father. Behold your sins are forgiven you. You are clean before me, therefore, lift up your heads and rejoice, let the hearts of your brethren rejoice and let the hearts of all my people rejoice, who have with their might, built this house to my name. For behold I have accepted this house and my name shall be here; and I will manifest myself to my people, in mercy, in this House, yea I will appear unto my servants and speak unto them with mine own voice, if my people will keep my commandments and do not pollute this Holy House.

Yea the hearts of thousands and tens of thousands shall greatly rejoice in consequence of the blessings which shall be poured out, and the endowment with which my servants have already been endowed and shall hereafter be endowed in this House. And the fame of this House shall spread to foreign lands, and this is the beginning of the blessing, which shall be poured out upon the heads of my people. even so Amen.

After this vision closed, the Heavens were again opened unto them and Moses appeared before them and committed unto them the keys of the gathering of Israel from the four parts of the Earth and the leading of the ten tribes from the Land of the North.

After this Elias[28] appeared and committed the dispensation of the gospel of Abraham, saying, that in them and their seed all generations after them should be blessed.

After this vision had closed, another great and glorious vision burst upon them, for Elijah, the Prophet, who was taken to Heaven without tasting death, also stood before them, and said,

behold the time has fully come which was spoken of by the Mouth of Malachi, testifying, that he[29] should be sent before the great and dreadful day of the Lord come, to turn the hearts of the Fathers to the children, and the children to the fathers, lest the whole earth be smitten with a curse. Therefore, the keys of this dispensation are committed into your hands, and by this ye may know that the great and dreadful day of the Lord is near, even at the doors

---

28. The mention of "Elias" appearing to Joseph Smith and Oliver Cowdery is curious since in a subsequent vision "Elijah" stood in their view. Elias is used for Elijah in the Greek NT. Whether this is a scribal error made in the journal entry is not known.
29. Elijah.

139. Concern Not Yourselves about Zion
From the William W. Phelps Journal, LDS archives
(cf. LDS D&C 111)

Revelation received at Salem, Massachusetts, on 6 August 1836

A revela[t]ion Salem (M[as]s.) August 6, 1836.

I the Lord your God am not displeased with your coming this Journey, not-withstandi[n]g your follies I have much treasure in this city for you, for the benefit of Zion; and many people in this city whom I will gather out in due time for the benefit of Zion, through your instrumentality. Therefore it is expedient that you should form acquaintance with men in this city, as you shall be led, and as it shall be given you.

And it shall come to pass, in due time, that I will give this city into your hands, that you shall have power over it, insomuch that they shall not discover your secret parts; and its wealth, pertaining to gold and silver, shall be yours. Concern not yourselves about your debts, for I will give you power to pay them. Concern not yourselves about Zion, for I will deal merciful[ly] with her.

Tarry in this place and in the regions round about, and the place where it is my will that you should tarry, for the main, shall be signalized unto you by the peace and the power of my Spirit, that shall flow unto you. This place you may obtain by hire &c. And inquire diligently concerning the more ancient inhabitants and founders of this city, for there are more treasures than one for you, in this city: Therefore, be ye as wise as serpents and yet without sin, and I will order all things for your good as fast as ye are able to receive them: Amen.

140. Rebel Not against My Servant Joseph
From SB (cf. LDS D&C 112; RLDS D&C 105)

Revelation received at Kirtland, Ohio, on 23 July 1837
for Thomas B. Marsh, President of the
Quorum of the Twelve Apostles[30]

A Revelation given Kirtland July 3rd 1837. The word of the Lord unto Thomas, B. Marsh concerning the twelve Apostles of the Lamb.

Verily thus saith the Lord unto you my servant Thomas [B. Marsh] I have heard thy prayers and thine alms have come up as a memorial before me in behalf of those thy brethren who were chosen to bear testimony of my name and to send it abroad among all nations kindreds tongues and people and ordained through the instrumentality of my servants.

---

30. The text of this revelation in the SB contains some alterations made at a later date. This transcription follows what was originally written in 1838 when it was copied into the SB.

Verily I say unto you there have been some few things in thine heart and with thee, with which I the Lord was not well pleased; nevertheless inasmuch as thou hast abased thyself thou shalt be exalted: therefore all thy sins are forgiven thee.

Let thy heart be of good cheer before my face and thou shalt bear record of my name not only unto the Gentiles, but also unto the Jews; and thou shalt send forth my word unto the ends of the earth.

Contend thou therefore morning by morning and day after day let thy warning voice go forth; and when the night cometh let not the inhabitants of the earth slumber because of thy speech.

Let thy habitation be known in Zion and remove not thy house, for I the Lord have a great work for you to do, in publishing my name among the children of men, therefore gird up your loins for the work. Let your feet be shod also for thou art chosen, and thy path lyeth [lieth] among the mountains and among many nations, and by thy word many high ones shall be brought low; and by thy word many low ones shall be exalted, thy voice shall be a rebuke unto the transgressor, and at thy rebuke let the tongue of the slanderer cease its perverseness.

Be thou humble and the Lord thy God shall lead thee by the hand and give thee answer to thy prayers. I know thy heart and have heard thy prayers concerning thy brethren. Be not partial towards them in love above many others, but let your love be for them as for yourself, and let your love abound unto all men and unto all who love my name. And pray for your brethren of the twelve. Admonish them sharply for my name's sake, and let them be admonished for all their sins, and be ye faithful before me unto my name; and after their temptations and much tribulation behold I the Lord will feel after them, and if they harden not their hearts and stiffen not their necks against me they shall be converted and I will heal them.

Now I say unto you, and what I say unto you, I say unto all the twelve. Arise and gird up your loins, take up your cross, follow me, and feed my sheep. Exalt not yourselves; rebel not against my servant Joseph [Smith, Jr.] for Verily I say unto you I am with him and my hand shall be over him; and the keys which I have given him, and also to youward shall not be taken from him untill I come.

Verily I say unto you my servant Thomas [B. Marsh], thou art the man whom I have chosen to hold the keys of my kingdom (as pertaining to the twelve) abroad among all nations, that thou mayest be my servant to unlock the door of the kingdom in all places where my servant Joseph [Smith, Jr.], and my servant Sidney [Rigdon], and my servant Hyrum [Smith], cannot come, for on them have I laid the burden of all the Churches for a little season: wherefore whithersoever they shall send you, go ye, and I will be with you and in whatsoever place ye shall proclaim my name an effectual door shall be opened unto you that they may receive my word. Whosoever receiveth my word receiveth me, and whosoever receiveth me receiveth those (the first presidency) whom I have sent, whom I have made counsellors for my name's sake unto you.

And again I say unto you, that whosoever ye shall send in my name, by the voice of your brethren the twelve, duly recommended and authorized by you, shall have power to open the door of my kingdom unto any nation whithersoever ye shall send them, inasmuch as they shall humble themselves before me and abide in my word and hearken to the voice of my spirit.

Verily! verily! I say unto you, darkness covereth the earth and gross darkness the minds of the people and all flesh has become corrupt before my face! Behold vengeance cometh speedily upon the inhabitants of the earth A day of wrath! A day of burning! A day of desolation! of weeping! Of mourning and of lamentation! And as a whirlwind it shall come upon all the face of the earth saith the Lord.

And upon my house shall it begin and from my house shall it go forth saith the Lord. First among those among you saith the Lord; who have professed to know my name and have not known me and have blasphemed against me in the midst of my house saith the Lord.

Therefore see to it that you trouble not yourselves concerning the affairs of my Church in this place saith the Lord but purify your hearts before me and then go ye into all the world and preach my gospel unto every creature who have not received it and he that believeth and is baptized shall be saved, and he that believeth not, and is not baptized shall be damned

For unto you (the twelve) and those (the first presidency) who are appointed with you to be your counsellors and your leaders, is the power of this priesthood given for the last days and for the last time, in the which is the dispensation of the fulness of times, which power you hold in connection with all those who have received a dispensation at any time from the beginning of the creation for verily I say unto you the keys of the dispensation which ye have received have come down from the fathers: and last of all being sent down from heaven unto you.

Verily I say unto you, Behold how great is your calling. Cleanse your hearts and your garments, lest the blood of this generation be required at your hands. Be faithful untill I come for I come quickly and my reward is with me to recompense every man according as his work shall be. I am Alpha and Omega:-Amen.

141. Things Which Are Not Pleasing in My Sight
From SB

Revelation received at Kirtland, Ohio, on 4 September 1837 concerning John Whitmer and William W. Phelps

Revelation to Joseph Smith Jr Given in Kirtland Geauga Co. Ohio Sept 4th 1837 Making known the transgression of John Whitmer [and] W. W. Phelps

Verily thus Saith the Lord unto you my Servent Joseph [Smith, Jr.]. My Servents John Whitmer & William W Phelps have done those things which are not pleasing in my sight Therefore if they repent not they shall be removed out of their places Amen

142. Awake My Shepherds and Warn My People
From a manuscript in LDS archives

Revelation received at Kirtland, Ohio, on 7 January 1838
for Edward Partridge

Thus saith the Lord, my servant Edward [Partridge] and his house shall be numbered with the blessed, and Abraham t[he]ir father, and his name [s]hall be had in sacred rememberance.

And again thus saith the Lord, let my people be aware of dissentiors [dissenters] among them, lest the enemy have power over them;

Awake my shepherds and warn my people! for behold the wolf[31] cometh to destroy them, — receive him not.

Kirtland Jan. 7th 1838

143. Let the First Presidency of My Church Be Held in Full Fellowship
From a manuscript in LDS archives

Revelation received at Kirtland, Ohio, on 12 January 1838
concerning trying the First Presidency
of the Church of the Latter Day Saints

Kirtland Ohio Jan. 12th 1838
In the presence of Joseph Smith Jr Sid[ney] Rigdon Vinson Knight & G[eorge]. W. Robin[son] at the French Farm, The following inquiry was made of the Lord

A question asked of the Lord concerning the trying of the first Presidency of the Church of Latter Day Saints for transgress[ions] According to the item of Law found [in the] third Sec[tion] of the Book of covenants 37 Verse[32] Whether the descision [decision] of Such an counsil [council] of one Stake Shall be conclusive for Zion and all the Stake[s][?]

Answer[:] Thus saith th[e] Lord the time has now come when a desisi[on] [decision] of Such an council would not answer for Zion and all her Stakes

[Question:] What will answer for Zion and all her Stakes[?]

Answer; Thus Saith the Lord let the first presidency of my Church be held in full fellowship in Zion and all her Stakes u[n]til they shall be found transg[ress]ors by Such an high Council as is named in the 3rd Sec. 37 Verse of the Book of Cove-

---

31. David W. Patten stated on 5 February 1838 that the wolf "was the dissenters in Kirtland" (Donald Q. Cannon and Lyndon W. Cook, eds., *Far West Record: Minutes of the Church of Jesus Christ of Latter-day Saints, 1830-1844* [Salt Lake City: Deseret Book Co., 1983], 138).
32. See document no. 126; LDS D&C 107; RLDS D&C 104.

nants, in Zion by 3 witnesses standing against each member of Said presidency and Said witnesses Shall be of long and faithful Standing and Such also as cannot be impeached by other witnesses before Said council and when a desision [decision] is had by such an council in Zion it Shall only be for Zion it Shall not answer for her Stakes but if Said desision [decision] be acknowledged by the Council of her Stakes, then it shall answer for her Stakes

But if it is not acknowledged by the Stakes then such Stakes may have [the] privilege of hearing for themselves. or if Said desision [decision] Shall be acknowledged by a majority of her Stakes then it Shal[l] answer for all her Stakes

And again the presidency of Said Church may be tried by t[he] voice of th[e] whole body of the Church of Zion, and the voice of a majority of all her Stakes, And again except a majority is had by the voice of the Church of Zion, and the majority of her Stakes, the charges will be considered not Sustained,

and in order to sustain such charge or charges before Said Church of Zion or her Stakes Such witnesses must be had as is named above, That is three witnesses &c each president that is of long & faithful st[anding] that can[not]³³ be impeached by other wit[nesses] befor[e] [the] Church of Zion or her Stakes, and all this Saith the Lord, because of wicked and asspi[r]ing [aspiring] men, let all your doings be in meekness and in humility before me even so amen

144. Except It Be Dedicated by This Presidency
From a manuscript in LDS archives

Revelation received at Kirtland, Ohio, on 12 January 1838 concerning appointing a stake of Zion

Kirtland Jan 12th 1838

[Question:] Can any branch of the Church of Latter Day Saints be considered a Stake of Zion u[n]till they have acknowledged the authority of the first Presidency, by a vote of Said Church,[?]

[Answer:] Thus Saith the Lord verily I say unto you nay

[Question:] How then[?]

Answer[:] No Stake shall be appointed except by the first presidency and this Presidency be acknowledged by the voice of the Same; Otherwise it shall not be counted as a Stake of Zion, And again except it be dedicated by this Presidency it cannot be acknowledged as a Stake of Zion, For unto this end, have I appointed them, in laying the foundation of and establishing my Kingdom³⁴

---

33. The SB has the word as "cannot."
34. The SB ends the text with the words "Even so Amen."

145. Get Out of This Place
From a manuscript in LDS archives

Revelation received at Kirtland, Ohio, on 12 January 1838
for the First Presidency

Thus Saith the Lord Let the presidency of my Church take their families as soon as it is practicable and a door is open for them and moove [move] unto the west[35] as fast as the way is made pla[in] before their faces and let their hearts be comforted for I will be with them

Verily I say unto you the time [has] come that your laibours [labors] are finished in this place, for a Season,

The[refore] arise and get yourselves unto a land which I Shall Show unto you even a land flowing with milk and honey you are clean from the blood of this people and wo unto those who have become your enimies [enemies] who have professed my name Saith the Lord, for their judgement lingereth not and their damnation Slumbereth not,

let all your faith[ful] friends arise with their families also and get out of this place And gather themselves together unto Zion and be at peace among yourselves O ye inhabitants of Zion or there Shall be no safety for you[36]

146. Put on the Authority of the Priesthood
From SB (cf. LDS D&C 113)

Explanation of Isaiah 11 and 52
given at Far West, Missouri, in [14-31] March 1838

Quest[ions]. on Scripture.

[Question] 1st. Who is the stem of Jessee [Jesse] spoken of in the 1st 2d 3d 4th and 5th verses of the 11th Chap[ter]. of Is[a]iah.[?]

Ans[wer]. Verely [Verily] thus saith the Lord It is Christ

Q[uestion]. 2d. What is the Rod spoken of in the 1st verse of the 11th Chap[ter]. that shou[l]d come of the stem of Jessee [Jesse].[?]

Ans[wer]. Behold thus saith the Lord it is a servant in the hands of Christ who is partly a descendant of Jessee [Jesse] as well as of Ephraim or of the house of Joseph, on whome [whom] thare [there] is laid much power.

Q[u]est[ion] 3d. What is the Root of Jessee [Jesse] spoken of in the 10th verse of the 11th Chap[ter].[?]

Ans[wer]. Behold thus saith the Lord; it is a descendant of Jessee [Jesse] as well as of Joseph unto whom rightly belongs the Priesthood and the kees [keys] of the

---

35. After financial trouble and internal dissent in Kirtland, the First Presidency moved to Far West, Missouri.
36. The SB ends the text with the words "Even so Amen."

Kingdom for an ensign and for the geathering [gathering] of my people in the Last days.

Questions by Elias Higby [Higbee][37]

1st Q[uestion]. What is me[a]nt by the command in Is[a]iah 52d Chap[ter] 1st verse which saith Put on thy strength O Zion and what people had I[sa]iah refer-ance [reference] to[?]

A[nswer]. He had reference to those whome [whom] God should call in the last day's who should hold the power of Priesthood to bring again zion and the re-demption of Israel. And to put on her strength is to put on the authority of the priesthood which she (Zion) has a right to by lineage: Also to return to that power which she had lost

Ques[tion]. 2d. What are we to understand by Zions loosing herself from the bands of her neck 2d verse.[?]

A[nswer]. We are to understand that the scattered remnants are exhorted to to return to the Lord from whence they have fal[l]en which if they do the promise of the Lord is that he will speak to them or give them revelation See 6th 7th and 8th verses The bands of her neck are the curses of God upon her or the remnants of Is-rael in their scattered condition among the Gentiles.

147. Others Shall Be Planted in Their Stead
From SB (cf. LDS D&C 114)

Revelation received at Far West, Missouri, on 11 April 1838
for David W. Patten

Revelation to D. W. Patten. given April 11th 1838

Verily thus Saith the Lord, it is wisdom in my Servant D[avid]. W. Patten, that he settle up all his business, as soon as he possibly can, and make a disposition of his merchandise, that he may perform a mission unto me next spring, in compa[n]y with others even twelve including himself, to testify of my name and bear glad tid-ings unto all the world,

for verrily [verily] thus saith the Lord that inasmuch as there are those among you who deny my name, others shall be planted in their stead and receive their bishoprick[38] Amen.

---

37. Elias Higbee was a member of the High Council of Zion at Far West, Missouri. See Can-non and Cook, *Far West Record*, 145-57.

38. Bishoprick (Bishopric) in this case means apostleship.

148. Provide for His Family
From SB

Revelation received at Far West, Missouri, on 17 April 1838
for Brigham Young

Revelation given to Brigham Young at Far West April 17th 1838.

Verrily [Verily] thus Saith the Lord, Let my Servant Brigham Young go unto the place which he has bought on Mill Creek and there provide for his family until an effectual door is op[e]ned for the sup[p]ort of his family untill I shall command [him] to go hence, and not to leave his family untill they are amply provided for Amen.

8. Early Church of
Jesus Christ of Latter Day Saints Period,
April 1838–November 1843

At Far West, Missouri, vacancies in the Quorum of Twelve Apostles, caused by
apostasy, were filled. A temple was considered for Far West. Joseph Smith, Jr.,
was arrested and brought to Liberty Jail in Clay County. In jail Smith wrote a
lengthy epistle in March 1839 detailing his prayer and supplication to God about
the persecution of the Saints. He learned to rely on his own experience and to ask
for revelation only when needed. After escaping from jail, Smith settled in Com-
merce (later Nauvoo), Illinois, next to the Mississippi River. Baptism for the dead
commenced in 1840. Church member John C. Bennett became a confidant of
Joseph Smith. Plans to build a temple and a boarding house in Nauvoo were
introduced to members. Newly developed doctrinal ideas were taught in public
and private. Plural marriage was introduced as a priesthood ordinance. A special
endowment ceremony and higher anointing were given to a few chosen men and
women. Still, Smith relied less on formal revelations, at least for specific solutions,
during the Nauvoo period.

149. The Ground upon Which Thou Standest Is Holy
From SB (cf. LDS D&C 115)

*Revelation received at Far West, Missouri, on 26 April 1838
concerning building a house unto the Lord*[1]

Revelation given in Far West, April 26th 1838. Making known the will of God,
concerning the building up of this place and of the Lord's House &c

Verrily [Verily] thus Saith the Lord unto you my Servant Joseph Smith Jr. and
also my Servant Sidney Rigdon, and also my Servant Hyrum Smith, and your
counsilors [counselors] who are and who shall be hereafter appointed, and also

---

1. This 26 April 1838 revelation commands the Saints to build a house (temple) at Far West.
On 15 November 1836 a building committee was appointed "to build the house of the Lord" in
Far West, Missouri (Donald Q. Cannon and Lyndon W. Cook, eds. *Far West Record: Minutes of
the Church of Jesus Christ of Latter-day Saints, 1830-1844* [Salt Lake City: Deseret Book Co.,

THE

DOCTRINE AND COVENANTS

OF

THE CHURCH OF JESUS CHRIST

OF

LATTER DAY SAINTS;

CAREFULLY SELECTED FROM THE REVELATIONS OF GOD.

BY JOSEPH SMITH,
PRESIDENT OF SAID CHURCH.

SECOND EDITION.

~~~~~~

NAUVOO, ILL.:
PRINTED BY JOHN TAYLOR.

1844.

Title Page of 1844 Doctrine and Covenants

unto my Servant Edward Partridge and his Councilors [Counselors], and also unto my faithfull Servants, who are of the High Council of my Church in Zion (for thus it shall be called) and unto all the Elders and people of my Church of Jesus Christ of Latter Day Saints, scattered abroad in all the world,

For thus shall my Church be called in the Last days even the Church of Jesus Christ of Latter Day Saints,

Verrily [Verily] I say unto you all; arise and shine forth that thy light may be a standard for the nations and that thy gathering to-gether upon the land of Zion and upon her stakes may be for a defence and for a reffuge [refuge] from the storm and from wrath when it shall be poured out without mixture upon the whole earth,

Let the City Far West, be a holy and consecrated land unto me, and it shall be called most holy for the ground upon which thou standest is holy Therefore I command you to build an house unto me for the gathering together of my Saints that they may worship me, and let there be a begin[n]ing of this work; and a foundation and a preparatory work, this following Summer; and let the begin[n]ing be made on the 4th day of July next; and from that time forth let my people labour diligently to build an house, unto my name, and in one year from this day, let them recommence laying the foundation of my house; thus let them from that time forth laibour [labor] diligently untill it shall be finished, from the Corner Stone thereof unto the top thereof, untill there shall not any thing remain that is not finished.

Verrily [Verily] I say unto you let not my Servant Joseph [Smith, Jr.] neither my Servant Sidn[e]y [Rigdon], neither my Servant Hyrum [Smith], get in debt any more for the building of an house unto my name. But let my house be built unto my name according to the pattern which I will shew unto them, and if my people build it not according to the pattern which I shall shew unto their presidency, I will not accept it at their hands. But if my people do build it according to the pattern which I shall shew unto their presidency, even my servant Joseph [Smith, Jr.] and his Councilors [Counselors]; then I will accept it at the hands of my people.

And again; Verrily [Verily] I say unto you it is my will, that the City Far West should be built up spe[e]dily by the gathering of my Saints, and also that other places should be appointed for stakes in the regions round about as they shall be manifested unto my Servant Joseph [Smith, Jr.] from time to time. For behold I will be with him and I will sanctify him before the people for unto him have I given the Keys of this Kingdom and ministry even so Amen.

1983], 102). A site was selected in 1837 where a temple would be built. On 7 April 1837 a meeting was held at Far West and the presidency of the church in Missouri (David Whitmer, John Whitmer, and William W. Phelps) was "appointed to superintend the building of the house of the Lord in this City Far West and receive Revelations Visions &c. concerning said house" (ibid., 103-104). Excavation for the temple began on 3 July 1837. Phelps wrote, "the day was beautiful, the Spirit of the Lord was with us, a cellar for this great edifice, 110 [feet] long by 80 [feet] broad was nearly finished" (*Latter Day Saints' Messenger and Advocate* 3 [July 1837]: 529; [Aug. 1837]: 560). But on 6 November 1837 at a meeting where Joseph Smith, Jr., was present, it was voted "that the building of the house of the Lord in this place be postponed till the Lord shall reveal it to be his will to be commenced" (*Far West Record*, 120).

150. Let the Twelve Be Organized
From SB (cf. LDS D&C 118)

Revelation received at Far West, Missouri, on 8 July 1838
concerning the Twelve Apostles

The following Revelation was given in Far West Mo July 8th 1838, and read this day in the congregation of the Saints,

Revelation Given to the Twelve Apostles July 8th 1838 in Far West Mo in the presence of J[oseph] Smith Jr. S[idney]. Rigdon, H[yrum]. Smith, E[ward]. Partridge I[saac]. Morl[e]y J[ared]. Carter, S[ampson]. Avard T[homas]. B. Marsh & G[eorge]. W. Robinson Making known the will of the Lord concerning the Twelve Show unto us thy will O. Lord concerning the Twelve.

Verily thus saith the Lord, Let a conference be held immediately, Let the Twelve be organized. Let men be appointed to supply the places of those who [have] fallen.

Let my servent Thomas [B. Marsh] remain for a season in the land of Zion, to publish my word let the residue continue to preach from that hour, and if they will do this in all Lowliness of heart in meekness and pureness and long suffering I the Lord God give unto them a promise, that I will provide for their families, and an effectual door shall be op[e]ned for them, from henceforth,

And next spring let them depart to go over the great waters, and there promulge [promulgate] my gospel in the fullness thereof, and to bear record of my name.

Let them take l[e]ave of my Saints in the City Far West, on the Twenty sixth day of April next, on the building spot of mine house saith the Lord,

Let my servent John Taylor,[2] and also my servant John E Page, and also my servent Willford Woodruff[3] and also my servant Willard Richards be appointed to fill the places of those who have fallen, and be officially Notified of their appointment[4] even so Amen

151. Their Former Standing Has Been Taken Away
From SB

Revelation received at Far West, Missouri, on 8 July 1838
concerning Frederick G. Williams and William W. Phelps

Revelation Given the same day, and at the same place, and read the same day in the congregation of the Saints Making known the duty of F[rederick]. G. Williams & Wm W. Phelps

---

2. John Taylor became third president of the LDS church in 1880.
3. Wilford Woodruff became fourth president of the LDS church in 1889.
4. These men were chosen to fill the vacancies in the Quorum of the Twelve as John F. Boynton, Luke S. Johnson, Lyman E. Johnson, and William E. McLellin were no longer church members by July 1838.

Verrily [Verily] thus Saith the Lord in consequence of their transgressions, their former standing has been taken away from them

And now if they will be saved, Let them be ordained as Elders, in my Church, to preach my gospel and travel abroad from land to land and from place to place, to gather mine Elect unto me Saith the Lord, and let this be their labors from hence forth Even So Amen

152. This Shall Be a Standing Law unto Them Forever
From SB (cf. LDS D&C 119; RLDS D&C 106)

Revelation received at Far West, Missouri, on 8 July 1838 concerning surplus property as a tithing

Revelation, Given the same day and read at the same time, of the preceeding ones July 8th 1838

[Question:] O! Lord, show unto thy servents how much thou requirest of the properties of thy people for a Tithing?

Answer. Verrily [Verily] thus saith the Lord, I require all their surpluss [surplus] property to be put into the hands of the Bishop of my Church of Zion, for the building of mine house, and for the Laying [of] the foundation of Zion, and for the priesthood, and for the debts of the presidency of my Church, and this shall be the begin[n]ing of the tithing of my people. and after that, those, who have thus been tithed, shall pay one tenth of all their interest an[n]ually. And this shall be a standing Law unto them forever, for my holy priesthood saith the Lord.

Verrily [Verily] I say unto you, it shall come to pass, that all those who gather unto the land of Zion, shall be tithed of their surpluss [surplus] properties, and shall observe this Law, or they shall not be found worthy to abide among you. And I say unto you, if my people observe not this Law, to keep it holy, and by this law sanctify the Land of Zion unto me, that my Statutes and my Judgements, may be kept thereon that it may be most holy, behold verrily [verily] I say unto you, it shall not be a land of Zion unto you, and this shall be an ensample [example] unto all the stakes of Zion, even so Amen.

153. It Shall Be Disposed Of
From SB (cf. LDS D&C 120)

Revelation received at Far West, Missouri, on 8 July 1838 concerning the disposition of property tithed

Revelation Given the same day July 8th 1838 Making known the disposition of the properties tithed, as named in the preceeding revelation

Verrily [Verily] thus saith the Lord, the time has now come that it shall be disposed of, by a council composed of the first Presidency of my Church and of the Bishop and his council and by my high Council, and by mine own voice unto them saith the Lord, even so Amen.

154. Let Them Settle Up Their Business
From SB (cf. LDS D&C 117)

*Revelation received at Far West, Missouri, on 8 July 1838
for William Marks, Newel K. Whitney, and Oliver Granger*

Revelation Given to Wm. Marks, N. K. Whitney Oliver Granger & others. Given in Zion. July 8th 1838

Verrily [Verily] thus saith the Lord unto my servent W[illia]m. Marks, and also unto my servent N[ewel]. K. Whitney, Let them settle up their buisness [business] spe[e]dily, and Journey from the land of Kirtland before I the Lord sendeth the snows again upon the ground, Let them awake and arise and come forth and not tarry for I the Lord command it, therefore if they tarry, it shall not be well with them, let them repent of all their sins and of all their covetous desires, before me saith the Lord. For what is property unto me saith the Lord.[?]

Let the properties of Kirtland be turned out for debts saith the Lord, Let them go; saith the Lord, and whatsoever remaineth let it remain in your hands saith the Lord,

for have I not the fowls of heaven and also the fish of the sea, and the bea[s]ts of the mountains,[?] have I not made the earth,[?] do I not hold the destinies of all the armies of the Nations of the earth,[?] therefore will I not make solitary places to bud, and to blossom, and bring forth in abundence [abundance] saith the Lord,[?]

Is there not room enough upon the mountains of Adam Ondi Awmen [Ahman], and upon the plains of Olah[a] Shinehah, or in the land where Adam dwelt;[5] that you should not covet that which is but the drop, and neglect the more weighty matters,[?] Therefore come up hither unto the Land of my people, even Zion,

let my servent Wm. Marks, be faithfull over a few things, and he shall be ruler over many. Let him preside in the midst of my people in the City Far West and let him be blessed with the blessings of my people.

Let my servant N[ewel]. K. Whitney be ashamed of the Nicholatine band, and of all their secret abominations,[6] and of all his littleness of soul before me saith the Lord and come up unto the land of Adam Ondi Awman [Ahman], and be a bishop

---

5. Smith taught that the biblical Adam lived in the present state of Missouri in America. About twenty-five miles north of Far West was a settlement called Adam-ondi-Ahman in Daviess County; here was discovered what was believed to be the remains of an altar on which Adam offered sacrifices.

6. This apparently refers to dissenters in the Kirtland, Ohio, area.

unto my people saith the Lord, not in name but in deed saith the Lord.

And again verrily [verily] I say unto you I remember my servent Oliver Granger, behold Verrily [Verily] I say unto him, that his name shall be had in sacred remembrance from Generation to Generation for ever and ever, saith the Lord. Therefore let him contend earnestly for the redemption of the first presidency of my Church saith the Lord, and when he falls he shall rise again for his sacrafice [sacrifice] shall be more sacred unto me, than his increase saith the Lord,

Therefore, let him come up hither spe[e]dily unto the land of Zion, and in due time he shall be made a merchent [merchant] unto my name saith the Lord, for the benefit of my people, Therefore let no man despise my servent Oliver Granger, but let the blessings of my people be upon him forever and ever,

and again verily I say unto you, let all my servents in the Land of Kirtland rem[em]ber the Lord their God, and mine house also, to keep and preser[v]e it holy, and to overthrow the money Changers in mine own due time saith the Lord, Even so Amen

155. Council of the Eternal God of All Other Gods

From an Epistle of Joseph Smith, Jr., et al., to the church, 20 March 1839, LDS archives (cf. LDS D&C 121-122)

Extracts from an Epistle of Joseph Smith, Jr.,
written at Liberty Jail, Clay County, Missouri,
on 20 March 1839 to the church at Quincy,
Illinois, and scattered abroad, and
to Bishop Edward Partridge[7]

[Prayer:] O God where art thou and where is the pavilion that covereth thy hiding place[?] how long shall thy hand be stayed and thine eye yea thy pure eye behold from the etearnal [eternal] heavens the [w]rongs of thy people and of thy servants and thine ear be penetrated with their cyes [cries][?] yea o Lord how long shall they suffer these [w]rongs and unlawfull oppressions before thine hart [heart] shall be softened towards them and thy bowels be moved with compassion towords [towards] them.[?]

O Lord God almity [almighty] maker of heaven earth and seas and of all things that in them is and who control[l]eth and subjecteth the devil and the dark and benig[h]ted dominion of shayole [sheol]. Streach [Stretch] forth thy hand let thine eye pierce let thy pavilion be taken up let thy hiding place no longer be covered let thine ear be inclined let thine hart [heart] be softened and thy bowels moved with compassion toward us let thine anger be kindle[d] against our enemi[e]s and in the

---

7. This epistle was dictated and signed by Smith and fellow prisoners Hyrum Smith, Lyman Wight, Caleb Baldwin, and Alexander McRae. Compare these extracts with the edited version of this epistle in the *Times and Seasons* 1 (May 1840): 100-103 and (July 1840): 131-32. For the complete letter, see Dean C. Jessee, ed., *The Personal Writings of Joseph Smith* (Salt Lake City: Deseret Book Co., 1984), 389-407.

fury of thine hart [heart] with thy sword avenge us of our [w]rongs remember thy
suffering saint[s] oh our God and thy servants will rejoyce in thy name for ever.

. . .

[Response:] then the voice of inspiration steals along and whispers my son
peace be unto thy soal [soul] thine advirsity [adversity] and thy afflictions shall be
but a small moment and then if thou indure [endure] it well God shall exalt the[e]
on high thou shalt tryumph [triumph] over all thy foes thy friends do stand by
the[e] and they shall hail the[e] again with warm harts [hearts] and friendly hands
thou art not yet as Job thy friends do not contend again[st] the[e] neither charge
the[e] with transgretion [transgression] as they did Job and they who do charge
the[e] with transgretion [transgression] there [their] hope shall be blasted and there
[their] prospects shall melt away as the hory [hoary] frost melteth before the burning rays of the rising sun

and also that God hath set to his hand and seal to change the times and seasons
and to blind their minds that they may not understand his marvilos [marvelous]
workings that he may prove them also and take them in there [their] own craftiness
also because their harts [hearts] are corrupt and the thing which they are willing to
bring upon others and love to have others suffer may come upon themselv[e]s to
the verry [very] utmost that they may be disappointed also and their hopes may be
cut off and not many years hence that they and their pasterity [posterity] shall be
swept from under heaven saith God that not one of them is left to stand by the wall

cursed are all those that shall lift up the heal [heel] against mine anointed saith
the Lord and cry they have sin[n]ed when they have not sin[n]ed before me saith
the Lord but have done that which was meat [meet] in mine eyes and which I commanded them but those who cry transgres[s]ion do it becaus[e] they are the servants of sin and are the children of disobediance themselv[e]s and those who swear
false[ly] against my servants that they might bring them unto bondage and death.

Wo unto them because they have offended my little ones they shall be severed
from the ordinances of mine house their basket shall not be full their houses and
their barnes [barns] shall famish and they themselv[e]s shall be dispised [despised]
by those that flattered them they shall not have right to the priesthood nor their
posterity after them from generation to generation it had been better for them that
a millstone had been hanged about their necks and they drown[e]d in the depth of
the see [sea]

wo unto all those that discomfort my people and drive and murder and testify
against them saith the Lord of host[s] a generation of viper[s] shall not escape the
damnation of hell behold mine eye seeth and knoweth all their works and I have in
reserve a swift judgement in the season thereoff [thereof] for them all for there is a
time appointed to ev[e]ry man according as his work shall be

. . .

[Instructions:] and now Bretheren [Brethren] after your tribulations if you do
these things, and exercise fervent prayer, and faith in the sight of God Always he
shall give unto you knowledge by his holy spirit yea by the unspeakable gift of the

holy-Ghost that has not been revealed since the world was untill now which our fathers have wa[i]ted with anxious expectation to be revealed in the last times which their minds were pointed to by the Angels as held in reserve for the fullness of their glory

a time to come in the which nothing shall be with held whither [whether] there be one god or many gods they shall be manifest all thrones and dominions princi-palities and powers shall be revealed and set forth upon all who have indured [en-dured] valiently [valiantly] for the gospel of Jesus Christ and also if there be bounds set to the heavens or to the seas or to the dry land or to the sun moon or starrs [stars] all the times of their revolutions all their appointed days month[s] and years and all the Days of their days, months and years, and all their glories laws and set times shall be reveal[e]d in the days of the dispensation of the fullness of times according to that which was ordained in the midst of the councyl [council] of the eternal God of all other Gods before this world was that should be reserved unto the finishing and the end thereoff [thereof] when ev[e]ry man shall enter into his eternal presants [presence] and into his im[m]ortal rest

· · ·

[Reflections:] How long can rowling [rolling] watters [waters] remain im-pure[?] what power shall stay the heavens[?] as well might man streach [stretch] forth his puny arm to stop the Missouri River in its dicread [decreed] cours[e] or to turne [turn] it up stream as to hinder the Almighty from pooring [pouring] down kno[w]ledge from heaven upon the heads of the Latter day saints

what is [Lilburn W.] Boggs[8] or his murderous party but wimbling willows upon the shore to catch the flood wood as well might we argue that watter [water] is not watter [water] because the mountain torants [torrents] send down mire and riles the cristle [crystal] stream altho[ugh] afterwords [afterwards] renders it more pure than before or that fire is not fire because it is of a quenchable nature by pooring [pouring] on the flood, as to say that our cause is down because runegadoes [rene-gades] lyers [liars] preasts [priests] theavs [thieves] and murderers who are all alike tenatious of their crafts and creeds have poord [poured] down from their spiritual wickednes[s] in high places and from their strong holds of the divi[ne] a flud [fluid] of dirt and mire and filthiness and vomit upon our heads no God forbid hell may poor [pour] forth its rage like the burning lavy [lava] of mount vesuvias [vesuvius] or of Etna or the most ter[r]ible of the burning mountains and yet shall mormon-ism stand.

watter [water], fire, truth, and god are all the same truth is mormonism God is the author of it he is our shield it is by him we receive our birth, it was by his voice that we were called to a dispensation of his gospel in the begin[n]ing of the fullness of times it was by him we received the book of mormon and it was by him that we remain unto this day and by him we shall remain if it shall be for our glory and in his almighty name we are determined to indure [endure] tribulation as good sol-diers unto the end

8. Lilburn W. Boggs was governor of Missouri and issued an "Extermination Order" on 27 October 1838.

. . .

[Instructions and Reflections:] Behold there are many called but few are chosen. And why are they not chosen? Because their hearts are set so much upon the things of this world and aspire to the honors of men that they do not learn this one lesson.

that the rights of priesthood are inseperably connected with the powers of heaven and that the powers of heaven cannot be control[l]ed nor handled only upon the principals [principles] of rightiousness [righteousness] that they may be confer[r]ed upon us it is tru[e] but when we undertake to cover our sins or to gratify our pride or vaine [vain] ambition or to exercise controle [control] or dominion or compulsion upon the souls of the children of men in any degree of unritiousness [unrighteousness] behold the heavens with draw themselves the spirit of the Lord is grieved and when it has withdrawn amen to the priesthood or the authority of that man behold ere he is aware he is left unto himself to kick against the pricks to persecute the saints and to fight against God.

We have learned by sad experiance [experience] that it is the nature and disposition of almost all men as soon as they get a little authority as they suppose they will im[m]ediat[e]ly begin to exercise unritious [unrighteous] dominion hence many are called, but few are chosen.

No power or influance [influence] can or ought to be maintained by virtue of the priesthood, only by persuasion by long suffering, by gentleness and meakness and by love unfaigned [unfeigned], by kindness by pure knowledge which shall geratly [greatly] enlarge the soul without highpocracy [hypocrisy] and without guile reproving betimes with sharpness when moved upon by the holy ghost and then showing forth afterwords [afterwards] an increas[e] of love to ward him whom thou hast reproved lest he esteem the[e] to be his enemy that he may know that thy faithfulness is stronger than the cords of death thy bowells [bowels] also being full of charity to ward all men and to the household of faith and virtue garnish thy thoughts unseasingly [unceasingly] then shall thy confidence wax strong in the presants [presence] of God and the doctrines of the priesthood destell [distill] upon thy soul as the dews from heaven

the Holy Ghost shall be thy constant companion and thy septer [scepter] an unchanging septer [scepter] of ritiousness [righteousness] and truth and thy dominion shall be an everlasting dominion and without compulsory means it shall flow unto thee for eve[r] and ever

the ends of the Earth shall inquire after thy name and fools shall have thee in derision and hell shall rage against thee while the pure in heart and the wise and the noble and the virtuous shall seak [seek] council [counsel] and authority and bles[s]ings constantly from under thy hand and thy people shall never be turned against thee by the testimony of traters [traitors] and although their influance [influence] shall cast the[e] into trouble and into barrs [bars] and walls thou shalt be had in honor and but for a small moment and thy voice shall be more ter[r]ible in the midst of thine enemies than the fierce Lion because of thy ritiousness [righteousness] and thy God shall stand by the[e] for ever and ever.

If thou art called to pass through tribulation if thou art in perel [peril] among false brethren if thou art in perel [peril] amongst robbers if thou art in peral [peril] by land or by sea if thou art accused with all man[n]er of false accusations if thine enemies fall upon the[e] if they tear the[e] from the society of thy father and mother and brethren and sisters and if with a drawn sword thine enemies tear the[e] from the bosom of thy wife and of thine off springs and thine elder son although but six years of age[9] shall cling to thy garmont [garment] and shall say my father O my father why can[']t you stay with us[?] o my father what are the men agoing to do with you[?] and if then he shall be thrust from the[e] by the sword and thou be drag[g]ed to prison and thine enemies prowl around the[e] like wolves for blood of the Lamb

and if thou shouldest be cast into the pit or into the hand of murdere[r]s and the sentance [sentence] of death pas[s]ed upon thee if thou be cast into the deep if the bil[l]owing surge conspire against thee if fearse [fierce] wind become thine enemy if the heavens gether [gather] blackness and all the elements combine to hedge up thy way and above all if the verry [very] jaws of hell shall gap[e] open her mouth wide after thee know thou my son that all these things shall give thee experiance [experience] and shall be for thy good The son of man hath des[c]ended below them all art thou greater than he[?]

therefore hold on thy way and the priesthood shall remain with thee for their bounds are set they cannot pass thy days are known and thy years shall not be numbered less therefore fear not what man can do for God shall be with you for ever and ever

156. I Am Well Pleased with Your Offering
From the 1844 D&C 103 (cf. LDS D&C 124)

Revelation received at Nauvoo, Illinois, on 19 January 1841
concerning writing a proclamation to the kings
of the earth, building a temple, and a
boarding house in Nauvoo, also
the organization of the priesthood quorums[10]

Revelation given to Joseph Smith, January 19, 1841.

Verily, thus saith the Lord unto you, my servant Joseph Smith, I am well pleased with your offering and acknowledgments, which you have made, for unto this end have I raised you up, that I might shew forth my wisdom through the weak things of the earth.

Your prayers are acceptable before me, and in answer to them I say unto you, that you are now called, immediately to make a solemn proclamation of my gospel,

---

9. Joseph Smith III was born on 6 November 1832 in Kirtland, Ohio. He became president in April 1860 of the Reorganized Church of Jesus Christ of Latter Day Saints.

10. This is Smith's longest revelation. John C. Bennett read it at the general conference on 7 April 1841 from the BLL. See *Times and Seasons* 2 (15 Apr. 1841): 386.

and of this stake which I have planted to be a corner-stone of Zion, which shall be polished with that refinement which is after the similitude of a palace.

This proclamation shall be made to all the kings of the world, to the four corners thereof—To the honorable President elect,[11] and the high-minded governors of the nation in which you live, and to all the nations of the earth, scattered abroad. Let it be written in the Spirit of meekness, and by the power of the Holy Ghost, which shall be in you at the time of the writing of the same; for it shall be given you by the Holy Ghost to know my will concerning those kings and authorities, even what shall befal[l] them in a time to come. For, behold! I am about to call upon them to give heed to the light and glory of Zion, for the set time has come to favor her.

Call ye, therefore, upon them with loud proclamation, and with your testimony, fearing them not, for they are as grass, and all their glory as the flower thereof, which soon falleth, that they may be left also without excuse, and that I may visit them in the day of visi[t]ation, when I shall unveil the face of my covering, to appoint the portion of the oppressor among hypocrites, where there is gnashing of teeth; if they reject my servants and my testimony which I have revealed unto them.

And again, I will visit and soften their hearts, many of them, for your good, that ye may find grace in their eyes, that they may come to the light of truth, and the Gentiles to the exaltation or lifting up of Zion. For the day of my visitation cometh speedily, in an hour when ye think not of, and where shall be the safety of my people? and refuge for those who shall be left of them?

Awake! O kings of the earth! Come ye, O! come ye, with your gold and your silver, to the help of my people, to the house of the daughters of Zion.

And aga[i]n, verily I say unto you, let my servant Robert B. Thompson help you to write this proclamation;[12] for I am well pleased with him, and that he should be with you; let him, therefore, hearken to your counsel, and I will bless him with a multiplicity of blessings; let him be faithful and true in all things from henceforth, and he shall be great in mine eyes; but let him remember that his stewardship will I require at his hands.[13]

And again, verily I say unto you, blessed is my servant Hyrum Smith, for I the

---

11. William H. Harrison was elected ninth president of the United States. He took the oath of office on 4 March 1841 and died a month later on 4 April 1841.

12. Robert B. Thompson, a scribe for Smith, died on 27 August 1841. On 22 December 1841 "Joseph the Seer commenced giving instructions to the scribe [Willard Richards] concerning writing the Proclamation to the Kings of the earth mentioned in the Revelation given January 19, 1841" (BLL, 36; Dean C. Jessee, ed., *The Papers of Joseph Smith: Journal, 1832-1842* [Salt Lake City: Deseret Book Co., 1992], 2:344; a manuscript draft of "A Religious Proclamation" is in LDS archives). This proclamation was not finished in Smith's lifetime.

13. William Law wrote concerning Thompson: "As scribe to Pres't. Joseph Smith, he discharged his duty faithfully and well. He it was who wrote from the mouth of the Prophet, those sacred revelations recently received, and in his dying hour gave a fearless testimony as to the truth of those things in which we believe; his soul was filled with the love of God, and he went forth rejoicing, to enter (as he said) upon a new course of labors" (*Times and Seasons* 2 [1 Sept. 1841]: 519-20).

Lord loveth him, because of the integrity of his heart, and because he loveth that which is right before me, saith the Lord.

Again, let my servant John C. Bennett, help you in your labor in sending my word to the kings and people of the earth, and stand by you, even you my servant Joseph Smith, in the hour of affliction, and his reward shall not fail, if he receive counsel; and for his love he shall be great; for he shall be mine if he do[es] this, saith the Lord. I have seen the work which he hath done, which I accept, if he continue, and will crown him with blessings and great glory.[14]

And again, I say unto you, that it is my will that my servant Lyman Wight should continue in preaching for Zion, in the spirit of meekness, confessing me before the world, and I will bear him up as on eagle's wings, and he shall beget glory and honor to himself, and unto my name, that when he shall finish his work, that I may receive him unto myself, even as I did my servant David Patten, who is with me at this time, and also my servant Edward Partridge, and also my aged servant Joseph Smith, sen., who sitteth with Abraham, at his right hand, and blessed and holy is he, for he is mine.

And again, verily I say unto you, my servant George Miller is without guile; he may be trusted because of the integrity of his heart; and for the love which he has to my testimony, I the Lord loveth him; I therefore say unto you, I seal upon his head the office of a bishoprick, like unto my servant Edward Partridge, that he may receive the consecrations of mine house, that he may administer blessings upon the heads of the poor of my people, saith the Lord. Let no man despise my servant George [Miller], for he shall honor me.[15]

Let my servant George [Miller], and my servant Lyman [Wight], and my servant John Snider, and others, build a house unto my name, such an one, as my servant Joseph [Smith] shall show unto them; upon the place which he shall show unto them also. And it shall be for a house for boarding, a house that strangers may come from afar to lodge therein: therefore, let it be a good house, worthy of all acceptation, that the weary traveller may find health and safety while he shall contemplate the word of the Lord, and the corner-stone have I appointed for Zion. This house shall be a healthy habitation if it be built unto my name, and if the governor, which shall be appointed unto it shall not suffer any pollution to come upon it. It shall be holy, or the Lord your God will not dwell therein.

And again, verily I say unto you, let all my saints [come] from afar; and send ye swift messengers, yea, chosen messengers, and say unto them, Come ye, with all your gold, and your silver, and your precious stones, and with all your antiquities; and with all who have knowledge of antiquities, that will come may come, and bring the box tree, and the fir tree, and the pine tree, together with all the precious trees of the earth; and with iron, with copper, and with brass, and with zinc, and

---

14. The First Presidency wrote concerning Bennett: "He is a man of enterprize [enterprise], extensive acquirements, and of independant [independent] mind, and is calculated to be a great blessing to our community" (*Times and Seasons* 2 [15 Jan. 1841]: 275). Bennett withdrew from the church after being a member nineteen months.

15. "George Miller has been appointed, by revelation, Bishop, in place of E[dward]. Partridge, deceased" (*Times and Seasons* 2 [1 Feb. 1841]: 310).

with all your precious things of the earth, and build a house to my name, for the Most High to dwell therein;

for there is not a place found on earth that he may come and restore again that which was lost unto you, or, which he hath taken away, even the fulness of the priesthood; for a baptismal font there is not upon the earth; that they, my saints, may be baptized for those who are dead:[16] for this ordinance belongeth to my house, and cannot be acceptable to me, only in the days of your poverty, wherein ye are not able to build a house unto me.

But I command you, all ye my saints, to build a house unto me; and I grant unto you a sufficient time to build a house unto me, and during this time your baptisms shall be acceptable unto me.

But, behold, at the end of this appointment, your baptisms for your dead shall not be acceptable unto me; and if you do not these things at the end of the appointment, ye shall be rejected as a church with your dead, saith the Lord your God.[17]

For, verily I say unto you, that after you have had sufficient time to build a house to me, wherein the ordinance of baptizing for the dead belongeth, and for which the same was instituted from before the foundation of the world, your baptisms for your dead cannot be acceptable unto me; for therein are the keys of the holy priesthood, ordained, that you may receive honor and glory. And after this time, your baptisms for the dead, by those who are scattered abroad, are not acceptable unto me, saith the Lord;[18]

for it is ordained that in Zion and in her stakes, and in Jerusalem, those places which I have appointed for refuge, shall be the places for your baptisms for your dead.

And again, verily I say unto you, how shall your washings be acceptable unto me, except ye perform them in a house which you have built to my name? For, for this cause I commanded Moses that he should build a tabernacle, that they should bear it with them in the wilderness, and to build a house in the land of promise,

---

16. Smith gave his first discourse on baptism for the dead on 15 August 1840. He wrote in December 1840: "The saints have the priviledge [privilege] of being baptised for those of their relatives who are dead, who they feel to believe would have embraced the gospel if they had been priviledged [privileged] with hearing it, and who have received the gospel in the spirit through the instrumentality of those who may have been commissioned to preach to them while in [spirit] prison" (Smith to the Quorum of the Twelve and Elders in England, 15 Dec. 1840, LDS archives).

17. In "An Epistle of the Twelve to the Saints of the Last Days," the Twelve wrote: "The building of the Temple of the Lord, in the city of Nauvoo, is occupying the first place in the exertions and prayers of many of the saints at the present time, knowing as they do, that, if this building is not completed, speedily, 'we shall be rejected as a church with our dead,' for the Lord our God hath spoken it; but while many are thus engaged in laboring, and watching and praying for this all important object, there are many, very many more, who do not thus come up to their privilege and their duty in this thing, and in many instances we are confident that their neglect arises from a want of proper understanding of the principles upon which this building is founded, and by which it must be completed" (*Times and Seasons* 3 [15 Dec. 1841]: 625, emphasis in original).

18. Besides baptizing for the dead in the Mississippi River, church members also performed proxy baptisms at Kirtland, Ohio, in May 1841 ("Minutes of a conference, held in Kirtland, Ohio, May 22nd 1841," *Times and Seasons* 2 [1 July 1841]: 460).

that those ordinances might be revealed, which had been hid from before the world was;

therefore, verily I say unto you, that your anointings and your washings, and your baptisms for the dead, and your solemn assemblies, and your memorials for your sacrifices, by the sons of Levi, and for your oracles in your most holy places, wherein you receive conversations, and your statutes and judgments, for the beginning of the revelations and foundation of Zion, and for the glory, honor and endowment of all her municipals, are ordained by the ordinance of my holy house which my people are always commanded to build unto my holy name.

And verily I say unto you, let this house be built unto my name, that I may reveal mine ordinances therein, unto my people; for I deign to reveal unto my church, things which have been kept hid from before the foundation of the world; things that pertain to the dispensation of the fulness of times; and I will show unto my servant Joseph [Smith] all things pertaining to this house, and the priesthood thereof; and the place whereon it shall be built: and ye shall build it on the place where you have contemplated building it; for that is the spot which I have chosen for you to build it.[19]

If ye labor with all your mights, I will consecrate that spot, that it shall be made holy; and if my people will hearken unto my voice, and unto the voice of my servants whom I have appointed to lead my people, behold, verily I say unto you, they shall not be moved out of their place. But if they will not hearken to my voice, nor unto the voice of these men whom I have appointed, they shall not be blest, because they pollute mine holy grounds, and mine holy ordinances, and charters, and my holy words, which I give unto them.

And it shall come to pass, that if you build a house unto my name, and do not do the things that I say, I will not perform the oath which I make unto you, neither fulfil[l] the promises which ye expect at my hands, saith the Lord; for instead of blessings, ye, by your own works, bring cursings, wrath, indignation, and judgments, upon your own heads, by your follies, and by all your abominations, which you practice before me, saith the Lord.

Verily, verily I say unto you, that when I give a commandment to any of the sons of men, to do a work unto my name, and those sons of men go with all their mights, and with all they have, to perform that work, and cease not their diligence, and their enemies come upon them, and hinder them from performing that work; behold, it beho[o]veth me to require that work no more at the hands of those sons of men, but to accept of their offerings; and the iniquity and transgression of my holy laws and commandments, I will visit upon the heads of those who hindered

---

19. At the general conference held at Nauvoo on 3 October 1840 it was reported: "president [Joseph Smith] then spoke of the necessity of building a 'House of the Lord' in this place" (*Times and Seasons* 1 [Oct. 1840]: 186). Smith wrote in an epistle, "You will observe by the 'Times & Season[s]' that we are about building a Temple for the worship of our God in this place ... we have secured one of the most lovely sites for it ... It is expected to be considerably larger and on a more magnificent scale than the one in Kirtland" (Smith to the Quorum of the Twelve and Elders in England, 15 Dec. 1840, LDS archives; published in *Times and Seasons* 2 [1 Jan. 1841]: 259-60).

my work, unto the third and fourth generation, so long as they repent not, and hate me, saith the Lord God.

Therefore for this cause have I accepted the offerings of those whom I commanded to build up a city and a house unto my name, in Jackson county, Missouri, and were hindered by their enemies, saith the Lord your God:[20] and I will answer judgment, wrath, and indignation, wailing, and anguish, and gnashing of teeth, upon their heads, unto the third and fourth generation, so long as they repent not, and hate me, saith the Lord your God.

And this I make an example unto you, for your consolation, concerning all those who have been commanded to do a work, and have been hindered by the hands of their enemies, and by oppression, saith the Lord your God; for I am the Lord your God, and will save all those of your brethren, who have been pure in heart, and have been slain in the land of Missouri, saith the Lord.

And again, verily I say unto you, I command you again to build a house to my name, even in this place that you may prove yourselves unto me, that ye are faithful in all things whatsoever I command you, that I may bless you, and crown you with honor, immortality, and eternal life.

And now, I say unto you, as pertaining to my boarding-house, which I have commanded you to build, for the boarding of strangers, let it be built unto my name, and let my name be named upon it, and let my servant Joseph [Smith] and his house have place therein, from generation to generation:

for this annointing [anointing] have I put upon his head, that his blessing shall also be put upon the head of his posterity after him; and as I said unto Abraham, concerning the kindreds of the earth; even so I say unto my servant Joseph [Smith], in thee, and in thy seed, shall the kindred of the earth be blessed. Therefore, let my servant Joseph [Smith] and his seed after him have place in that house, from generation to generation, forever and ever, saith the Lord,

and let the name of that house be called the Nauvoo House;[21] and let it be a delightful habitation for man, and a resting place for the weary traveler, that he may contemplate the glory of Zion, and the glory of this the corner-stone thereof; that he may receive, also, the counsel from those whom I have set to be as plants of renown, and as watchmen upon her walls.

---

20. This revelation states that the offer to build a city and a house (temple) in Independence, Jackson County, Missouri, was accepted. But the temple was not built because of the enemies of the Saints.

21. The *Times and Seasons* contained the following notice: "THE NAUVOO HOUSE ASSOCIATION, whose charter we publish in our present number, are zealously engaged in erecting a house for the accommodation of strangers, visiters [visitors], and the public, which for magnitude and splendor of workmanship, will stand unrivaled in the western country, and will be a lasting monument of the taste and enterprise of our citizens and friends. It is to be in L form, presenting a front on two streets of 120 feet each, 40 feet deep, and three stories high, exclusive of the basement story. It will be constructed principally of brick, and the estimated expense is $100,000." The charter states in section 3: "The said Trustees are further authorized and empowered to obtain by stock subscription, by themselves or their duly authorized agents, the sum of one hundred and fifty thousand dollars, which shall be divided into shares of fifty dollars each" (*Times and Seasons* 2 [1 Apr. 1841]: 369-70).

Behold! verily I say unto you, let my servant George Miller, and my servant Lyman Wight, and my servant John Snider, and my servant Peter Haws, organize themselves, and appoint one of them to be a president over their quorum for the purpose of building that house.

And they shall form a constitution whereby they may receive stock for the building of that house. And they shall not receive less than fifty dollars for a share of stock in that house, and they shall be permitted to receive fifteen thousand dollars from any one man for stock in that house; but they shall not be permitted to receive over fifteen thousand dollars stock, from any one man; and they shall not be permitted to receive under fifty dollars for a share of stock from any one man, in that house; and they shall not be permitted to receive any man as a stockholder in this house, except the same shall pay his stock into their hands at the time he receives stock; and in proportion to the amount of stock he pays into their hands, he shall receive stock in that house; but if he pay nothing into their hands, he shall not receive any stock in that house.

And if any pay stock into their hands, it shall be for stock in that house, for himself, and for his generation after him, from generation to generation, so long as he and his heirs shall hold that stock, and do not sell or convey the stock away out of their hands by their own free will and act: if you will do my will, saith the Lord your God.

And again, verily I say unto you, if my servant George Miller, and my servant Lyman Wight, and my servant John Snider, and my servant Peter Haws, receive any stock into their hands, in moneys, or in properties, wherein they receive the real value of moneys, they shall not appropriate any portion of that stock to any other purpose, only in that house; and if they do appropriate any portion of that stock any where else, only in that house, without the consent of the stockholder, and do not repay fourfold, for the stock which they appropriate any where else, only in that house, they shall be accursed, and shall be moved out of their place, saith the Lord God, for I the Lord am God, and cannot be mocked in any of these things.

Verily I say unto you, let my servant Joseph [Smith] pay stock into their hands for the building of that house, as seemeth him good; but my servant Joseph [Smith] cannot pay over fifteen thousand dollars stock in that house, nor under fifty dollars; neither can any other man, saith the Lord.

And there are others also, who wish to know my will concerning them; for they have asked it at my hands: Therefore I say unto you, concerning my servant Vinson Knight, if he will do my will, let him put stock into that house for himself and for his generation after him, from generation to generation, and let him lift up his voice, long and loud, in the midst of the people, to plead the cause of the poor and the needy, and let him not fail, neither let his heart faint, and I will accept of his offerings; for they shall not be unto me as the offerings of Cain, for he shall be mine, saith the Lord. Let his family rejoice, and turn away their hearts from affliction, for I have chosen him and anointed him, and he shall be honored in the midst of his house, for I will forgive all his sins, saith the Lord; Amen.

Verily I say unto you, let my servant Hyrum [Smith] put stock into that house, as seemeth him good, for himself and his generation after him, from generation to generation.

Let my servant Isaac Galland put stock into that house, for I the Lord love him for the work he hath done, and will forgive all his sins; therefore, let him be remembered for an interest in that house, from generation to generation. Let my servant Isaac Galland be appointed among you, and be ordained by my servant William Marks, and be blessed of him, to go with my servant Hyrum [Smith], to accomplish the work that my servant Joseph [Smith] shall point out to them, and they shall be greatly blessed.[22]

Let my servant William Marks pay stock into that house, as seemeth him good, for himself and his generation, from generation to generation.

Let my servant Henry G. Sherwood pay stock into that house, as seemeth him good, for himself and his seed after him, from generation to generation.

Let my servant William Law pay stock into that house, for himself and his seed after him, from generation to generation. If he will do my will, let him not take his family unto the eastern lands, even unto Kirtland; nevertheless I the Lord will build up Kirtland, but I the Lord have a scourge prepared for the inhabitants thereof. And with my servant Almon Babbitt there are many things with which I am not well pleased; behold, he aspireth to establish his council [counsel] instead of the council [counsel] which I have ordained, even the presidency of my church, and he setteth up a golden calf for the worship of my people.[23]

Let no man go from this place who has come here essaying to keep my commandments. If they live here let them live unto me; and if they die let them die unto me; for they shall rest from all their labors here, and shall continue their works. Therefore, let my servant William [Law] put his trust in me, and cease to fear concerning his family, because of the sickness of the land. If ye love me, keep my commandments, and the sickness of the land shall redound to your glory.

Let my servant William [Law] go and proclaim my everlasting gospel, with a loud voice, and with great joy, as he shall be moved upon by my spirit, unto the inhabitants of Warsaw, and also unto the inhabitants of Carthage, and also unto the inhabitants of Burlington, and also unto the inhabitants of Madison, and await patiently and diligently for further instructions at my general conference, saith the Lord.

If he will do my will, let him from henceforth hearken to the counsel of my ser-

---

22. The First Presidency wrote about Isaac Galland, "He is the honored instrument the Lord used, to prepare a home for us, when we were driven from our inheritances" in Missouri (*Times and Seasons* 2 [15 Jan. 1841]: 275).

23. At the church conference held at Nauvoo on 3 October 1840, it was "Resolved, that Elder Alman Babbit [Almon Babbitt] be appointed to preside over the church in Kirtland" (*Times and Seasons* 1 [Oct. 1840]: 186). Babbitt had been out of fellowship a number of times and had difficulty following the counsel of the First Presidency. On 22 May 1841 at a conference in Kirtland, he "resigned his office of president of this stake, that the conference might exercise its full right, and choose its own officers from head to foot." The minutes reported, "Elder Babbitt was then nominated for the president or presiding elder of the stake in Kirtland; but he declined, yet, after some discussion, was unanimously elected" ("Minutes of a conference, held in Kirtland, Ohio, May 22nd 1841" *Times and Seasons* 2 [1 July 1841]: 458).

vant Joseph [Smith], and with his interest support the cause of the poor, and publish the new translation of my holy word[24] unto the inhabitants of the earth; and if he will do this, I will bless him with a multiplicity of blessings, that he shall not be forsaken, nor his seed be found begging bread.

And again, verily I say unto you, let my servant William [Law] be appointed, ordained, and anointed, as a councillor [counselor] unto my servant Joseph [Smith], in the room of my servant Hyrum [Smith]; that my servant Hyrum [Smith] may take the office of priesthood and patriarch, which was appointed unto him by his father, by blessing and also by right,[25] that from henceforth he shall hold the keys of the patriarchal blessings upon the heads of all my people, that whoever he blesses shall be blessed, and whoever he curseth shall be cursed: that whatsoever he shall bind on earth shall be bound in heaven; and whatsoever he shall loose on earth shall be loosed in heaven; and from this time forth, I appoint unto him that he may be a prophet and a seer and a revelator unto my church,[26] as well as my servant Joseph [Smith], that he may act in concert also with my servant Joseph [Smith], and that he shall receive counsel from my servant Joseph [Smith], who shall shew unto him the keys whereby he may ask and receive, and be crowned with the same blessing, and glory, and honor, and priesthood, and gifts of the priesthood, that once were put upon him that was my servant Oliver Cowdery; that my servant Hyrum [Smith] may bear record of the things which I shall shew unto him, that his name may be had in honorable remembrance from generation to generation, forever and ever.

Let my servant William Law also receive the keys by which he may ask and receive blessings;[27] let him be humble before me, and be without guile, and he shall receive of my spirit, even the comforter, which shall manifest unto him the truth of all things, and shall give him in the very hour, what he shall say, and these signs shall follow him: he shall heal the sick, he shall cast out devils, and shall be delivered from those who would administer unto him deadly poison; and he shall be led in paths where the poisonous serpent cannot lay hold upon his heel, and he shall mount up in the imagination of his thoughts as upon eagle's wings; and what if I will that he should raise the dead, let him not withhold his voice. Therefore let my servant William [Law] cry aloud and spare not, with joy and rejoicing, and with

24. This revision of the King James Bible was not published during Smith's lifetime. A version of the "new translation" titled *The Holy Scriptures* was published by the RLDS church in 1867.

25. Joseph Smith, Sr., ordained his son Hyrum to be his successor as church patriarch during his last sickness in September 1840. The elder Smith died on 14 September 1840. Joseph Smith, Jr., wrote a letter to the Council of the Twelve and Elders in England, "Brother Hyrum succeeds him as him [sic] as patriarch of the Church, according to his last directions and benedictions" (Smith to the Quorum of the Twelve and Elders in England, 15 Dec. 1840, LDS archives; published in *Times and Seasons* 2 [1 Jan. 1841]: 260). Hyrum gave one of his first patriarchal blessings to John C. Bennett on 21 September 1840.

26. "Hyrum Smith who some time since received the appointment of Patriarch in the church in place of Joseph Smith, Sen., deceased, has recently, by revelation, been appointed a Prophet and Revelator" (*Times and Seasons* 2 [1 Feb. 1841]: 310).

27. "William Law has recently, by revelation, been appointed one of the first Presidency, in place of Hyrum Smith, appointed as above" (*Times and Seasons* 1 [1 Feb. 1841]: 310).

hosannas to him that sitteth upon the throne forever and ever, saith the Lord your God.

Behold I say unto you, I have a mission in store for my servant William [Law] and my servant Hyrum [Smith], and for them alone; and let my servant Joseph [Smith] tarry at home, for he is needed: the remainder I will shew unto you hereafter: even so; Amen.

And again, verily I say unto you, if my servant Sidney [Rigdon] will serve me and be councillor [counselor] unto my servant Joseph [Smith], let him arise and come up and stand in the office of his calling, and humble himself before me;[28] and if he will offer unto me an acceptable offering, and acknowledgments, and remain with my people, behold, I the Lord your God will heal him that he shall be healed; and he shall lift up his voice again on the mountains, and be a spokesman before my face. Let him come and locate his family in the neighborhood in which my servant Joseph [Smith] resides, and in all his journeyings let him lift up his voice as with the sound of a trump, and warn the inhabitants of the earth to flee the wrath to come; let him assist my servant Joseph [Smith]; and also let my servant William Law assist my servant Joseph [Smith], in making a solemn proclamation unto the kings of the earth, even as I have before said unto you.

If my servant Sidney [Rigdon] will do my will, let him not remove his family unto the eastern lands, but let him change their habitation, even as I have said. Behold, it is not my will that he shall seek to find safety and refuge out of the city which I have appointed unto you, even the city of Nauvoo.—Verily I say unto you, even now, if he will hearken unto my voice, it shall be well with him: even so; Amen.

And again, verily I say unto you, let my servant Amos Davis pay stock into the hands of those whom I have appointed to build a house for boarding, even the Nauvoo House; this let him do if he will have an interest, and let him hearken unto the counsel of my servant Joseph [Smith], and labor with his own hands that he may obtain the confidence of men; and when he shall prove himself faithful in all things that shall be entrusted unto his care; yea, even a few things, he shall be made ruler over many; let him therefore abase himself that he may be exalted: even so; Amen.

And again, verily I say unto you, if my servant Robert D. Foster will obey my voice let him build a house for my servant Joseph [Smith], according to the contract which he has made with him, as the door shall be open to him from time to time; and let him repent of all his folly, and clothe himself with charity, and cease to do evil, and lay aside all his hard speeches, and pay stock also into the hands of the quorum of the Nauvoo House, for himself and for his generation after him, from generation to generation, and hearken unto the counsel of my servants Joseph [Smith] and Hyrum [Smith] and William Law, and unto the authorities which I have called to lay the foundation of Zion, and it shall be well with him forever and ever: even so; Amen.

---

28. "We have to announce that Sidney Rigdon has been ordained a Prophet, Seer and Revelator" (*Times and Seasons* 2 [1 June 1841]: 431).

And again, verily I say unto you, let no man pay stock to the quorum of the Nauvoo House, unless he shall be a believer in the Book of Mormon, and the revelations I have given unto you, saith the Lord your God: for that which is more or less than this cometh of evil, and shall be attended with cursings and not blessings, saith the Lord your God: even so; Amen.

And again, verily I say unto you, let the quorum of the Nauvoo House have a just recompense of wages for all their labors which they do in building the Nauvoo House, and let their wages be as shall be agreed among themselves, as pertaining to the price thereof; and let every man who pays stock bear his proportion of their wages, if it must needs be, for their support, saith the Lord; otherwise their labors shall be accounted unto them for stock in that house: even so; Amen.

Verily I say unto you, I now give unto you the officers belonging to my Priesthood, that ye may hold the keys thereof, even the priesthood which is after the order of Melchisedek, which is after the order of my only begotten Son.

First, I give unto you Hyrum Smith to be a patriarch unto you to hold the sealing blessings of my church, even the Holy Spirit of promise, whereby ye are sealed up unto the day of redemption, that ye may not fall; notwithstanding the hour of temptation that may come upon you.

I give unto you my servant Joseph [Smith], to be a Presiding Elder over all my church, to be a translator, a revelator, a seer and prophet. I give unto him for councillors [counselors] my servant Sidney Rigdon, and my servant William Law, that these may constitute a quorum and first presidency, to receive the oracles for the whole church.[29]

I give unto you my servant Brigham Young, to be a president over the twelve travelling council, which twelve hold the keys to open up the authority of my kingdom upon the four corners of the earth, and after that to send my word to every creature;[30] they are: Heber C. Kimball, Parley P. Pratt, Orson Pratt, Orson Hyde, William Smith, John Taylor, John E. Page, Wilford Woodruff, Willard Richards, George A. Smith; David Patten I have taken unto myself, behold his priesthood no man taketh from him; but verily I say unto you, another may be appointed unto the same calling.[31]

And again, I say unto you, I give unto you a High Council, for the corner stone of Zion; viz: Samuel Bent, H[enry]. G. Sherwood, George W. Harris, Charles C. Rich, Thomas Grover, Newel Knight, David Dort, Dunbar Wilson; Seymour Brunson I have taken unto myself, no man taketh his priesthood, but another may be appointed unto the same priesthood in his stead, (and verily I say unto you, let

29. On 8 April 1841 "Gen[eral]. J[ohn]. C. Bennett was presented with the First Presidency as assistant president, until Pres't. [Sidney] Rigdon's health should be restored" (*Times and Seasons* 2 [15 Apr. 1841]: 387).

30. Smith stated at a special conference on 16 August 1841 that "the time had come when the twelve should be called upon to stand in their place next to the first presidency, and attend to the settling of emegrants [emigrants] and the business of the church at the stakes, and assist to bear off the kingdom victorious to the nations" (*Times and Seasons* 2 [1 Sept. 1841]: 521-22; conference minutes, 16 Aug. 1841, in LDS archives).

31. On 8 April 1841 Rigdon nominated Lyman Wight to fill the vacancy in the Quorum of the Twelve and Wight was unanimously accepted (*Times and Seasons* 2 [15 Apr. 1841]: 387).

my servant Aaron Johnson be ordained unto this calling in his stead,) David Ful[l]mer, Alpheus Cutler, William Huntington.

And again, I give unto you Don C. Smith to be a president over a Quorum of High-priests: which ordinance is instituted for the purpose of qualifying those who shall be appointed standing presidents or servants over different stakes scattered abroad, and they may travel also if they choose, but rather be ordained for standing presidents, this is the office of their calling saith the Lord your God. I give unto him Amasa Lyman and Noah Packard for councillors [counselors] that they made [may] preside over the quorum of high-priests of my church saith the Lord.

And again I say unto you, I give unto you John A. Hicks, Samuel Williams, and Jesse Baker which priesthood is to preside over the quorum of Elders which quorum is instituted for standing ministers, nevertheless they may travel, yet they are ordained to be standing ministers to my church, saith the Lord.

And, again, I give unto you Joseph Young, Josiah Butterfield, Daniel Miles, Henry Herriman, Zera Pulsipher, Levi Hancock, James Foster, to preside over the quorum of seventies, which quorum is instituted for travelling elders to bear record of my name in all the world, wherever the travelling high council, my apostles, shall send them to prepare a way before my face. The difference between this quorum and the quorum of elders is, that one is to travel continually, and the other is to preside over the churches from time to time, the one has the responsibility of presiding from time to time and the other has no responsibility of presiding, saith the Lord your God.

And again I say unto you, I give unto you Vinson Knight, Samuel H. Smith, and Shadrach Roundy if he will receive it to preside over the Bishopric, a knowledge of said Bishopric is given unto you, in the Book of Doctrine and Covenants.

And, again, I say unto you Samuel Rolfe and his councillors [counselors] for Priests, and the president of the Teachers and his councillors [counselors] and also the president of the Deacons and his councillors [counselors], and also the president of the Stake and his councillors [counselors]:[32]

the above offices I have given unto you, and the keys thereof for helps and for governments, for the work of the ministry, and the perfecting of my saints, and a commandment I give unto you that you should fill all these offices and approve of those names which I have mentioned or else disapprove of them at my general conference, and that ye should prepare rooms for all these offices in my house when you build it unto my name saith the Lord your God: even so: Amen.

---

32. The president of the Nauvoo Stake was William Marks. Austin Cowles and Charles C. Rich were ordained counselors in the stake presidency by Marks on 30 March 1841 (Nauvoo High Council Minutes, LDS archives).

157. Let Them Gather Themselves Together
From the Manuscript History, Book C-1:1,173 (cf. LDS D&C 125)

Revelation received at Nauvoo, Illinois, in [1-6] March 1841
concerning building a city to be named Zarahemla
in the Territory of Iowa[33]

[Question] What is the Will of the Lord concerning the Saints in the Territory of Iowa?

[Answer] Verily thus saith the Lord, I say unto you, if those who call themselves by my name, and are essaying to be my Saints, if they will do my will and keep my commandments concerning them; let them gather themselves together unto the places, which I shall appoint unto them by my servant Joseph [Smith], and build up cities unto my name that they may be prepared for that which is in store for a time to come.

Let them build up a city unto my name upon the Land opposite to the City of Nauvoo and let the name of Zarahemla be named upon it. And let all those who come from the East, and the West, and the North, and the South, that have desires to dwell therein, take up their inheritances in the same, as well as in the City of Nashville, or in the City of Nauvoo, and in all the Stakes which I have appointed saith the Lord.

158. Take Stock in the [Nauvoo] House
From the Manuscript History, Book C-1:1,173

Revelation received at Nauvoo, Illinois, on 20 March 1841
for William Allred and Henry W. Miller

Let my Servants William Allred and Henry W. Miller have an agency for the selling of Stock for the Nauvoo House, and assist my servants Lyman Wight, Peter Haws, George Miller, and John Snider, in building said house, and let my Servants William Allred, and Henry W. Miller take stock in the House, that the poor of my people may have employment, and that accommodations may be made for the Strangers who shall come to visit this place, and for this purpose let them devote all their properties, saith the Lord.

---

33. According to John Smith, Bishop Alanson Ripley had an interview with him on 6 March 1841. John Smith recorded that Ripley informed him "that Joseph [Smith] said it was the will of the Lord the brethren in general in Ambrosia [Territory of Iowa] should move in and about the city Zerehemla [Zarahemla] with all convenient [convenient] speed which the Saints are willing to do because it is the word of the Lord" (John Smith Journal, LDS archives).

159. Your Offering Is Acceptable to Me
From BLL (cf. LDS D&C 126)

Revelation received at Nauvoo, Illinois, on 9 July 1841
for Brigham Young[34]

Brigham Young, President of the Quorum of the twelve, arrived at his house in Nauvoo, July 1st 1841. from England, having been absent from his family since the 14th of September 1839, and the following Revelation was given at his house in Nauvoo City, July 9th 1841.[35]

Dear & well beloved Brother, Brigham Young, Verily thus saith the Lord unto you my servant Brigham [Young] it is no more required at your hand to leave your family as in times past for your offering is acceptable to me I have seen your labor and toil in journeyings for my name. I therefore command you to send my word abroad and take special care of your family from this time henceforth and forever, Amen.

Given to Joseph Smith this day.

160. I the Lord Will Bless Them
From BLL

Revelation received at Nauvoo, Illinois, on 2 December 1841
concerning Nancy Marinda Hyde[36]

A Revelation Given Dcr [December] 2d 1841. N. M. Hyde

Verily thus saith the Lord unto you my servant Joseph [Smith]. that inas much as you have called upon me to know my will concerning my handmaid Nancy Marinda Hyde Behold it is my will that she should have a better place prepared for her than that in which she now lives, in order that her life may be spared unto her;
Therefore go and say unto my servant Ebenezer Robinson, & To my handmaid his wife,[37] Let them open their doors and take her and her children into their house, and take care of them faithfully and kindly until my servant Orson Hyde returns from his mission or until some other provision can be made for her welfare & safety: Let them do these things and spare not and I the Lord will bless them & heal them. if they do it not grudgingly saith the Lord God. and she shall be a blessing unto them,

---

34. Quotation marks omitted.
35. This revelation was recorded in the BLL in December 1841.
36. Nancy Marinda Hyde (also known as Marinda Nancy Hyde), wife of Apostle Orson Hyde.
37. Angeline Robinson.

and let my handmaid Nancy Marinda Hyde hearken to the counsel of my servant Joseph [Smith] in all things whatsoever he shall teach unto her, and it shall be a blessing upon her and upon her children after her, unto her Justification saith the Lord.

161. A Mission to Preach My Gospel
From BLL

Revelation received at Nauvoo, Illinois, on 22 December 1841 concerning Amos Fuller

December 22d 1841

Verily thus saith the Lord unto my servants the Twelve, Let them appoint unto my servant Amos Fuller, a mission to preach my gospel unto the children of men, as it shall be manifested unto them by my Holy Spirit. Amen.

162. Beautify the Place of My Sanctuary
From BLL

Revelation received at Nauvoo, Illinois, on 22 December 1841 for John Snider

Nauvoo, — Dec[e]mber 22d 1841. The word of the Lord came unto Joseph the Seer,

verily thus saith the Lord, Let my servant John Snider take a mission to the Eastern continent,[38] unto all the conferences now sitting in that region, and let him carry a package of Epistles that shall be written by my servants the Twelve, making known unto them their duties concerning the building of my houses which I have appointed unto you[39] saith the Lord, that they may bring their gold, & their silver, and their precious stones, and the box-tree, and the Fir-tree, and all fine wood to beautify the place of my sanctuary saith the Lord; and let him return speedily with all means which shall be put into his hands, even so; Amen.

---

38. England.
39. The proposed Nauvoo temple and Nauvoo House.

163. Take in Hand the Editorial Department
From BLL

Revelation received at Nauvoo, Illinois, on 28 January 1842
concerning the Times and Seasons[40]

A Revelation to the twelve concerning the Times and Seasons.

Verily thus saith the Lord unto you my servant Joseph [Smith]. go and say unto the Twelve That it is my will to have them take in hand the Editorial department of the Times and Seasons according to that manifestation which shall be given unto them by the Power of my Holy Spirit in the midst of their counsel Saith the Lord. Amen

164. The Kingdom of God and His Law
From the William Clayton Journal, 1 January 1845

Revelation received at Nauvoo, Illinois, on 7 April 1842
concerning the Kingdom of God[41]

Verily thus saith the Lord, this is the name by which you shall be called, the kingdom of God and his law with the keys and power thereof and judgments in the hands of his servants Ahman Christ.

165. I Am the Lord Thy God
From BLL

Revelation received at Nauvoo, Illinois, on 19 May 1842
for Hiram Kimball[42]

1. o[']clock P.M. City council. The Mayor John C. Bennet[t] having resigned his office, Joseph [Smith] was Elected Mayor & Hyrum Smith Vice Mayor of Nauvoo. While the election was going forward in the council. Joseph received & wrote the following Rev[elation]—& threw it across the room to Hiram Kimball one of the Councillors.

---

40. Wilford Woodruff wrote under 3 February 1842: "After consulting upon the subject the quorum appointed Elders J[ohn]. Taylor & W[ilford] Woodruff of the Twelve to Edit the Times & Seasons & take charge of the whole esstablishment under the direction of Joseph the Seer" (Scott G. Kenney, ed., *Wilford Woodruff's Journal*, typescript, 1833-1898, 9 vols., 1983-85 [Midvale, UT: Signature Books], 2:153, original in LDS archives).

41. Quotation marks omitted. It is not known if this is the full text of the revelation. The date of this revelation is from the following note: "The name given this council on the day it was organized by the Lord. April 7, 1842" ([Joseph F. Smith] Minutes of Council of Fifty, 10 Apr. 1880, typed copy, Special Collections, Harold B. Lee Library, Brigham Young University, Provo, Utah).

42. Quotation marks omitted.

Verily thus saith the Lord unto you my servant Joseph [Smith] by the voice of my Spirit, Hiram Kimball has been insinuating evil. & forming evil opinions against you with others. & if he continue in them he & they shall be accursed. for I am the Lord thy God & will stand by thee & bless thee. Amen.

166. Shall Be Crowned upon Your Heads
From a manuscript in LDS archives

Revelation received at Nauvoo, Illinois, on 27 July 1842 for Newel K. Whitney concerning Sarah Ann Whitney to be a wife of Joseph Smith[43]

Wednesday 27th July 1842

Verily thus saith the Lord unto my se[r]vant N[ewel]. K. Whitney the thing that my se[r]vant Joseph Smith has made known unto you and your Famely [Family] and which you have agreed upon is right in mine eyes and shall be crowned upon your heads with honor and immortality and eternal life to all your house both old & young because of the lineage of my Preast [Priest] Hood saith the Lord it shall be upon you and upon your children after you from generation to generation By virtue of the Holy promise which I now make unto you saith the Lord.

these are the words which you shall pronounce upon my se[r]vant Joseph [Smith] and your Daughter S. A. [Sarah Ann] Whitney[44] they shall take each other by the hand and you shall say

you both mutu[al]ly agree calling them by name to be each others companion so long as you both shall live preser[v]ing yourselv[es] for each other and from all others[45] and also through [o]ut all eternity reserving only those rights which have been given to my servant Joseph [Smith] by revelation and commandment and by legal Authority in times passed [past]

If you both agree to covenant and do this then I give you S. A. [Sarah Ann] Whitney my Daughter to Joseph Smith to be his wife to observe all the rights betwe[e]n you both that belong to that condition I do it in my own name and in the name of my wife your mother and in the name of my Holy Progenitors by the right of birth which is of Priest Hood vested in me by revelation and commandment and

---

43. Smith commenced having women sealed to him at Nauvoo in a religious ceremony with an officiator in April 1841. His first marriage was evidently to Louisa Beaman on 5 April 1841, the ceremony being performed by Joseph B. Noble. By 27 July 1842 Smith had women who were members of the church sealed to him without the knowledge of his wife, Emma Smith. They are grouped as follows: two single women (Louisa Beaman and Eliza Roxey Snow), two widows (Agnes Coolbrith Smith and Delcena Johnson Sherman), and seven married women (including a mother and daughter, Patty and Sylvia Sessions).

44. Sarah Ann Whitney, age seventeen, daughter of Newel and Elizabeth Ann Whitney.

45. The 1835 D&C contains the following question as part of the marriage ceremony: "You both mutually agree to be each other's companion, husband and wife, observing the legal rights belonging to this condition; that is, keeping yourselves wholly for each other, and from all others, during your lives?" (1835 D&C 101)

promise of the liveing God obtained by the Holy Melchesdick[46] Gethrow[47] and other of the Holy Fathers commanding in the name of the Lord all those Powers to concentrate in you and through [you] to your po[s]terity for ever

all these things I do in the name of the Lord Jesus Christ that through this order he may be gloryfied [glorified] and [that] through the power of anointing Davied [David] may reign King over Iseral [Israel] which shall hereafter be revealed let immortality and eternal life henc[e]forth be sealed upon your heads forever and ever.

Part in the first reserection [resurrection] together with other blessings now added sunday 27st [21st] [48] day of augt [august] [18]42 myself[49] and wife I now also bless[ed] with part in the first reserection [resurrection] also with many other blessings together with the promise to all of my house the same day & of the same time

27 augt [august] [18]42 saturday evening myself and wife to[o] were Baptised for remission of sins[50]

Sunday in fore part of the day we were all confirmed & b[l]essed again[51] with all good things & eternal life in first reserection [resurrection] I was blessed above others with long life the Keys of the Priest Hood a double portion of t[he] spirit heretofore confer[r]ed upon my fellows with all gifts posses[s]ed by my prog[e]nitors who held the Priest Hood before me anciently.

167. I Shall Triumph over All My Enemies
From a manuscript letter in LDS archives (cf. LDS D&C 127)

*Letter from Joseph Smith to the church written
near Nauvoo, Illinois, on 1 September 1842
concerning baptism for the dead*

September 1st 1842
To all the saints in Nauvoo

Forasmuch as the Lord has revealed unto me that my enemies both of Mo [Missouri] and this State were again on the pursuit of me, and inasmuch as they pursue me without cause and have not the least shadow or coloring of justice or right on their side in the getting up of their prosecutions against me; and inasmuch as their pretensions are all founded in falsehood of the blackest die [dye], I have thought it expedient and wisdom in me to leave the place for a short season for my own safety and the safety of this people.

---

46. Melchizedek.
47. Jethro.
48. Another manuscript has the date as August "21st" which was the third Sunday of the month. This was the date when Newel and Elizabeth Whitney were sealed and received the blessings of the resurrection as they pertain to the new and everlasting covenant of marriage.
49. Newel K. Whitney.
50. Newel and Elizabeth Whitney were rebaptized on 27 August 1842.
51. On Sunday morning, 28 August 1842, Newel and Elizabeth Whitney received their confirmation blessings.

I would say to all those with whom I have business that I have left my affairs with agents and clerks who will transact all business in a prompt and proper manner and will see that all my debts are cancelled in due time, by turning out property or otherwise as the case may require, or as the circumstances may admit of. When I learn that the storm is fully blown over then I will return to you again.

And as for the perils which I am called to pass through they seem but a small thing to me, as the envy and wrath of man has been my common lot all the days of my life and for what cause it seems mysterious, unless I was ordained from before the foundation of the world for some good end, or bad as you may choose to call it. Judge ye for yourselves, God knoweth all these things whether it be good or bad, but nevertheless deep water is what I am wont to swim in, it all has become a second nature to me and I feel like Paul to glory in tribulation for unto this day has the God of my Fathers delivered me out of them all and will deliver me from henceforth for behold and lo I shall triumph over all my enemies for the Lord God hath spoken it.

Let all the saints rejoice therefore and be exceeding glad for Israel[']s God is their God and he will meet [mete] out a just recompense of reward upon the heads of all your oppressors.

And again verily thus saith the Lord let the work of my Temple and all the works which I have appointed unto you be continued on and not cease; and let your diligence and your perseverance and patience and your works be redoubled, and you shall in no wise lose your reward saith the Lord of Hosts. And if they persecute you so persecuted they the prophets and righteous men that were before you; for all this there is a reward in heaven.

And again I give unto you a word in relation to the Baptism for your dead. Verily thus saith the Lord unto you concerning your dead when any of you are baptised for your dead let there be a recorder, and let him be eye-witness of your baptisms; let him hear with his ears that he may testify of a truth, saith the Lord; that in all your recordings it may be recorded in Heaven, that whatsoever you bind on earth may be bound in heaven; whatsoever you loose on earth may be loosed in heaven; for I am about to restore many things to the Earth, pertaining to the Priesthood saith the Lord of Hosts.

And again let all the Records be had in order, that they may be put in the archives of my Holy Temple to be held in remembrance from generation to generation saith the Lord of Hosts.

I will say to all the saints that I desired with exceeding great desire to have addressed them from the stand on the subject of Baptism for the dead on the following sabbath but inasmuch as it is out of my power to do so I will write the word of the Lord from time to time on that subject and send it [to] you by mail as well as many other things.

I now close my letter for the present for the want of more time, for the enemy is on the alert and as the saviour said the prince of this world cometh but he hath nothing in me.[52]

---

52. John 14:30.

Behold my prayer to God is that you all may be saved and I subscribe myself your servant in the Lord, prophe[t] and Seer of the Church of Jesus Christ of Latter day Saints Joseph Smith[53]

168. The Key of Knowledge
From BLL (cf. LDS D&C 128)

Letter from Joseph Smith to the church written near Nauvoo, Illinois, on 6 September 1842 instructions about recording baptisms for the dead[54]

Journeying, Septr. 6th 1842.
To the Church of Jesus Christ of Latter-day Saints; Sendeth Greeting.

As I stated to you in my letter before I left my place, that I would write to you from time to time, and give you information in relation to many subjects: I now resume the subject of the baptism for the dead as that subject seems to occupy my mind, and press itself upon my feelings the strongest, since I have been pursued by my enemies.

I wrote a few words of Revelation to you concerning a Recorder. I have had a few additional views in relation to this matter, which I now certify; ie. [that is] It was declared in my former letter that there should be a Recorder who should be eye-witness, and also to hear with his ears that he might make a Record of a truth before the Lord.

Now, in relation to this matter; it would be very difficult for one Recorder to be present at all times and to do all the business. To obviate this difficulty, there can be a Recorder appointed in each ward of the City, who is well qualified for taking accurate minutes; and let him be very particular and precise in making his Record and taking the whole proceeding; certifying in his Record, that he saw with his eyes, and heard with his ears; giving the date, and names &c. and the history of the whole transaction, naming also some three individuals that are present, if there be any present who can at any time, when call'd upon, certify to the same; that in the mouth of two or three witnesses, every word may be established.

Then let there be a general Recorder to whom these other Records can be handed, being attended with certificates over their own signatures; certifying that the Record which they have made, is true. Then the General Church Recorder can enter the Record on the general Church Book with the Certificates and all the attending witnesses, with his own statement that he verily believes the above statements and Records to be true, from his knowledge of the general character and ap-

---

53. "When this letter was read before the brethren it cheered their hearts and evidently had the effect of stimulating them and inspiring them with courage, and faithfulness" (BLL, 190; Jessee, *Papers of Joseph Smith*, 2:457-58).

54. William Clayton wrote the original letter. Page 5 and a few lines on page 9 were not readable on a microfilm copy of the letter. The copy in the BLL is the text used here.

pointment of those men by the Church. And when this is done on the general Church Book; the Record shall be just as holy, and shall answer the ordinance just the same as if he had seen with his eyes and heard with his ears, and made a Record of the same on the general Book.

You may think this Order of things to be very particular: But let me tell you, that they are only to answer the will of God by conforming to the ordinance and preparation, that the Lord ordained and prepared before the foundation of the world for the salvation of the dead who should die without a knowledge of the Gospel.

And further, I want you to remember that John the Revelator was contemplating this very subject in relation to the dead, when he declar'd, as you will find recorded in Revelations Chap[ter]. 20th v. 12; ["]And I saw the dead, small and great, stand before God: and the books were opened: and another book was opened, which is the book of Life; and the dead were judg'd out of those things which were written in the books, according to their works.["]

You will discover in this quotation, that the books were opened, and another book was opened which is the book of Life; but the dead were judg'd out of those things which were written in the books according to their works; consequently, the books spoken of, must be the books which contained the record of their works, and refers to the Records which are kept on the earth: And the book which was the book of life, is the Record which is kept in heaven; the principle agreeing precisely with the doctrine which is commanded you in the Revelation contained in the letter which I wrote you previous to my leaving my place, "that in all your recordings it may be recorded in heaven."

Now the nature of this ordinance consists in the power of the Priesthood by the revelations of Jesus Christ, wherein it is granted that whatsoever you bind on earth, shall be bound in heaven, and whatsoever you loose on earth shall be loosed in heaven: Or in other words, taking a different view of the translation, whatsoever you record on earth shall be recorded in heaven; and whatsoever you do not record on earth, shall not be recorded in heaven; for out of the books shall your dead be judg'd according to their works, whether they, themselves have attended to the ordinances in their own propria persona,[55] or by the means of their own agents according to the ordinance which God has prepared for their salvation, from before the foundation of the world, according to the records which they have kept concerning their dead.

It may seem to some, to be a very bold doctrine that we talk of; a power which records, or binds on earth, and binds in heaven. Nevertheless, in all ages of the world, whenever the Lord has given a dispensation of the Priesthood to any man, by actual revelation, or any set of men; this power has always been given: Hence, whatsoever those men did in authority, in the name of the Lord, and did it truly and faithfully, and kept a proper and faithful record of the same, it became a law on earth and in heaven; and could not be annull'd according to the decree of the great Jehovah. This is a faithful saying: Who can hear it?

---

55. Latin for "one's own person."

And again for a precedent, Matt[hew]. chapter 16 verses 18, 19, "And I say also unto thee, that thou art Peter: and upon this rock I will build my church; and the gates of hell shall not prevail against it. And I will give unto thee, the keys of the kingdom of heaven; and whatsoever thou shalt bind on earth, shall be bound in heaven; and whatsoever thou shalt loose on earth, shall be loosed in heaven.["]

Now the great and grand secret of the whole matter, and the summum bonum[56] of the whole subject that is lying before us consists in obtaining the powers of the Holy Priesthood. For him, to whom these keys are given; there is no difficulty in obtaining a knowledge of facts in relation to the salvation of the children of men; both as well for the dead as for the living.

Herein is glory, and honor, and immortality and eternal life. The ordinance of baptism by water, to be immers'd therein in order to answer to the likeness of the dead, that one principle might accord with the other to be immers'd in the water, and come forth out of the water is in the likeness of the resurrection of the dead in coming forth out of their graves: hence, this ordinance was instituted to form a relationship with the ordinance of baptism for the dead; being in likeness of the dead.

Consequently, the baptismal Font was instituted as a simile of the grave, and was commanded to be in a place underneath where the living are wont to assemble, to show forth the living and the dead; and that all things may have their likeness, and that they may accord one with another; that which is earthly, conforming to that which is heavenly, as Paul hath declar'd, 1st Corinthians, Chap[ter]. 15, verses 46, 47 & 48.

"Howbeit, that was not first which is spiritual, but that which is natural, and afterward, that which is spiritual. The first man is of the earth, earthy: the second man, is the Lord from heaven. As is the earthy, such are they also that are earthy: and as is the heavenly, such are they also that are heavenly:["]

And as are the records on the earth in relation to your dead, which are truly made out, so also are the records in heaven. This, therefore, is the sealing and binding power; and in one sense of the word the keys of the kingdom, which consists in the key of knowledge.

And now my dearly and beloved brethren and sisters, let me assure you that these are principles in relation to the dead and the living; that cannot be lightly passed over, as pertaining to our salvation: for their salvation is necessary and essential to our salvation; as Paul says concerning the fathers, "That they without us, cannot be made perfect;" neither can we without our dead, be made perfect.[57]

And now, in relation to the baptism for the dead; I will give you another quotation of Paul, I Cor[inthians]. 15 chap[ter]. verse 29 "Else what shall they do which are baptized for the dead, if the dead rise not at all? Why are they then baptized for the dead?"

And again in connection with this quotation I will give you a quotation from one of the prophets, which had his eye fix'd on the restoration of the Priesthood—the glories to be reveal'd in the last days, and in an especial manner, this

---

56. Latin for the "greatest" or "supreme good."
57. See Heb. 11:40.

most glorious of all subjects belonging to the everlasting gospel, viz. the baptism for the dead; for Malachi says, last chap[ter].—verses 5 & 6. "Behold I will send you Elijah the prophet, before the coming of the great and dreadful day of the Lord: And he shall turn the hearts of the fathers to the children, and the hearts of the children to their fathers, lest I come and smite the earth with a curse."

I might have rendered a plainer translation to this, but it is sufficiently plain to suit my purpose, as it stands. It is sufficient to know in this case, that the earth will be smitten with a curse, unless there is a welding link of some kind or other, between the fathers and the children, upon some subject or other. And behold! what is that subject? It is the baptism for the dead.

For we without them, cannot be made perfect; neither can they, without us, be made perfect. Neither can they or us, be made perfect without those who have died in the gospel also; for it is necessary in the ushering in of the dispensation of the fulness of times; which dispensation is now beginning to usher in, that a whole, and complete and perfect union, and welding together of dispensations and keys, and powers and glories should take place, and be reveal'd, from the days of Adam even to the present time; and not only this, but those things that never have been reveal'd from the foundation of the world; but have been kept hid from the wise and prudent; shall be revealed unto babes and sucklings, in this, the dispensation of the fulness of times.

Now what do we hear in the gospel which we have received? A voice of gladness—a voice of mercy from heaven—a voice of truth out of the earth—glad tidings for the dead; a voice of gladness for the living and and the dead; glad tidings of great joy! How beautiful upon the mountains, are the feet of those that bring glad tidings of good things; and that say unto Zion, behold! thy God reigneth.[58] As the dews of Carmel so shall the knowledge of God descend upon them.

And again, What do we hear? Glad tidings from Cumorah! Moroni, an angel from heaven, declaring the fulfillment of the prophets—the book to be reveal'd!

A voice of the Lord in the wilderness of Fayette, Seneca County, declaring the three witnesses to bear record of the Book.

The voice of Michael on the banks of the Susquehanna, detecting the devil when he appeared as an angel of light.

The voice of Peter, James & John, in the wilderness, between Harmony, Susquehanna County, and Colesville, Broom[e] County, on the Susquehanna river, declaring themselves as possessing the keys of the kingdom, and of the dispensation of the fulness of times.

And again, the voice of God in the chamber of old father Whitmer in Fayette, Seneca County,[59] and at sundry times, and in divers places, through all the travels and tribulations, of this Church of Jesus Christ of Latter Day Saints.

And the voice of Michael the archangel—the voice of Gabriel, and of Raphael,

---

58. See Isa. 52:7.
59. At the home of Peter Whitmer, Sr., in June 1829 (Dean C. Jessee, ed., *The Papers of Joseph Smith: Autobiographical and Historical Writings* [Salt Lake City: Deseret Book Co., 1989], 1:239, 299).

and of divers angels, from Michael or Adam, down to the present time; all declaring, each one their dispensation, their rights, their keys, their honors, their majesty & glory, and the power of their Priesthood; giving line upon line; precept upon precept; here a little and there a little: giving us consolation by holding forth that which is to come confirming our hope.

Brethren, shall we not go on in so great a cause? Go forward and not go backward. Courage, brethren! and on to the victory. Let your hearts rejoice and be exceeding glad. Let the earth break forth into singing. Let the dead speak forth anthems of eternal praise to the king Immanuel, who hath ordain'd before the world was, that which would enable us to redeem them out of their prisons; for the prisoner[s] shall go free.

Let the mountains shout for joy, and all ye vallies [valleys] cry aloud; and all ye seas and dry lands tell the wonders of your eternal king: And ye rivers, and brooks, and rills, flow down with gladness. Let the woods and all the trees of the field praise the Lord: and ye solid rocks, leap for joy. And let the sun, moon, and the morning stars sing together; and let all the sons of God shout for joy: And let the eternal creations declare his name forever and ever.

And again, I say, how glorious is the voice we hear from heaven proclaiming in our ears, glory and salvation, and honor, and immortality and eternal life. Kingdoms, principalities and powers!

behold! the great day of the Lord is at hand, and who can abide the day of his coming, and who can stand when he appeareth? For he is like a refiner's fire, and like fuller's soap: and he shall sit as a refiner and purifier of silver, and he shall purify the sons of Levi, and purge them as gold and silver; that they may offer unto the Lord an offering in righteousness.[60]

And let us,[61] present in his holy Temple, when it is finished, a Book, containing the Records of our dead, which shall be worthy of all acceptation.

Brethren, I have many things to say to you on the subject; but shall now close for the present, and continue the subject another time.

I am as ever your humble servant, and never deviating friend, Joseph Smith.[62]

---

60. See Mal. 3:2–3.

61. The words "therefore, as a church and a people, and as Latter Day saints offer unto the Lord an offering in righteousness. And let us" were not included in this copy of the letter (Manuscript letter, 8, LDS archives).

62. "The important instructions contained in the foregoing letter [6 Sept. 1842] made a deep and solemn impression on the minds of the saints and they manifested their intentions to obey the instructions to the letter" (BLL, 201; Jessee, *Papers of Joseph Smith,* 2:475).

169. For Time and for All Eternity
From a manuscript in LDS archives (cf. LDS D&C 132)

Revelation received at Nauvoo, Illinois, on 12 July 1843
concerning biblical men having wives and concubines,
adultery, a commandment for Emma Smith,
the law of the priesthood[63]

Nauvoo; July 12th 1843[64]

Verily thus Saith the Lord, unto you my Servant Joseph [Smith], that inasmuch as you have inquired of my hand to know and understand wherein I the Lord justified my Servants, Abraham Isaac and Jacob; as also Moses, David and Solomon, my Servants, as touching the principle and doctrin[e] of their having many wives and concubines: Behold and lo, I am the Lord thy God, and will answer thee as touching this matter:

Therefore, prepare thy heart to receive and obey the instructions which I am about to give unto you, for all those, who have this law revealed unto them, must obey the Same; for behold I reveal unto you a new and an everlasting covenant, and if ye abide not that covenant, then are ye damned; for no one can reject this covenant and be permitted to enter into my glory; for all who will have a blessing at my hands, shall abide the law which was appointed for that blessing and the conditions thereof, as was instituted from before the foundation of the world: and as pertaining to the new and everlasting covenant, it was instituted for the fulness of my glory; and he that receiveth a fulness thereof, must and shall abide the law, or he shall be damned, saith the Lord God.

And verily I say unto you, that the conditions of this law are these: All covenants; contracts; bonds; obligations, oaths, vows, performances, connexions [connections], associations or expectations that are not made and entered into and Sealed by the Holy Spirit of promise of him who is anointed both as well for time

---

63. William Clayton, who was a clerk for Joseph Smith, recorded in his journal for 12 July 1843: "This A.M. I wrote a Revelation consisting of 10 pages on the order of the priesthood, showing the designs in Moses, Abraham, David and Solomon having many wives & concubines &c. After it was wrote [written] Prests. [Presidents] Joseph & Hyrum [Smith] presented it and read it to E. [Emma Smith] who said she did not believe a word of it and appeared very rebellious. J[oseph] told me to Deed all the unincumbered lots to E[mma]. & the children He appears much troubled about E[mma]" (William Clayton Journal, typed copy, LDS archives). Willard Richards wrote on this day: "Received a Revelation in the office in presence of Hyrum [Smith] & Wm Clayton" (Joseph Smith Journal, 12 July 1843, LDS archives). This revelation was first printed in *Deseret News Extra*, 14 Sept. 1852, 25-27, Great Salt Lake City, Utah Territory; published in the 1876 LDS D&C. Punctuation marks added to the manuscript are included.

64. Joseph C. Kingsbury wrote an eight-page manuscript copy of the revelatory document in July 1843. The handwriting on a microfilm copy of page 3 of Kingsbury's copy was difficult to read. Kingsbury described copying from the original dictated manuscript written by William Clayton: "Bishop Newel K. Whitney handed me the revelation above referred to on either the day it was written or the day following, and stating that it was asked me to take a copy of it. I did so, and then read my copy of it to Bishop Whitney, who compared it with the original which he held in his hand while I read to him" (Joseph C. Kingsbury Affidavit, 22 May 1886, published in *Historical Record* 6 [May 1887]: 226).

and for all eternity, and that too most holy, by Revelation and commandment, through the medium of mine anointed whom I have appointed on the earth to hold this power, (and I have appointed unto my Servant Joseph [Smith] to hold this power in the last days, and there is never but one on the earth at a time on whom this power and the keys of this priesthood is confer[r]ed) are of no efficacy, virtue or force, in and after the resurrection from the dead for all contracts that are not made unto this end, have an end when men are dead.

Behold, mine house is a house of order, Saith the Lord God, and not a house of confusion. Will I accept of an offering Saith the Lord, that is not made in my name[?] or, will I receive at your hands, that which I have not appointed[?] and will I appoint unto you, Saith the Lord, except it be by law, even as I and my Father ordained unto you, before the world was[?] I am the Lord thy God, and I give unto you this commandment, that no man shall come unto the Father but by me, or by my word, which is my law, Saith the Lord; and every thing that is in the world, whether it be ordained of men, by thrones, or principalities, or powers, or things of name whatsoever they may be that are not by me or by my word, Saith the Lord, Shall be thrown down, and shall not remain after men are dead, neither in nor after the resurrection Saith the Lord your God:

For whatsoever things remaineth are by me; and[65] [whatsoever things are not by me] Shall be [Shaken and destroyed There]fore, if a man marry him a wife in the world and he marry her not by me, nor by my word; and he covenant with her So long as he is in the world, and She with him, their covenant and marriage is not of force when they are dead and when they are out of the world; therefore, they are not bound by any law when they are out of the world; therefore, when they are out of the world, they neither marry nor are given in marriage, but are appointed angels in heaven, which angels are ministering Servants to minister for those who are worthy of a far more, and an exceeding, and an eternal weight of glory; for these angels did not abide my law, therefore they cannot be enlarged, but remain Separately and Singly without exaltation in their Saved condition to all eternity, and from henceforth are not Gods but are angels of God for ever and ever.

And again, verily I say unto you if a man marry a wife, and make a covenant with her for time and for all eternity, if that covenant is not by me, or by my word, which is my law, and is not Sealed by the Holy Spirit of promise, through him whom I have anointed and appointed unto this power, then it is not valid neither of force when they are out of the world, because they are not joined by me, saith the Lord, neither by my word; when they are out of the world, it cannot be received there, because the angels and the Gods are appointed there, by whom they cannot pass; they cannot, therefore, inherit my glory, for my house is a house of order, saith the Lord God.

And again, verily I say unto you, if a man marry a wife by my word, which is my law, and by the new and everlasting covenant, and it is sealed unto them by the Holy Spirit of promise, by him who is anointed, unto whom I have appointed this

---

65. Page 2 of the Kingsbury copy has a small lacuna. Wording has been added in brackets.

power, and the keys of this priesthood, and it shall be said unto them, ye shall come forth in the first resurrection; and if it be after the first resurrection, in the next resurrection; and shall inherit thrones, kingdoms, principalities, and powers, dominions, all heights, and depths, then shall it be written in the Lamb's Book of Life, that he shall commit no murder, whereby to shed innocent blood; and if ye abide in my covenant, and commit no murder whereby to shed innocent blood, it shall be done unto them in all things whatsoever my Servant hath put upon them, in time, and through all eternity; and shall be of full force when they are out of the world, and they shall pass by the angels, and the Gods, which are set there, to their exaltation and Glory in all things, as hath been sealed upon their heads, which glory shall be a fulness and a continuation of the seeds for ever and ever.

Then shall they be Gods, because they have no end; therefore shall they be from everlasting to everlasting, because they continue; then shall they be above all, because all things are subject unto them. Then shall they be Gods, because they have all power, and the angels are subject unto them.

Verily, verily I say unto you, except ye abide my Law, ye cannot attain to this glory; for strait is the Gate and narrow the way that leadeth unto the exaltation and continuation of the lives, and few there be that find it, because ye receive me not in the world, neither do ye know me. But if ye receive me in the world, then shall ye know me, and shall receive your exaltation, that where I am, ye shall be also. This is eternal lives to know the only wise and true God, and Jesus Christ whom he hath sent. I am he. Receive ye, therefore, my law. Broad is the gate and wide the way that leadeth to the deaths, and many there are that go in thereat, because they receive me not, neither do they abide in my law.

Verily, verily I say unto you, if a man marry a wife according to my word, and they are Sealed by the Holy Spirit of promise according to mine appointment, and he or She Shall Commit any Sin or transgression of the new and everlasting covenant whatever, and all manner of blasphemies, and if they commit no murder wherein they Shed innocent blood, yet they Shall come forth in the first resurrection, and enter into their exaltation; but they Shall be destroyed in the flesh, and Shall be delivered unto the buffetings of Satan unto the day of redemption, saith the Lord God.

The blasphemy against the Holy Ghost which Shall not be forgiven in the world, nor out of the world is in that ye Commit murder, wherein ye Shed innocent blood, and assent unto my death, after ye have received my new and everlasting covenant, Saith the Lord God; and he that abideth not this law, can in no wise enter into my glory, but Shall be damned, Saith the Lord.

I am the Lord thy God and will give unto thee the law of my Holy priesthood, as was ordained by me and my Father before the world was, Abraham received all things, whatsoever he received, by Revelation and Commandment, by my word, Saith the Lord, and hath entered into his exaltation, and Sitteth upon his throne.

Abraham received promises concerning his Seed and of the fruit of his loines [loins], from whose loins ye are, viz. my Servant Joseph [Smith], which were to continue So long as they were in the world; and as touching Abraham and his Seed out of the world, they Should continue, both in the world and out of the world

Should they Continue as innumerable as the Stars; or if ye were to count the Sand upon the Sea Shore, ye Could not number them.

This promise is yours also, because ye are of Abraham, and the promise was made unto Abraham, and by this law are the Continuation of the works of my Father where in he glorifieth himself. Go ye, therefore, and do the works of Abraham; enter ye into my law, and ye Shall be Saved. But if ye enter not into my law, ye Cannot receive the promises of my Father, which he made unto Abraham.

God commanded Abraham, and Sarah gave Hagar to Abraham to wife. and why did She do it? Because this was the law, and from Hagar Sprang many people. This Therefore, was fulfilling among other things the promises. Was Abraham, therefore, under condemnation? Verily, I say unto you, Nay, for I the Lord Commanded it. Abraham was Commanded to offer his Son Isaac; nevertheless, it was written you shalt not kill; Abraham however, did not refuse, and it was accounted unto him for righteousness.

Abraham received concubines, and they bare him Children, and it was accounted unto him for righteousness, because they were given unto him, and he abode in my law: as Isaac also, and Jacob did none other things than that which they were commanded; and because they did none other thing than that which they were commanded, they have entered into their exaltation according to the promises, and sit upon thrones, and are not angels, but are Gods.

David also received many wives and concubines, as also Solomon, and Moses my Servant; as also many others of my Servants from the beginning of Creation untill this time; and in nothing did they Sin, Save in those things which they received not of me.

David's wives and Concubines were given unto him, of me, by the hand of Nathan my Servant, and others of the prophets who had the keys of this power, and in none of these things did he Sin against me, Save in the case of Uriah and his wife, and therefore, he hath fallen from his exaltation, and received his portion; and he Shall not inherit them out of the world; for I gave them unto another, saith the Lord.

I am the Lord thy God, and I Gave unto thee, my Servant Joseph [Smith], an appointment, and restore all things; ask what ye will and it Shall be given unto you, according to my word; and as ye have asked Concerning adultery; Verily, verily I say unto you, if a man receiveth a wife in the new and Everlasting Covenant, and if She be with another man, and I have not appointed unto her by the holy anointing, She hath Committed adultery, and Shall be destroyed.

If She be not in the new and everlasting Covenant, and She be with another man, she has Committed adultery; and if her husband be with another woman, and he was under a vow, he hath broken his vow, and hath committed adultery; and if She hath not committed adultery, but is innocent, and hath not broken her vow, and She knoweth it, and I reveal it unto you, my Servant Joseph [Smith], then Shall you have power by the power of my Holy priesthood to take her, and give her unto him that hath not Committed adultery, but hath been faithful; for he Shall be made ruler over many; for I have conferred upon you the Keys and power of the priesthood, wherein I restore all things, and make known unto you all things in due time.

And Verily, verily I say unto you, that whatsoever you Seal on Earth Shall be Sealed in heaven, and whatsoever you bind on earth in my name, and by my word, Saith the Lord, it Shall be eternally bound in the heavens; and Whosesoever Sins you remit on earth, Shall be remitted eternally in the heavens; and Whosesoever Sins you retain on earth, Shall be retained in heaven.

And again, Verily I say, Whomsoever you bless, I will bless; and whomsoever you Curse, I will curse; Saith the Lord, for I the Lord am thy God.

And again, Verily I say unto you, my Servant Joseph [Smith], that whatsoever you give on earth, and to whomsoever you give any one on earth, by my word, and according to my law, it Shall be visited with blessings, and not cursings, and with my power Saith the Lord, and Shall be without condemnation on earth and in heaven; for I am the Lord thy God, and will be with thee even unto the end of the world and through all Eternity.

For Verily, I seal upon you, your exaltation, and prepare a throne for you in the Kingdom of my Father, with Abraham your Father. Behold, I have seen your Sacrifices, and will forgive all your Sins; I have seen your Sacrifices in obedience to that which I have told you: Go, therefore, and I make a way for your escape, as I accepted the offering of Abraham, of his Son Isaac.

Verily I say unto you, a commandment I give unto mine handmaid, Emma Smith, your wife, whom I have given unto you, that She Stay herself and partake not of that which I Commanded you to offer unto her.

For I did it, saith the Lord, to prove you all, as I did Abraham, and that I might require an offering at your hand by covenant and Sacrifice: and let mine handmaid, Emma Smith, receive all those that have been given unto my Servent Joseph [Smith], and who are virtuous and pure before me; and those who are not pure, and have Said they ware [were] pure Shall be destroyed, Saith the Lord God.

For I am the Lord thy God: and ye shall obey my voice; and I give unto my Servent Joseph [Smith], that he Shall be made ruler over many things, for he hath been faithfull over a few things and from henceforth I will Strengthen him.

and I command mine handmaid, Emma Smith, to abide and cleave unto my Servent Joseph [Smith], and to none else. But if She will not abide this commandment; She Shall be destroyed, saith the Lord; for I am the Lord thy God, and will destroy her, if She abide not in my law; but if She will not abide this Commandment, then Shall my Servent Joseph [Smith], do all things for her, even as he hath said, and I will bless him, and multiply him, and give unto him an hundred fold in this world, of fathers and mothers, brothers and Sisters, houses and lands, wives and children, and crowns of eternal lives in the eternal worlds.

And again, Verily I say, let mine handmaid forgive my Servant Joseph [Smith] his trespasses, and then Shall She be forgiven her trespasses, wherein She hath trespas[s]eth against me, and I the Lord thy God will bless her, and multiply her; and make her heart to rejoice.

and again I Say let not my Servant Joseph [Smith] put his property out of his hands, lest an enemy come and distroy [destroy] him, for Satan seeketh to distroy [destroy]; For I am the Lord thy God, and he is my Servent; and behold! and lo, I am with him as I was with Abraham, thy Father, even unto his exaltation and glory.

Now as t[o]uching the law of the priesthood, there are many things perta[i]ning thereunto. Verily, if a man be called of my Father, as was aaron, by mine own voice, and by the voice of him that Sent me, and I have endowed him with the Keys of the power of this priesthood, if he do any thing in my name, and according to my law, and by my word, he will not Commit Sin, and I will justify him. Let no one, therefore Set on my Servant Joseph [Smith] for I will justify him, for he Shall do the Sacrifice which I require at his hands for his transgressions, saith the Lord, your God.

&[66] again, as pertaining to the Law of the priesthood; if any man espouse a virgin, & desire to espouse another, & the first give her consent, & if he espouse the second, & they are virgins & have vowed to no other man, then is he justified; he cannot Commit adultery, for they are given unto him; for he Cannot Commit adultery with that, that belongeth unto him, & to none else; & if he have ten virgins given unto him by this Law, he Cannot Commit adultery, for they belong to him, & they are given unto him, therefore is he justified.

But if one, or either of the ten virgins, after she is espoused, Shall be with another man, she has Committed adultery, & Shall be distroyed [destroyed]; for they are given unto him to multiply & replenish the Earth, according to my Commandment, & to fulfill the promise which was given by my father before the foundation of the world, & for thine exaltation in the eternal worlds, that they may bear the Souls of men, for herein is the work of my father Continued, that he may be Glorified.

And again, Verily, verily I say unto you, if any man have a wife who holds the Keys of this power, & he teaches unto her the Law of my priesthood as pertaining to these things, then Shall She believe & administer unto him; or She Shall be distroy [destroyed], Saith the Lord your God; for I will distroy [destroy] her, for I will magnify my name, upon all those who receive & abide in my law.

Therefore, it Shall be lawful in me, if She receive not this law, for him to receive all things, whatsoever I the lord, his God, will give unto him, because She did not believe & administer unto him according to my word; & She then becomes the transgresser, & he is exempt from the law of Sarah, who administered unto Abraham according to the law, when I Commanded Abraham to take Hagar to wife.

And[67] now, as pertaining to this law, Verily, verily I say unto you, I will reveal more unto you hereafter; therefore, let this Suffice for the present. Behold, I am Alpha & Omega: Amen.

---

66. From here to the end of the text, it appears that the document may have been copied at another sitting. The handwriting is not as large, while use of the ampersand (&) instead of the word "and" also leads to this conclusion.

67. "And" written over "&".

170. Labor Diligently in Proclaiming My Gospel

From a letter of Brigham Young on behalf of the Quorum of the Twelve to Apostle John E. Page, 25 November 1843, RLDS archives

Revelation received at Nauvoo, Illinois, in [ca. 25] November 1843 for John E. Page[68]

the word of the Lord came through Joseph the Seer, - thus,

Let my Servant John E. Page take his departure speedily from the City of Boston, and go directly to the City of Washington, and there labor diligently in Proclaiming my Gospel to the inhabitants, thereof, and if he is humble and faithful, lo! I will go with him & will give him the hearts of the people, that he may do them good, and build up a chu[r]ch unto my name in that city.

---

68. Quotation marks omitted. The *Times and Seasons* reported, "Elder Page has gone to Washington, where he purposes proclaiming to the rulers of our nation, the great principles of eternal truth. We are pleased to know that he has gone there, for we think that he is the very man to 'counsel our counsellors, and to teach our senators wisdom'" (*Times and Seasons* 5 [1 Mar. 1844]: 458).

Conclusion

We have only a minimal understanding of Joseph Smith's view of the revelatory process. The written manuscripts and printed texts imply that the words received in most of the revelations were uttered in the name of Jesus Christ. Yet circumstances in 1834-35 motivated church leaders to change many of the revelations, demonstrating concern for more than just the original wording. Events that did not unfold as proposed in the revelations were revised. As priesthood ideas developed, changing the texts provided a way to revise original concepts to conform to an evolving theology.

The 1835 D&C committee consisted of Joseph Smith, Oliver Cowdery, Sidney Rigdon, and Frederick G. Williams. This committee was not reluctant to make changes, despite initial reservations expressed by Cowdery. In fact, the Kirtland Revelations Book contains revisions in Smith's own hand, showing that he for one did not consider the earlier texts definitive. Revisions were inserted in about a third of the early revelations, and when published, the revised texts were presented as what was said at the time and place where the original text was first received.

Since no record is known of the committee's reasons for making and arranging the revisions, we are left to examine the relevant material in order to understand the committee's reasons ourselves. And since the church leaders seemed to understand that the revelations were originally inspired, they undoubtedly considered the message to be the word and will of God as it came through Joseph Smith.

Most of the significant emendations occurred in preparing the 1835 D&C. Apparently the 1835 committee wanted to keep the message of the text alive and credible, and Smith as an editor/manager wanted both to accommodate the immediate past and present new insights to his followers. Except for the 1835 revision, the revelations afterwards followed for the most part the earliest known text. The events of 1834-35 that necessitated textual revisions—(1) a court case involving consecrated property, (2) the expulsion of church members from Jackson County, Missouri, (3) the failed redemption of Zion, and (4) the church's problems at Kirtland, Ohio—had passed.

To make significant changes and additions to any revelation was a serious matter. Since many of the revelations were given to individuals, one wonders if the 1835 committee received permission from those individuals to change the text. Besides this, many of the documents had been copied by church members and printed in *The Evening and the Morning Star*. While the pages of the BC manuscript (except eight pages) had been destroyed, copies had been made and preserved by faithful members. Other manuscripts of some of the revelations existed, so the committee had the basic wording of those early texts.

One of the first ways to amend a previous revelation was to revoke the earlier instructions with a new commandment.[1] When additional instructions were needed to clarify the law of the church,[2] revelations were directed to those needs and material was added to the previously written text.[3] Subsequent problems were sometimes solved through additional revelations, as well.

The Articles and Covenants was published in the *Evening and Morning Star* reprint in January 1835 with a note prior to the revised text that stated, "*With a few items from other revelations.*"[4] But there is no evidence of separate revelations received either to fill in additional text or to revise wording.

The majority of textual revisions were made to revelations from the period of the translation of the Book of Mormon to the establishment of the Kirtland High Council (1828-34). Before February 1834, the highest ecclesiastical group in the Church of Christ was the presidency of the high priesthood organized in March 1832. This presidency of three high priests was called the First Presidency in 1835.

According to the 1835 revision, Smith was told in March 1829 that he should be "ordained and go forth and deliver my words unto the children of men."[5] Mention was also made of three servants (witnesses) "whom I shall call and ordain, unto whom I will show these things." The 1835 text stated, "And you must wait yet a little while; for ye are not yet ordained."[6] These additions relating to ordination were inserted into the revelation after the events occurred.

How do these revisions relate to the pronouns "my" and "I" as God gave words of comfort in 1829? By retaining the March 1829 date in the 1835 version, the changes leave the impression that the altered text as now published was as Smith had originally received it. Like the three additions above, many of the other revisions indicate that the added words are those of Jesus Christ, something that readers accepted uncritically in 1835, not knowing that their history had been rewritten.

Changes were sometimes made in one document but not in another. For example, the Articles and Covenants (June 1830) has "The Elders are to conduct the meetings according as they are led by the Holy Ghost" to which were added in 1835 the words "to the commandments and revelations of God."[7] A March 1831 revelation also mentions that the elders of the church are "to conduct all meetings as they are directed and guided by the Holy Spirit,"[8] without the addition. Oliver

---

1. See document nos. 62, 64, 85; LDS D&C 56:4-6; 58:32; 75:6 and RLDS D&C 56:2; 58:6; 75:2.
2. Document no. 45; LDS D&C 42:1-73; RLDS D&C 42:1-19 (9 Feb. 1831).
3. See documents nos. 76, 78, 83, 98; LDS D&C 68:13; 107:59; 72:9, 24; 83:1; and RLDS D&C 68:2; 104:31; 72:3, 5; 82:1.
4. *Evening and Morning Star* (Kirtland reprint) 1 (June 1832): 2, reprinted January 1835, emphasis in original.
5. 1835 D&C 32:2; LDS D&C 5:6-7; RLDS D&C 5:2.
6. 1835 D&C 32:3; LDS D&C 5:11, 17; RLDS D&C 5:3.
7. 1835 D&C 2:9; LDS D&C 20:45; RLDS D&C 17:9.
8. Document no. 51; LDS D&C 46:2; RLDS D&C 46:1.

Cowdery asked Newel K. Whitney, church bishop in Kirtland, for the original text of the law of the church.[9] But when the revelation was republished, it appeared as an altered text.[10] Cowdery editorialized:

> Some have said, and still say, that this Church, "*has all things common.*" This assertion is meant, not only to falsify on the subject of property, but to blast the reputation and moral characters of the members of the same.
>
> The church at Jerusalem, in the days of the apostles, had their earthly goods in common; the Nephites, after the appearance of Christ, held theirs in the same way; but each government was differently organized from ours, and could admit of such a course when ours cannot.[11]

One problem here is how church members could obey a revised law given in 1835 as a "Revelation given February 1831." This could hardly be considered the same revelation since it required such different actions of the members. The laws of the church, especially the law of consecration and stewardship, would now require a radical alteration in lifestyle. The alterations in the text were not made because of transcription errors, but because of new circumstances. Rather than have members obey the old requirement, the law was changed due to the new conditions. These changes from early manuscripts and the BC text were made ostensibly because of typographical errors. But the changes were more substantive. The 1835 law of consecration was substituted for the original form of the law given in February 1831. The new language of the revelation made a difference in how the Saints were to follow the church law.

New insights and information inserted into the text of older revelations created a problem. While some may have considered that the new material brought the text up to date, others accepted the revised text as though it were the original. When republished in the *Evening and Morning Star*, the text was said to follow the original, so members did not expect the changes. Did the additions and omissions make the texts better? Did the variants in the documents merely correct typographical errors and follow the original texts?

A revelation given in November 1831 said that the commandments "were given unto my servants in their weakness, after the manner of their language, that they might come to understanding." It also stated that the commandments were "true and faithful." The message continued: "What I the Lord have spoken, I have spoken, and I excuse not myself, and though the heavens and the earth pass away, my word shall not pass away, but shall all be fulfilled, whether by mine own voice, or by the voice of my servants, it is the same."[12]

As the revelations were first given, the messages were presented in their own

---

9. Cowdery to Whitney, 4 Feb. 1835, Newel K. Whitney Collection, Special Collections, Harold B. Lee Library, Brigham Young University, Provo, Utah; reproduced in *BYU Studies* 11 (Summer 1971): 325.

10. *Evening and Morning Star* (Kirtland reprint) 1 (July 1832): 30-31, reprinted February 1835.

11. *Evening and Morning Star* (Kirtland reprint) 1 (Aug. 1832): 48, reprinted March 1835, emphasis in original.

12. Document no. 73; LDS D&C 1:24, 37-38; RLDS D&C 1:5, 7-8.

historical setting and time. Because of the changes, Smith's later views were mixed in with earlier instructions and practices, making it difficult to understand if the revelations were intended to come literally from God, in the sense of God speaking directly to Smith. What we find is that Joseph Smith and his associates were themselves responsible for altering the ideas in the revelations, commandments, and instructions, so that these documents seem more like directives to the church than the direct words of God.

That a number of Smith's revelations were altered means that revelations were changed with little regard to the integrity of the original text. For example, the role of Adam in LDS theology is an important topic.[13] When the revised revelations appeared in the 1835 D&C, the identification of Adam as Michael was introduced into the canon. Sidney Rigdon wrote, referring to the book of Daniel, "for who could the ancient of days be but our father Adam? surely none other: he was the first who lived in days, and must be the ancient of days."[14] The 1835 D&C included additional material concerning Adam: "and also with Michael, or Adam, the father of all, the prince of all, the ancient of days."[15] It had been established by September 1835 when the D&C was printed and bound that Michael[16] was the name of Adam and was the ancient of days.[17] Additional wording to what is now LDS D&C 78 and RLDS D&C 77 indicated that Michael held the "keys of salvation under the counsel and direction of the Holy One."[18] Joseph Smith taught by 8 August 1839 that "the Keys have to be brought from heaven whenever the Gospel is sent.—When they are revealed from Heaven it is by Adam[']s Authority."[19]

On 21 January 1836 Smith reported that he received visions and revelations while in a meeting. Warren Parrish recorded in the prophet's journal, "[I] saw father Adam, and Abraham and Michael and my father and mother, my brother Alvin that has long since slept[.]"[20] Smith's father was at this meeting and his mother was probably at home in Kirtland. As Smith and other church members came to understand that Michael and Adam referred to the same person—even though the original text indicates that Smith saw Adam and Michael as separate beings—the wording was changed so that now LDS D&C 137:5 reads, "I saw Father Adam and Abraham; and my father and my mother; my brother Alvin, that has long since

13. See Rodney Turner, "The Position of Adam in Latter-day Saint Scripture and Theology," M.A. thesis, Brigham Young University, 1953.
14. "Millen[n]ium," *The Evening and the Morning Star* 2 (May 1834): 154, Kirtland, Ohio.
15. 1835 D&C 50:2; LDS D&C 27:11; RLDS D&C 26:2.
16. See Dan. 10:13, 21; 12:1; Jude 1:9; Rev. 12:7.
17. See Dan. 7:9, 13, 22.
18. LDS D&C 78:16; RLDS D&C 77:3.
19. Andrew F. Ehat and Lyndon W. Cook, eds., *The Words of Joseph Smith: The Contemporary Accounts of the Nauvoo Discourses of the Prophet Joseph* (Provo, UT: Religious Studies Center, 1980), 8. See Joseph Smith et al., *History of the Church of Jesus Christ of Latter-day Saints*, ed. B. H. Roberts (Salt Lake City: Deseret Book Co., 1959), 3:386.
20. Joseph Smith 1835-36 Journal, 136, 21 Jan. 1836, LDS archives; Dean C. Jessee, ed., *The Papers of Joseph Smith: Journal, 1832-1842* (Salt Lake City: Deseret Book Co., 1992), 2:157. See also T. B. H. Stenhouse, *The Rocky Mountain Saints* (New York: D. Appleton and Co., 1873), 63-64; and Lyndon W. Cook, *The Revelations of the Prophet Joseph Smith* (Provo, UT: Seventy's Mission Bookstore, 1981), 303. See document no. 137.

slept." This deletion of "and Michael" was important to avoid contradicting the other revelations referring to Adam as Michael.

To further understand why the words "and Michael" are not in current editions of the D&C, we need to know about the revelation's textual history. Clearly, Smith said he saw in vision "Adam, ... and Michael." This entry was recopied into the Manuscript History by Willard Richards in 1843.[21] Then the Manuscript History, Book B-1, was later recopied into the duplicate history, Book B-2.[22] The vision was published in Salt Lake City in the *Deseret News* issue of 4 September 1852. At this time the words "and Michael" were dropped.[23] One reason for this is that President Brigham Young had in April 1852 proclaimed that Adam was Michael (Joseph Smith had taught the same) and that Adam was God.[24] The original journal entry was probably thought to be in error and the two words were dropped. This revised vision appeared as part of the "History of Joseph Smith" or "Life of Joseph Smith" and was later reprinted in the *Millennial Star*. The LDS *History of the Church* was edited by B. H. Roberts from the *Millennial Star* and published in 1904.[25]

In 1976, at a meeting of the First Presidency and Council of the Twelve Apostles in the Salt Lake temple, leaders voted to add the January 1836 vision to the official canon as part of the PGP. Later, in 1979, the church announced that the vision would be removed from the PGP and added as section 137 to the planned 1981 D&C. Thus the deletion of two words impacted future theology.

Additional problems can be created when textual emendations are considered important enough to be added to an earlier document. One concern is how the revised text would be interpreted when considered in the milieu from which it emerged. Adding ideas, phrases, and commentary to documents considered inspired of God creates misunderstandings of the historical setting and theological development of the early church.

With careful examination, we develop a better appreciation of the early history and of the Saints' need for receiving instructions from their founding prophet. We can now see things that they could not have seen, such as the historical problems caused by changing the wording of documents. Doctrinal teachings of another period now in revised form also show us that theological concerns have always been present in determining what to publish.

The benefits of having the early texts of these documents are, one, that they help promote an understanding of the historical situation at the time the original revelations were received. Second, they enable us to appreciate better the development of both the revelator Joseph Smith and of the early LDS church. The revela-

21. Manuscript History, Book B-1:695, LDS archives.
22. Manuscript History, Book B-2:618, LDS archives.
23. "Life of Joseph Smith," *Deseret News* 2 (4 Sept. 1852): [1], Great Salt Lake City, U.T. Manuscript History, Book B-1 or Book B-2, was used for printing the "Life of Joseph Smith" entry of 21 January 1836 in the *Deseret News*. The *Deseret News* contains the edited version.
24. Sermon delivered by Brigham Young on 9 April 1852, *Journal of Discourses*, 26 vols. (Liverpool, Eng.: Latter-day Saints' Book Depot, 1854-86), 1:50-51. For further discussion, see David John Buerger, "The Adam-God Doctrine," *Dialogue: A Journal of Mormon Thought* 15 (Spring 1982): 14-58.
25. *History of the Church*, 2:380.

tions trace the development of a new religious movement and illuminate the changing nature of its doctrines. From Smith's early beginnings as he dictated the Book of Mormon, he showed concern for the religious heritage he shared with other Christian denominations, for instance.

Just like a photograph that is meant to document experience, but is not the experience itself, a revelation is much the same. It is meant to express words and thoughts believed to have been inspired by Deity. In Mormon tradition the inspired words were written down as Joseph Smith dictated them to the person acting as his scribe. The scribe tried to write the words as exactly as possible, and what the scribe wrote became the original text. Other persons made copies. Differences in these copies were mostly minor. For instance, the BC manuscript was copied from the originals or early manuscripts in November 1831. When the revelations were prepared for publication, there were insignificant differences between the original texts and the prepared manuscript. Most of these variants had no impact on the meaning of the text.

So the history of the revelations as a living document shows them changing and growing. Every stage of the development provides us with valuable insights. Yet one cannot overemphasize the essential nature of the earliest texts in uncovering what is presumably nearest to the original intentions and meanings within the historical circumstances surrounding them. An early text leads to a greater appreciation of the early Restoration movement. As the 1981 LDS D&C states concerning the pseudonyms, "Since there exists no vital need today to continue the code names, the real names only are now used herein, as given in the original manuscripts."[26] The same applies to the texts of the revelations. The early texts preserve historical accuracy and help to uncover original meaning.

As Smith perceived the divine will, he revealed additional ordinances and doctrines that further set Mormonism apart from American Christian churches. Many ideas had their roots during the years of thought and reflection before the Nauvoo, Illinois, period of church and priesthood development, but then blossomed there.

Smith's projects in Illinois—the temple for the priesthood, the Nauvoo House for his family—were monumental tasks requiring strict obedience. But there are fewer explicit revelations during this period when the church president's instructions were considered inspired guidance to those privileged to hear them.

In Nauvoo the prophet's private teachings remained private. He felt a need to have members keep secret instructions regarding temple-related ordinances, including plural marriage. The revelation on marriage of 12 July 1843 is a long treatise on the subject, the next-to-last revelation Smith received (document 169 in this collection).

As a final note, I feel that Smith's revelations do not tell the full impact of the prophet's leadership, but they do show his growing desire to experience the divine will in times of need. With his death on 27 June 1844, his memory has been partly preserved in the revelations, especially in the originals but also in the later revisions.

26. Heading of LDS D&C 78; 1981 ed., 147.

ILLUSTRATIONS

Oliver Cowdery, early scribe, second elder, member of presidency
and Doctrine and Covenants committee.

Sidney Rigdon, early scribe, member of presidency and
Doctrine and Covenants committee.

Frederick G. Williams, assistant scribe, member of presidency and Doctrine and Covenants committee.

Early copy of a commandment given to Joseph Smith, Jr., concerning the sacrament, in the handwriting of Edward Partridge, LDS archives (Cf. document number 28; BC 28; LDS D&C 27; RLDS D&C 26).

Transcription:

Commandment to the Church AD 1830
Saying listen to the voice of Jesus Christ your Lord your God
[& your Redeemer whose word is q]uick & powerfull for behold I say
unto you that it mattereth not what ye [shall eat or] what ye shal[l]
drink when ye partake of the sacrament if it so be that y[e do it]
with an eye single to my glory remembering unto the Fathe[r my]
body which is laid down for you & my blood which was shed for [the]
remission of your sins wherefore a commandment I give unto you
that ye shall not purchase wine niether strong drink of your enemies wherefore
ye shall partake of none except it is made new among you yea in
this my Fathers kingdom which shall be built up on the earth
behold this is wisdom in me wherefore marvel not for the
hour cometh that I will drink of the fruit of the vine w[ith]
you on the earth & with all those whom my Father
hath given me out of the world wherefore lift up your
hearts & rejoice & gird up your loins & be faithfull untill
[I come even so amen]

THE EVENING AND THE MORNING STAR.

| Vol. I. | Independence, Mo. May, 1833. | No. 12. |

REVELATIONS.

☞ Having given, in a previous number, the Preface to the book of Commandments now in press, we give below, the close, or as it has been called, the Appendix. It affords us joy to lay before the saints, an article frought with so much heavenly intelligence, having previously published many from the same book for their instruction.

We hope that while they read it, they will remember, that it is a voice from him who spake as never man spake. We hope that while they are blessed with revelation upon revelation, with commandment upon commandment, and with precept upon precept, they will remember to do them. We hope that while they are thus blessed with the precious word of their Lord from heaven, in these last days, to fulfill that which was spoken in days of old, they will hearken to his counsels and lend an ear to all his precepts.

Indeed it is a source of joy to us, to know, that all the prophecies and promises which are contained in them, which have not been fulfilled, will come to pass. The saints may lift up their heads and rejoice, for their redemption will soon be perfected. Soon the curtain of heaven will be unfolded, as a scroll is unfolded after it is rolled up, and they will see their Lord face to face. In view of these coming scenes, they may lift up their heads and rejoice, and praise his holy name, that they are permitted to live in the days when he returns to his people his everlasting covenant, to prepare them for his presence.

The book from which this important revelation is taken, will be published in the course of the present year, at from 25, to 50 cents a copy. We regret that in consequence of circumstances not within our control, this book will not be offered to our brethren as soon as was anticipated. We beg their forbearance, and solicit an interest in their prayers, promising to use our exertions with all our means to accomplish the work.

HEARKEN, O ye people of my church, saith the Lord your God, and hear the word of the Lord concerning you; the Lord who shall come down upon the world with a curse to judgment; yea, upon all the nations that forget God, and upon all the ungodly among you.

For he shall make bare his holy arm in the eyes of all the nations, and all the ends of the earth shall see the salvation of their God:

Wherefore, prepare ye, prepare ye, O my people; sanctify yourselves; gather ye together, O ye people of my church, upon the land of Zion, all you that have not been commanded to tarry.

Go ye out from Babylon. Be ye clean that bear the vessels of the Lord. Call your solemn assemblies, and speak often one to another.

And let every man call upon the name of the Lord; yea, verily I say unto you, again, the time has come when the voice of the Lord is unto you, Go ye out of Babylon; gather ye out from among the nations, from the four winds, from one end of heaven to the other.

Send forth the elders of my church unto the nations which are afar off; unto the islands of the sea; send forth unto foreign lands; call upon all nations; firstly, upon the Gentiles, and then upon the Jews.

And behold and lo, this shall be their cry, and the voice of the Lord unto all people: Go ye forth unto the land of Zion, that the borders of my people may be enlarged, and that her stakes may be strengthened, and that Zion may go forth unto the regions round about:

Yea, let the cry go forth among all people: Awake and arise and go forth to meet the Bride-groom:

Behold and lo the Bride-groom cometh, go ye out to meet him. Prepare yourselves for the great day of the Lord. Watch, therefore, for ye know neither the day nor the hour.

Let them, therefore, which are among the Gentiles, flee unto Zion. And let them who be of Judah, flee unto Jerusalem, unto the mountains of the Lord's house.

Go ye out from among the nations, even from Babylon, from the midst of wickedness, which is spiritual Babylon.

But verily thus saith the Lord, let not your flight be in haste, but let all things be prepared before you: and he that goeth, let him not look back, lest sudden destruction should come upon him.

Hearken and hear O ye inhabitants of the earth. Listen ye elders of my church together, and hear the voice of the Lord, for he calleth upon all men and he commandeth all men every where to repent: for behold the Lord God hath sent forth the angel crying through the midst of heaven, saying: Prepare ye the way of the Lord, and make his paths strait, for the hour of his coming is nigh, when the Lamb shall stand upon mount Zion, and with him a hundred and forty-four thousand, having his Father's name written in their foreheads:

Wherefore, prepare ye for the coming of the Bride-groom: go ye, go ye out to

meet him, for behold he shall stand upon the mount of Olivet, and upon the mighty ocean, even the great deep, and upon the islands of the sea, and upon the land of Zion; and he shall utter his voice out of Zion, and he shall speak from Jerusalem, and his voice shall be heard among all people, and it shall be a voice as the voice of many waters, and as the voice of a great thunder, which shall break down the mountains, and the valleys shall not be found:

He shall command the great deep and it shall be driven back into the north countries, and the islands shall become one land, and the land of Jerusalem and the land of Zion, shall be turned back into their own place, and the earth shall be like as it was in the days before it was divided.

And the Lord even the Savior shall stand in the midst of his people, and shall reign over all flesh. And they who are in the north countries shall come in remembrance before the Lord, and their prophets shall hear his voice, and shall no longer stay themselves, and they shall smite the rocks, and the ice shall flow down at their presence.

And an high way shall be cast up in the midst of the great deep. Their enemies shall become a prey unto them, and in the barren deserts there shall come forth pools of living water; and the parched ground shall no longer be a thirsty land. And they shall bring forth their rich treasures unto the children of Ephraim my servants.

And the boundaries of the everlasting hills shall tremble at their presence.—And then shall they fall down and be crowned with glory, even in Zion, by the hands of the servants of the Lord, even the children of Ephraim; and they shall be filled with songs of everlasting joy.

Behold this is the blessing of the everlasting God upon the tribes of Israel, and the richer blessing upon the head of Ephraim and his fellows.

And they also of the tribe of Judah, after their pain, shall be sanctified in holiness before the Lord to dwell in his presence day and night for ever and ever.

And now verily saith the Lord, that these things might be known among you, O inhabitants of the earth, I have sent forth mine angel, flying through the midst of heaven, having the everlasting gospel, who hath appeared unto some, and hath committed it unto man, who shall appear unto many that dwell on the earth, and this gospel shall be preached unto every nation, and kindred, and tongue, and people, and the servants of God shall go forth, saying, with a loud voice:

Fear God and give glory to him: for the hour of his judgment is come: and worship him that made heaven, and earth, and sea, and the fountain of waters, calling upon the name of the Lord day and night, saying:

O that thou wouldst rend the heavens, that thou wouldst come down, that the mountains might flow down at thy presence. And it shall be answered upon their heads, for the presence of the Lord shall be as the melting fire that burneth, and as the fire which causeth the waters to boil.

O Lord, thou shalt come down to make thy name known to thine adversaries, and all nations shall tremble at thy presence. When thou doeth terrible things, things they look not for; yea, when thou comest down and the mountains flow down at thy presence, thou shalt meet him who rejoiceth and worketh righteousness, who remember them in thy ways:

For since the beginning of the world have not man heard nor perceived by the ear, neither hath any eye seen, O God, besides thee, how great things thou hast prepared for him that waiteth for thee.

And it shall be said, Who is this that cometh down from God in heaven with died garments; yea, from the regions which are not known, clothed in his glorious apparrel, travelling in the greatness of his strength?

And he shall say, I am he who spake in righteousness, mighty to save. And the Lord shall be red in his apparrel, and his garments like him that treadeth in the wine vat, and so great shall be the glory of his presence, that the sun shall hide his face in shame; and the moon shall withhold its light; and the stars shall be hurled from their places:

And his voice shall be heard, I have trodden the wine-press alone, and have brought judgment upon all people; and none was with me; and I have trampled them in my fury, and I did tread upon them in mine anger, and their blood have I sprinkled upon my garments, and stained all my raiment: for this was the day of vengeance which was in my heart.

And now the year of my redeemed is come, and they shall mention the loving kindness of their Lord, and all that he has bestowed upon them, according to his goodness, and according to his loving kindness, forever and ever. In all their afflictions he was afflicted.

And the angel of his presence saved them; and in his love, and in his pity, he redeemed them, and bare them, and carried them all the days of old; yea, and Enoch also, and they who were with him; the prophets which were before him, and Noah also, and they who were before him, and Moses also, and they who were before him, and from Moses to Elijah, and from Elijah to John, who were with Christ in his resurrection, and the holy apostles, with Abraham, Isaac and Jacob, shall be in the presence of the Lamb.

And the graves of the saints shall be opened, and they shall come forth and stand on the right hand of the Lamb, when he shall stand upon mount Zion, and upon the holy city, the New Jerusalem, and they shall sing the song of the Lamb day and night forever and ever.

Outside cover of manuscript volume "Kirtland Revelations,"
LDS archives.

appointed unto you to keep the church record and history continualy for thou I have appointed to an other office before it shall be given thee by the Comforter to write these things even So Amen

Kirtland Decer 4th 1831 Harken and listen to the voice of the Lord Oh ye who have assembled yourselves together who are the high Priest of my church to whom the kingdom and power is given for verily Saith the Lord it is expedient in me for a bishop to be appointed unto you or of you unto the Church in this part of the Lords vineard and verily in this thing you have done wisely for it is required of the Lord at the hand of every Steward to render an account of his Stewardship both in time and in Eternity for he who is faithful and wise in time is accounted worthy to inherit the mansions prepared for him of my Father verily I Say unto you the Elders of the Church in this part of my Vinyard shall render an account of their Stewardship unto the Bishop which shall be appointed of me in this part of my Vinyard these things shall be had on record to be handed over to the Bishop in Zion and the duty of the Bishop shall be made known by the commandments which have been given and by the voice of the Conference and verily I Say unto you my servent Newel Whitney is the man which shall be appointed and ordained unto this power this is the will of the Lord your God your redeemer even So Amen —

Kirtland December 4th 1831 = = = =
The word of the Lord in addition to the law which has been given making known the duty

The Twelve Apostles (1835–1837)

John F. Boynton

Orson Hyde

Luke S. Johnson

Heber C. Kimball

William E. McLellin

Orson Pratt

Parley P. Pratt

William Smith

Brigham Young

Photographs unavailable of Apostles
Lyman E. Johnson, Thomas B. Marsh, and David W. Patten

APPENDICES

Appendix A.
Corrected Dates and Locations of
Joseph Smith's Revelations

LDS D&C;	RLDS D&C	Traditional Date	Correct Date	Correct Location
23	21	Apr. 1830	6 Apr.1830	Manchester, NY
21	19	6 Apr. 1830		Manchester, NY
22	20	Apr. 1830	16 Apr. 1830	Fayette, NY
20	17	Apr. 1830	[1-9] June 1830	Fayette, NY
32	31	[ca.17] Oct. 1830		Manchester, NY
37	37	[30] Dec. 1830		Canandaigua, NY
56	56	June 1831	15 June 1831	
66	66	25 Oct. 1831	29 Oct. 1831	Hiram, OH
70	70	12 Nov. 1831		Hiram, OH
74	74	Jan. 1832	[ca. 17 Feb.– early Mar.] 1832	Hiram, OH
78	77	Mar. 1832	1 Mar. 1832	Kirtland, OH
80	79	Mar. 1832	7 Mar. 1832	
81	80	Mar. 1832	15 Mar. 1832	
99	96	Aug. 1832	29 Aug. 1832	Hiram, OH
94	91	6 May 1833	2 Aug. 1833	
107	104	28 Mar. 1835	[28-30] Apr. 1835	

Appendix B.
Book of Commandments Manuscript Fragments

The following transcript does not contain all of the handwritten corrections, punctuation marks, and verses that were made in preparing the BC (see reproductions). A complete transcription is located in RLDS archives. Words added above the line are indicated by angle brackets < >.

Four leaves (eight pages) of the original manuscript are extant. These pages contain the complete text of three revelations and portions of three others. In 1903 the RLDS church purchased what is known as the Book of Mormon Printer's Manuscript and other items including these eight manuscript pages. The dates, manuscript page numbers, and cross references for these revelations are as follows:

No. 1; 11 Sept. 1831
page 111; LDS D&C 64:32-43; RLDS D&C 64:6-8.

Note: The unfinished BC ends at line 8 at the word "Ephraim." The final words being "for verily I say that the rebelious are not of the blood of Ephraim." The remainder of the text continues beyond the BC printing.

No. 2; 29 Oct. 1831
pages 111-[112]; LDS and RLDS D&C 66.

No. 3; 30 Oct. 1831
page [112]; LDS and RLDS D&C 65.

No. 4; 3 Nov. 1831 [appendix to BC]
pages 117-120; LDS D&C 133:14-73; RLDS D&C 108:4-13.

No. 5; 16 Feb. 1832 [added to Nov. 1831 BC manuscript]
page [139]; LDS D&C 76:109-119; RLDS D&C 76:7-8.

No. 6; 15 Mar. 1832 [added to Nov. 1831 BC manuscript]
pages [139]-140; LDS D&C 81; RLDS D&C 80.

Reproduction of the eight pages is contained on the following pages with the BC manuscript on the left side and the transcript on the right.

to pass in its time; wherefore be not weary in well doing,
for ye are laying the foundation of a great work, & out of
small things proceedeth that which is great. behold, the Lord
requireth the heart, & a willing mind; & the willing & obedient
shall eat the good of the Land of Zion in these last days.
& the rebelious shall be cut off out of the Land of Zion, & shall be
sent away & shall not inherit the Land, for verily I say that the
rebelious are not of the blood of Ephraim, wherefore, they shall
be plucked out. Behold, I the Lord have made my Church in
these last days like unto a Judge, sitting on a hill, or in an
high place, to judge the Nations; for it shall come to pass, that
the inhabitants of Zion shall judge all things pertaining to Zion, & all liers, &
hypocrites shall be proved by them, & they which are not Apostles
& prophets shall be known. & even the Judge & his counsellors, if they are
not faithful in their stewardships, shall be condemned, & others
shall be planted in their stead. for behold I say unto you,
that Zion shall flourish, & the glory of the Lord shall be upon
her, & she shall be an ensign unto the People, & there shall
come unto her out of every Nation under heaven. & the
days shall come, when the Nations of the Earth shall
tremble because of her, & shall fear because of her terrible
ones; the Lord hath spoken it. amen.
    Given at Kirtland September the 11th 1831

    A Revelation to Wm E. McLelin Recd Oct 29th 1831
Behold thus saith the Lord unto you my Servant William E. McLelin, blessed
are you, in as much as you have turned away from your iniquities & have received
my truths; saith the Lord your redeemer, the Saviour of the World, of as many
as believe on my name; verily I say unto you, blessed are you for receiving mine everlasting
covenant, even the fullness of my gospel, sent forth unto the children of
men, that they might have life & be made partakers of the glories which are to be revealed
in the last days, as it was written by the Prophets & Apostles in days of old; verily I say unto
you, my servant Wm E. McLelin that you are clean but not all; repent therefore of those things
which are not pleasing in my sight, saith the Lord, for the Lord will shew them unto you.
repent & hearken, verily the Lord will shew unto you what I will concerning you, or
what is my will concerning you, behold, verily I say unto you, that it is my will that you
should proclaim my gospel from land to land, & from city to city, yea in those regions

No. 1; 11 Sept. 1831; Page 111

to pass in its time wherefore be not weary in well doing for ye are laying the foundation of a great work & out of small things proceedeth that which is great behold the Lord requireth the hearts & a willing mind & the willing & obedient shall eat the good of the Land of Zion in these Last days & the rebelious shall be cut off out of the Land of Zion & shall be sent away & shall not inherit the Land for verily I say that the rebelious are not of the blood of Ephraim wherefore they shall be plucked out Behold I the Lord have made my Church in these last days like unto a Judge on an hill or in an high place to Judge the Nations for it shall come to pass that the inhabitants of Zion shall Judge all things <pertaining to Zion> & all liars & hypocrites shall be proved by them & they which are not Apostles <& prophets> shall be known & even the Judge & his counsellors if they are not faithfull in their stewardships shall be condemned & an others shall be planted in their stead for behold I say unto you that Zion shall florish & the glory of the Lord shall be upon her & she shall be an ensign unto the People & there shall shall come unto her out of every Nation under heaven & the days shall come when the Nations of the Earth shall tremble because of her & shall fear because of her terable ones the Lord hath spoken it amen

Given at Kirtland September the 11th. 1831

No. 2; 29 Oct. 1831

A Revelation to Wm. E Mc lelin Recd. Oct. 29th. 1831

Behold thus saith the Lord unto my Servant William (E.) Mc lellin) blessed are you in as much as you have turned away from your iniquities & have received my truths saith the Lord your redeemer the Saviour of the World <even> of as many as believe on my name verily I say unto you blessed are you for receiving mine everlasting truth Covenant even the fullness of my gospel sent forth unto the children of men that they might have life & be made partakers of the glories which was <are> to be revealed in the last days, as it was written by the Prophets & Apostles in days of old verily I say unto you my Servant Wm. (E.) that you are Clean but not all repent therefore of those things which are not pleasing in my sight saith the Lord for the Lord will shew <them> unto you what I [] & now verily I the Lord will shew unto you what I will concerning you or what is my will concerning you Behold verily I say unto you that it is my will that you should proclaim my Gospel from land to land & from City to City yea in those regions

1. (Opposite). Book of Commandments manuscript page 111 in the handwriting of John Whitmer, RLDS archives. Courtesy Library-Archives, Reorganized Church of Jesus Christ of Latter Day Saints, Independence, Missouri.

this place, go not up unto the land of Zion till that as much as you can send ^10 otherwise think not of thy property ^11 unto the eastern lands, bear testimony ^12 while [crossing?] ~~way people~~ in any thing in the synagogues, reasoning with the people.

let my servant ^13 [Sidney?] ~~[go]~~ with you, & forsake him not, ^14 give him thine instructions, ^15 he that is faithfull shall be made strong in every place, & the Lord will go with you ^16 lay your hands upon the sick, & they shall recover ^17 return not untill I the Lord shall send you ^18 be patient in afflictions ^19 ask & ye shall receive; knock & it shall be opened unto you ^20 seek not to be cumbered ^21 forsake all unrighteousness, commit not adultery, a temptation with which thou hast ~~been~~ troubled ^22 keep these ^23 sayings ~~for they are~~ [faithfully?], & these shall magnify thine office ^24 push many people to Zion with songs of everlasting joy upon their heads ^25 continue in these things, even unto the end, & you shall have a crown of eternal life on the right hand of my father who is full of grace & truth ^26 verily thus saith the Lord your God your redeemer even Jesus Christ. AMEN.

A Revelation (No 3) Oct 30th 1831

Hearken & lo a voice as one but sent down from on high who is mighty & powerfull whose going forth is unto the ends of the earth yea whose voice is unto men prepare ye the way of the Lord make his paths straight the keys of the kingdom of God are committed unto man on the earth & from ~~thence~~ shall the gospel roll forth unto the ends of the earth as the stone ~~cut out~~ [which] is cut out of the Mountain without hands shall roll forth untill it has filled the whole earth yea a voice crying prepare ye the way of the Lord prepare ye the supper of the Lamb make ready for the Bridegroom pray unto the Lord call upon his holy name make known his wonderfull works among the people call upon the Lord that his kingdom may go forth upon the earth that the inhabitants thereof may receive it & be prepared for the days to come in the which the son of man shall come down in heaven clothed in the brightness of his glory to meet the kingdom of God which is set up on the earth wherefore may the kingdom of God go forth that the kingdom of heaven may come that thou O God may be glorified in heaven so on earth that thine enemies may be subdued for thine is the ~~kingdom~~ honour power & glory forever & ever. Amen.

No. 2; 29 Oct. 1831, Continued; Page [112]

[round] about where it ~~hath~~ <has> not been proclaimed tarry not many days in this place go not up unto the land of Zion <as yet> but in as much as you can send send otherwise think not of thy property go unto the Eastern lands bear testimony ~~unto every people~~ & in every Place <unto every people> & in their synagagues reasoning with the people let my Servant Samuel <H Smith> go with you & forsake him not & give him thine instructions & he that is faithfull shall be made strong in every place & I the Lord will go with you lay your hands upon the sick & they shall recover return not untill I the Lord shall send you be patiant in afflictions ask & ye shall receive knock & it shall be opened unto you seek not to be Cumbered forsake all unrighteousness commit not Adultry a temptation with which ~~thus hast~~ <~~you have~~ thou hast> been troubled keep these sayings <for they are> true & faithful & ~~thou shall~~ <~~you shall~~ thou shall> magnify ~~thine~~ <~~your~~ thine> office & push many people to Zion with songs of everlasting Joy upon their heads continue in these things <even> unto the end <even> & you shall have a crown of eternal life on the right hand of my father who is full of grace & truth verily thus saith the Lord your God your redeemer even Jesus Christ Amen

No. 3; 30 Oct. 1831

Revelation Oct. 30th. 1831

Hearken & lo a voice as one sent down from on high who is mighty & powerfull whose going forth is unto the ends of the Earth yea whose voice is unto men prepare ye the way of the Lord make his paths strait The keys of the kingdom of God are committed unto man on the Earth & from hence shall the gospel roll forth unto the ends of the Earth as the stone which is ~~hewn from~~ <cut out of> the Mountain without hands shall roll forth until it ~~hath~~ <has> filled the whole Earth yea a voice crying prepare ye the way of the Lord prepare ye the supper of the Lamb make ready for the Bridegroom pray unto the Lord call upon his holy name make known his wonderfull works among the people call upon the Lord that his kingdom may go forth upon the Earth that the inhabitants thereof may received it & be prepared for the days to come in the which the Son of man shall come down in heaven Clothed in the brightness of his glory to meet the kingdom of God which is set up on the Earth Wherefore may the kingdom of God go forth that the kingdom of heaven may come that thou O God may be glorified in heaven so on Earth that thine enemies may be subdued for thine is the ~~kingdom~~ honour power & glory for ever & ever Amen

2. (Opposite). Book of Commandments manuscript page 112.
Courtesy Library-Archives, Reorganized Church of Jesus
Christ of Latter Day Saints, Independence, Missouri.

from the midst of wickedness; which is spiritual Babylon.
12 But verily thus saith the Lord, let not your flight be in haste, but let all things be prepared before you: & he that goeth, let him not look back a lest sudden distruction shall come upon him.
13 Hearken & hear oh ye inhabitants of the Earth ✳ listen ye Elders of my Church together, & hear the voice of the Lord, for he calleth upon all men & he comandeth all men every where to repent: for behold, the Lord God hath sent forth the Angel crying through the midst of heaven; saying: prepare ye the way of the Lord, & make his paths straight, for the hour of his coming is nigh, when the Lamb shall stand upon Mount Zion, & with him an hundred & forty four thousand, having his father's name written in their foreheads:
15 wherefore, prepare ye for the coming of the Bridegroom: go ye, go ye out to meet him, for behold, he shall stand upon the Mount of Olivet, & upon the mighty Ocean, even the great deep & upon the Islands of the Sea, & upon the land of Zion — & he shall utter his voice out of Zion, & he shall speak from Jerusalem, & his voice shall be heard among all people, & it shall be the voice of many waters, & as the voice of a great thunder which shall break down the Mountains, & the vallies shall not be found; 16 he shall command the great deep & it shall be driven back into the North countries; & the Islands shall become one land; & the land of Jerusalem & the land of Zion, shall be turned back into their own place; & the earth shall be like as it was in the days before it was divided; 17 & the Lord even the Saviour shall stand in the midst of his people, & shall reign over all flesh; & they which who are in the North countries shall come in remembrance before the Lord; & their Prophets shall hear his voice, & shall no longer stay themselves & they shall smite the rocks, & the ice shall flow down at their presence 18 & an high way shall be cast up in the midst of the great deep; their enemies shall become a prey unto them; & in the barren deserts there shall come forth pools of living water; & the parched ground shall no longer be a thirsty land; & they shall bring forth their rich treasures

No. 4; 3 Nov. 1831; Page 117

From the midst of wickedness which is spiritual Babylon But verily thus saith the Lord let not your flight ~~not~~ be in haste but let all things be prepared before you & he that goeth let him not <look> back - lest sudden distruction shall come upon him Hearken & hear oh ye inhabitants of the Earth & listen ye Elders of my Church together & hear the voice of the Lord for he calleth upon all men & he commandeth all men every where to repent for behold the Lord God hath sent forth the Angel ~~with the everlasting gospel~~ crying through the midst of Heaven saying prepare ye the way of the Lord & make his paths strait for the hour of his coming is nigh when the Lamb shall stand upon Mount Zion & with him ~~a~~ <an> hundred & forty-four thousand having his fathers name written in their foreheads wherefore prepare ye for the coming of the Bride-groom Go ye [go] ye out to meet him for Behold he shall stand upon the Mount of Olivet & upon the mighty Ocean even the great deep & upon the Islands of the Sea & upon the Land of Zion - & he shall utter his voice out of Zion & he shall speak from Jerusalem & his voice shall be heard among all people & it shall be <a voice ┼ > as the voice of many waters & as the voice of a great thunder which shall break down the Mountains & the valies shall not be found he shall command the great deep & it shall be drive[n] back into the North countries & the Islands shall become one land & the land of Jerusalem & the Land of Zion shall be turned back into their own place & the earth shall be like as it was in the days before it was ~~before it was~~ divided & the Lord even the Saviour shall stand in the midst of his people <& shall reign> over all ~~the Earth~~ flesh & they ~~which~~ who are in the North countries shall come in remembrance before the Lord & their Prophets shall hear his voice & shall no longer stay themselves & they shall smite the rocks & the ice shall folow down at their presence & an high way shall be cast up in the midst of the great deep their enemies shall become a pray unto them & in the barren deserts there shall come forth pools of living water & the parched ground shall <no> longe[r] be a thirstly land & they shall bring forth their rich treasures

3. (Opposite). Book of Commandments manuscript page 117.

unto the Children of Ephraim my servants, & the boundaries
of the everlasting hills shall tremble at their presence. & they
shall fall down & be crowned with glory, even in
Zion, by the hands of the servants of the Lord, even the Chil-
-dren of Ephraim; & they shall be filled with songs of ever-
-lasting joy. Behold this is the blessing of the everlasting God
upon the toilers of Israel, & the richer blessing
upon the head of Ephraim & his fellows. & they also of the
tribe of Judah, after their pain, shall be sanctified in
holiness before the Lord to dwell in his presence day & night
forever & ever. & now verily saith the Lord, that these things
might be known among you, oh inhabitants of the
Earth, I have sent forth mine Angels, flying through the
midst of heaven, having the everlasting Gospel, who hath
appeared unto some, & hath committed it unto many, who shall
appear unto many that dwell on the Earth, & this gospel
shall be preached unto every Nation, & kindred, & tongue, &
people, & the servants of God shall go forth, saying, with a loud
voice, Fear God & give glory to him: for the hour of his judgement
is come: & worship him that made heaven, & earth, & the sea,
& the fountains of waters, calling upon the Lord day & night,
saying, Oh that thou wouldst rend the heavens, that thou
wouldest come down, that thy mountains might flow
down at thy presence & it shall be answered upon
their heads for the presence of the Lord shall be as the
melting fire burneth & as the fire which causeth the
waters to boil. Oh Lord thou shalt come down to make
known thy name to thine adversaries & all nations shall
tremble at thy presence. When thou doest terrible things,
things they look not for; yea, when thou camest down
& the Mountains flowed down at thy presence, thou shalt
meet him who rejoiceth & worketh righteousness, who remembereth
thee in thy ways: for since the beginning of the world have not
man heard nor perceived by the ear, neither hath the eye seen
O God, besides thee, have great things thou hast prepared for him who
awaiteth, for things thou shalt be sent unto us that that cometh

No. 4; 3 Nov. 1831, Continued; Page 118

unto the Children of Ephraim my servents & the boundaries of the everlasting hills shall tremble at their presence & these shall ~~thy~~ <they> fall down & be crowned with glory even in Zion by the hands of the Servents of the Lord even the children of Ephraim & they shall be filled with songs of everlasting Joy Behold this is the blessing of the everlasting God upon the ~~heads of the~~ tribes of Israel & the richer blessing upon the head of Ephraim & his fellows & they also of the tribe of Judah after their pain shall be sanctified in holiness before the Lord to dwell in his presence day & night for ever & ever & now verily saith the Lord that these things might be known among you oh inhabitants of the Earth I have sent forth mine Angel flying throug[h] the midst of heaven having the everlasting Gospel who hath appeared unto some & hath committed it unto man who shall appear unto many that dwell on the Earth & this gospel shall be preached unto every Nation & kindred & tongue & People & the Servents of God shall go forth saying with a loud voice fear God & give glory to him for the hour of his Judgment is come & worship him that made Heaven & earth & ~~the~~ sea & the fountains of waters calling upon the Lord day & night saying Oh that thou wouldst rend the heavens that thou wouldest come down that the mountains ~~would~~ <might> flow down at thy presence & it shall be answered upon their heads for the presence of the Lord shall be as the melting fire that burneth & as the fire ~~that~~ <which> causeth the waters to boil Oh Lord thou shalt come down to make ~~known~~ thy name <known> to thine advsaries & all nations shall trembl[e] at thy presence When thou doest teribl[e] things things ~~that~~ <[——]> they look not for yea when thou comest down & the Mountains flow down at thy presence thou shalt meet him ~~that~~ <who> rejoiceth & worketh reighteousness who remember thee in thy ways for since the begining of the world have not men heard nor perceived by the Ear neither hath ~~the~~ <any> eye seen O God besides thee how great things thou <hast> prepared for him that waiteth for thee & <it> shall be said who is this that cometh

down from god in heaven with his garments; yea,
from the regions which are not known, clothed in his glorious
apparel, traveling in the greatness of his strength; & I
shall speak I am he who spoke in righteousness, mighty to save,
& the Lord shall be red in his apparel, & his garments
like him that treadeth in the wine vat; & so
great shall be the glory of his presence, that the Sun
shall hide his face in shame; & the moon shall withhold its
light; & the stars shall be hurled from
& his vine shall be trod, I have trodden
alone, & have brought judgement upon other
people; & none were with me; & I have trampled
them in my fury, & I did tread upon them in
anger; & their blood have I sprinkled upon my garments,
& I have stained all my raiment; for this was the day
of vengeance which was in my heart; & now the year
of my redeemed is come; & they shall mention the loving
kindness of their Lord, & all that he hath bestowed upon
them according to his goodness, & according to his loving
kindness, forever & ever; in all their affliction he was afflicted,
& the angel of his presence saved them; & in his love &
his pity, he redeemed them, & he bear them, &
them all the days of old; yea, & Enoch also, & they who
were with him; the prophets that were before him
& Noah also, & they who were before him & Moses also,
& they who were before him, & from Moses to Elijah
& from Elijah to John, who were with Christ in his
resurrection, & the Holy Apostles, with Abraham, Isaac,
& Jacob, shall be in the presence of the Lamb; & the graves
of the saints shall be opened, & they shall come forth & stand
on the right hand of the Lamb, when he shall stand upon
mount zion; & upon the Holy City, the new jerusalem, &
& they shall sing the song of the lamb day & night for ever
& ever—for this cause, that men might be partakers
of the glories which is to be revealed, the Lord sent forth the
fullness of his gospel, his everlasting covenant,

No. 4; 3 Nov. 1831, Continued; Page 11[9]

down from god in heaven with ~~thy~~ <died> garments yea from the regions ~~that is~~
<which are> not known clothed in his gloriou[s] appearl travling in the greatness of his
strength & he ~~speak~~ <say> I am he <who spake> in righteousness mighty to save & the
Lord shall be ~~read~~ read in his appearl & his garments like him that treadeth in the wine
~~path~~ <vat> & so great shall be the glory of his presence that the Sun shall hide his face
in shame & the moon shall ~~be blown out~~ <with hold its light> & the stars shall be hur-
relled from their place ~~sockets~~ & his voice shall be heard I have trodden the p[———]
~~winepress~~ <vat press> alone & have brought Judgment upon all people & none ~~was~~
<were> with me & I have trampelled them in my fury & I did tread upon them in
mine anger & their blood have I sprinkled upon my garments & ~~have~~ stained all my raiment for this was the day of vengeance which was in my heart & now the year of my
redeemed is come & they shall mention the loving kindness of their Lord & all that he
~~hath~~ <has> bestowed upo[n] them according to his goodness & according to his loving
kindness forever & ever in all their afflictions he was afflicted & the angel of his presence saved them & in his love & in his pity he redeemed them & ~~did~~ <he> bear them &
~~did~~ carried them all the days of old yea & Enoch also & they ~~which~~ <who> were with
him the Prophets ~~which~~ <that> were before him & Noah also & they ~~which~~ <who>
were before him & ~~Elijah~~ <Moses> also & they ~~which~~ <who> were before him &
from ~~Elijah~~ <Mosses> to ~~Moses~~ <Elijah> & from ~~Moses~~ <Elijah> to John who were
with Christ in his resurrection & the Holy Apostles with Abraham Isaac & Jacob shall
be in the presence of the lamb & the graves of the saints shall be opened & they shall
come forth & stand on the right hand of the Lamb when he shall stand upon mount
Zion & upon the Holy City the New Jerusalem ~~wh[——]~~ & they shall sing the Song of
the lamb day & night for ever & ever & for this cause that men might be <made> per-
takers of the glories which were <to be> revealed the Lord sent forth the fullness of ~~the~~
<his> gospel ~~& the~~ <his> everlasting covenant

420

appearing in plainness & simplicity, to prepare the weak
for those things which are coming <del>upon</del> on the earth; & for
the Lords <del>command</del> in the day when the weak <ins>shall</ins> <del>& little</del> confound the wise are before
a strong nation, & two should put their tens of thousand
to flight; & by the weak things of the earth, the Lord should
thresh the Nations <del>of the earth</del> by the power of his Spirit.

[& for this cause these commandments were given; they
were commanded to be kept from the world in the
<del>time that they</del> were given, but now are to go forth unto all]³⁹

[flesh]¹⁴ & this according to the mind & <del>the</del> will of the Lord;
<del>and wheresoever</del> over all flesh & unto him that repenteth
& sanctifieth himself before the Lord shall be given eternal
life; <del>and upon them</del> that harken not to the voice of the Lord, shall
be <del>fulfilled</del> that which was written by the Prophet
<del>Moses</del> <del>saith</del> that they should be cut off from among the
people.³⁴ & also that which was written by the Prophet, Malachi

for Behold the day cometh that <del>shall burn</del> shall <del>be</del> as an Oven; & all
<del>the proud</del> & they that do yet, & all that do wickedly, shall be
<del>stubble</del> & the day that cometh shall burn them up saith the
<del>Lord of hosts</del> that it shall leave them neither root nor
<del>branch.</del>³⁵ wherefore this shall be the answer of the
<del>Lord</del> unto them that day when I came unto my own, as man
among you received me, & <del>ye</del> were driven out; when I
called again there was none of you to answer; yet
my arm was not shortened at all, that I could not
redeem, neither my power to deliver;³⁶ Behold at my
rebuke I dry up the Sea, I make the Rivers a wilderness; their fish stinketh, & dieth for thirst. I
clothe the Heavens with blackness, & make Sackcloth
their covering;³⁷ & this shall ye have of my hand, ye shall
lie down in sorrow;³⁸ Behold & lo there are none to deliver
you, for ye obeyed not my voice, when I called unto you out
of the Heavens; ye believed not my Servants; & when they
were sent unto you ye received them not; wherefore they
sealed up the testimony, & bound up the law, & ye were
delivered up unto darkness; these shall go away into outer

No. 4; 3 Nov. 1831, Continued; Page 120

Reasoning in plainess & simplicity to prepare the weak for those things which are coming ~~upon~~ on the earth & for the Lords Errand in the ~~days~~ when the <weak should confound the wise> & the little one become a strong nation & two shall put their tens of
thousands to flight & by the weak things of the Earth the Lord should thresh the Nations ~~of the Earth~~ by the power of his spirit & for this cause these commandments were
given they were commanded to be kept from the world in the day <that> they were
given but now are to go forth unto all flesh & this according to the mind & ~~the~~ will of
the Lord who ~~reigneth~~ <ruleth> over all flesh & unto him that repenteth & sanctifieth
himself before the Lord shall be given eternal life & ~~they~~ <upon them> that harken not
to the voice of the Lord shall be fulfilled that which was written by the Prophet Moses -
that they should be cut off from among the people & also that which was written by the
Prophet Malachi for Behold the day cometh that ~~burneth~~ <shall burn> as an oven & all
the proud ~~& they that do~~ yea & all that do wickedly shall be stuble & the day that
cometh shall burn them up saith the Lord of hosts that it shall leve them neither root
nor branch wherefore this shall be the answer of the Lord <unto them> in that day
when I came unto my own no man among you received me & you ~~are~~ <were> driven
out when I called again there was none of you to answer yet my arm was not shortened
at all that I could not redeem neither my power to deliver Behold at my rebuke I dry up
the Sea I make the rivers a wilderness their fish stinketh & dieth for thirst I Clothe the
Heavens with blackness ⋆ make sackCoth their covering & this shall <ye> have ~~at~~ of
my hand ye shall lie down ~~with~~ <in> sorrow Behold & lo there are none to deliver you
for ye obeyed not my ~~Voice~~ <voice> when I called ~~unto~~ you out of the Heavens ye believed not my Servants & when they were sent unto you ye received them not wherefore they sealed up the testimony & bound up the Law & ye were delivered ~~up~~ <~~H~~
over> unto darkness these shall go away into outer

presence of Heaven, for as the Lord exp[...] the see store, &
hear the voice of the Lord saying; their all shall bow the knee,
& every tongue shall confess to him who sitteth upon the throne
[...] & ever; for they shall be judged according to their works;
& every man shall receive according to his own works, & his own
dominion, in the mansions which are prepared; & they shall be
servants of the most high, but where god & Christ dwells they
cannot come, worlds without end; this is the end of the vision
which we were commanded to write while we were yet in
the spirit.

But great & marvelous are the works of the Lord & the mysteries
of his Kingdom which he shewed unto us, which surpasseth all
understanding in glory, & in might, & in dominion, which he
commanded us we should not write, while we were yet
in the spirit, & are not lawful for man to utter; neither
is man capable to make them known, for they are only to
be seen & understood by the power of the holy Ghost, which God
bestows on them who love him & purify themselves before
him, to whom he grants this privilege of seeing & knowing for
themselves; that through the power & manifestation of the spirit
while in the flesh, they may be able to bear his presence in
the world of glory. ≡ to god & the Lamb be glory, & honor, &
dominion, forever & ever, amen.

83 REVELATION given to ~~F. G. Williams~~ Hiram

Portage Co. March 15, 1832 Co. Ohio

Verily I say unto you my servant ~~Frederick~~ listen to the word of
him who speaketh, to the word of the Lord your God, & hearken to
the calling wherewith you are called, even to be a high Priest in
my church & counsellor unto my servant Joseph, unto whom
I have given the keys of the Kingdom which belong always to
the presidency of the high Priest hood; therefore verily I acknowledge him & will bless him, & also thee, in as much as thou
art faithful in counsel, in the office which I have appointed
unto you, & in prayer always vocally & in thy heart in public
& in private, also in thy ministry, in proclaiming the
gospel in the land of the living, & among thy brethren;

No. 5; 16 Feb. 1832; Page [139]

firmanment of Heaven or as the sand upon the sea shore & heard the voice of the Lord saying these all shall bow the knee & every tongue shall confess to him who sitteth upon the throne forever & ever for they shall be judged according to their works & every man shall receive according to his own works & his own dominion in the mansions which are prepared & they shall be servants of the most high but where God & Christ dwells they cannot come worlds without end this is the end of the vision which we <saw which we> were commanded to write while we were yet in the Spirit But great & marvelous are the works of the Lord & the mysteries of his kingdom which he shewed unto us which surpaseth all understanding in glory & in might & in dominion which he commanded us ~~that~~ we should not write while we were yet in the Spirit & are not Lawful for men to utter neither is man capable to make them known for they are only to be seen & understood by the power of the holy Gohost which God bestows on those who love him & purify themselves before him to whom he grants this privilege of seeing & knowing for themselves that through the power & manifestation of the Spirit while in the flesh they may be able to bear his presence in the world of glory & to God & the Lamb be glory & honor & dominion forever & ever amen

No. 6; 15 Mar. 1832

Revelation given to ~~Jesse Gause~~ <F G Williams> Hiram Portage # March 15. 1832 # Co. Ohio
Verily <verily> I say unto you my servant ~~Jesse~~ <Frederick G Williams> listen to the voice of him who speaketh, to the word of the Lord your God, & hearken to the calling wherewith you are called, even to be a high Priest in my Church & counsellor unto my Servant Joseph, unto whom I have given the keys of the Kingdom which belongs always to the presidency of the high Priest Hood, therefore verily I acknowledge him & will bless him, & also thee, in as much as thou art faithful in Counsel, in the office which I have appointed unto you, & in prayer always vocally & in thy heart in publick & in private also in thy ministry, in proclaiming the gospel in the Land of the Living & among thy brethren;

7. (Opposite). Book of Commandments manuscript page 139.
Courtesy Library-Archives, Reorganized Church of Jesus
Christ of Latter Day Saints, Independence, Missouri.

and in doing these things thou wilt do the greatest good
unto thy fellow beings, & will promote the glory of him
who is your Lord. wherefore be faithful, stand in the office
I have appointed you, succor the weak, lift up the hands
which hang down, & strengthen the feeble knees; & if thou
art faithful unto the end thou shalt have a crown
of immortality & eternal life in the mansions which
I have prepared in the house of my father behold & lo
these are the words of Alpha & Omega even Jesus
Christ AMEN

No. 6; 15 Mar. 1832, Continued; Page 140

and in doing these things thou wilt do the greatest good unto thy fellow beings, & will promote the g<lo>lory of him who is your Lord. wherefore be faithful, stand in the office I have appointed you succor the weak, lift up the hands which hang down, & strengthen the feeble knees; & if thou art faithful unto the end thou shalt have a crown of immortality & eternal life in the mansion which I have prepared in the house of my father behold & lo these are the words of Alpha & Omega even Jesus Christ Amen

8. (Opposite). Book of Commandments manuscript page 140.
Courtesy Library-Archives, Reorganized Church of Jesus
Christ of Latter Day Saints, Independence, Missouri.

Appendix C.
Revelations Printed in
The Evening and the Morning Star[1]

Document Number	LDS D&C	RLDS D&C	Date, Page Number, and Consecutive Page Numbers		BC [in press]
5	7:1-3	7:1	May 1833	6; 94	6:1
23	22	20	June 1832	1-2; 1-2	23
24	20	17	June 1832	1; 1	24
	20	17	June 1833	1-2; 97-98	24
28	27	26	Mar. 1833	6; 78	28
29	29	28	Sept. 1832	2; 26	29
	29:16-20	28:4-5	June 1833	7; 103	29:19-23
41	38	38	Jan. 1833	5-6; 61-62	40
	38:31-33	38:7	Apr. 1833	4; 84	40:27-29
45	42:11-72	42:4-19	July 1832	1; 9	44:12-54
	42:30-31	42:8	Nov. 1832	6; 46	44:26
46	43:15-35	43:4-8	Oct. 1832	2-3; 34-35	45:14-44
48	42:78-93	42:21-23	Oct. 1832	2; 34	47:1-20
49	42:74-77	42:20	July 1832	1; 9	47:21-24
50	45:1-67, 71	45:1-12, 14	June 1832	2; 2	48:1-60, 67
51	46	46	Aug. 1832	1; 17	49
	46:2, 7-9	46:1, 3-4	May 1833	3; 91	49:2, 9
	46:13-16	46:5-6	May 1833	2; 90	49:14-16
54	49	49	Nov. 1832	7; 47	52
55	50	50	Aug. 1832	1; 17	53
64	58:1-11	58:1-3	Mar. 1833	4; 76	59:1-14
	58:35-36	58:7	Nov. 1832	6; 46	59:45-47
	58:55-56	58:12	June 1832	2; 2	59:68-69
65	59	59	July 1832	1; 9	60
	59:1-4	59:1	Feb. 1833	5; 69	60:1-7

---

1. Document nos. 23-24, 28, 30 (LDS D&C 28; RLDS D&C 27), 38 (LDS D&C 35; RLDS D&C 34), and 45 were published in *The Telegraph* (Painesville, Ohio) in 1831-32. This was prior to publication in the *Evening and the Morning Star* at Independence, Missouri.

Document Number	LDS D&C	RLDS D&C	Date, Page Number, and Consecutive Page Numbers		BC [in press]
67	61	61	Dec. 1832	5; 53	62
	61:24-25	61:4	Nov. 1832	6; 46	62:26-27
69	63:1-64	63:1-16	Feb. 1833	6-7; 70-71	64:1-76
72	65	65	Sept. 1832	2; 26	
73	1	1	Mar. 1833	6; 78	1
	1:17-23	1:4	Dec. 1832	6; 54	1:4
76	68	68	Oct. 1832	3; 35	
	68:25-28	68:4	Mar. 1833	5; 77	
77	133	108	May 1833	1-2; 89-90	
	133:12-15	108:5	June 1832	2; 2	
78	69:5-6	69:2	Aug. 1832	7; 23	
82	72:1-8	72:1-2	Dec. 1832	5-6; 53-54	
83	72:9-26	72:3-5	Dec. 1832	6; 54	
	72:16-19	72:4	July 1833	7; 111	
	72:24-26	72:5	June 1832	2; 2	
88	76	76	July 1832	2-3; 10-11	
	76:50-70	76:5	Dec. 1832	3; 51	
	76:99-108	76:7	Feb. 1833	5; 69	
98	83	82	Jan. 1833	6; 62	
100	84:99-102	83:17	Jan. 1833	3; 59	
101	85		Jan. 1833	5; 61	
104	88:117-26	85:36-38	Feb. 1833	5; 69	
105	88:127-37	85:39-44	Mar.1833	6; 78	

Appendix D.
Locations of Manuscript Revelations

The following list of manuscripts in the possession of the LDS church does not include copies recorded in the Manuscript History or pre-1841 revelations in the Book of the Law of the Lord.

Document Number	Published LDS D&C	RLDS D&C	Date	Manuscripts NKW	KRB Page #	Books A	B	C	LDS archives
2	4	4	Feb.1829						X
3	5	5	Mar. 1829	X					
5	7	7	Apr. 1829						X
14	17	15	June 1829		119-20				
22	21	19	6 Apr. 1830						X
23	22	20	16 Apr. 1830				X		X
24	20	17	June 1830			X	X		X
28	27	26	4 Sept. 1830						X
29	29	28	Sept. 1830	X					
35	32	31	Oct. 1830		83-84				
36	33	32	Oct. 1830						X
38	35	34	Dec. 1830						X
39	36	35	Dec. 1830						X
44	41	41	4 Feb. 1831		93-94				
45	42	42	9 Feb. 1831			X	X		X
48	42	42	23 Feb. 1831			X			X
49	42	42	23 Feb. 1831		117-18	X			X
50	45	45	7 Mar. 1831						X
52	47	47	8 Mar. 1831		12-13				
55	50	50	9 May 1831			X	X		
56	51	51	20 May 1831		87-89		X		
57			May 1831		91-92				
58	52	52	June 1831						X
59	53	53	June 1831	X			X		
62	56	56	15 June 1831						X
63	57	57	20 July 1831		89-91		X		
65	59	59	7 Aug. 1831	X		X			
67	61	61	12 Aug. 1831				X		

Document Number	Published LDS D&C	Published RLDS D&C	Date	Manuscripts NKW	KRB Page #	Books A	B	C	LDS archives
69	63	63	30 Aug. 1831	X			X		
70	64	64	11 Sept. 1831	X		X	X		X
71	66	66	29 Oct. 1831		95-97				X
72	65	65	30 Oct. 1831		87				X
78	107	104	Nov. 1831	X	84-86				
81	71	71	1 Dec. 1831	X	11-12				
82	72	72	4 Dec. 1831	X	13	X			X
83	72	72	4 Dec. 1831	X	13-15	X			X
84	73	73	10 Jan. 1832	X					
85	75	75	25 Jan. 1832	X		X			
86	75	75	25 Jan. 1832	X		X			
87	76	76	16 Feb. 1832		1-10	X	X		
88			27 Feb. 1832		10				
89	74	74	Feb.-Mar. 1832		94-95, 117				
90	78	77	1 Mar. 1832	X	15-17				
91	80	79	7 Mar. 1832		18-19				
92			Mar. 1832	X					
93	79	78	12 Mar. 1832		12				
94	81	80	15 Mar. 1832		17-18				
95	77		Mar. 1832						X
96			20 Mar. 1832	X	19				
98	83	82	30 Apr. 1832	X	93		X		
99	99	96	29 Aug. 1832		19-20				
100	84	83	22-23 Sept. 1832	X	20-31				
101	85		27 Nov. 1832						X
102	86	84	6 Dec. 1832		31-32		X		
103	87		25 Dec. 1832	X	32-33		X		X
104	88	85	27-28 Dec. 1832		33-46		X		X
105	88	85	3 Jan. 1833		47-48				
106			6 Jan. 1833						X
107			27 Feb. 1833		48-49				
108	89	86	27 Feb. 1833		49-51		X		X
109	90	87	8 Mar. 1833	X	51-55				
110	91	88	9 Mar. 1833		55		X		
111	92	89	15 Mar. 1833		55				X
112	93	90	6 May 1833	X	56-59				
113	95	92	1 June 1833		59-60				
114	96	93	4 June 1833		60-61				
115	97	94	2 Aug. 1833		61-64				X
116	94	91	2 Aug. 1833		64-66				X

Document Number	Published LDS D&C	Published RLDS D&C	Date	Manuscripts NKW	KRB Page #	Books A	B	C	LDS archives
117	98	95	6 Aug. 1833		66–71				X
118	100	97	12 Oct. 1833	X	71–72				
119	101	98	16 Dec. 1833		73–83				X
120	103	100	24 Feb. 1834	X	108–111			X	X
121	104	101	23 Apr. 1834		100–107		X		
122			28 Apr. 1834		111		X		
123	105	102	22 June 1834	X	97–100				X
124	106	103	25 Nov. 1834		116				
125			5 Dec. 1834						X
126	107	104	Apr. 1835	X	84–86				

Document Number	Published LDS D&C	Published RLDS D&C	Date	Manuscripts JS Journal 1835-36	SB	BLL	LDS archives
127			27 Oct. 1835	X			
128			1 Nov. 1835	X			
129			2 Nov. 1835	X			
130			3 Nov. 1835	X			
131			7 Nov. 1835	X			
132			8 Nov. 1835	X			
133			14 Nov. 1835	X			
134			16 Nov. 1835	X			
135			16 Nov. 1835	X			
136	108		26 Dec. 1835	X			
137	137		21 Jan. 1836	X			
138	110		3 Apr. 1836	X			
139	111		6 Aug. 1836				X
140	112	105	23 July 1837		X		X
141			4 Sept. 1837		X		
142			7 Jan. 1838				X
143			12 Jan. 1838		X		X
144			12 Jan. 1838		X		X
145			12 Jan. 1838		X		X
146	113		Mar. 1838		X		
147	114		11 Apr. 1838		X		
148			17 Apr. 1838		X		X
149	115		26 Apr. 1838		X		X
150	118		8 July 1838		X		X

Document Number	Published LDS D&C	RLDS D&C	Date	Manuscripts JS Journal 1835–36	SB	BLL	LDS archives
151			8 July 1838	X			
152	119	106	8 July 1838	X			X
153	120		8 July 1838	X			
154	117		8 July 1838	X			X
155	121–22		20 Mar. 1839				X
156	124		19 Jan. 1841		X		X
159	126		9 July 1841		X		
160			2 Dec. 1841		X		
161			22 Dec. 1841		X		
162			22 Dec. 1841		X		
163			28 Jan. 1842		X		
164			7 Apr. 1842				X
165			19 May 1842		X		
166			27 July 1842				X
167	127		1 Sept. 1842		X		X
168	128		6 Sept. 1842		X		X
169	132		12 July 1843				X

Key

NKW	=	Newel K. Whitney Collection
KRB	=	Kirtland Revelations Book
A	=	"Book of Commandments, Law and Covenants; Book A"
B	=	"Book of Commandments, Law and Covenants; Book B"
C	=	"Book of Commandments, Law and Covenants; Book C"

JS Journal:

1835–36	=	Joseph Smith Journal, 1835–36
SB	=	Scriptory Book of Joseph Smith
BLL	=	Book of the Law of the Lord

Appendix E.
Six Additional Revelations
Given through Joseph Smith

1. Canadian copyright revelation received ca. January 1830

One incident which occurred while the Book of Mormon was at the printer throws light on the importance Joseph Smith placed on his copyright to that book. Hiram Page, one of the eight witnesses to the book, states that Smith sent Oliver Cowdery, himself, and two others to Canada to sell the copyright to the Book of Mormon in that country. However, they returned empty-handed. It is not known if the text of this revelation is extant.[1]

Page related his experience to William E. McLellin in 1848, eighteen years later. In his letter Page criticized Joseph Smith because the expected outcome of their trip was unfulfilled. Page wrote (original spelling retained):

> Joseph [Smith, Jr.] he[a]rd that there was a chance to Sell a copyright in canada for any useful book that was used in the States Joseph thought this would be a good opertunity to get a handsom[e] Sum of money which was to be (after the expencis [expenses] were taken out) for the exclusive benefit of the Smith famaly [family] and was to be at the disposal of Joseph accordingly Oliver Cowdery Joseph Knights, Hiram Page and Joseah Stoel [Josiah Stowell] were chosen ([illegible words] by revilation) to do the buisanse [business]; we were living some 30 to 100 miles apart the neces[s]ary preperation was made (by them) in a Sly manor [manner] So as to keep martin Har[r]is from drawing a Share of the money, it was told me we were to go by revilation but when we assembled at father Smiths; there was no revilation for us to go but we were all anctious [anxious] to get a revilation to go; and when it came we were to go to kingston where we were to Sell if they would not harden their hearts; but when we got their [there]; there was no purchaser neither were they authorized at kingston to buy rights for the provence [province]; but little york was the place where Such buisanse [business] had to be done; we were to get 8,000 dollars we were treated with the best of respects by all we met with in kingston — by the above we may See learn how a revilation may be rece[i]ved and the one person rece[i]ving it not be benefited[2]

Eight thousand dollars was a great deal of money in Smith's time. It is unlikely that anyone would have invested such a large amount of money for a copyright. Page said they went to Kingston, Ontario, Canada, and "were treated with the best of respects." He indicated, however, that Smith was "not benefited."

---

1. G. T. Harrison published a purported copy of the revelation in 1954, but he appears to have made up the text. See *Mormons Are Peculiar People* (New York: Vantage Press, 1954), 74-75.

2. Page to McLellin, 2 Feb. 1848, Fishing River, Missouri, photocopy, RLDS archives. Thanks to Ronald E. Romig, RLDS archivist, for proofing the letter.

Page did not see anything wrong with Smith wanting to sell the copyright. David Whitmer, who recounted the event many years later, did not seem concerned either, but was disturbed because Smith received a revelation through the seer stone that did not come to pass.[3] The revelation to sell the copyright in Canada was written down and recorded but never published. McLellin, who joined the church in August 1831, wrote in 1872 the following:

> But again, Joseph [Smith, Jr.] had a revelation for Oliver [Cowdery] and friends to go to Canada to get a copy-right secured in that Dominion to the Book of Mormon. It proved so false that he never would have it recorded, printed or published, I have seen and read a copy of it, so that I know it existed. So do all those connected with him at the time. ... But in the spring of 1830 the revelation relative to the Canada mission was certainly untrue.[4]

McLellin's comment that the revelation was not recorded evidently refers to its being recorded for the BC manuscript. There was no plan to have it published in that compilation. McLellin also mentioned that he read the revelation in manuscript form. He wrote in 1877, "J[oseph] Smith's revelation for Cowdery to go to Canada was never printed. M[artin]. Harris had the copy that I read in Manuscript."[5] Additionally, McLellin commented:

> When the Book [of Mormon] was translated, and at the printer's with the copy-right secured, Joseph [Smith, Jr.] delivered a long revelation for O[liver]. Cowdery and others to go to Kingston in Canada, and get a copy-right in that dominion to the book, in order to sell it and make money out of its sale. They went, but, did not succeed, and the revelation proved so false, that Joseph never would have it printed or put with his other revelations either.[6]

David Whitmer in 1887 also mentioned the Canadian revelation. He wrote:

> Joseph [Smith, Jr.] looked into the hat in which he placed the stone, and received a revelation that some of the brethren should go to Toronto [sic], Canada, and that they would sell the copy-right of the Book of Mormon. Hiram [P]age and Oliver Cowdery went to Toronto [sic] on this mission, but they failed entirely to sell the copy-right, returning without any money. Joseph was at my father's house [in Fayette] when they returned. I was there also, and am an eye witness to these facts. Jacob Whitmer and John Whitmer were also present when Hiram Page and Oliver Cowdery returned from Canada. Well, we were all in great trouble; and we asked Joseph how it was that he had received a revelation from the Lord for some brethren to go to Toronto [sic] and sell the

3. David Whitmer in an interview published in the *Des Moines Daily News*, 16 Oct. 1886, and David Whitmer, *An Address to All Believers in Christ* (Richmond, MO: author, 1887), 30-31.

4. McLellin to Joseph Smith III, commenced July 1872, RLDS archives. McLellin also related that the revelation was received in 1829. See Joseph Fielding Smith, comp., *Life of Joseph F. Smith, Sixth President of The Church of Jesus Christ of Latter-day Saints* (Salt Lake City: Deseret News Press, 1938), 240, and in a Notebook (21), J. L. Traughber Collection, Manuscript 666, Manuscripts Division, J. Willard Marriott Library, University of Utah, Salt Lake City.

5. McLellin to John L. Traughber, 7 May 1877, copied by Traughber, Traughber Collection, Accession 1446, Box 2, Marriott Library.

6. McLellin to John L. Traughber, 19 Feb. 1877, copy by Traughber, Traughber Collection, Box 2. See also letter of John L. Traughber, no date, in W. Wyl [Wilhelm Ritter von Wymetal], *Mormon Portraits or The Truth about the Mormon Leaders from 1830 to 1886* (Salt Lake City: Tribune Printing and Publishing Co., 1886), 311.

copy-right, and the brethren had utterly failed in their understanding. Joseph did not know how it was, so he enquired of the Lord about it, and behold the following revelation came through the stone: *"Some revelations are of God: some revelations are of man: and some revelations are of the devil."*[7] So we see that the revelation to go to Toronto [sic] and sell the copy-right was not of God, but was of the devil or of the heart of man.[8]

John L. Traughber had information from both McLellin and Whitmer concerning the revelation. He wrote:

Dr. William E. McLellan, who was one of the original Mormon "Twelve," has stated to me time and again that he saw and read a long revelation which Joseph Smith delivered to Oliver Cowdery and Hiram Page to go to Kingston, Canada and get out a copyright for the Book of Mormon under that dominion, and sell it for the purpose of paying E.B. Grandin of Palmyra, New York, for printing the first edition of the Book of Mormon. Dr. McLellan stated emphatically that the revelation promised complete success to Cowdery and Page in their mission to Canada. In September, 1879, I closely questioned David Whitmer as to the facts concerning the revelation on the copyright. He stated that it was delivered in January, 1830, and that Cowdery and Page crossed the lake on the ice and went to Kingston, and did just as the revelation required them to do; but they completely failed in their endeavor to get a copyright.[9]

2. REVELATION RECEIVED WEST OF JACKSON COUNTY, MISSOURI, ON 17 JULY 1831

In July 1831 after the arrival of Joseph Smith, Jr., and others in Jackson County, Missouri, plans were made to preach to the Native Americans. Smith received a directive on intermarriage with the Indians. At a later date William W. Phelps wrote, evidently from memory, what he claimed was part or the substance of this revelation:

Part — of a revelation by Joseph Smith Jun. given over the boundary, west of Jackson Co. Missouri, on Sunday morning, July 17, 1831, when Seven Elders, viz: Joseph Smith Jun. Oliver Cowdery, W.W. Phelps, Martin Harris, Joseph Coe, Ziba Peterson and Joshua Lewis united their hearts in prayer, in a private place, to inquire of the Lord who should preach the first sermon to the remnants of the Lamanites and Nephites, and the people of that Section, that should assemble that day in the Indian country, to hear the gospel, and the revelations according to the Book of Mormon.

Among the company, there being neither pen, ink or paper, Joseph [Smith, Jr.] remarked that the Lord could preserve his words as he had ever done, till the time appointed, and proceeded:

Verily, verily, saith the Lord your Redeemer, even Jesus Christ, the light and the life of the world, ye can not discerne [discern] with your natural eyes, the design and the purpose of your Lord and your God, in bringing you thus far into the wilderness for a trial of your faith, and to be especial witnesses, to bear testimony of this land, upon

7. A March 1831 revelation says, "that ye may not be seduced by evil spirits, or doctrines of devils, or the commandments of men, for some are of men, and others of devils" (see document no. 51, LDS D&C 46:7; RLDS D&C 46:3).

8. Whitmer, *An Address to All Believers in Christ*, 31, emphasis in original. See also interview with Whitmer in the *Omaha Herald*, 17 Oct. 1886; reprinted in Lyndon W. Cook, ed., *David Whitmer Interviews: A Restoration Witness* (Orem, UT: Grandin Book Co., 1991), 203.

9. J. L. Traughber, "False Prophecies," 1, Traughber Collection, Box 2, folder 43. McLellin changed the way he spelled his last name to McLellan.

which the zion of God shall be built up in the last days, when it is redeemed.

Verily, inasmuch as ye are united in calling upon my name to know my will concerning who shall preach to the inhabitants that shall assemble this day to learn what new doctrine you have to teach them, you have done wisely, for so did the prophets anciently, even Enoch, and Abraham, and others: and therefore, it is my will that my servant Oliver Cowdery should open the meeting with prayer; that my servant W. W. Phelps should preach the discourse; and that my servants Joseph Coe and Ziba Peterson should bear testimony as they shall be moved by the Holy Spirit. This will be pleasing in the sight of your Lord.

Verily I say unto you, ye are laying the foundation of a great work for the salvation of as many as will believe and repent, and obey the ordinances of the gospel, and continue faithful to the end: For, as I live, saith the Lord, so shall they live.

Verily I say unto you that the wisdom of man in his fallen state, knoweth not the purposes and the privileges of my holy priesthood. but ye shall know when ye receive a fulness by reason of the anointing: For it is my will, that in time, ye should take unto you wives of the Lamanites and Nephites, that their posterity may become white, delightsome and Just, for even now their females are more virtuous than the gentiles.

Gird up your loins and be prepared for the mighty work of the Lord to prepare the world for my second coming to meet the tribes of Israel according to the predictions of all the holy prophets since the beginning; For the final desolation, and decrees upon Babylon: For, as the everlasting gospel is carried from this land, in love for peace, to gather mine elect from the four quarters of the earth, for Zion,— even so shall rebellion follow after speedily, with hatred for war until the consumption decreed hath made a full end of all the kingdoms and nations that strive to govern themselves by the laws and precepts, and force and powers of men under the curse of sin, in all the world.

Verily I say unto you, that the day of vexation and vengeance is nigh at the doors of this nation, when wicked, ungodly and daring men will rise up in wrath and might, and go forth in anger, like as the dust is driven by [a] terrible wind; and they will be the means of the destruction of the government, and cause the death and misery of man[y] souls, but the faithful among my people shall be preserved in holy places, during all these tribulations.

Be patient, therefore, possessing your souls in peace and love, and keep the faith that is now delivered unto you for the gathering of scattered Israel, and lo, I am with you, though ye cannot see me, till I come: even so. Amen.

Reported by W.W.P. [William W. Phelps]

About three years after this was given, I asked brother Joseph [Smith, Jr.] privately, how "we," that were mentioned in the revelation could take wives from the "natives"—as we were all married men? He replied instantly "In th[e] same manner that Abraham took Hagar and Katurah [Keturah]; and Jacob took Rachel Bilhah and Zilpah: by revelation—the saints of the Lord are always directed by revelation."[10]

While the text of this revelation was not written in July 1831, intermarriage with the Indians was discussed. Four months later Ezra Booth wrote:

10. Manuscript in LDS archives; versification omitted. See also Phelps to Brigham Young, 12 Aug. 1861, LDS archives. The wording "until the consumption hath made a full end of all the kingdoms and nations" and "death and misery of man[y] souls" is similar to LDS D&C 87:1, 6. The mention of "the destruction of the government" may indicate when Phelps recorded the revelation—near the start of the American Civil War which commenced on 12 April 1861. For expectation of the end time during this period, see James B. Allen, *Trials of Discipleship: The Story of William Clayton, a Mormon* (Urbana: University of Illinois Press, 1987), 304-308.

In addition to this, and to co-operate with it, it has been made known by revelation, that it will be pleasing to the Lord, should they form a matrimonial alliance with the Natives; and by this means the Elders, who comply with the thing so pleasing to the Lord, and for which the Lord has promised to bless those who do it abundantly, gain a residence in the Indian territory, independent of the agent.[11]

Phelps included a copy of this revelation in a letter to LDS church president Brigham Young. Commenting on the letter to Young, David J. Whittaker wrote:

Several things are apparent: (1) While the Book of Mormon strongly teaches that God removes the curse of the dark skin, this document implies that intermarriage can; (2) Some scholars think that this revelation was the initial impetus for plural marriage, as some of the missionaries had wives in Ohio; and (3) This document seems to have begun the Mormon practice of marrying native Americans. Some of the contents of the document better fit an 1861 context and it is possible that Phelps added his own understanding thirty years later. Ezra Booth confirms early talk about marrying Indians, but the reasons for doing so probably did not include polygamy or even changing skin color, but rather facilitating entrance into the reservation for missionary work ...[12]

3. REVELATION RECEIVED AT KIRTLAND, OHIO, CA. NOVEMBER 1836 FOR IRA AMES

Joseph [Smith, Jr.] received the Word of the Lord about as follows. Verily thus saith the Lord unto my servant Ira [Ames] it is not my will that you should go up to the land of Missouri until the residue of my church go.[13]

4. REVELATION RECEIVED AT KIRTLAND, OHIO, ON 5 JANUARY 1837 REGARDING THE KIRTLAND SAFETY SOCIETY

Wilford Woodruff, an elder in the church, wrote:

I visited the office of the Kirtland Safety Society & saw the first money that was issued by the Treasurer or Society. It was given to Brother [Jacob] Bump (in exchange for other notes) who was the first to Circulate it.

I also he[a]rd President Joseph Smith jr. declare in the presence of F[rederick G.] Williams, D[avid]. Whitmer, S[ylvester?]. Smith, W[arren]. Parrish, & others in the Deposit Office that he had received that morning the Word of the Lord upon the Subject of the Kirtland Safety Society. He was alone in a room by himself & he had not ownly [only] the voice of the Spirit upon the Subject but even an audable [audible] voice. He did not tell us at that time what the LORD said upon the subject but remarked that if we would give heed to the Commandments the Lord had given this morning all would be well.[14]

11. Booth to Rev. Ira Eddy, 6 Dec. 1831, *Ohio Star* 2 (8 Dec. 1831): 1.

12. David J. Whittaker, "Mormons and Native Americans: A Historical and Biographical Introduction," *Dialogue: A Journal of Mormon Thought* 18 (Winter 1985): 35. See also Richard S. Van Wagoner, *Mormon Polygamy: A History*, 2nd ed. (Salt Lake City: Signature Books, 1989), 12-13.

13. "Journal and Record of the Life & Family of Ira Ames," microfilm #A-311, Utah State Historical Society, Salt Lake City, written ca. 1858, original in LDS archives.

14. Woodruff then recorded his prayer: "May the Lord bless Joseph [Smith, Jr.] with all the Saints & support the above named institution & Protect it so that every weapen [weapon] formed against it may be broaken [broken] & come to nought while the Kirtland Safety Society

Joseph Smith wrote the following in the January 1837 issue of the *Messenger and Advocate*:

> In connexion [connection] with the above Articles of Agreement of the Kirtland Safety Society, I beg leave to make a few remarks to all those who are preparing themselves, and appointing their wise men, for the purpose of building up Zion and her Stakes. It is wisdom and according to the mind of the Holy Spirit, that you should call at Kirtland, and receive counsel and instruction upon those principles that are necessary to further the great work of the Lord, and to establish the children of the Kingdom, according to the oracles of God, as they are had among us. And further, we invite the brethren from abroad, to call on us, and take stock in our Safety Society.[15]

5. REVELATION RECEIVED AT KIRTLAND, OHIO, ON 4 JUNE 1837 FOR HEBER C. KIMBALL

Heber C. Kimball wrote in his journal:

> June the 4- 1837 Kirtland The word of the Lord to me through Joseph [Smith] the prophet [was] that I should gow [go] to England to open the dore [door] of procklamation [proclamation] to that nation and to hed [head] the same[16]

6. REVELATION RECEIVED AT NAUVOO, ILLINOIS, CA. 27 AUGUST 1842 CONCERNING PREACHING AGAINST STATEMENTS MADE BY JOHN C. BENNETT

Wilford Woodruff recorded:

> During my sickness [10 August to 19 September 1842] there was some important things transpired in the Church. We received the word of the Lord Concerning the Elders of the Church (through Joseph the Seer). The Lord manifested that it was his will that the first presidency, the Twelve, The High Council The quorum of High Priest[s], and the Elders quorum as a general thing Should go into the vineyard. The instructions were for the Elders to confine themselves to the free States & mostly to New England & the canidas [and] not to go to any of the indians or Slave States.[17]

This word of the Lord related to problems caused by disaffected church member John Cook Bennett's letters published in the *Sangamo Journal* (Springfield, Illinois) exposing Nauvoo iniquities. To counter his charges, a broadside was published titled *AFFIDAVITS AND CERTIFICATES, Disproving the Statements and Affidavits Contained in John C. Bennett's Letters. Nauvoo[.] Aug. 31, 1842.*

Eliza R. Snow establishes the approximate date of the revelation:

> Last evening [27 August] Prest. S. [Joseph Smith] was at home and met in the large drawing room with a respectable number of those considered trustworthy - counsel'd them to go out forthwith to proclaim the principles of truth.[18]

---

shall become the greatest of all institutions on EARTH" (Scott G. Kenney, ed., *Wilford Woodruff's Journal*, typescript, 1833-1898, 9 vols., 1983-85 [Midvale, UT: Signature Books], 1:120, entry of 5 Jan. 1837, original in LDS archives).

15. *Latter Day Saints' Messenger and Advocate* 3 (Jan. 1837): 443.

16. Heber C. Kimball Journal, LDS archives.

17. Kenney, *Wilford Woodruff's Journal*, 2:186-87, original in LDS archives.

18. Maureen Ursenbach [Beecher], ed., "Eliza R. Snow's Nauvoo Journal," *BYU Studies* 15 (Summer 1975): 398. William Clayton recorded for 27 August 1842, "In the large room over

Hyrum Smith spoke at a church conference on 29 August 1842:

the people abroad had been excited by John C. Bennett[']s false statements and that letters had frequently been received inquiring concerning the true nature of said reports; in
consequence of which it is thought wisdom in God that every Elder who can, should
now go forth to every part of the United States, and take proper documents with them
stating the truth as it is and also preach the gospel, repentance, Baptism & salvation and
tarry preaching untill they shall be called home.[19]

---

the Store with some of the Twelve and others who were preparing affidavits for the press" (Dean
C. Jessee, ed., *The Papers of Joseph Smith: Journal, 1832-1842* [Salt Lake City: Deseret Book Co.,
1992], 2:444).

19. Jessee, *Papers of Joseph Smith*, 2:444.

Appendix F.
A Commandment to Oliver Cowdery
Received in 1829

This commandment is included here because it is an early historical document that contains material similar to what was included in the Articles and Covenants of the church accepted in June 1830 (Document no. 24; LDS D&C 20; RLDS D&C 17). Footnotes show source ideas for Cowdery's commandment.[1]

A Commandment from God unto Oliver [Cowdery] how he should build up his church & the manner thereof

Saying Oliver [Cowdery] listen to the voice of Christ your Lord & your God & your Redeemer & write the words which I shall command you concerning my Church my Gospel my Rock & my Salvation.[2] Behold the world is ripening in iniquity & it must needs be that the children of men are stirred up unto repentance both the Gentiles & also the House of Israel[3] for behold I command all men every where to repent & I speak unto you even as unto Paul mine apostle for ye are called even with that same calling with which he was called[4] Now therefore whosoever repenteth & humbleth himself before me & desireth to be baptized in my name shall ye baptize them[5]

And after this manner did he command me that I should baptize them Behold ye shall go down & stand in the water & in my name shall ye baptize them And now behold these are the words which ye shall say calling them by name saying Having authority given me of Jesus Christ I baptize you in the name of the Father & of the Son & of the Holy Ghost Amen And then shall ye immerse them in the water & come forth again out of the water & after this manner shall ye baptize in my name[6] For behold verily I say unto you that the Father & the Son & the Holy Ghost are one & I am in the Father & the Father in me & the Father & I are one.[7]

And ye are also called to ordain Priests & Teachers according to the gifts & callings of God unto men[8] & after this manner shall ye ordain them Ye shall pray unto the Father in my name & then shall ye lay your hand[s] upon them & say In the name of Jesus Christ I ordain you to be a Priest or if he be a Teacher I ordain you to be a Teacher to preach re-

1. Manuscript in LDS archives. See Robert J. Woodford, "The Historical Development of the Doctrine and Covenants," Ph.D. diss., Brigham Young University, 1974, 287-90.
2. Wording similar to BC 15:3, 19; LDS D&C 18:4, 17; RLDS D&C 16:1, 4 (June 1829).
3. BC 15:5; LDS D&C 18:6; RLDS D&C 16:2.
4. BC 15:11; LDS D&C 18:9; RLDS D&C 16:3.
5. Wording similar to 1830 BOM, 478; LDS 3 Ne. 11:23/RLDS 5:24 and BC 24:30; LDS D&C 20:37; RLDS D&C 17:7.
6. 1830 BOM, 478; LDS 3 Ne. 11:23-27/RLDS 5:24-27 and BC 24:52-54; LDS D&C 20:73-74; RLDS D&C 17:21.
7. 1830 BOM, 478; LDS 3 Ne. 11:27/RLDS 5:27.
8. 1830 BOM, 575; LDS Moro. 3:4/RLDS 3:3; BC 15:35; LDS D&C 18:32; RLDS D&C 16:5 and BC 24:42; LDS D&C 20:60; RLDS D&C 17:12.

pentance & remission of sins through Jesus Christ by the endurance of faith on his name to the end Amen[9]

And this shall be the duty of the Priest He shall kneel down & the members of the Church shall kneel also[10] which Church shall be called The Church of Christ & he shall pray to the Father in my name for the church & if it so be that it be built upon my Rock I will bless it And after that ye have prayed to the Father in my name ye shall preach the truth in soberness casting out none from among you but rather invite them to come[11]

And the Church shall oft partake of bread & wine & after this manner shall ye partake of it The Elder or Priest shall minister it & after this manner shall he do he shall kneel with the Church & pray to the Father in the name of Christ & then shall ye say O God the Eternal Father we ask thee in the name of thy Son Jesus Christ to bless & sanctify this bread to the souls of all those who partake of it that they may eat in remembrance of the body of thy Son & witness unto thee O God the Eternal Father that they are willing to take upon them the name of thy Son & always remember him & keep his commandments which he hath given them that they may always have his spirit to be with them Amen[12]

And then shall ye take the cup & say O God the Eternal Father we ask thee in the name of thy Son Jesus Christ to bless & sanctify this wine to the souls of all those who drink of it that they do [it] in remembrance of the blood of thy Son which was shed for them that they may witness unto thee O God the Eternal Father that they do always remember him that they may have his spirit to be with them Amen[13]

And now behold I give unto you a commandment that ye shall not suffer any one knowingly to partake of my flesh & blood unworthily when ye shall minister it for whoso eateth & drinketh my flesh & blood unworthily eateth & drinketh damnation to his soul Therefore if ye know that a man is unworthy to eat & drink of my flesh & blood ye shall forbid him nevertheless ye shall not cast him out from among you but ye shall minister unto him & shall pray for him unto the Father in my name & if it so be that he repenteth & is baptized in my name then shall ye receive him & shall minister unto him of my flesh & blood but if he repenteth not he shall not be numbered among my people that he may not destroy my people For behold I know my Sheep & they are numbered nevertheless ye shall not cast him out of your Synagogues or your places of worship for unto such shall ye continue to minister for ye know not but what they will return & repent & come unto me with full purpose of heart & I shall heal them & ye shall be the means of bringing Salvation unto them Therefore keep these sayings which I have commanded you that ye come not under condemnation for wo unto him whom the Father condemneth[14]

And the church shall meet together oft for prayer & sup[p]lication casting out none from your places of worship but rather invite them to come And each member shall speak & tell the church of their progress in the way to Eternal life[15] And there shall be no pride nor envying nor strifes nor malice not idoletry [idolatry] nor witch crafts nor

9. 1830 BOM, 575; LDS Moro. 3:2-3/RLDS 3:2.

10. 1830 BOM, 575; LDS Moro. 4:2/RLDS 4:3.

11. 1830 BOM, 507; LDS 3 Ne. 27:8/RLDS 12:19-20. Cf. 1830 BOM, 492; LDS 3 Ne. 18:22-25/RLDS 8:53-56.

12. 1830 BOM, 575; LDS Moro. 4:1-3/RLDS 4:1-4 and BC 24:56-57; LDS D&C 20:76-77; RLDS D&C 17:22.

13. 1830 BOM, 575-76; LDS Moro. 5:1-2/RLDS 5:2-3 and BC 24:59; LDS D&C 20:79; RLDS D&C 17:23.

14. 1830 BOM, 492; LDS 3 Ne. 18:28-33/RLDS 8:60-66.

15. Cf. 1830 BOM, 492, 576; LDS 3 Ne. 18:22-25; Moro. 6:5/RLDS 3 Ne. 8:53-57; Moro. 6:6.

whoredoms nor fornications nor covetiousness [covetousness] nor lying nor deceits nor no manner of iniquity & if any one is guilty of any or the least of these & doth not repent & show fruits meat for repentance they shall not be numbered among my people that they may not destroy my people[16]

And now I speak unto the Church Repent all ye ends of the Earth & come unto me & be baptized in my name which is Jesus Christ & endure to the end & ye shall be saved Behold Jesus Christ is the name which is given of the Father & there is none other name given whereby men can be saved Therefore all men must take upon them the name which is given of the Father for in that name shall they be called at the last day Therefore if they know not the name by which they are called they cannot have place in the Kingdom of my Father[17] Behold ye must walk uprightly before me & sin not & if ye do walk uprightly before me & sin not my grace is sufficient for you that ye shall be lifted up at the last day[18]

Behold I am Jesus Christ the Son of the living God I am the same which came unto my own & my own received me not I am the light which shineth in darkness & the darkness comprehendeth it not[19] these words are not of men nor of man but of me[20] Now remember the words of him who is the first & the last the light & the life of the world[21] And I Jesus Christ your Lord & your God & your Redeemer by the power of my Spirit have spoken it Amen[22] – And now if I have not authority to write these things judge ye behold ye shall know that I have authority when you & I shall be brought to stand before the judgment seat of God[23] Now may [the grace] of God the Father & our Lord Jesus Christ be & abide with you all & [lacuna in MS] save you Eternally in his Kingdom through the Infinite atonement which is in Jesus Christ Amen[24]

Behold I am Oliver [Cowdery] I am an Apostle of Jesus Christ[25] by the will of God the Father & the Lord Jesus Christ Behold I have written the things which he hath commanded me for behold his word was unto me as a burning fire shut up in my bones & I was weary with forbearing & I could forbear no longer[26] Amen

Written in the year of our Lord & Saviour 1829 — A true Copy of the articles of the Church of Christ O.C.

---

16. Cf. 1830 BOM, 500; LDS 3 Ne. 21:19/RLDS 9:105; and BC 4:5. 1830 BOM, 492; LDS 3 Ne. 18:31/RLDS 8:63 and 1830 BOM, 211; LDS Mosiah 26:32/RLDS 11:141.

17. BC 15:23-26; LDS D&C 18:22-25; RLDS D&C 16:4.

18. Wording similar to BC 15:34; LDS D&C 18:31; RLDS D&C 16:5 and LDS D&C 17:8; RLDS D&C 15:3.

19. Cf. BC 5:10; LDS D&C 6:21; RLDS D&C 6:10; BC 9:15; LDS D&C 10:57; RLDS D&C 3:14 and BC 10:12; LDS D&C 11:28-29; RLDS D&C 10:12.

20. BC 15:37; LDS D&C 18:34; RLDS D&C 16:5.

21. Wording similar to BC 9:19; LDS D&C 10:70; RLDS D&C 3:18.

22. BC 15:50; LDS D&C 18:47; RLDS D&C 16:7.

23. Cf. 1830 BOM, 548; LDS Ether 5:6/RLDS 2:5.

24. Cf. 1830 BOM, 566; LDS Ether 12:41/RLDS 5:41; 1830 BOM, 577; LDS and RLDS Moro. 7:2; 1830 BOM, 585; LDS Moro. 9:26/RLDS 9:28; 1830 BOM, 79; LDS 2 Ne. 9:7/RLDS 6:15-16; and 1830 BOM, 319; LDS Alma 34:12/RLDS 16:213.

25. LDS D&C 20:3; RLDS D&C 17:1.

26. Ezra Booth, a former member of the church, wrote in 1831, "Cowdery's desires for this work were so keen and excessive, as, to use his own language, it 'was unto me a burning fire shut up in my bones, and I was weary with forebearing, and I could forbear no longer;' and he did in fact, issue some productions" (Booth to Rev. Ira Eddy, 24 Nov. 1831, Ohio Star 2 [8 Dec. 1831]: 1).

SELECT BIBLIOGRAPHY

I. Histories and Manuscripts

Smith, Joseph. Manuscripts, LDS archives. The Joseph Smith Journals, Manuscript History, and the Revelation Collection are available on microfilm at LDS archives, Salt Lake City, Utah; RLDS archives, Independence, Missouri; and Special Collections, Harold B. Lee Library, Brigham Young University, Provo, Utah.

_____. *Book of Mormon.* Palmyra [NY]: E.B. Grandin, 1830. Current editions include Salt Lake City: Church of Jesus Christ of Latter-day Saints, 1981. Independence, MO: Reorganized Church of Jesus Christ of Latter Day Saints, 1908 [Authorized Edition] and 1966 [Revised Authorized Edition, 1992]; Church of Christ (Temple Lot), 1990.

_____. *A Book of Commandments, for the Government of the Church of Christ.* Zion [Independence, MO]: W.W. Phelps & Co., 1833. [in press 1833]

_____. Compiled by Joseph Smith, Junior, Oliver Cowdery, Sidney Rigdon, Frederick G. Williams. *Doctrine and Covenants of the Church of the Latter Day Saints: Carefully Selected from the Revelations of God.* Kirtland, OH: Frederick G. Williams & Co., 1835.

_____. *The Doctrine and Covenants of the Church of Jesus Christ of Latter Day Saints.* Nauvoo, IL: John Taylor, 1844.

Kirtland Revelations Book (manuscript book containing some of Joseph Smith's revelations, LDS archives) published under the title *Joseph Smith's Kirtland Revelation Book.* Salt Lake City: Modern Microfilm Co., 1979 [reproduction of entire manuscript book].

Joseph Smith Journals, LDS archives. See Dean C. Jessee, ed., *The Papers of Joseph Smith: Journal, 1832-1842,* Vol. 2 (Salt Lake City: Deseret Book Co., 1992); and Scott H. Faulring, ed., *An American Prophet's Record: The Diaries and Journals of Joseph Smith* (Salt Lake City: Signature Books in association with Smith Research Associates, 1987).

Kirtland Council Minute Book, 3 December 1832-27 November 1837, LDS archives, typescript.

Nauvoo High Council Minutes, LDS archives, typescript.

Cannon, Donald Q., and Lyndon W. Cook, eds. *Far West Record: Minutes of The Church of Jesus Christ of Latter-day Saints, 1830-1844.* Salt Lake City: Deseret Book Co., 1983. Manuscript titled "The Conference Minutes and Record Book of Christ's Church of Latter Day Saints." Manuscript in the possession of the LDS church.

Cook, Lyndon W. and Milton V. Backman, Jr., eds. *Kirtland Elders' Quorum Record 1836-1841.* Provo, UT: Grandin Book Co., 1985. Original record in RLDS archives.

Flint, B. C. *An Outline History of the Church of Christ (Temple Lot).* Independence, MO: The Church of Christ (Temple Lot), 1953.

Searle, Howard C. "Early Mormon Historiography: Writing the History of the Mormons, 1830-1858." Ph.D. diss., University of California, Los Angeles, 1979.

Smith, Joseph, et al. *History of the Church of Jesus Christ of Latter-day Saints.* 6 vols. Introduction and Notes by B. H. Roberts. Salt Lake City: Deseret Book Co., 1959. Behind this revised history are preliminary manuscripts and the bound books of the compiled Manuscript History of Joseph Smith, also known as the Manuscript History of the

Church, LDS archives. Most of the revelations in this manuscript from 1828 to 1834 were copied from the 1835 D&C. The history portion up to 27 November 1832 (except revelation texts) has been published in Dean C. Jessee, ed., *The Papers of Joseph Smith: Autobiographical and Historical Writings,* Vol. 1 (Salt Lake City: Deseret Book Co., 1989).

Smith, Joseph III and Heman C. Smith, eds. *The History of the Reorganized Church of Jesus Christ of Latter Day Saints.* 4 vols. Lamoni, IA: Herald House, 1897-1903. Reprinted 1967.

Westergren, Bruce N., ed. *From Historian to Dissident: The Book of John Whitmer.* Salt Lake City: Signature Books, 1995. "The Book of John Whitmer Kept by Commandment," original manuscript in RLDS archives.

II. ARTICLES AND BOOKS

Aland, Kurt and Barbara. *The Text of the New Testament, An Introduction to the Critical Edition and to the Theory and Practice of Modern Textual Criticism.* Grand Rapids, MI: Eerdmans/E.J. Brill, 1987.

Allen, James B. and Glen M. Leonard, *The Story of the Latter-day Saints.* Salt Lake City: Deseret Book Co., 1976; rev. ed., 1992.

Beecher, Maureen Ursenbach. "Discover Your Heritage: 'They Will Kill Us!'," *New Era* 4 (Sept. 1974): 36-37.

Beecher, Maureen Ursenbach and Lavina Fielding Anderson, eds. *Sisters in Spirit: Mormon Women in Historical and Cultural Perspective.* Urbana: University of Illinois Press, 1987.

Black, Susan Easton. "The Importance of the Individual in the Lord's Revelations," in *The Heavens Are Open: The 1992 Sperry Symposium on the Doctrine and Covenants and Church History* (Salt Lake City: Deseret Book, 1993), 48-58.

_____. *Who's Who in the Doctrine & Covenants.* Salt Lake City: Bookcraft, 1997.

Black, Susan Easton and Charles D. Tate, Jr., eds. *Joseph Smith: The Prophet, The Man.* Provo, UT: Religious Studies Center, Brigham Young University, 1993.

Brugger, William. "The Doctrine and Covenants as Literature," *New Perspectives* 11 (Apr. 1994): 22-30.

Church History in the Fulness of Times: The History of the Church of Jesus Christ of Latter-day Saints. Salt Lake City: Church of Jesus Christ of Latter-day Saints, 1989.

Compier, Don H. "Canonization in the Reorganized Church of Jesus Christ of Latter Day Saints." In Maurice L. Draper, ed., *Restoration Studies III* (Independence, MO: Herald Publishing House, 1986), 178-83.

Conkling, J. Christopher. *A Joseph Smith Chronology.* Salt Lake City: Deseret Book Co., 1979.

Cook, Lyndon W. "The Far West Record and the Doctrine and Covenants," in *The Seventh Annual Sidney B. Sperry Symposium: The Doctrine and Covenants* (Provo, UT: Brigham Young University, 1979), 129-39.

_____. *The Revelations of the Prophet Joseph Smith: A Historical and Biographical Commentary of the Doctrine and Covenants.* Provo, UT: Seventy's Mission Bookstore, 1981.

Cooper, Rex Eugene. *Promises Made to the Fathers: Mormon Covenant Organization.* Salt Lake City: University of Utah Press, 1990.

Cowan, Richard O. *The Doctrine and Covenants: Our Modern Scripture.* Salt Lake City: Bookcraft, rev. ed., 1984.

Crawley, Peter. "A Bibliography of The Church of Jesus Christ of Latter-day Saints in New York, Ohio, and Missouri" [1830-39], *BYU Studies* 12 (Summer 1972): 465-537.

_____. "Joseph Smith and A Book of Commandments," *Princeton University Library*

Chronicle 42 (Autumn 1980): 18-32.

Draper, Maurice L. "The 1835 General Assembly and the Doctrine and Covenants," *Saints Herald* 132 (Aug. 1985): 12-13, 16.

Fitzgerald, John W. "The Doctrine and Covenants," *Improvement Era* 44 (Oct. 1941): 586-87, 630-32.

Flake, Chad J. "The Newell K. Whitney Collection," *BYU Studies* 11 (Summer 1971): 322-28.

Garrett, H. Dean. "The Coming Forth of the Doctrine and Covenants." In Milton V. Backman, Jr., ed., *Regional Studies in Latter-day Saint Church History: Ohio* (Provo, UT: Department of Church History and Doctrine, Brigham Young University, 1990), 89-103.

Godfrey, Kenneth W., Audrey M. Godfrey and Jill Mulvay Derr. *Women's Voices: An Untold History of the Latter-day Saints, 1830-1900.* Salt Lake City: Deseret Book Co., 1982.

Grandstaff, Mark R. "Having More Learning Than Sense: William E. McLellin and the Book of Commandments Revisited," *Dialogue: A Journal of Mormon Thought* 26 (Winter 1993): 23-48.

Grunder, Rick. *Mormon Parallels: A Preliminary Bibliography of Material Offered for Sale 1981-1987.* Ithaca, NY: Rick Grunder Books, 1987.

Ham, Wayne, ed. *Publish Glad Tidings: Readings in Early Latter Day Saint Sources.* Independence, MO: Herald Publishing House, 1970.

Hansen, Klaus J. *Mormonism and the American Experience.* Chicago: University of Chicago Press, 1981.

Hearken, O Ye People: Discourses on the Doctrine and Covenants. Sandy, UT: Randall Book Co., 1984.

Hicks, Michael. *Mormonism and Music: A History.* Urbana: University of Illinois Press, 1989.

Hill, Donna. *Joseph Smith: The First Mormon.* Garden City, NY: Doubleday, 1977.

Hill, Marvin S. *Quest for Refuge: The Mormon Flight from American Pluralism.* Salt Lake City: Signature Books, 1989.

Howard, Richard P. *Restoration Scriptures: A Study of Their Textual Development.* Independence, MO: Herald Publishing House, 1969; 2nd ed., 1995.

Hurd, Jerrie W. *Our Sisters in the Latter-day Scriptures.* Salt Lake City: Deseret Book, 1987.

Jackson, Kent P., comp. and ed. *Joseph Smith's Commentary on the Bible* Salt Lake City: Deseret Book Co., 1994.

Jessee, Dean C., ed. "Joseph Knight's Recollection of Early Mormon History," *BYU Studies* 17 (Autumn 1976): 29-39.

_____. comp. and ed. *The Personal Writings of Joseph Smith.* Salt Lake City: Deseret Book, 1984.

_____. ed. *The Papers of Joseph Smith: Autobiographical and Historical Writings.* Vol. 1. Salt Lake City: Deseret Book Co., 1989.

_____. ed. *The Papers of Joseph Smith: Journal, 1832-1842.* Vol. 2. Salt Lake City: Deseret Book Co., 1992.

Lambert, Asael C. Asael Carlyle Lambert Collection, Manuscript 35. Boxes 1-3, 6-12, Manuscripts Division, J. Willard Marriott Library, University of Utah, Salt Lake City, Utah.

_____. "The Book of Doctrine and Covenants," *Improvement Era* 54 (Oct. 1951): 714-15, 734.

Lancaster, James E. "'By the Gift and Power of God': The Method of Translation of the Book of Mormon," *Saints Herald* 109 (15 Nov. 1962): 798-802, 806, 817. Reprinted in *John Whitmer Historical Association Journal* 3 (1983): 51-61; *Restoration Studies III* (Independence, MO: Herald Publishing House, 1986), 220-31; and Dan Vogel, ed., *The Word of God: Essays on Mormon Scripture* (Salt Lake City: Signature Books, 1990), 97-112.

La Rue, William Earl. *The Foundations of Mormonism: A Study of the Fundamental Facts in the History and Doctrines of the Mormons from Original Sources.* New York: Fleming H. Revell Co., 1919.

Launius, Roger D. and Linda Thatcher, eds. *Differing Visions: Dissenters in Mormon History.* Urbana: University of Illinois Press, 1994.

Ludlow, Daniel H., ed. *Encyclopedia of Mormonism: The History, Scripture, Doctrine, and Procedure of the Church of Jesus Christ of Latter-day Saints.* New York: Macmillan Publishing Co., 1992, 1:138, 404-27.

Lyon, T. Edgar. "How Authentic Are Mormon Historic Sites in Vermont and New York?" *BYU Studies* 9 (Spring 1969): 341-50.

Marquardt, H. Michael. "Early Texts of Joseph Smith's Revelations, 1828-1833," *Restoration* 1 (July 1982): 8-11.

McDonnell, John. Letter to the Editor, *Saints Herald* 124 (Dec. 1977): 44.

McKiernan, F. Mark, Alma R. Blair, and Paul M. Edwards, eds. *The Restoration Movement: Essays in Mormon History.* Lawrence, KS: Coronado Press, 1973.

Metzger, Bruce M. *The Text of the New Testament, Its Transmission, Corruption, and Restoration.* 3rd ed. New York: Oxford University Press, 1992.

_____. *A Textual Commentary on the Greek New Testament.* 2nd. ed. Stuttgart, Ger.: German Bible Society, 1994.

Millet, Robert L. and Kent P. Jackson, eds. *Studies in Scripture, Volume 1: The Doctrine and Covenants.* Sandy, UT: Randall Book, 1984.

Newell, Linda King, and Valeen Tippetts Avery. *Mormon Enigma: Emma Hale Smith.* 2nd ed. Urbana: University of Illinois Press, 1994.

Olson, Earl E. "The Chronology of the Ohio Revelations," *BYU Studies* 11 (Summer 1971): 329-49.

Parkin, Max H. "Kirtland, A Stronghold for the Kingdom," in McKiernan et al., *The Restoration Movement,* 63-98.

Petersen, Melvin J. "Preparing Early Revelations for Publication," *Ensign* 15 (Feb. 1985): 14-20.

Porter, Larry C. "The Church in New York and Pennsylvania, 1816-1831," in McKiernan et al., *The Restoration Movement,* 27-61.

_____ and Susan Easton Black, eds., *The Prophet Joseph: Essays in the Life and Mission of Joseph Smith.* Salt Lake City: Deseret Book, 1988.

Pratt, Parley P. [Jr.], ed. *Autobiography of Parley P. Pratt.* Salt Lake City: Deseret Book Co., 1994.

Shipps, Jan. *Mormonism: The Story of A New Religious Tradition.* Urbana: University of Illinois Press, 1985.

_____ and John W. Welch, eds. *The Journals of William E. McLellin 1831-1836.* Provo, UT: BYU Studies; Urbana: University of Illinois Press, 1994.

Smith, Joseph [III]. "Editorial. Request for explanations in regard to the Doctrine and Covenants," *Saints Herald* 49 (15 Jan. 1902): 41-43.

Smith, W[alter]. W. "The Book of Doctrine and Covenants," *Saints Herald* 68 (9 Feb. 1921): 125-29.

_____. "The Doctrine and Covenants; Its Contents and Publication," *Journal of History* 14 (Apr. 1921): 129-60.

Traughber, John Logan. J. L. Traughber Collection, Accession 1446, Box 2, Manuscripts

Division, J. Willard Marriott Library, University of Utah, Salt Lake City.

Turner, J[onathan]. B. *Mormonism In All Ages*. New York: Platt & Peters, 1842.

Van Wagoner, Richard S. *Sidney Rigdon: A Portrait of Religious Excess*. Salt Lake City: Signature Books, 1994.

Van Wagoner, Richard S., Steven C. Walker and Allen D. Roberts, "The 'Lectures on Faith': A Case Study in Decanonization," *Dialogue: A Journal of Mormon Thought* 20 (Fall 1987): 71-77.

Walker, Steven C. "The Voice of the Prophet," *BYU Studies* 10 (Autumn 1969): 95-106.

Watson, Elden J., comp. *The Orson Pratt Journals*. Salt Lake City: comp., 1975.

Welch, John W. "Topically Speaking: A Look at the Impressive Doctrine and Covenants," *Ensign* 15 (Sept. 1985): 20-25.

Weldon, Clair E. "Two Transparent Stones: The Story of the Urim and Thummim," *Saints Herald* 109 (1 Sept. 1962): 616-20, 623.

Woodford, Robert J. "The Story of the Doctrine and Covenants," *Ensign* 14 (Dec. 1984): 32-39.

_____. "How the Revelations in the Doctrine and Covenants Were Received and Compiled," *Ensign* 15 (Jan. 1985):27-33.

III. Latter-day Saint Concept of Inspiration, Revelation, and the Nature of Scripture

Allen, James B. "Line Upon Line," *Ensign* 9 (July 1979): 32-39.

Arbaugh, George B. *Revelation in Mormonism: Its Character and Changing Forms*. Chicago: University of Chicago Press, 1932.

Collins, William P. "Thoughts on the Mormon Scriptures: An Outsider's View of the Inspiration of Joseph Smith," *Dialogue: A Journal of Mormon Thought* 15 (Autumn 1982): 49-59.

Crouch, Brodie. *The Myth of Mormon Inspiration*. Shreveport, LA: Lambert's Book House, 1968.

Crowther, Duane S. *Thus Saith the Lord: The Role of Prophets and Revelation in the Kingdom of God*. Bountiful, UT: Horizon Publishers, 1980.

Dunford, Kent. "The Limits of Revelation," *Sunstone* 7 (Nov.-Dec. 1982): 30-32

Dunn, Scott. "The Dangers of Revelation," *Sunstone* 7 (Nov.-Dec. 1982): 25-29

Free, Jack. *Mormonism and Inspiration*. Concord, CA: Pacific Publishing Co., 1962.

Hansen, Lorin K. "Some Concepts of Divine Revelation," *Sunstone* 5 (Jan.-Feb. 1980): 12-18. Reprinted in *Sunstone* 10 (May 1985): 51-57.

Howard, Richard P. "Latter Day Saint Scriptures and the Doctrine of Propositional Revelation," *Courage: A Journal of History, Thought and Action* 1 (June 1971): 209-25. Reprinted in Dan Vogel, ed., *The Word of God: Essays on Mormon Scripture* (Salt Lake City: Signature Books, 1990), 1-18.

_____. "Adjusting Theological Perspectives to Historical Reality," *Saints Herald* 129 (1 Sept. 1982): 28.

_____. "The Problem of History and Revelation," *Saints Herald* 129 (1 Oct. 1982): 30.

_____. "Protective and Learning Images in Latter Day Saint Revelation," *John Whitmer Historical Association Journal* 6 (1986): 3-9.

Jalovick, David A. "Adapted to the Circumstances: Joseph Smith and Divine Revelation in Early Mormon History, 1830-1844," *Studies in History* (Buffalo, NY: State University of New York at Buffalo, 1983-84), 40-61

Ralson, Colleen. *Dissecting the Doctrine and Covenants*. St. Louis, MO: Personal Freedom

Outreach, 1990.

Oakman, Arthur A. "Divine Revelation," in *A Decade of the Best* (Independence, MO: Herald Publishing House, 1972), 113-44.

Oaks, Dallin H. "Revelation," *New Era* 12 (Sept. 1982): 38-46.

Olson, Kathryn. "A Reappraisal of Canonization in the [RLDS] Doctrine and Covenants," *Courage: A Journal of History, Thought and Action* 2 (Winter 1972): 345-52.

Reynolds, George. "Revelation - Inspiration," *Juvenile Instructor* 37 (1 Mar. 1902): 129-31.

Scott, Hazel M., ed. *Restoration Scriptures: Doctrine and Covenants.* Independence, MO: Temple School Center, Reorganized Church of Jesus Christ of Latter Day Saints, 1995.

Shumway, Nicolas. "Ambiguity and Language of Authority," *Dialogue: A Journal of Mormon Thought* 16 (Summer 1983): 52-56.

Sloan, Clark P. "Revelation: Reflection of the Divine," *Saints Herald* 138 (Apr. 1991): 11-12.

Spencer, Geoffrey F. "A Reinterpretation of Inspiration, Revelation and L.D.S. Scriptures," *The University Bulletin* [Graceland College, Lamoni, Iowa] 20 (Winter 1968): 41-51, 103. Reprinted in Dan Vogel, ed., *The Word of God: Essays on Mormon Scripture* (Salt Lake City: Signature Books, 1990), 19-27.

_____. "Revelation and the Restoration Principle," in Maurice L. Draper and A. Bruce Lindgren, eds., *Restoration Studies II* (Independence, MO: Herald Publishing House, 1983), 186-92.

_____. "According to the Scriptures," *Saints Herald* 132 (Aug. 1985): 5-7, 26.

Vlahos, Clare D. "A Question of Methodology," *Courage: A Journal of History, Thought and Action* 2 (Spring 1972): 464-66.

_____. "Joseph Smith Jr.'s Conception of Revelation," in Maurice L. Draper and A. Bruce Lindgren, eds., *Restoration Studies II* (Independence, MO: Herald Publishing House, 1983), 63-74.

Welch, Sharon. "Revelation in the Restoration Movement," *Commission,* Sept. 1979, 27-32.

IV. BOOK OF COMMANDMENTS/DOCTRINE AND COVENANTS CONTROVERSY

Curtis, J. F. "The Holloway-Wheaton Discussion," *Saints Herald* 74 (7 Dec. 1927): 1,437-39.

_____. *Our Beliefs Defended.* Independence, MO: Herald Publishing House, 1928.

Elvin, Robert M. "Book of Commandments," *Saints Herald* 31 (30 Aug. 1884): 563.

Haldeman, John R., ed. *The Evening and Morning Star* 12 (Aug. 1911): 1-4. Independence: MO: Church of Christ (Temple Lot).

_____. "Changes in Articles and Covenants," *The Evening and Morning Star* 12 (Oct. 1911): 1, 3-4.

_____. "Unreliable 'History,'" *The Evening and Morning Star* 13 (June 1912): 1-4.

Housknecht, Gary. *An Introduction to the Book of Commandments* N.p., 1977 [Church of Christ (Temple Lot); Independence, MO].

Lambert, J. R. *Objections to the Book of Mormon and the Book of Doctrine and Covenants Answered and Refuted.* Lamoni, IA: Herald Publishing House [n.d.].

MacGregor, Daniel. *Changing of the Revelations.* Milwaukee, WI [1927].

McKay, Patrick S., Sr. "Doctrine and Covenants Versus Book of Commandments," *Restoration Foundation* 2 (Third Quarter 1988): 1-4.

McLellin, William E. Letter to Joseph Smith III, 10 Jan. 1861, RLDS archives.

_____. Letter to D.H. Bays, 24 May 1870, *The True Latter Day Saints' Herald* 17 (15

Sept. 1870): 553-57.

_____. Letter to M. H. Forscutt, Oct. 1870, *The True Latter Day Saints' Herald* 19 (15 July 1872): 435-37; 19 (1 Aug. 1872): 472-74.

_____. Letter to Joseph Smith III, commenced July 1872, RLDS archives.

_____. Notebook, J. L. Traughber Collection, Manuscript 666, Manuscripts Division, J. Willard Marriott Library, University of Utah, Salt Lake City.

Mintun, J. F. "The Correct History of the Book of Commandments and the Truthfulness and Authority of the Book of Doctrine and Covenants," (Part 2), *Saints Herald* 73 (6 Jan. 1926): 6-8.

Page, Hiram. Letters to William E. McLellin, 2 Feb., 4 Mar., 6 June 1848, RLDS archives.

Petersen, Melvin J. "Editing the Revelations for Publication," *Courage: A Journal of History, Thought and Action* 1 (Mar. 1971): 172-79.

Schrader, Amy. "The Book of Commandments," *Zion's Advocate* 61 (Mar. 1984): 41-42.

Sheldon, William A. "Restoration Teachings Examined: A Treatise on the Book of Commandments, The Evening & The Morning Star, and the Doctrine & Covenants," *Zion's Advocate* 74 (Oct. 1997): 178-82.

Smith, Israel A. "Book of Commandments Versus Doctrine and Covenants," *Upon This Rock* (Independence, MO: Herald Publishing House, 1953), 98-120.

Smith, Joseph [III]. "Book of Commandments," *Saints Herald* 39 (23 Jan. 1892): 50-52; reprinted as *Book of Commandments and Book of Doctrine and Covenants* by the Late President Joseph Smith [III]. Independence, MO: Herald Publishing House, n.d.

Smith, Joseph [III] and W. W. Blair, eds. "Questions and Answers," *Saints Herald* 33 (25 Dec. 1886): 802-803.

Smith, Joseph III and Heman C. Smith, eds. *The History of the Reorganized Church of Jesus Christ of Latter Day Saints*. Lamoni, IA: Herald House, 1897, 1:578-81.

The Wheaton-Curtis Debate. Independence, MO: DupliCraft Co., 1970. [A debate held in 1928 at De Kalb, Illinois, between Clarence L. Wheaton and James F. Curtis.]

Wheaton, Clarence L. "The Book of Commandments," *Zion's Advocate* 2 (15 July 1925): 5-7.

_____. "The Book of Commandments," *Zion's Advocate* 48 (July 1971): 86-89.

Wheaton, Clarence L. and Angelia Wheaton. *The Book of Commandments Controversy Reviewed*. Independence, MO: Church of Church (Temple Lot), 1950.

Whitmer, David. Letter of David Whitmer to "Dear Brethren," ca. 9 Dec. 1886, *Saints Herald* 34 (5 Feb. 1887): 90-93.

_____. *An Address to Believers in the Book of Mormon*. Richmond, MO: author, April 1887.

_____. *An Address to All Believers in Christ*. Richmond, MO: author, April 1887.

V. Textual Changes in Joseph Smith's Revelations

Comprehensive Comparison of Changes to the Revelations. Independence, MO: Church of Christ (Temple Lot), 1978.

Anderson, Creg. *The Doctored Covenants Why All the Changes?* (n.p., n.d.) [ca. 1964].

Best, Karl F. "Changes in the Revelations, 1833 to 1835," *Dialogue: A Journal of Mormon Thought* 25 (Spring 1992): 87-112.

Fitzgerald, John William. "A Study of the Doctrine and Covenants." Unpublished Master's thesis, Brigham Young University, 1940.

"A Comparative Study of A Book of Commandments for the Government of the Church of Christ [Organized] According to Law, On the 6th of April, 1830[,] Independence, Missouri, 1833, and Doctrine and Covenants of The Church of the Latter Day Saints:

Carefully Selected from the Revelations of God[,] Kirtland, Ohio 1835, Department of History, Reorganized Church of Jesus Christ of Latter Day Saints, Independence, Missouri, July, 1966." RLDS archives.

Howard, Richard P. *Restoration Scriptures: A Study of their Textual Development.* Independence, MO: Herald House, 1969, chaps. 10-12; 2nd ed., 1995, chaps. 8-11.

Pardo, John [pseud.]. *Comparisons of the Book of Commandments with the Doctrine & Covenants.* St. George, UT: comp., 1989 [1991].

Petersen, Melvin J. "A Study of the Nature of and the Significance of the Changes in the Revelations as Found in a Comparison of the Book of Commandments and Subsequent Editions of the Doctrine and Covenants." Unpublished Master's thesis, Brigham Young University, 1955.

Raveill, Jack. *The Revelation Revisions of 1835.* Blue Springs, MO: author. [RLDS edition, 1981; LDS edition, 1983/1984.]

_____. *The Fulness of the Gospel.* Blue Springs, MO: author, 1981.

Tanner, Jerald and Sandra Tanner. *The Case Against Mormonism.* Salt Lake City: Modern Microfilm Co., [1967-68], 1:131-91.

Woodford, Robert J. "The Historical Development of the Doctrine and Covenants." Unpublished Ph.D. diss., Brigham Young University, Provo, UT, 1974.

_____. "A Survey of Textual Changes in the Doctrine and Covenants," *The Seventh Annual Sidney B. Sperry Symposium* (Provo, UT: Brigham Young University, 1979), 27-36.

VI. Use of Biblical Phrases in Joseph Smith's Revelations

Rasmussen, Ellis T. "Textual Parallels to the Doctrine and Covenants and Book of Commandments as Found in the Bible." Unpublished M.A. thesis, Brigham Young University, 1951.

Smutz, Lois Jean. "Textual Parallels to the Doctrine and Covenants (Sections 65 to 133) as Found in the Bible." Unpublished M.R.E thesis, Brigham Young University, 1971.

VII. Commentaries, Manuals, and Compendiums on the Doctrine and Covenants

Doctrine and Covenants Section 1 through 102, Gospel Doctrine Teacher's Supplement. Salt Lake City: Church of Jesus Christ of Latter-day Saints, 1978.

Doctrine and Covenants and Church History. Salt Lake City: Church of Jesus Christ of Latter-day Saints, 1979.

The Doctrine and Covenants Student Manual (Religion 324-325. Salt Lake City: Church of Jesus Christ of Latter-day Saints, 1981.

Edwards, F. Henry. *The Edwards Commentary on the Doctrine and Covenants.* Independence, MO: Herald House, 1986.

Ham, Wayne A. *Restoration Scriptures Part Three: Doctrine and Covenants.* Independence: MO: Reorganized Church of Jesus Christ of Latter Day Saints, Temple School, General Leadership Program, 1983.

Scott, Hazel M. *Restoration Scriptures: Doctrine and Covenants.* Independence, MO: Reorganized Church of Jesus Christ of Latter Day Saints, Temple School Center, 1995.

Smith, Hyrum M. *The Doctrine and Covenants, containing revelations given to Joseph Smith, Jun., the Prophet.* Liverpool, Eng.: Printed and Published by Hyrum M. Smith, 1916. Revised edition with Janne M. Sjodahl. Salt Lake City: Deseret Book Co., 1951.

Sperry, Sidney B. *Doctrine and Covenants Compendium.* Salt Lake City: Bookcraft, 1960.

Stevens, Thelona D. *Research Notes on Doctrine and Covenants - Church History.* Independence, MO: author, 1976.

VIII. BACKGROUND ARTICLES ON AUTHORITY, DOCTRINE, AND
PRIESTHOOD

Alexander, Thomas G. "The Reconstruction of Mormon Doctrine: From Joseph Smith to Progressive Theology," *Sunstone* 5 (July-Aug. 1980): 24-33. Reprinted in *Sunstone* 10 (May 1985): 8-18; and Gary James Bergera, ed., *Line Upon Line: Essays on Mormon Doctrine* (Salt Lake City: Signature Books, 1989), 53-66.

Cannon, Brian Q., et al., comp., "Priesthood Restoration Documents," *BYU Studies* 35 (1995-96): 163-207.

Cannon, M. Hamlin, "Angels and Spirits in Mormon Doctrine," *California Folklore Quarterly* 4 (1954): 343-50.

Conrad, Larry W. "Scripture in the Reorganization: Exegesis, Authority, and the 'Prophetic Mantle'," *Dialogue: A Journal of Mormon Thought* 24 (Summer 1991): 65-80.

Crawley, Peter. "The Passage of Mormon Primitivism," *Dialogue: A Journal of Mormon Thought* 13 (Winter 1980): 26-37.

De Pillis, Mario S. "The Quest for Religious Authority and the Rise of Mormonism," *Dialogue: A Journal of Mormon Thought* 1 (Spring 1966): 68-88. Reprinted in D. Michael Quinn, ed., *The New Mormon History: Revisionist Essays on the Past* (Salt Lake City: Signature Books, 1992), 13-35.

Hale, Van. "The Doctrinal Impact of the King Follett Discourse," *BYU Studies* 18 (Winter 1978): 209-25.

_____. "The King Follett Discourse: Textual History and Criticism," *Sunstone* 8 (Sept.-Oct. 1983): 4-12.

Harrell, Charles R. "The Restoration of the Priesthood ([LDS] D&C 13 and 27)," in Robert L. Millet and Kent P. Jackson, eds., *Studies in Scripture, Volume 1: The Doctrine and Covenants* (Sandy, UT: Randall Book, 1984), 86-99.

Hartley, William G. "'Upon You My Fellow Servants': Restoration of the Priesthood," in Larry C. Porter and Susan Easton Black, eds., *The Prophet Joseph: Essays on the Life and Mission of Joseph Smith* (Salt Lake City: Deseret Book, 1988), 49-72.

Irving, Gordon. "The Mormons and the Bible in the 1830s," *BYU Studies* 13 (Summer 1973): 473-88.

Lindgren, A. Bruce. "The Development of the Latter Day Saint Doctrine of the Priesthood, 1829-1835," *Courage: A Journal of History, Thought and Action* 2 (Spring 1972): 439-43. Reprinted in *Restoration* 2 (Jan. 1983): 21-23.

Petersen, LaMar. *Problems in Mormon Text.* Salt Lake City: author, 1957.

Prince, Gregory A. *Power From On High: The Development of Mormon Priesthood.* Salt Lake City: Signature Books, 1995.

Quinn, D. Michael. "The Evolution of the Presiding Quorums of the LDS Church," *Journal of Mormon History* 1 (1974): 21-38.

_____. *The Mormon Hierarchy: Origins of Power.* Salt Lake City: Signature Books in association with Smith Research Associates, 1994.

Russell, William D. "The Latter Day Saint Priesthood: A Reflection of 'Catholic' Tendencies in Nineteenth Century American Religion," in Maurice L. Draper and Clare D. Vlahos, eds., *Restoration Studies I* (Independence, MO: Herald Publishing House, 1980), 232-41.

Van Orden, Bruce A. "Important Items of Instruction ([LDS] D&C 129-131)," in Robert L. Millet and Kent P. Jackson, eds., *Studies in Scripture, Volume 1: The Doctrine and Covenants* (Sandy, UT: Randall Book Co., 1984), 497-511.

_____. "Items of Instruction: [LDS] Sections 130 and 131," in *Hearken, O Ye People: Discourses on the Doctrine and Covenants* (Sandy, UT: Randall Book Co., 1984), 231-49.

Vogel, Dan. "The Earliest Mormon Concept of God," in Gary James Bergera, ed., *Line Upon Line: Essays on Mormon Doctrine* (Salt Lake City: Signature Books, 1989), 17-33.

Vogel, Dan and Brent Lee Metcalfe, "Joseph Smith's Scriptural Cosmology," in Dan Vogel, ed., *The Word of God: Essays on Mormon Scriptures* (Salt Lake City: Signature Books, 1990), 187-219.

IX. PSEUDONYMS IN REVELATIONS

Pratt, Orson [Sr.], ed. "Explanation of Substituted Names in the Covenants," *The Seer* 2 (Mar. 1854):227-29, Washington, D.C.

West, Wm. S. *A Few Interesting Facts, Respecting the Rise[,] Progress and Pretensions of the Mormons.* Warren?, OH: author, 1837.

Whittaker, David J. "Substituted Names in the Published Revelations of Joseph Smith," *BYU Studies* 23 (Winter 1983): 103-12.

X. ARTICLES ON *The Evening and the Morning Star* (INDEPENDENCE, MISSOURI)

Banks, Loy Otis. "The Evening and the Morning Star," *Missouri Historical Review* 43 (July 1949): 319-33.

Howard, Richard P. "Restoration Journalism: The Evening and the Morning Star," *Saints Herald* 117 (May 1970): 47.

Jennings, Warren A. "Factors in the Destruction of the Mormon Press in Missouri, 1833," *Utah Historical Quarterly* 35 (Winter 1967): 57-76.

Romig, Ronald E. and John H. Siebert, "First Impressions: The Independence, Missouri, Printing Operation, 1832-33," *John Whitmer Historical Association Journal* 10 (1990): 51-66.

Smith, Heman C. "Independence Publications," *Journal of History* 5 (Apr. 1912): 144-55.

Smith, Walter W. "The Periodical Literature of the Latter Day Saints," *Journal of History* 14 (July 1921): 257-60.

XI. REPRINTS OF *The Evening and the Morning Star*

The Evening and the Morning Star, a reprint copy by the Church of Christ (Temple Lot) in their publication *The Evening and Morning Star* 12 (July 1911) to 15 (June 1913), Independence, MO.

The Evening and the Morning Star, reprint, Salt Lake City: Modern Microfilm Co. [1964].

The Evening and the Morning Star, reprint published in West Germany for Eugene Wagner, 1969.

The Evening and the Morning Star, reprint of 1969 Wagner printing. Independence, MO: Price Publishing Company, 1994.

The Evening and the Morning Star, reprint, Orem, UT: Grandin Book Company, 1995.

XII. REPRINTS OF *A Book of Commandments*

Book of Commandments, published by the *Salt Lake Tribune,* Salt Lake City, 1884.

Book of Commandments, published by the Tribune Printing Co., Salt Lake City, 1903.

Book of Commandments, published by C.A. Wickes, Lamoni, IA, 1903.

Book of Commandments, published by Charles F. Putnam and Daniel MacGregor, Independence, MO, 1926.

Book of Commandments, published by the Church of Christ (Temple Lot), Independence, MO, 1960.

Book of Commandments, published by Woodruff Printing Co. for Jerald Tanner, Salt Lake City, 1961.
Book of Commandments in *Joseph Smith Begins His Work*, Vol. 2, published for Wilford C. Wood by Deseret News Publishing Co., Salt Lake City, 1962.
Book of Commandments, reprint, Independence, MO: Herald House, 1972.

XIII. REPRINTS OF THE 1835 EDITION OF THE DOCTRINE AND COVENANTS

Doctrine and Covenants in *Joseph Smith Begins His Work*, Vol. 2, published for Wilford C. Wood by Deseret News Publishing Co., Salt Lake City, 1962.
Doctrine and Covenants, reprint, Independence, MO: Herald House, 1971.
The following histories use or refer to the 1835 or a later edition of the Doctrine and Covenants:
1. John Whitmer's History
2. Joseph Smith's Draft History (1839) and Joseph Smith's Manuscript History (1839-44)
3. Lucy Smith's History (1844-45)
4. Joseph Knight, Sr.'s History
5. Newel Knight Journal
6. Newel Knight Autobiography
7. Joseph Knight, Jr.'s Incidents of History from 1827 to 1844 [1846].

XIV. PUBLICATIONS THAT INCLUDE REVELATIONS OF JOSEPH SMITH

The Doctrine and Covenants of The Church of Jesus Christ of Latter-day Saints. Salt Lake City: Church of Jesus Christ of Latter-day Saints, 1981.
Book of Doctrine and Covenants. Independence, MO: Herald Publishing House, 1990. Published by the Reorganized Church of Jesus Christ of Latter Day Saints.
A Book of Commandments. Independence, MO: Church of Christ, Temple Lot, 1960.
Collier, Fred C., comp. *Unpublished Revelations of the Prophets and Presidents of the Church of Jesus Christ of Latter-day Saints*, Vol. 1. Salt Lake City: Collier's Publishing Co.; 2nd ed., 1981.
Heidt, Stephen C., comp. *The Un-Canonized Revelations of the Prophet Joseph Smith*. Magna, UT: Oquirrh Mountain Publishing Co., 1993.
Reay, David M. and Vonda S. Reay. *Selected Manifestations*. Oakland, CA: compilers, 1985.
Book of Doctrine and Covenants. Independence, MO: Price Publishing Co., 1996.
Commandments and Covenants, from original sources, for order in the Lord's House, of the Church of Christ. Lamoni, IA: Ricky Donovan Leonard, comp., 1993.
The Articles and Covenants for the Government of the Church of Christ: A Book of Remembrance. New Jerusalem [Independence, MO]: The Firm Press, 2nd printing, 1990.
The Book of Commandments and Covenants. Independence, MO: The Church of Jesus Christ, 1978.
The Stick of Ephraim. Independence, MO: The Restored Church of Jesus Christ, 1987.

XV. STUDIES OF CERTAIN SECTIONS OF THE DOCTRINE AND COVENANTS

Document no. 3; LDS and RLDS D&C 5 (March 1829)

Howard, Richard P. "More Light and Truth in the Development of Section 5:3, 1829-1835," *Saints Herald* 129 (1 June 1982): 28.

Document no. 5; LDS and RLDS D&C 7 (April 1829)

Howard, Richard P. "Peter, James, and John in Light of the Revision of Sections 7 and 26," *Saints Herald* 129 (1 May 1982): 28.

Document no. 6; LDS and RLDS D&C 8 (April 1829)

Howard, Richard P. "Changing Modes of Revelation as Seen in the Revision of Section 8:3b-f," *Saints Herald* 129 (1 Aug. 1982): 28.

Document no. 8; LDS D&C 10; RLDS D&C 3 (May 1829)

Parkin, Max H. "A Preliminary Analysis of the Dating of Section 10," *The Seventh Annual Sidney B. Sperry Symposium* (Provo, UT: Brigham Young University, 1979), 68-84.

Document nos. 17-24; LDS D&C 23, 21-22, 20; RLDS D&C 21, 19-20, 17 (6, 16 April, June 1830)

Anderson, Richard L. "The Organization Revelations (D&C 20, 21, and 22)," in Robert L. Millet and Kent P. Jackson, eds., *Studies in Scripture, Volume 1: The Doctrine and Covenants* (Sandy, UT: Randall Book Co., 1984), 109-23.

Howard, Richard P. "Clarity of Doctrine, Language, and Polity Grounds for the Revision of Section 17," *Saints Herald* 129 (1 July 1982): 28.

Marquardt, H. Michael. "An Appraisal of Manchester as Location for the Organization of the Church," *Sunstone* 16 (Feb. 1992): 49-57.

Woodford, Robert J. "The Articles and Covenants of the Church of Christ and the Book of Mormon," in *Doctrines for Exaltation: The 1989 Sperry Symposium on the Doctrine and Covenants* (Salt Lake City: Deseret Book Co., 1989), 262-73.

Document no. 26; LDS D&C 25; RLDS D&C 24 (July 1830)

Madsen, Carol Cornwall. "The 'Elect Lady' Revelation: The Historical and Doctrinal Context of Doctrine & Covenants 25," in *The Heavens Are Open: The 1992 Sperry Symposium on the Doctrine and Covenants and Church History* (Salt Lake City: Deseret Book Co., 1993), 208-21.

Document no. 28; LDS D&C 27; RLDS 26 (4 Sept. 1830)

Howard, Richard P. "Peter, James, and John in Light of the Revision of Sections 7 and 26," *Saints Herald* 129 (1 May 1982): 28.

Document no. 30; LDS D&C 28; RLDS D&C 27 (Sept. 1830)

Barry, Louise. *The Beginning of the West: Annals of the Kansas Gateway to the American West 1540-1854.* Topeka: Kansas State Historical Society, 1972.

Caldwell, Martha B. *Annals of Shawnee Methodist Mission and Indian Manual Labor School.* Topeka: Kansas State Historical Society, 1977.

Gentry, Leland H. "Light on the 'Mission to the Lamanites,'" *BYU Studies* 36 (1996-97): 226-34.

Howard, Richard P. "Traces of Our First Mission to the Indians," *Saints Herald* 120 (July 1973): 53.

Jennings, Warren A. "The First Mormon Mission to the Indians," *Kansas Historical Quarterly* 37 (Autumn 1971): 288-99.

Romig, Ronald E. "The Lamanite Mission," *John Whitmer Historical Association Journal* 14 (1994): 25-33.

Stott, G. St. John. "New Jerusalem Abandoned: The Failure to Carry Mormonism to the Delaware [Indians]," *Journal of American Studies* 21 (1987): I, 71-85.

Document nos. 45, 48-49; LDS and RLDS D&C 42 (Feb. 1831)

Arrington, Leonard J., Feramorz Y. Fox and Dean L May. "Communitarianism under Joseph Smith: The Law of Consecration and Stewardship," in *Building the City of God* (Salt Lake City: Deseret Book Co., 1976), 15-40, 427-38.

Backman, Jr., Milton V. "Clothed with Bonds of Charity: The Law of Consecration and Stewardship in Ohio 1830-1838," in *Regional Studies in Latter-day Saint Church History:*

Ohio (Provo, UT: Department of Church History and Doctrine, Brigham Young University, 1990), 93-104.

Cook, Lyndon W. *Joseph Smith and the Law of Consecration.* Provo, UT: Grandin Book Co., 1985.

DePillis, Mario S. "The Development of Mormon Communitarianism, 1826-1846." Unpublished Ph.D. diss., Yale University, 1960.

Haldeman, John R., ed. "First Steps Toward Tithing," in *The Evening and Morning Star* 12 (August 1911):1-4. Independence: MO: The Church of Christ (Temple Lot).

Howard, Richard P. "Historical Perspective on Section 42:4," *Saints Herald* 128 (1 Nov. 1981): 28.

_____. "Historical Dialogue with Section 42:8-11," *Saints Herald* 128 (1 Dec. 1981): 29.

_____. "Further Reflections on Section 42:4," *Saints Herald* 129 (1 Feb. 1982): 26.

_____. "Resuming the Scriptural Dialogue: Sections 51:1b,e and 42:8-11," *Saints Herald* 129 (1 Apr. 1982): 24.

Johnson, Clark V. "The Law of Consecration: The Covenant That Requires All and Give Everything," in *Doctrines for Exaltation: The 1989 Sperry Symposium on the Doctrine and Covenants* (Salt Lake City: Deseret Book Co., 1989), 97-113.

Moser, Dorothy. "Zion Building - Yesterday and Today?" *Saints Herald* 111 (1 Mar. 1964): 4-8, 22.

Nelson, William O. "To Prepare a People," *Ensign* 9 (Jan. 1979): 18-23.

Romig, Ronald E. and Anne L. *Stewardship Concepts and Practices* (Studies in Restoration History). Independence, MO: Herald Publishing House, 1992.

Romig, Ronald E. "Law of Consecration: Antecedents and Practice at Kirtland, Ohio," in Wayne Ham, ed., *Restoration Studies VI* (Independence, MO: Herald Publishing House, 1995), 191-205.

Smith, Walter W. "History of Stewardships and Consecration as Practiced by the Latter Day Saints," *Journal of History* 16 (July 1923): 257-93.

Van Orden, Bruce A. "The Law of Consecration," in Robert L. Millet and Larry E. Dahl, eds., *The Capstone of our Religion: Insights into the Doctrine and Covenants* (Salt Lake City: Bookcraft, 1989), 81-94.

Document no. 54; LDS and RLDS D&C 49 (March 1831)

Flake, Lawrence R. "A Shaker View of a Mormon Mission," *BYU Studies* 20 (Fall 1979): 94-99.

Meader, Robert F. W. "The Shakers and the Mormons," *The Shaker Quarterly* 2 (Fall 1962): 83-96.

Perkins, Keith W. "The Ministry to the Shakers (D&C 49, 51, 54)," in Robert L. Millet and Kent P. Jackson, eds., *Studies in Scripture, Volume 1: The Doctrine and Covenants* (Sandy, UT: Randall Book Co., 1984), 211-24.

Document no. 56; LDS and RLDS D&C 51; (20 May 1831)

Howard, Richard P. "Resuming the Scriptural Dialogue: Sections 51:1b,e and 42:8-11," *Saints Herald* 129 (1 Apr. 1982): 24.

Document no. 63; LDS and RLDS D&C 57 (20 July 1831)

Parkin, Max H. "The Courthouse Mentioned in the Revelation on Zion," *BYU Studies* 14 (Summer 1974): 451-57.

Document no. 72; LDS and RLDS D&C 65 (30 Oct. 1831)

Welch, John W. and Trevor Packer, "The Document Corner: The Newly Found Manuscript of Doctrine and Covenants Section 65," *BYU Studies* 33 (1993): 331-36.

Document no. 87; LDS and RLDS D&C 76 (16 Feb. 1832)

Hicks, Michael. "Joseph Smith, W. W. Phelps, and the Poetic Paraphrase of 'The Vision,'" *Journal of Mormon History* 20 (Fall 1994): 63-84.

Nyman, Monte S. "Six Visions of Eternity: Section 76," in *Hearken, O Ye People: Discourses on the Doctrine and Covenants* (Sandy, UT: Randall Book Co., 1984), 105-18.

Document no. 94; LDS D&C 81; RLDS D&C 80 (15 March 1832)

Quinn, D. Michael. "Jesse Gause: Joseph Smith's Little-Known Counselor," *BYU Studies* 23 (Fall 1983): 487-93.

Woodford, Robert J. "Jesse Gause, Counselor to the Prophet," *BYU Studies* 15 (Spring 1975): 362-64.

Document no. 100; LDS D&C 84; RLDS D&C 83 (22-23 Sept. 1832)

Millet, Robert L. "A Revelation on Priesthood (D&C 84)," in Robert L. Millet and Kent P. Jackson, eds., *Studies in Scripture, Volume 1: The Doctrine and Covenants* (Sandy, UT: Randall Book Co., 1984), 309-25.

Document no. 103; LDS D&C 87 (25 Dec. 1832)

Andrus, Hyrum L. *Anticipations of the Civil War in Mormon Thought and Joseph Smith and the West.* Provo, UT: Extension Publications, Brigham Young University, 1966.

Cannon, Donald Q. "A Prophecy of War (D&C 87)," in Robert L. Millet and Kent P. Jackson, eds., *Studies in Scriptures, Volume 1: The Doctrine and Covenants* (Sandy, UT: Randall Book Co., 1984), 335-39.

Howard, Richard P. "Christmas Day, 1832: Joseph Smith Responds to the Nullification Crisis," *Saints Herald* 116 (May 1969): 54.

Madison, R. Ben. "'Beginning at the Rebellion of South Carolina': Joseph Smith's 1832 'Civil War Prophecy,'" in Joni Wilson and Ruth Ann Wood, eds., *Restoration Studies VII* (Independence, MO: Herald Publishing House, 1998), 73-85.

Morris, Bates. *Joe Smith's Prophecy on the Rebellion Examined and Found Wanting.* Chicago: author, 1927.

Document nos. 104-105; LDS D&C 88; RLDS D&C 85 (27-28 Dec. 1832; 3 Jan. 1833)

Matthews, Robert J. "The Olive Leaf (D&C 88)," in Robert L. Millet and Kent P. Jackson, eds., *Studies in Scriptures, Volume 1: The Doctrine and Covenants* (Sandy, UT: Randall Book Co., 1984), 340-57.

Document no. 108; LDS D&C 89; RLDS D&C 86 (27 Feb. 1833)

Alexander, Thomas. "The Word of Wisdom: From Principle to Requirement," *Dialogue: A Journal of Mormon Thought* 14 (Fall/Autumn 1981): 78-88.

Arrington, Leonard J. "An Economic Interpretation of the 'Word of Wisdom,'" *BYU Studies* 1 (Winter 1959): 37-49.

Bergera, Gary J. "Has the Word of Wisdom Changed Since 1833?" *Sunstone* 10 (July 1985): 32-33.

Brown, Kenneth J. "Early Nineteenth Century Health Views and the Word of Wisdom (D&C 89)," in *The Seventh Annual Sidney B. Sperry Symposium* (Provo, UT: Brigham Young University, 1979), 255-73.

Bush, Lester E. "The Word of Wisdom in Early Nineteenth Century Perspective," *Dialogue: A Journal of Mormon Thought* 14 (Fall/Autumn 1981): 46-65; reprinted in Dan Vogel, ed., *The Word of God: Essays on Mormon Scripture* (Salt Lake City: Signature Books, 1990), 161-85.

Petersen, LaMar. *Hearts Made Glad: The Charges of Intemperance Against Joseph Smith the Mormon Prophet.* Salt Lake City: author, 1975.

Tyree, Alan D. "The Use of Wisdom," *Saints Herald* 124 (Aug. 1977): 46-50.

Document no. 112; LDS D&C 93; RLDS D&C 90 (6 May 1833)

Garrard, LaMar E. "The Origin and Destiny of Man (D&C 93)," in Robert L. Millet and Kent P. Jackson, eds., *Studies in Scripture, Volume 1: The Doctrine and Covenants* (Sandy, UT: Randall Book Co., 1984), 365-78.

Document no. 137; LDS D&C 137 (21 Jan. 1836)

Backman, Milton V., Jr. "Witnesses of the Glories of Heaven: The historical background of Doctrine and Covenants 137," *Ensign* 11 (Mar. 1981): 59-61.

Document no. 139; LDS D&C 111 (6 Aug. 1836)

Cannon, Donald Q. "Joseph Smith in Salem (D&C 111)," in Robert L. Millet and Kent P. Jackson, eds., *Studies in Scripture, Volume 1: The Doctrine and Covenants* (Sandy, UT: Randall Book Co., 1984), 432-37.

Godfrey, Kenneth W. "More Treasures Than One: Section 111," in *Hearken, O Ye People: Discourses on the Doctrine and Covenants* (Sandy, UT: Randall Book Co., 1984), 191-204.

Proper, David R. "Joseph Smith and Salem," *Essex Institute Historical Collections* 100 (Apr. 1964): 88-97.

Document nos. 150, 154; LDS D&C 118, 117 (8 July 1838)

Boone, David F. "A Time For Commitment (D&C 117 and 118)," in Robert L. Millet and Kent P. Jackson, eds., *Studies in Scripture, Volume 1: The Doctrine and Covenants* (Sandy, UT: Randall Book Co., 1984), 445-55.

Document no. 155; LDS D&C 121-122 (20 March 1839)

Woodford, Robert J. "Letters from Liberty Jail," in *Hearken, O Ye People: Discourses on the Doctrine and Covenants* (Sandy, UT: Randall Book Co., 1984), 219-29.

Document no. 156; LDS D&C 124 (19 Jan. 1841)

Arrington, J. Earl. "William Weeks, Architect of the Nauvoo Temple," *BYU Studies* 19 (Spring 1979): 337-59.

Brown, Lisle G. "The Sacred Departments for Temple Work in Nauvoo: The Assembly Room and the Council Chamber," *BYU Studies* 19 (Spring 1979): 361-74.

Cloward, Robert A. "Revelations in Nauvoo (D&C 124-126)," in Robert L. Millet and Kent P. Jackson, eds., *Studies in Scripture, Volume 1: The Doctrine and Covenants* (Sandy, UT: Randall Book Co., 1984), 476-89.

Kimball, Stanley B. "The Nauvoo Temple," *Improvement Era* 66 (Nov. 1963): 974-84.

Document nos. 167-168; LDS D&C 127-128 (Sept. 1842)

Ashenhurst, Harry J., Bruce Graham, Bob Mesle and Dale Tripp, "Baptism for the Dead: A Scriptural Perspective," *Saints Herald* 117 (Apr. 1970):22-23, 25.

Bishop, Guy M. "'What Has Become of Our Fathers?' Baptism for the Dead at Nauvoo," *Dialogue: A Journal of Mormon Thought* 23 (Summer 1990): 85-97.

Launius, Roger D. "An Ambivalent Rejection: Baptism for the Dead and the Reorganized Church Experience," *Dialogue: A Journal of Mormon Thought* 23 (Summer 1990): 61-84.

Underwood, Grant. "Baptism for the Dead: Comparing RLDS and LDS Perspectives," *Dialogue: A Journal of Mormon Thought* 23 (Summer 1990): 99-105.

Document no. 169; LDS D&C 132 (12 July 1843)

Backman, Danel W. "The Authorship of Doctrine and Covenants Section 132," in *The Eighth Annual Sidney B. Sperry Symposium: A Sesquicentennial Look at Church History* (Provo, UT: Brigham Young University, 1980), 27-44.

Compton, Todd. *In Sacred Loneliness: The Plural Wives of Joseph Smith.* Salt Lake City: Signature Books, 1997.

Foster, Lawrence. *Religion and Sexuality: Three American Communal Experiments of the Nineteenth Century.* New York: Oxford University Press, 1981.

Roberts, B. H., ed. *History of the Church of Jesus Christ of Latter-day Saints.* Salt Lake City: Deseret Book Co., 1959. Introduction, 5:XXIX-XLVI.

Van Wagoner, Richard S. *Mormon Polygamy: A History.* 2nd ed. Salt Lake City: Signature Books, 1989.

XVI. ATLAS AND PHOTOGRAPHS

Brown, S. Kent, Donald Q. Cannon, and Richard H. Jackson, eds. *Historical Atlas of Mormonism.* New York: Simon & Schuster, 1994.

Holzapfel, Richard Neitzel and Jeffery T. Cottle, *Old Mormon Palmyra and New England: Historic Photographs and Guide.* Santa Ana, CA: Fieldbrook Productions, 1991.

_____. *Old Mormon Kirtland and Missouri: Historic Photographs and Guide.* Santa Ana, CA: Fieldbrook Productions, 1991.

_____. *Old Mormon Nauvoo 1839-1846: Historic Photographs and Guide.* Provo, UT: Grandin Book Co., 1990.

_____. *A Window to the Past: A Photographic Panorama of Early Church History and the Doctrine and Covenants.* Salt Lake City: Bookcraft, 1993.

Holzapfel, Richard Neitzel, Jeffery T. Cottle, and Ted D. Stoddard, eds. *Church History in Black and White: George Edward Anderson's Photographic Mission to Latter-day Saint Historical Sites 1907 Diary, 1907-8 Photographs.* Provo, UT: Religious Studies Center, Brigham Young University, 1995.

Further Readings

CHURCH RECORDS

Bitton, Davis and Leonard J. Arrington. *Mormons and Their Historians.* Salt Lake City: University of Utah Press, 1988.

Jessee, Dean C. "The Writing of Joseph Smith's History," *BYU Studies* 11 (Summer 1971): 439-73.

_____. "Joseph Smith and the Beginning of Mormon Record Keeping," in Larry C. Porter and Susan Easton Black,, eds., *The Prophet Joseph: Essays on the Life and Mission of Joseph Smith* (Salt Lake City: Deseret Book Co., 1988), 138-60.

_____. "Sources for the Study of Joseph Smith," in David J. Whittaker, ed., *Mormon Americana: A Guide to Sources and Collections in the United States* (Provo, UT: BYU Studies, 1995), 7-28.

Peterson, Paul H. "Understanding Joseph: A Review of Published Documentary Sources," in Susan Easton Black, and Charles D. Tate, Jr., eds., *Joseph Smith: The Prophet, The Man* (Provo, UT: Religious Studies Center, 1993), 101-16.

Searle, Howard C. "Authorship of the History of Joseph Smith: A Review Essay," *BYU Studies* 21 (Winter 1981): 101-22.

Van Orden, Bruce A. "William W. Phelps's Service in Nauvoo as Joseph Smith's Political Clerk," *BYU Studies* 32 (Winter/Spring 1992): 81-94.

NEW YORK ERA OF CHURCH HISTORY

Bushman, Richard L. *Joseph Smith and the Beginnings of Mormonism.* Urbana: University of Illinois Press, 1984.

Marquardt, H. Michael and Wesley P. Walters. *Inventing Mormonism: Tradition and the Historical Record.* San Francisco: Smith Research Associates, 1994.

Porter, Larry C., Milton V. Backman, Jr. and Susan Easton Black, eds., *Regional Studies in Latter-day Saints Church History: New York*. Provo, UT: Department of Church History and Doctrine, Brigham Young University, 1992.

Vogel, Dan, ed. *Early Mormon Documents*. Vol. 1. Salt Lake City: Signature Books, 1996.

OHIO ERA OF CHURCH HISTORY

Anderson, Karl Ricks. *Joseph Smith's Kirtland: Eyewitness Accounts*. Salt Lake City: Deseret Book Co., 1989.

Anderson, Richard L. "The Impact of the First Preaching in Ohio," *BYU Studies* 11 (Summer 1971):474-96

Anderson, Richard L. and Peter Crawley, "The Political and Social Realities of Zion's Camp," *BYU Studies* 14 (Summer 1974): 406-20.

Backman, Milton V., Jr., ed., *Regional Studies in Latter-day Saint Church History: Ohio*. Provo, UT: Department of Church History and Doctrine, Brigham Young University, 1990.

_____. *A Profile of Latter-day Saints of Kirtland, Ohio and Members of Zion's Camp 1830-1839*. Provo, UT, 1982.

_____. *The Heavens Resound: A History of the Latter-day Saints in Ohio 1830-1838*. Salt Lake City: Deseret Book Co., 1983.

Bradley, James L. *Zion's Camp 1834: Prelude to the Civil War*. Salt Lake City: Publishers Press, 1990.

Hill, Marvin S., C. Keith Rooker, and Larry T. Wimmer, "The Kirtland Economy Revisited: A Market Critique of Sectarian Economics," *BYU Studies* 17 (Summer 1977): 391-482.

_____. "Cultural Crisis in the Mormon Kingdom: A Reconsideration of the Causes of Kirtland Dissent," *Church History* 49 (Sept. 1980): 286-97.

Launius, Roger D. *Zion's Camp: Expedition to Missouri, 1834*. Independence, MO: Herald Publishing House, 1984.

Partridge, Scott H. "The Failure of the Kirtland Safety Society," *BYU Studies* 12 (Summer 1972): 437-54.

Rowley, Dennis. "The Ezra Booth Letters," *Dialogue: A Journal of Mormon Thought* 16 (Autumn 1983): 133-37.

Sampson, D. Paul and Larry T. Wimmer, "The Kirtland Safety Society: The Stock Ledger Book and the Bank Failure," *BYU Studies* 12 (Summer 1972): 427-36.

Van Orden, Bruce A. "Zion's Camp: A Refiner's Fire," in Larry C. Porter and Susan Easton Black, eds., *The Prophet Joseph: Essays on the Life and Mission of Joseph Smith* (Salt Lake City: Deseret Book Co., 1988), 192-207.

_____, ed. "Writing to Zion: The William W. Phelps Kirtland Letters (1835-1836)," *BYU Studies* 33 (1993):542-93.

MISSOURI ERA OF CHURCH HISTORY

Anderson, Richard L. "New Data for Revising the Missouri 'Documentary History,'" *BYU Studies* 14 (Summer 1974): 488-501.

Dyer, Alvin R. *The Refiner's Fire: The Significance of Events Transpiring in Missouri*. Rev. ed. Salt Lake City: Deseret Book Co., 1968.

Garr, Arnold K. and Clark V. Johnson, eds. *Regional Studies in Latter-day Saint Church History: Missouri*. Provo, UT: Department of Church History and Doctrine, Brigham Young University, 1994.

Jennings, Warren A. "Isaac McCoy and the Mormons," *Missouri Historical Review* 61 (Oct.

1966): 62-82.

Johnson, Clark V., ed. *Mormon Redress Petitions: Documents of the 1833-1838 Missouri Conflict*. Provo, UT: Religious Studies Center, Brigham Young University, 1992.

LeSueur, Stephen C. *The 1838 Mormon War in Missouri*. Columbia: University of Missouri Press, 1987.

Lyon, T. Edgar. "Independence, Missouri, and the Mormons, 1827-1833," *BYU Studies* 13 (Summer 1973): 10-19.

Parkin, Max H. "Zion's Camp Cholera Victims Monument Dedicated," *Missouri Mormon Frontier Foundation Newsletter*, No. 15 (Fall 1997): 2-6.

Romig, Ronald E. *Early Independence, Missouri "Mormon" History Tour Guide*. Independence: Missouri Mormon Frontier Foundation, 1994.

_____. *Early Jackson County, Missouri: The "Mormon" Settlement on the Big Blue River*. Independence: Missouri Mormon Frontier Foundation, 1996.

Wilcox, Pearl. *The Latter Day Saints on the Missouri Frontier*. Independence, MO: author, 1972.

ILLINOIS ERA OF CHURCH HISTORY

Allen, James B. "One Man's Nauvoo: William Clayton's Experience in Mormon Illinois," *Journal of Mormon History* 6 (1979): 37-59.

[Beecher], Maureen Ursenbach, ed. "Eliza R. Snow's Nauvoo Journal," *BYU Studies* 15 (Summer 1975): 391-416.

Ehat, Andrew F. "'It Seems Like Heaven Began on Earth': Joseph Smith and the Constitution of the Kingdom of God," *BYU Studies* 20 (Spring 1980): 253-79.

Ehat, Andrew F. and Lyndon W. Cook, eds. *The Words of Joseph Smith: The Contemporary Accounts of the Nauvoo Discourses of the Prophet Joseph*. Provo, UT: Religious Studies Center, Brigham Young University, 1980.

Flanders, Robert Bruce. *Nauvoo Kingdom on the Mississippi*. Urbana: University of Illinois Press, 1965.

Garrett, H. Dean, ed. *Regional Studies in Latter-day Saint Church History: Illinois*. Provo, UT: Department of Church History and Doctrine, Brigham Young University, 1995.

Hallwas, John E. and Roger D. Launius, eds., *Cultures in Conflict: A Documentary History of the Mormon War in Illinois*. Logan: Utah State University Press, 1995.

Hartley, William G. "Nauvoo Stake, Priesthood Quorums, and the Church's First Wards," *BYU Studies* 32 (Winter/Spring 1992): 57-80.

Holzapfel, Richard Neitzel and Jeni Broberg Holzapfel. *Women of Nauvoo*. Salt Lake City: Bookcraft, 1992.

Howard, Richard P. "The Joseph Smith Store: Church Headquarters at Nauvoo?" *Saints Herald* 118 (Oct. 1971): 34.

Kimball, James L., Jr. "A Wall to Defend Zion: The Nauvoo Charter," *BYU Studies* 15 (Summer 1975): 491-97.

Kimball, Stanley B. "Nauvoo," *Improvement Era* 65 (July 1962): 512-17, 548-51.

Launius, Roger D. and John E. Hallwas, eds., *Kingdom on the Mississippi Revisited: Nauvoo in Mormon History*. Urbana: University of Illinois Press, 1996.

Leonard, Glen M. "Picturing the Nauvoo Legion," *BYU Studies* 35 (1995): 95-135.

Lyon, T. Edgar. "Doctrinal Development of the Church During the Nauvoo Sojourn, 1839-1846," *BYU Studies* 15 (Summer 1975): 435-46.

Madsen, Carol Cornwall. *In Their Own Words: Women and the Story of Nauvoo*. Salt Lake City: Deseret Book Co., 1994.

Marquardt, H. Michael. *The Strange Marriages of Sarah Ann Whitney to Joseph Smith the Mor-*

mon Prophet, Joseph C. Kingsbury and Heber C. Kimball. Salt Lake City: Modern Microfilm, 1973; rev. ed., Salt Lake City: Utah Lighthouse Ministry, 1982.

Miller, David E. and Della S. Miller. *Nauvoo: The City of Joseph*. Santa Barbara: Peregrine Smith, 1974; reprinted Salt Lake City: Publishers Press, 1996.

Quinn, D. Michael. "The Practice of Rebaptism at Nauvoo," *BYU Studies* 18 (Winter 1978): 226-32.

Smith, Andrew F. *The Saintly Scoundrel: The Life and Times of Dr. John Cook Bennett*. Urbana: University of Illinois Press, 1997.

MILLENARIAN WORLD VIEW

Anderson, Richard L. "Joseph Smith and the Millenarian Time Table," *BYU Studies* 3 (Spring-Summer 1961): 55-66.

Erickson, Dan. *"As a Thief in the Night": The Mormon Quest for Millennial Deliverance*. Salt Lake City: Signature Books, 1998.

Leonard, Glen M. "Early Saints and the Millennium," *Ensign* 9 (Aug. 1979): 43-47.

Norman, Keith E. "How Long, O Lord? The Delay of the Parousia in Mormonism," *Sunstone* 8 (Jan.-Apr. 1983): 48-58.

Staker, Susan, ed. *Waiting For World's End: The Diaries of Wilford Woodruff*. Salt Lake City: Signature Books, 1993.

Stein, Stephen J. "Sign of the Times: The Theological Foundations of Early Mormon Apocalyptic," *Sunstone* 8 (Jan.-Apr. 1983): 59-65.

Underwood, Grant. *The Millenarian World of Early Mormonism*. Urbana: University of Illinois [Press], 1993.

ZION AND TEMPLES

Andrew, Laurel B. *The Early Temples of the Mormons: The Architecture of the Millennial Kingdom in the American West*. Albany: State University of New York Press, 1978.

Buerger, David John. *The Mysteries of Godliness: A History of Mormon Temple Worship*. San Francisco: Smith Research Associates, 1994.

Bushman, Richard L. "New Jerusalem, U.S.A.: The Early Development of the Latter-day Saint Zion Concept on the American Frontier." Unpublished Honors thesis, Harvard College, 1955.

Higdon, M. Elizabeth. "Eyes to the Glory: The History of the Heavenly City of Zion," in Maurice L. Draper, ed., *Restoration Studies I: Sesquicentennial Edition* (Independence, MO: Herald Publishing House, 1980), 269-77.

Lindgren, A. Bruce. "Zion as a Doctrine of Providence," *Restoration Studies I* (1980): 287-95.

Marquardt, H. Michael. "The Independence Temple of Zion," *Restoration* 5 (Oct. 1986): 13-17.

Morgan, D. J. *Temples. Important Facts about the building of Temples by Latter Day Saints*. Independence, MO: author, 1930[?].

Olson, Steven L. "Zion: The Structure of a Theological Revolution," *Sunstone* 6 (Nov.-Dec. 1981): 21-26.

Romig, Ronald E. "Temple Lot Discoveries and the RLDS Temple," in Garr, Arnold K. and Clark V. Johnson, eds., *Regional Studies in Latter-day Saint Church History: Missouri* (Provo, UT: Department of Church History and Doctrine, Brigham Young University, 1994), 313-35.

Romig, Ronald E. and John H. Siebert, "Jackson County, 1831-1833: A Look at the Development of Zion," in Maurice L. Draper and Debra Combs, eds., *Restoration Studies*

III (Independence, MO: Herald Publishing House, 1986), 286-304.

_____. "The Genesis of Zion and Kirtland and the Concept of Temples," in Marjorie B. Troeh and Eileen M. Terril, eds., *Restoration Studies IV* (Independence, MO: Herald Publishing House, 1988), 99-123.

JOSEPH SMITH'S CORRECTION OF THE KING JAMES VERSION BIBLE

Barney, Kevin L. "The Joseph Smith Translation and Ancient Texts of the Bible," *Dialogue, A Journal of Mormon Thought* 19 (Fall 1986): 85-102; reprinted in Dan Vogel, ed., *The Word of God: Essays on Mormon Scriptures* (Salt Lake City: Signature Books, 1990), 143-60.

Harris, James R. "Changes in the Book of Moses and Their Implications Upon a Concept of Revelation," *BYU Studies* 8 (Summer 1968): 361-82.

Howard, Richard P. *Restoration Scriptures: A Study of Their Textual Development.* Independence, MO: Herald House, 1969, chaps. 5-9; 2nd ed., 1995, chaps. 4-7.

Hutchinson, Anthony A. "The Joseph Smith Revision and the Synoptic Problem: An Alternative View," *John Whitmer Historical Association Journal* 5 (1985): 47-53.

Knecht, Stephen R. *The Story of Joseph Smith's Bible Translation: A Documented History.* Salt Lake City: Associated Resea[r]ch Consultants Publication, 1977.

_____, ed. "The New Translation of the Old and New Testaments." The Book of Genesis, unpublished manuscript, 1984. RLDS archives.

_____. "Three Interesting Aspects of the Joseph Smith Translation Manuscripts and History," *Restoration* 4 (Oct. 1985): 20-24.

Matthews, Robert J. "The 'New Translation' of the Bible, 1830-1833: Doctrinal Development During the Kirtland Era," *BYU Studies* 11 (Summer 1971): 400-22.

_____. *"A Plainer Translation:" Joseph Smith's Translation of the Bible, A History and Commentary.* Provo, UT: Brigham Young University Press, 1975.

_____. "Some Relationships between Joseph Smith's Translation of the Bible and the Doctrine and Covenants," in *The Seventh Annual Sidney B. Sperry Symposium, The Doctrine and Covenants* (Provo, UT: Brigham Young University, 1979), 1-16.

_____. "The Joseph Smith Translation: A Primary Source for the Doctrine and Covenants," in *Hearken, O Ye People: Discourses on the Doctrine and Covenants* (Sandy, UT: Randall Book Co., 1984), 79-92.

Mesle, C. Robert. "Reinterpreting the Inspired Version," in Maurice L. Draper, ed., *Restoration Studies III* (Independence, MO: Herald Publishing House, 1986), 254-58.

Millet, Robert L. "Joseph Smith's Translation of the Bible and the Synoptic Problem," *John Whitmer Historical Association Journal* 5 (1985): 41-46.

_____. "From Translations to Revelations: Joseph Smith's Translation of the Bible and the Doctrine and Covenants," in Larry C. Porter, Milton V. Backman, Jr., and Susan Easton Black, eds., *Regional Studies in Latter-day Saint Church History: New York* (Provo, UT: Department of Church History and Doctrine, Brigham Young University, 1992), 215-34.

Millet, Robert L. and Robert J. Matthews, eds. *Plain and Precious Truths Restored: The Doctrinal and Historical Significance of the Joseph Smith Translation.* Salt Lake City: Bookcraft, 1995.

Nyman, Monte S. and Robert L. Millet, eds. *The Joseph Translation: The Restoration of Plain and Precious Things.* Provo, UT: Religious Studies Center, Brigham Young University, 1985.

INDEX

A

Aaron, 212, 218, 268, 328; gift of Aaron (1835), 36-37; literal descendants of (1835), 171-72, 178, 268, 271

Aaronic priesthood (1835), 76, 267-68

Abraham, 212, 278, 284, 301, 304, 323, 325-28, 334

accountability, years of, 48, 65, 278

Adam (see also Michael), 73-74, 82-83, 232, 269-70, 278, 294n5, 322, 334-35; ancient of days, 73, 79n58, 334; father of all, 73, 334; first man, 212; Michael, 73, 79n58, 270, 334; in the valley of Adam-ondi-Ahman, 197, 270; prince of all, 73, 334

Adam-ondi-Ahman (1835), 197-98; Adam bestowed last blessing in, 270; Daviess County, Missouri, 294n5

adultery, 108, 118-20, 156, 164, 326, 328

Albany, New York, 217

Allred, William, 311

Ames, Ira, 16, 376

Amherst, Ohio, 184-85

Anderson, William, 87

Apocrypha, 236

apostle (see Twelve apostles)

Articles and Covenants, 62, 108, 177, 194, 379; Doctrine and Covenants, 260; keep them, 93

Ashley, Major N., 184

Avard, Sampson, 292

B

Babbitt, Almon W., 306

Baker, Jesse, 310

Baldwin, Caleb, 295n7

Baldwin, Wheeler, 137

baptism, manner of, 65; of John the Baptist in the womb, 213, 217-18; shall be baptized when eight years old, 170; for the dead, 302, 317-18, 320-21

Barlow, Philip L., 78n48

Basset, Heman A., 138

Beaman, Louisa (daughter of Alvah and Sarah Beaman [also spelled Beeman]), 315n43

Bennett, John C., 289, 299, 301, 307n25, 309n29, 314, 377-78

Bent, Samuel, 309

Bible, 40n25; and Book of Mormon, 108; copyright, 258; Joseph Smith's translation (correction) of, 98n99, 112, 123n29, 183, 186, 192-93, 194n29, 198, 204n65, 206, 220n15-16, 234n25, 236, 239, 307

Billings, Titus, 157

Boggs, Lilburn W., 297

Book of Abraham, 276n20

Book of Commandments, 4-5; appendix, 5n15, 173-76, 343, 354-61; manuscript fragments, 349-65; paper for, 6, 206-207; preface, 4-5, 165-67; printing, 4-7, 207, 216, 231; testimony to, 168-69; unfinished, 7, 349-51

Book of Mormon, 297, 309; alteration of manuscript pages, 38; book of Lehi (lost manuscript pages), 23, 38; copyright, 258; Lamanites, 40n24; Moroni has keys of the stick of Ephraim (1835), 72, 74; plates of Nephi, 39-40; record of the Nephites, 26, 167; sell copyright, 372-74; translated lost manuscript pages, xiii, 38-39; translation, 43; view of the plates, 49-50

Booth, Ezra, 49n34, 70n19, 137, 144, 149n65, 158n72, 159, 375-76, 381n26

Boston, Massachusetts, 217, 329

Boynton, John F., 268n7, 292n4

Brunson, Seymour, 185, 309

Bump, Jacob, 376

Burlington, Territory of Iowa, 306

Burnett, Stephen, 185, 198

Burroughs, Philip, 90

Butterfield, Josiah, 310

C

Cahoon, Reynolds, 137, 154, 185, 202n47, 244, 273

Canadian copyright revelation, 372-74

Canandaigua, New York, 97
Cannon, Brian Q., 80n59
Carter, Gideon H., 185
Carter, Jared, 138, 200, 244, 292
Carter, Simeon, 137, 185
Carter, William, 137
Carthage, Illinois, 306
Caswall, Henry, 18n80
celestial kingdom, 222-23, 263-64; Joseph
    Smith's vision of (1836), 278-79
celestial world, 195-96, 222
Chandler, Michael H., 276n20
Chariton, Missouri, 154
children, begin to become accountable, 83;
    shall be baptized when eight years old,
    170
church, abominations in, 130; laws, 107, 112,
    134; of Enoch, 188; of the first born,
    186n20, 188-90, 196, 206, 222, 238, 268;
    organized in Manchester, New York, 57-
    58; out of the wilderness, 29, 93; repent of
    their sins, 158; two priesthoods in, 267;
    under condemnation, 214, 266
Clark, William, 87-88
Clayton, William, 318n54, 323n63-64, 377-
    78n18
Coe, Joseph, 140, 374-75
Colesville, New York, 69, 98, 321
Coltrin, Zebedee, 8, 137, 200n41, 231n23
command and revoke, 141, 146, 332
commandment to Oliver Cowdery in 1829,
    379-81
commentary on text, (D&C 4), 26; (D&C
    5), 29-31; (D&C 7), 34-35; (D&C 8),
    36-37; (LDS D&C 17), 49-51; (LDS
    D&C 19), 54; (LDS D&C 20), 67-68;
    (LDS D&C 23), 57-59; (LDS D&C 27),
    73-80; (LDS D&C 28), 85-89; (LDS
    D&C 33), 93-94; (D&C 39), 102; (D&C
    41), 106; (D&C 42), 112-15; (D&C 48),
    127; (D&C 50), 132; (D&C 51), 134-35;
    (D&C 57), 143-44; (D&C 64), 161;
    (D&C 65), 165; (D&C 68), 171-72;
    (D&C 76), 191-93; (LDS D&C 78), 197-
    98; (LDS D&C 81), 201-204; (LDS
    D&C 83), 209-210; (LDS D&C 84),
    217-19; (LDS D&C 88), 230; (LDS
    D&C 104), 260
Compier, Don H., 15-16
congregations of the wicked, 151, 153-55,
    169, 194

consecration, law of, 265, 333
Cook, Lyndon W., 138n47
Copley, Leman, mission to Shakers, 128
copyright, for 1835 Doctrine and Covenants,
    10, 13, 258; sell for Book of Mormon,
    372-74
Corrill, John, 14, 108n6, 131, 136
Covill, James, 101-103
Cowdery, Oliver, xiii, 4-6, 15, 17-18, 23,
    31-33, 35-37, 46, 48-49, 57, 69-71, 80,
    83, 90, 98, 126, 138, 140,143, 148, 150-
    51, 153, 157-58, 170, 179, 208, 220n14,
    256-57, 274, 307, 332, 372-75; angel
    Michael is Adam, 74, 278n22; arrange
    church covenants, 10, 260; command-
    ment to in 1829, 379-81; editorial com-
    ments, 10-12; Gabriel is Noah, 74; gift of
    working with the rod, 36-37; hath a gift,
    31; member of 1835 D&C committee,
    12, 331; mission to Native Americans,
    85-89, 92; ordained an elder, 58, 61; rod
    of nature, 36n21; scribe for Joseph Smith,
    Jr., 31n13; steward over the revelations,
    5, 180, 182-83; visions in Kirtland tem-
    ple, 279-80
Cowdery, Warren A., 266, 279n26
Cowdery, William, 256n48
Cowles, Austin, 310n32
Cummins, Richard, 87
Cutler, Alpheus, 310

D

David, 323, 326
Davis, Amos (also spelled Davies), 308
debts, 110, 115, 160, 182, 259, 281, 293-94,
    317
dissenters, 284, 294n6
Doctrine and Covenants, canonization in
    1835, 15-16; committee work (1835) ac-
    cepted, 15; copyright, 13, 258; edition of
    1844, 17; General Assembly, 13-16; revi-
    sions in 1835 edition, 16, 18; (LDS D&C
    3), 25; (D&C 4), 25-26; (D&C 5), 28-
    29; (D&C 7), 33-34; (D&C 8), 36; (LDS
    D&C 10), 41; (LDS D&C 18), 48; (LDS
    D&C 19), 53-54; (LDS D&C 20), 66-67;
    (LDS D&C 27), 72-73; (LDS D&C 28),
    84; (LDS D&C 30), 90; (LDS D&C 33),
    93; (D&C 39), 102; (D&C 41), 106;
    (D&C 42), 110-12, 119-20; (D&C 43),
    117-18; (D&C 47), 126; (D&C 48), 127;
    (D&C 50), 132; (D&C 51), 134; (D&C

57), 143; (D&C 64), 160-61; (D&C 65), 165; (D&C 68), 170-71; (D&C 76), 190-91; (LDS D&C 78), 196-97; (LDS D&C 81), 201; (LDS D&C 83), 209; (LDS D&C 84), 217; (LDS D&C 88), 229-30; (LDS D&C 104), 259-60; (LDS D&C 107), 178-79

Dodds, Asa, 184

Dort, David, 309

E

Eames, Ruggles, 185

Egyptian papyri, 276n20

Elias, 72, 76-79, 205-206; Elijah, 76-77; Gabriel (Noah), 74, 77, 79; John (the Baptist), 77, 78; Jesus, 77, 78n51; John the Revelator, 77, 79; preparer, 77; restorer of all things, 72, 76n36; vision of, 280

Elijah, 73-74, 76, 95, 175, 321; vision of, 280

endowment, Kirtland, 264-65, 280; Nauvoo, 289

England, 377

Enoch, 175, 198, 212, 231-32, 270; God of, 121; Zion of, 98

Ephraim, 286; blood of, 160n74, 350-51; children of, 174; loins of, 160n74, 164

evangelical ministers (patriarchs), 269

Evening and the Morning Star (Independence), 3, 343; printing office shut down by mob, 7; published revelations each month, 6; revelations printed in, 366-67

Evening and Morning Star (Kirtland reprint), editorial comments, 10-12, 333

exaltation, 325

F

Far West, Missouri, 286-89, 291-94

Far West temple, 289, 291-93

Fayette, New York, 23, 44-46, 49, 55, 62, 69, 71n22, 75, 83, 89-92, 94-95, 97-98, 101-102, 321; first church conference in, 58; second church conference, 80n60; third church conference, 98n100

first elders, 226, 264-65

First Presidency, 171-72, 282-86, 294-95, 309

Fishing River, Missouri, 263

Fort Madison, Territory of Iowa, 306

Foster, James, 310

Foster, Robert D., 308

Freedom, New York, 266

French, Peter, 241

Fuller, Amos, 313

Fuller, Edson, 137

Fullmer, David, 310

G

Gabriel, 74, 76, 79, 321

Galland, Isaac, 306

Gates, Thomas, 15

gathering, 221, 280, 287; to Ohio, 98, 100-101; to Far West, Missouri, 291; to Missouri, 142-43, 148, 212, 249, 251, 264, 291

Gause, Jesse, 208n69, 362-63; counselor to Joseph Smith, 199n40, 200-204; traveled to Independence (1832), 6

Gilbert, Algernon Sidney, 138n48, 142, 152, 159-60, 208, 235, 252; establish a store, 143; send goods to the Lamanites, 143-44

gods, may become, 325; plurality of, 297

Gould, John, 248

Grandin, Egbert B., 374

Granger, Oliver, 294-95

Great Britain, 221

Griffin, Selah J., 137, 141

Grover, Thomas, 309

H

Hagar, 326, 328

Hancock, Levi W., 137, 310

Hancock, Solomon, 137

Harmony, Pennsylvania, 23, 25-26, 31, 33, 35, 37-38, 42-43, 69-72, 75, 321

Harris, Emer, 185

Harris, George W., 309

Harris, Lucy (wife of Martin Harris), 23

Harris, Martin, xiii, xvi, 6, 24n2, 26n4, 27-28, 30-31, 48n33, 49, 51, 54, 65n11, 107n4, 137, 207, 208n69, 256, 372, 374; baptism in Manchester, New York, 58; had copy of Canadian copyright revelation, 373; humble himself, 27; lay money before bishop, 147; lost manuscript pages, 23, 38n23; pay printer's debt, 53; repent of his sins, 147; steward over the revelations, 5, 180, 182-83

Harris, William, 18

Harrison, G. T., 372n1

Harrison, William H., 300n11

Haskins, Lincoln, 194

Haws, Peter, 305, 311

Herriman, Henry, 310
Hicks, John A., 310
Higbee, Elias, 287
high council: in Kirtland, 269, 332; in Missouri (Zion), 269, 284-85, 287n37, 291, 294; in Nauvoo, 309-10
high priesthood, 177, 195, 200, 213-14, 220, 271-72; president of, 177-78, 184n19
high priests, 170, 177, 181, 206, 214, 217, 229, 232, 267-68, 270-71, 310
Hiram, Ohio, 55, 163-65, 167-69, 173, 177, 179-81, 183, 186, 194, 198-200, 204, 206, 211
Holmes, Erastus, 277
House of the Lord (Kirtland temple), accepted, 280
Howard, Richard P., 5n20, 11
Humphrey, Solomon, 138
Huntington, William, Sr., 310
Huntsburg, Ohio, 267n6
Hyde, Nancy Marinda (wife of Orson Hyde), xii, 312-13
Hyde, Orson, 169, 184, 194n28, 248, 255, 268n7, 274, 309, 312

I

Independence, Missouri, 207, 209, arrival of missionaries to Native Americans, 86; center place, 142; courthouse, 142n53; place of the city of Zion and the gathering, 142
Independence temple, cornerstone for, 148n62, 149n65; offering accepted, 304; reared in this generation, 212-13; spot lying westward, 142, 149n65; temple lot, 212
Indians (see Native Americans)
Isaac, 326-27

J

Jackman, Levi, 15
Jackson County, Missouri (Zion), 145, 149-50, 304; redemption of, 250, 253-54, 263-64, 265n3; purchase land, 251, 265
Jacob, 326
Jacques, Vienna, xii, 235
James, George F., 138
Jesus, Elias, 77-78
Jew (Native Americans), 142n54
Jews, 122-23, 194-95, 206, 212-13, 245
John the Baptist, 76-77, 175; at transfiguration, 78; baptized in the womb, 213, 217-19; filled with Holy Ghost, 213; ordained Smith and Cowdery (1835), 72-74; spirit and power of Elias (Elijah), 76-77; understood as Elias (Elijah), 77-78
John the Beloved Disciple, parchment written and hidden by, 33-34
Johnson, Aaron, 310
Johnson, John, Sr., 55, 241, 256-57
Johnson, Luke S., 169, 184, 268n7, 292n4
Johnson, Lyman E., 169, 184, 268n7, 292n4
Judah, tribe of, 174

K

keys of the kingdom, 200, 202, 234
Kimball, Heber C., 197, 268n7, 309, 377
Kimball, Hiram, 314-15
Kingsbury, Joseph C., 323n64
Kingston, Canada, trip to sell copyright of Book of Mormon, 372-74
Kirtland, Ohio, 55, 105, 107, 112, 115, 118, 120-21, 124, 126-28, 130, 135-36, 138-40, 155, 158, 181-82, 195, 212, 219-22, 229, 231-32, 234, 236-37, 239, 241, 243-44, 248, 253, 255, 260, 266-67, 273-79, 281, 283-86, 294-95, 302n18, 306; city of my saints, 257; stronghold in land of, 159, 265n3
Kirtland High Council, 332
Kirtland Revelations Book, handwritten corrections in, 12; manuscript copies of revelations in, 8
Kirtland Safety Society, 376-77
Knight, Joseph, Sr., 43, 60, 149n66, 372; at church organization, 58
Knight, Newel, 137, 139, 141, 309
Knight, Polly Peck, 149n66
Knight, Vinson, 284, 305, 310

L

Lamanites (see Native Americans)
Law, William, 300n13, 306-309
Lectures on Theology (Lectures on Faith), 12, 15-16
Levitical priesthood, 267
Lewis, Joshua, 148n63, 374
Liberty Jail, Clay County, Missouri, 289, 295
location of manuscript revelations, 368-70
Lord's day, 149-50
Lyman, Amasa M., 310

M

Madison (see Fort Madison)

Malachi, 176, 280, 321

Manchester, New York, 51, 55, 57-60, 69, 86, 92; baptisms in, 58; church organized in, 57-58

Marks, William, 294, 306, 310n32

marriage, new and everlasting covenant, 323-26; for time and all eternity, 324

Marsh, Thomas B., 91, 137, 141, 185, 268n7, 281-82, 292

Matthews, Robert J., 78n51

McIllwaine's Bend, Missouri, 152

McLellin, William E., xvin13, 5n12, 8, 29, 97n98, 160n74, 163-64, 169, 184, 203n55, 235, 267n6, 268n7, 274, 279, 292n4, 350-51; on Canadian copyright revelation, 373-74; process of revelation, xiv

McRae, Alexander, 295n7

Melchizedek priesthood, 171-72, 267-68

Michael (see also Adam), 73, 81-82, 197-98, 228, 270, 278, 321-22, 334-35

Miles, Daniel S., 310

millennium, 117

Miller, George, 301, 305, 311

Miller, Henry W., 311

Missouri, land for the gathering, 142-43, 251; land of promise, 142; land of your enemies, 138; land of your inheritance, 138; place for the city of Zion, 142, 304; purchase lands, 142, 156, 251

money (moneys, monies), 70, 136, 139, 141-42, 151, 157, 179, 206, 216, 235, 250, 256, 258-59, 264, 274, 305; to purchase land, 127, 147-48, 251, 254

Morley, Isaac, 108n6, 137, 159, 275, 292

Moroni (son of Mormon), 72, 74, 321

Moses, 175-76, 213, 218, 302, 323, 326; vision of, 280

Mount Zion (in Missouri), 175, 212-13

Murdock, John, 136, 154, 211

N

Nashville, Territory of Iowa, 311

Nathan, 326

Native Americans, 40n24; blossom as the rose, 129; goods to, 143-44; intermarriage with, 374-76; mission to, 85-89

Nauvoo, Illinois, 289, 299, 308, 311-16, 318, 323, 329

Nauvoo High Council, 309-10

Nauvoo house (boarding house), 289, 299, 301, 304, 313; quorum, 305, 308-309;

shares in, 304n21; stock in, 305, 311

Nauvoo temple, 289, 299, 302-304, 310, 313, 317, 322

new and everlasting covenant of marriage, 316n48, 323-24

New Jerusalem (in Missouri), 55, 108-110, 112-14; called Zion, 124; city of, 84n62, 85, 107, 127, 138, 142, 175, 212, 304; dedicated, 148n62; gathering of the saints, 212; land of peace, 124; lay the foundation of the city, 127; offering accepted, 304; purchase the lands, 127; spot of the temple, 148, 149n65; temple to be built, 4, 86, 142, 304

new song, 216

New Translation of the Bible (see Bible)

New York, New York, 217

Noah, 74, 76, 79, 175, 212, 270

Noble, Joseph B., 315n43

O

Ohio, go to, 98, 100-101

organization of priesthood quorums, 268-69, 309-10

P

Packard, Noah, 310

Page, Hiram, 84-85, 372-74

Page, John E., 292, 309, 329

Palmyra, New York, 58

Parkin, Max H., 14n57

Parrish, Warren, 263, 276, 334, 376

Partridge, Edward, xvin13, 14, 95n95, 97, 105-107, 113, 119, 127, 132-34, 137-38, 142n53, 148, 151, 159, 172, 208, 219n14, 275, 284, 291-92, 295, 301; divide unto the saints their inheritance, 143; judge in Israel, 146

patriarchs, 269n10

Patten, David W., 268n7, 274, 284n31, 287, 301, 309

Perrysburg, New York, 247

Peter, James, and John, 73-74, 77, 321; keys of ministry (1835), 35, 73; ordained Smith and Cowdery (1835), 73, 79-80

Peterson, Ziba, 148, 374-75; mission to Native Americans, 85-89, 92

Phelps, William W., xv, 3-4, 6, 14-18, 50n41, 140n49, 147, 152, 198, 208, 219, 220n15, 231n23, 275, 283, 291n1, 292-93, 374-76; assisted 1835 D&C committee, 13; printer unto the church, 143;

steward over the revelations, 5, 180, 182-83

plural marriage, 289, 323-28; and Sarah Ann Whitney, 315-16; distinguishes gods from angels, 325-26; law of the priesthood, 328

Post, Stephen, 279n27

Pratt, Orson, 94, 137, 184, 202, 255, 259n49, 268n7, 309

Pratt, Parley P., 131, 137, 242, 254-55, 268n7, 309; mission to Native Americans, 85-89, 92; mission to Shakers, 128; process of revelation, xiv

presidency of the high priesthood, 199-200, 267, 271, 332

president of the high priesthood, 177-78, 184n19 , 271-72

priesthood, Aaronic, 267-68; and apostates, 220, 296; greater, 212-13; lesser, 213, 216, 268; Levitical, 267; lineage, 221; literal descendants of Aaron (1835), 171-72, 178, 268, 271; literal descendants of the chosen seed, 269; Melchizedek, 267-68; of Aaron (1835), 76; order of Enoch, 188; order of Melchizedek, 188, 267, 269, 309; order of the Son of God, 267

proclamation to the kings, 299-300, 308

Pulsipher, Zera, 310

Q

Quincy, Illinois, 295

R

Raphael, 321

redemption of Zion, 250-51, 253-54, 263-65, 279; date, 265n3

restoration of all things, 73, 221

revelation(s), came through Joseph Smith, 3, 12, 331; Canadian copyright, 372-74; central to Mormonism, xi; changes in text, 12, 16-19, 331; copy furnished us, 11; corrected dates and locations, 348; earliest text, 19; first person, xiii; Kirtland Safety Society, 376; location of manuscripts, 368-71; manuscript copies, 8; on parchment hidden by John the Beloved Disciple, 33n14; on the order of the priesthood, 323n63; original text, 3, 17; print, 258; process of, xiv; so different from original, 11; textual sources used, 9; typographical errors, 10; withheld from the public, xvi

Rich, Charles C., 309, 310n32

Richards, Willard, 192n22, 292, 309, 323n63, 335

Rigdon, Sidney, 9-10, 14, 55, 86, 95, 97, 102, 105n1, 106-107, 118-19, 136-40, 148, 151, 153, 181, 183, 184n19, 195, 202, 208, 234-35, 239, 241, 254-56, 282, 284, 289, 291-92, 308-309, 334; arrange church covenants, 10, 260; counselor to Joseph Smith, 199n40; member of 1835 D&C committee, 13, 331; mission to Shakers, 128; ordained a prophet, seer and revelator, 308n28; scribe for Bible revision, 77-78, 96n96; spokesman unto this people, 247; steward over the revelations, 5, 180, 182-83; traveled to Independence (1832), 6; vision of three degrees of glories, 186-93; worked on Lecture on Faith, 13; write a description of the land of Zion, 147, 158n72

Riggs, Burr, 184

Ripley, Alanson, 311n33

Robinson, Angeline (wife of Ebenezer Robinson), 312

Robinson, Ebenezer, 16, 312

Robinson, George W., 284, 292

Rockwell, Sarah Witt (wife of Orin Rockwell), baptism in Manchester, New York, 58

rod, gift of working with, 36; of nature, 36-37

Rolfe, Samuel J., 310

Romig, Ronald E., 372n2

Roundy, Shadrach, 310

Ruland, John, 87

Ryder, Symonds, 138n47

S

sacrament, 65n11, 72, 233, 342

Salem, Massachusetts, 281

salvation of the dead, 319

Sarah, 326, 328

school of the prophets, 230, 234, 240

Scott, Jacob, 137

seer stone, 51; revelations received through, xiii, 23n1, 94n94, 373-74

Sessions, Patty (wife of David Sessions), 315n43

Sessions, Sylvia (daughter of David and Patty Sessions), 315n43

seventy, 268-69, 272, 310

Sharp, Thomas, 18n79

Sherman, Delcena Johnson (widow of

Lyman R. Sherman), 315n43

Sherman, Lyman R., 277-78

Sherwood, Henry G., 306, 309

Smith, Agnes Coolbrith (widow of Don Carlos Smith), 315n43

Smith, Alvin (brother of Joseph Smith), 278, 334

Smith, Don Carlos (brother of Joseph Smith), 273, 310

Smith, Eden, 185, 199

Smith, Emma Hale (wife of Joseph Smith), xii, 23, 105n1; an elect lady, 70; and plural marriage, 315n43, 323n63; cleave unto Joseph Smith and to none else, 327; receive those given to Joseph Smith, 327; select sacred hymns, 71n20

Smith, George A., 309

Smith, Hyrum (brother of Joseph Smith), 10, 42, 46n32, 58-59, 136, 154, 185, 244, 255, 282, 289, 291-92, 295n7, 300-301, 305-306, 308-309, 314, 323n63, 378; appointed a prophet and revelator, 307n26; ordained by father as church patriarch, 307n25; patriarch, 309

Smith, John, 15, 311n33

Smith, Joseph, Jr., 9-10, 17-19, 26, 46, 60, 69, 71, 95, 97, 102, 118, 126, 183, 199, 219, 221n17, 247, 279, 295, 303n19, 334; alteration of manuscript pages, 38; appoint another in his stead, 115; Book of Commandments, 5; Canadian copyright revelation, 372-74; chosen to do the work of the Lord, 24; church organization, 57-58; corrected revelations, 6n26, 8, 331, 345; date for redemption of Zion, 265n3; Emma Smith to abide and cleave unto, 327; exaltation sealed, 327; forgiveness of sins, 63, 159, 234, 327; gift to translate, 26, 28; give heed unto all his words, 3, 61; intermarriage with Indians (Native Americans), 376; keys of the mystery, 96; Kirtland Revelations Book, 8, 12, 331; Kirtland Safety Society, 376-77; letter to Edward Partridge, 113; lost gift, 38; member of 1835 D&C committee, 12, 331; no other gift, 26, 28-30; not kept the commandments, 239; ordained prophet and seer, 58, 60n6; power and keys of this priesthood, 324-25, 328; president of the high priesthood, 184n19, 201-202; process of reve-

lation, xiv; received the laws, 107n4; repent, 27; revelations through seer stone, 23n1, 94n94; Sarah Ann Whitney sealed to, 315; song in the gift of tongues, 231-32; steward over the revelations, 5, 180, 182-83; transgressed, 24; translated from parchment, 33n14; translation (correction) of the Bible, 98n99, 123n29; trip to Michigan in Aug. 1835, 14n57; trip to Salem, Mass., in Aug. 1836, 281; understanding of Elias, 76-79; vision of celestial kingdom, 278-79; vision with Sidney Rigdon of three degrees of glories, 186-93; visions with Oliver Cowdery in Kirtland temple, 279-80; well pleased with your offering, 299; women sealed to, 315n43

Smith, Joseph, Sr. (father of Joseph Smith), 25-26, 60, 135, 235, 278, 301, 307n25, 334, 372; baptism in Manchester, New York, 58

Smith, Joseph III (son of Joseph Smith), 299n9

Smith, Lucy Mack (mother of Joseph Smith), 278, 334; baptism in Manchester, New York, 58

Smith, Mary Bailey (wife of Samuel H. Smith), xii, 273

Smith, Samuel Harrison (brother of Joseph Smith), 10, 59, 137, 154, 163, 184, 194n28, 273, 310

Smith, Susanna Bailey (daughter of Samuel H. and Mary Smith), 273n16

Smith, Sylvester, 185

Smith, William (brother of Joseph Smith), 268n7, 274, 309

Snider, John (also spelled Snyder), 301, 305, 311, 313

Snow, Eliza Roxey (daughter of Oliver and Rosetta Snow), 315n43, 377

Sodom and Gomorrah, 27

Solomon, 323, 326

song by the gift of tongues, 231-32

South Carolina, 221

Stanton, Daniel, 185

stock in Nauvoo House, 305, 311

Stowell, Josiah, 372

study it out in your mind, 37

Sweet, Northrop, 92, 94

T

Taylor, John, 292, 309

telestial kingdom, 223
telestial world, 189-90
temple, Far West, 289, 291-93; Independence, 142, 148, 149n65, 212, 242, 304; Kirtland, 239-41, 243-44, 265, 279-80; Nauvoo, 289, 302-304, 310, 313, 317, 322
Teraphim, 50
terrestrial kingdom, 223
terrestrial world, 189
textual criticism, 17-18
textual revisions, 331-36
textual sources used, 9
Thayer, Ezra (also spelled Thayre), 92, 94, 135, 137, 141, 185
Thompson, Ohio, 133, 139, 141
Thompson, Robert B., 300
Times and Seasons, 314
tithing, 112, 114, 159, 242, 293-94
Traughber, John L., 374
treasure in Salem, Massachusetts, 281
Turner, Jonathan B., 18-19, 29
Twelve apostles, 48n33, 68, 267n6, 268-70, 278-79, 282-83, 287, 289, 292, 302n17, 309, 313-14; humble themselves, 274
twelve disciples, 46-47
two priesthoods, 213, 267

U

United Firm, 9-10, 55, 195, 207-208, 241, 255-61; treasuries, 258-59
Uriah, 326
Urim and Thummim, 41, 49-51

V

Van Wagoner, Richard S., 14n57

W

Wakefield, Joseph H., 131, 137
wars, 100, 122-23, 156, 221
Warsaw, Illinois, 306
Washington, D.C., 329
Welton, Micah B., 185
Whitlock, Harvey G., 137, 154, 276-77
Whitmer, David, xiv, 5n12, 29-30, 44n29, 46, 48-49, 89, 137, 154, 291n1, 373-74, 376
Whitmer, Jacob, 373
Whitmer, John, 3, 6, 15, 45n30, 71, 90, 94n94, 179, 208, 219n12, 275, 283, 291n1, 373; church historian, 12, 126, 219; steward over revelations, 5, 180, 182-83

Whitmer, Peter, Jr., 45; mission to Native Americans, 85-89, 92
Whitmer, Peter, Sr., 23, 44n29, 321n59
Whitney, Elizabeth Ann (wife of Newel K. Whitney), 315-16
Whitney, Newel K., 8-9, 11, 105n1, 138n48, 157, 160, 181-82, 195, 208, 217, 239, 241, 257, 294-95, 315-16, 323n64, 332-33
Whitney, Sarah Ann (daughter of Newel and Elizabeth Whitney), xii, 315
Whittaker, David J., 376
Wight, Lyman, 108n6, 136, 254-55, 295n7, 301, 305, 309, 311
Williams, Frederick G., 8-10, 191, 201, 203-204, 211n1, 220n15, 231, 234-39, 241, 255-56, 273-74, 292-93, 362-63, 376; accompanied missionaries to Native Americans, 86-87; farm owned by, 135, 159; member of 1835 D&C committee, 13, 331; trip to Michigan in August 1835, 14n57
Williams, Samuel, 310
Wilson, Calves, 184
Wilson, Lewis Dunbar, 309
wife, cleave unto her and none else, 108; one, 129
wives and concubines, 323
women sealed to Joseph Smith, 315n43
Woodford, Robert J., 210n72
Woodruff, Wilford, 16, 292, 309, 314n40, 376-77
word of wisdom, 232-33

Y

Young, Brigham, 268n7, 279, 288, 309, 312, 335, 376
Young, Joseph, 310

Z

Zarahemla, Territory of Iowa, 311
Zion (of Enoch), 98
Zion (in Missouri), 55; land of, 251; of God shall stand, 145; offering accepted, 304; place for the city of, 142; redemption of, 250-51, 253-54, 263-65, 279; shall not be moved, 249; stakes, 249; temples, 242n37; the pure in heart, 243; to with songs of everlasting joy, 124, 164, 249
Zion's Camp, 253n45, 263
Zomar (original word for Zion), 149n65

ABOUT THE AUTHOR

H. Michael Marquardt is co-author of *Inventing Mormonism: Tradition and the Historical Record*, author of *The Strange Marriages of Sarah Ann Whitney*, *The Book of Abraham Revisited*, and editor of *Joseph Smith's Diaries*. His essays have appeared in the *Journal of Pastoral Practice*, *Restoration*, and *Sunstone*. He and his wife Dorothy reside in Sandy, Utah, and are the parents of five children.